The SAGE
Handbook of
Philosophy of
Education

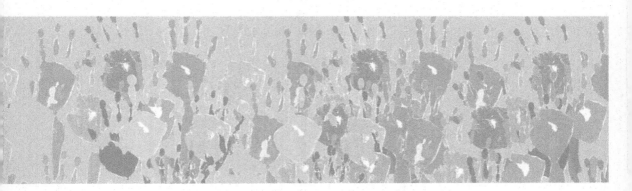

The SAGE
Handbook of
Philosophy of
Education

Edited by
Richard Bailey
Robin Barrow
David Carr and
Christine McCarthy

Los Angeles | London | New Delhi
Singapore | Washington DC

First published 2010

SAGE Publications Ltd
1 Oliver's Yard
55 City Road
London EC1Y 1SP

SAGE Publications Inc.
2455 Teller Road
Thousand Oaks, California 91320

SAGE Publications India Pvt Ltd
B 1/I 1 Mohan Cooperative Industrial Area
Mathura Road
New Delhi 110 044

SAGE Publications Asia-Pacific Pte Ltd
3 Church Street
#10-04 Samsung Hub
Singapore 049483

Library of Congress Control Number: 2009928797

British Library Cataloguing in Publication data

A catalogue record for this book is available from the British Library

ISBN 978-1-84787-467-2
ISBN 978-1-44627-041-7 (pbk)

Typeset by Glyph International, Bangalore, India
Printed and bound by CPI Group (UK) Ltd, Croydon, CR0 4YY
Printed on paper from sustainable resources

FSC
www.fsc.org
MIX
Paper from
responsible sources
FSC® C013604

Contents

Contributors

Briana Allen has been a Technology Instructor and Coordinator for 8 years, working with K-12 students and teachers in the use and integration of technology. She coordinates with colleagues to create integrated technology projects which compliment students' core curriculum, emphasizing project- and problem-based activities. Her interests include how to seamlessly integrate technology into the classroom, how best to train teachers in the integration of technology and how technology's use in schools changes the roll of educator and student.

Brenda Almond is Emeritus Professor of Moral and Social Philosophy at the University of Hull, where she was for several years Reader in Education and Philosophy. She has lectured widely both in the UK and worldwide and is the author of many articles and books on philosophy and on education. She was Joint Founding Editor of the *Journal of Applied Philosophy* and is President of the Philosophical Society of England. Her books include *Education and the Individual* (1981, as Brenda Cohen), *Educational Thought: an Introduction* (1993), *Exploring Ethics: A Traveller's Tale* (1998), *Exploring Philosophy: the Philosophical Quest* (1995) and *The Fragmenting Family* (Oxford University Press, 2006).

Richard Bailey is a writer and theorist on education and sport. He has been a Professor at Canterbury, Roehampton and most recently Birmingham universities. He has studied Philosophy, Physical Education and Anthropology, and continues to work in these areas, especially with regard to their relevance for learning and the development of expertise. He is the author of *Education in the Open Society: Karl Popper and Schooling* (Ashgate), editor of *The Philosophy of Education: an Introduction* (Continuum), and is author/editor of 13 other books on theoretical and practical aspects of schooling and sport. He also edits the 25-volume *Continuum Library of Educational Thought*.

Robin Barrow is Professor of the Philosophy of Education at Simon Fraser University, Canada, where he was also Dean of Education from 1992 to 2002. Prior to that he was Reader in the Philosophy of Education at the University of Leicester, UK. A past Vice-Chair of the Philosophy of Education Society, GB, and past President of the Canadian Philosophy of Education Society, he is the author of some 25 books in the fields of philosophy, education and classics, the most recent of which are *Plato* (Continuum) and *An Introduction to Moral*

Philosophy and Moral Education (Routledge). In 1996 he was elected a Fellow of the Royal Society of Canada.

Michael Bonnett is currently Reader in Philosophy of Education at the University of Bath and Senior Research Fellow at the University of London Institute of Education, and was formerly Senior Lecturer in the Philosophy of Education in the University of Cambridge. He is author of numerous published articles, including several on environmental education and sustainability. His book on environmental concern and education *Retrieving Nature. Education for a Post-Humanist Age* was published in 2004. His earlier book *Children's Thinking* (1994) explored the significance of a poetic dimension to human understanding and the process of education.

David Carr is Professor of Philosophy at Education at the University of Edinburgh. He is author of *Educating the Virtues* (1991), *Professionalism and Ethics in Teaching* (2000) and *Making Sense of Education* (2003), as well as of many philosophical and educational papers. He is also editor of *Education, Knowledge and Truth* (1998), co-editor (with Jan Steutel) of *Virtue Ethics and Moral Education* (1999), and (with John Haldane) of *Spirituality, Philosophy and Education* (2003).

James C. Conroy is Professor of Religious and Philosophical Education and Dean of the Faculty of Education at the University of Glasgow. He is the author of numerous publications on religious and moral education, citizenship education, the philosophy of education and the place of literature and the arts in the work of liberal education. He is visiting and adjunct Professor at Fordham University, New York, and previously held visiting Senior Research Fellowships at Australian Catholic University and the Federal University of Rio Grande do Sul, Porto Alegre, Brazil. He is currently President of the Association for Moral Education, Secretary and Treasurer of the *Journal of Moral Education* Trust, Board Member of the General Teaching Council for Scotland, Member of the Teacher Workforce Planning Group for Scotland, and member of the Commissioning Panel AHRC/ESRC Programme on Religion and Society. He occupies officer and editorial board positions on a number of academic associations and learned journals, including EERA, PESGB, *Journal of Policy Futures in Education, Ethics and Education, International Journal of Catholic Education*. He is the author of the *Betwixt and Between: the Liminal Imagination, Education and Democracy* (New York: Peter Lang, 2004).

Craig A. Cunningham is Associate Professor in the Integrated Studies in Teaching, Technology, and Inquiry Department at National-Louis University in Chicago, where he teaches courses in technology integration, curriculum design and the philosophy of education. A member of the Philosophy of Education Society (U.S.) and the John Dewey Society, Professor Cunningham is the author (with Marty Billingsley) of *Curriculum Webs: Weaving the Web into Teaching and Learning,* 2nd edition (Allyn and Bacon, 2006), and has also written about

John Dewey's aesthetics, metaphysics and theory of the self as well as the history of character education in America.

Andrew Davis taught in primary schools before lecturing in philosophy of education and mathematics education at Cambridge University before moving to Durham. He has published extensively on the topics of learning and educational assessment. He is currently editing *New Philosophies of Learning* with Ruth Cigman, to appear as a special issue of the *Journal of Philosophy of Education* and as a book published by Wiley-Blackwell.

Robert A. Davis is Professor of Religious and Cultural Education at the University of Glasgow. He has taught, written and broadcast widely on literature, religion, folklore, music, education and the cultural history of childhood. He has held visiting positions at several international institutions, including Ireland, Australia and Sweden. His literary critical work includes the preparation of standard editions of several of the works of Robert Graves and studies of the children's writers Alan Garner and Philip Pullman. His educational work includes examinations of the place of imaginative literature in moral education, the future of education for religious literacy and the history of faith-based schooling. He is co-investigator for the AHRC/ESRC Religion and Society project on the effectiveness of Religious Education in British secondary schools and is also co-authoring a new intellectual biography of the nineteenth century educational reformer and philanthropist, Robert Owen. He occupies editorial board positions on several international journals, including the *Journal of the Philosophy of Education* and the *Journal of Policy Futures in Education.*

Michael Degenhardt studied economics at the London School of Economics (LSE), where he discovered (too late) that philosophy was more worthwhile. He did his teacher training and taught history for several years in what was then Southern Rhodesia. On returning to England he continued to teach in schools and colleges and began part-time studies in philosophy with Richard Peters. In 1978 he was appointed to lecture in Education at the University of Tasmania. Now retired in Surrey he enjoys reading history of ideas and writing in the area of culture, values and curriculum.

Frederick S. Ellett, Jr was born in Elmira, New York, in 1945. He attended Cornell University where he received a B.S. (Electrical Engineering), 1967; a M.S. (Electrical Engineering), 1970; and a Ph.D. (Philosophy of Education), 1977 (Kenneth A. Strike chaired the Ph.D. Committee). He taught philosophy of education at UCLA's Graduate School of Education from 1976 to 1988, and since 1988 he has been Associate Professor, Philosophy of Education, Faculty of Education, University of Western Ontario, London, Ontario, Canada. His interests include the conceptual, epistemological and ontological aspects of educational policy and assessment, with special interests in theories of rationality and morality.

Penny Enslin is Professor of Education at the University of Glasgow, where she is Director of the Ed D programme. Until July 2006 she was a Professor in the School of Education at the University of the Witwatersrand, Johannesburg, where she now holds the position of Professor Emeritus. Her research and teaching interests lie in the area of political theory and education, with particular interests in democracy and citizenship education. She has published internationally on deliberative democracy and education, liberalism, gender and feminist theory, nation building, African philosophy of education, and higher education.

David P. Erikson is Professor of Philosophy of Education and Educational Policy in the Department of Educational Foundations, College of Education, at the University of Hawaii at Mānoa in Honolulu, Hawaii. He has research interests in philosophy of the social sciences, moral and political education, educational policy studies, and comparative/international education. He currently serves as Director of International Education in the College of Education.

John Halliday began his working life as a telecommunications engineer following a degree in Physics and Mathematics. He went on to teach in a number of colleges of further education before obtaining degrees in philosophy and education. Since entering higher education he has published widely in the areas of philosophy of education and teacher education, including five books. He is perhaps best known for his work on the philosophy of vocational education, but currently is writing a new book exploring new perspectives on disadvantage and achievement from an analysis of informal learning.

Mark Halstead is a Research Professor in the School of Education at the University of Huddersfield. He has written widely in the field of moral education, including *Education in Morality* (co-edited with Terence H. McLaughlin, 1999), *Values in Education and Education in Values* (co-edited with Monica J. Taylor, 1996) and *Citizenship and Moral Education* (co-authored with Mark Pike, 2006). He has also edited Special Issues of the *Journal of Moral Education on Philosophy* and *Moral Education: the Contribution of John Wilson* (2000) and *Islamic Values and Moral Education* (2007). He has a special interest in Muslim education and multicultural education.

David T. Hansen is Professor and Director of the Program in Philosophy and Education at Teachers College, Columbia University. His research interests include the philosophy and practice of teaching, the criticism of educational values, and cosmopolitanism as an educational mode of being. He has published widely in these fields, including books such as *The Call to Teach* and *Exploring the Moral Heart of Teaching*. He has served as President of the John Dewey Society and the Philosophy of Education Society (North America).

Graham Haydon is Reader in Philosophy of Education at the Institute of Education, University of London. Much of his work has been on moral and citizenship education in plural societies, including the relationship between Personal and Social Education and Citizenship Education. His publications include *The Importance of PSHE: a Philosophical and Policy Perspective on Personal, Social and Health Education* (Philosophy of Education Society of Great Britain 2005) and *Values in Education* (Continuum 2006).

Nicki Hedge is the Director of Learning Innovation in the Faculty of Education at the University of Glasgow. She teaches, mainly, on the Doctorate in Education programme in which she runs courses in Advanced Research Methods and on Masters courses in Modern Educational Thought. Originally an applied linguist, and more recently responsible for distance education at the University of Glasgow, her current research is focussed on social justice, with particular attention to knowledge and education as global public goods. Previous nationally and internationally funded projects include work on inclusion, e-learning and distance education, assessment and adult literacy.

Dr. Stephen Johnson lectures in Politics and Ethics on the Social Policy degree course of the University of Warwick, at North Warwickshire college. He has taught in primary and secondary schools, sixth form colleges and further and higher education. He has published articles in the *Journal Philosophy of Education,* the *British Journal of Educational Studies* and the *Journal of Further* and *Higher Education.* He is on the Editorial Advisory Board of the *Journal Further and Higher Education.* He is author of *Teaching Thinking Skills,* impact 8, published in 2001 by the Philosophy of Education Society of Great Britain. He is co-author, with Professor Harvey Siegel, of a forthcoming book on thinking skills. He was Secretary of the Philosophy of Education Society of Great Britain for 10 years.

James Scott Johnston is Assistant Professor of Philosophy and Education, Faculty of Education, Queen's University, Kingston, Ontario, Canada. His current research interests are pragmatism (John Dewey); pragmatism and continental philosophy in conversation; and modes of inquiry. Dr. Johnston has recently written two books – *Inquiry and Education: John Dewey and the Quest for Democracy* and *Regaining Consciousness: Self-Consciousness and Self-Cultivation from 1781–Present* – and he has another book, *Deweyan Inquiry: from Educational Theory to Practice*, also from SUNY Press. He has recently published articles in Educational Theory, Transactions of the Charles S. Peirce Society, and Studies in the Philosophy of Education.

Constantin Koopman is a teacher and researcher at Walden University (USA). After having completed his studies in musicology and philosophy at Utrecht University, he specialized in music education and aesthetic education at Radboud University Nijmegen (The Netherlands). In the past years, he has also worked at the universities of Auckland and Cologne, and at The Royal Conservatoire of The Hague. His publications on aesthetics and aesthetic education have appeared in various international journals, including the *Journal of Philosophy of Education,*

Educational Philosophy and Theory, the *Journal of Aesthetic Education* and the *Journal of Aesthetics and Art Criticism.*

Megan J. Laverty is Associate Professor in the Philosophy and Education Program at Teachers College, Columbia University. She is the author of *Iris Murdoch's Ethics: A Consideration of her Romantic Vision* and co-editor of *Playing with Ideas: Modern and Contemporary Philosophies of Education.* Her research interests include: the history of philosophy of education; moral philosophy and its significance for education; philosophy of dialogue and dialogical pedagogy; and philosophy with children and adolescents in schools.

Christine McCarthy is Associate Professor in the Department of Educational Policy and Leadership Studies, Social Foundations Program at the University of Iowa. Her research has focused on Deweyan conceptions of the nature of knowledge, of mind, and of art. Her current research interests are in the relations of art-making, mind and consciousness.

Mike McNamee is Professor of Applied Ethics in the School of Health Science at Swansea University where he teaches medical ethics. Having completed a PhD in the Philosophy of Physical Education he has pioneered the development of sports ethics as an area of study and research over the last 20 years. He is a former President of the International Association for the Philosophy of Sport and is Editor of the journal *Sport Ethics and Philosophy.* His latest book is *Sports, Virtues and Vices* (Routledge, 2008).

Robert Manery is a doctoral candidate in the Curriculum Theory and Implementation program in the Faculty of Education at Simon Fraser University. His research interests include philosophy of education, hermeneutic theory, moral philosophy, literature and language arts education. He has published a book of poetry entitled *It's Not As If It Hasn't Been Said Before* (Tsunami Editions, 2001).

Jack Martin is Burnaby Mountain Endowed Professor of Psychology at Simon Fraser University. His research interests are in philosophy and history of psychology, social-developmental psychology, and educational psychology, with particular emphasis on the psychology of selfhood and personhood. Author of over 150 scholarly articles and book chapters, his most recent books include *Psychology and the Question of Agency* (2003, with Jeff Sugarman and Janice Thompson) and *The Psychology of Human Possibility and Constraint* (1999, with Jeff Sugarman), both published by SUNY Press. A new book (with Suzanne Kirschner), entitled *The Sociocultural Turn in Psychology,* will soon be published by Columbia University Press.

Nathan Martin is a Ph.D. candidate in musicology at McGill University. His dissertation, 'Rameau and Rousseau: Harmony and History in the Age of Reason,' concerns the reception of Jean-Philippe Rameau's Theory of Harmony in Rousseau's musical writings.

Cris Mayo is an associate professor in the Gender and Women's Studies and Department of Educational Policy Studies at the University of Illinois at Urbana-Champaign. Her publications in queer studies and philosophy of education include *Disputing the Subject of Sex: Sexuality and Public School Controversies* (Rowman and Littlefield, 2004, 2007) as well as articles in *Educational Theory, Philosophy of Education, Review of Research in Education, Educational Philosophy and Theory*, and *Sexuality Research and Social Policy.*

Francine Menashy is a Ph.D. candidate at the Ontario Institute for Studies in Education of the University of Toronto, in the Philosophy of Education program and collaborative program in Comparative, International and Development Education. Her dissertation focuses on international education policy and privatization of schooling. Previous work has been published in the *Journal of Educational Thought* and the *McGill Journal of Education.*

D.C. Phillips is Professor (Emeritus) of Education, and, by courtesy, of Philosophy, at Stanford University. He is a member of the U.S. National Academy of Education, and a past President of the Philosophy of Education Society of America. He writes on topics in the history of late-nineteenth and twentieth-century thought; recently, he has focused on philosophical issues in educational research, an area that he approaches from the perspective of philosophy of science. He has authored or edited 11 books and about 140 essays in books and journals.

John P. Portelli is Professor, Co-Director of the Centre for Leadership and Diversity, and Associate Chair of the Department of Theory and Policy Studies at OISE, University of Toronto. His research and teaching focus on: issues of democratic theory and educational policy, leadership and pedagogy; student engagement and the curriculum of life; analysis and critique of neo-liberalism in education. He has published eight books (including two collections of poetry). He is a former editor of *Paiduesis: The Journal of the Canadian Philosophy of Education Society.*

Richard Pring is presently Lead Director of the Nuffield Review of 14–19 Education and Training for England and Wales, a £1 million research project funded by the Nuffield Foundation. Previously, from 1989 to 2003, he was Professor of Educational Studies and Director of the Department of Educational Studies at the University of Oxford. His most recent book is *'John Dewey: Philosopher of Education for the 21st Century?'* (Continuum).

Timothy Reagan has served on the faculties of Gallaudet University, the University of Connecticut, Roger Williams University, and the University of the Witwatersrand in South Africa. He is currently Professor of Educational

Leadership at Central Connecticut State University. His research interests are focused primarily on issues of language and culture in education. His latest book is *Language Matters*, published by International Age Publishers (2009).

Andrew Reid studied philosophy at the University of Glasgow and was, until his retirement, Senior Lecturer in Education at the University of Edinburgh, where he taught mainly in the area of Philosophy of Education. He has published in the *Journal of Philosophy of Education* and elsewhere on issues and problems concerning the nature and aims of education. His interest in T.S. Eliot as an educational and cultural thinker is part of a wider concern to defend a traditional view of education, teaching and learning against its detractors.

Claudia Ruitenberg is Assistant Professor, Philosophy of Education, in the Department of Educational Studies at the University of British Columbia. She has published in the *Journal of Philosophy of Education, Studies in Philosophy and Education* and the *Philosophy of Education* yearbooks. Current research interests include poststructuralist perspectives on hate speech and censorship in education, and radical democratic perspectives on citizenship and political education. She teaches educational theories, philosophical methods and critical thinking.

Harvey Siegel is Professor and Chair of the Department of Philosophy at the University of Miami. His areas of specialization include epistemology, philosophy of science and philosophy of education. He is the author of *Relativism Refuted: A Critique of Contemporary Epistemological Relativism* (Springer 1987), *Educating Reason: Rationality, Critical Thinking, and Education* (Routledge 1988), and *Rationality Redeemed?: Further Dialogues on an Educational Ideal* (Routledge 1997). He is editor of (among other things) *The Oxford Handbook of Philosophy of Education* (Oxford 2009).

Richard Smith is Professor of Education at the University of Durham, UK, where he was for many years Director of the Combined Degrees in Arts and Social Sciences. He is Editor of the new journal *Ethics and Education* and Associate Editor of the *Journal of Philosophy of Education*. His most recent authored book is (with Paul Smeyers and Paul Standish) *The Therapy of Education* (Palgrave Macmillan, 2006). His principal research interests are in the philosophy of education and the philosophy of social science.

Hugh Sockett is a Professor of Education in the Department of Public and International Affairs at George Mason University. His books include *The Moral Base for Teacher Professionalism* (1993), *Transforming Teacher Education* (with Diane Wood and Pamela LePage, 2005), *Educational Reconciliation* (with Pamela LePage, 2002), and *Teacher Dispositions* (2006: as editor). He is currently working on a book entitled *Knowledge and Virtue in Teaching*, which builds on his article 'Dispositions as virtues: the complexity of the construct', in the *Journal of Teacher Education*.

Barbara Stengel is a Professor of Educational Foundations, Philosophy and Women's Studies at Millersville University. She brings a feminist perspective and a gender analysis to issues in teacher education and knowledge, the moral dimensions of teaching and learning, Dewey studies and the play of emotion in education.

Daniel Vokey is Associate Professor, Philosophy of Education, in the Department of Educational Studies at the University of British Columbia. His current research interests include comparing perspectives on the development of practical wisdom from both Western and Eastern traditions. A recent publication by Daniel in this area is 'Hearing, contemplating, meditating: in search of the transformative integration of heart and mind,' in C. Eppert and H. Wang, (eds), *Cross-cultural Studies in Curriculum: Eastern Thought, Educational Insights*. Mahwah, NJ: Lawrence Erlbaum, pp. 287–312.

Ieuan Williams lectures in philosophy at Swansea University. His main teaching and research interests have been in the philosophy of mind and language. In recent years he has developed a special interest in Plato's philosophy and its enduring value in relation to contemporary moral and political issues. He has recently published articles on Plato and Media Theory and on Plato, Citizenship and Political Justice in Contemporary Society. He is currently writing an updated version of Richard Crossman's 1938 classic *Plato Today*.

Kevin Williams is Senior Lecturer in Mater Dei Institute of Education, Dublin City University, and is a former president of the Educational Studies Association of Ireland. His recent books include *Education and the Voice of Michael Oakeshott* (2007), *Faith and the Nation: Religion, Culture and Schooling in Ireland* (2005) and *Why Teach Foreign Languages in Schools? A Philosophical Response to Curriculum Policy* (2000).

Preface

The SAGE Handbook of the Philosophy of Education is designed primarily to be useful to students studying the philosophy of education in the context of the study of educational foundations or theory. It is also designed to be of use to practising teachers who wish to gain easy access to current philosophical thinking on particular contemporary educational issues, and to educationalists of all types who want a guide to questions relating to the nature, the history, and the current state of the art of philosophy of education.

We have sought to balance the handbook in three particular ways. First, we have sought to give fair weight to different styles of philosophy or modes of philosophizing about education. Secondly, we have tried to give due recognition to both past and present educational philosophizing. Thirdly, we have endeavoured to give even-handed attention both to the general 'perennial' issues in educational philosophy and to a set of more narrowly focused issues of contemporary educational concern.

To this end, we have dedicated Section 1 specifically to addressing different conceptions of philosophy of education, and to exploring its appropriate concerns and methodologies. This section also examines the vexed relationship of educational philosophy to other fields of educational theory, and to the problems and circumstances of educational practice.

Section 2 is devoted to certain thinkers who, in our judgement, are either especially significant in the development of the discipline and its concerns, such as Plato, Jean-Jacques Rousseau and John Dewey, or are influential in current philosophical discussions, such as the phenomenologists and the post-structuralists. Here, we have also gathered matter pertaining more generally to the history of the philosophy of education. It hardly needs saying that the problem of selection is great. There are many different criteria we might have adopted and differences of opinion as to who most obviously satisfies them. We have not attempted to come up with a list simply of those whom we think most worthy of study. Instead, we have focused on those figures who may most obviously be said to have produced, through something recognizable as philosophical reasoning, a coherent overall view of education and its practices. In the various chapters we have focused either on an individual or on a cluster of individuals (sometimes over a span of time) who can clearly be identified as representing some kind of school of thought. In each case, in order to highlight continuities and to help the reader to see connections, developments and patterns and to find their way through the literature, the text refers to ongoing influences and relationships. At the end of this section, there is a concise biographical dictionary of educational thinkers that provides brief reference to a group of individuals, not otherwise treated in this volume, who have nonetheless made some important or significant contribution to educational thought, indicating their focus and where to locate it in their works.

Section 3 is dedicated to contemporary philosophical thought on education; this body of thought provides the basis and reference point for a philosophical treatment of certain particular contemporary problems. Here we have attempted to address a common criticism of earlier handbooks (and textbooks) on philosophy of education, namely that they have given insufficient attention to the needs and interests of non-philosophical colleagues. We believe it is vitally important to include discussions of topics that, though not exclusively, nor even primarily, philosophical, nonetheless do raise philosophical issues. It will become apparent that numerous discussions of educational concerns have a philosophical character. Indeed, it is difficult to imagine any educational issue that is not related to assumptions about knowledge or values, or which would not benefit from critical consideration of key concepts. This final section seeks to explore the contribution that philosophy can make to educational practice; it seeks to show that parents, teachers and policy-makers, just as much as academics, can benefit from the philosophy of education. Thus our aim is, on the one hand, to accommodate the desire for a handbook inclusive enough to bring together both contemporary and traditional reflections on the nature of education, and to draw on the relevant work of both philosophers and educational theorists. We have tried, on the other hand, to fulfil the hope that this broad coverage will go beyond a superficial survey of the field, and that it will offer insightful and relatively detailed examinations of certain central subjects. For convenience, the chapters in this section are arranged into four groups: 'Teaching and general education'; 'Knowledge, learning and curriculum'; 'Social principles in education'; and 'Aspects of education'.

Our hope is that the reader of this handbook will realize, through philosophically informed discussion of a range of educational thinkers and topics, the relevance of philosophical enquiry for all of those studying education. Indeed, if the key question for sound educational policy making and practice is, as has often been supposed, 'What kind of a curriculum would ensure a better future and quality of life in moral and spiritual as well as material and economic terms for generations to come?', we urgently need to bring to our deliberations a philosophical clarity, as well as a depth of thought and argument, that is too often missing from educational debate. However, we would be disappointed if the reader put down this handbook with the impression that philosophy was only, or even mainly, handmaiden to other disciplines or sciences associated with educational thinking and practice. Philosophy (from the Greek for the love of knowledge or wisdom) requires thinkers to think for themselves. This is why Immanuel Kant asserted that it is not possible to learn philosophy; it is only possible to learn how to philosophize. This does not mean that the philosopher ought to live a life of solitary contemplation, but it does mean that the philosopher is compelled to think for him or herself. This is perhaps why philosophical conversations often seem characterized by ambiguity and perplexity. Important questions are rarely resolved with simple answers unless, of course, we choose to borrow uncritically the dogmas and doctrines of others. For Bertrand Russell, the person who does decide to live so uncritically 'goes through life imprisoned in the prejudices derived from common sense, from the habitual beliefs of his age or his nation, and from convictions which have grown up in his mind without the cooperation or consent of his deliberate reason'. So, we suggest, philosophy is fundamental. The perennial debates of philosophers who have written about education have an intrinsic interest and value, but they also have considerable utility.

Richard Bailey
Robin Barrow
David Carr
Christine McCarthy

Educational Philosophy and Theory

1

What is Philosophy of Education?

D.C. Phillips

As any parent of a 3- or 4-year-old child knows, 'What is ...?' questions are extremely troublesome, in large measure because it is rarely clear what answer would satisfy the questioner. Indeed, the common experience is that the youngster is satisfied by nothing, since any answer that is given is likely to be followed by a series of further questions. The situation is even worse if the questioner (this time an adult) is interrogating a philosopher, as it is virtually certain that the first answer that is received – and very possibly the later ones as well – will be unsatisfactory. For the philosopher's instinct, when asked 'What is X?', is not to discourse about the nature of X, but to begin by analyzing the question itself. The questioner is sometimes bamboozled, then, to have the simple-seeming query answered by 'Well, it is not clear what you are asking for, when you ask what is X'. Warming up, the philosopher may point out that the questioner might be seeking a verbal definition of X, alternatively could be after a fuller description of X that would allow cases of X to be identified, or perhaps would be satisfied merely by being given an example of X; some questioners might be searching for the 'essence' of X, or wish to find out what X *ought* to be, or why X is worth bothering about at all.

It might be thought that the situation could not possibly deteriorate any further – but when the 'what is?' question that is directed to a philosopher contains the word 'philosophy' itself, all hope of receiving a quick, simple and direct answer has to be abandoned, for the philosopher will suggest that the question cannot be answered until the meaning of 'philosophy' has been clarified – and the nature of philosophy is 'essentially contested'. And of course this is a very reasonable position to take, and certainly is the one that will be the starting point for the present chapter.

What follows, then, is the slow, complex and indirect answer given by a philosopher to the apparently simple question: 'What is philosophy of education?' And, as indicated, the discussion must start with the nature of philosophy itself – for it should be obvious that individuals holding different conceptions of what constitutes philosophy will give quite different accounts of philosophy of education, and sadly there do indeed exist a number of divergent views about this underlying matter.

Before proceeding, several preliminary issues need to be resolved. First, the dictionary definition is of no help whatsoever. My copy of *Webster's II New Riverside* is particularly circular, defining 'philosophize' as 'to speculate or reason like a philosopher', the problem being that when one turns to 'philosopher' the entry is 'an expert or student in philosophy'. This is followed by a second and equally uninformative definition, 'someone who thinks deeply', which is untenable for two reasons. First, almost everyone thinks deeply about at least some issues, and yet it seems strange to say that everyone is a philosopher; and secondly, not everyone who aspires to think deeply (including the philosopher) actually succeeds in doing so – and it also seems strange to say that a philosopher who labours unsuccessfully is on that occasion *not* being a philosopher.

It is important to stress that I am not disputing the fact that many (although certainly not all) philosophers of education think deeply; it is simply that this characteristic cannot be the basis of a definition that purports to demarcate philosophy of education from other activities. Nor is it being denied that there is an enormous number of complex educational issues that it is important to think deeply about. Hopefully the discussion that follows – and indeed this whole book – will make clear the particular contribution that can be made by deep philosophical reflection.

I should make explicit what was left implicit in the discussion above: namely, that there are two broad usages of the word 'philosophy' and its cognates – and these should not be confused. The first of these is the vapid non-technical usage according to which anyone who thinks abstractly about an issue or pursuit that is valued within a society may be called a philosopher; this is what the lexicographers for *Webster's* had in mind when they crafted the account I cited earlier. I recall having heard the (late) brilliant coach of my local professional American football team being called a philosopher (presumably because of the depth of his analyses of the game); and I have heard the term used to describe certain TV personalities who give lifestyle advice to those who are less fortunate than themselves. Other examples of this usage of the term can be found by browsing in the 'Philosophy' section of your nearest mega-bookstore. I will not pursue this any further here (but see Phillips, 1985), for it is my purpose in this present discussion to illuminate – at least in a preliminary way that will be built upon in subsequent chapters – the second, more technical usage of 'philosophy' (and relatedly of course 'philosophy of education'); this is the sense of the term that would apply to work done in university departments of philosophy or programmes in philosophy of education (although I do not want to suggest that this type of philosophy is pursued only in universities and colleges). And, as hinted earlier, this will be a difficult task enough, for in this world of technical philosophy there are strong differences of opinion about what it is that philosophy can achieve and about appropriate standards of rigour and the like; Lucas captured this aspect of philosophy well when he wrote 'Someone once remarked sarcastically that if all the philosophers in the world were stretched end to end they would still not reach an agreement' (Lucas, 1969, p. 3).

A second preliminary matter that needs to be disposed of before we proceed concerns another approach that might be taken to the task of defining philosophy (and perforce, philosophy of education), but which turns out to be as frustrating as consulting the dictionary (although, as will become evident below, I will adopt a variant of this strategy myself). 'Philosophy is what philosophers do', it might be suggested, 'so let us simply take a few examples of philosophers at work and base our account on what we see there'. The problem with this approach is easy to detect: How does one go about selecting whom to study? How will you decide who counts as being a philosopher? Elsewhere I have called this the foxtrot problem: suppose you ask what the foxtrot is, and are told it is a ballroom dance and if you want to learn more about it you should watch someone actually doing it. But unless you already know what the dance is, how are you going to select whom to watch, and when? And it is not satisfactory to ask the dancers whether they (it takes two to foxtrot) are doing the foxtrot, for they may claim to be doing so but may be in error. Similarly, many people may claim to be doing philosophy, or philosophy of education, but isn't it possible that they are mistaken? (Maybe they are guilty of wishful thinking.)

Although this may seem rather fanciful, it actually is an important issue. If you were to hear the football coach (mentioned earlier) referred to as a philosopher, and as a result were to base your conception of the field on his ruminations about gridiron, you would have quite a different view of the field than if you were to base your conception on, say, the work of Ludwig Wittgenstein or Karl Popper. But even if you realized that there were the two senses of the term 'philosophy' and 'philosopher', and restricted yourself to the technical sense (according to which both Wittgenstein and Popper were philosophers, and the coach was not) the problem still does not abate. For there are remarkably different traditions in technical philosophy – one emanating by and large from the Continent, but by no means restricted to that geographical locale (see Smeyers, 1994), and another having evolved more or less in the English-speaking world, but also not restricted to there; philosophers working in either of these traditions often have little (if any) tolerance of work done in the other – so that one's choice of a philosopher to emulate will not be universally endorsed. (This can be illustrated by reference to the nomination of Jacques Derrida, the prominent French 'deconstructionist' philosopher, for an honorary degree at Cambridge in 1992. This proved to be so controversial, that after a period of heated public debate in which his philosophy was derided as a sham and as an 'anti-philosophy' philosophy, by opponents, and praised as groundbreaking by supporters, the entire faculty of the university had to vote on the matter. The honour was approved by just a small margin. Indeed all the philosophers at Cambridge, stretched end to end, could not reach an agreement!)

By way of illustration, here is a description of work within a philosophical tradition that I would probably not point to if you asked me to provide an exemplar of (technical) philosophy – not so much because I do not consider it philosophy (its concern with language and concepts, with critique of assumptions, and so on, seem to me to clearly place it within the domain of philosophy), but because it is a tradition I am not at home in, and because the way in which these concerns are pursued strikes me as sometimes being problematic:

> As a general trend, poststructuralism highlights the centrality of language to human activity and culture – its materiality, its linguisticality, and its pervasive ideological nature. Poststructuralism emphasizes the self-undermining and self-deconstructing character of discourse ... . Above all, it provides new practices of 'reading' – both texts and text analogues – and new and experimental forms of 'writing'. [It] ... offers a range of *theories* (of the text), *critiques* (of institutions), *new concepts*, and *new forms of analysis* (of power) ... . (Peters and Burbules, 2004, p. 5)

Despite the force of the discussion above (which, incidentally, is itself an example of a philosopher's mind at work), this chapter needs to start somewhere. So in the following I focus on the technical sense of the term 'philosophy' and its cognates, and I give my personal account of what philosophical work entails – but it is an account that I can (and will) support with references to the technical literature. (It will be obvious that I am firmly based in the broad English-speaking tradition mentioned above – although I would probably have voted, with reservations, for Derrida being given that honorary degree. Other views about the nature of philosophy and philosophy of education, no doubt, will be found lurking behind some of the other chapters in this volume.) So, with preliminaries behind us, it is time to throw as much light as possible on philosophy, and philosophy of education.

BRIEF INTRODUCTORY EXAMPLES

Because discussions of the different intellectual traditions within the domain of philosophy run the risk of becoming quite rarified, it seems a counsel of wisdom to start with some concrete examples (all of which shall be educationally relevant, and all of which I will eventually clarify enough to assure the reader that I have dodged the 'foxtrot problem'). While they will of necessity be developed only briefly (some will be dealt with in a more satisfactory way in subsequent chapters), they will be adequate enough for me to draw upon by way of illustration of the points that I will make later on about the scope of the philosophical terrain. And the reader should be warned that at least one of these examples will appear at first to be quite puzzling – but, after all, we are entering a puzzling domain.

Constructivism

Many curriculum experts, especially in the fields of science and mathematics education, together with individuals involved in teacher training and along with large numbers of teachers themselves, subscribe to a perspective on learning and teaching that they call *constructivism*. The so-called 'radical constructivism' promulgated by Ernst von Glasersfeld has been particularly influential (Glasersfeld, 1995, 2007), but it is pertinent to note that the education journals of the last two decades contain a staggering number – many thousands – of citations pertaining to the broad constructivist perspective that includes his work but much else besides. The problem that has arisen over time is this: no clear account has emerged of the essentials of this position, and it was difficult to determine what an individual was committed to in virtue of being identified as 'a constructivist'. Indeed, the situation was such that 'there is a very broad and loose sense in which all of us these days are constructivists' (Phillips, 1995, reprinted in Curren, 2007, p. 399).

The common element in all forms of constructivism is that knowledge is not found or discovered but rather is made or constructed by humans; however, this formulation papers over a number of complex issues, and it has been interpreted in different ways by different groups of constructivists. An important early statement that appears to embody this position was published by Immanuel Kant (1781), but it is noteworthy that he wrote a long, abstract book in his attempt to deal with some of these embedded complexities:

> But though all of our knowledge begins with experience, it does not follow that it all arises out of experience. For it may well be that even our empirical knowledge is made up of what we receive through impressions and of what our own faculty of knowledge ... supplies from itself. (Kant, 1959, p. 29)

Some interesting issues arise here: If much (all?) of our knowledge is built up from our own faculty or capacity for knowledge-construction, is it credible to believe that what we construct is in some way isomorphic or in correspondence with the 'reality' that exists in the universe outside of ourselves? Furthermore, if the knowledge that each of us possesses has been built by ourselves, is there any assurance that the knowledge I have constructed is identical with, or compatible with, the knowledge that you have constructed? And is there any guarantee that the knowledge a student constructs is the same as the knowledge the teacher has constructed? Perhaps everyone in a classroom (teacher and each of the individual students) inhabits a world constructed by themselves, with no genuine contact possible with the worlds of others – a scenario that constructivist teachers apparently take quite seriously, but which several philosophers have shown to be an untenable holdover from seventeenth-century epistemology (theory of knowledge).

In addition to the issues above, the recent lively discourse over modern forms of constructivism allowed several quite different theses to become entangled, leading to a great deal of confusion until some analytic work by philosophers came to the rescue. (The following account is based upon Phillips, 1995/2007, 2000.) In the first place, when it is said that humans construct their own knowledge, one or other or both of two quite different processes might be the focus of attention:

1   The individual learner or knower constructing his or her cognitive understandings of the material being learned or of the stimuli being received; for the purposes of discussion, this has been labelled the 'individual psychology' focus of constructivism.
2   The construction of the publicly available disciplines or bodies of knowledge – such things as physics, biology, history, and economics; these are human constructions to the development of which many individuals have contributed throughout the course of human intellectual history. This has been labelled the 'public disciplines' focus.

This distinction paves the way for further clarification, for it becomes apparent that in discussions of each of these quite different processes there have been scholars who stressed the role of individual constructive activity, while there have been others who stressed that the activity of individuals is influenced by social or communal forces. (There has been a confusing tendency to treat individual construction of understanding in individualistic terms, and construction of bodies of knowledge in social–communal terms.) Consider, as an example, the 'individual psychology' focus. The great developmental psychologist Jean Piaget was (among other things) interested in how individual learners develop logical principles and construct bodies of knowledge about their environment; almost all of his attention was on the young, individual inquirer and what was happening within his or her cognitive apparatus – his model often seemed to be the young inquirer engaged in a solitary struggle to achieve understanding. The social psychologist Lev Vygotsky was also interested in how individuals construct their understanding of the world around them, but he stressed the role played by social mechanisms in fostering this individual learning. Turning to the second broad focus – the development of the public disciplines – a similar distinction can be drawn, for there have been some scholars who focused on the contributions of individual inquirers while others have focused on the social construction of knowledge, i.e., upon the social or communal processes and forces that have shaped the public disciplines.

One of several consequences of accepting these distinctions is that it is clear now that the frequently used expression – 'the social construction of knowledge' – is misleading if left unmodified, for there are scholars in both the 'individual psychology' and 'public disciplines' camps who stress the importance of social processes.

Explaining human actions: behaviour versus states of mind

The Harvard psychologist B.F. Skinner (1904–1990) was something of a 'Renaissance man'; in addition to being one of the two or three major figures in the development of the position known as 'behaviourism' during the twentieth century, he was a gifted author (see his novel *Walden Two*, first published in 1948 [Skinner, 1962], and his multi-volume autobiography), a fearsome controversialist, an iconoclast with respect to the nature of scientific inquiry, and he had a capacity for seeing the deeper social and theoretical implications of his orientation towards psychology.

Skinner's behaviourist psychology was inspired in part by the (apparent) headway psychologists were making in the study of animal behaviour, where of course only observational and experimental methods were feasible (animals cannot be interviewed!); but in addition his work was shaped by his strongly held views about the nature of science, which in turn had been shaped by the logical positivist philosophy that was influential in the USA and elsewhere at the time he was a graduate student. (Most of the central figures in the development of logical positivism originally came from backgrounds in the sciences or mathematics or logic.) This philosophical position was hostile towards metaphysics, on the grounds that if a concept could not be defined in observational or behavioural terms then it was meaningless. Thus, for example, in the view of logical positivists the metaphysical concept 'soul' is meaningless, for it cannot be defined observationally – which means that there is no evidence available to settle a dispute between a person who claims all humans (and only humans) have a soul, and on the other hand a person who believes that there is no such entity; put another way, there is no way in which truth can be distinguished from error in metaphysics. The logical positivists would acknowledge that metaphysical terms like 'soul' may have an 'emotive' meaning, but they have no substantive meaning – they are meaningless noises.

Skinner applied this perspective to the study of human behaviour, especially to inquiries directed at discovering the causes of what people do; he argued that a science of behaviour was possible, if it were based on observing both the behaviour itself and the conditions under which it occurs (such things as the reinforcing or dampening effect of the consequences of behaviour). Such a science would entail moving beyond 'pre-scientific' ways of explaining behaviour in terms of unseen (and un-seeable) internal states or events such as desires or feelings; he had harsh things to say about these supposed 'psychic inner causes' that were attributable to the actions of a psychic or mental inner agent that each of us harbours (and which he called 'autonomous man'; see Skinner, 1972, Ch. 9). In his classic book *Science and Human Behaviour* (1953) he wrote:

> The inner man is regarded as driving the body very much as the man at the steering wheel drives a car. The inner man wills an action, the outer executes it. The inner loses his appetite, the outer stops eating … . The inner has the impulse which the outer obeys … . The inner man is sometimes personified clearly, as when delinquent behaviour is attributed to a 'disordered personality,' or he may be dealt with in fragments, as when behaviour is attributed to mental processes, faculties, and traits. (Skinner, 1953, p. 29)

The 'experimental analysis of behaviour' now makes it possible for us to abandon these unproductive ways of explaining human behaviour that are carry-overs from the past; we can move (as the title of one of his later books puts it) 'beyond freedom and dignity' (beyond, that is, using these concepts in an explanation of human behaviours). The following is typical of his analyses:

> Man's struggle for freedom is not due to a will to be free, but to certain behavioural pro-cesses characteristic of the human organism, the chief effect of which is the avoidance of or escape from so-called aversive features of the environment. (Skinner, 1972, p. 42)

Behaviourism has had a pronounced impact on educational practice. It is of course common for teachers and parents to reinforce such things as giving correct responses to questions, and the following of commands or directives – the reinforcing agent (reward) may be praise, special classroom privileges, the awarding of 'gold stars', the receiving of an 'A' grade; and the attempt also is made to extinguish or at least lower the frequency of disruptive or uncooperative behaviour, by the use of negative reinforcement or punishment. The programmed instruction and teaching machines of some decades ago worked on Skinnerian principles, in that correct responses to questions were acknowledged and praised virtually instantly. Many elements of behaviourism are still to be found in the work of some contemporary educational researchers, who 'operationally define' their concepts (that is, define them in observable terms), and who use so-called 'objective measures' that they believe do not rely on making judgments about the subjective beliefs and commitments of those who are being studied.

'Education according to nature', and the progressive movement

On a hot summer day in 1749, Jean-Jacques Rousseau was walking to visit the philosopher Diderot (who was in detention), when, in a newspaper he was browsing through to pass the time on the way, he came across the announcement of an essay competition being held by the Dijon Academy. The topic: 'Has the progress of the sciences and arts done more to corrupt morals or improve them?' Rousseau was overcome; he 'beheld another universe', and descended into 'a state of agitation bordering on delirium' (Rousseau, 1781/1953, p. 328). In a letter to a correspondent he said he collapsed under a tree, and wept uncontrollably. For it had suddenly become clear to him that – contrary to popular opinion – progress in these fields contributes nothing to human virtue or happiness, but was a source of corruption or distortion. He realized that the arts and sciences served to mask or suppress man's natural proclivities instead of allowing them to follow the path to unhindered expression, an insight that he modelled with his romantic abandonment to his (natural) emotions under that tree! To his surprise he won the first prize, and became famous – and with this recognition there started 'the long chain of my misfortunes' (Rousseau, 1953, p. 326). He was – at least as he depicted himself in his autobiography – the epitome of a tragic, Romantic hero. Little did he know that one of the several books and essays in which he developed this summer insight would come to be regarded as a master-piece of philosophy of education, that because of it he would be known as the 'liberator of the child', and that the book would be burned by the public hangman and banned in many places in Europe.

The book in question, *Emile, or On Education* (1762), was a novel that depicted episodes in the life of the hero from his infancy until he reached manhood and started a family. The theme is announced in the memorable opening sentences:

> God makes all things good; man meddles with them and they become evil. He forces one soil to yield the products of another, one tree to bear another's fruit. He confuses and confounds time, place, and natural conditions. He mutilates his dog, his horse, and his slave. He destroys and defaces all things; he loves all that is deformed and monstrous; he will have nothing as nature made it, not even man himself, who must learn his paces like a saddle horse, and be shaped to his master's taste like the trees in his garden. (Rousseau, 1955, p. 5)

Because society harbours the arts and the sciences, as well as social conventions and the like, and because these things swamp or distort the child's natural tendencies, the educator has a forced choice – either the man can be educated (that is, the person as he naturally is), or the citizen (the man who lives in, and is shaped by, his society). Rousseau wrote that 'harmony becomes impossible. Forced to combat either nature or society, you must make your choice … you cannot train both'. (Rousseau, 1955, p. 7)

Emile's parents allow the child to be taken by a tutor (who of course has the wisdom of Rousseau himself) to the family's country estate, where unencumbered by the forces of civilized society, his natural tendencies are allowed to express themselves. Emile learns to read when he desires to learn (he has a party invitation to read, for example) – and because he wants to acquire this skill, it comes easily; he learns other subjects when the local environment triggers an appropriate interest; he acquires a moral code by suffering the natural consequences of his actions (if he lies, people on the estate start to mistrust him); and he acquires some religious understanding not by reading the Good Book but by studying the 'book of nature' (and also via a lengthy conversation with a 'Savoyard Priest' he meets while rambling through the countryside). It was the de-emphasis on Scripture, and on the formal teachings of the Church, that was in part responsible for the suppression of the novel in many places. In short, Emile learns from *things*, not from books – indeed, the only book available for him to read for several years is (on reflection, no surprise) *Robinson Crusoe*; this is, of course, the account of a resourceful man alone on an island learning to thrive without the trappings of civilization – or so it might seem.

Later in the novel Emile meets his soul mate, Sophy, whose education Rousseau also sketches; compared to Rousseau's forward-looking account of Emile's education, the path he lays down for Sophy is truly astounding. The sense can be conveyed in just a few words: '… it follows that woman is specially made for man's delight … she ought to make herself pleasing in his eyes and not provoke him to anger; her strength is in her charms … .' (p. 322)

In Rousseau's time there were some disastrous attempts to use *Emile* as an educational blueprint, but the author was disdainful – the novel was intended to be a graphic presentation of the principles that should be at work in education, and clearly was not a practical handbook. But over many decades the idea of 'education according to nature' flourished and became one of the central themes of the progressive education movement of the late nineteenth and twentieth centuries. Rousseau's ideas influenced the educational philosophy of the great American philosopher and educationist John Dewey; and left their imprint on the famous British 'free school' *Summerhill*. The founder and principal of this school, A.S. Neill, claimed in 1960 that he had never read Rousseau; but nevertheless he was working and reading and discussing education in contexts where Rousseau's ideas were well-known – intellectual influence can be real but indirect. The following passage reveals clearly enough Neill's use of Rousseau's ideas, even if he did not get them directly from J-J. himself:

> When my first wife and I began the school, we had one main idea: *to make the school fit the child* – instead of making the child fit the school … . We set out to make a school in which we should allow children freedom to be themselves. In order to do this, we had to renounce all discipline, all direction, all suggestion, all moral training, all religious training. (Neill, 1960, p. 4)

DIFFERENT CONCEPTIONS OF PHILOSOPHY

With the background now in place, the discussion can return to the long-delayed main issue: What is philosophy, and – in the light of answers to that question – what is philosophy of education? There are a number of different ways of describing the work of philosophers, and these can be illustrated by reference to the three examples discussed above. And just as several *different* but not *incompatible* descriptions can be given of some event (a political rally, for example) because they focus on different aspects, so it is with the descriptions or accounts of philosophy given below.

(1) The discussion should start with what probably was the most puzzling example, namely the second; for B.F. Skinner was a major psychologist, and although he was a Harvard man (and therefore well-rounded) he nevertheless did not hold an appointment in the Philosophy Department. So why does he appear as an example? Simply because there is an important conception of philosophy according to which he was, indeed, doing philosophy in at least the two books of his that were cited above.

Consider a group of scholars doing research or otherwise practicing within their specialized field – perhaps they are economists, or physicists, or historians, or teachers of mathematics, or artists. The bulk of the scholarly interactions between them, that in some cases may lead to breakthroughs or discoveries that enhance that field, may be considered as 'level one' or 'object-level' discourse. Thus, the discourse of physicists at this level might contain references to temperature, pressure, Brownian motion, molecules, velocity of light, simultaneity of events, the ether, universal gravitation, and so on; and to the laws or theories that link some of these things; and to experiments or observations involving these and other physical entities and quantities. Philosophers who work in these domains – philosophers of science, of economics, of mathematics, of history, and so on – are not making substantive contributions to the discourse at the object level between the practitioners of that field (for, to stick with the same example, philosophers of physics are philosophers, not physicists); instead, to use rather fanciful language, they are at a 'higher' or more abstract level, and are gazing down at the level one or object-level discourse between the practitioners, and are raising questions or problems about this discourse. In brief, they are working at a *meta-level*, and are raising *meta-questions* about the object level of the domain they are studying. Thus, philosophers of physics might discuss such questions as

'What do physicists mean, in their object-level discourse, when they say two events are simultaneous – and how do they ascertain this?'
'In studying the gravitational forces existing between two astronomical entities, what assumptions are being made about the nature of the space between these objects? Is it assumed that this space is Euclidean?'
'Is the so-called string theory that is advocated by some physicists in any conceivable way testable? And if not, is it a metaphysical theory rather than a scientific one?'
'Even in their most abstract theories, physicists postulate the existence of entities of various kinds; in what sense (or senses) can it be supposed that such entities are "real", or are they just "convenient fictions"?'

This account of philosophers working at a meta-level applies to many, but perhaps not to all; certainly most philosophy departments these days (at least in the English-speaking world) have some members who are philosophers of science, or of mathematics, or of social science, and so on, who analyze, clarify, or otherwise ruminate upon discourse at the object-level in their respective fields. The crucial point that needs to be stressed, however, is that some leading scholars/ researchers in these disciplines – like Skinner, for example – also on occasion ascend from the object-level to the meta-level, and look 'down' and reflect on the very same kinds of issues that philosophers cogitate about. (In fact, it might be the case that it is *because* these individuals can distance themselves somewhat from the object-level in order to reflect upon it, that they *are* 'leading scholars' in their fields.) In physics, it seems incontrovertible that Newton and Einstein sometimes operated at a meta-level. In a sense, then, at the meta-level the distinction between 'philosophers of field X' and 'practitioners or researchers in field X' tends to fade. In this context it is interesting to note that Blackwell's *A Companion to the Philosophy of Science* (Newton-Smith, 2000) – a reputable reference book in philosophy – contains essays on the scientists Bohr, Darwin, Einstein, Galileo, Leibniz, Mach, Newton, and Whewell, and many others are referenced in the index.

So, to return to Skinner: it should now be obvious that I am suggesting he was raising meta-questions about the field of 'explanation of human behaviour'. Looking down on this field, he was convinced that he saw behaviour being investigated in terms of metaphysical entities like 'interests', 'desires', 'inner drives', 'autonomy', and so forth, and he was pointing out that there was no apparent way to confirm or disconfirm accounts that were given in terms of such unobservables. Skinner was doing meta-psychology, and at the same time he was doing philosophy. And, in the opinion of this author, he was doing it all very creditably – although I judge him in the end to have been quite wrong. (For what it is worth, I should point out that the Blackwell volume on philosophy of science mentioned above contains a brief positive comment about one aspect of Skinner's negative position on the issue of intentions being used for prediction and explanation of behaviour – so he *must* have been doing philosophy!)

There is a little more to say about Skinner, and the discussion will return to him in due course. Before moving on, however, it might be as well to restate as pithily as possible the two points about philosophy that have been made above – first, much philosophical activity takes place at the meta-level, where issues are raised (and sometimes dealt with) about the object-level; and secondly, a few scholars in a field from time to time adopt a vantage point where they, too, focus on meta-issues about their field – and to the extent that they do this, they can be regarded as doing philosophy.

(2) There is a completely different way of thinking about philosophy, one that focuses upon the type of work that is done (whether at the meta-level or not). The account above left this issue vague. (To say that I have a perch from which I can look down and ask questions or make comments about what my neighbours are doing in their backyards, is – perhaps – to say that I am making meta-comments, but it is completely uninformative about *what kind of questions* or comments I am generating.)

The distinguished moral philosopher William Frankena (a former president of the American Philosophical Association, who also had a strong interest in philosophy of education), identified three types of activity one or more of which philosophers have traditionally pursued:

> Looking back over its history, it appears that philosophy has done three sorts of things. It has sought to work out a conception of the universe as a whole in all of its aspects, and of man's place in it. In this endeavour it has been synthetic … . [Also] philosophers have sought to afford some wisdom in the conduct of human affairs. That is, they have tried to provide … a guide to action … by discovering and formulating goals, norms or standards … . [Third] philosophers have often been engaged in a less exciting but still essential kind of enquiry – analysis or criticism. This includes a critical evaluation of the assumptions and methods used by philosophers, as well as by scientists and common sense people … . (Frankena, in Lucas, 1969, p. 287)

These three activities may be labelled speculative/metaphysical (I have taken the liberty here of adding the second term to Frankena's label), normative, and analytical. And of course they are not entirely discrete. To consider a simple case, if you are going to be normative and provide a guide for action for your friends, this guide will need to be backed-up by something, for those who are receiving guidance no doubt will be anxious to know what gives *you* the right to tell them how to live; often the guidance you (as a philosopher) will provide is derived in some way from, and is warranted or justified by, the analytic or speculative/metaphysical work that you have done. It is worth pointing to the parallel here with parenting: for of course parents are frequently normative when dealing with their children, not only putting forward guidelines but also insisting that these be followed. And at least some parents have warrants or groundings for their normative demands – these are not mere whims, but gain support from such things as the parents' depth of experience of life, from their years of study and reflection, or from their social and religious convictions.

Frankena's typology can be illustrated by reference to the cases presented earlier. The first of those, concerning constructivism, was intended to demonstrate that careful analytic work can contribute to the work of scholars or researchers or practitioners by making clear that the important if not revolutionary position that they were pursuing was in fact an amalgam of several quite different positions that needed to be distinguished and treated separately. (Whether or not this example also illustrates Frankena's point that analytic work is 'less exciting' I will leave to the reader to decide.)

Turning to Rousseau, it is apparent that *Emile* is packed with normative advice about what to do and what not to do in child-rearing, and about what the aims of the educational process ought to be. Thus: do not interfere with or suppress the natural tendencies of the child; only teach something when the child is ready to learn it; do not make book-learning the dominant mode of education for a youngster; let the child primarily learn from 'things'; do not treat the acquisition of moral knowledge differently from the acquisition of other types of knowledge; and so forth. And what justified or warranted or served as the grounding for this advice? Simply, it was Rousseau's speculative/metaphysical theory that 'what is natural is good' – the theory so beautifully summarized in his novel's opening lines. But it is also noteworthy that Rousseau was not a rigorous thinker, in the sense that careful analytic work, avoidance of contradictions, and so forth, was not the way he approached the development of his ideas – this one in particular. Thus, the pioneer of modern analytic philosophy of education, C.D. Hardie, in a monograph first published in 1941, had a 'field day' teasing apart the various things that might have been meant by 'education according to nature', and showing that each of these was indefensible (see Hardie, 1941/1962, Ch. 1).

Skinner's work also had strong normative elements. He had decided views about the nature of scientific investigation – views that, apparently, were derived from the analyses of the logical positivists; and he stressed time and again that when studying humans or animals, the only focus was what was observable, namely behaviour and its consequences. This position was grounded in his analytic work, wherein he showed (at least to his own satisfaction), that explanation of behaviour in terms of inner processes and entities was meaningless.

An interesting philosophical meta-question arises here about Skinner's vehement rejection of metaphysics, with its associated claim that certain commonly referred to entities were in fact non-existent and that explanations that made reference to them were at best vacuous and at worse meaningless. Was this far-reaching position *itself* a type of metaphysical theory? And whether or not he was doing metaphysics, he certainly was being speculative in Frankena's sense of the term.

In his novel *Walden Two* he gave an account of a utopian society that was organized entirely on behaviourist psychological principles. He showed how a society that ran on these principles would allow individual citizens to pursue goals of
their own choosing, and the format of the novel allowed him to answer sceptical
questions asked by an 'outsider'. (If Rousseau is to count as a philosopher
because of *Emile*, in addition to his other writings, then Skinner must also count
because of *Walden Two* – not to mention his other work!)

(3) Finally, there is a way of describing philosophy that will be familiar to anyone
who has ever glanced at the catalogue of an academic publisher, or at a listing of
courses in a university Department of Philosophy; in general it cuts across or is
orthogonal to the tripartite division of philosophical activities described in the
section above, although there is some overlap with both it and with the depiction
of philosophy given in Section (1). The focus here is not *the type of activity*
(metaphysical/speculative, normative, or analytical), or the *level* (meta-level
versus object-level), but *the domain* in which these philosophical activities are
being pursued – are questions or issues about knowledge the focus, or morality
and ethics, or beauty, or citizenship and individual and group rights in a pluralistic society ... . The well-regarded Blackwell reference series 'Companions to
Philosophy' is organized in this way. There are separate volumes on, among
others, epistemology, ethics, aesthetics, political philosophy, philosophy of mind,
metaphysics, logic, philosophy of science, philosophy of language, philosophy
of religion, feminist philosophy, and cognitive science.

Once again the three examples discussed earlier can provide some enlightenment.
First, constructivism is a (confused) set of views about human knowledge – the
main concern of which is the ways in which it is built up, but many constructivists
also address the issue of whether the beliefs that are constructed (by whatever
means) are appropriately classified as being 'true'. (To use the word 'knowledge'
is to imply that the beliefs in question *are* true.) So probably the best way to classify philosophical (and analytic) discussions of constructivism is under the rubric
of *epistemology*. Secondly, the ambit of Skinner's work was so broad that different parts of it can be classified in different ways. His views on how research
should be pursued in psychology clearly fit under *philosophy of science* (and even
more precisely the sub-field of *philosophy of social and behavioural science*), and
his attacks on mental entities such as the 'autonomous man' and the 'inner homun-
culus' fit squarely with topics discussed within the field of *philosophy of mind*,
and even within *metaphysics*. Finally, *Emile* – with its devastating analysis of the
source of social problems, with its negative evaluation of the impact of progress
in the sciences on life in modern societies, and with its suggested solutions – is
recognized to be an important work in *political philosophy*.

AN IMPORTANT QUALIFICATION

Before turning – at last! – to philosophy of education, it is important to stress
once again that the three ways of describing the nature of philosophy that were

discussed above are not mutually exclusive. (More than one way of describing a field can be valid.) Thus, a philosopher of science might be doing meta-level work in that domain, but he or she might also (and at the very same moment) be doing analytic work – the point of which is to clarify some issues about, say, how knowledge claims are warranted or supported within this field (which is an epistemological issue); and the philosopher might hope that on the basis of this analysis some normative advice could be given to practicing scientists about their knowledge-testing procedures. With only slight hyperbole it might be said that the philosopher is like a hunter, who – armed with a variety of skills – refuses to be fenced in by arbitrary boundaries, but roams at will, seeking challenging game wherever the spoor may lead!

SO, WHAT IS PHILOSOPHY OF EDUCATION?

In the light of the preceding accounts of the nature of philosophy, it seems natural to conclude that philosophy of education is a domain of activity roughly comparable to philosophy of science or political philosophy. (Clearly the editors of Blackwell's philosophical companions, referred to above, have this view, for they recently added 'philosophy of education' to their series; see Curren, 2003.) But this does not seem adequate; the field of education is so broad and complex, and is intertwined with so many other aspects of society, and is of such fundamental social importance, that the direction philosophical work can take is almost limitless. My (speculative) suggestion is that as a field philosophy of education is on a par in complexity not with any one branch of philosophy, but with the *whole field* of philosophy.

Thus, within the domain of philosophy of education the whole range of activities outlined in the course of this chapter can be found. Some philosophers of education – and some educational researchers, curriculum theorists and others – ask meta-questions and pursue meta-issues (arising from the object-level interactions and discourse between educational researchers, or between teachers and principals, or between a teacher and a group of learners); some do normative work (about the aims of education, about how children ought to be treated, about the kind of just society we ought to be striving to bring about – using education as the means); some pursue issues that are epistemological (what knowledge should be taught in schools, and how much of the justification or warrants for this knowledge should be taught; is there a place in the curriculum for bodies of belief that are not well-established enough to be regarded as knowledge; are the warrants that researchers in, say, educational psychology offer for their purported discoveries in fact adequate); some work on issues that also are central in political philosophy (what rights to an education do children possess; if the interests of the developing child come into conflict with the rights of the parents to 'control' the education of their children – assuming there is such a right – then whose rights and interests should prevail; can a child develop personal autonomy and at the same time become incorporated into a community of faith); and yet other philosophers of education focus on ethical issues (classroom interactions between teacher and students, and between students themselves; treatment of individuals who are 'research subjects').

In the opening paragraph several different possibilities were identified that might lie behind the question 'What is philosophy of education?' If a dictionary-type definition was being sought, then the following is probably circular enough to satisfy everyone: 'Philosophy of education is a field where philosophical inquiry is pursued that focuses upon issues arising within the domain of education'. If what was wanted was an account of what (collectively) philosophers of education do, then the summary in the paragraph above is my best shot. If what was desired was an example of a philosopher of education at work, then (hesitantly) I offer this whole chapter. But, finally, perhaps the concern lying behind the 'What is?' question was 'Why does philosophy of education (as so-described) matter?' To ask this is tantamount to asking why it is important – to be reflective about our practices, to avoid inconsistencies in our beliefs, to be aware of what we are committed to as a consequence of holding the principles we claim to hold, and to expand our horizon of possibilities by considering alternative goals and ideals that might never have occurred to us were it not for the work of some philosopher of education. If none of these reasons is persuasive, then I am afraid you have purchased the wrong book!

REFERENCES

Curren, R. (2003) (Ed.) *A Companion to the Philosophy of Education*. Oxford: Blackwell.
Curren, R. (2007) (Ed.) *Philosophy of Education: An Anthology*. Oxford: Blackwell.
Frankena, W. (1969) Toward a philosophy of the philosophy of education. Reprinted in C. Lucas (Ed.), *What is Philosophy of Education?* Toronto: Macmillan, pp. 286–91.
Glasersfeld, E. von. (1995) *Radical Constructivism: A Way of Knowing and Learning*. London: Falmer Press.
Glasersfeld, E. von. (2007) (Ed.) *Key Works in Radical Constructivism*. [(Ed.)] Mary Larochelle. Rotterdam: Sense Publishers.
Hardie, C. (1962) *Truth and Fallacy in Educational Theory*. New York: Teachers College Bureau of Publications.
Kant, I. (1959) *Critique of Pure Reason*. London: Dent/Everyman.
Lucas, C. (1969) (Ed.) *What is Philosophy of Education?* Toronto: Macmillan.
Neill, A. (1960) *Summerhill: A Radical Approach to Child Rearing*. New York: Hart.
Newton-Smith, W. (2000) (Ed.) *A Companion to the Philosophy of Science*. Oxford: Blackwell.
Peters, M. and Burbules, N. (2004) *Poststructuralism and Educational Research*. Lanham, MD: Rowman and Littlefield.
Phillips, D. (1985) Philosophy of education. In T. Husen and N. Postlethwaite (Eds), *International Encyclopedia of Education*. Oxford: Pergamon.
Phillips, D. (2000) (Ed.) *Constructivism in Education: Opinions and Second Opinions on Controversial Issues*. 99th Yearbook of the NSSE. Chicago: University of Chicago Press.
Phillips, D. (2007) The good, the bad, and the ugly: the many faces of constructivism. Reprinted in R. Curren (Ed.), *Philosophy of Education: An Anthology*. Oxford: Blackwell, pp. 398–409.
Rousseau, J-J. (1953) *The Confessions of Jean-Jacques Rousseau*. (trans.) J. Cohen. London: Penguin Books.

Rousseau, J-J. (1955) *Emile*. (trans. B. Foxley). London: Dent/Everyman.

Skinner, B. (1953) *Science and Human Behaviour*. New York: Free Press.

Skinner, B. (1962) *Walden Two*. New York: Macmillan.

Skinner, B. (1972) *Beyond Freedom and Dignity*. London: Jonathan Cape.

Smeyers, P. (1994) Philosophy of education: Western European perspectives. In T. Husen and N. Postlethwaite (Eds), *The International Encyclopedia of Education*, 2nd edition. Oxford: Pergamon, pp. 4456–61.

2

Schools of Thought in Philosophy of Education

Robin Barrow

SOME DIFFERENT APPROACHES TO TEACHING PHILOSOPHY OF EDUCATION

There are a number of ways in which the field of philosophy of education might be organized, whether for purposes of study or teaching. For example, one might study prominent philosophers who have something to say relevant to education, in their historical order (e.g., Plato, Rousseau); one might study prominent educational thinkers, whether philosophers or not, in a philosophical manner (e.g., Pestalozzi, Freire); or one might focus on particular branches of philosophy and their implications for education (e.g., moral philosophy and moral education, philosophy of science and science teaching). Some argue that, ideally, philosophy of education should involve a systematic inquiry into ultimate questions about the nature of being or existence (metaphysics), allied to a theory of knowledge or what can be known (epistemology) and concern for questions of value of various kinds, be it moral, aesthetic, economic, etc. (axiology), which in practice makes philosophy of education barely distinguishable from philosophy generally. By contrast some would focus more on specific contemporary educational issues that give rise to the philosophical questions (e.g., Is a policy of inclusion educationally desirable? Is it morally required? What is the relationship between a moral and an educational imperative?). And then again, there is the view that we should concentrate on examining key educational concepts in a critical manner (e.g., What is it to be educated? What is the nature of knowledge? What is worth knowing?).

One approach, particularly popular in the United States in the mid-twentieth century, and still widespread, is one that is based on what are commonly referred to as 'schools of thought' or, sometimes, more colloquially, 'isms', such as Idealism and Realism.[1] There are problems, to which we shall return below, in differentiating between a school of thought and a specific philosophical doctrine, theory, or method, in differentiating between a school of thought and an ideology, in distinguishing between logically distinct kinds of –ism or school of thought, and in separating specifically philosophical and broader educational perspectives. The difficulty of making such distinctions in a clear and consistent way has led to a variety of textbooks and syllabi that contain rather different lists of 'schools of thought'. Sometimes, of course, this is simply a matter of judgment and selection. But sometimes it is a result of confusion over what exactly constitutes a school of thought.

Nonetheless, there are certain schools of thought that are more or less invariably referred to, and these would include Idealism, Realism, Naturalism and Pragmatism. Further distinctions may be made within these categories, as between, e.g., Idealism and Religious Idealism or Realism and Theistic Realism (sometimes referred to as Thomist Realism, after Thomas Aquinas). There may also be a place for more contemporary 'isms' or schools of thought, such as Marxism, Existentialism, Postmodernism, or, more specifically, Phenomenology and Hermeneutics. Less common, but still to be noted, are Reconstructionism, Behaviourism, and variants of Eastern Philosophy.

Importantly, the quite common practice of including Philosophical Analysis as a distinct school of thought should be noted. For nothing pinpoints the problematic nature of such listings more clearly than the inclusion of Philosophical Analysis under the general heading of 'Schools of Thought'. Whatever else is to be said, it is apparent (as will be discussed more fully below) that Philosophical Analysis, even if it refers to a particular kind of analytic approach, is not the same kind of thing as Realism (Naturalism, Idealism, etc.): the former may be based upon certain beliefs, but it is in itself nothing more than a view of the task to be undertaken (namely, analyzing concepts), while Realism embodies a set of substantive beliefs about the nature of things and has nothing to say directly about the philosopher's method. Thus, Philosophical Analysis and Realism are not distinct or competing schools of thought; rather, if 'school of thought' is to mean anything, it is incorrect to refer to them both as schools of thought.

For those readers who are as yet unfamiliar with some of the schools of thought mentioned, it is perhaps worth stressing the two fundamental general points asserted here and to be discussed more fully below: first, the various 'isms' or schools of thought that are commonly listed alongside one another as if they were all essentially different species of the same genus are in fact sometimes of a quite different genus; that is to say, they are not simply different organizations of thought but different kinds of ways in which to organize thought. Secondly, and in particular, it will be argued that Philosophical Analysis is not a school of thought or an 'ism' that is in any significant way parallel to or of the same kind as, say, Realism or Idealism.

Finally, by way of introduction, it should be noted that my argument in this chapter is overall rather critical of the 'schools of thought' approach. That being so, I should acknowledge at the outset that a study of various 'isms' or schools of thought can clearly have some advantages. To these we now turn.

SOME SPECIFIC SCHOOLS OF THOUGHT AND THE ADVANTAGES OF TEACHING THEM

The school of thought approach to philosophy of education does have certain advantages, particularly when the focus is on reasonably familiar schools. Idealism, for example, referring essentially and paradigmatically to the Platonic view that reality resides in ideas or in the mind, rather than in the material world and physical sense perceptions, introduces us to both the beginning of systematically recorded Western philosophy and a viewpoint that in one form or another has persisted strongly to the present day. To introduce Idealism is to introduce a central and hugely influential part of Plato's philosophy; to study it is to come to grips with a powerful and enduring philosophical 'ism'. It is also to approach a set of questions that ultimately any philosophy of education should face: What is the nature of reality? What is truth? In what does true knowledge consist?

Likewise Realism, construed as the view that it is the material world that is real and our sense perceptions that are primary, the antithesis of Idealism, has had and continues to have a wide following, and should obviously be given consideration alongside Idealism, if our object is to take the question of reality, truth and knowledge seriously.

There is also value in the historical story that is generally associated with the schools of thought approach. Though Realism can be associated with, for example, John Locke, it is often introduced by reference to Aristotle and his emphasis on empirical observation and deducing general laws from study of particulars, while making various specific criticisms of Plato's Theory of Ideas (or Forms). And there is something to be said for recognizing that philosophical viewpoints as much as anything else often develop out of and in reaction to the past. Thus, it is interesting to consider the emergence of Religious Idealism as a result of the development of Plato's philosophy in the work of Christian Neo-Platonists and the towering figure of St. Augustine. Similarly, we see the emergence of Religious Realism, as individuals such as Thomas Aquinas develop an Aristotelian viewpoint through the prism of Christianity.

The views of Jean-Jacques Rousseau represent something of an historical shift, for the Naturalist school of thought is associated with his thesis that truth and goodness are to be discerned in a state of nature or by growing up in a natural environment. In principle, of course (and we shall return to this), one could hold this view while being either an Idealist or a Realist, since Rousseau does not present his argument as an argument about the nature of reality or even knowledge; his focus is rather on the claim that a certain kind of upbringing will lead to a certain kind of knowledge, awareness and character. In other words his *Emile* (a book named after its central character, whose upbringing is described in detail) is an educational thesis, with implications about knowledge and truth, whereas Plato's Theory of Ideas is an epistemological thesis, perhaps with implications for education (see below). Just as there is an undoubted need for the philosopher of education to think about reality and truth, so it is important to think about nature, which is widely recognized as one of the most elusive of concepts. (Incidentally, though logical connections can be made, Rousseau's thesis is not directly related to his contemporary David Hume's view that no 'ought' can be derived from an 'is', nor to G.E. Moore's subsequent warnings against committing the 'naturalistic fallacy'.) (Moore, 1962, Bk 3, Part 1, Sec 1). There are, however, difficulties in working out precisely what Rousseau's various claims about 'nature' and 'natural' amount to, and also in determining just what is natural in any given sense and how it should relate to education. After all, there is at least one straightforward sense in which one could argue that education neither is nor should be natural; rather it is a process whereby one's 'nature' becomes cultured and civilized. This is not necessarily to support such a thesis; merely to recognize the complexity of the concept of nature and hence the school of Naturalism (see Ch. 7).

Pragmatism, associated particularly with philosophers at the end of the nineteenth century such as Charles Peirce, William James and John Dewey, attempts to link truth to what is useful or what yields results. This is a peculiarly American viewpoint (possibly partly the product of America's supposed frontier mentality). We are thus reminded forcibly that ideas seldom if ever emerge simply from abstract thought alone but are partly the product of circumstance. Danger lies both in ignoring that fact and equally in assuming that ideas are nothing more than the product of the times in which they are born.

Briefly, to complete initial comments on some possible schools of thought, Marxism takes the view just criticized that all ideas (including values, religious and moral beliefs) are simply the product of particular social and economic structures. To reduce a rich tradition of thought such as Marxism to such a bare summary of course runs the risk of distortion. But here we see the beginnings of one of the problems to be considered below: either hundreds of diverse Marxist intellectuals have to be classified together in terms of a lowest common denominator, or we do justice to their various differences, in which case we do not have one recognizable 'school of thought' of any significance. Existentialism may be defined, in Jean Paul Sartre's phrase, as the view that human 'existence precedes essence', or, slightly more broadly, the view that we are not given but that rather we create our own natures, characters and futures (cf. Rousseau), and therefore are ultimately responsible for being what we are; it may be further argued that this knowledge leads to feelings of futility, alienation, and angst. Postmodernism and other more contemporary 'isms' or schools of thought need to be given separate consideration (see Relativism section below), because they really do not fit the model of 'school of thought' so far discussed; however, we may generalize here by saying that they tend towards a relativistic viewpoint to the effect that knowledge in the conventional or traditional sense is not possible.

To approach the philosophy of education, then, through a study of schools of thought or the 'isms' has the advantages of introducing some major philosophical ideas in an order that reveals continuity, perhaps development. Many of the individual philosophers encountered in this approach are names of considerable philosophical importance; many of the ideas are also of central significance to philosophy; and some at least are crucial to those who wish to think about education. Those who want to study and understand education do indeed need to consider the nature of truth and knowledge, what it is to be human, what constitutes reality, what is natural in all of that word's various senses, and what aspects of nature we should be concerned about.

SOME PROBLEMS WITH THE CLASSIFICATION OF SCHOOLS OF THOUGHT

Now the problems start. The first and most obvious one, already alluded to, is that none of these schools of thought is in fact a homogeneous whole. 'Marxism' is not the only label that covers a wide variety of (sometimes incompatible) positions. One only has to review a few of the various textbooks based on the schools of thought approach to see that (1) different authors associate different schools with different philosophers and that (2) the various individuals classified under a particular 'ism' in a given book do not usually hold particularly similar, let alone identical views, and indeed are sometimes more at a variance with each other than with outsiders. (One thinks, for example, of Marxism and the battle between Trotskyites and other sub-sects, or of the tension between the pagan Realism of Aristotle and the Realism of the Christian Aquinas.) Idealism is invariably associated with Plato, but some would add reference to Bishop Berkeley, perhaps, or Kant or Hegel, not to mention a number of lesser known more contemporary figures (e.g., Herman Horne, J. Donald Butler). There is nothing wrong with grouping such individuals together for certain purposes, but they do not hold identical views, or even sometimes particularly similar views, even on the specific matter at issue, let alone in their wider philosophical position. Kant, to put it bluntly and simply, believes in something different from Plato's Theory of Ideas. Berkeley's view that 'to be is to be perceived' is not Plato's view (still less would the latter accept the 'reality' of the physical world on the grounds that it is eternally perceived by God) (Berkeley, 1934). While the notion that Hegel's epistemology is comparable to Plato's in any detailed and serious way is quite untenable. To pursue the point: surely this system of classification is suspect when one author presents Rousseau as a Pragmatist (e.g., Ozmon and Craver, 2008), another claims that his 'romantic naturalism was akin to idealism' (Neff, 1966, p. 28), and a third presents him as a representative of Naturalism (alongside Herbert Spencer who surely cannot plausibly be placed alongside Rousseau either philosophically or educationally) (Gutek, 1988). Such divergent and disparate classifications can be made and such incongruous bedfellows found only because the categories (the labels) are so broad as to be effectively meaningless.

Perhaps enough has been said to illustrate the general point that the 'schools of thought' are very imprecise categories and that, as a result, many individuals are classified differently by different people. It would surely make more sense and prove more useful to proceed by examining the particular positions of individuals, such as Plato, Berkeley, and Kant, rather than trying to see them as part of a single coherent school of thought. They may have something in common, they might perhaps be said to belong to one tradition rather than another, but they are not proponents of the same thesis. It might be argued against this that, for example, no more are all so-called Utilitarian philosophers of a single mind. Indeed, they may not be in all respects, but, if they are correctly classified as 'Utilitarians', then they do have a doctrine in common. (How detailed the common doctrine is depends upon the classification scheme: to say that A and B are both 'Rule-Utilitarians' is to say something more precise than that they are both 'Utilitarians'. Similarly, we might add qualification by reference to 'Hedonistic' or 'Ideal' Utilitarians.) But to say that Bentham and J.S. Mill were both Utilitarians is to say something much more precise and significant than it is to say that Hegel and Berkeley were both Idealists.

Nor is this lack of precision in the categorization of various 'isms' particularly surprising since to some extent the business of grouping things together or classifying them is dependent on one's purpose or interest. The botanist's rationale for classifying various plants may be quite different from that of the home-owner who wants a certain colour combination or to plant by reference to height. Similarly, any two philosophers might be more or less suitably linked together depending on whether our interest and focus is on their epistemology, their moral views, their political intent, or their pedagogic tenets, and so on and so forth.

The second rather more serious concern is that the logical status of the 'isms', or the nature of the schools of thought, varies once we pass beyond the basic distinction between, say, Idealism and Realism. Even in respect of the basic distinction, it may be doubted whether we need to and whether anybody actually does believe in their complete polarization. It may be a useful pedagogical device to contrast one with the other, but in point of fact it is misleading to say simply that Plato did not believe in the reality of the material world or that Locke did not believe in the reality of thought. Each of them, along with any other person of sense, would acknowledge a degree of truth in both schools of thought. Plato's point was not that there are no sticks or that a stick couldn't impinge on you by poking your eye out; his point, clearly and explicitly expressed, was simply that appearances change and deceive and that, if we want to understand the nature of say, justice, we need to think about it – not try to proceed by observing instances of it. Aristotle inclined rather to emphasizing the latter procedure. But that does not mean that they took a diametrically different view of reality. (And, in fact, they didn't. The classification of Aristotle as a Realist obscures the fact that, despite some particular criticisms, as far as we know he never repudiated the Theory of Ideas and might therefore be classified as an Idealist, at any rate more easily than Hegel.)

But my point here is that whereas Idealism, Realism, and Pragmatism are directly comparable in that each one is a specific philosophical thesis about reality and truth, Naturalism is a different kind of animal. 'Naturalism', at least if it is supposed to be embodied in the diverse work of Rousseau, Pestalozzi and Spencer, is indeed 'difficult to define' (Gutek, 1988, p. 68); more than that it does not present a thesis about nature in the way that Plato presents a thesis about Ideas. If we move from Realism to Thomist Realism we do not simply modify the basic idea that sense perceptions are primary; we move away from a theory of knowledge to the quite different realm of a theory of substantive belief. In place of a reasoned thesis relating to knowledge we have an unreasoned thesis relating to the existence of a God and the truth of a religion.

Marxism takes us close to what many would call an 'ideology' rather than a 'school of thought', for Marxism involves not simply an explanation, nor a method, nor even a set of conclusions; it is an explanatory system. An Idealist may believe in Plato's Theory of Ideas, but nothing in that belief tells him how to inquire into other matters or guarantees that he will retain that belief. But Marxism as a school of thought entails taking any situation or question and responding to it with a given form of explanation. In principle, anyone can deliver the Marxist explanation of anything and everything, just as they can, in principle, deliver the Catholic account, regardless of who they are and what they believe.

It is interesting in this connection that one book based on the Schools of Thought approach is entitled *Philosophical and Ideological Perspectives on Education* (Gutek, 1988). It includes Liberalism, Conservatism, Utopianism, Marxism, and Totalitarianism as ideologies, and then throws in Existentialism, Perennialism, Progressivism and Social Reconstructionism as 'theories of education'. But it is by no means clear what the difference between a theory, an ideology, and a philosophical perspective (= school of thought?) may be. Nor is it clear why we have chapters on Existentialism and Perennialism, for example, but not one on Utilitarianism, Cartesianism or Feminism. Equally interesting is that Marxism is an ideology for Gutek but a philosophical 'ism' for Ozmon and Craver (2008); and why is existentialism classified by Gutek as a theory of education? It all seems to reinforce the point that most if not all of this classification into schools of thought is rather arbitrary and proceeds without any clear or consistent criteria for selection. The question that is being raised here is not whether or not some or indeed all of these 'schools of thought' are worthy of thought and study, but whether this is an effective organization scheme, a meaningful one, and one that does justice to the history of ideas. Again, I suggest that studying individuals would be a great deal more productive.

THE RELATIONSHIP BETWEEN SCHOOLS OF THOUGHT AND EDUCATIONAL THEORY

But now we come to the crucial question, which is not about the value of the 'isms' approach to the history of ideas or even to philosophy, but about its value for the philosophy of education. What is the relationship between the various schools of thought and education? The truth is, as D.C. Phillips has remarked, 'there is no simple one-to-one correspondence between a person's ... philosophical commitments – for example, to idealism, realism, or pragmatism – and his or her everyday beliefs and actions' (Husen and Postlethwaite, 1994, Vol. 8, p. 4451). Being an Idealist doesn't necessarily mean anything in particular in terms of being a teacher or an educational theorist. An Idealist and a Realist can quite coherently have identical views about education. In which case, it may be asked, how is it that textbooks often explicitly refer to the implications of being committed to a given school of thought for such things as one's educational aims, and views on curriculum and methods of teaching? The answer, I fear, is that they strain at a gnat.

What seems to happen is that, having established a broad conception of philosophical Idealism (Realism, Pragmatism, etc.), textbooks then proceed to create a rather different conception of Educational Idealism (Realism, Pragmatism, etc.), either by stipulation or by extrapolating from the views of contemporary educationalists who either classify themselves as Idealists (Realists, etc.) or are so classified by others. There is often what might be termed a family resemblance between the 'ism' in question and the educational view ascribed to it, but seldom if ever a clear logical connection. In fact about the only certain educational dictum to be drawn from any of the 'isms' is that each would expect the 'ism' in question to be treated as the truth. What, for example, follows for education from Plato's Idealism (i.e. Theory of Ideas)? Nothing follows directly, other than the conclusion that, in so far as it is true, students should ultimately come to study and learn the Theory of Ideas. It is a mistake to proceed as if the various educational views that Plato has follow from his Idealism, for they do not. Thus, it has been said that Idealists tend to be educational elitists. But even if Plato is an educational elitist, that is not because he is an Idealist; rather, it is because he holds the quite separate belief that few can attain to knowledge of the Ideas. But that belief is not itself part of his or anyone else's Idealism. We cannot assume that Berkeley and Hegel, still less Rousseau for those who see him as a Romantic Idealist (e.g., Neff, 1966), would be elitists (though they might be). One might reason that given Plato's Idealism, it follows that he would want an abstract intellectual curriculum and, more particularly, that he would want mathematics studied. But even that doesn't follow automatically from his Idealism: it involves the further premise that as a matter of fact people will find conceptual work easier if they approach it by way of prior study of mathematics. Are we to assume that, being Idealists, Berkeley and Hegel lead the campaign for more mathematics in the curriculum? Besides it seems clear that, while he thought the intellectual life the best, Plato was actually in favour of professional or vocational education for the majority. We may not like such differentiation, but that is neither here nor there: an Idealist today, so far as his Idealism goes, can quite coherently favour or oppose comprehensive schools, streaming/tracking, sex education, history, PE or auto mechanics. All his Idealism commits him to is belief in the significance of mind in relation to reality.

What tends to happen is that our overall perception of the philosophy of various individuals in general dictates the educational concept. Philosophical Idealism is closely allied to the Platonic Theory of Ideas, but Educational Idealism is allied to what is taken to be Plato's educational philosophy (often erroneously, but that's another story). The confusion is apparent when we see that, while in general terms, Idealists are presumed to favour study of the best that has been thought and said, firm discipline, and character formation, Plato is nonetheless perceived by some as an advocate of progressive teaching methods such as discovery learning and dialogue. Two things contribute to this confusion: first, the use of phrases such as 'realizing one's full potential', 'encouragement of truth-seeking', 'the teacher as a model', 'unfolding what is latent in the child', 'teaching to think', and 'holistic study' in order to explicate the educational implications of a given school of thought such as Idealism. What do these phrases mean? Who is going to oppose them? Above all, why are they presumed to depend on Idealism? Well, in fact they clearly don't, since identical or similar phrases are used to explicate most other educational 'isms'.

Secondly, the various 'isms' are often of a different logical order. One cannot deduce a great deal about the educational implications of Naturalism per se, because the label covers so many distinct species of Naturalism, sometimes involving quite contradictory theses. But from Rousseau one can deduce quite a lot. This is because *Emile* is primarily an educational thesis. There may still be confusion over the concept of nature, but Rousseau has written a treatise embodying a theory of education: Naturalism, then, at least in the case of Rousseau, is an educational theory. Idealism, however, is not, although Plato also had an educational theory. Nothing at all follows from Hegel's philosophy for education unless one improperly takes it as an argument for teaching by means of presenting a thesis, then an antithesis, and finally a synthesis. And it is a commonplace of criticism that, when, for example, Kant and Locke do write about education, what they have to say owes little or nothing to their philosophy.

PHILOSOPHICAL ANALYSIS CONTRASTED WITH 'ISMS'

As noted above, many schools of thought approaches include Philosophical Analysis or Analytic Philosophy as if it were an 'ism' comparable to any other. But it is not; it is distinct from all the other 'isms', ideologies and schools of thought that have been mentioned, and this fact is extremely important for making sense of philosophy of education.

The paradigm 'isms' might be more fully and accurately described as particular philosophical viewpoints on particular issues. To subscribe to them is to hold a view about the matter in question. Others, such as Marxism, differ in that they involve a view about the appropriate kind of answer to give to any question: it provides an explanatory system deemed to fit all situations. Inasmuch as it had not previously been accorded proper recognition, Marx's insight that economic conditions often determine beliefs was in its time most valuable. It is still important to recognize it as one kind of explanation relevant to some questions. It is uncritical and complacent (and fairly obviously wrong) to continue to treat it as the only appropriate explanation for any event.

But analytic philosophy defined as an activity, namely inquiry into concepts in order to delineate and discriminate them more sharply, involves neither a particular viewpoint (nor theoretical perspective on any problem in philosophy) nor a particular method, nor an explanatory system (least of all a monolithic one). On the issue of method, some confusion is caused by the widespread tendency to confuse philosophical analysis with some particular way of doing it (e.g., linguistic, ordinary language, or late Wittgensteinian philosophy) and sometimes even with a genuine 'ism' such as logical positivism. But analytic philosophy is not to be identified with either linguistic analysis or logical positivism. It is an activity to be defined solely in terms of the task before it: to analyze, explicate or seek a fuller and more coherent understanding of concepts. This has relevance beyond the observation that it therefore has no place in books based on schools of thought. For, the conclusion that the schools of thought approach may have less to recommend it as a way of approaching philosophy of education than is sometimes supposed leads to the further assumption, implicit in this Handbook overall, that if we want to understand education we would be well advised to focus on analyzing the key concepts in education, rather than focusing on a confused mélange of logically distinct kinds of philosophical position. There is sense in focusing on a particular individual's educational views or on particular philosophical claims, as in Section 2 of this Handbook, and also in focusing on the educational problems and concepts considered in Section 3. But there really isn't much to be said for approaching the critical study of education through various philosophical schools of thought, even were the list of such 'isms' to be revised and pruned to avoid some of the shortcomings noted. Every educational philosopher ideally needs to focus on key educational concepts, with as little prior commitment to any particular school of thought as possible.

RELATIVISM AND SOME CURRENT SCHOOLS OF THOUGHT

There is one issue that runs through the history of philosophy that is central and important to philosophy of education and educational practice – namely, relativism. I regard relativism as the view that truth is relative to societies, and subjectivism as the view that it is relative to persons. However, for present purposes that distinction is not particularly important: what is important is the question of the tension or potential conflict between relativistic and objectivist stances in relation to the possibility of truth and knowledge in various areas; what is important is our view of whether in all, some or any fields there is objective truth, such that in principle we may be said to know some things. It is in relation to this issue that we need finally to give consideration to some contemporary 'isms' and schools of thought.

Throughout the history of philosophy an argument has persisted over whether there are or are not truths about the world, whether we can perceive them, and, if so, how; and that debate is of fundamental importance for education since, on any view, education is concerned with distinguishing truth from falsehood, opinion from knowledge, the correct from the incorrect, and the better from the worse. Even the most extreme relativist seems to want others to adopt relativism, and presumably relativists want the education system to provide some kind of guidance through the myriad beliefs and opinions on offer. What matters in this respect, therefore, is not whether, say, the Pragmatic theory of truth is more or less plausible than others, but the contrast between any theory that presumes a distinction between truth and falsity and hence allows for the possibility of a distinction between knowledge and opinion, and those that don't. Idealism, Realism, and Pragmatism all presume that there is truth and, for the most part, from the point of view of education that means that, despite their disagreements as to the theoretical foundation of knowledge, they can (and in practice often do) agree on the distinct question of what some of the more important things we know and wish to pass on may be. In Rousseau's case it is not entirely clear what his view on the relationship between nature and truth is, but it is clear that he too believes there are truths to be discovered. In other words, educational arguments about such important questions as to whether, why and in what way science or the arts should be studied are not affected by one's position as an Idealist, Realist, etc. Only if one takes the position that there is no truth, but only differing individual perceptions, are there obviously serious consequences for one's educational views. And that raises the question of whether any 'ism' or school of thought, despite appearances, actually does maintain such a thesis.

And so we come to such schools of thought as Postmodernism, Existentialism, certain Eastern Philosophies, Hermeneutics, and Phenomenology. Clearly, here again we have a group of 'isms' of quite diverse nature, but they do have in common a tendency to be wary of or uncomfortable with the idea that we can place very much reliance on our 'knowledge'. I shall not comment on Eastern Philosophies as a school of thought, beyond remarking that the study of such world views as Buddhism, Confucianism, Taoism, and Zen Buddhism, though in itself it might be very educational, would seem to have as little to do with an argument for this or that educational practice as would a study of Mormons, Methodists or Moonies. Of course, in each case, a society committed to the viewpoint in question will have an educational system that in various ways reflects that viewpoint. That is merely to say something along the lines of 'Catholics want to bring up their children to believe in Catholicism and in accordance with Catholic belief'. But that says absolutely nothing about the questions that are central to philosophy of education such as 'Is there any reason to believe in the truth of any given religion?' and 'What are the educational implications of an answer to that question?', let alone 'Is trigonometry worth studying?', 'Should schooling be compulsory?' or 'What should an educated person understand?'

Existentialists, who often differ markedly from one another in point of specifics, even in respect of fundamental beliefs such as whether they believe in God or not, nonetheless make a plausible point to the effect that much of what we become in life depends upon ourselves; however, they do not have any clear view to offer on the nature of truth, knowledge or learning. Nothing follows necessarily for education from Existentialism other than the fact that, assuming we are existentialists, we shall want to teach people that Existentialism is true.

'Postmodern' is a label that means nothing and much. One is aware that those who classify themselves as Postmodern often feel that they are being misunderstood or even caricatured, but it would appear to be a simple matter of fact that the label has no fixed meaning and can at best be said to refer to one or more of a set of historically familiar relativist claims. This is not to say that a given individual such as Foucault does not have some specific things to say about punishment or love, and this is not the place to question how much of what he says is plausible. But Foucault's position on love is not the same thing as his postmodernism and that position has no obvious bearing on education. Even his views on punishment yield no obvious clear answer to the educational question of whether it is appropriate or advisable to punish particular children for particular misdemeanours in particular ways. What is of some concern in the context of philosophy of education is that some, seemingly confusing sociology of belief with epistemology, argue in the name of postmodernism for an extreme relativism, impervious to the obvious contradiction in asserting the truth of the proposition that there is no truth. But to believe sincerely that everything is just a matter of subjective opinion would, if taken seriously, have major educational consequences, for it would undermine the basic assumption shared by virtually all other schools of thought: namely, that we wish to pass on valued and well-founded knowledge of the way of the world, whatever that may consist of. Fortunately, postmodern educationalists never seem to draw this or indeed any other specifically educational conclusion. Their theoretical position seems strangely but savagely divorced from any particular educational position. (Clearly, this account of postmodernism will be deemed – ironically – 'incorrect' by many, and the reader's attention is drawn to the fact that there are separate chapters below which have more to say on, for example, Post-structuralism and Phenomenology.)

Hermeneutics is a strange beast, the main problem here being not so much any specific 'hermeneutical' beliefs as the question of what use the label serves. What does it mean to claim to be a hermeneutic? Historically, it referred to a particular method, a would-be science, if you like, of studying the scriptures. But, though founded as a method, Hermeneutics now seems to eschew any particular method(s). So are they just 'inquirers' as the term suggests etymologically? Does the label simply refer to those who cautiously search for the truth? Gadamer, who sees himself, and is widely seen by others, as engaging in hermeneutics or hermeneutical inquiry, has argued convincingly in *Truth and Method* (1996) that there is in many areas of life an objective reality but that our grasp of it is necessarily and always perspectival or filtered through our minds. I would argue that this is a position that Plato, Aristotle and Kant certainly, and Rousseau possibly, would happily endorse, although they did not make it their business to state it explicitly. But the question we are concerned with here is what exactly does claiming that Gadamer's inquiry was a hermeneutic one add to the story? It is in fact difficult to see Hermeneutics as a school of thought. It is also difficult to see its connection to any implications for education, except in so far as one might need to counter some of the wilder excesses of postmodernism or some extreme Idealist or Realist position that maintained, respectively, a refusal to study the material world or the conceptual world at all.

Phenomenology likewise, though sometimes seen as a school of thought, seems rather a label to describe an attitude to humanistic inquiry or a basic belief in the value of studying the phenomena of consciousness and the development of personal meaning. (Classifying the meaning of this term is not helped by the fact that many, but not all, associate Phenomenology closely with Existentialism.) The lack of any delineation of particular methods and the lack of clarity as to what exactly is meant by, for instance, 'studying the phenomena of consciousness', makes the notion of a phenomenological school of thought somewhat opaque and its implications for education once again obscure, although Phenomenology, unlike all the other 'schools of thought' referred to, is regarded by some as itself providing the key to a particular form of pedagogy.

CONCLUSION

The analytic thrust of this volume is predicated on the idea that, notwithstanding sociological and psychological factors, and the possibility that we may at all times be mistaken in our perceptions of reality, and may indeed be merely partaking in someone else's dream, we should continue to live our lives on the assumption that there are certain truths and a distinction to be drawn between truth and falsity, and that we should continue to seek for the truth by rejecting those beliefs that for one reason or another seem clearly to be unfounded, and that education is fundamentally concerned with helping to develop people's understanding of the world and life in its broadest sense. There is no reason to reject this basic set of premises, save only if one embraces an extreme form of subjectivity, under whatever name, that maintains there are no truths and that understanding cannot be distinguished from viewpoint, however acquired. If one sincerely held such a view, then one might be expected to lose interest in the very idea of education. Fortunately, the few who do subscribe to such a view seem nevertheless, albeit inconsistently, to continue to value education. For most of us such a view seems quite implausible, to the extent that subscribing to it might even seem to involve bad faith: we none of us live our lives other than as if we presume that there are truths and falsehoods.

Approaching philosophy of education through schools of thought of course remains a possibility, but the advantages are not obviously great or confined exclusively to this approach, and the concerns are many and deep. It would seem wiser, if the historical element or the introduction of certain great thinkers is deemed important, to study various individuals, rather than loosely and often misleadingly group them together in somewhat vague 'isms' or schools of thought. It would also seem advisable to give more thought to the educational significance of what various individuals have to say, rather than simply to their stature as philosophers.

But perhaps better still would be to eschew an emphasis on either history of philosophy or particular individuals, and to focus on examining educational concepts, programmes, policies, and practices themselves, with a view to aiming at some clear concepts and coherent arguments. We are well aware that an entirely independent, theory-free and, more broadly, influence-free inquiry is not possible, but one can be more or less willing and able to try for, and more or less successful in aiming at and achieving, a clearer, better explicated and defended understanding of educational priorities, even in the face of our unavoidable perspectives.

What seems particularly pointless in the pursuit of truth is to adopt any position or perspective that automatically yields entirely predictable answers. The thinking goes into adopting, say, a Utilitarian position in ethics. Once I have convinced myself that I am a Utilitarian, there is not a great deal of philosophical interest or difficulty in determining the Utilitarian answer to moral problems (even if it does not always yield a simple definitive answer). But once I have adopted Utilitarianism and am merely applying it to problems, I cease to be doing moral philosophy. In the same way, to adopt Marxism is to cease thinking critically. Other schools of thought we have referred to may be less constricting, but fundamentally it remains the case that to consider an educational problem through the prism of an 'ism' is to severely limit your options.

NOTE

1 In a review of the *Philosophy of Education* Hirst (1983), R.S. Peters wrote:
'Before then [sc. 1965] philosophy of education had been unco-ordinated and variously interpreted. There was, first of all, the pattern adopted by many working at it in American Colleges of Education, who were determined to convince their colleagues in the Faculties of Arts that they were genuinely doing philosophy. They intended to take schools of thought such as Idealism, Realism, Pragmatism and to probe their implications for education. Indeed, when I was first introduced to the subject, the most widely canvassed question was that of the "implications" of philosophy for education.'

REFERENCES

Berkeley, George (1934) *A Treatise Concerning the Principles of Human Knowledge*. London: J.M. Dent.

Gadamer, Hans-Georg (1996) *Truth and Method*. New York: Continuum.

Gutek, Gerald L. (1988) *Philosophical and Ideological Perspectives on Education*. New Jersey: Prentice Hall.

Hirst, Paul H. (1983) *Educational Theory and its Foundational Disciplines*. London: Routledge and Kegan Paul.

Hume, David (1962) A *Treatise of Human Nature*. London: J.M. Dent.

Husen, T. and Postlethwaite, N. (1994) (Eds) *The International Encyclopedia of Education*, 2nd edn. Oxford: Pergamon.

Moore, G.E. (1962) *Principia Ethica*. Cambridge: Cambridge University Press.

Neff, Frederick C. (1966) *Philosophy and American Education*. New York: The Center for Applied Research in Education, Inc.

Ozmon, Howard A. and Craver, Samuel M. (2008) *Philosophical Foundations of Education*, 8th edn. Columbus, OH: Pearson, Merrill/Prentice Hall.

Peters, R.S. (1983) Philosophy of education. In Paul H. Hirst (Ed.), *Educational Theory and Its Foundation Disciplines*. London: Routledge and Kegan Paul.

3

The Philosophy of Education and Educational Theory

David Carr

THE CHANGING FACE OF EDUCATIONAL THEORY

The main obstacle to understanding the relationship of educational philosophy to educational theory is that both of these terms have undergone shifts of meaning over the years. Still, it seems safe to say that some of the earliest systematic Western theorizing about education was broadly philosophical. Indeed, one pioneering attempt to make coherent sense of education and teaching is credited by Plato to the founding father of Western philosophy, Socrates. More precisely, the key ethical question that Socrates appears to have addressed in such Platonic dialogues as *Gorgias*, *Meno* and *Republic* (Hamilton and Cairns, 1961) – that of how to determine the good or virtuous life and/or what might help us to live that life – is also a fairly obvious educational question. It also seems that the first great post-Socratic philosophers approached this issue in a recognizably modern philosophical way, via mostly a priori clarification of received usage. So, notwithstanding that Plato and Aristotle's rather different approaches to the issue of how we might conceive or teach others how to live the good life are broadly 'anthropological' – concerned, that is, to explore the question of what it is to be distinctively human – their method is nevertheless more philosophical than (as in modern anthropology) empirical scientific. Thus, for example, Plato seems to have derived his suspicion of democracy and associated educational policies from his largely conceptual analysis of human personality as more significantly implicated in non-material psychic, spiritual or intellectual than in material or physical nature. Likewise, though Aristotle (by contrast with Plato) understands moral virtue in more naturalistic terms, his guiding perspective on the soul as the form of the body and his practical conception of moral wisdom are also mainly the products of a priori rather than empirical reflection (McKeon, 1941).

It would appear, however, that a major turning point in the study of education occurs with the general Western European shift towards a more experimental or empirical approach to enquiry in the seventeenth and eighteenth centuries. Indeed, it is arguable that the pivotal figure here is the so-called founding father of progressive education Jean-Jacques Rousseau. To be sure, the Rousseau of the Social Contract (1973) is primarily a political philosopher and, despite much psychological speculation in his *Emile* (1974), it is hardly the (experimental) psychology of modern textbooks. Thus, though Rousseau has a four-stage theory of child development that predates Jean Piaget's by two centuries, his analysis is mostly a priori and he provides little in the way of real empirical support for such speculations. That said, there is clearly some recognition in Rousseau of the need to pay attention to actual developmental features of real as opposed to virtual children. Moreover, such appreciation becomes increasingly apparent in the work of those eighteenth century progressive educationalists most immediately influenced by Rousseau – such as Pestalozzi and Froebel – for whom the development of something like empirically grounded principles of human psychological and other development is evidently becoming a significant investigative desideratum.

Whereas the seventeenth century had little in the way of developed psychological science to offer the likes of Pestalozzi and Froebel, the view that the study of human cognitive, emotional and social growth and learning ought to be scientifically grounded clearly gained educational momentum in the nineteenth and twentieth centuries. At the end of the nineteenth and beginning of the twentieth centuries, for example, the impact of Freud's pioneering clinical work on psychoanalysis is clearly evident in the progressivism of Homer Lane, A.S. Neill and their various disciples. But perhaps the greatest boost to the scientific aspirations of educational theory was provided by early twentieth century (behaviourist) learning theory. Indeed, despite the disrepute into which it has nowadays largely fallen, the work of early behaviourists exerted a powerful influence on all shades of educational theorizing – precisely in so far as it appeared to provide an experimentally testable science of learning upon which a systematic 'technology' of pedagogy might be constructed: stimulus–response theories promised to provide a reliable basis for the re-modelling of animal learning in general and human learning in particular. In this light, many major twentieth century pioneers of educational reform – including such distinguished thinkers as Bertrand Russell and John Dewey (see Perry, 1967) – were warmly receptive to the new behavioural science (which also meshed well with the associationist epistemology of Russell and the evolutionary naturalism of Dewey). Indeed, though a philosopher, Dewey in particular played a key role in generating that widespread sympathy for the social sciences – especially psychology – which was to be widespread among his many twentieth century (particularly North American) followers.

To be sure, one could not fairly regard Dewey as any kind of crude reflex psychologist – and, in any case, contemporary psychologists of education would not be slow to insist that psychological science has been overtaken by any number of major developments since its behaviourist heyday. Thus, for most teachers of at least the past half-century the names of Piaget, Bruner, Ausubel, and other psychologists of cognitive development are likely to be rather more familiar than those of Watson, Thorndike or Skinner. Beyond these pioneers, moreover, cognitive psychology has itself clearly moved on in diverse directions – either towards various forms of social constructivism (Vygotsky, Bandura) or in the more naturalistic directions of cognitive neuroscience. Still, notwithstanding the complex and sophisticated nature of such developments, it seems safe to say that these and other predominantly empirical or experimental approaches to the study of the mind continue to be viewed by most contemporary educational theorists and practitioners as principal sources of evidential support for the development of new and improved approaches to pedagogy and instruction. It would therefore seem that over the course of the last century the idea that serious educational theorizing needs to be grounded in something like the experimental evidence of social or other scientific research came very much into its own.

MODERN DEVELOPMENTS IN PHILOSOPHY: THE ANALYTICAL 'REVOLUTION'

As seen, many past theorists of education (such as Plato, Aristotle, Rousseau and Dewey) were nothing if not philosophers: few could seriously doubt the philosophical nature and significance of the issues and questions they raised – most, if not all, of which continue to be staples of respectable present-day philosophy courses. Since it is also true that many if not most of the questions they raised were educational questions (or at least questions with clear educational implications) it is no less surprising that space was often devoted to such thinkers in courses of professional teacher education, and in the textbooks of educational philosophy and theory created for such courses (see, for example, Rusk, 1979) – even though such philosophical ideas would often be mixed in fairly indiscriminately with the more empirically focused social scientific theory and research also recently noticed. But philosophy – no less than other branches of enquiry – moves on. From this viewpoint, for example, although Dewey's life and work covered the best part of a century (1859–1952), and although his influence on mid-twentieth century American analytical pragmatists continued to be substantial (see, for example, Quine, 1969), his philosophical approach would surely have appeared rather dated to many if not most professional academic philosophers by the time of his death.

The main development in academic philosophy of the first half of the twentieth century (at least in Anglophone cultures) was a move – the so-called 'semantic ascent' – towards conceiving traditional philosophical problems primarily as linguistic confusions or 'grammatical' mistakes. To be sure, previous philosophers had already shown that serious philosophical errors are liable to follow from misunderstanding the grammatical functions of terms: Kant, for example, had shown that past philosophers (such as Anselm and Descartes) had been seriously mistaken in taking the word 'exists' in 'God exists' to be a kind of (property attributing) adjective (Kant, 1968). However, nothing short of a revolution in philosophical analysis occurred with the virtual reconstruction of traditional logic by the German logician Gottlob Frege (1848–1925). Frege's so-called 'predicate calculus' (Geach and Black, 1966) provided a way of disclosing the deep logical structure or grammar of our ordinary (and often misleading) ways of speaking, that quickly delivered (with the aid of such followers of Frege as Russell [1956]) spectacular results in terms of the clarification of previously intractable philosophical puzzles about truth, meaning, existence and other concepts.

Whereas much of the work of Frege and Russell was highly formal and technical – and therefore not always to the tastes of philosophers concerned with issues and problems beyond the rarefied atmosphere of logic and mathematics – the key idea that philosophical mistakes were at heart confusions of language had nevertheless a profound impact on the general drift of Anglophone philosophy in the early years of the twentieth century. Generally, Frege's logical insights and developments seemed to be much more in tune with the down to earth 'scientific' temper and tendencies of the long established British empiricist and emerging American pragmatist traditions of philosophy than with the more high flown idealist and other metaphysical speculations of many philosophers in his own German (and more generally European continental) homeland. But for many British and American philosophers (as well as for those of former British dominions where the influence of English culture and language remained pervasive) Frege's close philosophical attention to the logical grammar and semantics of particular forms of human discourse offered to yield surer, albeit more modest, results than the ideology, rhetoric and sweeping generalization of Hegelians, Marxists, Nietzscheans and other 'continental' European thinkers.

Perhaps the most significant 'methodological' principle to undergo effective transfer from the more particular Fregean context of concern with logic and mathematics to the broader domain of philosophy was Frege's advice that one should look for the meaning of a term only in the context of a proposition (Frege, 1978). This idea was very much taken to heart by Frege's (arguably) most important philosophical successor – the Austrian philosopher Ludwig Wittgenstein – particularly after Wittgenstein's appointment as Professor of Philosophy at Cambridge University in 1929. In his later philosophy – particularly in his influential *Philosophical Investigations* (1953) – Wittgenstein effectively adapts and extends Frege's principle in his famous observation that the *meaning* of (philosophically problematic and other) terms is to be found in their *use*. In this regard, Wittgenstein was more than likely the principal architect of that influential twentieth century Anglophone philosophical trend (though it was perhaps more influential in Britain and its former spheres of colonial influence than in the USA) known as 'ordinary language philosophy'. At all events, despite some diversity of approach, such 'leaders' of the so-called ordinary language movement as Wittgenstein, and the Oxford philosophers Gilbert Ryle and J.L. Austin, sought to 'dissolve' many traditional puzzles and paradoxes of philosophy by showing how past thinkers had been 'bewitched' or misled by the surface grammar of ordinary usage into various philosophical errors.

Wittgenstein (whose own work was mainly on the theory of meaning) himself sought to expose the basic incoherence of a central tenet of much traditional (rationalist and empiricist) philosophy that humans make sense of experience by acts of reference to 'inner' or subjective psychological states: on the contrary, Wittgenstein (1953) argued, any knowledge we might have of such subjective states must itself depend upon a public language for the common expression and identification of such experiences. Relatedly, Ryle set out to show in his *Concept of Mind* (1949) that a widely held 'Cartesian' view of the mind as a bastion of 'occult' non-material states (to which the 'subjects' of such states have privileged access) rests mainly on mistaking certain 'psychological' and/or action verb phrases – actually meant for the identification of behavioural dispositions of flesh and blood human agents – for quasi-names of mysterious psychic objects or things (such as thoughts or desires). Generally, however, such attention to usage could be used to expose conceptual errors in a wide variety of philosophical fields. It could be used to show that past philosophers (from Plato to G.E. Moore) had been mistaken in their search for a single 'moral' definition of the term 'good'. For, in so far as the grammatical function of the term 'good' in the greeting 'Good morning!' is clearly different from its role in the sentence 'That was a good risotto', no such unitary or 'essential' definition of 'good' exists to be found.

Following the logic of this method, however, we could hardly fail to see that the term 'philosophy' is itself liable to diverse usage – so that 'philosophy' in this new post-Fregean 'analytical' sense might here mean something rather different from its use in talk of Plato's, Marx's or Uncle Tom Cobley's 'philosophy'. For whereas this second sense of 'philosophy' would normally be taken to pick out a particular set of views (held by Plato, Marx or Cobley), the first sense seems to identify something closer to a method of investigation or analysis. In this sense, to be sure, someone might well *do* philosophy without *having* any particular philosophy whatsoever. Moreover, given this apparent ambiguity, there is clearly scope for a related distinction between senses of 'philosophy of education'. For whereas the study of educational philosophy had formerly meant (in, say, the training of teachers and other educational professionals up until the middle of the twentieth century) some kind of acquaintance with the 'doctrines of the great educators' (such as Plato, Rousseau and Dewey), the new analytical techniques developed by Frege, Russell, Wittgenstein and others clearly signalled a new approach to educational philosophy – or philosophizing – as a valuable method for the professional clarification of educationally problematic usage.

THE NEW PHILOSOPHY OF EDUCATION

The first serious attempts to apply the new analytical techniques to the language of educational theory, policy and professional practice were made during the period of post-Second World War settlement. The two philosophers most widely credited with having spearheaded this general trend are the British philosopher Richard S. Peters (1966) and the American Israel Scheffler (1960). It is likely that Peters' work represented the sharpest break with previous professional uses of philosophy in his own context – since, as already noticed, the new analytical approach was at some variance with the study of 'doctrines of the great educators' previously prevalent in teacher training in the United Kingdom. Peters, along with colleagues at the London Institute of Education, also had wide influence on those (former colonial) educational systems that continued to be heavily influenced by British academic and professional culture. However, despite the significant degree of continuity of Scheffler's work with a home-grown American tradition of philosophical pragmatism (which explicitly acknowledged debt to Dewey), it was probably no less radical in its own application to contexts of professional theory, policy and practice of new analytical philosophical approaches that would not have been widely familiar beyond the philosophical academy.

It should also be noted that the new analytical philosophy of education emerged in a post-war climate of social, political and economic reconstruction in which hope of human social and other improvement was widely held to turn on significant educational reform. First, of course, there was a clear imperative to promote the knowledge and skills upon which any economic reconstruction would depend. However, having also emerged from a dark era in which various forms of ideological manipulation had brought Western civilisation to the brink of collapse, there was doubtless also some awareness (at least in Western democracies) of the need for adequate educational insurance against such totalitarian mind control. At all events, the British 1944 Education Act raised the school leaving age to fifteen – securing compulsory secondary education for all young people – and the 1963 Robbins Report set in motion a programme of educational expansion that widely extended access to higher and university education. Alongside this, there was renewed attention to the generally parlous and outdated state of teacher education and training – particularly for primary and secondary schools – not least to the prospect of raising the academic standard of professional preparation for teaching to degree-level.

Indeed, R.S. Peters and other British analytical philosophers of education were key players in developing a new academic conception of degree-level professional studies for teachers. Here, not surprisingly, it was held that philosophy of education might play a central role in such professional studies – not primarily for the purpose of acquainting teachers with the educational perspectives of such past philosophers as Plato, Rousseau and Dewey, but by equipping them with a range of analytical skills apt for the clarification of educational discourse and for the detection of ambiguities or fallacies in educational proposals and arguments. Indeed, Peters and his followers held that much of the error and bad practice to which teachers and educational planners were liable was not so much the consequence of lack of information or ignorance of practical pedagogical techniques, but of failures to understand clearly what they were about – which was often due to conceptual confusion of teaching with indoctrination, authority with authoritarianism, freedom with license, and so on. Peters' own pioneering analyses sought to bring some clarity to much loose talk of education and, by close and careful attention to usage, to draw significant and valuable distinctions between education and other concepts, such as training, socialization and therapy, with which it seemed often to be confused (Peters 1966, 1973).

To be sure, Peters, Scheffler and their followers did not hold that the skills of analytical educational philosophy were all that educational professionals required to be effective teachers, classroom assistants, curriculum planners and so on. Indeed, notwithstanding the enduring influence in some quarters of (Deweyan and other) pragmatism, much new philosophy of education was rooted in a traditional empiricist distinction between the a priori or conceptual concerns of philosophy and the a posteriori or empirical business of natural and social scientific enquiry. R.S Peters himself explicitly argued in his influential work *Ethics and Education* (1966) that appropriate professional education and training would need to draw upon a range of academic disciplines and skills more or less sharply distinguished in this way. Thus, besides the philosophical expertise needed for the clarification of the basic aims and objectives of education, teachers would also need the more practically useful knowledge provided by the social sciences of psychology and sociology for the development of managerial and pedagogical skills and techniques. In like vein, the influential Oxford theorist of moral education John Wilson argued that while it was the job of the philosophical researcher into moral education to clarify the meaning of such basic terms as 'moral' or 'good', it was up to psychologists and sociologists to discover (empirically) the best means, methods and contexts for the promotion of moral qualities and dispositions (Wilson, et al., 1967).

At all events, it was around some such view of the professional division of labour that the new college of education degree-level programmes of studies in education were often constructed. Thus, in addition to time-honoured courses in teaching methods – linked to teaching experience in schools – students would be required to undergo systematic academic study of (largely analytical) philosophy of education, psychology of education, educational sociology, history of education and so on. In short, the new view of educational theory that prevailed in many (Anglophone) contexts of pre-service teacher education in the 1960s and 1970s was: first, that professional theory ought to be an academically balanced diet of a priori philosophical analysis, and (albeit secondhand) empirical social scientific (psychological and sociological) theorizing – perhaps with some history of education thrown in for good measure; secondly, that the overall justification of such theory – bearing in mind the practical conception of philosophical analysis at work here – could only lie in its application to the hard practical business of education and teaching. Further to this, it would appear that for many educational theorists of this time (such as Wilson and Peters), the relationship between philosophy of education in particular and educational theory in general might best be characterized (in the eighteenth century English philosopher John Locke's term) as an 'under-labourer view'. On this view, it would fall to educational philosophers to clear away the 'conceptual rubble' – the linguistic untidiness – in received educational usage, so that the empirical (social) scientists might then get on with the practical business of working out the most effective means and methods of instruction.

THE POST-WAR ANALYTICAL PARADIGM UNDER FIRE

However, it was not long before a number of interrelated objections to this general picture of educational theory as applied science, and to the associated under-labourer view of educational philosophy, emerged. For a start, not a few educational philosophers were unhappy with the dualism between theory and practice (already rejected by Dewey) that this picture implied. To many, there was something fundamentally incoherent about the very idea of relating theory to practice: for did this not imply that there might be something describable as 'practice' that was conceptually distinct from any (educational or other) 'theory', and which would depend upon such independently established theory for its justification or rationale? Such unease with the theory–practice distinction also seemed consistent with the difficulties that some educational philosophers – increasingly attracted to the idealist and constructivist intellectual traditions of Marxist, post-structuralist and other European philosophical trends – began to have with Anglophone conceptual analysis. For was not the problem with this approach that it took the concepts it sought to analyse to be (perhaps in the spirit of Plato) somehow timelessly or universally independent of any and all social or cultural conditions or contexts? But had not the likes of Hegel and Marx shown convincingly that concepts and theories were no less constructions of society and culture than other human products?

For many, indeed, the view that concepts themselves are the products of locally formed minds and circumstances – and that their meanings may therefore vary from place to place – were conclusively confirmed by the investigations of historians, sociologists and anthropologists. In this light, we could not assume that ancient or contemporary Greek understandings of (say) virtue, freedom or democracy were the same as or similar to (say) modern British interpretations of such terms. Indeed, we should be clear that on such historicist or constructivist views there could be no firm line between theory and practice, precisely because – rather than independently justifying practice – theory could itself be little more than the post hoc rationalization of local practices. It should also be apparent that such perspectives make it therefore difficult if not impossible to draw any clear or meaningful line between philosophy and social (or other) science – or between claims about what it is proper for people to believe and observations about what they do in fact happen to believe. Moreover, in its more radical forms, such constructivism brooks no exceptions. It is held to apply no less to the so-called 'hard' sciences of physics and mathematics than to such more 'value-laden' fields of human enquiry as history or anthropology. Thus, from a radical constructivist perspective (see, e.g., Kuhn, 1970), the theories of physical scientists are no less the creations of their time and place than the religious beliefs of a community of faith – and are therefore no less vulnerable to error, sophistry and illusion.

Although such historicist or constructivist scepticism about the 'objectivity' of theory is nowadays widespread in educational and other philosophy it would be hard to find a clearer case of its direct application to the particular 'problem' of educational theory than the work of the British philosopher of education (one must, on his own terms, hesitate to refer to him as a 'theorist') Wilfred Carr. Carr's work is certainly eclectic and has over the years drawn fairly liberally on the ideas of Aristotle, Dewey, Habermas, Richard Bernstein and Alasdair MacIntyre, among others. Still, in a long-running series of influential papers (one recently [2006] and significantly entitled 'Education without theory') Carr argues that we should indeed have serious doubts about the value or use of so-called 'educational theory' for understanding the practice of education, and that the more general and lately noticed philosophical scepticism about the very possibility of objective knowledge or theory provides the most compelling grounds for such doubts. However, while conceding that there may be some justice in Carr's case against educational theory, it is of no less present importance – in the interests of (amongst other things) accuracy of diagnosis – to ask whether the case against educational theory in particular is well supported, if at all, by historicist or constructivist doubts about theory as such.

CARR'S CRITIQUE OF 'FOUNDATIONALISM'

Carr is faithful to many of his more modern influences in basing his case against both educational theory and theory as such on rejection of what he calls 'foundationalism'. The main trouble here (as elsewhere, as we shall see, in Carr's work) is that this term is somewhat ambiguous – or, at any rate, liable to diverse and shifting interpretations. First, from one possible 'anti-foundationalist' viewpoint, there is something mistaken or naïve (perhaps naively positivist) about supposing that there can be unproblematic (inductive) inference from this or that body of theory-neutral empirical observations to more meaningful interpretation of such observations or to practical policies or prescriptions based on them. There can be

little doubt that such anti-foundationalism correctly identifies a significant problem about certain past empiricist or positivist conceptions of the relationship of
theory to practice – not least in such professional fields as education. Explanation
and prescription are clearly underdetermined by data (see Quine, 1969) and one
cannot safely move directly from observations that things are thus and so, to
accounts of why they are so, or to judgements about whether they should (or
should not) be so. However, a stronger form of 'anti-foundationalism' seems
committed to the claim that since all perspectives are imbued with or 'infected'
by the socially constructed interests and purposes of particular constituencies,
there cannot be any rationally objective grounds for human theory or practice
that are free from such local interests and concerns: on this view, all theory and
explanation is tainted with human (subjective) bias.

On this second view, in short, it is held that because our theories and explanations have local social histories, we have to doubt whether there can be any real
grasp of the truth of things at all. From a logical viewpoint, however, such inference is so clearly fallacious (it is effectively a form of the 'genetic' fallacy) – and
the claim that it is taken to support is so obviously implausible – that one can
only wonder why it seems to have been so widely endorsed. The fact that I have
been raised in this rather than that culture has no bearing whatsoever on whether
what I am typing this chapter on is a computer, or on the truth of any current
scientific explanation (which may of course be *mistaken*) of how the contraption
works – other than, of course, that such truth reflects the achievements and is
expressed in the language of that culture. If, after shipwreck, my computer is
washed up to a cargo cult who believe this device to be a physical incarnation
of their great god 'Ibok', their regarding it as such clearly does not make it so.
Since the item is *in fact* a computer and there is no god Ibok, the cargo cult is
simply confused and mistaken. Here is the philosopher John Cottingham (2005)
on those who regard the 'objectivity' and 'rationality' of modern science as
simply reflecting the local cultural perspective of 'children of the Enlightenment':

> ... it is one thing to say that none of our evaluations can float entirely free from the particu-
> larities of history, and quite another to say that there can be no good reasons for defending
> a particular tradition or methodology. We may be unable to escape from the boat on which
> we sail the ocean, but that does not stop us being confident that the improvements of
> navigation that have been developed over the past two or three centuries do indeed enable
> us to steer better than the earlier mixture of luck and guesswork. The values of the Enlight-
> enment cannot in good faith be seen as a temporary aberration, or as a dubious passing
> phase, but are part of the long journey of the human mind towards an ever fuller and more
> accurate understanding of the natural order.

There is not therefore much to be said for such radical anti-foundationalism
and little serious warrant for the blanket historicist or constructivist scepticism
about the possibility of objective knowledge on which it is based. The great
modern advances in technology that have demonstrably improved the human lot
in respect of economic productivity, communications, travel and so on have all
rested on experimentally tried and tested scientific theory – notwithstanding the

provisional nature of such science. Thus, to say (rightly) that we see through a glass darkly is not to say that we do not see at all, and – as often noted – the most vocal of post-modern epistemic sceptics seem to be no less reliant than the rest of us on computers and mobile phones and no more nervous of their mortal prospects while collecting their air-miles on global lecture tours. But while it is clearly throwing out the baby with the bath-water to ground doubts about educational theory in a general scepticism about theoretical objectivity as such, this is not to say that Carr is mistaken in his more particular scepticism about whether any and all rational educational practice needs to be grounded in some sort of 'applied' science. Here, however, it may be that Carr fails to see the wood (of the problem) of educational theory, for the trees of his larger anti-foundationalist scepticism about theory as such.

Oddly enough, what lies at the root of Carr's misperception of the problem of educational theory is a failure of conceptual analysis. It is common for philosophers hailing from the general quarters from which Carr draws many of his criticisms to object to such analysis on the grounds that it mistakenly takes such problematic terms as 'truth', 'knowledge', 'justice', 'virtue' and 'education' to have universal meanings that can be fixed by strict definitions. Ironically, this is just what good conceptual analysis *does not do* – and what all too many post-whatever critics of conceptual analysis often do. Indeed, we have already noticed that the founding father of analytical philosophy Gottlob Frege insisted as a key methodological principle that the meaning of a term is revealed only in the context of a proposition, and his pupil Wittgenstein – whom Carr at one point invokes in some support of his anti-foundationalist position – urges that we should look for the meaning in the *use*. But this is just the advice that Carr seems not to have heeded at any point (so far as one can see) in his own attempts to address this issue. To this extent, his analysis of theory – so far as it goes – seems to be quite 'essentialist'. In short, he seems to assume that the term 'theory' has one invariant meaning in all contexts – presenting this as the composite Aunt-Sally for his 'anti-foundationalist' critique – and fails to see that it has a variety of (faster and looser) uses in significantly different contexts of educational or education-related discourse. For reasons of space, we may here distinguish just two of these.

First, then, when students of education are asked what they expect to study in their classes of 'educational theory', they may mention a range of academic disciplines – such as Psychology of Education, Sociology of Education, History of Education and so on – of precisely the kind that were introduced into post-war teacher education programmes. However, when politicians are heard in the media decrying the latest 'barmy theory' they may not have such disciplines in mind at all. The 'theories' they will often be denouncing are not so much the results of social scientific research, but more generally the kinds of ideologies, policies or prescriptions that often go under such (loose) labels as 'progressive education', 'traditional education', 'child-centred education', 'de-schooling', 'liberal education' and so on. Now a very important and telling point already emerges from such difference of usage. To begin with, 'educational theory' in the first sense identifies a set of disciplines that are of a generally (and genuinely) theoretical (often experimental scientific) character – though they are not obviously or especially educational disciplines. Piaget's cognitive stage theory and Gardner's theory of multiple intelligence are widely regarded (rightly or wrongly) as relevant to educational practice and as useful to teachers; however, they are, speaking strictly, not so much educational as psychological theories. For example, the fact that there are different kinds of intelligence (if there are) says nothing at all about what we should do with such knowledge in the classroom.

On the other hand, whereas 'child-centred education', 'liberal education' and 'de-schooling' have much of a principled nature to say about how we should go about educating or promoting the learning of young people, they are not obviously scientific theories – though they may make some appeal to the findings of social science to justify some of their prescriptions. Moreover, as already noted, such prescriptions are frequently underdetermined – if determined at all – by empirical evidence. Whereas Plato grounded his decision to devote the lion's share of educational resources to the most able in alleged differences of intelligence, others have cited such differences in support of devoting more time and resources to the less able (see White, 1973). The key point here is that proponents of (say) child-centred education are less – or at least not primarily – likely to make their case for greater attention to children's interests or for more freedom in the classroom on any alleged 'value-neutral' empirical facts of human development in the way that aviation designers would aspire to base aeroplane construction on the experimentally grounded principles of aeronautical science. In short, while the psychological or sociological theories studied in 'educational theory' would have some (true or false) claim to be science – though they are not in any obvious sense *educational* science – the 'educational theories' derided by politicians and the media may well constitute principled perspectives on education, though they are not so obviously instances of (at least experimental or empirical) science.

EDUCATIONAL PHILOSOPHY AND THEORY: SCIENCE OR ETHICS?

The predictable response to these observations from those of 'post-analytic' (or post-whatever) temper is that they rest entirely on an outdated empiricist distinction between the factual (the domain of science) and the evaluative or prescriptive (the domain of ethics) and that this distinction – no less than that between theory and practice (of which the fact–value distinction is sometimes taken to be a special case) – has been shown (by Dewey and others) to be bogus, false or otherwise untenable. In response, however, it is arguable that such claims are mere unexamined slogans that need careful scrutiny if not outright resistance. Once again, the trouble with most general complaints about the theory–practice distinction (which we shall not further pursue here) is that – as in the case of objections to foundationalism – it is seldom clear just which of several different versions of this distinction is being taken to task. Although some implausible or unhelpful uses may have been made of this distinction, it should also be clear that it is a valuable if not indispensable one for many (theoretical) purposes. The same may be said for distinctions between descriptive statements or statements of fact, and evaluative or prescriptive judgements, for which there is a fairly clear warrant in usage and which have proved invaluable in modern philosophy for clarifying many central questions of ethics. On the other hand, it is a fair complaint – rightly made by modern neo-naturalists – that the sharp logical separation between facts and values observed by Hume and his positivist heirs (see, for example, Ayer, 1967) is untenable to the point of making it difficult to see why we have the values we have. So, for example, human beings (even sadists) generally regard torture as cruel and would mostly condemn it: but, of course, to regard something as cruel is intelligible only in the knowledge that sentient beings suffer pain under certain conditions and that such pain is unpleasant. One reason why children often appear cruel is that they are not aware of this *fact*.

Moreover, clear reflection on these issues is apt to be occluded by some failure to separate a number of different distinctions that have been unhelpfully elided in post-Enlightenment ethics since Hume and Kant. Thus, for example, despite common assumptions to the contrary, it is not obvious that the fact–value distinction is identical with the is–ought distinction. For although our values are invariably rooted in our experience of the world and human nature – in our knowledge of what circumstances are or are not conducive to the flourishing of human agents as part of that nature – it should be no less clear that such agents (for instance, surgeons operating to save a mother and her unborn baby) may agree completely in their values and about the facts while disagreeing about what they should do for the best. In short, inference from 'is' to 'ought' is often less clear than from fact to value – and much confusion about this has been conspicuous in modern moral philosophy. Thus, for example, utilitarians who (rightly) rejected empiricist and Kantian logical separation of values from facts seem to have assumed (wrongly) that such rejection would licence direct argument from 'is' to 'ought' (of which the principle of utility is itself a clear instance). On the other hand, later moral 'prescriptivists' seem to have (rightly) taken to heart the point that there is no direct inference from description to prescription, but to have concluded from this (wrongly) that human values are entirely separate from or independent of factual knowledge (see Carr, 1995).

As it also happens, these key distinctions appear to have been recognized in Aristotle's ethics. First, Aristotle clearly appreciates that human values and virtues are not disconnected from our understanding of human life and experience as part of that natural order which is also the topic of various kinds of scientific (physiological, biological, psychological) study. That said, Aristotle also recognizes that there are kinds of deliberation and judgement – about, for example, what to do in the case of conflict between equally compelling values and virtues – with which scientific study is not (at least by itself) well placed to assist us. There is, in short, a significant difference between the sort of reflection involved in truth-focused scientific observation, enquiry and explanation and the kind of deliberation required to help us act for the best in morally uncertain or problematic circumstances. In this light, it is not that there is no difference between fact and value or description and prescription: on the contrary, facts can help us understand and clarify our values and accurate description of the particular circumstance of moral dilemma may be indispensable to good judgement and wise prescription. Indeed, it should be clear from all this that what is here really required is the careful mapping of a range of complex conceptual distinctions and contrasts between description, evaluation and prescription; it is therefore nothing short of philosophically irresponsible to shirk this task in the name of meaningless post-whatever repudiation of such distinctions. Moreover, such repudiation is especially odious in the shape of any neo-idealist or radical constructivist assimilation of facts to values that would effectively confine human communities to the subjective circle of their own self-validating prejudices.

Returning to Carr's particular problem about educational theory, however, it should be clear that these observations about different forms of human enquiry do raise genuine issues about the theoretical status of educational enquiry – not least regarding the educational merit of those forms of social scientific (psychological and sociological) enquiry that were earlier distinguished (using the old analytical distinction between a priori and a posteriori investigation) from philosophy by reference to their empirical or experimental content. For, as we saw, there has been a growing modern tendency to conceive the study of education in terms of gradual movement towards more precise empirical scientific understanding of the processes of pedagogy – which, if it has not entirely replaced philosophical reflection, has very much relegated it to a back seat. On this view, educational philosophy might still have some vestigial role to play by virtue of the conceptual policing of common usage or the clarification of general ethical principles (in the interests of fair distribution of educational resources); however, the core of educational research and enquiry in any modern study of education would have to be scientific and empirical. In short, on this view, the main advances in modern educational thought have been made on the basis of close empirical observation of learning and/or the testing of educational methods, and educational theory has to be regarded – indeed, has come to be widely regarded (as the prevailing drift of university MSc programmes in Education indicates) – as a branch of social science.

We have seen that it is not reasonable to doubt the objective utility and power of empirical science in general. In this respect, in so far as the great technological developments of the modern age are clearly the direct consequence of powerful Enlightenment advances in our knowledge and understanding of the basic workings of nature, post-whatever scepticism about scientific objectivity is largely beneath serious notice. The question of present concern, however, is whether all or any alleged advances in the study of human learning or pedagogy constitute 'scientific' progress of this kind – and there is some reason to doubt this. For, to be sure, we also began this chapter by noticing that the major questions about education raised by such philosophers as Plato and Rousseau were questions about justice (Are all entitled to equal education regardless of apparent differences of ability?) and freedom (To what extent is it appropriate to manipulate the processes of human development?). Indeed, if what such great philosophers as Aristotle and Kant have said (in their rather different ways) about the key differences between empirical or other science and moral enquiry is so – and many if not most educational questions are moral issues – then scientific descriptions or analyses could have only limited bearing on the resolution of such questions. How, for example, might empirical research settle the question between (some) traditionalist educationalists and (some) progressives about the status and place of authority and discipline in the lives of children? Indeed, might it not be a simple (category) mistake to look for *any* general causal law determining what is right or suitable for all children in these or other respects?

Moreover, it is worth noting that much of the allegedly modern scientific or 'empirical' work of supposed educational relevance is apt to look less scientific on closer scrutiny. There can be little doubt that much twentieth century theory of learning and development has been (conceptually or empirically) mistaken – which, given the contemporary view that good science is always provisional and liable to disconfirmation – is both understandable and forgivable. But it seems less often appreciated that the main problems to which much of such theory has been prone are ethical, rather than empirical. Behaviourist learning theories would be morally objectionable even if we *could* effectively condition people to do what we might wish them to (which to some extent we can in fact do). Again, denying educational opportunities to the less able might be morally objectionable even we could prove scientifically that some are genetically inferior to others. In many if not most cases what lies at the root of bad educational thinking is not so much bad (empirical) science as bad or corrupt ethical deliberation – and, indeed, the questionable science has often enough turned out to be no more than a spurious prop for better or worse moral philosophy. An interesting case in point here is the influential (for at least half a century) theory of moral development of the American cognitive psychologist Lawrence Kohlberg (1981) – which, in the wake of Piaget's pioneering field investigations, made much of its empirical credentials. In short, Kohlberg claimed that his basically Kantian conception of moral development as progress through a series of earlier 'heteronomous' stages of moral development to a stage of independent self-legislating moral maturity was conclusively confirmed by his own close observation of children's responses to key questions at different age-related stages.

Whereas Kohlberg's work has been criticized from a variety of philosophical and empirical research perspectives – it has been pointed out (for example, by feminist ethicists of 'care': see Gilligan, 1982) that the constituency whose opinions Kohlberg polled was gender biased – the present author has elsewhere argued that empirical 'evidence' plays little or no coherent or substantial role in Kohlberg's theory and that his account is effectively normative 'all the way down' (Carr, 2002). On closer scrutiny, it seems that many modern social scientific theories of some educational influence are often little more than normative or moral accounts in thin empirical disguise. In fact, given the fairly central concern of education and teaching with questions of what constitutes human flourishing and of what we might best do to promote such flourishing, none of this should appear particularly surprising – and Plato and Aristotle could put us right about this from the outset. To be sure, this is not to say that ethical enquiry is in and of itself sufficient for the resolution of pressing educational issues and problems, or that empirical work can offer no useful contribution to thinking clearly about what we should or might do. Whereas statistical and qualitative research into educational questions is ever vulnerable to the time-honoured philosophical complaint that it seems all too often no more than the laborious and expensive demonstration of trivial truths, it can sometimes provide useful (and occasionally surprising) evidence for educational policy and prescription. We have also seen that in order to avoid dangerous constructivist or neo-idealist (or relativist) assimilation of knowledge to opinion, we should heed the Aristotelian advice that wise moral deliberation is ultimately rooted in an understanding of human nature to which empirical science no less than literary and other sources of human wisdom can usefully contribute. But the present chapter does point to the need for a shift of gravity regarding what seems to be the prevailing modern conception of the proper relationship of philosophical (or ethical) to empirical work in the field of educational studies. On this view, despite current trends, the empirical tail might be better or more wisely wagged by the philosophical or ethical dog.

REFERENCES

Ayer, A.J. (1967) *Language, Truth and Logic*. London: Gollancz.

Carr, D. (1995) 'The primacy of virtues in ethical theory: Part 1', *Cogito*, 9, 238–244.

Carr, D. (2002) 'Moral education and the perils of developmentalism', *Journal of Moral Education*, 31, 1, 5–19.

Carr, W. (2006) 'Education without theory', *British Journal of Educational Studies*, 54, 2, 136–159.

Cottingham, J. (2005) *The Spiritual Dimension: Religion, Philosophy and Human Value*. Cambridge: Cambridge University Press.

Frege, G. (1978) *The Foundations of Arithmetic: A Logico-Mathematical Enquiry into the Concept of Number*. Oxford: Blackwell.

Geach, P.T. and Black, M. (eds) (1966) *Translations from the Philosophical Writings of Gottlob Frege*. Oxford: Blackwell.

Gilligan, C. (1982) *In a Different Voice: Psychological Theory and Women's Development*. Cambridge, Mass: Harvard University Press.

Hamilton, E. and Cairns, H. (eds) (1961) *Plato: The Collected Dialogues*. Princeton: Princeton University Press.

Kant, I. (1968) *The Critique of Pure Reason*. London: Macmillan.

Kohlberg, L. (1981) *Essays on Moral Development: Volume 1*. New York: Harper and Row.

Kuhn, T.H. (1970) *The Structure of Scientific Revolutions*, 2nd edn. Chicago: University of Chicago Press.

McKeon, R. (Ed.) (1941) *The Basic Works of Aristotle*. New York: Random House.

Perry, L.R. (1967) *Bertrand Russell, A.S. Neill, Homer Lane, W.H. Kilpatrick: Four Progressive Educators*. London: Collier-Macmillan, Educational Thinkers Series.

Peters, R.S. (1966) *Ethics and Education*. London: George Allen and Unwin.

Peters, R.S. (1973) Aims of education, in R.S. Peters, (ed.), *The Philosophy of Education*. Oxford: Oxford University Press.

Quine, W.V.O. (1969) *Ontological Relativity and Other Essays*. New York: Columbia Press.

Rousseau, J-J. (1973) *The Social Contract and other Discourses*. London: Dent.

Rousseau, J-J. (1974) *Emile*. London: Dent.

Rusk, R. R. (1979) *Doctrines of the Great Educators*. London: Macmillan.

Russell. B. (1956) *Logic and Knowledge: Essays 1901–1950*. London: George Allen and Unwin.

Ryle, G. (1949) *The Concept of Mind*. London: Hutchinson.

Scheffler, I. (1960) *The Language of Education*. Springfield, IL: Thomas Press.

White, J.P. (1973) The curriculum mongers, in R. Hooper (ed.), *The Curriculum: Context, Design and Development*. Edinburgh: Oliver and Boyd.

Wilson, J., Williams, N. and Sugarman, B. (1967) *Introduction to Moral Education*. Harmondsworth: Penguin.

Wittgenstein, L (1953) *Philosophical Investigations*. Oxford: Blackwell.

4

The Philosophy of Education and Educational Practice

Richard Pring

INTRODUCTION: THINKING PHILOSOPHICALLY

There is a puzzle. On the one hand, few university departments or schools of education now provide a philosophical perspective on educational questions; people with philosophical training are rarely appointed. And yet, on the other hand, philosophical problems – at least to the discerning eye – permeate so many of the educational questions which worry us. Furthermore, policy solutions to perceived problems are quite clearly muddled because they have not addressed questions which philosophers from time immemorial have been asking. It is the job of philosophy to scratch beneath the surface of 'agreed meanings' – the 'self-evidently true' pronouncements – and to show that life is much more complicated than is assumed. And so one task of philosophy is to make people, especially those who think they have the right answer, uncomfortable.

A very good example of this is provided by Plato in the *Republic*. The rather arrogant Thrasymachus defines 'justice or right' as 'what is in the interest of the stronger party'.[2] Socrates sees a problem in that definition. What is meant by 'in the interest of'? Socrates enlarges on his puzzlement.

> For instance, Polydamas the athlete is *stronger* than us, and it's *in his interest* to eat beef to keep fit; we are *weaker* than him, but you can't *mean* that the same diet is *in our interest* and so right for us?'

Thrasymachus now gets irritated as he refines his original definition to embrace the state or government as the stronger party. In other words, those in power are the ones who define what is right and just – which, in fact, would often seem to be the case. Socrates presses on with the possible objections to this definition, providing counter-examples. Eventually, Thrasymachus exits in a fit of temper. What seemed straightforward had been proved not to have been so.

There are now few examples of heads of education departments exiting in fits of temper because there are fewer philosophers of education appointed to ask awkward questions – about the meaning of education underpinning the educational practices, or about the point of teaching particular subject content, or about the basis for the teacher's authority, or about the meaning of evidence in evidence-based research.

But Plato (or Socrates) was not simply going through the mechanical motions of asking 'What do you mean?' whenever someone said something he disagreed with.

First, he was aware of ambiguity in words which were playing a pivotal role in the other person's argument. A lot hung on a particular and contestable interpretation. By giving counter-examples, he was able to bring this out – and, in this particular case, was able to reveal the distinctively moral nature of the discourse about what is right and just.

Secondly, however, that verbal probing led inexorably to deeper questions about the nature of the state and its relations to the individual members of the state – indeed, to the constitution of the Republic and to the form of education appropriate to the future citizens of the Republic. There is an interconnection of 'meanings', a mosaic of concepts through which we understand the social world and act intelligently within it. One task of the philosopher, and of the philosopher of education in particular, is to examine critically the understandings embodied in the language of the social world which affect the policy and practice of education.

This chapter is designed to illustrate this: to penetrate some of the language through which we talk about education and to examine critically the implications of that language.

THE NUFFIELD REVIEW

Plato, in speaking through the mouth of Socrates, was addressing real and pressing issues in moral discourse (as that engaged in by the influential Sophists) and in arguments about the constitution of the state. Likewise, to philosophize about education is to address real and pressing problems about educational policy-making and educational practice. It needs to be rooted in the practice of education and in the descriptions and justifications of that practice.

As an example, let us consider the Nuffield Review of Education and Training 14–19 for England and Wales which was set up to be an independent, comprehensive and evidence-based review of the education system for students between the ages of 14 and 19.[3] But immediately the philosophically minded will detect problems. 'Comprehensive' from what point of view?

'Comprehensive' is an interesting word. It signifies that every aspect has been taken into account – quality of learning, curriculum, assessment, role of the teacher, system performance, qualifications framework, institutional provision, progression – and indeed these did serve as the headings for various chapters. But there is an infinite number of possible 'aspects', and the ones which one picks out depend on the point of view from which one is doing the review. That 'point of view' was shaped by the understanding the directorate had of an educated person. Therefore the key question addressed was: What counts as an educated person in this day and age?

The significance of that can be seen from the consideration of a quite different question which might have shaped the Review: namely, 'What learning is required for the economic prosperity of the country?' After all, that does seem to be the implicit question behind many of the changes which are affecting the education and training of 14–19 year olds.

CONCEPT OF EDUCATION

However, the changes affecting young people are made under the guise of *educational* reform, and understandably so, because education is associated with that development of persons which would not occur through sheer physical adaptation and growth. We don't talk about the education of donkeys (only the training of them), but we do talk about the education of human beings.

Furthermore, as Peters argued many years ago (1965), the dominant use of 'education' is essentially evaluative – the valuing of development as leading to a better state of being. In that sense, so he argued, the 'logic' of the word 'education' is somewhat like that of 'reform'. To say someone is reformed is to say that he or she has changed for the good – what previously was judged bad has now been overcome and replaced by a better state of mind or moral character. And one way of criticizing, say, a government's 'reform agenda', is not so much by referring to the facts (as when one might say the changes claimed have not taken place) as by pointing out that things have not changed for the better. It is a change but not a reform.

So too, one might criticize educational reforms on the grounds that they are regarded as not educational (that is, they do not meet the evaluative criteria picked out by our use of the word 'education') or they are 'mis-educational' (that is, they get in the way of educational development).

However, what should be those 'evaluative criteria' whereby an activity is valued as educational? To answer that we need, as Peters argued, to attend a little more carefully to the particular aspects of development which are normally picked out by our use of the word – not any sort of improvement is *educationally* worthwhile (for example, one might improve as a pickpocket). 'Education' would pick out those improvements which are concerned with the development and learning of what is distinctively human – the capacities to live distinctively human lives.

Of course, there lies the difficulty (often unacknowledged) which permeates all educational discourse: namely, disagreement over what counts as a distinctively human life and human fulfilment. And the Nuffield Review therefore had to tackle that difficulty because answers to the question posed above are implicit in the very content of the curriculum, in the way in which young people are expected to learn, in the relationships between the teachers and the taught, and in the organizational arrangements for education and training. If you separate children at the age of 11 to give them different sorts of learning experience, then you are subscribing to different educational aims for different children. If you make some subjects part of a core curriculum and not others (e.g. the arts and the humanities), then you are in fact saying that the former subjects have more educational value than the others. Therefore, clarity about the different and often competing aims of education and about the values which they embody was important for the Review.

But what are the aims of education – or, philosophically, how does one set about answering that question?

ESTABLISHING THE AIMS OF EDUCATION

One popular answer, and embedded in the key government 14–19 document (DfES, 2004), is that it is to enable all young people 'to realize their potential'. This oft-repeated wisdom always receives solemn nods of agreement. But let us 'do a Socrates' and look for a counter-example. My eldest grandson at the age of 5 took my handkerchief without my knowing it from my pocket and put it down the lavatory. He demonstrated great potential for being a Fagin. Do I want him to realize his potential? Well, some potentials and not others. We have potential for both good and bad, and simply to recommend the realization of potential is to dodge the ethical issues. Which potentials do we want realized and in what ways, in the light of the cultural resources we have inherited, do we want them to be realized?

Therefore, by examining the meaning of the word 'education' – by clarifying how it is used in our language – we come to realize that we are engaged in an ethical form of discourse with all the difficulties that that entails. What are the criteria by which one might judge the educational worth of a person's so-called education? People have different values.

LANGUAGE MATTERS

In this, as in so much else, language matters and so do the metaphors we employ in thinking about educational aims. Language shapes our thinking. It embodies how we see and experience the world. It is very noticeable that pursuing the relevance of education to the economic world has given rise to the increasing use of a particular sort of 'management language', where the performance of schools and colleges is described and evaluated in terms usually used of business organizations. Where have these changes come from, and what lies behind them?

Much of the answer to that undoubtedly lies in the increased central control of education, which brings with it the language of effectiveness and efficiency – the most effective way of attaining some pre-specified goal. Enter the language of performance management: for example, *levers* and *drivers* of change, and *public service agreements* as a basis of funding. The language through which we describe, evaluate and justify 'educational activities' has changed. The *consumer* or *client* replaces the learner. The curriculum is *delivered*. *Stakeholders* shape the aims. Aims are spelt out in terms of *targets*. *Audits* (based on *performance indicators*) measure success, defined in terms of hitting the targets. Cuts in resources are euphemistically called '*efficiency gains*'. Education, in its descriptive sense, becomes that package of activities (or *inputs*) which are largely determined by government, assisted, in England, by a *delivery unit* at No. 10, whose *management models* for running education include that of *command and control* – a process well described in Seddon's (2008) paper on 'deliverology'.

As the language of performance and management has advanced, so we have proportionately lost a language of education which recognizes the intrinsic value of pursuing certain sorts of question, of trying *to make sense of* reality (physical, social, economic and moral), of *seeking* understanding, of *exploring* through literature and the arts what it means to be human or what Plato, in *The Symposium*, referred to as the 'desire and pursuit of the whole'. In that respect the distinctive features of 'school' are being obscured.

How different the provision of education and training might be if we employed different metaphors, for the words we use embody the way in which we conceive the world, other people, the relationships between them and the way in which they should be treated. Oakeshott referred to education as an *initiation into the world of ideas*, a world of ideas which had arisen from *the conversation between the generations of mankind*, in which the young person is introduced to the different voices in that conversation – the voices of poetry, of science, of history, of philosophy. There is an *engagement* between learners and teachers who are able to relate that conversation to the interests and needs of the learner (Oakeshott, 1972, 1990).

Yet other metaphors enable one to conceive of education differently. The American philosopher, John Dewey (1916), seeing the danger of the 'false dualism' of 'academic' (the transmission of knowledge) and 'vocational' (the narrowly conceived training to hit a target) emphasized the integration of practice with the world of ideas ('the accumulated wisdom of the race') as the young person adapted to new situations, faced problems that need to be solved, endeavoured to make sense of experience and learned to extend and benefit from relations within the wider community. Education as growth and adaptation was the metaphor.

These and other different understandings of education and its aims, each with its own distinctive metaphors, compete for allegiance: one which sees teaching as *delivering* knowledge and skills in order to meet targets; another as an *engagement* between teacher and learners in order to help them to enter into a *conversation* and to appreciate the world of ideas; and yet a further as a continuing and intelligent adaptation to reality as problems arise and are solved, though drawing upon the knowledge and experience of previous investigations.

The danger is that, in seeking wholesale 'reform' of 14 to 19, we shall depend upon an uncritical use of language and of metaphors – a language which lends itself more to effective control and management than to an engagement between minds.

Language continues to bewitch policy and practice in other ways too: for example, in the questionable distinction between academic and vocational. Upon analysis this dichotomy not only does not make sense but also is extremely dangerous for practice. It excludes important activities, especially in the arts, which have been 'disapplied' from the National Curriculum post-14. Are these academic or vocational? They can become 'academic' (theorizing about drama or studying the history of art), but then they lose their distinctively practical and aesthetic character. Again the meaning of 'vocational', as indeed that of 'skill', is so 'elastic' as to stretch from very narrow skills training to intellectually demanding apprenticeships in engineering, through which young people can move into higher education.

AN EDUCATED PERSON

In sorting out the aims of education and training for 14–19 year olds, we need to look at the development of the person as a whole – those qualities and attainments which make him and her distinctively human and the ways in which those qualities might be enhanced. There is a danger otherwise of having too narrow a view of the aims. The following sets out the characteristics of being a person, which need to be nurtured or developed if each is to live a distinctive human form of life – exercising the different human qualities to the greatest extent possible. But, of course, in spelling them out, I am laying myself open to criticism from those who might wish to argue for a different understanding of human fulfilment. There is never a final end to ethical argument. Yet argue one must if one is to justify what to teach, how to teach and where to teach.

Intellectual development

There is a common association between 'education' and the initiation into the different forms of knowledge which constitute what it means to think intelligently – the acquisition and application of key concepts, principles and modes of enquiry to be found in the physical and the social sciences, in the study of literature and history, in mathematics, and in language and the arts. It is concerned with the development of the intellect, and thus with the capacity to understand, to think critically about the physical, social, economic and moral worlds we inhabit, and to act intelligently within them. It is, as Stenhouse (1983) argued, to 'value the emancipation of pupils through knowledge'. It is to enter into the world of ideas. But such entry can be achieved at different levels – no one need be excluded.

Such a view, however – seeing the link between education and the development of the capacity to think intelligently (what Dewey referred to as the 'intelligent management of life') demands yet further philosophical thinking about 'thinking intelligently' – the different forms of thinking with their distinctive concepts and modes of enquiry, their different tests for the truth of what has been said and the interrelationships between the different modes of thinking.

Practical capability

However, as the Royal Society of the Arts (RSA) pointed out in its 1986 Manifesto *Education for Capability*, the pursuit of 'intellectual excellence' can create an imbalance between theoretical knowledge and practical competence – a different form of 'intelligent management of life'. As the Manifesto declared

> The idea of the educated person is that of a scholarly individual who is able to understand but not act … . Education should … also include the exercise of creative skills, the competence to undertake and complete tasks and the ability to cope with everyday life… . Educators should spend more time preparing people for a life outside the education system.

The RSA represents a broader view of excellence where theory and practice are integrated in intelligent doing and making, and in giving recognition to 'competence, coping, creativity and co-operation with others'. Practical *know how* is not reducible to *knowing that* – practical intelligence to theoretical knowledge. There is a need to recognize and respect practical capability, that capacity to face and to solve practical problems, including working intelligently with one's hands, that integration of 'brain and hands', reflected particularly in the achievements of great engineers such as Morris (later Lord Nuffield) and Brunel, but seen also in the intelligent problem-solving of countless craftsmen and women.

Community participation

Dewey argued strongly that one could not separate the individual from the community through which he or she had come to see the world in a particular way. Our own growth in understanding and dispositions cannot be disconnected from the interactions with other people through which prevailing understandings are challenged and our experiences transformed. Therefore, the development of that 'intelligent management of life' requires the development of a sense of community – of the practical know-how and the disposition both to learn from the experiences and criticisms of the wider community and to contribute to its further growth.

That sense of community – acknowledging common needs, recognizing the importance to personal growth of common enlightenment and pursuing common enjoyment – lies at the centre of education for citizenship. The community shapes the lives of each of us, but is itself shaped by the thinking and activity of its members. Hence, the importance of education for democracy and the embodiment of democratic principles in the life of school and college. Part of that would be the acquisition of the knowledge and skills whereby each individual was able to contribute fruitfully to the community.

Moral seriousness

Part of what is distinctive to being a person is the capacity to shape one's life according to what one believes to be right – to take responsibility for the direction of one's life. Young learners can, and should be helped to, reflect on how they should live their lives, commit themselves to notions of justice, care about the environment and other social and moral issues. It is a matter of *seriousness* in asking what kind of life is worth living, what is worth pursuing in leisure or career and what obligations are to be considered sacred. It is to have certain moral virtues (e.g. concern for those in trouble) and intellectual virtues (e.g. openness to evidence, argument and criticism).

One important aspect of that moral seriousness must be a concern about the 'the big issues' which affect the wider society into which the young person is entering – those concerning the conflicts which so easily arise, the capacity of a multicultural society to live in harmony, the steps which need to be taken to confront ecological and climate change. It is not enough to have knowledge; one needs also the dispositions to apply that knowledge in the creation of a better world.

Pursuit of excellence

Schools have often seen part of their educational mission to be that of inspiring young people with ideals which enable them to aim high, to pursue excellence in its different forms and to reach beyond the present situation inspired by the ideals of what might be achieved in academic work, sport, the arts or even in a task or job which, though lowly, provides the scope for a sense of achievement. This need not be something remote, but that sense of achievement is open to all.

Self-awareness

'Know thyself' instructed Socrates. Knowledge of oneself, of one's strengths and weaknesses, of what one might aspire to, of the contribution one might make to the wider community and of what one would find fulfilling, must be at the heart of education. Such self-knowledge and exploration is achieved in many ways – through the arts, drama and literature, through group activities and individual pursuits. Confidence in oneself, though tempered by realistic appraisal and resilience in the face of failure, are part of the educational ideal for all young people, irrespective of background or ability.

That then is the educated 19 year old: one who has a sufficient grasp of those ideas and principles to enable him or her to manage life intelligently, who has the competence and skills to tackle practical tasks including those required for employment, who has a sense of community and the disposition to make a contribution to it, who is morally serious in the sense that he or she cares about fairness and responsibility to others, who is inspired by what has been done by others and might be done by oneself, and who has a sense and knowledge of self-confidence and resilience in the face of difficulty. Such an educational aim is open to everyone, irrespective of ability or background. Such an aim should shape the education for the future.

At least, that is the 'educated 19 year-old' as the Nuffield Review sees it. But the philosopher will no doubt want to probe more deeply – to question the concept of intelligence, to seek further clarity of the concept of practical knowledge, to extend the concept of 'self-knowledge' or to push the analysis of community to the deeper considerations of those in social philosophy who have argued for this as a central educational aim (see, for example, Tawney, 1931).

But all this needs to be argued and there would be something questionable about the argument and analysis if there were no competing views contesting it. After all, the practice of so much education finds little room for the practical intelligence or the moral seriousness. The educated products of many universities use their educational achievements for bad ends – very skilfully. Would they, bereft of moral seriousness, be regarded as educated persons?

Social justice

Much of what has been said would seem to focus simply on the educated individual, although such a person would, as it was said, develop the kind of knowledge and dispositions to contribute to the wider community – to become a good and active citizen. But that does not quite do justice to the aim of producing the just society which Plato's Republic was supposed to embody. There are deep-seated philosophical arguments about the relation of the individual to the wider society. How far should education be geared to individual autonomy and advancement, and how far to the realization of the common humanity through which the individual is able to find his or her fulfilment? That important question – affecting the arguments for and against the 'common school' – is resolvable only through a consideration of what it means to be a person and to be one more fully. For Dewey, one realizes one's potential only within a community and a common educational experience is therefore crucial.

PHILOSOPHY OF EDUCATION AND EDUCATIONAL PRACTICE

The implications of this way of thinking – which I have but introduced and thereby shown the need for a more extensive and deeper questioning of 'What do you mean?' – are considerable for educational practice. That practice is dominated by targets and performance indicators, but such indicators should be logically related to the aims one is aspiring to realize. Change the aims and one must change the indicators of success accordingly. Or, put another way, a narrow set of indicators implies a narrow set of educational aims which well may not tally with the ones spelt out above. Many schools working in difficult social and economic contexts have been publicly charged with failing, when, set against these broader educational aims, they might well be regarded as highly successful. Or, again, given the range of aims (that is, the range of qualities, dispositions and understandings which are part and parcel of what it means to be human and to manage life intelligently), does the curriculum reflect them all – for instance, the 'practical capability' emphasized by the RSA – and do the practices of the school community demonstrate the moral seriousness which one seeks to develop in all young people?

WHO DECIDES UPON THE AIMS?

What has been written in this chapter is essentially contestable. By which I mean that, such is the disagreement in ethical or moral discourse, people are bound to differ about the aims of education – about the weight to be given to this or to that kind of knowledge, or to the authority of the teacher and to the freedom of the child. Given the controversial nature of the questions, who is to decide what is worth learning? Who are the moral experts?

Plato had an answer. Certain people, by reason of their background and education, had reached a stage of wisdom such that they were able to distinguish between what is true and what is false, between what is good and what is bad. A selective form of education picked out and educated the guardian class and the philosopher kings. And such a platonic ideal shaped the education of the ruling class in England in the nineteenth century – the creation through the public school system of what Coleridge referred to as 'the clerisy'. But such an understanding of moral wisdom would not find too many defenders today. How then might one find a solution to the important questions which divide rather than unite?

There are many voices in the deliberations about the aims of education and about the implementation of those aims in practice. Reconciliation of differences or the accommodation of differences within the system as a whole or within the school or college is, as with all moral discourse, a matter of constant deliberation. But it requires the right sort of forum, both nationally and locally, for such deliberations to take place. No one voice, not even the government's, should be allowed to drown out the others.

CONCLUSION

I have tried to illustrate the role of philosophy in the development of educational policy and practice.

First, those with a philosophical frame of mind see puzzles in the use of language where very often others do not. What seems to be a straightforward description or evaluation of events turns out not to be so. Language can be deceptive. Certain words hide important differences of meaning – differences which embody different understandings of how the physical, social and moral worlds we inhabit should be seen. The philosopher, much to the annoyance of some people, keeps asking 'What do you mean by that?' But in pursuing those questions one comes to realize that the use of a word depends on the connotations of that word from quite different contexts. The use of 'skill' in educational discourse is a good example. The development of skills is a clarion call for much educational policy, but the word is used very elastically to cover the physical dexterity of the carpenter, language skills, cognitive skills and so on – often as though what is meant in one context can be transferred without change of meaning to another, with all the implications that has for the 'training in skills'. The Nuffield Review therefore had to make fine and not so fine distinctions between the knowledge and skills (with which it is often equated) in order to see the range of factors to be included in the idea of an educated 19 year old.

Secondly, however, in pursuing such uninspiring looking questions systematically, one would be forced (as Plato was in *The Republic*) to deeper questions with which philosophers have been grappling since Plato – concerning the nature of knowledge, the sort of life worth living, thereby the ultimate aim of education, the quality of learning, or the authority of the state in deciding what is worth learning.

Not only are these puzzles not faced by policy-makers, but also they are not considered by teachers, who increasingly see their role (under the shadow of particular metaphors) to 'deliver' what is demanded by those policy-makers and their civil servants and agents. Rarely in the past has the philosophical spirit been so required amongst teachers and their mentors as it is at present.

NOTES

2 Plato the *Republic*, Part I, Book I, 338. Such a view was common amongst the Sophists of the day.

3 The Nuffield Review was funded by the Nuffield Foundation and its Report was published in May 2009, *Education for All: the Future of Education and Training for 14–19 Year Olds*. London: Taylor and Francis. I was privileged to be lead director of the Review.

REFERENCES

Dewey, J. (1916) *Democracy and Education*. New York: Free Press.

DfES (2004) *Education and Training 14–19*. London: DfES.

Oakeshott, M. (1972) Education: its engagements and its frustrations. In T. Fuller, (Ed.), *Michael Oakeshott and Education*. London: Yale University.

Oakeshott, M. (1990) A place of learning. In T. Fuller (Ed.), *Michael Oakeshott and Education*. London: Yale University.

Peters, R.S. (1965) *Ethics and Education*. London: Allen and Unwin.

RSA (1986) *Education for Capability*. London: Royal Society of the Arts.

Seddon, J. (2008) Deliverology: the science of delivery, or dogmatic delusion? In *Systems Thinking in the Public Sector*. Axminster: Triarchy Press.

Stenhouse, L. (1983) *Authority, Education and Emancipation*. London: Heinemann.

Tawney, R.H. (1931) *Equality*. London: Allen and Unwin.

Some Key Historical Figures in the Philosophy of Education

Some Key Historical Figures
in the Philosophy of
Education

5

Plato and Education

Ieuan Williams

The chosen candidate to be minister of education, and those who choose him, should appreciate that this is by far the most important of all the supreme offices in the state. (Plato, *Laws* 765)

Education – interpreted in the broadest possible sense – has a claim to be considered perhaps the greatest preoccupation of the *Republic* and the *Laws* alike. (Malcolm Schofield, 2006)

INTRODUCTION: PLATO, POLITICS AND EDUCATION, IN HIS WORLD AND OURS

Plato invented the philosophy of education as we know it today. He identified the fundamental questions that constitute this area of inquiry and in doing so offered a wholly persuasive account of its great interest and importance. These questions included issues connected with learning, understanding and knowledge, with such features of human mentality as rationality, intelligence, emotion and desire, with moral aspects of education essentially bound up with virtue and citizenship, and, finally, with the distinctive social and political functions of education which connect it with justice. Plato is almost unique among philosophers, and certainly among political philosophers, in taking so much interest in the topic of education,[4] and for reasons that deserve brief comment.

Plato was born in Athens in 427 BC and died there in 347 BC. He spent almost his entire working life in that city, principally directing and teaching in the Academy he founded some time early in the fourth century. Athens, in decline during most of Plato's lifetime, was a city famous for its art and culture and for being the first democracy, a political system which Plato did not admire. Plato came from an aristocratic family and, like most young men of aristocratic birth, expected to enter the political life of the city. What is of particular interest to this review is why Plato was so hostile, not only to democracy, but to every other political system he was familiar with. His disillusion with Athenian politics, particularly after the execution of his teacher Socrates in 404 BC, is important to understanding the questions and issues to which he devoted serious and prolonged philosophical attention. His reflections eventually led him to the conclusion, defended in great detail in the *Republic*, that 'the troubles of mankind will never cease until either true and genuine philosophers attain political power or the rulers of states by some dispensation of providence become genuine philosophers.'[5] The fact that this form of government will not be democratic, and certainly not liberal as we now understand that concept, has laid Plato open to the charge that he was advocating a form of authoritarian, even totalitarian, state, and that his views on education can be dismissed because of this.[6] Such a negative response to Plato's work is short-sighted. Although democracy is a political system that is now widely championed and routinely claimed to be superior to its rivals, Plato believed that Athenian democracy was an unstable and excessively competitive society that fell far short of the ideal of justice he championed in a number of his works. We certainly should not expect his vision of the aims, practice and content of education to be consistent with the kind of democratic and liberal ethos that continues to prevail in many modern nation states. However, the fact that the democratic ethos, and the institutions and structures that sustain it, are perennially fragile and in constant need of defence and reinforcement, makes Plato's views on the political dimensions of education of serious interest. Plato's moral and political anxieties are remarkably similar to our own, for in spite of quite obvious differences of geographical scale, size of population, and in the technology of production, communication and culture, there are real and telling similarities between the Greek city-states of Plato's day and many contemporary societies: much human behaviour continues to be motivated by self-interest, there is widespread preoccupation with wealth and pleasure, large numbers of people succumb to the pervasive influence of techniques of persuasion, relativism is widely accepted in matters of belief, there are persistent social divisions and inequalities, and, in general terms, perceptions and values are guided by appearance rather than the reality which Plato believed to be discernible to human intelligence. It is against this background that Plato's distinctive, albeit highly contentious, views on education may greatly assist critical examination of contemporary assumptions and practices.

Although one of Plato's last works, the *Laws*, has much to say about the provision and practice of education, and once again offers a very clear indication of the great importance Plato attached to it, it is his best known work, the *Republic*, which contains his most sustained philosophical treatment of the topic, The key to understanding the role of education in *Republic* is what we will call its central argument.

EDUCATION AND JUSTICE: THE CENTRAL ARGUMENT

For Plato, education should play an essential role in creating and sustaining a just society. This implies that the content of education, and the pedagogical practices through which that content engages the interest and activity of young people, must be carefully selected and arranged to ensure that these can successfully achieve their principal purpose. Because Plato assumes there to be the closest possible parallel between the well-being of the individual soul and that of the well-ordered polity, he adopts the strategy of first analysing the latter for the purpose of greater understanding of the former. This strategy is of much importance to his account of the purposes that education is to fulfil, both in relation to society and to individual citizens.[7]

Justice in the State

The starting point of Plato's inquiry is the assumption that because both soul and State have the same structure, justice in both State and individual soul takes the same form. Plato's conception of justice is not that of a society designed to ensure 'the disproportionate happiness of any one class but the greatest happiness of the whole' (420b).[8] Justice prevails in both soul and the State when they are internally well ordered, and the key to understanding that order is the idea of virtue. In contrast to a modern conception of happiness, which at best recognizes a contingent relationship between virtue and happiness – nineteenth century utilitarianism is the paradigm of such a theory – Plato insists that the relationship between the two is one of necessity: according to Plato's philosophical framework only the virtuous can achieve happiness. However, such happiness is not to be defined by reference to pleasure – here Plato is going against the view of happiness prevalent in ancient Athens – but in terms of the distinctively Greek idea of *eudaimonia*; for Plato, that of a virtuous life free from the temptations of all forms of sensory indulgence and personal corruption. Thus we may say that if a just community is ordered for the purpose of realizing virtue in the lives of its individual citizens, then the main vehicle of that order will be education. However, the nature of the education designed to achieve that purpose will be significantly different from that found in Plato's Athens. It will be compulsory, its content will be carefully selected and arranged, and the whole system will be rigorously supervised by those in political authority.

As Plato's (often ironic) spokesman in the *Republic*, Socrates initiates the central argument with the observation that any human community has needs. Given that individuals are not self-sufficient, the very existence and survival of a community will depend on the cooperation of individuals in meeting basic needs for food, clothing and shelter. Plato insists that cooperation here works best when each person engages in the kind of work or occupation for which he or she is naturally fitted. This assumption, which might be called the principle of specialization, is crucially important to the central argument of the *Republic*.

Although the aptitudes and propensities with which Plato is concerned have their origins in nature, they provide the basis of a Platonic principle requiring each to engage in practices best suited to their inherited qualities. This principle has wide-ranging implications for Plato's account of the relationship between education and justice.[9]

However, human communities have more than material needs. They are prone to threats of invasion and conquest and to the forms of internal disunity and conflict that subvert justice and the well-being of citizens. This observation leads Socrates in the *Republic* to identify two further needs – for military strength and security and for good government. In this regard, just as able craftsmen and other workers are required for meeting the material needs of a community, so another class of courageous and well-trained personnel will be required for effective defence, and a further one of naturally qualified and appropriately educated rulers will be required, for the just legislation, that Plato contrasted with its counterfeit forms in Greek tyrannies, oligarchies and democracies.

Who is to belong to these three classes will be determined in accordance with the principle of specialization, which ensures that 'every person is not a plurality but a unity', and ultimately that 'the community as a whole will be a unity and not a plurality' (423c–d, W). This principle is so important for Plato that he regards it as nothing less than the foundation of a just society (4342, W), one which implies what is perhaps the most arresting claim in the *Republic*, that the unity and order of a just society can only be maintained if it is governed by a specially educated class – Plato calls them Guardians – who are qualified for this role by virtue of intellect, temperament and character. However, although the ultimate aim of education is the selection and training of potential Guardians, there will be no individuals in Plato's community who are deprived of an appropriate form of education (424a, 425b–c): it is to the moral development of individual souls that educational practices are to be directed.

Virtue and justice in the soul

In the *Republic* Plato takes the soul to be more complex, both in its internal structure and in its relation to the social environment, than the dualism he had defended in dialogues such as the *Phaedo*. In order to understand the role of education in the *Republic* we have to see how the soul is conceived, not as a single entity but as three parts or aspects of human being. This change brings with it a further difference of great interest to the kind of impact education can have on the soul: the kind of moral and spiritual disorder that Plato characterized as a lack of virtue is no longer seen to occur between soul and body but between internal parts of the soul. Indeed it is the frequent occurrence of this kind of inner disorder that, for Plato, shows that the soul does consist of different parts. A desire seeks its object: thirst, for example, is directed at its object, the drink that would quench it. But if we imagine that the soul 'resists the pull of thirst', then, Socrates argues, it must be a separate part of the soul that is exerting such resistance: in short, a desire cannot resist itself. This leads Socrates to distinguish between an appetitive part of the soul that moves it towards the satisfaction of desires, and a rational part by which the soul is able, through critical reflection, to choose the actions that conduce to its welfare (439d). The third spirited or passionate part of the soul that Socrates identifies[10] is inspired by attention to certain common ways in which human agents react emotionally in various circumstances. Human agents generally experience a range of morally significant reactive emotions – anger and resentment are, for Plato, the two most significant – prompted by perceived threats to the integrity and existence of the self. Plato's point here is that such reactions, like desires, can run beyond an agent's control, most typically to acts of aggression and violence, and thus need to be 'recalled by reason within' (440c–d): only through such restraint will the spirited aspect be able to preserve the existence and integrity of the soul. The importance of spirit can be fully appreciated, however, only through its proper relationship to reason. Although spirit seems at first a kind of desire, it can also seem to be, 'when not corrupted by bad education', 'a natural auxiliary of reason' (441a): a person's experiences may overcome her reason and cause that person to vent her anger 'at the source of the compulsion within'. Here it may seem that there are two factions at war within the person and that in this struggle between what she wants to do and what she rationally believes she should not, do, the spirited part is allied with rationality (440b). Nevertheless, spirit and reason remain distinct aspects of the life of the soul, and it is the distinctiveness and independence of reason, determined by its capacity for knowledge and wisdom, that enables it to fulfil its proper function of care of the soul with spirit as its ally.

The picture that emerges in this part of the *Republic* is of the soul as vulnerable to various forms of conflict, both within itself and with the social environment in which it is placed.[11] Such conflict is endemic in unjust societies and implies the absence of those virtues of character that Plato regarded as necessary to happiness. Justice and virtue may be restored to the soul when right reason governs each part of the soul and ensures that it fulfils its proper function in relation to the well-being of the whole: the ultimate function of reason, via its own characteristic virtue of wisdom, is to ensure that the other parts of the soul conform to the virtues (rather than the vices) characteristic of their natures – temperance in the case of appetite, courage in that of spirit (441c–e).

EDUCATION: JUST CITIZENS FOR A JUST SOCIETY

Plato's inquiry has reached the stage at which it can be agreed that 'the same principles which exist in the State also exist in the individual' (441c) and that in both cases it is a unifying harmony between the parts under the rule of reason. The question is now that of how Plato understood the crucial role of education in the preparation of just citizens for a just society. His inquiry turns on the assumption that individual aptitudes and propensities are unequally distributed across the human population.[12] Some children are born with enhanced rational capacities; others inherit the qualities of character and temperament associated with spirit; and others, perhaps the largest number, will naturally possess stronger appetites, and, thereby (Plato wrongly assumes) both lower degrees of courage and intelligence and an aptitude for practical skills. These differences lie at the root of the conflict, disorder and disunity that is injustice, both in the State and in the individual. Given that a State will be just only if its citizens are just, it must be the fundamental purpose of education to create just citizens. We can appreciate how education can do this only if we recognize that the three virtues that comprise the moral unity of the soul depend on the governance of appetite and spirit by reason. Yet many individuals will lack sufficient capacity for the rational thought required for such restraint. Plato concludes from this that since there are individuals who cannot by themselves achieve self-restraint, the only alternative is for the State to ensure that restraint occurs through education and just social control. In brief: productive individuals will live temperate lives in conformity with the tasks, traditions and practices for which they are suited by nature, as well as education and training. The members of the class that Plato calls auxiliaries – who are the spirited elements of the community – will be brave, and honourable, in accordance with their executive role.[13] The Guardians, by virtue of their capacity for rational reflection, and their prolonged and rigorous education, will rule with wisdom and authority.

THE PROVISION AND PRACTICE OF EDUCATION

As noted, Plato's curricular recommendations departed significantly from contemporary Athenian educational custom: for Plato, education was to be both compulsory and exclusively provided by the State; neither the content of the curriculum nor the social function of education could be left to what would today be called the private sector.[14] According to the system prescribed by the *Republic* there will be a point at which the natural aptitudes and qualities of temperament of individual pupils (in Plato's imagery whether their souls have a preponderance of gold, silver or bronze) are appropriately formed for their various purposes.[15] It is on the basis of some such educational programmes that individual children may be directed towards the kinds of work to which they are best suited, and ultimately towards their proper social class. However, Plato did not believe that children would inevitably be confined to the same social group as their parents. Thus, offspring of the productive class may have the natural potential to become Guardians or auxiliaries and, if so, should be given the education appropriate to this station. On the other hand, the offspring of Guardians, both male and female,[16] may not have the qualities that would qualify them for political rule and would in that case be relegated to either the auxiliary or the productive classes (423c–d).[17]

It is on the education of the Guardians that Plato concentrates in greatest detail and the two most important areas of the curriculum that they will follow are music and gymnastics (398b–412b). The educational value accorded to both music and poetry – the two went closely together in sung poetry and musically accompanied recitation – is very great in Plato's scheme. Yet, despite certain radical features, that scheme is mostly conservative. Recognizing that music enters very deeply into the soul (401d–e), and that poetry can have effects, for better or worse, on a person's moral understanding and sensibility, Plato insists that the kinds of rhythm and melody – as well as the content of the poetry to which young children are exposed – must be carefully selected for their value in promoting admirable qualities of character and intellect. Since beauty, grace and truth are the salient values here, it is important to discourage undesirable qualities of ugliness, insensitivity and shallowness of character.

Plato's strict censorship of the curriculum has been subject to intense criticism. Although the idea that educationists might select works of literature and music judged to be beneficial to pupils and students is hardly in itself objectionable; what is questionable, in the context of a liberal and democratic society, is the selection of artistic forms that represent only virtuous qualities, on the assumption that works of this kind might promote imitation of such qualities. Plato seems unable to see that art may deepen understanding by exploring the moral complexity of human life. Plato's insistence on such selection, moreover, threatens a regime of cultural censorship that would hardly be acceptable in any modern liberal democracy.

COMPLETING THE CENTRAL ARGUMENT

Plato musters two powerful images in support of the protracted and academically advanced education destined for his guardians.

The allegory of the cave

This allegory (524a–517c) pictures the condition of individuals in societies that are necessarily unjust or devoid of the virtues that only an adequate system of education can foster (514a). We are to imagine human beings imprisoned in an underground cave in which they are able only to see moving images projected on the cave wall. The fact that the prisoners are manipulated[18] into perceiving appearances rather than real things symbolizes their lack of the kind of education Plato outlines in the *Republic*: the lives of the cave-dwellers are dominated by mere images, opinions and vain desires.[19] Moreover, although a significant number of prisoners may hope for some release from the cave's illusions and vain desires, relatively few may hope to bear the dazzling sunlight of the world beyond the cave. These few are those who are able to contemplate the true nature of reality (516b), and, having acquired knowledge and wisdom, become qualified to return to the cave to care for the souls of those who remain imprisoned. They are the philosophers who have apprehended, not what masquerades as reality in the sensory world, or in conventional morality, but the actual ideas or forms through which the world, both as it is and how it might be, can be fully comprehended. Those individuals, 'the best minds of the community', will have achieved the greatest knowledge of all, 'the vision of the good'. However, once their education is complete, they will not be permitted to remain in this intellectual 'world' but compelled to return to the world of 'sensible' experience. True Guardians should also be happy to play this role, and to accept the conditions of guardianship (no private property, no marriage partners and communal existence) in so far as their education has prepared them to do so: having seen through the illusions of vain desire that defined life in the cave, they have become virtuously indifferent to them.

The simile of the divided line

Though placed before the allegory of the cave in the text of the *Republic*, the simile of the cave (509d–510e) is intended to represent both the nature of the Guardians' educational development and their relationship to those over whom they have political authority. We are to imagine a vertical line divided into two, the lower half signifying the visible or sensory realm and the upper half representing the intelligible realm, each half itself divided into two further sections. The line, therefore, represents four stages of cognitive ascent, beginning with the lowest and ending at the highest. What is crucially important, however, is that on one side of each section Plato locates an experiential or cognitive capacity of the soul that is then matched on the other side to the appropriate 'object' of that capacity. These 'objects' are arranged from lower to higher according to their inherent clarity, while the forms of experience and cognition that engage with them are arranged by virtue of being able, in varying degrees, to respond to and appreciate the relative clarity of those objects. In the two lower sections Plato places objects of sense experience, images, shadows and reflections (such as those seen projected on to the wall of the cave) at the lowest level, and objects themselves, rather than their reflections and representations, at the level above. Such objects are clearer than their images and reflections; they are experienced as they really are and human agents may form objective beliefs about them.[20] The second section of the lower half of the line represents the liberated condition of those in the cave who are no longer in thrall to images and illusions. The upper section of the line representing the intelligible realm, the realm of knowledge and understanding, is itself divided into higher and lower sections. The lower represents scientific inquiry: the kind of knowledge that intellect achieves when, for example, it grasps how the sun causes the temporal intervals of days, seasons and years or the validity of a geometric proof. Although this level indicates some advancement of the intellect from the level of belief to more abstract and complex forms of thought, cognition remains tied to the visible nature of objects and to various kinds of sign. At the highest level of cognition, the intellect is able to contemplate directly what were previously given in visible form; these are the forms or ideas that objects, signs, relationships and processes exemplify. Such forms are real in the sense that they are discovered rather than created by human beings; they are unchanging in contrast to the sensible particulars falling under them, and are, in contrast to objects of perception, absolutely clear and fully grasped – both in themselves and in relation to other forms – 'by the eye of the mind' (510e). The capacity to apprehend the true reality, the forms of things, is the final and absolutely necessary stage in the Guardians' education. It is only from this perspective that they are able to apprehend the form of the good, a perspective analogous to physical vision of the sun outside the cave. The concept of illumination is morally and politically important at this point in Plato's inquiry: at this stage the soul is finally able to grasp the true nature of the just State and how its citizens ought to live and be educated. Ultimately, it is the ability to apprehend and apply forms, and most significantly the form of genuine rather than conventional justice, that qualifies the Guardians for the task of legislating and educating for a just society. For Plato, moreover, once this system has been established it should not be allowed to change in any significant way (424b).

The images of the line and the cave are immensely important to Plato's philosophy of education. Whereas the allegory of the cave powerfully evokes the human condition prior to liberation from the bondage of illusion – one of the primary aims of education – the simile of the divided line reflects the structure and character of the education that will be required for maintaining a class of properly qualified Guardians. However, it is also important to see that the two images are not exclusively concerned with the education of the Guardians, given that a society can only be just if education affects the souls of all its citizens. The key point of the allegory of the cave is that no-one generally needs to remain in the condition described at the beginning of the allegory. Through participating in the right kind of education, the condition of the entire citizenry may be transformed. As C.D.C. Reeve rightly argues,[21] in opposition to the view advanced by Terence Irwin (1997), everyone in the new community receives an education, either in the crafts or in music and gymnastics, which promises to purge them of those vain desires that undermine virtue – which introduces the grim thought, which Plato ascribes to Socrates, that those who fail to respond to their education will be put to death (409e–410a).

Our account of the central argument of Plato's *Republic* shows how Plato's conception of a just society depends upon a system of education that ultimately aims to instil virtue in the character of individual citizens. Although Plato's political system and the practices that he held to follow from it may be found variously objectionable, his overall educational aim might be considered the most worthy that educationists could conceive.

Attractions

Plato's philosophical inquiries into education are of enduring value, not because his principal ideas, theories and recommendations should command universal approval, but because of the manner in which they challenge many current educational assumptions and orthodoxies. The philosophy of education is in perpetual need of renewal, and dialogue with a great philosopher of the past can be of vital importance in stimulating such renewal. Among the many issues that emerge in studying the *Republic*, the following may be numbered among the most fundamental and urgent.

(1) Plato's inquiries in the *Republic* indicate the necessity of integrating the central concerns of philosophy of education into a larger philosophically coherent whole. In this connection Plato's attempt to ground his educational ideas in a metaphysically, epistemologically, politically, ethically and psychologically unified system sets a demanding but valuable task. The central argument of the *Republic* precisely shows the need for educational philosophy to connect with and draw upon other aspects of philosophical reflection. Thus, although we may disagree with Plato's views, his concern with the larger philosophical integrity of the philosophy of education is an example that present-day educational philosophers might do well to follow.

(2) Plato's treatment of education, principally in the *Republic*, the *Statesman* and the *Laws*, attaches great importance to moral education, precisely understood as the education of virtuous character – an aim, which if achieved, has profound implications for the continuing stability of society (424a). Even though moral education and its importance in the school curriculum has been a topic of great interest to modern philosophers of education, this still remains a matter of uncertainty and confusion in democratic, liberal and pluralistic societies. Plato's profound concern with individual moral education, his own account of moral virtue, and the very idea that all education is of moral significance, continues to offer a corrective to more modern technicist conceptions of education.

(3) Plato is the first philosopher of education to give aesthetic and cultural education a key place in the curriculum. Educational thought and policy-making is in perennial danger of adopting an instrumental or utilitarian perspective, of favouring vocational and economic aims and of neglecting the value of aesthetic and cultural studies for the development of virtuous character. Plato may have been hostile to the kind of freedom enjoyed by artists and 'communicators' in democratic societies, but the value he attaches to aesthetic and cultural education, however conservatively he may have conceived this part of the curriculum, is central to his contemporary legacy.

(4) For Plato, the ultimate aim of education is good citizenship. In recent years there has been a revival of interest in citizenship and in the question of how an education system might serve to promote good citizenship.[22] The questions central to this area of interest – e.g. What constitutes good citizenship? What are the ethical beliefs and qualities that underpin good citizenship in an ethnically and culturally diverse society? What should be the role of schools in the promotion of good citizenship? – are not well understood and require considerable clarification. Plato responds directly and positively to such questions, and although the

views he defends may not today be acceptable, they may again prompt serious discussion. Following Plato, it might be suggested that in so far as citizenship, in the fullest sense, only seems possible in a just society, it should be the main aim of citizenship education to create such a society.[23]

Dangers

Since the *Republic* is a philosophically provocative book, a distinguished example of the kind of work belonging to the tradition of *Politeia* (citizenship) writing with which Plato was familiar, it should be read with considerable caution. Plato is a seductive writer, well capable of enticing the reader into assuming that he intends us to believe everything to which he gives Socratic voice in the *Republic*. However, it needs to borne in mind that despite Plato's reputation as the arch-enemy of rhetoric, he was himself a master of this art and that his own work is often playful and ironic – a stimulus to further thought rather than the last word on any issue. Plato would not have wanted to silence further discussion, but to raise it to the highest level of rigour and seriousness.

(1) Whatever might be said for the idea that comprehensive philosophical inquiry into education should include an account of human psychology, Plato's theory of the tripartite soul does not provide a particularly persuasive picture of human mentality. It does not adequately explain mental conflict, the function of reason in restraining excessive desire and spirit, or the promotion of virtues within the soul. Moreover, the idea that human mentality may be separated into three distinct kinds of capacity is seriously misleading as an account of the relationships between desire, emotion and rationality. Indeed, it can be argued that Plato's model of human mentality is unduly pessimistic in suggesting that the great majority of human beings are by nature largely incapable of controlling their desires and achieving virtue. Nevertheless, Plato teaches the valuable lesson that any acceptable account of human psychology would have to encompass a normative or moral dimension and could not, therefore, be a matter for purely naturalistic (or empirical) scientific study.

(2) Plato's conception of human society as divided into three distinct classes also seems unacceptably authoritarian and inegalitarian. Plato is committed to a rigid stratification of society into separate groups subject to a 'top-down' system of political authority that rules out the possibility of fostering further moral and political development, whether in individuals or in the community.[24] Plato's stance on social and cultural change may be attractive to modern conservatives who are similarly sceptical regarding the possibility of moral and cultural progress, yet the assumptions and arguments which Plato deploys in its defence are not generally persuasive. The assumption that any kind of change, once a just political and social order is in place, must inevitably mean decline and deterioration seems more a matter of Platonic prejudice rather than an evidentially supported claim.

(3) We come finally to the idea of justice with which the *Republic* is ultimately concerned. The principle that justice requires citizens to remain committed to the specialist occupation and social status marked out for them by nature, a principle to which educational provision must conform, is not convincingly defended and incorporates variously implausible assumptions. One such problem is the claim that children who inherit stronger desires than others ought to devote themselves to the skills of craftsmanship and productivity: strong appetites are not obviously a condition of possessing practical skills and expertise. Plato recognized that humans exhibit significant individual differences, but the complex nature and origins of these differences fails to reflect the simplistic relationship between education and social stratification envisaged in the *Republic*. There is a clear danger here that Plato's view of the social function of education may appeal to those who have lost faith in liberal values and the principles and practices of democratic politics. Plato condemned the Athenian democracy that he lived through as an unstable and excessively competitive society in which the self-interested majority paid scant regard to social justice and to the personal virtues that they held to be mere conventions. Such sceptics miss the point: Plato does not share the belief, widely held by modern conservatives, that because the ideal of a universal virtuous citizenship is impossible, the majority of mankind are destined to live lives that are inferior in quality to the superior and fortunate few. Plato is sufficiently optimistic to believe, both that tyranny can be avoided and that a society can be properly ordered in accordance with an ideal of justice rather than, as in the case of numerous contemporary societies, function through transitory conventions that work to the advantage of those who are stronger, cleverer and richer than the majority.

Thus, as hostile to democracy and liberal values as he undoubtedly was, Plato's provocative and polemical arguments continue to represent a serious and challenging voice in the ongoing dialogue of philosophy of education.[25]

NOTES

4 Rousseau and John Dewey come closest to following Plato's example in giving serious attention to education in the context of their inquiries into human nature, ethics and justice. Hobbes has very little to say about education in *Leviathan*, and, while Locke did regard education as a natural right, he does little by way of integrating his views on education with his theories of sovereignty and rights. Rawls (1971), perhaps the most influential contemporary work of political philosophy, barely mentions education.

5 Plato, *Phaedrus and Letters VII and VIII*, 1973, pp. 112–114. The occurrence of the word 'cure' in this passage is of great interest in revealing how Plato understood political corruption and injustice to be analogous to illness and how, in consequence, he understood the right kind of education to be an essential part of their cure.

6 Plato's ideas on politics and education had their greatest influence in Britain during the Victorian and Edwardian eras. This influence declined in the aftermath of the First World War, particularly after the rise of fascism, and very dramatically after the Second World War. Thus, Richard Crossman, then a lecturer in philosophy at Oxford and later to become a prominent Labour MP, in his brilliant and entertaining book *Plato Today*, published in 1937, accused Plato of carrying out 'the most blatant and profound attack upon liberal ideals that history can show'. (1937, p. 84), and Karl Popper, in his *The Open Society and Its Enemies* (1945) asserted 'that Plato's political programme, far from being morally superior to totalitarianism, is fundamentally identical with it' (p. 87).

7 The priority Plato gives to the State in his inquiry does not mean that Plato regards political justice as being more important than justice in a person's soul. The relationship between them is so close as to make any talk of priority

misplaced: a just State depends on there being just individuals, and there can only be just individuals if there are appropriate educational policies and arrangements provided and supervised by the State. The principle that the State should control and supervise the provision of education is one of Plato's most significant recommendations: education is far too important to be a matter of private arrangements between individuals and profiteering and inadequately qualified teachers such as the Sophists. The private educational arrangements that prevailed in Plato's Athens were to serve the advantage of individuals in later life rather than the well-being of society.

8 References to Plato's works are given by the page number of the original Greek followed by the letter, generally a, b, c, d, and e, indicating the section of the page being quoted or referred to. I have followed two translations: the classic translation by Benjamin Jowett and the recent translation by Robin Waterfield. Waterfield's is the more readable but Jowett's retains the greater philosophical clarity. References to Waterfield's translation are indicated by the letter W. All other references are to Jowett's translation.

9 The movement of individuals from one form of work to another Plato regards as undesirable and destructive, permitted in unjust societies such as oligarchies and democracies.

10 Benjamin Jowett in his great translation of the *Republic* favoured the term 'spirit' to characterize this feature of the soul, while Robin Waterfield, in a very recent translation, uses the term 'passion'. Jowett's practice is to be preferred because it captures more clearly what Plato is elucidating, and allows for the fact that characteristic expressions of spirit can in fact be characterized by passion.

11 Jonathan Lear rightly emphasizes the importance of the interactive relationship between the soul and the kinds of environment in which a citizen lives (1998, pp. 219–246).

12 This principle was very much at work in the recommendations of the Butler Report, which resulted in the Education Act of 1948. The central principle of the Act was that different kinds of school were to be established – in practice it turned out to be two, grammar schools and secondary modern schools – for different types of pupil. The more intellectually gifted, selected by an examination after the age of eleven, were placed in the grammar schools and those deemed to be more practical in their aptitudes placed in the secondary modern schools. This division of secondary education into two kinds of school, together with the selection process by which it functioned, was abolished in 1965.

13 Plato is mindful of the tendency among the military, as common in modern times as in Plato's own, to instigate coups through which they gain power but not legitimate political authority. Plato regarded the kind of rule resulting from military take-over as disastrous, invariably resulting in corruption, inefficiency and misery for the population. Some things do not change.

14 For excellent accounts of education as it existed in Greek states, see Freeman, 1970, Ch. 4, and Hornblower and Spawforth, 1998, pp. 244–250.

15 This is suggested at 425b–c where it is stated that it will be education that will determine the direction a person's life will take.

16 One example of Plato's radicalism in the *Republic* is that he believes that men and women are equal and should perform the same tasks, except where difference of strength precludes it. These tasks include that of Guardianship.

17 Plato believed that this policy must be carried out quite ruthlessly for the good of the community.

18 The word 'manipulate' is appropriate here, given that allegory of the cave is intended, in part at least, to represent the way in which unjust rulers seek to deceive and influence the opinions and desires of the subjects over which they have power. The fact that the models that are used to project images on to the wall of the cave are carried by human beings also suggests that the seated spectators are being intentionally deceived.

19 C.D.C Reeve (1988) in his brilliant analysis of the line and cave images emphasizes the link Plato makes between education and the elimination of what may be called vain and excessive desires, the desires that lead a person away from virtue and real happiness.

20 The point here is that when objects themselves are perceived the perception is not necessarily deceptive, principally because the critical intellect is also engaged; hence, the formation of beliefs.

21 Reeve (1988) pp. 286–287, note 7. Irwin's view is expressed in 1977, p. 221.

22 See Callan (1997), and McDonough and Feinberg (2002).

23 This entails the interesting consideration that unjust societies abuse citizenship, and actually raise obstacles to good citizenship rather than encouraging it.

24 It is this that drew criticism from the American philosopher John Dewey, one of the most important philosophers of education in the twentieth century. While praising Plato for the clarity with which he understood the social function of education, Dewey, in the context of modern American democracy in the early twentieth century, was severely critical of the manner in which Plato tied the public function of education to the aim of arresting, rather than facilitating, social change. See Dewey, 1944, pp. 88–93.

25 Annas (2003) is an excellent overview of Plato's life and work, and Annas (1981) is a fine introductory guide to the *Republic*, devoting considerable attention to education. Pappas (1995) is a well-constructed, but not

always easy, guide to the *Republic*. Guthrie (1975) offers an extremely clear and reliable study of the *Republic* and its background. Volume four of the same work contains excellent accounts of the *Statesman* and the *Laws*. Schofield (2006) is brilliant discussion of Plato's political philosophy which brings out very clearly the centrality of education to Plato's work. Reeve (1988) provides an outstanding and original account of the *Republic* that rewards careful study. Ferrari (2007) is valuable collection of essays on the *Republic*, almost all of which are connected with Plato's views on education. Blackburn (2006) is a critical and largely unsympathetic response to the *Republic*. Popper's *The Open Society and Its Enemies* (1945) is a severe and, in places, intemperate condemnation of Plato's alleged totalitarianism. Crossman's *Plato Today* (1937), published before the Second World War, and now dated in certain respects, remains an immensely stimulating and entertaining book on Plato's philosophy. The chapter 'Plato Looks at British Education' remains of great interest to students of education. Finally, Lane (2001) provides an exceptional study of Plato's historical reception and influence.

FURTHER READING

Plato's major works on education are the *Republic* (Oxford World's Classics, trans. Robin Waterfield, 1994) and the *Laws* (Penguin Classics, trans. T.J. Saunders, 1970). Julia Annas, *An Introduction to Plato's Republic* (Oxford University Press, 1981) includes a fine account of education in Plato's *Republic*. W.K.C. Guthrie, *A History of Greek Philosophy, Vol. IV* (Cambridge University Press, 1975) remains an excellent study of the *Republic* and its background. Malcolm Schofield's brilliant, *Plato: Political Philosophy* (Oxford University Press, 2006) brings out very clearly the centrality of education to Plato's political philosophy. Simon Blackburn's *Plato's Republic* (Atlantic Books, 2006) is a challenging discussion. Karl Popper's attack on Plato in *The Open Society and Its Enemies* (Routledge, 1945) remains valuable. Richard Crossman's 1937 classic *Plato Today* (Unwin, 1937) includes a stimulating discussion of Plato's views on education in the context of British society prior to the 1948 Education Act.

REFERENCES

Plato

Plato, *Republic* (trans. Robin Waterfield). Oxford: Oxford University Press, 1994.
Plato, *Republic* (trans. Benjamin Jowett). London: Sphere Books, 1970.
Plato, *Laws* (trans. T.J. Saunders). Harmondsworth: Penguin Classics, 1970.
Plato, *Statesman* (trans. J.B. Skemp). London: Routledge, 1952.
Plato, *Phaedrus and Letters VII and VIII* (trans. Walter Hamilton). Harmondsworth: Penguin Books, 1973.

Other references

Annas, Julia (1981) *An Introduction to Plato's Republic*. Oxford: Oxford University Press.
Annas, Julia (2003) *Plato: a Very Short Introduction*. Oxford: Oxford University Press.
Blackburn, Simon (2006) *Plato's Republic: a Biography*. London: Atlantic Books.
Callan, Eamonn (1997) *Creating Citizens*. Oxford: Oxford University Press.
Crossman, Richard (1937) *Plato Today*. Oxford: Oxford University Press.
Dewey, John (1966) *Democracy and Education*. London: The Free Press, Collier Macmillan. (Originally published in 1916; revised in 1944.)
Ferrari, G.R.F. (Ed.) (2007) *The Cambridge Companion to Plato's Republic*. Cambridge: Cambridge University Press.
Freeman, Kathleen (1970) *God, Man and State: Greek Concepts*. Westport, CT: Greenwood Press.

Guthrie, W.K.C. (1975) *A History of Greek Philosophy, IV: Plato: the man and his dialogues: earlier period*. Cambridge: Cambridge University Press.

Hornblower, Simon and Spawforth, Antony (Eds) (1998) *The Oxford Companion to Classical Civilization*. Oxford: Oxford University Press.

Irwin, Terence (1977) *Plato's Moral Theory*. Oxford: Clarendon Press.

Lane, Melissa (2001) *Plato's Progeny*. London: Duckworth.

Lear, Jonathan (1998) Inside and outside the *Republic*. In *Open Minded: Working Out the Logic of the Soul*. Cambridge, MA: Harvard University Press.

McDonough, Kevin and Feinberg, Walter (Eds) (2002) *Citizenship and Education in Liberal-Democratic Societies*. Oxford: Oxford University Press.

Pappas, Nicholas (1995) *Plato and the Republic*. London: Routledge.

Popper, Karl (1945) *The Open Society and Its Enemies*, Vol. 1, *Plato*. London: Routledge.

Rawls, John (1971) *A Theory of Justice*. Cambridge, MA: The Belknap Press of Harvard University Press.

Reeve, C.D.C. (1988) *Philosopher-Kings: The Argument of Plato's Republic*. Princeton, NJ: Princeton University Press.

Schofield, Malcolm (2006) *Plato: Political Philosophy*. Oxford: Oxford University Press.

6

Rousseau's 'Émile' and Educational Legacy

Jack Martin and Nathan Martin

Perhaps no single volume, with the exception of Plato's *Republic*, has exerted as much influence on the subsequent history of educational thought and practice as has Jean-Jacques Rousseau's (1979) *Émile*. Although Rousseau's writings on education are not exhausted by this single work, *Émile* contains all of the ideas that dominate Rousseau's educational thought and legacy. Consequently, we devote the first half of this chapter to a close reading of *Émile* before tracing its influence on subsequent developments in education and schooling.

READING *ÉMILE*

Émile begins with an important, schematic discussion that clearly delineates the kind of education Rousseau proposes. Education, Rousseau stipulates, comes from three sources: from nature, from men, and from things. What Rousseau means by 'education from things' is fairly intuitive: it is the knowledge that we gain through our interaction with our physical environment. 'Education from men' is what we acquire when we internalize the beliefs and opinions of others. What 'education from nature' entails, however, is less immediately obvious. In this context, 'nature' is 'the internal development of our faculties and our organs' (p. 38). 'Education from nature,' therefore, is what individuals learn from their own mental and physical growth.

For education to be well-ordered, Rousseau continues, these three sources must be harmonized. Since our psycho-physical development is unalterable, 'education from men' and 'education from things' must be made to conform to 'education from nature.' Rousseau's curriculum presents an education closely tailored to the mental and physical development of the individual.

In one sense, Rousseau regards this development as something common to all: each of us, in the normal course of things, grows taller, learns to talk, goes through puberty, and so on. At the same time, such generic patterns leave considerable latitude for individual variance, and Rousseau – perhaps more than any previous thinker – is acutely sensitive to such differences. It is perhaps for this reason that, rather than presenting his theory of education in the abstract, Rousseau instead decides to illustrate its application by giving himself an imaginary pupil: Émile.

Rousseau's stated goal of harmonizing the three sources of education, however, runs into an immediate difficulty. To educate a man[26] according to his nature, Rousseau asserts, is to raise him for himself. Human societies, however, require that men be raised for others, that they be molded into good subjects or good citizens. Rousseau concludes, therefore, that there are two distinct and incompatible kinds of education – 'the one, public and common; the other, individual and domestic' (p. 40). True public education, he continues, could be instituted only in conjunction with a comprehensive restructuring of civil society such as Rousseau proposes in the *Social Contract*.[27] *Émile* will be concerned solely with 'domestic education or the education of nature' (p. 41).

Thus, Émile will receive a natural education from the hands of Rousseau. His education, that is to say, will be closely tailored to each stage in his mental and physical growth. In Book I, Émile is an infant; in Book II, a child; in Book III, a prepubescent adolescent; in Book IV, he goes through puberty; and in Book V, he is a man. At each point, Rousseau emphasizes that both the objects Émile studies and the manner in which they are introduced be appropriate to his pupil's level of development.

The aim of Rousseau's instruction is to make Émile happy, self-sufficient, and free – three terms that, in Rousseau's conceptual vocabulary, are almost interchangeable. The question that *Émile* attempts to answer, therefore, is how, within the existing social order, a man can be raised to be happy, free, and self-sufficient. In this respect, *Émile* offers one possible solution to a problem that Rousseau (1964) had posed in his *Discourse on the Origins of Inequality* (Second Discourse).

What the Second Discourse most fundamentally offers is an aetiology of civilization's discontents. 'Social man' (*l'homme policé*), according to Rousseau, is a complex of voracious and ultimately insatiable desires. He is miserable because his 'needs' outstrip his powers. Because he cannot satisfy these needs himself, he requires the services of others and so becomes dependent on them. In return for their services, he contracts obligations to them, and his freedom is compromised. As a foil to the civilized man's frustrations, Rousseau holds up the liberty and felicity of 'natural man' (*l'homme naturel*). Living alone in the depths of the woods, with no social ties and no language, humans – according to Rousseau – originally desired nothing beyond their natural needs for food, sleep, and sex. Such needs, moreover, were easily met: when hungry, the natural man foraged; when tired, he slept; when aroused, he sought out trysts with passing females. Because his needs were proportioned to his powers, natural man was self-sufficient. He incurred no obligations to others and so felt only physical constraints. In consequence, he was free, independent, and happy.

The essential goal of Rousseau's instructional program is to resuscitate, within the context of civilized modernity, the spiritual equilibrium of natural man: Émile is to be a natural man for modern times. With that end in view, Rousseau's most fundamental concern is to prevent his pupil from acquiring any needs beyond his own capacities. All such needs, Rousseau is convinced, are socially induced, and so to prevent their taking root, Émile must at first be kept apart from human society. As an infant and a child, he will be raised in rural isolation, with only his nurse, his tutor, and their servants for company. It is only later, once he has been adequately prepared, that Émile will be introduced to society.

Of course, despite his pastoral retreat, Émile is not really alone. Nor is he self-sufficient: he depends on his tutor, his nurse, their cook, and so on. To keep Émile in the illusion of independence, therefore, the tutor must employ considerable artifice. Despite being enmeshed in a web of complex social relations, Émile must think that he is free of all social constraint. His actual 'dependence on men' must be disguised so that it appears to him to be 'dependence on things.' Only in this way can Émile be kept in his natural state.

The tutor, accordingly, will never command or enjoin Émile to do anything, nor will he forbid any course of action. Instead, he will present Émile with physical obstacles that compel him to act in certain ways. If Émile errs, the tutor will not lecture or scold, but will arrange matters so that Émile's punishment seems to stem naturally from his action. If, for instance, Émile breaks the window in his bedroom, the tutor will not object. But neither will he replace the glass promptly, and Émile, shivering in the cold, will learn not to break windows.

In this way, Émile will be kept in near total ignorance of social relations throughout his childhood. This isolation from social influences is Rousseau's primary goal in the first part of his curriculum. His ancillary goal is to begin forming Émile's judgment. For if he is to be able, one day, to enter society without becoming its dupe, Émile must develop his powers of observation and judgment.

Though Émile's capacity for reasoning will not develop until the age of 12, preparatory work can be done throughout his childhood. Since sensation is the foundation of all knowledge,[28] it is imperative that Émile's senses be honed. For his senses to be acute, his body must be healthy. From the end of his infancy to the age of 12, therefore, Émile's time will be divided between physical activity and exercises in sense perception.

To train his eyes, Émile will learn to draw;[29] to train his ears, he will learn to sing. Much of the work of training his senses, however, will be done in an impromptu manner in the course of long walks in the surrounding countryside. During these walks, for instance, Émile will learn to estimate distances by sight. The end result of all these exercises will be to form Émile's powers of observation, powers that will later provide the foundation for his ability to judge.

At the age of 12, Émile reaches the age of reason. Now he will begin to study assiduously. He will begin with the natural sciences. His knowledge of them will not, however, be acquired from books but rather from observation and experiment: '[Émile will] not learn science but discover it' (p. 168). To awaken his interest in the sciences, Émile's tutor takes him to observe various natural phenomena. Master and pupil go, for instance, to watch the sun rise in the summer; the tutor asks Émile how it is possible that the sun rises opposite to where it sets. They go again in winter and notice that the sun rises in a different place. In this way, Émile's interest in astronomy is awakened. Similarly, the tutor takes Émile one day to a country fair, where a magician attracts a wax duck by waving a piece of bread. The tutor asks Émile how the trick is done, then takes him home and shows him the properties of magnets. With Émile's interest in the sciences awakened, the two begin to perform experiments in order to better understand the phenomena they have observed. Throughout, 'Émile has no book other than the world, no instruction other than the facts' (p. 168). Rousseau's intention throughout is that Émile learns how to investigate matters for himself.

The sciences, however, will not be Émile's only study. He should also learn a trade. To that end, Émile and his tutor go once or twice a week to spend the day with a master carpenter: 'we get up at his hour, [are] at work before him, eat at his table, work under his orders, and after having had the honour of supping with his family, return, if we wish, to sleep in our hard beds' (p. 201).

Between the ages of 12 and 15, to summarize, Émile divides his time between the sciences and his trade. By 15, his senses have been honed, his judgment formed. It is now time to begin introducing Émile to society. 'After having begun by exercising his body and his senses, we have exercised his mind and his judgment. Finally, we have joined the use of his limbs [i.e. in his trade] to that of his faculties. We have made an active and a thinking being. It remains for us, in order to complete the man, only to make a loving and feeling being' (p. 203). Doing so is the work of the remainder of the treatise.

At 15 years of age, however, Émile's physical development intervenes. He begins to go through puberty.[29] Now the tutor must take care to manage Émile's nascent passions, his sexual desire in particular. The only truly natural passion, Rousseau believes, is *amour de soi-même* (self-love), the innate impulse towards self-preservation that impels us to meet our natural needs. All other passions are modifications or transformations of this one primitive passion and emerge only once human beings begin to form social bonds. One transformation of self-love that Rousseau regards as particularly harmful is *amour-propre* (vanity, or self-regard), a kind of insidious desire for social comparison and preferment. As, in effect, a desire for social status, *amour-propre* plays itself out in a zero-sum game: I can only have more social status if you have less, and vice versa.[30] In both the Second Discourse and *Émile*, Rousseau implies that one of the earliest and most powerful manifestations of *amour-propre* is in erotic love. In its original form, the need for sex was not tied to any particular object: for the natural man, any natural woman would do. In its socially conditioned form, however, sexual desire comes to be fixed on particular individuals. In being thus transformed into erotic love, desire comes to demand reciprocation – the beloved must recognize the lover as worthy of her love. With that, *amour-propre* comes into play, for such recognition flatters the lover's self-image.

The tutor's principal endeavor, in this fourth stage of Rousseau's program, is to restrain Émile's burgeoning sexual desire. To do so, he employs his usual tactics of diversion and delay. In fact, thanks to the tutor's offices, Émile's first passion will not be erotic love but 'friendship' (*amitié*), by which Rousseau seems to mean not so much personal friendship as a kind of generalized benevolence towards other people. This sentiment, Rousseau believes, can best be nurtured by showing Émile people who are less fortunate than he is, a sight that will awaken his sense of pity (*pitié*).

At the same time, the tutor will begin to introduce Émile to the whole sphere of social relations. At first, however, he will do so only in the abstract, by having Émile read history. Up to now, Émile has read only one book: *Robinson Crusoe*, in whose isolated and independent existence he recognizes his own (obviously idealized) self-portrait. Now Émile will read. But his reading will not be indiscriminate. He will ignore modern historians, who moralize and make judgments, and instead read ancient writers, who report the facts without judging them.[31] For the goal, here as before, is to teach Émile to rely on his own judgment rather than relying on the opinions of others. Rousseau recommends in particular that Émile read Thucydides and Plutarch – the former will show him the actions of men, the latter their hearts. The end result of this reading, Rousseau believes, is that Émile will come to pity the great as he earlier learned to pity the poor and the weak.

In considering other men, therefore, Émile discovers that both those more fortunate and those less fortunate than he are miserable. He alone is happy. There is, however, one further lesson that Émile must learn if his sense of compassion (*pitié*) is to be complete. For the danger is that Émile, in preferring his lot to that of others, will conclude that he is superior to others. Émile must be made to feel his own weakness. Having learned that others are wretched, Émile now learns that his own good fortune is precarious: by his own errors, or the malice of others, he himself can easily be made wretched too.

The only 'traps' from which Rousseau proposes to preserve his pupil entirely are 'those of courtesans' (p. 246). The tutor's aim, after all, in developing Émile's compassion has been to delay the onset of his sexual maturity. Indeed, Rousseau's two great fears, at this point in his program, are that Émile will be seduced by a woman or that Émile will begin to masturbate. It is time, therefore, for a frank talk. Rousseau's sex-ed lesson, though, requires careful preparation. Rousseau proposes that Émile be kept physically active so that, exhausted by his exercise, he will be able to listen tranquilly to his tutor's lecture and the tutor will be able 'to depict [sexual desire] without exciting it' (p. 321). The talk itself must be handled carefully:

> This new instruction is important, and it is advisable to go back and pick up the thread from a more general point of view. This is the moment to present my accounts to him, so to speak: to show him how his time and mine have been employed; to disclose to him what he is and what I am, what I have done, what he has done, what we owe each other, all his moral relations, all the commitments he has contracted, all those that have been contracted for him, what point he has reached in the progress of his faculties, how much of the road he still has to cover, the difficulties he will find there, the means of getting over these difficulties, what I can help him with, and finally, the critical point at which he stands, the new perils which surround him, and all the solid reasons which ought to oblige him to keep an attentive watch over himself before listening to his nascent desires. (p. 318)

The end result, Rousseau believes, will be that Émile, at the very moment his tutor proposes to relinquish his authority, will seek his tutor's guidance and propose that the tutor take up his authority once again under a new and now explicit contract.[32]

Having studied men in the abstract, having learned compassion, and fore-warned of 'the new perils which surround him,' Émile is now ready to enter society. Émile and his tutor will go to Paris. The tutor, however, has one further ruse. To inoculate his student against the charms of Parisian women, he presents Émile with the image of an ideal woman, whom he names Sophie. All other women, Rousseau is convinced, will pale in comparison to Sophie, and Émile will therefore be 'disgusted with those that could tempt him' (p. 328).

In Paris, Émile will have his first direct experience in human society. His time there will acquaint him with its norms and form his taste. At the same time, Émile will begin to read widely, not only in the Latin classics (whose language he will now learn) but also in literature's 'sewers in the reservoirs of modern compilers, newspapers, translations, and dictionaries' (p. 344). The only thing Émile will not find in Paris is Sophie. And after having exhausted their time in the capital, Émile and his tutor will return to the countryside to find her.

In the fifth and final book of Rousseau's treatise, Émile finds his Sophie, courts her, and eventually marries her, all thanks to his tutor's contrivances. Book five begins with a long digression on the kind of education appropriate to women before progressing to a miniature sentimental novel.[33] It ends, however, with one final lesson for Émile: 'One morning, when they have not seen each other for two days, I enter Émile's room with a letter in my hand; staring fixedly at him, I say, "What would you do if you were informed that Sophie is dead?" ' (p. 442). Émile is understandably perturbed. Now that he has his pupil's attention, the tutor pro-ceeds to explain that Émile is too much governed by his passion. Though the tutor has made Émile good, he has not yet made him virtuous, for 'virtue belongs only to a being that is weak by nature and strong by will.'[34] Émile must learn to 'extend the law of necessity to moral things' (p. 446) – that is, to respond to the constraints and misfortunes resulting from his inescapable 'dependence on men' – with the same equanimity with which he bows to natural necessity ('dependence on things'). Sophie, after all, might fall ill, might die, or might leave him for another. Unless Émile learns to accept such misfortunes resolutely and to govern his passions, how will he be able to live happily and wisely?

The practical upshot is that Émile must leave Sophie for a time. He and his tutor will travel for 2 years, and at the end of that term, if he and she still wish it, Émile will return and marry Sophie. Émile's travels will allow him to observe men in all their conditions and estates, to learn their languages and customs. In particular, he will take note of the different governments men live under, and judge which of these is most conducive to a happy life. When, at 22, he returns and marries Sophie, which he does at the book's conclusion, he will know where in the world they will most likely be able to live in peace and tranquillity.[35]

Rousseau's *Émile* bowled over some of its first readers.[36] A modern reader is likely to react far more sceptically. What Rousseau seems to have offered, such a reader might conclude, is a bizarre recipe for a kind of cultish home-schooling. That conclusion is not entirely misguided. Rousseau's precepts, at least, have probably never been systematically applied in their entirety. Whatever its strengths as a work of moral or political philosophy, however much insight it offers into Rousseau, the book is simply too strange, too fanciful in many of its episodes, to serve as a workable blueprint for instruction. Nevertheless, its main ideas and themes, in many cases abstracted from the agenda they serve in Rousseau's version, have exerted a considerable influence on subsequent educational theory and practice.

ROUSSEAU'S EDUCATIONAL LEGACY

Whether or not it is appropriate to consider Rousseau as an educational theorist, let alone educator, has been much debated. Certainly, it is just as possible to interpret *Émile* (despite the alternative title, '*On Education*') as an imaginary, idealized upbringing in relation to political positions such as those found in Rousseau's *Social Contract* (in many ways a 'twin' volume to *Émile*) and *Discourse on the Origins of Inequality*, as it is to understand it as a theory of education organized by stages of personal development. Even in his later *Letter to the Government of Poland*, wherein he proposed a national system of education for citizenship (one which included vigorous physical activity), politics clearly can be argued to predominate. Nonetheless, if the appropriate criterion is documented influence on educational theory and practice, it is noteworthy that almost all writings on the history and philosophy of education mention Rousseau and his ideas.

The natural development and nurturing of the Rousseauian self are most clearly evident in progressive, child-centerd, and humanistic theories and practices in education. However, many behaviorists, Adlerians, and instructional designers also have responded to Rousseau's insistence that children be free to experience directly the contingent necessities and natural consequences that attend their worldly actions, and have been happy to accept the role of 'arranging tutor' that so clearly typifies Rousseau's ideal educator. More generally, developmental theorists in education recognize a stage theory of ontogenetic development in Rousseau's *Émile* that anticipates the influential stage theory developed nearly 200 years later by another Swiss, Jean Piaget. For their part, some psychoanalytically inclined educationists have located pre-Freudian conceptions of psychodynamic processes like sublimation in Rousseau's musings on the origins of some of our higher pursuits in the arts and philosophy. Still another line of influence frequently traced to Rousseau, perhaps paradoxically, concerns Rousseau as an originator of collectivist movements within education. Marxists, deconstructionists, and critical theorists all have been struck by the Rousseauian arguments that individual distinctions result in inequality and that inequality of social circumstances ought not be confused with what is natural. In what follows, the most salient of these various lines of influence will be considered separately.

Progressive and alternative education

Although there is considerable debate concerning the precise nature of agreements and disagreements among various educational doctrines that might be included under the banners of progressive and alternative education (e.g., Adelman, 2000), it is most often held that Rousseau's ideas initiated and, in many ways, sustained these movements. 'Pestalozzi, Herbart, Froebel, the Macmillans, Montessori, Caldwell, Cook, Dewey are his [Rousseau's] successors; and such devices as the Nursery School [Kindergarten], the Dalton Plan, the Play Way, and the Project Method are the practical results of what they taught' (Jacks, 1950). In particular, his emphasis on the interests, activities, and development of pupils gradually became enshrined in a general form of education that focused on the whole person, individual differences in interests and abilities, and learning by doing, especially through play and concrete, problem-solving situations. Perhaps even more influential was his overarching concern for the authentic self-esteem of the learner as a buffer against the potentially invidious comparisons with others that are encouraged by traditional modes of education and society in general.

It was Johann Bernhard Basedow[37] who, a mere six years after the publication of *Émile* and 10 years before Rousseau's death, published an influential call for educational reform based, in part, on Rousseau's ideas. Subsequently, well-known educators like Pestalozzi, Herbart, and Froebel established the first non-traditional schools and kindergartens in Switzerland and Germany in the late 1700s and early 1800s, and developed a variety of neo-Rousseauian educational theories and methods that, in different ways and with different emphases, all grappled with the tensions between nature and society, self and others, and personal freedom and civic duty/virtue. Moreover, like Rousseau, they all argued that education should be transformed from a ruthless installation of intellectual and social discipline to a facilitative harmonizing of the untrammeled, organic nature of children with the inescapable demands of social existence.

Johann Heinrich Pestalozzi was among the first of Rousseau's disciples to apply his ideas directly to the schooling of children. Pestalozzi attempted to systematize the natural, progressive unfolding of children's inborn powers by bringing what he regarded as basic elements of knowledge into contact with the faculties of the mind in a way that proceeded from what was near in the child's experience to that which was distant. He understood education as supporting an organic process of human development through interaction with everyday objects within a loving environment. It was primarily through Joseph Neff, an associate of Pestalozzi who was contracted by William Maclure to assist with the education of children in New Harmony, Indiana (an experimental community founded by Robert Owen and William Maclure), that Pestalozzianism found its way to the United States (Gutek, 1978). Neff used Pestalozzi's methods, and pioneered the 'field trip,' in opposition to harsh discipline and rote memorization. Against the unquestioned authority of the teacher, Neff encouraged his students to question and reason on the bases of their own senses and understanding. Pestalozzi's ideas were advocated widely by Amos Bronson Alcott, who has been called the Pestalozzi of America (Shepard, 1938).

In Europe, it was Friedrich Wilhelm August Froebel, who had spent time at Pestalozzi's school at Yverdun, Switzerland, who adopted many of Pestalozzi's methods against what he regarded as the harsh and culturally narrow educational views of his Prussian contemporaries. Extending Pestalozzi's use of everyday objects to what he called 'gifts' (basic geometric shapes, sand, paper, songs, etc.), and pursuing a much more theistic, metaphysical, and nationalistic agenda, Froebel desired to build a new German nation through a rejuvenated form of education that would start with the kindergarten. Since many of Froebel's educational concerns were highly moral and political, several of his followers arrived in the USA around 1868 as refugees from political ferments in Europe in which their educational ideas were interpreted as threats to church and state (Adelman, 2000). In the USA and the UK, Froebel's ideas[38] quickly began to supplant the educational reforms of Pestalozzi. However, in France, Germany, and Scandinavia, both Pestalozzi and Froebel were equally celebrated and studied (Adelman, 2000).[39]

The moral and political tenor of the educational thought and practice of Rousseau and the early European progressives received an influential hearing in the educational writings of John Dewey, who together with his wife Alice, daughter Evelyn, and colleagues like George Herbert Mead and Jane Adams, became immersed in a variety of educational experiments, including the establishment and running of the famous Laboratory School sponsored by the University of Chicago. The educational plan adopted in the Chicago Laboratory School was based initially on Froebel's kindergarten, albeit with a more explicitly social and pragmatic rendering, and consisted largely of following and responding to the child's nature (Deegan, 1999). Dewey was primarily concerned with achieving a social democratic middle ground between what too frequently are cast as oppositional polarities, such as curriculum content versus learner interest, and self versus community.

For Dewey (1938), starting with the life experience and interests of the child in no way precludes ending with the organized subject matter of the established disciplines. Most of Dewey's educational writings are concerned with describing in theoretical detail the conditions and processes involved in such educational transformations.[40] His social progressivism strived to escape the more extreme forms of tension between self and society with which Rousseau struggled both intellectually and personally.[41] On the other hand, many radical and progressive educators (before and after Dewey) in both North America and Europe adopted and implemented educational policies and practices that encouraged much more radical forms of individual freedom on the parts of students and teachers.

During the general cultural upheaval that was the 1960s, alternative education became widely recognized as a distinctive educational movement, with innovations such as open classrooms, integrated curricula, democratic education, and school choice being adopted and implemented in many traditional public school systems. Alternative schools and alternative programming in regular schools drew inspiration not only from the ideas of Rousseau Pestalozzi, Froebel, and Dewey but also from the psychoanalytically informed educational practices of Homer Lane and A.S. Neill (founder of the famous, Summerhill), from the Montessori schools established and championed by Maria Montessori, and from the Waldorf system of education founded by Austrian philosopher Rudolf Steiner. The Montessori school emphasized student freedom, optional attendance, and student equality in educational decision making. The Waldorf school was insistent that the inner needs of the child not be thwarted by the self-interest of adults, but be fully and lovingly met (although not without being subjected to natural and social necessity). The Waldorf school understood education as an art form, dedicated to 'the awakening of what is actually there within the human being' (Steiner, 1967, p. 23). With the reassertion of traditional values in politics and education during the 1980s, this heyday of alternativism in education has passed. Nonetheless, many of the pedagogical ideas of Rousseau (and of those he influenced, such as Pestalozzi and Dewey) are readily evident in almost all contemporary classrooms that continue to make use of what have come to be known as the orientations and methods of discovery learning and inquiry-based teaching.

Child-centered and psychological education

Progressive emphases on the nature, development, and self-esteem of the child also held considerable attraction to the developing discipline of psychology. In the 1950s and 1960s, humanistic psychologists like Abraham Maslow (1954) and Carl Rogers (1957) reacted against the prevailing behaviorism of the day, and spearheaded a renewed focus on internal processes in psychology, with an emphasis on individually unique, affectively laden experiences. In place of

Rousseau's designing tutor, Rogers advocated a nurturing facilitator so attuned to the natural goodness and individual uniqueness of each learner that she was able to provide learners with what Rogers regarded as both necessary and sufficient psychological conditions that would guarantee worthwhile educational experiences. Such conditions included freedom to experience the world in safety and pursue individual interests without censor or imposition, and to be in receipt of a genuinely respectful, positive, and unconditional regard and concern from the teacher. Thus, freed from societal conditions of worth, Rogers argued that students would be guided primarily by a natural self-actualizing tendency that worked simultaneously for the benefit of themselves and others (a psychological form of *amour de soi-même*).

But, it is perhaps in developmental psychology, especially as applied to education, that Rousseau's legacy has been most persistent. Here, it must be remembered that prior to Rousseau, the 'educational psychologies' of thinkers like Plato and Locke displayed almost no developmental theses. With Rousseau came the ideas that children were not simply miniature adults, but went through various predictable stages of development typified by distinctive ways of thinking and learning that were specific to those stages. Rousseau's developmental perspective and Hegel's mediational syntheses of Rousseau's conflicts between nature and society, and self and community were picked up not only by Dewey but also by George Herbert Mead, Jean Piaget, and Lev Vygotsky in ways that subsequently influenced entire generations of developmental, educational psychologists. The continuing influence of Rousseau is readily evident in the theories of such psychologists concerning the graduated differentiation and emergence of children's' cognitive categories and intellectual capabilities through activity with others in the world of objects and social practices, and in their insistence that educators must arrange and facilitate educational and psychological experiences appropriate to children's current stages of development within a developmental trajectory that is natural, but in need of the proper kinds of social promotion and encouragement. Of particular importance in this regard is the promotion of the self-esteem and self-concepts of schoolchildren and adolescents in ways thought to be consistent with self-discovery, self-expression, and self-fulfilment.

Critical theory and deconstructionism

A third line of influence running from Rousseau to contemporary critical theory and deconstructionism is more speculative and less specific. However, given the extent to which much contemporary philosophy of education has experienced a turn to Continental ideas from the likes of Marx, Weber, Foucault, and Derrida, it is important not to forget that Rousseau, that champion of self-expression and authenticity, was not only a scathing critique of societal degeneration, but an advocate of certain kinds of collectivity. For Rousseau was a hero to both Kant and Hegel, and at least a few scholars like Allan Bloom (1990) have concluded that

Rousseau's 'critique of modern economics and his questions about the legitimacy of private property are at the root of socialism, particularly Marxism' (p. 211). Moreover, although not a revolutionary himself, Rousseau clearly despised bourgeois society, was frequently rhapsodic concerning peasant life, and advocated a kind of post-Marxist critical theory that predicted a powerful role for an intellectual elite with a superior intelligence capable of discovering 'the rules of society best suited to nations' (1762/1975, p. 35). 'In short, it is the best and most natural arrangement for the wisest to govern the multitude' (p. 59).

These ideas find considerable resonance in the critical theory developed by the Frankfurt School (including Theodor Adorno, Walter Benjamin, and Herbert Marcuse). Similarly, the deconstructionism of French post-Marxists like Jacques Derrida, Jacques Lacan, and Michel Foucault, may be seen to reflect certain aspects of Rousseau's social and political analyses. And, so too does much of the writings of educational critics like Paul Goodman, Jonathon Kozol, Herbert Kohl, Paulo Freire, Henry Giroux, and Ivan Illich, all of whom advocate radical educational reforms, and some of whom may be read as advocating the abolishment of schools altogether. For example, when Illich says that 'School enslaves more profoundly and more systematically, since only school is credited with the principal function of forming critical judgment' (1972, p. 68), one cannot help but hear echoes of Rousseau's societal enchainment of free persons, perhaps with a Foucaultian twist of self-captivity. Indeed, many contemporary critical theorists and deconstructionists in education, like Rousseau before them, seem convinced that individual distinctions result in inequality and that inequality of social circumstances ought not be confused with what is natural.

CONCLUDING REMARKS

It would be foolish to make strong claims in support of a solely Rousseauian genesis for the general lines of continuing influence that have been considered. However, there can be little doubt that Rousseau's highly innovative and idiosyncratic life, work, and writings constitute important sources of many of these educational ideas and practices. The obvious example here concerns Rousseau's pivotal role in articulating the natural, organic unfolding of a human nature that can be subverted and/or twisted by the imposition of improper educational and psychological conditions. Many have critically disparaged such a delicate naturalism, and the organic metaphors it has inspired (e.g., Egan, 2002). Nonetheless, no one who reads Émile is likely to omit the personal development of students from whatever educational perspective she or he subsequently adopts. And, none who have witnessed and experienced first hand the excesses of bureaucratic proceduralism and social engineering in the academy, schools, and everyday life can help but experience a 'natural' resonance to the siren call of the old Master, as weird and wooly as he undoubtedly was, to take a more solitary walk, or at least to maintain a healthy distance from it all.

ACKNOWLEDGMENTS

We gratefully acknowledge the generous assistance of librarians and curators at the Bibliothèque Publique et Universitaire in Geneva for facilitating our access to materials from their Jean-Jacques Rousseau Archives, and thank the Burnaby Mountain Endowment Fund, Simon Fraser University for supporting our work on this chapter.

NOTES

26 'Man' is used here in the exclusive sense: the education Rousseau sketches over the course of Émile is for boys and men; his (reactionary) thoughts on women's education come near the end of the book.

27 For its model, Rousseau refers us to Plato's *Republic*.

28 Here, Rousseau follows both Locke and Condillac.

29 Puberty came later in the eighteenth century.

30 For a more nuanced interpretation of *amour-propre*, see Dent (1988, pp. 20–21 and 113–167). According to Dent, it is dominating forms of *amour-propre*, which encourage subservient dependence on others, that are especially invidious.

31 'The worst historians for a young man are those who make judgments. Facts! Facts! And let him make his own judgments,' p. 239.

32 I do not doubt for an instant that [Émile] will come by himself to the point where I want to lead him, that he will eagerly put himself in my safekeeping, that he will be struck by the dangers with which he sees himself surrounded, and will say to me with all the warmth of his age, 'O my friend, my protector, my master! Take back the authority you want to give up at the very moment that it is most important for me that your retain it. You had this authority up to this time only due to my weakness; now you shall have it due to my will, and it shall be all the more sacred to me. Defend me from all the enemies who besiege me, and especially from those whom I carry within myself and who betray me. Watch over your work in order that it remain worthy of you. I want to obey your laws; I want to do so always. This is my steadfast will. If ever I disobey you, it will be in spite of myself. Make me free by protecting me against those of my passions which do violence to me. Prevent me from being their slave; force me to be my own master and to obey not my senses but my reason.' (p. 325)

33 In the manner of Roussseau's novel, *La Nouvelle Héloïse*.

34 Who, then, is the virtuous man? It is he who knows how to conquer his affections; for then he follows his reason and his conscience; he does his duty; he keeps himself in order, and nothing can make him deviate from it. Up to now you were only apparently free. You have only the precarious freedom of a slave to whom nothing has been commanded. Now be really free. Learn to become your own master. Command your heart, Emile, and you will be virtuous. (pp. 444–445).

35 Readers interested in a more extensive overview of Émile might wish to consult Dent (2005; pp. 81–123).

36 Kant, for example.

37 Interestingly, Basedow's life displayed significant similarities to that of Rousseau in that he ran away from home as a boy, reacted strongly against the harsh punishment he experienced at the hands of would-be educators, and worked as a tutor for a wealthy aristocratic family. Basedow also advocated the development of 'laboratory schools' that would train teachers in new methods – methods that eventually were adopted widely in German public schools.

38 These were ideas that married an educational philosophy emphasizing the uniqueness of the whole person and reflection on learning by doing with an almost utopian fervor for social reform.

39 Elizabeth Peabody, who worked as an assistant to the American Pestalozzi, Amos Bronson Alcott, became a well-known educator in her own right, and went on to found American kindergartens based on Froebel's methods.

40 It has been said that Rousseau grounded education in nature, and Dewey grounded it in society. However, given that both men understood the necessity of both, it might be better to say that whereas Rousseau leaned toward nature, Dewey inclined toward society.

41 Having said this, it must be remembered that some colleagues and disciples of Dewey, such as William Heard Kilpatrick and George S. Counts, took very seriously Dewey's social interests, and understood the purpose of the school as serving 'to free society from its inherited evils by identifying itself with social and democratic life' (Mulhern, 1959, p. 486).

FURTHER READING

In addition to numerous, good translations of Rousseau's major writings into English, there are two comprehensive sources concerning the life and works of Jean-Jacques Rousseau: the Pléiade edition of his *Oeuvres Complètes*, compiled by B. Gagnebin, M. Raymond, and others, and the Voltaire Foundation edition of his *Correspondance Complète* by R.A. Leigh. More recently, two additional and important reference works have appeared: the *Dictionnaire de Jean-Jacques Rousseau* and the chronology *Jean-Jacques Rousseau au Jour le Jour*, both edited by Raymond Trousson and Frédéric S. Eigeldinger. Also noteworthy are Jean Starobinski's *La Transparence et l'Obstacle* (*Jean-Jacques Rousseau: Transparency and Obstruction*), Maurice Cranston's *The Noble Savage: Jean-Jacques Rousseau*, Raymond Trousson's *Jean-Jacques Rousseau*, and Arthur Melzer's overview of Rousseau's thought, *The Natural Goodness of Man*. A very recent biography, *Jean-Jacques Rousseau: Restless Genius* by Leo Damrosch, brilliantly mines Rousseau's *Confessions, The Social Contract,* and *Émile*. With respect to Rousseau's philosophy of education, Alan Bloom's introduction to, translation of, and notes on Rousseau's *Émile*, and Nicholas Dent's treatment of *amour-propre* in *Émile* (in *Rousseau: An Introduction to his Psychological, Social, and Political Theory*) are especially compelling.

REFERENCES

Adelman, C. (2000) Over two years, what did Froebel say to Pestalozzi? *History of Education,* 29, 103–114.

Bloom, A. (1990) *Giants and Dwarfs: Essays 1960–1990.* New York: Simon and Schuster.

Deegan, M. J. (1999) Play from the perspective of George Herbert Mead. In M.J. Deegan (ed.), *Play, School, and Society by George Herbert Mead.* New York: Peter Lang, pp. xix–cxii.

Dent, N. (1988) *Rousseau: An Introduction to His Psychological, Social, and Political Theory.* Oxford: Blackwell.

Dent, N. (2005) *Rousseau.* London: Routledge.

Dewey, J. (1938) *Experience and Education.* New York: Macmillan.

Egan, K. (2002) *Getting it Wrong from the Beginning: Our Progressivist Inheritance from Herbert Spencer, John Dewey, and Jean Piaget.* New Haven, CT: Yale University Press.

Gutek, G. L. (1978) *Joseph Neff: The Americanisation of Pestalozzianism.* Tuscaloosa, AL: The University of Alabama Press.

Illich, I. (1972) *Deschooling Society.* New York: Harper and Row.

Jacks, M. L. (1950) *Modern Trends in Education.* London: Melrose.

Maslow, A.H. (1954) *Motivation and Personality.* New York: Harper.

Masters and J.R. Masters, trans. New York: St. Martin's Press. (Original works published 1750 and 1755.)

Mulhern, J. (1959) *A History of Education: A Social Interpretation,* 2nd edn. New York: Ronald.

Rogers, C. R. (1957) The necessary and sufficient conditions of therapeutic personality change. *Journal of Consulting Psychology,* 21, 95–103.

Rousseau, J. J. (1964) *The First and Second Discourses.* R.D. Masters (Ed.) R.D.

Rousseau, J. J. (1975) The social contract. In L. Bair (trans)., *The Essential Rousseau.* New York: Penguin, pp. 1–124. (Original work published 1762.)

Rousseau, J. J. (1979) *Émile, or on Education.* A. Bloom, trans. New York: Basic Books. (Original work published 1762.)

Shepard, O. (1938). *Pedlar's Progress: The Life of Bronson Alcott.* London: Williams and Norgate.

Steiner, R. (1967). *Discussions with Teachers.* London: Rudolph Steiner Press.

7

John Dewey and Educational Pragmatism

James Scott Johnston

INTRODUCTION

John Dewey (1859–1952) is the best known and frequently cited philosopher of
education in America and maintains a large following elsewhere in the world.
Indeed, it is not too much of a stretch to say that because of Dewey's attention to
education and his philosophically like-minded students populating the faculty at
Columbia University's Teachers' College, the discipline of philosophy of education began in earnest. Dewey wrote prolifically on education. He also wrote on a
broad range of other social and political topics, as well as on all major branches
of philosophy. Dewey lived a very long life (92 years), and was witness to the
American Civil War (as a child), two World Wars, and the introduction of life-
changing technologies such as the telephone, automobile, airplane, radio, television, blood transfusions, and penicillin. Indeed, one of Dewey's aims was to
persuade his readers of the importance of technologies as means to improve their
lives. Dewey steadfastly championed science and scientific inquiry throughout
his many writings, and felt that refining our inquiries and improving our
technologies were among the best ways to mitigate social problems.

Progressive education generally, and Dewey's philosophy of education in particular, at least in North America, have always been popular in teachers' colleges
and with faculties of education. Having said this, pragmatism, and particularly
Dewey's pragmatism, was ignored for many years by Anglo-American philosophers and it was not until quite recently that pragmatism's star rose again, thanks

in large part to American philosopher Richard Rorty's celebration of Dewey (along with Ludwig Wittgenstein and Martin Heidegger). Since then, pragmatism generally, and Dewey's philosophy in particular, have enjoyed a renaissance of sorts. I shall discuss Dewey's educational pragmatism by first presenting a brief biography, followed by a general discussion of his philosophical commitments, and following this, his philosophy of education. I will then address some issues and controversies surrounding Dewey's philosophy of education. I provide a brief, annotated biography at the end of the discussion.

BRIEF BIOGRAPHY

John Dewey was born into a middle-class family in Burlington, Vermont, on October 20, 1859. He did quite well in school, and eventually matriculated at the University of Vermont, taking his degree in 1882. He taught high school for two years, first in Oil City, Pennsylvania, and then in Charlotte, Vermont. Dewey's first love was philosophy, and in an attempt to see if he was of the right philosophical mind, he sent an article to the editor of *The Journal of Speculative Philosophy* (William Torrey Harris), asking if Harris would consider reading it over in order to provide feedback as to whether there was a philosophical future for Dewey. There was indeed, Harris acknowledged, and he published the article, entitled, 'The metaphysical assumptions of materialism'. Dewey decided to attend Johns Hopkins University in 1882. He received his PhD in philosophy in 1884, under the supervision of G.S. Morris.

Morris was one of the 'new Hegelians' who brought Hegel's philosophy of spirit to American shores. Dewey imbibed this idealism, and his earliest articles and books discussed traditional philosophical topics in an idealist spirit. Dewey's other influence was physiological and experimental psychology, particularly the psychology of Wilhelm Wundt by way of Wundt's pupil, G. Stanley Hall. Hall would go on to write one of the the the defining texts of American psychology – *Adolescence*.

Dewey began his teaching career at the University of Michigan in 1885 and remained until 1894, with one year's absence in 1889 to take the Chair in Philosophy at the University of Minnesota after the death of his beloved advisor, G.S. Morris, who had moved from Johns Hopkins to occupy the position by that time. It was at Michigan that Dewey met, and married, Alice Chipman and the couple's first child was born while Dewey was still at Michigan. Dewey was to lose two of his biological children to illness. Alice, it is said, was never able to overcome her losses, and as she became older, her melancholy deepened and her temperament soured.

Dewey moved to the University of Chicago in 1894, at the insistence of the university's first president, William Rainey Harper. It was here, at the University of Chicago, that Dewey's involvement in pedagogy and educational theory began in earnest. It was at Chicago that he began to discuss public education seriously. Dewey was responsible for the management of the Laboratory School and, at one point, Alice Dewey was the school's principal. Dewey's investigations in the

Laboratory School resulted in his most famous publication, *School and Society*, in 1899. The lessons Dewey learned in the Laboratory School would be drawn on repeatedly in his subsequent educational writings.

Dewey also began what would become a life-long interest in social democracy while at Chicago. Dewey witnessed first hand the gritty industrialization of Chicago, the masses of immigrants subjected to low wages and abysmal working conditions, the poverty and squalor of vast stretches of neighbourhoods, the failure of the schools to accommodate vast numbers of immigrant children, and the attempts at amelioration through organizations such as Jane Addams's Hull House. Indeed, Dewey was a frequent guest at Hull House, and gave lectures on various topics while there. Henceforth, Dewey began to write on social and political issues.

A fall-out with William Rainey Harper led to Dewey resigning his positions at the University of Chicago. Dewey left Chicago for Columbia in 1904, and remained there until his retirement in 1929. Dewey's influence began to be felt worldwide during his tenure at Columbia. He travelled extensively to such places as Turkey, China, Japan, and the Soviet Union, toured these nations' educational institutions, and gave hundreds of lectures and talks. He published many of his most famous educational writings during this period, including *Interest and Effort in Education* (1914), *Schools of Tomorrow* with his daughter, Evelyn (1915), and *Democracy and Education* (1916) – a favourite of Dewey's, which he once evaluated as the best overall statement of his philosophy. Dewey began to write even more forcefully on issues of politics. Though Dewey retired from Columbia in 1929, he did not slow down. If anything, he wrote more furiously than ever. Retirement gave Dewey the opportunity to expand on his earlier, philosophical interests: especially art and logic. Dewey was re-married in 1945 to Roberta Grant, Alice having passed away in 1927. Dewey collaborated with his old friend Arthur Bentley on *Knowing and the Known* in 1949, and was in the midst of revising his landmark text on metaphysics, *Experience and Nature*, when he died of pneumonia on June 1, 1952, in New York City, aged 92 years.

DEWEY'S PRAGMATIC PHILOSOPHY

Interestingly, Dewey did not call himself a pragmatist until well into his philosophical career. Pragmatism was the term William James associated with him, when he footnoted Dewey and his University of Chicago colleagues in his book, *Pragmatism* (1907), with regard to their work on logic. James famously credited Charles Saunders Peirce with coining the term, though Peirce himself could not recall doing so. The terms Dewey generally used to describe his phases of thought were 'absolutist', 'instrumentalist', and 'experimentalist'. He has also called his philosophy a 'direct realism', as well as a "naturalistic empiricism' or 'empirical naturalism'. These are in addition to pragmatism. During his tenure at Michigan, Dewey embraced the idealism of his advisor, G.S. Morris. Dewey would be led to call his early philosophical approach, 'absolutism'. This he held from 1885 to 1894. He melded this with insights gained from the newly minted discipline of experimental psychology. In fact, Dewey's 'new Hegelianism' was an amalgam of an absolute self with lessons learned from experimental studies on attention, perception, emotion, behaviour and cognition. Helpful to Dewey in this was the work of William James. James's *Psychology*, published in 1890, confirmed many of Dewey's nascent suspicions about the self, particularly with regard to the role of the 'mental'. The tension between Dewey's absolutism on the one hand, and experimental psychology on the other was ultimately resolved in favour of experimental psychology – though a 'Hegelian bacillus', as Dewey has called it, remains in his philosophy. We see evidence of Dewey's turn to functional–psychological understandings of human behaviour most clearly in his famous article, 'The reflex-arc concept in psychology' (1896). Here, Dewey criticizes behaviourists who insist that behaviour operates according to a reflex-arc mechanism. Instead of a pure stimulus-response reflex on the part of the subject, Dewey suggests a reflex circle, in which an organic connection between environmental stimuli, the sensory organs, the brain and spinal cord, and the resultant behaviour of the subject, take place. This accounts for the change in behaviour called 'learning' better than the reflex-arc theory.

Dewey and other scholars have named his second phase 'instrumentalism'. This period lasted approximately from 1898 to 1918. The term 'instrumentalism' is largely based on his work completed at the University of Chicago, particularly in logic. This innovative work was published as *Essays in Logical Theory* in 1903. Crudely put, instrumentalism insists on there being a qualitative or quantitative difference in the outcome of any inquiry for genuine knowledge to have occurred. We might say, with William James, that for recognition, 'there has to be a difference that makes a difference'. For Dewey and his students, logic was functional and developed and fulfilled its purpose in solving problems. However, there was nothing absolute, metaphysical or transcendental about logic, despite the reverence in which philosophers (especially Dewey's critics) seemed to hold it. Dewey would continue to write on the topic of logic, producing his masterpiece, *Logic: the Theory of Inquiry*, in 1938, at the age of 78.

Dewey's final phase of activity he labels, 'experimentalism'. Dewey thought this a better term to describe his overall approach than instrumentalism, which had overly materialistic and utilitarian connotations. By the time Dewey wrote *Reconstruction in Philosophy* (1920), which called for a philosophy sensitive to 'the problems of men', by which he meant problems of communities, economics, politics, society, and state, he had envisioned the chief business of philosophy and allied disciplines as experimenting with natural and social phenomena in a quest to solve human problems. This carried through to the end of his life.

As I have suggested, Dewey's philosophy of pragmatism shares affinities with a number of other thinkers, including G.W.F. Hegel, Wilhelm Wundt, and with the pragmatists William James, Charles Saunders Peirce, and George Herbert Mead. Dewey differs from Hegel and Mead, however, in his emphasis on the importance of *scientific* inquiry, and in the case of Wundt, Peirce, and James, on the importance of attending to communal and social ties and bonds. Dewey would often urge his readers to adopt (and persuade others to adopt) scientific inquiry as the means by which to solve human problems. This went hand in hand with his further call for democracy and democratic living. Dewey saw scientific inquiry and democratic living as of a piece. Dewey did not believe in absolutes (after 1895), supernatural beings, transcendental principles, Platonic forms or kinds, the irrefutability of logic, or the certainty of ideas. Instead, Dewey thought that the attention paid to these by contemporary philosophy was equivalent to 'putting old wine in new bottles'. Philosophy had to overcome the shibboleths of the past, and ensure that these are not reintroduced in ongoing reconstruction of philosophy, if it is to be of benefit to human problems.

Much of Dewey's effort, then, was spent on combating these hidden but never-theless, dangerously regressive tendencies in various branches and systems of philosophy. This we might call Dewey's 'negative' project. His 'positive' project, by contrast, was to push philosophy to help solve human or social problems, chiefly through theorizing ways to break down barriers such as class, race, geography, and gender that keep people apart. Communication and democratic living were always central strategies for Dewey. In the *Public and Its Problems* (1927), he lamented that the great American public was 'lost', and 'bewildered', and he felt that the solution for this was to marshal the forces of shared, social inquiry in a quest to solve social problems such as those mentioned above. The schools, needless to say, were to play a central role in this.

In the last phase of Dewey's philosophical thinking, he developed a novel philosophy of experience. Beginning with *Experience and Nature* (1925) and extending to *Art as Experience* (1934), and *Experience and Education* (1938), Dewey formulated an organic and naturalistic model of experience that placed the individual and her environment in a transactional relationship in which each reciprocally transforms the other. All organisms, human or otherwise, transact. There is a to and fro, whereby the organism is transformed by the environment and the environment transformed by the organism. On the part of the person, this transaction manifests as an experience. Experiences, Dewey claimed, were immediate. We have and undergo them. What is vital and unique to the human organism is selecting the qualities of satisfying experiences, and subjecting these to reflection in the quest for an end we anticipate will come about through our selection and reflection. When we do this, we begin to form intelligent habits, including the 'habits' of thinking, ordering, and controlling. These are the habits of inquiry. In time, we are able to inquire and use the habits of inquiry to achieve selected ends, leading to more and better experiences. This is as much a social and community undertaking as it is personal. Problems are better solved and satisfaction more easily achieved if problems are worked through in conjunction with others. In saying this, Dewey insists that problems are largely social. Individual problems have indirect bearing on social situations, as they take place in social contexts and generally involve one's conduct. Problems distanced from social situations, Dewey says, are often pseudo-problems. This is not to say that

Dewey eschewed abstract fields or disciplines such as mathematics. It is Dewey's reminder that all legitimate problems have social import or connection, including the problems of philosophy.

Experience may also have an aesthetic element; those experiences that are most satisfying Dewey labels 'aesthetic', because they result in a 'qualitatively immediate and unified, whole'. What counts as aesthetic for Dewey, then, is the quality of the transaction we have with the art object and the resultant experience we undergo. The work of art is the medium through which we have a 'consummatory' experience. These experiences are educationally the most valuable. They often manifest for the student as the 'aha' moment, when the task, problem, subject under discussion, or art 'come together', and 'make sense'. These are very often the experiences students remember, reproduce, and (most importantly for the context of education) from which students learn. These experiences stimulate a child on to further investigation and experimentation.

Dewey's final 'positive' philosophical task was to complete his theory of logic. He had consciously worked on this task for over 40 years, but was unable to commit fully until 1935. The result was an intellectual *tour de force*. Dewey's *Logic: the Theory of Inquiry* (1938) is his final and complete statement on the role of logic in problem solving, including problem solving in the contexts of ordinary living, laboratory science, mathematics, and social science. It is also a treatise on logic in its own right. Dewey's thesis is that logic is not an abstract, formal, irrefutable system, but a series of conclusions of investigations, built up over time, that remain susceptible to ongoing inquiry. For Dewey, logic, like all forms of inquiry, corrects itself: it remains attuned to the existential aims and goals for which it is used, and it adjusts itself when anticipated outcomes or solutions are not met. Of course, not all see logic this way, and Dewey was often pushed to defend his non-mathematical, non-symbolic accounting of logic. Dewey's reply was forceful and direct. He castigates formal logic for remaining abstract and aloof from the everyday personal and social problems of peoples, and those philosophers of formal logic (Dewey has Russell and Whitehead in mind) for perpetuating the 'myth' about the absoluteness of logic. In place of this, Dewey provides a context-sensitive logic; differing (logical) methods will have to be used in differing circumstances. For example, the methods of mathematics that are crucial in certain physical experiments are often unnecessary in social science contexts. Dewey also focuses on the function, rather than the necessity, of traditional philosophical topics such as concepts, objects, and ideas. These, Dewey says, are tools having their worth in experimental outcomes. If they cannot help solve the problems under consideration, their utility is questionable at best.

DEWEY'S PHILOSOPHY OF EDUCATION

It was at the time of his tenure at the University of Chicago that Dewey became involved with the newly developed Laboratory School. Dewey was given two departments to run – the department of philosophy and the newly opened department of pedagogy. Dewey gave courses in both. Among his responsibilities as head of the pedagogy department was to develop, then manage, a Laboratory School, beginning in 1896. This school was composed largely of children of the staff and faculty at the university. Dewey observed the children, oversaw the curriculum, took charge of the operating budget, and assumed overall responsibility of the school. He likened the school to a 'living physiology laboratory', which would yield valuable information on the psychological and social development of children. Dewey published a series of lectures given to parents under the title, *School and Society* (1899) and this sparked nothing short of a revolution in educational theory.

Prior to Dewey, educational theory in America consisted of traditional pedagogical methods such as rote, drilling, memorization, and recitation, together with the 'new' theories of Johann Heinrich Pestalozzi, Johann Friedrich Herbart, and Friedrich Wilhelm August Froebel. These were child-centred theories that played down the importance of traditional methods, but often (especially in the case of Froebel) emphasized grand metaphysical speculations on the nature of the child and the purposes of education. Dewey rejected these as well, reminding his readers that there was no need to invoke supernatural or transcendental ideals, aims, and purposes for the benefit of educating children well. These were superfluous at best and intrusive at worst.

Dewey emphasized several key elements in what has come to be called 'progressive education'. Chief among these is the breaking down of dualisms common to educational theory and practice. We might follow the example in the previous section, and call this his 'negative' philosophy of education. These included the dualism between the child and her physical and social environment, the child and the curriculum, the child's interest and effort, together with the general opposition of the individual and society. Dewey commented on each of these dualisms in *School and Society, and Democracy and Education* (1916) and other educational writings, suggesting that the way we think of the relationships between ourselves and the environment, others, and the curriculum, and individuals and society, is at the root of our malaise. In place of these dualisms, Dewey advocated an organic, even holistic, education; one in which the child is in a thoroughgoing relationship with her community, society, and curriculum. What Dewey hoped for from schools was an educational community that would nurture a child by providing her with opportunities to explore her everyday world, introducing new topics through connection to the old, and stressing interpersonal and relational dimensions of her development through shared activities. This extended to the curriculum: a child was not able to begin with abstract, formal, or in any event, unfamiliar content without great risk of boredom or misunderstanding. This sort of curriculum has to be worked up to. Dewey did admit that some rote and memorization had to take place in certain contexts (French classes at the Laboratory School were good examples), but he always emphasized the importance of introducing the curriculum by degrees, and through building up to formal and abstract subject matters.

Dewey considered the child a bio-psycho-social organism. Unlike most animals, we are born helpless, and only gradually come to maturation with the intensive support of our families. We are also irreducibly social creatures who learn in the context of our families and communities, through speech-groups, by way of habits proceeding from the simple (crawling) to complex (solving quadratic equations). We are, developmentally speaking, in a state of ongoing growth. This growth is biological, but it is also personal, emotional, and social: in short, it involves all aspects of the person. Dewey famously said that the aim of education was growth, and this led many to speculate on what was meant by growth. Dewey pointed to the ceaselessness of the to-and-fro responses between ourselves and our environments: we never stop growing until we stop transacting with our world. Positive or legitimate growth occurs when we are able to exploit this reciprocal relationship to our advantages, and enrich our experiences – both personal and social – thereby.

The other key characteristic Dewey discussed at length was inquiry, and we may profitably call this appeal to inquiry Dewey's 'positive' philosophy of education. Inquiry was central to the child and central to the school in helping the child develop. Inquiry is the key to growth, because inquiry is the tool that helps us to control and ultimately bring ourselves into constructive reciprocal relationships with our environments. We do this by problem solving. The school helps to facilitate this problem solving: first, by identifying children's interests and matching these with ordinary, everyday problems that need solving; secondly, by gradually increasing the complexity and abstractness of problems and solutions. As this is happening, the child's powers of inquiry become formalized. The pinnacle of inquiry, so to speak, is scientific inquiry – the sort of inquiry that is done under controlled, experimental conditions, often in laboratories. A child may never practice inquiry at such a formal stage in her future career: however, it is important to introduce this level of inquiry to children so that they might gain an appreciation of it.

Dewey's educational pragmatism was wildly popular. His two most famous books, *School and Society* and *Democracy and Education*, were staples of teacher education programmes across the country and abroad. Indeed, Dewey was a central figure in what became the progressive education movement. This was spearheaded by several of Dewey's ex-students from Columbia University, especially William Heard Kilpatrick. So powerful was the progressive education movement that Dewey was eventually led to play down its rhetoric in his last book-length manuscript on education, *Experience and Education* (1938). Dewey never claimed to be fully child-centred. He insisted, rather, on consideration of the interests of the child in developing educational aims. Likewise, Dewey never suggested that children be granted the permissiveness, both with regard to discipline and curriculum, that some progressive educators were demanding. In fact, Dewey claimed, freedom could only arise in contexts where some element of social control exists to guide children. Freedom is only possible if a child is able to develop and practice the habit of self-discipline, and this requires a context with rules and obligations. Attending to a child's experiences and not merely her outward behaviour, Dewey said, was the key to educating.

SOME CRITICISMS OF DEWEY

Not everyone was or is elated with Dewey's philosophy of education. Issues and concerns regarding the ability of progressive education, and Dewey's philosophy of education in particular, have long been raised. I shall discuss three of these. The first concern, that Dewey's philosophy of education leaves little room for imagination or emotion, was raised by the analytic philosopher Israel Scheffler. The second concern, that Dewey's philosophy of education sidelines, or even denigrates, abstract and intellectual thought, was a charge raised by the historian and liberal social critic Richard Hofstadter in the 1950s, the British philosopher Anthony O'Hear in the 1980s, and more recently by historian Diane Ravitch in the 1990s. It has recently resurfaced, in the work of Henry Edmunson III. A third concern is that Dewey's philosophy of education, and his understanding of the role of the schools in particular, is unable to challenge and overcome corporatism and the monopolies of vested interests. His philosophy of education is romantic, idealistic, and ill prepared for the reality of power in institutions. This is a concern shared by a number of past and present thinkers, supporters as well as critics of Dewey, who worry that progressive education is unable to shoulder the burden of dissolving entrenched systems of power. Some have even suggested that Dewey's pragmatism is complicit in maintaining the capitalist status quo. Supporters of Dewey who worry over such issues include the philosopher John Stuhr. Detractors have included notable philosophers of education as varied as Eamon Callan, R.S. Peters, Chet Bowers, and Kieran Egan.

The first allegation is that Dewey leaves little room for the imagination and the emotions. This is because his concern, through his writings, seems to be the promotion of the scientific method to students. This is tantamount, critics complain, to producing mechanized pupils, able to experiment in a wide variety of settings, but unable to draw on their imaginations or emotions. Dewey's retort is found in several works, most notably *How We Think*, 2nd edn (1933), and *Art as Experience*. In the former, Dewey discusses imagination as the necessary ingredient for 'deliberative rehearsal' – the forecasting of tentative solutions in inquiry. Far from imagination being absent in inquiry, Dewey says it is a vital element. Emotion is treated most fully in Dewey's *Art as Experience*. Here, Dewey claims emotions are a complex of reflex and desire, and arise in an existential situation or experience. Emotions exist only in the context of desire or repulsion. Artists can evoke emotion by drawing out desires. Indeed, this is part of what makes an aesthetic experience 'consummatory', in Dewey's words: to evoke emotion (especially through desire) is to ensure a (more) satisfying experience.

The second allegation concerns the underestimation or denigration of intellectual thought. This is an old, yet frequently repeated, charge against Dewey.

In concert with those who criticize Dewey for having little role for imagination are those who attack him for ignoring or downplaying ideas, concepts, and logic. These, critics say, are vital to the student's intellectual development, and to cast them aside in favour of scientific method is to ensure the impoverishment of children. This is a charge common to both American philosopher Israel Scheffler and British philosopher R.S. Peters. Some thinkers, such as Edmundson and O'Hear, also argue for a return to a more traditional education – in O'Hear's case, with attention to contemporary social problems. Dewey's response to these allegations is blunt: concepts, ideas, and logic are tools that can be profitably used, but are not to be made absolute, permanent, or fixed. Traditional education reifies rote, and bears little connection to present-day issues and problems. A traditional education paired with attention to contemporary issues would be self-contradictory: one would give way to the other. When some critics complain of the supposed denigration of concepts, ideas, and logic, what they are often getting at is the unwillingness of Dewey to place these on a pedestal.

In fact, concepts, ideas, and logic are given much attention in Dewey's writing. In his final account of logic, Dewey reserves several chapters for discussion of concepts. Concepts (including mathematical abstractions) are vital to carry out inquiries. Concepts organize disparate sets of data; they categorize relations among complex phenomena; and this allows us to understand and make these phenomena meaningful. Concepts are also necessary tools for formulation of potential hypotheses and their resultant testing. We cannot, for example, hypothesize that a balloon filled with gas lighter than air will rise unless we understand something of gravity (a concept), and air and gases and their laws (more concepts). Likewise, we cannot easily conclude that an eight-legged arthropod is not an insect if we do not have the concept of arachnid.

The final allegation is the most difficult of all. How is progressive education, and Dewey's philosophy of education in particular, to thwart what seems to be entrenched systems of power, privilege, and the co-optation of the schools for interests other than those of parents and children? This question is similar to the question Dewey himself asks in *The Public and Its Problems*: that of where is the public? For Dewey, only the public coming together in community, to solve its problems, is able to rescue the institution of education from its less than noble controllers. However, schools are often said to be precisely the institutions designed to provide the intelligent thinkers and problem-solvers needed to think and bring the public together in the spirit of shared inquiry.

It hardly needs to be said that there are no easy answers to this question. Dewey often thought that if we could persuade people to communicate with one another and help one another to share problems, they would find their lives less burdensome and difficult, and a robust public might emerge. Dewey wrote many books for the public, urging people to try intelligent social inquiry. He castigated those who stood in the way of such inquiry, particularly those who wished to return to a supposed 'golden age' free of social problems, or to imaginary timeless values, truths, or principles. In the end, what Dewey had to offer was persuasion: only if we, in various communities, organizations, and institutions, can operate democratically, and share and solve one another's problems, in a spirit of reciprocity, will we find the common ground we need to begin developing 'The Great Community'. It is fair to argue that Dewey's faith in the public and, particularly, the schools, as a way towards fully democratic living, is naïve. However, it remains to be seen whether those who are critical of Dewey's hope are able to offer a better model.

FURTHER READING

There is no substitute for reading Dewey. Key texts include *Democracy and Education* (1916), *How We Think*, 2nd edn (1933), and *Experience and Education* (1938). In my opinion, the best introduction to Dewey in the context of teacher education is by Dougles J. Simpson, Michael J.B. Jackson, and Judy C. Aycock: *John Dewey and the Art of Teaching: Toward Reflective and Imaginative Practice* (2005). For philosophers of education and those with an artistic or aesthetic interest, my recommendation is James Garrison: *Dewey and Eros: Wisdom and Desire in the Art of Teaching* (1997). The best biography is Robert Westbrook: *John Dewey and American Democracy* (1991). Those interested in the Laboratory School should examine Laurel Tanner: *The Dewey School: Lessons for Today* (1997). Readers interested in various criticisms against Dewey, together with a response, may wish to look at James Scott Johnston: *Inquiry in Education: John Dewey and the Quest for Democracy* (2006).

REFERENCES

Dewey, John (1969) The metaphysical assumptions of materialism. In *John Dewey: The Early Works, 1882–1898, Vol. 1: 1882–1888*, 1–14, edited by Jo Ann Boydston. Carbondale, IL: Southern Illinois University Press.

Dewey, John (1972) The reflex-arc concept in psychology. In *John Dewey: The Early Works, 1882–1898. Vol. 5: 1895–1898*, 96–110, edited by Jo Ann Boydston. Carbondale, IL: Southern Illinois University Press.

Dewey, John (1976) *School and Society*. In John *Dewey: The Middle Works, 1899–-1924. Vol. 1, 1899–1901*, 1–110, edited by Jo Ann Boydston. Carbondale, IL: Southern Illinois University Press.

Dewey, John (1976) *Studies in Logical Theory*. In *John Dewey: The Middle Works, 1899–1924. Vol. 2, 1902–1903*, 293–378, edited by Jo Ann Boydston. Carbondale, IL: Southern Illinois University Press.

Dewey, John (1985) *Interest and Effort in Education*. In *John Dewey: The Middle Works, 1899–1924. Vol. 7, 1912–1914*, 151–198, edited by Jo Ann Boydston. Carbondale, IL: Southern Illinois University Press.

Dewey, John (1980) *Democracy and Education*. In *John Dewey: The Middle Works, 1899–1924. Vol. 9, 1916*, edited by Jo Ann Boydston. Carbondale, IL: Southern Illinois University Press.

Dewey, John (1980) *The Need for a Recovery of Philosophy*. In *John Dewey: The Middle Works, 1899–1924. Vol. 10, 1916–1917*, 3–48, edited by Jo Ann Boydston. Carbondale, IL: Southern Illinois University Press.

Dewey, John (1981) *Experience and Nature*. In *John Dewey: The Later Works, 1925–1952. Vol. 1, 1925*, edited by Jo Ann Boydston. Carbondale, IL: Southern Illinois University Press.

Dewey, John (1982) *Reconstruction in Philosophy*. In *John Dewey: The Middle Works, 1899–1924. Vol. 12, 1920*, 77–202, edited by Jo Ann Boydston. Carbondale, IL: Southern Illinois University Press.

Dewey, John (1984) *The Public and Its Problems*. In *John Dewey: The Later Works, 1925–1952. Vol. 2, 1925–1927*, 235–372, edited by Jo Ann Boydston. Carbondale, IL: Southern Illinois University Press.

Dewey, John (1988) *From Absolutism to Experimentalism*. In *John Dewey: The Later Works, 1925–1952. Vol. 5, 1929–1930*, 147–160, edited by Jo Ann Boydston. Carbondale, IL: Southern Illinois University Press.

Dewey, John (1986) *Experience and Education*. In *John Dewey: The Later Works, 1925–1952. Vol. 13, 1938–1939*, 1–62, edited by Jo Ann Boydston. Carbondale, IL: Southern Illinois University Press.

Dewey, John (1986) *Logic: the Theory of Inquiry*. In *John Dewey: The Later Works, 1925–1952. Vol. 12, 1938*, edited by Jo Ann Boydston. Carbondale, IL: Southern Illinois University Press.

Dewey, John (1987) *Art as Experience*. In *John Dewey: The Later Works, 1925–1952. Vol. 10, 1934*, edited by Jo Ann Boydston. Carbondale, IL: Southern Illinois University Press.

Dewey, John (1988) *How We Think*. In *John Dewey: The Later Works, 1925–1952. Vol. 8, 1933*, 105–352, edited by Jo Ann Boydston. Carbondale IL: Southern Illinois University Press.

Dewey, John and Dewey, Evelyn (1985) *Schools of Tomorrow*. In *John Dewey: The Middle Works, 1899–1924. Vol. 8, 1915*, 205–404, edited by Jo Ann Boydston. Carbondale, IL: Southern Illinois University Press.

Dewey, John and Bentley, Arthur (1991) *Knowing and the Known*. In *John Dewey: The Later Works, 1925–1952. Vol. 16, 1949–1952*, 1–294, edited by Jo Ann Boydston. Carbondale, IL: Southern Illinois University Press.

8

T.S. Eliot, Education and Culture

Andrew Reid

INTRODUCTION: BEFORE ELIOT

In setting out to explore the educational thought of T.S. Eliot (1888–1965), we may be inclined initially to locate his views in relation to some familiar conceptual framework or theoretical system; and what comes most readily to hand will almost certainly be that convenient apparatus, the traditional–progressive dichotomy. Eliot is surely a traditionalist; he famously wrote, after all, about tradition and the individual talent, placing particular emphasis on the former term. And he is unmistakeably an anti-progressivist, if a progressivist is one to whom human progress is a secular ideal, and education one of the chief tools for its realization.

Caution would be advisable, however, for the distinctive character of Eliot's thought is unlikely to be captured within any device so rudimentary as this. Tradition and culture must be preserved and transmitted; so far Eliot is undoubtedly with the traditionalist. But in his own critical and artistic practice he appears, paradoxically, as a disruptive influence; as one of the founders, and of those perhaps the most representative, of modernism in literature. Likewise, the creativity of the talented individual needs to be fostered: here is one point, certainly, on which Eliot and the progressivist appear to agree. But how? Eliot's answer, as it turns out, offers little encouragement to the progressivist, but it has the depth and authority of a figure who, by common consent, was himself one of the great creative artists of the twentieth century. And, to complicate matters still further, where education itself is concerned, Eliot's thought reveals a scepticism more profound than any traditionalist is likely to feel at ease with.

Views of this nature are likely, then, to resist comfortable encapsulation within the structures familiar to educational theorists; but they are nonetheless capable of elucidation, and as a step towards that goal it will be useful to place them in their historical and intellectual contexts. In what follows, I shall briefly expound Eliot's views on education, and then attempt to show how they are related to his wider intellectual, and specifically philosophical, preoccupations. But first I shall outline a little of the historical background from which his views may be said to emerge; and this means locating Eliot within a movement of modern educational thought which can plausibly claim Matthew Arnold (1822–1888) as a founding member.

Arnold's place in educational thought, and his status as a significant figure in the history of educational reform, rests largely on the part he played in the controversies surrounding the nature and aims of education in mid-Victorian Britain. The issue which provided the impetus for his first major foray into educational and social polemic was the Revised Code, issued by the government in 1862. The main feature of this set of regulations was a reduction in state funding to elementary schools, and the requirement that this funding would henceforth be determined by the performance of pupils on tests of reading, writing and arithmetic; such was the system of payment by results. Arnold was at that point an Inspector of Schools, and the reports which he produced in that capacity show him to have been an unusually sympathetic and enlightened member of his profession. His reaction to the Revised Code was to subject it to fierce attack as a piece of mean-spirited economizing designed to satisfy what he saw as the narrow-minded, materialistic and philistine opponents of culture, opponents later to be excoriated at length by him in his best-known work *Culture and Anarchy*. Culture, according to Arnold, is 'sweetness and light', or 'the study and pursuit of perfection', as represented by 'the best that has been thought and said' (Arnold [1869]: in Collini 1993: 81, 190); it should be spread as widely as possible, with elementary education having a role to play in this process. School should not be seen as '... a mere machine for teaching reading, writing and arithmetic, but as a living whole with complex functions, religious, moral and intellectual'. (Arnold [1862]: in Sutherland 1973: 37).

In contrast to the emphasis placed by his opponents on material achievement, on economic development, on 'machinery' or the belief in technological or administrative solutions to human problems, culture for Arnold is essentially an inward condition, characterized by a balanced and harmonious synthesis of our intellectual, aesthetic, spiritual and moral capacities. And what is conspicuously lacking in the social values of his time, he argues, is precisely this kind of balance or wholeness. One-sidedness and fanaticism are the dominant features of public discourse. Nonconformist religion is strong on self-righteousness and moral fervour, but it needs to be balanced by a breadth of wisdom and humane idealism. Industrial capitalism has put knowledge to work in transforming the material conditions of life and creating great wealth, but it has made the world a cruder and uglier place. The aesthetic and intellectual values of the enjoyment of beauty for its own sake and the pursuit of knowledge for its own sake need to be affirmed vigorously if the spiritual aspirations of human beings are to be fulfilled; and it is these aspirations that make life worth living.

The idea of culture as the best that has been thought and said may strike the contemporary reader as problematic in at least some respects, but it would have seemed compelling to a product of the English public school and university (in his own case, Rugby and Oxford), and of upper-middle class Victorian society, such as Arnold. What it meant was the high culture of Western civilization: the great tradition of art, thought and literature which, rooted in ancient Greece and Rome and in mediaeval Christendom, had reached full maturity in the centuries following the Renaissance. Arnold well understood, though, that this view of culture, and the conception of human perfection defined in terms of its values and achievements, would be questioned and criticized. The status of more recent developments, in particular of the rise of science in the seventeenth and eighteenth centuries, was, in relation to this picture, as yet unclear. In his own time, some of Arnold's critics would see, in the appeal to culture, a reluctance to face the challenges of modernity; in particular, the apparent threat posed to religion by science and the social changes brought about by industrialism. Other critics of the culture-transmission view of education, in Arnold's time and later, would note the significant coincidence of high culture and high social class. But for Arnold himself the urgent task was to promote the diffusion of sweetness and light throughout the whole of society; and in particular to acquaint the middle and lower classes, so far as it could be done, with an image of the fuller possibilities of life, a glimpse of a spiritual ideal transcending the limitations of their material condition.

ELIOT ON EDUCATION

On the question of the relation between education and culture, Eliot follows the route pioneered by Arnold. Maintaining the continuity of the culture, he declares, is an aim of education; and that means promoting 'what Matthew Arnold spoke of as "the knowledge of the best that has been thought and said in the world" (and, I might add, the best that has been done in the world, and that has been created in the arts in the world)' (Eliot 1978: 119). But if Eliot is to that significant extent a follower of Arnold, he is nonetheless a critical follower. The criticisms go deep, and they imply a view of education as an agency of cultural transmission considerably less positive and optimistic than that of his Victorian predecessor. Eliot believes that Arnold's conception of culture is essentially 'facile', prefiguring the fashionable aestheticism of the later Victorian period, rather than one in which the profound *anthropological* significance of culture as a way of life is fully understood (Eliot 1951: 434–436; 1962: 28). Arnold had thought of culture as an edifying substitute for the religious belief which he believed to be in decline in his own time; for Eliot, culture and religion are essentially inseparable – in some sense even the same thing, seen perhaps in different aspects (Eliot 1962: 31). Both are concerned with the fundamental question of how we are to live, of what gives life meaning and value. Eliot had become a member of the Anglican Church in 1927, and the major preoccupation of his social criticism thereafter was with how social and political questions could be treated from the standpoint of a rigorously orthodox Christian belief.

Thus, Eliot remarks on the 'thinness' of Arnold's account, which is 'partly due to the absence of social background to his picture' (Eliot 1962: 22); and in setting out to rectify that deficiency in his own analysis, he offers a distinctive view of the connection between culture, social structure and education. It is this strand in Eliot's thought which, as we shall see, places him well to the right in the conventional political spectrum. Eliot's political inclinations, if unorthodox, are unmistakeably conservative: and his writings on education turn out, in consequence, to consist largely of attacks on what he takes to be the progressivist platitudes upon which the typical educational policies of the time are founded. In his 1950 lectures on The Aims of Education, for example, much of the discussion is taken up with criticism of 'current fallacies of educational theory' (Eliot 1978: 62). The overall tendency is to reinforce the impression that Eliot's view of education is essentially a negative, sceptical and pessimistic one.

Likewise, in his book *Notes towards the Definition of Culture*, Eliot questions the 'prevalent assumption' that it is necessary to discuss education in terms of its aims or purposes. It is in this context that, surprisingly it may seem, he *criticizes* the idea that the purpose of education is culture transmission. It quickly becomes clear, however, that the target of his attack is not the idea of culture transmission as such, but rather the notion that the education system has preponderant responsibility for this task; in which case 'culture' is simply identified with whatever can be taught in schools. The problem here, Eliot believes, is that culture in the anthropological sense – the sense which Arnold fails adequately to grasp – cannot be made fully explicit; its effects are felt for the most part at a deep level, beyond the reach of conscious articulation, and it is this which gives it its power to express or represent a *whole* way of life (and not merely the conscious aesthetic and intellectual preferences of a privileged minority). To confine the idea of culture to whatever can be made the subject of lessons, or government educational policy, is to deny it this depth and distort its true significance. More generally, since so much that shapes a culture and thereby informs a society's way of life lies deep below the level of conscious awareness and control, it is absurd for governments to try to legislate for it by means of 'cultural policies' and the like. Eliot, moreover, wishes to attack the idea that education can legitimately be used as an instrument of government policy, a tool for promoting various social or political goals. In this context, talk of 'aims' is invariably a way of insinuating non-educational purposes into educational policy and practice; but the true concern of education is with the promotion of wisdom, knowledge and learning (Eliot 1962: 99). What makes all such talk of the aims of education problematic, then, is a failure to grasp correctly the nature and value of education.

There follows a critical examination of such claims as that the function of education is to serve the needs of the age; that it promotes happiness; and that it is widely desired. Eliot's way with commonplaces of this sort is to subject them to a fairly withering debunking. Thus, 'We are left wondering who is to determine what are the needs of the age ...' (Eliot 1962: 97); it is possible to be made extremely unhappy by education; and people can be persuaded to want almost anything. In his lectures on The Aims of Education (Eliot 1978: 61–124) the tone is less acerbic; but, attempts to itemize educational aims in terms of, for example, personal development, education for citizenship and preparation for employment are criticized as showing a tendency to disregard both the interrelation of such items, and the possibilities of conflict between them. Differing views on these items, moreover, require us to acknowledge the deeper question underlying them: 'What is Man?' (Eliot 1978: 109); and our differences on this question 'will turn out in the end to be religious differences'. It is in his treatment of the claim that education 'should be organised so as to give "equality of opportunity"' (Eliot 1962: 100), however, that Eliot's views may be said to diverge, in a spectacular way, from what would later come to be regarded as a generally accepted principle of educational thought and practice. 'Education should help to preserve the class and to select the elite ... the ideal of a uniform system such that no one capable of receiving higher education could fail to get it, leads imperceptibly to the education of too many people, and consequently to the lowering of standards to whatever this swollen number of candidates is able to reach'. (Eliot 1962: 100–101). 'What I wish to maintain is a point of view from which it appears more important – if we have to choose, and perhaps we do have to choose – that a small number of people should be educated well, and others left with only a rudimentary education, than that everybody should receive a share of an inferior quality of education, whereby we delude ourselves into thinking that whatever there can be the most of, must be the best' (Eliot 1978: 119–120).

Such views are, as Eliot recognizes, simply irreconcilable with the 'prevalent assumption' in favour of educational equality as a fundamental principle of democratic society. And if we were to leave it at that point, his educational thought would perhaps have little more than historical or biographical interest in a world where, as he finds himself obliged (somewhat grudgingly) to concede, credible alternatives to democracy are not to be found (Eliot 1962: 98; 1978: 86). But we need to pursue the matter a little further, in order to reach the foundations of Eliot's views on the relations between education, culture and society.

Eliot rejects the idea of equal opportunity in education because he sees in it a threat to the hierarchical class structure of society; and he believes that this class structure is necessary for the continuity of culture. Equal opportunity aims to allow the most intellectually able pupils, whatever their social background, to advance to the highest positions; the result, according to Eliot, would be to 'disorganise society, by substituting for classes, elites of brains, or perhaps only of sharp wits'. (Eliot 1962: 101). That the emergence of such elites may be an unavoidable feature of modern society is not in dispute; but what they cannot hope to do is to replace the social class as the primary agency of cultural transmission. Elites, for Eliot, are characteristic of an 'atomic' pattern of society (Eliot 1962: 37). They are selected according to the limited and highly specific abilities and purposes shared by their members; their position is transient and their membership subject to fluctuation. They thus lack the internal cohesion and continuity over time that is characteristic of a society based on a stable, integrated and enduring class structure: the 'organic' society (Eliot 1962: 15). The basis of the class system in the organic society is heredity; and this means that the *family* is, for Eliot, the 'primary channel of the transmission of culture' (Eliot 1962: 43). Culture transmission, in short, is a matter of upbringing rather than formal education or schooling, which can thus assume at best a secondary role in this respect. The classes which compose the organic society, moreover, have distinctive parts to play in its culture, and it is the harmonious interdependence of these functions which gives the society its character as an organism, a balanced whole within which diversity is contained and reconciled. So far as the culture *can* be expressed in a conscious articulation of its beliefs, ideas, meanings and values, this function is performed by elites – intellectual, literary, artistic and so on – which will, in general, tend to attach themselves to the dominant social class. For the remainder, the culture is expressed in customs, rituals, habits and traditions whose formation and internalization proceed in ways which are for the most part unconscious. Where education has a role in culture transmission, then, it must be largely aimed at the minority who are able to respond to it at a conscious level. Better, Eliot believes, to concentrate resources on this task, than to squander them in offering, in the name of equality, a diluted and adulterated substitute to the masses, an enterprise matched in its futility only by its worthlessness.

THE PHILOSOPHICAL BACKGROUND

Eliot's view of education, then, appears disquietingly negative and pessimistic, an attitude decidedly at odds with the general tenor of much contemporary educational thinking. But we should resist any temptation to dismiss this as merely a temperamental peculiarity. Eliot's educational thought is rooted, as I shall now try to show, in philosophical ideas which deserve to be examined seriously and assessed on their intellectual merits. As we have seen, its most distinctive features are an unorthodox political conservatism (even to otherwise sympathetic commentators, Eliot is a 'reactionary') and a rigorous religious orthodoxy, specifically regarding the doctrines of Anglo-Catholic Christianity. Many Anglicans, it should be noted, might differ from Eliot in their view of the relation between these two sets of beliefs. The Church of England has in the past, admittedly, been characterized satirically as the Tory Party at prayer; and its status as an Established church, with the monarch as its head, might seem to support the view of it as an essentially conservative force. But such a view would have little plausibility in the twenty-first century, and in any case has no real bearing on the particular relation between political and religious thought that we encounter in the case of Eliot.

Eliot had some involvement in reactionary politics, it is true, in the period before his conversion to the Anglican form of Christianity in 1927. And to characterize it in this way as conservative or reactionary is to place his thought within a secular political framework; as being 'right wing', say, as opposed to 'left wing'. But his mature political beliefs derive from his religious outlook; and from that standpoint, *all* secular political doctrines, whatever their location on the conventional left–centre–right spectrum, are viewed with scepticism, insofar as they share the belief that the deepest problems of human life can be solved by political methods. By contrast, Eliot's view is that such problems are, if approached in purely secular terms, fundamentally insoluble: he thus rejects *any* form of humanist, progressivist or utopian politics, right wing or left, on the grounds that all such doctrines are based on a false view of the human condition (Eliot 1951: 489–490; 1939: 95–96). Eliot's political scepticism, then, assumes a reactionary form, in terms of the conventional categories of political doctrine. Likewise, his rejection of progressivist politics reflects what appears to be a profound pessimism about the human situation and the prospects for its improvement. But again, since Eliot's is the standpoint of Christianity rather than secular political thought, this pessimism cannot be regarded as ultimate or constitutional, since for Christians the possibility of relief is held to be available in the doctrine of Redemption.

As a Christian, Eliot is committed to the belief that the human condition can only be fully grasped in terms of the Fall, and the consequent necessity of salvation or redemption. And while there are undoubtedly many Christians for whom religious faith is primarily a matter of celebration, it is worth stressing that Eliot's emphasis on the grim predicament in which humanity finds itself is, on its own terms, doctrinally sound: for if we need to be rescued, it is precisely because we are in a desperate situation. Human life includes an ineradicable element of wretchedness, suffering and injustice, and our only hope of relief lies in grasping that we are, beyond a certain level, powerless to help ourselves. In its fallen state, human kind is marked by a radical flaw, an imperfection or deformation of will and understanding so profound that, failing redemption, it is condemned endlessly to frustration and disappointment in its efforts to find fulfilment and success, and despair at the meaningless futility of existence. The clear implication of this bleak doctrine is that any political or secular scheme designed to relieve the *fundamental* insecurity and hopelessness of the human condition is doomed to failure. This is not to say, of course, that politicians and governments should not do everything in their power to make life better for people; and clearly this becomes in many cases a matter of urgent and inescapable obligation. But from a political standpoint we may be tempted by the delusion that progress and improvement without limit are possible, provided we command the necessary instruments of power. And this leads in turn to utopian dreams of a society in which all human needs are met, all aspirations fulfilled, all unhappiness abolished, and all lives made meaningful. There can be little doubt that such notions have been entertained, particularly in the twentieth century; and few surely would dispute the verdict that the results have been, to put it mildly, generally disappointing. For Christians of Eliot's stamp, such results are entirely predictable. The State may set out its plans for the earthly paradise, but its power to fulfil them is another matter. Delusive belief in such possibilities will always find adherents, however; 'human kind cannot bear very much reality' (Eliot 1969).

Eliot's view of the futility of utopian political schemes is one aspect of a general scepticism regarding any form of humanist or progressivist social thought, and a particular aversion to the commonplaces of educational progressivism noted earlier. The view of the human condition from which such wishful thinking is derived provides the basis for a familiar set of attitudes: liberal, individualist, and, in terms of art and literature, Romantic. Thus, it is characteristic of liberal or progressive political thought to present itself as innovative, a radical departure from the past, from history or tradition. These are typically depicted as an oppressive burden of stale custom and stagnant ritual serving only to perpetuate privilege and injustice, and to stifle the freedom, vitality and rights of the present and future; the dead past crushing the living present. In art and literature, the counterpart of the progressive movement is the Romantic cult of the free expression of emotion, the defiantly creative individual personality, the iconoclastic disrupter of bourgeois convention. Eliot detects in this Byronic pose a rather unconvincing impersonation or reflection of the diabolic pride and wilful disobedience to which Christianity attributes the fallen state of humankind (Eliot 1957: 194–195); his response is to argue for the classical values of balance, reason, harmony and restraint, and, most notably in his 1919 essay 'Tradition and the Individual Talent' for a view of individual creativity as depending upon a highly developed awareness of and accommodation to cultural tradition (Eliot 1951: 13–22). As a poet, and particularly in what is probably his best-known work, *The Waste Land*, his response is to depict the horrors of social, personal and spiritual disintegration in what he saw as the decaying European civilization of the early 1920s. In this work, a world reminiscent of Dante's *Inferno* is revealed in a seemingly disconnected succession of enigmatic and disturbing images, of mysterious disembodied voices, and of fragmentary scenes glimpsed fleetingly in the dim and eerie light of a nightmarish hallucination.

Eliot's political and social thought, then, is rooted in the Christian doctrine of human nature as essentially flawed and fallible, and thus as standing in need of the authority, order and correction provided by tradition; and the predominantly sceptical or negative aspect of his educational thought, his anti-progressivism, is perhaps best understood in this way. But there is another source to which his ideas can be traced, one which is of particular importance in explaining their more positive features, their specific intellectual shape and overall theoretical consistency: that is, the philosophy of F.H. Bradley (1846–1924), a subject on which Eliot completed his doctoral dissertation in 1916. Bradley's formidably obscure and difficult philosophy is now perhaps largely forgotten, having been consigned to virtual oblivion by the rise of the analytic movement whose origins can, to some extent, be traced to a conscious reaction against it on the part of Bertrand Russell and G.E. Moore. But his style of thought was still sufficiently potent in the years before World War I to exercise a considerable influence on the young Eliot.

A convenient entry point to the Bradleyan philosophy is provided by the reasonably familiar idea that nothing in the normal course of experience can be *fully* understood on its own, in isolation or abstraction from its context. Insofar, then, as we find it (for example) useful to single objects out from their background and connections with other objects, say for the purposes of scientific investigation, any understanding of them which we derive thereby is necessarily limited, conditional, or incomplete. This line of thought leads quickly to the conclusion that nothing short of a grasp of the *whole* of reality as a unified system will suffice to give us the final truth about anything. Bradley's name for this ultimate and unconditional totality is the *Absolute*. His philosophy, then, can be described as a form of *metaphysical holism*. Reality is, ultimately, One; and anything short of this is therefore to some degree *unreal*.

Eliot's study of Bradley focussed on a particular issue: namely, the *epistemological* question of how knowledge of this ultimate totality might be possible. Bradley believed that our ordinary forms of understanding, and the concepts and categories employed in the scientific account of the world, were indispensable tools which enable us to get through life in a practical sense; but they achieve this by allowing us to deal effectively only with the superficial appearance of things, and afford no grip whatever on the underlying reality. The characteristic mode of the intellect is to abstract, to discriminate and classify, to analyse and relate; but since reality is one and indivisible, the intellectual route will not finally lead us to it. Is there, then, any way of coming to know reality? The answer, perhaps surprisingly, is that there is. Experience itself, at its most primordial, allows us to encounter the absolute: and this *immediate experience*, to use Bradley's term, is, precisely, an experience of the essential wholeness of reality, underlying and prior to any intellectual process of division or abstraction: the differentiation, for example, of subject (or self) and object (or external world). In this primordial encounter with reality, moreover, there is as yet no trace of what subsequently becomes the familiar distinction between *feeling* (in the sense both of emotion and of sensory awareness) and *thought* (in the sense of our intellectual or cognitive grasp of things).

Bradley's metaphysical and epistemological doctrines undoubtedly play an important part in Eliot's thought. The great issue for Eliot, in both his literary and his social criticism, is the danger of atomism or fragmentation; the disintegration of the whole which signals the loss of reality and decline into chaos. In particular, the idea of culture as an organically integrated totality is, as we noted earlier, essential to his thought. Culture embraces the whole of society, and it is a fatal error to think of it as the exclusive possession of a particular class or elite; to mistake the part for the whole. Each class, certainly, has its special function to perform in relation to this totality; and it is this differentiation of cultural function which, according to Eliot, gives rise to the hierarchy of classes in the first place. The more advanced the society, the more elaborate the pattern of such differentiation (Eliot 1962: 25). The meanings and values which are consciously expressed in the art, literature and religious thought of the highest class are the same meanings and values which manifest themselves in the customary practices and rituals of the lower levels; the culture thus expresses a distinct way of life which is inherited and shared. But cultural specialization also carries with it the danger of cultural disintegration, particularly where 'the artistic sensibility is impoverished by its divorce from the religious sensibility' (Eliot 1962: 26).

This concept of *sensibility* is central to Eliot's thought. In his earlier essays, it is the capacity which comes into play in aesthetic experience, and particularly in relation to poetry. And while Eliot nowhere explicitly defines his use of the term, it seems fairly clear that he intends it to refer to something like the Bradleyan notion of immediate experience, and the fusion of thought and feeling implied in that notion. But in his later critical works, which include his social and educational writings, the concept of sensibility takes on a wider and deeper significance: the sensibility which responds to poetry and the arts is increasingly attuned to the religious or spiritual significance of experience; ultimate reality being, for Eliot in his post-conversion phase, essentially spiritual (Eliot 1951: 388; 1934: 45–46). As we have seen, for Eliot culture and religion are in some sense *the same thing*, experienced perhaps from different standpoints. In his earlier literary-critical work, Eliot had spoken of a *dissociation of sensibility* in which the Bradleyan fusion of thought and feeling had been weakened, to the detriment of English poetry. In his later social criticism, a similar fragmentation of religious and aesthetic sensibility threatens the organic wholeness of the culture.

In the light of this, the importance of the concept of culture transmission in Eliot's thought emerges more clearly. Aesthetic experience cannot be separated finally from moral and spiritual considerations. In particular, the test of significance and value in literature is its ability to enlarge, deepen and refine our grasp of the moral and spiritual meaning of human experience. The sensibility which enables these modes of responsiveness is, like other human capacities, subject both to variation among individuals and to development or refinement within individuals. And the degree to which this sensibility is developed in an individual or society marks the degree of personal growth or maturity, the extent to which we approximate to the authentically adult human condition in respect of our capacity for aesthetic, moral and spiritual experience. Culture transmission is thus the key to the fundamental educational goal of *development as a person*.

Education, then, understood as a conscious and systematic process of culture transmission and preservation, must be a matter of vital importance. In preserving and passing on its cultural traditions to new generations, a society keeps alive its way of life, its deepest convictions about what matters for human beings, what is ultimately real. The culture must be consciously preserved, for its survival, far from being automatically guaranteed, is always under threat; and it must be transmitted, for its achievements constitute an inheritance of supreme significance and value which belongs to all, and which operates for the benefit of all. But for Eliot, as we saw earlier, only a minority can be supposed realistically to possess the capacities for conscious appropriation of this inheritance, insofar as it *can* be consciously appropriated. It follows that we must not harbour unrealistic expectations of education. And it also follows that education is necessarily a *selective* process, whereby the minority capable of articulate and developed sensibility are identified and enabled to advance. Eliot is thus prepared to say that, so far as the organization of education is concerned, the selection of this minority is more important than any other consideration; for on it depends the survival and development of the culture. This is not a view that would achieve popular support in a modern, liberal, egalitarian, democratic world; and popular support was not something that Eliot set out to obtain for his views.

CONCLUSION: AFTER ELIOT

Eliot's educational doctrines have not, on the face of it, fared well with the passage of time. The reactionary tenor of his thought, and in particular his hostility towards the idea of equality in education, seem out of touch with changing social attitudes, and ill-adapted to the demands and expectations of democratic societies as they have evolved since 1948, when *Notes towards the Definition of Culture* was published. This is conceded even by a sympathetic commentator, G.H. Bantock, who acknowledges that we might find Eliot in this respect 'unrealistic'; and that so far as the education of the 'less able' is concerned, 'Eliot is no help at all' (Bantock 1970: 44, 112). Likewise, Eliot's excursions into anthropology, and especially his belief that social class differentiation emerges as a consequence of cultural specialization, have struck some later critics as eccentric. Raymond Williams, for example, finds that Eliot's treatment of class and culture, excluding as it does any consideration of economic factors, 'is not, when historically viewed, such as will give us complete confidence in his subsequent reasoning' (Williams 1963: 232). And, for still more recent commentators, Eliot's thoughts on education, culture and society might seem to have at best an antiquarian interest in a world in which traditional assumptions about meaning and value have been subject to radical criticism by the apparently irresistible rise of postmodernism and the doctrine of cultural relativism.

Is there anything, then, that can be salvaged from Eliot's educational thought? I shall, by way of conclusion, briefly suggest two ways in which continuing significance might be claimed for it. The first of these relates to the concept of sensibility, discussed in the previous section. For Arnold and Eliot, the study of literature, the arts and humanities has a central place in education. How is this justified? The answer is that if education is concerned fundamentally with the development of *persons*, then this requires us to give careful attention to the philosophical (or, for Eliot, religious) problem of human nature. As Eliot argues in his lectures on The Aims of Education, the central question for educational theory must be 'What is Man?' Now, according to the culture-transmission view of education, the deepest and most compelling explorations of that question, and those therefore which bear most significantly on the development of the distinctively human qualities, are contained in the classic art, literature and thought of Western culture. Personal development depends ultimately on the balanced cultivation of our aesthetic, intellectual, moral and spiritual sensibilities, and it is to that task that the study of the culture's greatest achievements is dedicated. Eliot's educational thought, then, deals with matters of permanent and vital interest: with fundamental questions about the nature of education and with what this implies in terms of priorities in the curriculum.

But this returns us to a problem briefly touched on above. In a culturally pluralistic and relativistic world, how can the claims of Western culture be represented as possessing anything more than local validity? This leads to the second and final suggestion which I wish to make on behalf of Eliot in particular and the culture-transmission view of education in general. When Eliot spoke of the Christian culture of Europe as 'the highest culture that the world has ever known' (Eliot 1962: 33), and when he spoke approvingly of Arnold's view of culture as 'the best that has been thought and said in the world', he was delivering value judgements which, from a standpoint *within* Western culture, claimed *universal* authority. Is a claim of this sort intelligible? How could it be justified? And on what specific grounds are the central achievements of Western culture judged superior to any other? An answer to these questions would require us to examine, in philosophical terms, the very ideas of objective rational justification and absolute value; and thus to consider seriously the possibility that cultural relativism, which presupposes their falsity, is at least in some respects mistaken. That would be a salutary step, if not an entirely novel one, for modern philosophy of education, and one which T.S. Eliot challenges us to take.[42]

NOTE

42 Matthew Arnold's writings are available in various editions. Page references above are to the selections edited by Gillian Sutherland and titled *Arnold on Education* (1973), and by Stefan Collini and titled *Culture and Anarchy and Other Writings* (1993). The brief account of F.H. Bradley's philosophy given here is based on two main sources: (1) Bradley (1897); (2) his 1909 essay 'On Our Knowledge of Immediate Experience', which is reprinted in Allard and Stock (1994). Eliot's 1916 dissertation is published as Eliot (1964).

FURTHER READING

Eliot's life and career are examined at length in Ackroyd, Peter: *T.S. Eliot* (Hamish Hamilton, 1984) and Gordon, Lyndall: *T.S. Eliot: An Imperfect Life* (Vintage, 1998). The philosophical aspect of his work is extensively discussed in Childs, Donald J: *From Philosophy to Poetry. T.S. Eliot's Study of Knowledge and Experience* (The Athlone Press, 2001); Freed, Lewis: *T.S. Eliot: The Critic as Philosopher* (Purdue University Press, 1979); Freed, Lewis: *T.S. Eliot: Aesthetics and History* (Open Court, 1962); and Thompson, Eric: *T.S. Eliot: The Metaphysical Perspective* (Southern Illinois University Press, 1963). Eliot's social and political views have been the subject of close examination, much of it fairly hostile: see, for example, Asher, Kenneth: *T.S. Eliot and Ideology* (Cambridge, 1995); Menand, Louis: *Discovering Modernism: T.S. Eliot and His Context* (Oxford, 2007); Ricks, Christopher: *T.S. Eliot and Prejudice* (Faber, 1988); and Eagleton, Terry: *The Idea of Culture* (Blackwell, 2000). Witnesses for the defence include Raine, Craig: *T.S. Eliot* (Oxford, 2006); Scruton, Roger: *A Political Philosophy* (Continuum, 2006) and Kirk, Russell: *Eliot and his Age: T.S. Eliot's Moral Imagination in the Twentieth Century* (ISI Books, 2008). On education, Eliot's most notable follower has been G.H. Bantock; in addition to the references given above, his book *Education, Culture and the Emotions* (Faber, 1967) should be mentioned, as should *T.S. Eliot's Social Criticism* (Faber, 1971) by Roger Kojecky.

REFERENCES

Allard, J.W. and Stock, G. (1994) *F.H. Bradley. Writings on Logic and Metaphysics*. Oxford: Oxford University Press.

Arnold, Matthew (1862) *The Twice-Revised Code*. London: Clowes.

Arnold, Matthew (1869) *Culture and Anarchy*. Cambridge: Cambridge University Press.

Bantock, G.H (1970) *T.S. Eliot and Education*. London: Faber and Faber.

Bradley, F.H. (1897) *Appearance and Reality*, 2nd edn. Oxford: Oxford University Press.

Collini, Stefan (ed.) (1993) *Arnold: Culture and Anarchy and Other Writings*. Cambridge: Cambridge University Press.

Eliot, T.S. (1934) *After Strange Gods*. New York: Harcourt, Brace and Company.

Eliot, T.S. (1939) *The Idea of a Christian Society*. London: Faber and Faber.

Eliot, T.S. (1951) *Selected Essays*, 3rd edn. London: Faber and Faber.

Eliot, T.S. (1957) *On Poetry and Poets*. London: Faber and Faber.

Eliot, T.S. (1962) *Notes towards The Definition of Culture*. London: Faber and Faber. (First published in 1948.)

Eliot, T.S. (1964) *Knowledge and Experience in the Philosophy of F.H. Bradley*. New York: Farrar, Straus and Company.

Eliot, T.S. (1969) *The Complete Poems and Plays of T.S Eliot*. London: Faber and Faber.

Eliot, T.S. (1978) *To Criticize The Critic*. London: Faber and Faber.

Sutherland, Gillian (ed.) (1973) *Arnold on Education*. Harmondsworth: Penguin Books.

Williams, Raymond (1963) *Culture and Society 1780–1850*. New York: Columbia University Press.

9

R.S. Peters: Liberal Traditionalist

M . A . B .   D e g e n h a r d t

ROOTS AND CONTEXT

Some people become celebrated as 'great educators' by innovating a doctrine on what education ought to achieve and how, and by getting this translated into practice. Richard Peters has strong views on how to improve education, and he has not been without influence on practice. However, his educational importance is of a different kind. During the 1960s he became a leading member of a loosely affiliated group of thinkers in various countries who sought to establish higher standards of philosophical care in educational thinking. In Britain, C.D. Hardie had already worked alone to this end and, in America, Israel Scheffler and others had formed an association, held conferences and launched a journal. Peters studied educational doctrines and practices as they already existed, as well as the tradition of Western philosophy. But he is no doctrinaire traditionalist convinced that wisdom and good sense can be found only in what has already faced the test of time. He is a *liberal* traditionalist: drawing on, evaluating and developing ideas that can be described as 'liberal' in one or other of two distinct meanings:

1. The expression 'liberal education' is usually attributed to Isocrates, a Greek thinker of the fourth century BCE. It indicated the kind of education thought fitting for a *liber* or free man, for one who was not just a non-slave but who also partook of the rights and responsibilities of citizenship. Rather than restricted learning equipping one for a trade or craft, such persons should have a 'non-servile' education in the bodies of learning that were developing at the time.

These could be valued as both intrinsically rewarding for the mind of one free to do things for their own sake, regardless of whether they served some further end, and also as affording the largeness or 'liberality' of thought that equips ruling citizens to judge complex matters of practical polity. Evolved versions of this view became important to Greek and Roman culture, and in the Christian Middle Ages were standardized into a seven liberal arts curriculum. The Renaissance and the rise of science both stimulated lively debate about just which arts were liberal and which mechanical. By the nineteenth century, reform of British education for the 'upper classes' was thought to be urgent. Thomas Arnold of Rugby School developed one version of liberal learning that emphasized history, classics and Christianity. In 1852 Cardinal Newman's *On the Scope and Nature of a University Education* (1915) appealed for broader liberal studies. But their elitist presuppositions became increasingly unpopular with some. It began to seem as if the notion of liberal education might have to be abandoned unless transformed into something that could be more widely available. Britain's first chief inspector of schools, Arnold's poetical son Matthew, aimed at something like this in his commitment to education in culture for all as a preliminary to vocational studies. Such ideas were debated in educational reports over many years. Partly in response to this, Paul Hirst began in the 1960s to develop a conception of liberal education that could be made available to all by distinguishing and teaching the modes of thinking appropriate to the various forms of knowledge. Peters often worked closely with Hirst and, like him, favoured curricula that could be intrinsically satisfying and also enlarge minds as appropriate to democratic citizenship. This non-elitist version of liberal education was more compatible with the second tradition of liberalism on which Peters drew.

2. Political liberalism had ancient progenitors but only took shape as a body of reforming ideas in the seventeenth century. It came in various forms, but recurrent themes were high valuations of freedom, democracy, equality of opportunity, respect for individuals plus optimism for human improvement through the free development of opinions and knowledge. From the late eighteenth century onwards many, not all, educational reformers drew on these ideas. Some of their schools were labelled 'libertarian' and evidenced less interest in the passing on of bodies of knowledge and more concern to understand children and free them to develop their individuality and natural inclinations.

Liberal thinking is often evident on both sides of the knowledge-centred versus child-centred divide that has developed in education since the eighteenth century. Peters can be read as attempting to accommodate the best of the two approaches. This was not easy. By 1962, when he became professor of philosophy of education at London University, the differences had hardened into bitter, doctrinaire confrontations, with each party regarding the other as perniciously mistaken. However, he had already published a volume of broadcast talks, *Authority, Responsibility and Education* (1960) designed to shed light rather than pour oil on these troubled waters. In this, as in much of his work, one can witness him making good use of both kinds of liberal thinking.

While his educational writings came to exhibit a striking unity, as well as shifts and developments, Peters did not seek to expound an educational doctrine, whole and complete. Rather he wanted to have more people understanding, and engaging in, the kind of inquires that he exemplified. To this end he had to write things for people to discuss but also to ensure that educators learned to appreciate and participate in educational philosophizing. He worked at this with amazing flair and energy, and for a while managed to persuade British politicians and school inspectors of the importance of philosophy in teacher education. He helped plan the new BEd degree and was active in securing appointments of qualified philosophers to colleges of education. He initiated the establishment of the Philosophy of Education Society of Great Britain, edited its journal, and encouraged philosophers to write about education.

CONCEPT AND PROGRAMME

Peters came to his chair well equipped to promote understanding between warring educational doctrines. He had taught in school, university and adult education, and done youth work. He had lectured and written on the history of philosophy and psychology, and on social, political and ethical theory. In his inaugural lecture (*Education as Initiation,* 1964) he adumbrates a view of what should be the concerns of philosophy of education and indicates matters for later inquiry. He first notes how teachers can come to conceive their work in terms of some enterprise other than education, such as socialization, or economic investment. He allows that sometimes teachers should attend to such matters, but fears 'conceptual blight' when they confuse these with their role as educators. They may, for example, come to think that their primary task is to socialize or to 'gentle the masses' by helping pupils to achieve and be contented with simple jobs, healthy hobbies and happy homes, and so neglect things like fostering independent thought.

In his inaugural lecture, and later and more fully in Chapter I of *Ethics and Education* (1966), Peters uses examples and analysis to show that education is not a concept marking out any particular process like training or instruction. Rather, in its central uses, the concept encapsulates three criteria that such processes must satisfy if they are to count as educating:

1   Something must be transmitted that can be considered worthwhile for its own sake, quite apart from any instrumental value it may have. And learners must become committed to it.
2   It must involve knowing and understanding by the learner with some 'cognitive perspective' or active awareness of its links to other knowledge and to people's lives.
3   It must not be passed on by procedures like indoctrination that deprive learners of any element of wittingness or voluntariness. (This does, of course, leave room for appropriate kinds of guidance and compulsion.)

In short, if I teach something that is worthless, or that my pupils do not come to care for in itself, or if they fail to see its links to other matters, or if I stifle their ability to evaluate it for themselves, then I am not educating.

Peters did not intend this as a personal expression of what he would like education to be. He offers it as an account of what, in its central usages, the word 'education' means. This leaves it open for anyone to say, 'Well if that is what education means, then leave me out'. On their own, he believes, analyses of concepts carry no prescriptions for practice. However, they may do more than help us get clear what we are talking about. Peters would sometimes tell students that the value of analysing a concept cannot be known in advance. 'You must wait and see what pops up'. And in his analysis of 'education' important points do emerge. Thus, as noted, education is not a 'process word' but a 'criteria word', for evaluating processes and activities with pretensions to being educational – a healthy reminder for those who aspire to value-free educational inquiry and planning. Also it emerges that educating does involve aims but not as something extrinsic. For education *means* the bringing about of desirable states. It is not always inappropriate, say, to develop educational policies to foster economic improvement. But when such instrumental talk becomes standard, then we slip into utilitarian or moulding models of education. These have us view education as a number of procedures which can be used and adjusted to achieve particular chosen ends. Growth models of education are intended to correct this error by seeing the mind as the source of its own development. But they slip into another error. Seeing education as largely a product of the learner's own nature, they blind us to the need for carefully deliberated choice of purposes in any educational programme. The analysis also brings out important points about knowledge in education. Not only must what is passed on include elements of knowledge (beliefs and skills alone do not constitute education) but also the knowledge learned must be active in learners' minds. Its connection to other knowledge and to the world must be understood so that one's outlook in general can be transformed by it. This is cognitive perspective.

VALUES AND JUSTIFICATION

Anyone trying to teach Peters' ideas will probably encounter a protest from some students: 'But this is all value judgements!' Indeed it is, but the mooting of this point as an objection is a manifestation of the value scepticism presently flourishing in our culture. Such scepticism views value judgements as necessarily involving lapses into emotive irrationality and the world of unknowability. Peters is aware of the harm this scepticism does to educational thinking. What kind of educational theorizing would it be that was not designed to help us judge what is the most valuable education we can give pupils? His conceptual analysis pinpoints the kinds of value questions that must arise from educational concerns and about which he needs to demonstrate the possibility of objective reasoning. This he attempts in *Ethics and Education.*

The inaugural lecture continues with a fuller account of the concept of 'education', consistent with the three criteria and developed dialectically out of the already noted weaknesses in moulding and growth models. Education, Peters now says, is *initiation*. Beginning with initiation into public traditions of language and basic skills, it gradually leads on to participation in distinct traditions that constitute forms of knowledge like science, history and mathematics, or in religious and aesthetic appreciation, or in practical kinds of knowledge involved with moral, prudential or technical modes of thought and action. Persons are not born with minds. Minds develop through gradual initiation into these modes which our ancestors took centuries to develop. Each generation in turn has to learn them with time and determination, before there is any possibility of developing them further.

In *Ethics and Education* he elucidates this by noting links between changes in Western understanding of the human mind and different models of education (p. 46ff). Empiricist thought represented us as born with a *tabula rasa* or blank slate, which receives sense impressions, and has an ability to remember and classify them. On this basis alone we are said to form an understanding of our world and ourselves. This view of the mind as largely passive or receptive has invited moulding models of education in which teachers shape children's minds by arranging for them to have the appropriate experiences. Behaviourist learning theories are modern versions. Kant criticised empiricism on the grounds that such a limited view of our minds could hardly account for our abilities to use experience to develop concepts and categories like space, time and causality, with which to order the flux of experience. Piaget's psychological investigations of such developments in children, and his contention that these happen independently of adult instruction, gave strength to growth models, according to which education can come about largely by learners' own natural development. In different ways, Hegel and Marx charged such understanding of minds with neglecting the social aspect of learning. We could hardly develop minds, as we clearly do, unless we were born into cultures with socially inherited modes of understanding embedded in institutions like language, science and social relations. This is an objective inheritance in so far as it does not depend on the thought of any one of us. It is a world of understanding into which we have to be initiated – not one just dependent on personal whims. Only by this do we develop minds through which we can cooperate with others in thinking for ourselves. This vital impersonal element in education can normally be acquired only from teachers who already have it and who, if they are to be fine teachers, must also evidence respect for persons, enlivened by fraternity. Peters emphasizes this because many approaches to education neglect it and threaten what D.H. Lawrence called 'the holy ground' between teacher and taught (quoted in Peters, 1964, p. 37 and 1966, pp. 52 and 54).

These ideas reveal something of the context from which Peters sets out in *Ethics and Education* to show the possibility of reasoned deliberation on educational values. Some of these values concern right and wrong ways of treating learners, and require attention to themes in moral, social and political philosophy. Others concern the selection and justification of the components of a curriculum.

These are particularly difficult for Peters given his contention that, to qualify as educational, subjects taught must have intrinsic as well as instrumental worth. He finds both merits and inadequacies in some classical ethical theories, and then seeks help in Kant's notion of argument by transcendental deduction. The central idea here is that when a question is raised about the justification of a belief, we can transcend or probe behind that question to see what must be presupposed for it to be even possible and meaningful to ask it.

There is room here to attend to just two of the values which Peters explores in this way. For what I take to be his reasons, I shall choose the two with which he starts. First is the idea of equality or fairness in education. This is not an easy topic, but it is a good topic for showing transcendental deduction at work (Peters, 1966, Ch. IV).

The principle of equality is often misleadingly expressed as 'All humans are equal', which sounds like an obviously false factual assertion. Understood more reasonably as expressing a view about how humans ought to be treated, it is still problematic, since treating everyone the same often involves obvious injustices. Moreover, educational measures designed to promote equality often seem to clash with other goods such as freedom. Peters' first move here is to note that to ask 'Why treat people equally?' is to request reasons. So presupposed in the question, or transcending it, is a commitment to rationality. One mark of rational thinking is precisely a refusal to make differentiations in thought or conduct, unless there are sound reasons for doing so. Thus, a rational principle of equality says it is irrational to treat people differently unless there are good reasons for making exceptions. It can, for example, be quite rational to make differential educational provisions to take account of special problems such as handicaps that make it difficult for a child to cope with the standard curriculum. This, of course, still requires decisions as to what are relevant grounds for differential educational provision. Differences in eyesight can clearly be relevant but not so differences in eye colour. In many familiar cases, however, things are not so clear. Peters goes on to illustrate how thinking through such cases can involve difficult judgements, often involving findings from other disciplines. A transcendental deduction cannot solve all problems of equality in education. It does provide a framework that enables reasoned deliberation on concrete cases.

Peters next considers the justification of judgements of activities as having intrinsic value or worthwhileness that earns them a place in the curriculum. Here, he allows, the helpfulness of transcendental deductions is less clear. But he cannot ignore the topic precisely because he contends that *educational* learning must involve appreciating the intrinsic worth of what is learned. Again he starts by trying to make explicit what someone must be already committed to when they ask questions like 'Why do this rather than that?'. For someone to be able to seriously ask such a question they must, he says, already see things in a certain way and already have certain commitments. There are, he believes, considerations intrinsic to some activities which constitute reasons for pursuing them, though some people have not even learned to consider this possibility. They can only think of any activity as good as a means to something else: typically to the satisfaction of basic human needs and appetites. To learn to see intrinsic values in some activities is to learn to see that they can be appraised not only for what they lead onto but also for standards inhering in them. This can only be learned by participating in activities having their own standards of excellence and by seeing how, in various ways, they can display qualities like elegance, ingenuity, neatness and cogency. These are long-evolved refinements out of primitive activities like hunting and making shelter. Learn to recognize such qualities and we are likely to prefer those activities which give scope for achieving them, especially if they are mutually compatible and contain elements of unpredictability to challenge skills and hold interest.

This, however, is not enough for Peters as it all applies equally to the best games as to realms of inquiry and creativity. And the latter do have something that games generally lack. In various ways they throw light on the nature of the world and of ourselves as we ask questions and make choices in that world. So one who asks 'Why do this rather than that?' will favour such studies and activities because in different ways they are all relevant to thinking about the question itself. Peters, however, is still not satisfied. Valuing areas of knowledge, inquiry and creativity, as telling us things that can help us understand and make choices, still seems like valuing them instrumentally. But at this point, he says, the intrinsic/instrumental distinction may lose its appropriateness. Then comes the final step in his deduction: the reason why the various areas of knowledge can have their special worthwhileness is that they all share in a serious concern for truth. This passionate concern was expressed when Socrates said that for man the unexamined life is not worth living.

> It lies at the heart of all rational activities in which there is a concern for what is true or false, appropriate or inappropriate, correct or incorrect. Anyone who asks seriously the question 'Why do this rather than that?' must already possess it; for it is built into the sense of 'serious'. It is impossible to give any further justification for it; for it is presupposed in serious attempts at justification. (Peters, 1966, p. 165)

In stark summary, the moment we start to think seriously about why some activities are worthwhile, we are committed to using reason in the pursuit of answers – a commitment so profound and general that it must extend to other attempts at the rational pursuit of truth, as found in activities like history, science and mathematics as well as philosophy. Unlike the passion of the dogmatist's concern for particular truths, it is an overall passion for truth and the principles for pursuing it. Nothing more can or need be said in favour of it. It is an attitude that does not come naturally to us and is mainly caught from those who already possess it and exhibit it in their teaching.

These two sketches of Peters' use of transcendental deductions on specific questions are intended to give some idea of how he seeks to use such arguments. He also uses them to defend principles of truth telling, consideration of interests, and freedom. Then, drawing together earlier themes, he discusses respect for persons, and matters of education and social control, such as authority and democracy (Peters, 1966, *passim*).

Education as Initiation and *Ethics and Education* are indebted to a variety of thinkers, yet together present a unified view of what philosophy of education should be, and a programme for further inquiry. To fulfil this, Peters wrote prolifically over two decades: eight books (one jointly with Paul Hirst), over 60 papers, and eight edited collections. (There is a good bibliography in Cooper, 1986, pp. 215–218.) Detailed treatment of all this is not possible and I now turn to consider some responses to his work, and some of his responses to these.

PETERS AND SOME CRITICS

Emotion

A once common complaint, sometimes from influential writers, was that Peters' concern for reason was matched by a hostile neglect of the feelings. This is absurdly inaccurate. Through a number of scattered pieces he develops a rich and helpful view of emotion, as appropriate to one whose understanding of 'education' specified learners becoming committed to what they learn. His *Reason and Compassion* (Peters, 1973a) proscribes any educational neglect of emotion. It rejects the common view of reason and emotion as mutually opposed faculties of mind whereby one or other can prevail in individual persons and also in disciplines of study – whence the common assumption that different curriculum subjects each cater mainly either for rational or for emotional development. Rather, he argues, emotions inevitably involve knowledge, belief and reasoning because how we feel about anything depends upon how we understand it. Conversely, there can be no development of reason without the 'rational passions', without a love of rational thinking and a hatred of irrationality. In trying to get things right, scholars and practical persons must, for example, care passionately for clarity and abhor contradiction, inconsistency and arbitrariness; they must dislike appeals to authority, revelation and tradition, but favour appeals to good reasons.

Thus, the use of reason is a passionate business while emotions can be more or less reasonable. Precisely how reason and passion interact can vary greatly but if they do, then education of the emotions is possible and important. If our feelings are linked to how we understand things, then what we learn can change both our understanding and our feelings. In an earlier work, 'The education of the emotions' (in Peters et al., 1972, Ch. 26), Peters rebukes psychologists for conducting no empirical studies on the best ways to achieve this, and makes one suggestion of his own. Literary studies are important because language is central to how we appraise and feel about the world. Entering into descriptions of people and their feelings, as given by fine writers, extends our own capacity for appraisal and response.

Peters' interest in emotion links to his interest in psychology generally, and to moral development in particular. No empirical investigator himself, he has studied philosophical and methodological differences between rival schools of psychology. These, he believes, can result in inattention to questions of educational moment. He is often less concerned to judge between schools than to reveal their perspectives as complimentary and needing integration. As early as 1960 he proposed, in *Freud's Theory of Moral Development in Relation to that of Piaget*, that the two psychologists were interested in distinguishable but inseparable aspects of moral development. Later papers argued similarly for other schools and inquirers (all collated in Peters, 1974, Part 3).

Just an analyst?

Peters has sometimes been dismissed as just another analytical philosopher. The burden of this complaint is not clear. In the last 100 years many philosophers have been concerned to clarify the usages and meanings of philosophically important words, though differing in purpose and style of doing this. Understandably, philosophers back to Socrates have seen conceptual clarification as a preliminary to more momentous enquiries. Others, however, have seen analysis as philosophy's main concern. It is this latter view that gets criticized as rendering philosophy dry and inconsequential, and deflecting attention from big questions for human living.

So is Peters an analytic philosopher and in what way? Certainly he does engage in conceptual analysis, and his analysis of 'education' is central to his thought. At least once his own self-description indicates that analysis is his way of doing philosophy. Early in the inaugural lecture he makes the conventional acknowledgement of his predecessors' work and contrasts it with his own:

> Louis Arnaud Reid was a synthetic thinker who was most at home in aesthetics and metaphysics. He was sympathetic to the layman's view that the task of the philosopher is to provide some kind of synoptic directives for living. In the field of education, therefore, he explored with great sensitivity the possibility of deriving educational policies from philosophical reflection. My training, on the other hand, has been in the analytic tradition, and I am most at home in social philosophy and philosophical psychology – those branches of philosophy ... in which concrete problems of human nature and human conduct loom largest. It has usually been the feeling of being very muddled about some fairly concrete issue in this field that has driven me into philosophical reflection. In comparison with my predecessor, therefore, I feel a very mundane fellow whose eyes are more likely to be fixed on the brass-tacks on or under the teacher's desk than on the Form of the Good. (Peters, 1964, p. 8)

Analysis follows this, but when it is done there is a style shift and the lecture ends with a quotation from Whitehead plus three stirring sentences:

> 'There is a quality of life that lies beyond the mere fact of life.' The great teacher is he who can convey this sense of quality to another, so that it haunts his every endeavour and makes him sweat and yearn to fix what he thinks and feels in a fitting form. For life has no one purpose; man imprints his purposes upon it. It presents few tidy problems; mainly predicaments that have to be endured or enjoyed. It is education that provides that touch of eternity under the aspect of which endurance passes into dignified wry acceptance, and animal enjoyment into a quality of living. (Peters, p. 48)

This is great stuff, but hardly the work of a 'mere analyst' who had learned nothing from the likes of the Stoics, Spinoza or Oakeshott. Indeed it is hard to believe that anyone who educated himself in the history of philosophy as well as Peters did, could actually believe that twentieth century fashions for analysis were the only ones for him to follow. Clearly he believed that new approaches could be helpful but not that they were the last word, nor that there was little to be learned from what had gone before. Later on, in his preface to *Psychology and Ethical Development,* he offers a more rounded self-portrait:

> I belong to the perhaps old fashioned school of thought that maintains that arguments matter, that one should listen carefully to what people say and consider what grounds they produce for the position they adopt. In philosophy generally, too, I hold ... that conceptual analysis (whatever that may be) is only a part of philosophy and that those who concentrate on it should constantly ask themselves whether anything of importance depends upon the distinctions that are being made. (Peters, 1974, p. 20)

Why, then, did he earlier represent himself as primarily an analyst? Perhaps because, given what often passed for philosophy of education at the time, he wanted to stress his interest in a rigorous and distinct field of inquiry. Perhaps he thought it important for philosophy of education to mark out its own preserve by establishing some key concepts. Hirst (in Cooper, 1986, p.11 ff) suggests he was anxious to make good use of modern analytical approaches though not sure how much to expect from them. He did hope that deeper understanding could be achieved by exploring interconnections between various concepts that feature in our educational thinking. R.K Elliott (in Cooper, 1986, pp. 41–68) ventures a more dramatic explanation: that Peters himself did not correctly understand what he was doing and that he was really 'a philosopher in the older style'. He did sometimes revert to an older style, says Elliott, and that when we recognize this element in all his writing his philosophy can be seen as an authentic revelation of himself. Then, he says, it emerges as a fresh, powerful expression of the Stoic mind-set: no mere latter day imitation but a new creation on the grand scale. This interpretation merits further exploration.

One concept of education?

More specific criticisms concern Peters' centrally important analysis of 'education'. From its first presentation, commentators argued that in setting out his three criteria he proposed a key analysis which reduced to one the diversity of ways in which we actually talk of education. This marginalizes important usages that do not fit his criteria. Peters notes such diversity but is held to have made inadequate allowance for it, as if he thought he had got to the essence of a term that actually has diverse meanings. Such charges gain weight from an oft cited passage where he asks '. . . have I already put my foot on the primrose path that leads to essentialism?' and answers 'Frankly I do not much mind if I have. What would be objectionable would be to suppose that certain characteristics could be regarded as essential, irrespective of context and the question under discussion' (Peters, 1964, p. 11). This did encourage complaints that, underestimating diversity, he also focuses on values that do not actually inhere in all uses of the concept. So, unintentionally, he overemphasizes his own values. Many usages of 'education' do not imply 'cognitive perspective', 'wittingness' or 'intrinsic worth'.

Peters' responses to such disquiets include adjustment of his own position. In 'Education and the educated man' (1970), and in a postscript to a symposium on Aims of Education – A Conceptual Inquiry with J. Woods and W.H. Dray (included in Peters, 1973b, pp. 49–57), he distinguishes 'education' as a family of processes and gives new emphasis to 'educated ' as a quality of persons. Only from the nineteenth century, it seems, was the expression 'educated man' used to characterize what had hitherto been known as a cultivated person of all-round moral, intellectual and spiritual development, with 'education' still being used less demandingly to refer to the upbringing of children, animals and even silkworms. This allows more status to usages that he previously found marginal. The concept he now sees as very fluid, along a continuum between two poles. The idea of the 'educated man' he still regards as a well-established ideal but now allows the older, less-differentiated idea to be more widespread than he first proposed. This revised position, he now says, enables those who believe in the more refined concept and its associated values to present those values more clearly and to encourage others to give them weight. To know whether one is right in this preference, one must investigate further into ethics and social philosophy.

However, in the year when the above symposium first saw general publication, Abraham Edel's paper, 'Analytical philosophy of education at the crossroads' (in Doyle, 1973, Ch. 14) considered a related matter. Referring to various analyses of educationally important concepts (including Peters on 'education') he urged the need to acknowledge pluralities of concepts. He argued, with illustrations, that while analysis tries to get clear about concepts by carefully isolating them from value judgements and empirical facts, in reality educational issues are inextricably involved with values and purposes in a world of facts. Hence, words like 'education' have many and varying usages. To maximize educational enlightenment, educational thinkers should attend to these too. This would involve cooperation between various experts. (Hardly surprisingly, it has not happened.)

In similar vein, R.F. Dearden later argued (Cooper, 1986, pp. 76–80) that Peters failed to give an adequate analysis of the concept of education because he took insufficient account of the diversity of concepts built into different educational philosophies, and overestimated the usefulness of analysing one supposed general concept. But, unawares, he did something more worthwhile: he elucidated one very important concept – that of 'liberal education'. Philosophers should also elucidate other concepts of education present in other philosophies: Christian, Islamic, fascist, Gandhian, Marxist, Deweyan and so on. (Amusingly, Peters had earlier discerned three understandings of 'liberal education' present in contemporary discussions ['Ambiguities in liberal education and the problems of its content', in Strike and Egan, 1978, Ch. I].)

Transcendental deductions

Peters' use of transcendental arguments to justify educational values has been much debated and in discussion he never hid his own misgivings. Some philosophers question whether such arguments ever work, and in education it has been doubted whether they even hit the target. As has been remarked, to love poetry because it instantiates rationality is not to love poetry. Charles Taylor concludes a general discussion on *the validity of transcendental deductions* with 'A valid transcendental deduction is indubitable, yet it is hard to know when you have one, at least one with an interesting conclusion. But then that seems true of most arguments in philosophy' (Taylor, 1995, p. 33). On the other hand, Jurgen Habermas has several times acknowledged debts to Peters' transcendental arguments, though proposing that they would be stronger if, instead of asking ad hoc questions about what is presupposed in particular moral argumentation, he had pushed deeper and asked:

> For anyone capable of speech and action, what normative presuppositions necessarily hold for them as soon as they enter into any discourse examining claims to validity? For example, the conditions of rational argument include allowing a voice to all. Any discussion would just not be rational if some rational voices were excluded. (Habermas, 1992, pp. 83–4)

Indeed, he concludes that Peters makes just this last point when he says that the conditions of argument include letting any rational being contribute to a public discussion.

Could it be that Peters' especial difficulty with the use of transcendental deductions to show the intrinsic worthwhileness of some activities originates elsewhere than with transcendental deductions? We might agree that there is something chilling in the thought of someone being very well taught to become a great pianist, a fine joiner or an accomplished philosopher, who yet tells us, truthfully, that they only find these activities worthwhile as means to some further end. But does it follow that there is reason to expect and look for a single account of what makes a range of different activities capable of having intrinsic worth for their practitioners? Perhaps no argument, transcendental or otherwise, could yield one reason for attributing intrinsic value to them all.

Peters offers a final defence of his position in one of his more difficult pieces, 'The justification of education' (in Peters, 1973b, Ch. XII). And transcendental arguments may still be helpful in thinking about some topics in education. Moreover, carefully following through Peters' developments of them does offer rewarding insights along the way. Like all powerful tools they should be used with care, ever bearing in mind the disquiet of Kevin Harris (1979) and others that both conceptual analysis and transcendental deductions have conservative tendencies because, in attempting to elucidate present thinking they actually offer more endorsement than critique – though perhaps, returning to Habermas, this only threatens if the enquiry does not probe deeply enough.

LEGACY

It is now nearly 50 years since Peters began to write and teach about education. People still find benefit in reading his work, but he no longer has the immediate impact on educational thought and policies that he once had. Several reasons for this can be discerned. Ours has become a less thinking culture (though book sales and university applications indicate widespread philosophical appetites). In retirement he can no longer maintain influential contacts with politicians and school inspectors. Nor can he personally inspire students by evidencing his earnest commitment to clarity and understanding in the service of learning. Another factor is something that he actually worked for: a huge increase in publications of philosophy of education books and journals. Many of these are in what might be loosely called a Peters style, using ordinary language to argue carefully and guide practice within a framework of liberal democratic values. But they advocate diverse opinions. Indeed the subject has now gone quasi multicultural, with new approaches deriving from previously less-studied thinkers like Nietzsche, Heidegger, Ortega, Weil, Sartre, Foucault and Derrida. All of these are 'Western', but philosophy of education has grown to a point where it is inconceivable that it be dominated by one or two thinkers, however powerful. Notwithstanding his achievements, however, educational policies in Britain and elsewhere have developed in managerial and technicist modes unpalatable to Peters. Under strong political direction, teachers now enjoy little room or encouragement to reflect on principles informing their work, or to exercise judgement and imagination. Curricula are increasingly geared to limited practical ends and liberal learning is marginalized. These are, of course, trends that might be reversed, and future educators may yet turn to Richard Peters among others in search of insights, wisdom and other good things that have been lost. If they do this they may be surprised to notice how much the form and content of contemporary philosophy of education owes to his work.

REFERENCES

Works by R.S. Peters

Peters, R.S. (1960) *Authority, Responsibility and Education.* London: Allen and Unwin (revised 1973).
Peters, R.S. (1964) *Education as Initiation* (inaugural lecture). London: Evans Brothers.
Peters, R.S. (1966) *Ethics and Education.* London: Allen and Unwin.
Peters, R.S. (1970) Education and the educated man: some further reflections. In *The Proceedings of the Annual Conference, Volume IV.* Cambridge: Philosophy of Education Society of Great Britain.
Peters, R.S. (1972) *Education and the Development of Reason* (edited with R.F. Dearden and P.H. Hirst). London: Routledge and Kegan Paul.
Peters, R.S. (1973a) *Reason and Compassion: The Lindsay Memorial Lectures.* London: Routledge and Kegan Paul.
Peters, R.S. (Ed.) (1973b) *The Philosophy of Education.* Oxford: The University of Oxford Press.
Peters, R.S. (1974) *Psychology and Ethical Development.* London: Allen and Unwin.
Peters, R.S. (1977) 'Ambiguities of liberal education and the problem of its content', in *Ethics and Educational Policy* (Eds K.A Strike and K. Egan). London: Routledge and Kegan Paul.

Works by other writers

Cooper, D. (Ed.) (1986) *Education, Values and Mind: Essays for R.S. Peters.* London: Routledge and Paul.

Edel, A. (1973) Analytical Philosophy at the Crossroads. In *Educational Judgments*, Ed. J.F. Doyle. London: Routledge and Kegan Paul.

Habermas, J. (1992) *Moral Consciousness and Community Action* (trans. C. Lenhardt and S.W. Nicholson). Cambridge: Polity Press.

Harris, K. (1979) *Education and Knowledge*. London: Routledge and Kegan Paul.

Newman, J.H. (1915) *On the Scope and Nature of University Education*. London: Dent. (First published in 1851.)

Taylor, C. (1995) *Philosophical Arguments*. Cambridge, MA: Harvard University Press.

10

Poststructuralism, Postmodernism and Education

Richard Smith

The purpose of this chapter is to give the reader a basic understanding of the terms structuralism and poststructuralism, as well as of the terms modernity, postmodernity and postmodernism. Naturally the reader will expect this to relate to education: in fact, I shall argue that the connection of these terms and the ideas they bring in their train is inseparable from fundamental ideas about education. I also want to show that these 'post-' ideas matter. In fact I believe that responding to them is one of the most important tasks that philosophy of education is currently confronted with. Some sense of this will I hope emerge, though there is not space to argue for this fully.

It is impossible to understand why some writers and thinkers have taken the 'postmodern turn' without understanding what is meant by the 'modernity' against which they are reacting. This requires a short historical overview. It is usually said that we in the West have been living in the era of 'modernity' for roughly 400 years. There is no precise agreement about when we should date the beginning of modernity. Lawrence Cahoone (1996, pp. 12–13) summarizes different views on the question:

> Did modernity in the West begin in the sixteenth century with the Protestant reformation, the rejection of the universal power of the Roman Catholic Church, and the development of a humanistic scepticism epitomised by Erasmus and Montaigne? Or was it in the seventeenth century with the scientific revolution of Galileo, Harvey, Hobbes, Descartes, Boyle, Leibniz and Newton? Or with the republican political theories and revolutions of the United States and France in the eighteenth century?

Some, then, date the beginning of modernity from the era of scientific revolutions that spans the end of the sixteenth century and the first decades of the seventeenth, a period characterized by the discovery (or rediscovery) of the circulation of the blood by William Harvey, the formulation of laws concerning gases and springs by Boyle and Hooke, respectively, work on magnetism by William Gilbert, and advances in anatomy that followed from the work of Andreas Vesalius. Others prefer to think of modernity as having earlier origins, perhaps going back as far as 1543 when Vesalius published *De Humani Corporis Fabrica* (*On the Fabric of the Human Body*) and Nicolaus Copernicus published his astronomical treatise *De Revolutionibus Orbium Coelestium* (*On the Revolutions of the Heavenly Spheres*).

What is central to modernity, however, whatever view one takes about dates and origins, is the idea of what we would now call *science*. So powerful and so productive were the discoveries and inventions of 'scientists', then usually called 'natural philosophers', that experimental science, and the logic and mathematics that underpinned it, became the model of respectable, rigorous knowledge. As we know only too well in our own time, to say 'scientists have discovered that', or to introduce a news item with footage of a scientist in a white coat in a laboratory, is to imply a claim to truth and objectivity and lull the critical faculties of the listener. Two other factors were crucial in the establishment of this view of the best kind of knowledge.

First, there was the ambition to formulate an account of scientific *method*: to set out systematic procedures for acquiring knowledge that could be used by anyone who went to the trouble of learning them. This project goes back at least as far as Francis Bacon, who wanted to find a new inductive method which all systematic thinkers could use to support their efforts. The book in which he set out his efforts is called, tellingly, the *Novum Organum*. This means 'The New Manual' (or 'The New Handbook'): it was intended precisely to be a manual of method, and to replace the old *Organum*, the manual of Aristotelian logic that had been in use since the Middle Ages and which Bacon considered dry and sterile (it could be used to establish whether a logical argument was sound, but it could not be used to find new knowledge). Bacon was enormously influential: he inspired the founding of the Royal Society in the 1660s. His interest in finding the 'right method' is mirrored in the work of the philosopher Descartes. Descartes, as well as being the author of a *Discourse on Method* 17 years after the publication of the *Novum Organum*, wrote *Rules for the Direction of the Mind* about a decade previously, and stated flatly in Rule 4 that 'We need a method if we are to investigate the truth of things'.

Secondly, there was, it is often claimed, a craving for certainty, and to understand this too we need some grasp of contemporary historical events. The first half of the seventeenth century saw conflict throughout Europe on a cataclysmic scale. The Thirty Years' War, essentially contesting the supremacy of Catholicism or Protestantism, lasted from roughly 1618 until the Peace of Westphalia in 1648. Armies, largely comprising mercenaries, marched back and forth across the centre of the continent until, it has been estimated, around one-third of the population of Germany had been slaughtered for no other offence than having the wrong religion. Meanwhile in England between 1642 and 1651 there was the English Civil War, during which King Charles I, a ruler by divine right in his own eyes, as well as in the eyes even of many who opposed him, was executed. Roughly 10% of the adult male population of England died in the English Civil War: a much greater proportion than in either World Wars of the twentieth century.

A conclusive case for connections between historical events and intellectual movements can never be fully made, but the case here is persuasive. What fundamental certainty could be found, beyond the murderous religious schisms and doctrines, that might serve as the basis for universal agreement and peace? In England many predicted the end of the world. If God permitted one of his elected Kings to be beheaded, what else might not be safe? The stability of the solar system became an issue of absorbing interest. What guarantee was there that the planets, Earth included, would keep to their orbits around the sun and not spin off into whatever void lay beyond? More, even, than the solar system was at stake: its regularity and security was taken as an assurance that the natural world reflects the rationality of God. Thus it was that Newton in England, Leibniz in Germany, and many others following them, looked for the most rigorous and certain way of demonstrating the stability of the solar system and the rationality of its creator: and that way was mathematical. Newton's enormous reputation rested in large part on his discovery of the law of physics – the inverse square law of universal gravitation – that held the sun, the Earth and the other planets in place, and would continue to hold them; and so men might be reassured that God too was in His place, presiding over a rational universe.

It is time to pull together the lines of this historical overview. The successes and anxieties of the seventeenth and eighteenth centuries both worked to entrench the idea that science, and the mathematical and geometrical way of reasoning that were taken to lie at its basis, were the one true road to knowledge: the only game in town, as we might now say. Galileo had said that the Book of Nature could only be read by mathematicians. Newton had shown that he was right: God spoke Newtonian, and the method that Bacon had been looking for had, in principle, been found. It is not difficult, but would extend this historical survey unnecessarily, to show how this idea ran through the 'long eighteenth century' that we call the Enlightenment and into the nineteenth, with successive writers and thinkers across a whole range of subjects and disciplines wanting to be the Bacon or Newton of their field.

This is the mind-set that we, in the twenty-first century, in what some call the era of late modernity, have inherited. It is a mind-set that is still automatically inclined to think science is the best or perhaps the one and only real kind of knowledge, that for every human activity there must be a method for doing it right, if only one can find it, and that precise measurement will give us the answers we want. The veneration of science is almost too obvious to require examples.

The advertisements during a couple of hours of television are usually enough to show how many products – from yoghurt and toothpaste to cat food and engine oil – are marketed as 'scientifically proven', or we are told 'science has shown', or there is footage of people in white coats in laboratories, peering into microscopes or holding test-tubes. Our critical faculties are anaesthetized by the mention of science, or allusion to it. Another example is supplied by academic nomenclature: most universities have a faculty of 'social science', yet the issues and problems studied there are hardly a matter of any kind of *science*, in the sense in which physics and chemistry are scientific.

Education provides many examples of the obsession with method. (And with handbooks: the reader will not need to look far for an example.) There is a vast self-help literature promising to set out the right way to bring up children, from settling a baby into a sleeping routine to 'managing those teenage years'. Yet it is doubtful whether family life is best thought of as a matter of organizing and managing, rather than as learning to be with, building trust, cultivating the capacity to listen, giving each other space – aspects of relationships which are not best thought of as any kind of method. If that is not obvious, consider another kind of relationship, that of one person becoming attracted to another, and becoming attractive to him or her in return. There could only be a 'method' to this kind and phase of a relationship if it was reduced to a crude business of seduction techniques; and such is the power of the idea that there must be a method for everything (and such too perhaps is the fear of being lonely and unattractive) that there are those who perform the reduction: Neil Strauss markets what he calls the 'Annihilation Method'[43] and there are numerous other methods on sale, including Magnus Huckvale's tapping programme,[44] marketed as a solution to everything from procrastination to making people fall for you. Formal education is constantly plagued by the idea that some new method will bring the millennium: all will be well once children learn about happiness, or when teachers implement the latest way of teaching children to read, or when the gap between school and university is filled by the teaching of 'threshold concepts'.

Measurement and quantification are also rife in education. Schools are ranked by league tables, as if what constituted good education was a matter of performing calculations on the basis of children's scores in public tests and examinations. Teachers' careers are made or broken on the basis of such scores. Universities plan their futures with an eye on what will make them a 'top ten' university in the tables compiled by national newspapers. Educational research becomes assimilated to the medical – i.e. scientific – model, in which the 'gold standard' is randomized control trials designed to establish 'what works', with outcomes expressed in percentage improvements on standardized tests and tasks, naturally. Measurement, it seems, offers certainty. Databases give our age the reassurance it craves.

What I have done so far is attempt to give a sketch of some of the characteristics of our late-modern condition, and an account of the development of modernity, that is of how we got here. Now the crucial point about so-called postmodern writers is this: they offer a very fundamental and far-reaching critique of modernity, particularly of its obsessions with science, method and measurement, and of the conceptions of knowledge, language, art and, in general, of being human that lie beneath these obsessions. They offer us some release from the mess we are in, at least to the extent of helping us to understand it. This is why they are important. They ask us to think outside the framework of our usual modernistic ways of thinking, and this makes them challenging, sometimes upsetting and often difficult.

Some remarks about terminology are needed at this point. As I shall use these words, we live in the era of modernity, or late modernity: some writers call this postmodernity, or refer to it as our postmodern condition. Virtually no writer describes himself or herself as a postmodernist (partly because this would imply that they subscribed to a distinctive *method*: it should be clear enough from what I have written above why they find this unattractive). Nevertheless it is helpful to describe as 'postmodernists' those thinkers and writers who offer a systematic, roughly philosophical critique of postmodernity (or late modernity). 'Postmodernism', as I understand the term, is a loose and rather unsatisfactory way of referring to the ideas of postmodernists – unsatisfactory, because it might be taken to imply a degree of homogeneity, even predictability and safeness, in these ideas.

In the rest of this chapter I shall focus on just two writers who are generally thought of as in the vanguard of postmodernism. The first is Jean-François Lyotard, who published *La condition postmoderne: rapport sur le savoir* in 1979. The English translation, *The Postmodern Condition: A Report on Knowledge*, was published in 1984. The text was originally commissioned by the Quebec government as a report on the influence of technology on the way knowledge is conceived in advanced societies. Lyotard is concerned that in the computer age learning and knowledge are becoming reconceived as information: i.e. solely or entirely as what can be translated into bits and bytes and stored on a computer – as data that can be mined and manipulated. Then other kinds of knowledge and understanding begin to seem merely quaint. Another effect is the complex phenomenon that Lyotard calls 'performativity'. The collection and analysis of data that computers make possible leads to more and more demands for efficiency, conceived as the extraction of maximum results for minimum input, in the way that teaching might appear to be more efficient if the class size is doubled without any lowering of examination results. 'The true good of the system … is the optimisation of the global relationship between input and output' (Lyotard, 1984, p. 11). This in turn leads to ready identification of people who are not 'performing' efficiently by comparison with their peers.

This is of course the world of results-driven education, league tables and 'teaching to the test' that we have come to live in. Notice that it requires a degree of uniformity; otherwise, comparative judgements (between schools, universities and so on) could not be made. It is no use complaining that your university – committed perhaps to widening participation and outreach work with local industry – simply isn't trying to do the same thing as the University of Oxford: it will be judged by the same criteria and appear (no doubt much lower) on the same league table nevertheless. The cost of not being 'commensurable', as Lyotard puts it, is high:

> The legitimization of power is based in optimizing the system's performance – efficiency. The application of this criterion to all our games necessarily entails a certain level of terror, whether soft or hard: be operational (that is, commensurable) or disappear (Lyotard, 1984, p. xxiv).

Why do we permit this dismal state of affairs to continue? Part of the answer is that there is another aspect of our unreflective, modernist mind-set. We expect science to offer knowledge as a unified and coherent system (no doubt characterized by a single 'method'). Think of the 'tree of knowledge' as presented in a now rather old-fashioned encyclopaedia. Rationality, perhaps, constitutes the trunk; this divides into science, conceived as empirical knowledge of the real world, and calculative reason (that is, mathematics and logic). Somewhere out among the further leaves and branches are such uncertain ways of knowing as politics, literature and art. There are various versions of this, but the basic idea is that knowledge is always and everywhere the same kind of thing, and behind this lurks the assumption that all knowing will follow the model of naïve science: to know the world is to represent it as it really is. For reasons we cannot go into here this is a naïve idea, if only because it neglects the extent to which we always see the world from a perspective highly coloured by our own theories and prejudices. It certainly becomes very problematic when we move outside the physical sciences to areas like mathematics and poetry. Knowledge thought of in this way lends itself to being centrally controlled by those who arrogate to themselves the right to determine what counts as 'reality' and thus what counts as a good representation of it. Postmodern knowledge, by contrast, is

> not simply a tool of the authorities; it refines our sensitivity to differences and reinforces our ability to tolerate the incommensurable. Its principle is not the expert's homology, but the inventor's paralogy (Lyotard, 1984, p. xxv).

Where knowledge is conceived in scientific, modernist terms – i.e. the ideal is the 'expert's homology' – we expect the experts in the field to agree, for the most part, on what is the right answer. When Lyotard writes that the principle of postmodern knowledge is 'the inventor's paralogy' he means the introduction of dissent where there has been comfortable consensus, and the discovery of new ideas that go against the prevailing wisdom. If this sounds anarchic, it is important to reflect that many of the ideas we now take for granted – that species evolve, rather than their number being fixed by God for all time, that the earth goes round the sun and not vice versa, that capitalism can be exploitative and damaging – only have the status they do because there were 'inventors' (here Darwin, Galileo and Karl Marx, respectively) who were prepared to disrupt the orthodoxy of the time by the development of a 'paralogy'.

When Lyotard writes (above) that 'postmodern knowledge refines our sensitivity to differences and reinforces our ability to tolerate the incommensurable' he asks us to reconceive the nature of knowledge itself. We might think here of a severely autistic child. On one, conventional, view this child lacks various capacities that we take for granted in the case of the 'normal' individual. Teachers who work with such children often report how unjust it seems to look at the autistic child in terms of deficit, particularly when the child may have all sorts of unusual abilities that children who are not thus 'handicapped' do not possess. An autistic child may for example have highly developed artistic abilities: there are grounds for detecting symptoms of autism in the childhoods of Beethoven and Vincent Van Gogh. To categorize such a child as merely 'working towards level 1' in the terminology of the National Curriculum seems absurd. In Lyotard's way of putting it, this shows no sensitivity to how this child is *different*, not commensurable with other children. And of course the same is true for children whose differences are less obvious. Any one of us can feel a profound sense of injustice when what makes us different, a unique individual, cannot make itself heard against the totalizing system that treats us as members of this and that category.

We now move to a different thinker, the French philosopher Jacques Derrida. It is usual to call Derrida a poststructuralist rather than a postmodernist. Again some explanation of terms is required. The Swiss linguist Ferdinand de Saussure (1857–1913) is usually thought of as the founder of structuralism. He was interested in just how language has meaning. It would be reassuring to think that the meaning of a word is given by what it labels: the meaning of 'table' is given by the physical object, in this case the table on which my laptop rests. This does not however work for language all the time. For instance it does not work for 'the' or 'however' or 'Monday', and it doesn't work for 'table' a lot of the time – consider the Table of the Elements, or tabling a motion at a political conference. Saussure tells us not only that language does not mirror the world but also that in general language has meaning via relations of difference. Language is a system of signs and of differences. 'Man' has its meaning because 'man' is not 'woman'. 'Tuesday' is not 'Wednesday'. There is no Tuesdayness for it to reflect. The meaning of 'dog' is in part 'not cat'. Interestingly, this is how children learn the word: the small child usually starts by calling all small and medium-sized animals 'dog', and only later begins to distinguish some of them as cats, sheep and so on. A rose by any name, to quote Shakespeare, would smell as sweet since there is nothing intrinsically sweet-smelling about the word 'rose'. The sign (rose) joins the signifier (word) and signified (concept) in entirely arbitrary ways. What we call a rose we might have called a glunck or a wooznum. There is no essential relation between the word and the thing. We like to think that some words at least display that essential relation in the form of onomatopoeia, but in Britain dogs say 'woof woof', while in France they say 'oua, oua', and in China 'mung mung'. Or we might like to imagine there is some other kind of intrinsic relationship between a word and what it indicates. We write 'giraffe' on the board and for the children's benefit we turn the two letters 'f' into tall animals side by side. Look, children!

And the very word look – doesn't it seem to have two eyes at its centre? We can write that on the board as well, and dots in each letter 'o' make everything clear.

Derrida is a poststructuralist in the sense that he takes Saussure's views much further, arguing that language is radically unstable, and in the sense that he opposes what he takes to be structuralism's project of describing final, closed systems as if they were perfect maps. Meaning is always postponed, Derrida tells us. It can never be finalized: there is no 'closure', no point at which meaning is established once and for all. If this point seems abstruse, consider the meaning of 'Stalin'. Does it mean the paranoid dictator who was responsible for the deaths (by starvation, in the gulags, by execution) of millions of his fellow-countrymen? Or does it mean the heroic leader of Soviet Russia in its resistance to, and defeat of, Nazi Germany? It is no more than commonsense to respond that we are still waiting for history's final verdict, and that there will never be a final verdict since the changing circumstances of the world mean that each age will have its own, different, Stalin (Winston Churchill, and no doubt Bush and Blair as well).

Not only is language a system of differences: the system itself is constantly in flux. For instance, we are inclined, when we note differences between two terms, to think of one of the pair – the binary – as somehow superior to the other. 'Man' is different from 'woman', but we all know how easy it is to assume superiority here, not least by gendered language (such as talk of the 'master bedroom' of a house). Consider other binaries: reality/appearance, presence/absence, heterosexual/homosexual, literal/metaphorical. We readily conceive the first term as prior and the second as derivative or secondary. Derrida offers us readings of texts where, at the touch of a careful reading, these binaries turn through a hundred and eighty degrees, or fall apart altogether. These readings are the kind of criticism that he calls 'deconstruction'. As an example of deconstruction, Derrida (1981) offers a reading of Plato's dialogue, *Phaedrus*. Here, among many other themes, is that of the supremacy of speech over writing (another binary: speech/writing). It is easy to imagine that the spoken (and heard) word is somehow prior to the written word, and that writing is an attempt (necessarily second-rate) to capture its immediacy. (Notice how tempting it may be to write 'What Wordsworth is trying to *say*'. . . .) Speech, so Socrates tells (speaks to) the young man, Phaedrus, bears a closer relation to thought than writing. When you write something down you often have a sense of 'that's not what I meant to say'; you cannot question writing in the way that you can ask a speaker what he meant. And of course this is why the *Phaedrus* is written, as all of Plato's texts are, as a dialogue. But it is *written* as a dialogue, as Plato would hardly not have noticed. It is full of literary tropes: metaphor, figurative language, rhetorical devices. At the point where we thought we were establishing the supremacy of speech over writing, the quality of the writing that appeared to be persuading us of the strength of the case shows the precise opposite. The speech/writing binary is turned, dizzyingly, upside down.

The broad concern of Jacques Derrida can be summed up as what he, and others, call 'logocentrism'. That labels the tendency to search for some guarantee of the meaning of a text, or of discourse, in something outside itself: in a notion of 'rationality' or 'reason' (one of the primary meanings of *logos*), in the word of God ('In the beginning was the Word', we read in the Bible, and the word translated as 'word' is also *logos*), in the author's intentions in writing ('What Wordsworth is trying to say', above) or the speaker's in speaking, in 'the real world', in something we call 'truth'. All of these, and others, are candidates for reassuring us that meaning can be pinned down, made certain, rendered stable beyond all possibility of destabilization. Recall here that quest for certainty that I identified above as one of the defining features of modernity.

The relevance of all of this to education may not be obvious at first sight. But think how people constantly try to justify education by reference to some version of reality that they claim, implicitly or explicitly, to have authoritative knowledge of. The purpose of education is often said to be to equip young people with skills 'for the real world', as if there were – in some dimension of genuine reality – such a thing, to be known so indubitably that we could stipulate what skills might be required to deal with it, rather than, inevitably, interpretations of and perspectives on it. Sometimes the real world in this context is taken to be a distinctively social place, for which the key skills (skills are usually called 'key' as another claim to ontological status: they open the door to the real world) are those of the good citizen who knows how to live in harmony with others. Sometimes the real world is taken to be that of the economy (globalized: this world is real in the same way everywhere) to which the individual must learn to contribute. Generally the real world is understood to be a harsh and unforgiving place, so we tell ourselves it would be irresponsible if we did not teach children how to buckle down and keep their noses clean. Now as a matter of fact (as I would of course put it) I have noticed that in the real world (if that comprises all that adults do after they have left formal education) people plant crocuses, read poetry and learn to play the harpsichord. When I politely enquire why education should not prepare young people for *this* reality, the reply tends to be – well, that I don't live in the real world. Perhaps the reader has had the same kind of experience as me: when people tell me I need to live in the real world it's usually the case that they want me to do something that I don't.

There has been a long-standing tendency in the UK to set up a contrast or binary between the 'real', 'practical' world on the one hand and, on the other, a shadowy world of bugaboos and nameless Others, variously characterized as trendy teachers, progressivists, theorists, academics and rhetoricians. Thus, we come across fearless speakers of the Plain Truth, defending all that we hold dear against subversive elements. History supplies depressing predecedents in which Jewish intellectuals were cast in this role in Nazi Germany and 'leftist' ones targeted in the McCarthyite witch-hunts in the post-war USA. At the time that I write this, one candidate for the vice-presidency of the USA is trying to make political capital out of the fact that she is by no means one of those tricky, un-American creatures, an Eastern, élitist intellectual, but a plain-speaking, moose-shooting hockey mum. The underlying binaries here are very similar.

Examples from education in the UK are of course less dramatic. But there sometimes seems to be a class of educationists employed specifically to insist on the priority of the practical and literal, and to denigrate the other side of the binary. I have in an earlier piece (Smith, 2000) offered deconstructive readings of material published by the (now former) Her Majesty's Chief Inspector of Schools in England and Wales, Christopher Woodhead. I repeat here some of my analysis of his 1998 lecture, 'Blood on the tracks: lessons from the history of education reform'. In para. 25 Mr Woodhead is writing about in-service training and preparation for Headship.

> Seeing is often believing in professional development. A course tutor who is teaching or leading a school himself has a credibility which is in itself very important. In-service training ought, moreover, to be rooted firmly in the practicalities of the particular task. This is not to adopt a deliberately anti-intellectual stance, it is rather to recognize both what teachers themselves want and what the inspection evidence confirms. Good training helps teachers solve the problems they face. It has an immediacy and a relevance. Bad training is strong on the academic rhetoric, the theorizing, the either/or let a thousand flowers bloom [sic] ... . How many times have each of us been asked to organize ourselves into groups and share our experience? Put bluntly, do we want 'reflective practitioners' or teachers who can teach children to read?

The binary contrasts one set of ideas with another. On the one side are phrases suggestive of simple reality and uncomplicated common sense: seeing is believing, rooted firmly, evidence confirms. On the other side, are the bugaboos: 'the academic rhetoric, the theorizing' – mere words, empty speechifying.

When we read the paragraph carefully, however, the binary begins to fall apart. The opening sentence does not say that the crucial feature of training is what it practically *does* but what it *appears* to do ('seeing is very often believing'): a reading confirmed by the second sentence, where what is described as 'very important' is not the course tutor's *ability* to lead professional development but his or her *credibility*. One might of course be credible ('She must be good – she's been in the job 20 years') but in fact entirely useless. The voice of common sense, having been thus established, attempts to confer its distinctive authority on the rest of the paragraph. We are to 'recognize both what teachers themselves want and what the inspection evidence confirms'. But what teachers want has just been identified as *credibility*, with all its problems; in any case what they want is subordinated to what the Chief Inspector 'recognizes', and is sandwiched between that all-seeing wisdom and the 'inspection evidence' which, since it is presumably the basis of what he recognizes, amounts to the same thing (and since it is thus doubly important we might expect to be told – but aren't – just what this 'evidence' is).

If all this is becoming a little complicated, it is a relief to meet the next two sentences that state what is what. 'Good training helps teachers solve the problems they face. It has an immediacy and a relevance'. The directness and simplicity have considerable rhetorical force after what has gone before. The next sentence is that most classical of rhetorical devices, the ascending tricolon

('Friends, Romans, countrymen . . .'), in which each leg of the colon is longer than the one before. Here the ascent is not too neat or glib: 'the academic rhetoric', 'the theorizing', 'the either/or let a thousand flowers bloom'. The paragraph finishes with two questions that do not expect an answer: they are *rhetorical* questions.

Thus, the paragraph begins to collapse under the strain of a close reading. Far from being straightforward and commonsensical, it is highly *rhetorical*. It displays many of the characteristic tricks of the trade of the speech-maker. It actively denies its own rhetoricity both by making implicit appeal to the language of common sense and by asserting that it is those on the other side of the binary whose discourse is mere 'academic rhetoric'.[45]

The significance of this aspect of Derridaean poststructuralism should now be clear. It is a powerful challenge to those who claim to have authoritative knowledge of educational 'reality' and assume the right to silence those whom they position on the other and inferior side of the binary. The Derridaean interest in subverting the binary in which 'text' and textuality, literature and theory are subordinated to 'practice' and 'reality' can seem odd until we recall that history provides many examples of people who burned the texts of those whose ideas did not fit comfortably with their own; and they did not stop with the books. The poststructuralist strand in 'postmodern' thinking, with its fascination with texts, and its denial that there is any easy recourse to anything outside of texts, a 'real world' independent of the wishes and ambitions of those who would bully us into conforming to their version of it, offers a kind of liberation and a glimpse of light in what have been dark times for education.[46]

NOTES

43 http://en.wikipedia.org/wiki/Neil_Strauss#The_Annihilation_Method
44 http://www.tapping.com/
45 This analysis draws on my earlier one (Smith, 2000).

FURTHER READING

The historical background to the quest for certainty is set out in Stephen Toulmin, *Cosmopolis: The Hidden Agenda of Modernity* (New York: The Free Press, 1990), which I follow in the first couple of pages above. Stuart Parker, *Reflective Teaching in the Postmodern World* (Buckingham: Open University Press, 1997), gives an excellent overview of a Derridaean approach. John D. Caputo, *Deconstruction in a Nutshell* (New York: Fordham University Press, 1997) is very readable on this aspect of Derrida's writings, but the reader should not expect to find anything in a nutshell there. Nigel Blake, Paul Smeyers, Richard Smith and Paul Standish, *Thinking Again: Education after Postmodernism* (Westport: Bergin and Garvey, 1998), offer a critical perspective on a range of 'postmodern' ideas. There is no substitute for reading Lyotard and Derrida themselves, especially Lyotard's *The Postmodern Condition* (1984) and Derrida's *Of Grammatology* (trans. Gayatri Chakravorty Spivak) (Baltimore: Johns Hopkins University Press, 1974). Neither constitutes a handbook, nor an easy read.

REFERENCES

Blake, Nigel, Smeyers, Paul, Smith, Richard and Standish, Paul (1998) *Thinking Again: Education after Postmodernism*. Westport, CT: Bergin and Garvey.

Cahoone, Lawrence (1996) *From Modernism to Postmodernism: an Anthology*. Oxford: Blackwell.

Derrida, Jacques (1974) *Of Grammatology* (trans. Gayatri Chakravorty Spivak). Baltimore: Johns Hopkins University Press.

Derrida, Jacques (1981) Plato's pharmacy. In *Dissemination* (ed. and trans. Barbara Johnson). London: Athlone Press.

Lyotard, Jean-François (1984) *The Postmodern Condition: A Report on Knowledge* (trans. G. Bennington and B. Massumi). Manchester: Manchester University Press.

Parker, Stuart (1997) *Reflective Teaching in the Postmodern World*. Buckingham: Open University Press.

Smith, Richard (2000) Another space. In Pradeep Dhillon and Paul Standish (Eds), *Lyotard: Just Education*. London: Routledge.

Toulmin, Stephen (1990) *Cosmopolis: The Hidden Agenda of Modernity*. New York: The Free Press.

11

Feminism and Education

Cris Mayo and Barbara Stengel

Many a woman has experienced vividly at first hand that demolition, that shaking of established belief, which Descartes thought necessary for the acquisition of knowledge – and it happened not because she is a philosopher, retreating to a room of her own, but because she is a woman in the wide world. (Langton, 2000: 127)

Over the past four decades, feminist scholars in increasing numbers have taken up their pens and keyboards to respond to issues raised about social life and education and to raise issues that have been ignored. They started from a missing point of view: their own experience of living as women 'in the wide world.' Whereas gendered identity was their point of departure, that standpoint itself quickly became a focus of critical scrutiny and theorizing. Both the gendered perspective and the perspective that interrogates the construction of gendered experience can be characterized as feminist in that each acknowledges the diversity of gendered perspectives and assumes that those perspectives are worthy of investigation. This simple shift in philosophical starting point has created much constructive mischief – prompting previously unasked questions, opening up new conceptual paths, and sometimes employing unorthodox modes of inquiry. Feminist scholars, including people of all gender identities, have advanced the cause of philosophy of education at the same time that they have troubled some of its most widely and dearly held assumptions.

Feminism creates a tension of category and method for feminist philosophers. When feminist philosophers accept 'women' as their conceptual starting point, they rely on a sex-gender framework that differentiates men from women (as the only two human possibilities) and renders women 'other.' By seeking to decenter the male experience using Enlightenment-based modes of inquiry they then rely on the conceptual apparatus that put male modes of being and thinking in the center to begin with. This strategy is potentially self-defeating. As poet Audre Lorde famously put it, 'The master's tools will never dismantle the master's house' (1984, 112).

Feminist explication of women as rational, moral beings, of 'women's ways of knowing' or of the 'ethics of care' ultimately push in the direction of critique of the imbalanced gender dualism that prompted the inquiry in the first place. Achieving balance is not possible because the sex-gender system and the criteria for knowing and acting built into it is the source of the imbalance. Eventually the system itself – and the narratives that legitimate and support it – comes under scrutiny. This is the story told here. From roots in late Renaissance, Enlightenment and American Progressive thinking to the multivocal, multiperspectival philoso-phizing of today, feminist philosophers have struggled with the tension inherent in the notion of a gendered point of view, while recognizing the pragmatic, polit-ical and philosophical difficulties in assuming either a generic human point of view or a view from nowhere.

Feminist philosophers of education – as do all feminist theorists – root their thinking in the pragmatic and political dimensions of the socio-historical move-ment for better lives for women, and for people of all genders. Whereas some critics contend that this pollutes the purity of their thinking, feminists respond that *all* forms of thinking are rooted in some pragmatic, political agenda and that they are simply acknowledging theirs. Reference to this particular practical ideal has not prevented feminist theorists from a vibrant internal critique and dialogue. Feminist theory is not so much a school of thought as a mode of thinking into action marked by a common conceptual, existential and pragmatic point of departure. Feminist philosophers of education employ analytic, herme-neutic, phenomenological, pragmatist, and poststructuralist tools in the service of careful thought about the education of all.

In what follows, we do two things. First, we examine the roots of feminist philosophy of education by attending to the work of several historical foremothers whose thinking shapes feminist philosophy still. Secondly, we trace the develop-ment of feminist philosophy of education in the contemporary era. Both strands illuminate the ways in which a feminist starting point – the lived experience of women in the world – prompts a continual overturning of assumptions and a sub-sequent turn to varied modes of inquiry and representation. What is for some an effort to insure that women's ways of knowing and being in the world are part of the philosophical and educational picture is for others a project involving multiple and complex critiques of the very categories that give shape to our shared reality.

THE ROOTS OF FEMINIST PHILOSOPHY OF EDUCATION

Whereas it is not true that the history of women thinking about education is lim-ited in time or scope, it *is* true that such thinking has developed rapidly in the century since women's suffrage captured the political stage and the political imagination. The gender-focused educational, social and political activism that began with women's participation in abolitionist movements and shifted into suffrage movements in the USA and Europe always understood the links between exclusion from education and political equality. From early activists, who insisted on the rights of all people to learn to the organized women's movements of the 1960s demanding federal laws protecting women's right to employment, education and political participation to women's roles in the black power movement, gay liberation, and the Chicano movement, education and attention to gender concerns were inextricably linked. Increasingly, women's political and educational activism has critiqued Western dominance and worked toward engaging global and transnational issues. We replicate this Western-oriented intellectual and political history by situating our discussion of feminist philosophy of education firmly within the Western canon, although we note the rise of transnational and global theorizing.

DEEP ROOTS

Four women exemplify the deep roots of feminist philosophy of education: Frenchwoman Christine de Pizan in the fourteenth century, Englishwoman Mary Wollstonecraft in the eighteenth century, and Americans Charlotte Perkins Gilman and Anna Julia Cooper in the early twentieth century. These four ask the same kind of potentially disruptive questions raised by feminist activists, philosophers and philosophers of education today, offering carefully considered, well-argued and sometimes counterintuitive answers. Each imagines a social world in which both men and women contribute morally and intellectually, each expands the notion of economic contribution to include 'women's work,' and each offers a vision of education that includes women's moral, intellectual and economic growth. In short, they all attend to gender as a category used to differentiate political, social and economic role and status and are critical of its use. Combining philosophical argumentation and narrative and literary devices they create distinctly gendered philosophical methods and arguments.

Christine de Pizan: the affinity of women and learning

In the best known of her more than 20 authored works, *The Book of the City of Ladies* (1982), Christine de Pizan utilizes an imagined conversation with Reason, Rectitude and Justice to illustrate the double bind in which women find themselves: women who accept a limited societal role accept as well limitations on their own development. Their acceptance of a stifling and confining role then justifies the continued lack of education for women. The 'City of Ladies' that de Pizan is charged to construct represents a multilayered argument that clarifies women's positive, intelligent contributions to human living. She begins this early exercise in the new scholarship on women with a description of her own life of the mind and her puzzlement as to why male writers so malign women. With a pragmatic understanding of the social construction of the self and a pointed description of the danger of what we would now call 'internalized oppression' (1982: 5), de Pizan articulates her narrator's self-doubt – until visitors arrive. Through Reason's interrogation the narrator comes to understand that learned men debate critical issues without resolution, that important matters of human understanding resist certainty, and that she should not sacrifice her own experience and judgment to those whose experience and judgment is also limited. Rectitude and Justice aid de Pizan's narrator in affirming her experience of the 'natural sense' and intelligence of women (86–87). She finds, through the stories of other women, that women can achieve moral excellence – that blend of prudence given as a gift of God with knowledge acquired through effort over time. Thus, she grounds her case for education on the link between education and virtue.

De Pizan achieves argumentative brilliance by making use of the implied (Christian) values and goals that undergird various societal institutions and turning those claims back on typical male and female behavior in an effort to overcome oppression in all forms. She does not react against or apologize for the flaws that males identify in women. Instead, she articulates an affirmative argument for women's contributions to shared social and political life and, in the process, carefully deconstructs what she calls 'masculine myth.'

Christine de Pizan accepts that men (public) and women (private) have separate domains and functions, but she rejects utterly the notion that education should be limited to social function or that intelligence is limited by sphere. Thus, the significant impact of *The Book of the City of Ladies* is rooted in the way in which form matches content: de Pizan is a highly educated and literate woman, articulating through allegory and historical inquiry a philosophy of education. As translator Earl Jeffrey Richards notes, 'the affinity of women and learning is both its vehicle and its message and the one is inseparable from the other' (xlv).

Mary Wollstonecraft: virtue and the exercise of reason

Several centuries – and the Enlightenment – separate the secular Mary Wollstonecraft from the Christian Christine de Pizan. Where de Pizan accepts the ideal of a Christian worldview, Wollstonecraft is critical of new forms of secular sociopolitical institutions in the making. But both focus on the common moral profile of the human person and both link the importance of education to the achievement of moral personhood.

Mary Wollstonecraft's feminist philosophy of education unfolds in *Vindication of the Rights of Woman*, a statement of political philosophy that is inextricably tied to educational concerns. For Wollstonecraft, a participant in the tumultuous political debates of the late eighteenth century, rights have no value – individual or societal – in the absence of the education that equips citizens to enact those rights.

The requisite education is one that recognizes the link between intellectual development and moral action. Wollstonecraft puts it this way: '... the most perfect education, in my opinion, is such an exercise of the understanding as is best calculated to strengthen the body and form the heart. Or, in other words, to enable the individual to attain such habits of virtue as will render it independent' (Poston, 1988: 21).

Wollstonecraft's feminism is a product of frustration with the failure of women to resist male domination combined with recognition of the socializing power of relations of dominance and submission. Startled by the response to her *Vindication of the Rights of Man*, Wollstonecraft realized that her words, though published by a woman, were interpreted widely as a defense of the rights of men (i.e., male human beings) rather than the rights of 'man' (i.e., all human beings). Wollstonecraft quickly penned *Vindication of the Rights of Woman* as a clarification. But she went further to articulate how education shapes the nature of men and of women and why education for intelligent citizenship must be afforded to all.

Wollstonecraft pursues the ideal of independence in a way that her foil, Rousseau, does not. Rousseau's treatment of Émile's life articulates autonomy but depicts Émile's dependence on Sophie. For Rousseau, Émile and Sophie are a unit; his autonomy requires her socio-economic dependence – which, Rousseau admits, is something of a mask for his sexual dependence on her. Wollstonecraft calls Émile and Sophie 'an absurd unit,' claiming that it is precisely the tyranny of men that renders women foolish or vicious. She argues instead for actual independence for both men and women, but defines independence in a way that acknowledges the social responsibility that accompanies women's reproductive capacity.

Like Christine de Pizan, Wollstonecraft argues that determinations of women's 'nature' – as unintelligent, as lacking character, as capricious in behavior, as subject to 'head strong passions and groveling vices' – will inevitably miss the mark until men and women are evaluated on the basis of a common education. Thus, Wollstonecraft challenges tradition doubly, arguing for the education of women's intellect and again arguing strongly for coeducation.

Charlotte Perkins Gilman: the economic value of 'women's work'

As is true of de Pizan and Wollstonecraft, Charlotte Perkins Gilman's theoretical methodology includes argumentation and narrative. Her thinking about education is tied to her understanding of women's experience and women's place not only in the social, political and economic world but also in the more intimate spaces of personal interaction. Gilman's work centers on key feminist issues: the origins of women's subjugation; the struggle to achieve both autonomy and intimacy in human relationships; the central role of work as a definition of self; and new strategies for rearing and educating future generations to create a humane and nurturing environment (Lane, 1990, 3–40).

That Gilman's work extends and intensifies the critique of the function that a gender distinction serves in modern society is unsurprising given her historical location in an era shaped by scientific advance and evolutionary theory. Gender's 'dense prejudice' (Gilman, 1898: 226) comes to Gilman's attention early in *Women and Economics*. Gilman argues that extant gender stereotypes, particularly but not only as applied to women, are hindering social progress. She begins by articulating the economic value of women's work even in the private sphere as 'housekeepers' and mothers and moves to suggest that changes in the patterns of family living and social intercourse – brought on by the advances of industrialization – demand a 'permanent provision for the needs of individuals, disconnected from the sex-relation.' She proposes communal living arrangements to ensure shared responsibility for housekeeping. For Gilman, it is meaningful work, not simply virtue or education of the intellect, that enables women to be and become fully human. But education, broadly considered, creates the conditions for this wholesome life of one's own – and Gilman sketches out an elaborate vision of women's education in her utopian novel *Herland* (1915/1998).

Herland tracks the daily life of a colony of women stranded for generations by war and natural disaster; we encounter these women through the eyes of three male explorers who happen upon them. That the men are utterly unable to understand how a colony of women can possibly be orderly and operational is a source of considerable humor and a clear indicator of the content and pervasiveness of male stereotypes about females.

In *Herland*, Gilman creates a society in which the nurturing that we associate with motherhood is extended and intensified to all aspects of social interaction for multiple educational purposes. Thus, the efforts more obviously, and more narrowly, 'educational' – like learning to communicate, or discovering the natural world or mastering one's field of economic endeavor – are situated experiences, woven into the patterns of communal living and excised of the competition, blame and deprivation that marked schooling then and now. For Gilman, a woman's work – in and outside the home – is both her source of meaning and the promise of societal betterment.

Anna Julia Cooper: race and gender intersect

In the post-Civil War era in the USA, the education – and the humanity – of African-Americans commanded the attention of public intellectuals, educators and policy-makers. Anna Julia Cooper turned the full force of her philosophical attention to gender and class as intersecting analytic lenses on this social reality. As Manning Marable says of her, Cooper may be the founding figure in contemporary writings bringing together race, class, and gender (Lemert and Bhan, 1998). That intersectionality is a key feature of much feminist analysis today has roots in Cooper's, and other early black feminist, efforts.

Cooper's thought is grounded in her lived experience – both personal and professional, a trait that marks feminist theory generally. She conveys an understanding of deconstructive concepts like discursive space, and offers a complex structural-ist critique of an American society that privileges the economically advantaged white male while colonizing the other (black, Native American, female). Cooper's incisive naming and nuanced theorizing of the life of the Black Woman as well as her explicit claim to an education of the mind solidify her place in the development of the feminist philosophy of education.

Cooper speaks as 'a Black Woman of the South' in the series of speeches and occasional pieces that became *Voice from the South*. She answers those – male and/or white – who would prescribe the treatment of black women by offering the 'witness of one who lives there.' It is the Black Woman's decentered status – as a nonentity in a society structured to maintain (white, wealthy) privilege – that grounds her moral vision and responsibility, that renders her 'better qualified to weigh and judge and advise because not herself in the excitement of the race' (Lemert and Bhan, 1998: 114).

Cooper creates a layered discursive space for women of color, not only black women, but all who 'have been crushed under the iron heel of Anglo-Saxon power and selfishness' (Lemert and Bhan, 1998: 108) by speaking as herself, as the narrator, and as the Black Woman. Through this narrative device, she explores the ways women of color are invited to speak and prohibited from speaking in a caste-based society. Though critical of the essentializing of white feminists, Cooper herself invites all women to accept their foundational and educational position as the makers and keepers of the home. While she understands the home as the center to which a woman's self and work are tethered, she does not confine women to a separate sphere. She employs the language of home and manners not only to argue for a critical moral role for women but also to illustrate the 'structural fault lines' (Lemert and Bhan, 1998: 42) of the intrasocietal colo-nizing that marked the America of her time and of ours. 'Woman versus the Indian' is as acute a critique of the play of race, gender and class in American society as one can find. Cooper meditates on the moral merit of white feminists, the cultural baggage of Southern women, the ascendant position of ladies – Southern or Northern – who favor social equality and civility until their own privilege is endangered, the oppression of the Black Woman, and the predomi-nance of Southern ideals in the nation's psyche as she argues for common cause among woman, the Indian and the Negro in uncovering and resisting structural oppression.

These four early feminist philosophers of education exemplify the inherent ten-sion that marks more contemporary work on gender and education. Each offers an argument for women's entrance into rationality and, thus, into the traditional domain of education, and each employs a gendered analysis, situated against the social and cultural norms defining femininity in her own time. At the same time, each is critical of the limitations of gendered analysis and of the traditional tools of analysis and modes of expression that reinscribe gender inequities. We see the development of these tensions in the next section as we present a progression in philosophy of education that begins in acceptance of the sex-gender system as a lens for analysis and proceeds through a critique of that system toward new gendered possibilities.

PHILOSOPHY OF EDUCATION IN WOMEN'S WORDS AND VOICES

Contemporary feminist approaches to philosophy of education, like feminisms in general, are diverse, ranging from singular women calling particular theories to account for their male biases and omission of women to broader collaborations seeking to redefine how knowledge is constructed and disseminated. Given the still-extant tendency to overlook the centrality of gender in shaping educational theory and practice, it is important that we represent the sheer volume and quality of that work as well as its diversity.

Gendered analysis highlights both the political *and philosophical* nature of the questions at the heart of the feminist philosophy of education. What is gender and what difference does the difference of gender make? These are philosophical questions that, like most philosophical questions, have political and empirical ramifications. Centering gender in philosophy of education raises questions that blur the lines between philosophy and empirical inquiry, raising questions about fairness in educational access, about the intellectual, moral and pedagogical implications of philosophical approaches, about the race and class privilege that may have allowed some women access and kept others out, and about the possibility that gendered analysis reifies problematic gender norms.

Women's entrance into what had been a male-dominated conversation in philosophy of education challenged the terms of that conversation by focusing work on women's particular embodied experiences (Leach, 1991). The philosophical implications of the women's movement first made it onto the Philosophy of Education Society (PES) program in 1972 – in a symposium featuring Barbara Arnstine, Maxine Greene, and Elizabeth Steiner Maccia (Leach, 1991). Several years later, in 1976, President Maxine Greene, just the second woman to serve as PES President, employed her trademark literary and existential perspectives to analyze 'the multiple, often mysterious devices [American] women invented for achieving their own education' in *Phi Delta Kappan*.

The first *Educational Theory* article that addressed gender as a central analytic category was Linda Nicholson's 'Women and schooling' in 1980. Taking radical critics of educational institutions to task for their omission of gender, Nicholson argued that not only are the functions of schooling gendered in ways that mirror other institutions but also that schools, by separating public and private, have been constitutive of the sex-role system that maintains gender difference. Nicholson's Marxist feminist analysis and Leach's later critique of phallogocentrism each shifted the focus of conversation on women from individualized exclusion to deeper scrutiny of the systematic formation of gender difference through, respectively, social and economic institutions, and the structure of discourse itself.

At the same time, other scholars were analyzing women's experience for affirmative models of educational possibility.

THE DIFFERENCE WOMEN MAKE

Nel Noddings' work on caring examines not the specificities of particular locations and identities of women but rather what the strengths of the role women play as caregivers might bring to ethics and education. The caring ethic, she contends, is 'essentially feminine,' and by centralizing relations, Noddings shifts the very ground of ethics away from judgment to affect-laden interaction as the key to moral action (1984: 8). Like Carol Gilligan's work in moral psychology (1982), Noddings reasserts the difference gender can make to ethics and ontology. Her work takes for granted what feminist philosophers have argued through the ages – that the autonomous, judging agent of philosophy had someone to raise him and feed him, that he talked and engaged with others, and thus his claim to isolated thought is untenable. Through her phenomenological analysis of the 'natural caring' evident in women's social roles, Noddings uncovers indicators that can be used to assess the presence or absence of caring relations in less intimate circumstances. 'Ethical caring,' with its focus on dialogue, has particularly strong implications for the organizations of schools and learning.

In *Reclaiming a Conversation*, Jane Roland Martin (1985) highlights the difference that women make by recovering and re-presenting the thinking of often ignored women philosophers and by reconsidering the centrality of gender to key works in philosophy of education. She demonstrates that women have made significant and distinctive contributions to philosophy and philosophy of education *and* that gender difference has historically been a key feature of even canonical works on philosophy of education. Redrawing our attention to these women and to sexual difference, and 'redress[ing] the harm done when women are excluded as objects and subjects of educational thought' (Martin, 1984: 344), Martin calls for an understanding of the interdependence of women and men, as well as recognition of the relationships between productive and reproductive processes (Martin, 1985: 183). In a later work, Martin, still dissatisfied with the masculinist bent of philosophy of education, calls for more attention to the domestic realm (Martin, 1995) and, like Noddings' use of maternal relations as a starting point for an ethics of care, Martin shifts the institution of school away from civics and into the domestic, using the institution of the home as her touchstone (Martin, 1995). The 1980s and 1990s saw not only the growth of feminist work but also the attention to what counts as philosophy of education, suggesting that the latter question was already present but perhaps exacerbated by the introduction of feminist philosophy of education (Kohli, 2000). Mary Leach argues that the introduction of 'un-ease' caused by feminist work can produce 'animated exchanges that continue to challenge us with a process of "coming to terms with" but never arriving at any final state,' signally a shift from recovery of women's voice to cautions on exclusionary discourses (1991: 298). But exclusions continued to matter as philosophers examined the gendered labor of teaching and the relative dearth of women educational theorists (Laird, 1998: 129; Hicks, 1999).

Jo Anne Pagano examines this gendered and embodied practice of teaching in 'Teaching women':

> The story of the art of teaching, when it is practiced by women, and when it is practiced in the teaching of women, must begin by producing difference, by acknowledging what women know … . The stories we tell are not our own. The impulse to the art of women teaching and the art of teaching women begins in that recognition. The impulse is triggered by the recognition that our public standing, our excellence as scholars and teachers exacts from us a different sort of pain, the pain of personal self-effacement. (1988: 339)

While some feminist philosophers of education examined what a gendered analysis brought to methods of inquiry or to critical and feminist pedagogy, other feminist philosophers simply shifted the focus of argumentation to gender itself. Barbara Houston, for instance, through careful reasoning and marshalling of empirical evidence, demonstrates that 'gender-free' education would continue gender bias. Drawing on Jane Roland Martin, Houston contends that education should aim toward 'gender-sensitive goals' that understand gender as an identity formed in power relations. Houston contends that a gender-sensitive perspective asks higher-order questions than a gender-free perspective, shifting gender for an individual attribute to a social system. The questions entailed by such a perspective, she argues, are 'Is gender operative here? How is it operative? What other effects do our strategies for eliminating bias have?' (1994: 131).

These feminist interventions into philosophy of education did spark a new conversation, both caring and critical. Ann Diller, marking both criticism of and support for Noddings' ethics, contends that it is a domain ethic: i.e., relationality does not translate well into globalized relations or political concerns. Diller notes that critics are further concerned that it is a 'dangerous ethic,' requiring 'either servility or supererogation' and that it potentially stabilizes gender relations as they are (1996: 81–104).

Weaving together feminist philosophy with narrative methods, Lynda Stone (1995) argues that methodological innovation has been central to feminist work, and that literature, personal observation, and phenomenology augment, enhance, and expand philosophy's depth of engagement. Centralizing new discourses in philosophy of education, this shift in methodology echoes Jane Roland Martin's critique of the masculinist 'separation of reason from feeling and emotion and of the self from other' (1984: 346).

DIFFERENCE/FEMINISMS

Newer feminist work, including work indebted to woman of color feminism (Combahee River Collective, 1982; Collins, 1990; Anzaldúa, 1990), shifts away from 'the' female body as the site of difference and examines the intersections of difference, collisions of race, class, and sexuality. Poststructural feminism describes regulatory regimes of gender identity and their concomitant slippages and subversions. Rather than returning to mythic forms of femininity, they examine the inadvertent openings in discourse and practice that show gender and sexual norms to be considerably more unstable and complex than they might appear. Mary Leach and Bronwyn Davies contend that feminist postmodernism 'problematizes the vital issues of subjectivity, language and power that have too often remained undertheorized in most modernist projects to bring about sex equity in schools' (1990: 322). Whereas 'women' and 'gender' remained uncertain categories throughout all of the foregoing work, by the late 1980s and early 1990s, the instability of the category of gender was affected by intersectional analyses that insisted on gender as a process involving racialization, sexuality and other forms of difference. C. Alejandra Elenes advocates for a borderlands' perspective, troubling essentialist identities and centering the conflicted and contested knowledges with which subordinated people – in her example, Chicana/os – can highlight the critical and creative process of education (1997: 375).

A growing interest in poststructural work meant that gender-based critiques were also themselves explicitly and centrally critiquing the category of gender itself, as well as bringing in other forms of difference. Megan Boler's *Feeling Power: Emotions and Education* signals this shift and examines not simply the place of emotion in thinking but how emotion is itself a category produced through material relations, as well as relations of difference. Shifting away from seeing emotion and affect as largely feminine realms, Boler's (1999) work simultaneously engages the challenges and potentials of multiculturalism, demonstrating the problematics of reifying feeling without examining their strategies and production. Suzanne De Castell and Mary Bryson's edited collection, *Radical In<ter>ventions: Identity, Politics, and Differences* examined how educational institutions and processes operated from the perspective of the marginalized and excluded, shifting discussion from the singularity of gendered exclusion to the intersections of race, class, gender, HIV/AIDS, sexuality and other interlocked vectors of difference. Bryson and de Castell's examination of gender equity projects in higher education provides one context in dire need of shifts in thinking about gender and marginalization. As they put it, such projects:

> risk consolidating and reifying those very problems which they are officially sanctioned to champion, both by reifying and nominally solidifying categories with a shaky, partial, contingent, and positioned ontology (for example, gender, sex, and equity); and by obscuring the vastly unequal power relations within which such discursive 'turf' is contested. (Bryson and de Castell, 1993: 341)

Deborah Britzman (1995), moving beyond gender to sexuality, examines how queer theory can shift understandings of reading practices, as well as teaching and learning in general, asserting key uses of queer theoretical concepts in educational discourse.

Audrey Thompson notes in her 1998 article, 'Not the color purple: black feminist lessons for educational caring', that while moves from Martin and Noddings to challenge masculinist bias recenter 'women', they universalize white women's experiences as standing in for all women. Critiques like Thompson's are a simultaneous indication of anti-essentialist moves in feminist philosophy of education and the related emphasis on the intersectionality and relationality of identities and communities. Practices central to feminism provide resources for people of all gender identities to rethink not only gender but also experience and knowledge. For instance, Thompson and Gitlin (1995) call for a return to the conversational practices of consciousness raising as a way to refigure knowledge, insist on difference and reconstruct knowledge. While consciousness raising can helpfully uncover the hidden biases and practices that structure identity, the excesses – aspects of identities, practices, and knowledges that are not contained in descriptive terms – also provide resources for rethinking pedagogy and knowledge construction (Orner et al., 1996). More recently, Morwenna Griffiths has argued that the feminization of teaching provides an opportunity to theorize what gender brings to practice. Arguing that the practice of teaching is 'leaky' and 'viscous,' she contends that these qualities encourage the kind of diverse interactions that can mitigate 'social stratification' and improve 'conviviality' (2006: 396). Urging a link between feminist political organizing and theorizing, Maureen Ford takes up the feminist practice of coalition building and argues for the implications of that political practice for rethinking teaching and philosophy of education (2007).

DIFFERENT CONTEXTS FOR GENDERED ANALYSIS

Increasingly, feminist philosophers of education have turned their attention to globalized gender difference and environmental sustainability. Barbara Thayer-Bacon (2003), focusing on environmentalism, argues that the cultural link between women and nature has implications for how feminists critique power relations in ecological contexts. Huey-li Li examines ecofeminism as a movement where strategic essentialism and diverse localities merge into a 'pedagogical project emphasizes ethical activism within oppressive contexts' even if the same conception of gender is not shared cross-culturally (2007: 368).

Turning to globalization as a gendered issue, Penny Enslin cautions that feminist political theories have yet to take globalized inequities into account. Enslin contends that 'Globalisation without the development of equal capacities among the worlds peoples to resist and work with it will surely exacerbate its now painfully apparent accompanying inequalities.' (Enslin, 2006: 63) Enslin argues that while noninterference may be a good goal that avoids Western dominance, nonetheless Western feminists do need to politically advocate for global educational improvement (Enslin, 2006: 66–67). But as Jill Blackmore points out, feminists have not yet developed 'sophisticated theories and global strategies for dealing in and through a "world polity," or even sophisticated ways of theorizing in the space between nation-states, the new regionalized states, NGOs, and a sense of the world polity – and how this all plays out in education' (Blackmore, 2000: 486).

THE FUTURE OF FEMINIST PHILOSOPHY OF EDUCATION

Our survey of historical and contemporary feminist philosophy of education, though woefully brief, establishes a key feature of the work: that it is constantly and rapidly reshaping itself and reshaping as well the field of inquiry it inhabits. To use gender as an analytic lens in a careful, thorough way is to push against the constraints of the system that supports the category. And pushing against the dominant system of thought and action requires questioning the very conceptual and logical tools that enable the identification of gender and its inequities. Some argue that we have entered a 'post-feminist' era in educational thought and practice. But it remains true that women's lives potentially offer a starting point for philosophy that cannot be subsumed into the male perspective. Even as feminist philosophers of education frame issues in new ways, they remain rooted in the concerns that have always prompted feminist theorizing: insuring better lives for people of all genders.

Are we correct to claim that feminist scholars have advanced the cause of philosophy of education at the same time that they have troubled some of its most widely (and dearly) held assumptions? Consider the claims made by feminist philosophers of education from Christine de Pizan to the present day:

- Gender matters.
- Women – as women – matter.
- Bodies matter.
- Relations are primary; interaction is educative.
- Disembodied rationality is not the only path to knowledge; feelings are also resources for knowledge.
- Knowledge and truth are plural, situated and narrative in construction, and power relations are implicated in knowledge and truth claims.
- Reliance on gender differences obscures other important (intracultural) differences such as race and class; i.e., essentializing is dangerous and intersectionality is vital.
- Thus, the category 'woman' is problematic as is the sex-gender system that frames it.
- Education can't be understood, let alone enacted, without taking each of these claims into account.

Note that these claims are not merely claims about women but are claims that address some of the abiding questions in philosophy and philosophy of education. It is easy to see why these claims might disrupt philosophers' business as usual. Modern philosophy, bound to define knowledge and delimit knowers and to prescribe ethical action, faces the suggestion that women (and all 'Others') might know differently or be socially constructed as divergent from a male ideal with the accusation of special pleading. Any shift away from the (masculine-defined) universal and enduring risks dismissal as trivial and even non-philosophical.

Although philosophy of education has opened its doors to diversity over the last few decades, there is still an understandable fear that the taints of 'identity' are diluting the strong stuff of philosophy, shifting its discourse from strong argument and enduring truth to the seemingly foundationless issues of political theory, poststructuralism, and even qualitative interpretative inquiry. Given the shifts entailed by centralizing gender, and, increasingly, race and sexuality, some philosophers of education fear the end of the field as they know it.

Feminist theory has altered methodological approaches to philosophy of education as well as shifted its focus, so perhaps this fear is well-grounded. As pioneer women's historian Gerda Lerner argued, when gender is centralized in the study of history, the mode of inquiry already dominant in history could not simply 'add women and stir' but rather required a 'new angle of vision' (Lerner, 1979). Yes, there has been an attempt to recover missing women philosophers and broaden how the philosophical canon is defined in order to return attention to women intellectuals, and we do that here, but even bringing those women into philosophy can highlight the ways in which women's perspective or epistemological standpoint challenges dominant modes and topics of philosophy. Women's experience as Other resonates with that of the colonized and the excluded and opens feminist theorizing to new interpretative, conceptual and theoretical terrain. Grappling philosophically with gender, race, class and sexuality, as well as relationality and embodiment, has meant that philosophers of education who recenter (and then critique) gender may – perhaps must – do so by returning to the 'interdisciplinary' strategies employed by those philosophers who began the philosophical tradition that feminists continue to engage but are compelled to challenge.

FURTHER READING

Readers who go directly to texts by de Pisan (1405/1982), Wollstonecraft (Poston [Ed.], 1988), Gilman (1898, 1915/1998), and Cooper (Lemert and Bhan [Eds], 1998) can see for themselves that contemporary feminist thinking in philosophy of education has a long and interesting history. The works of Maxine Greene (1976), Jane Roland Martin (1984, 1985) and Nel Noddings (1984) mark the turning point for an expanded feminist presence in philosophy of education and are well worth reading. To deepen one's understanding of the development of contemporary feminist-inspired philosophy of education, we recommend Mary Leach's excellent essay (1991), and the anthologies edited by Stone (1994) and Diller et al. (1996). It is wise to keep in mind that feminist philosophers of education are constantly in conversation with feminist theorists in other fields of study, including but not limited to philosophy. To understand the conversation in philosophy of education, it is helpful to be familiar with broader feminist discussions and debates. While there are a number of anthologies that would allow a reader to 'sample' feminist theory, we recommend Kolmar and Bartkowski's *Feminist Theory: A Reader* (2009, 3rd edn. Boston: McGraw-Hill) for its historical approach and cross-cultural sampling.

REFERENCES

Anzaldúa, Gloria (1990) 'La conciencia de la mestiza: towards a new consciousness' in Gloria Anzaldúa (ed.), *Haciendo Caras: Making Face, Making Soul*. San Francisco, California: Aunt Lute Books.

Blackmore, Jill (2000) 'Warning signals or dangerous opportunities? Globalization, gender, and educational policy shifts.' *Educational Theory*, 50 (4): 467–486.

Boler, Megan (1999) *Feeling Power. Emotions and Education*. New York: Routledge.

Britzman, Deborah (1995) 'Is there a queer pedagogy? Or, stop reading straight,' *Educational Theory*, 45 (2): 151–165.

Bryson, Mary and de Castell, Suzanne (1993) 'En/gendering equity: on some paradoxical consequences of institutionalized programs of emancipation,' *Educational Theory*, 43 (3): 341–355.

Collins, Patricia Hill (1990) *Black Feminist Thought. Knowledge, Consciousness, and the Politics of Empowerment*. New York: Routledge.

Combahee River Collective (1982) 'A black feminist statement,' in Barbara Smith, Patricia Bell Scott and Gloria T. Hull (eds), *All the Women are White, All the Men are Black, But Some of Us are Brave: Black Women's Studies*. Old Westbury, New York: The Feminist Press, pp. 13–22.

de Pizan, Christine (1405/1982) *The Book of the City of Ladies*. New York: Penguin Classics.

Diller, Ann, Houston, Barbara, Pauly Morgan, Kathryn and Ayim, Maryann (eds) (1996) *The Gender Question in Education: Theory, Pedagogy, and Politics*. Boulder, CO: Westview Press.

Elenes, C. Alejandra (1997) 'Reclaiming the borderlands: Chicana/o identity, difference, and critical pedagogy,' *Educational Theory*, 47 (3): 359–375.

Enslin, Penny (2006) 'Democracy, social justice and education: feminist strategies in a globalising world,' *Educational Philosophy and Theory*, 38 (1): 57–67.

Ford, Maureen (2007) 'Situating knowledges as coalition work,' *Educational Theory*, 57 (3): 307–323.

Gilligan, Carol (1982) *In a Different Voice*. Cambridge, MA: Harvard University Press.

Gilman, Charlotte Perkins (1898) *Women and Economics*. Boston: Small, Maynard and Company.

Gilman, Charlotte Perkins (1915/1998) *Herland*. Mineola, New York: Dover.

Greene, Maxine (1976) 'Honorable work and delayed awakenings: education and American women,' *Phi Delta Kappan*, 58 (1):25–30.

Griffiths, Morwenna (2006) 'The feminization of teaching and the practice of teaching: threat or opportunity?' *Educational Theory*, 56 (4): 387–405.

Hicks, Deborah (Spring 1999) 'The particular and the feminine: gendered accounts in educational theorizing,' *Educational Theory*, 49 (2): 251–264.

Houston, Barbara (1994) 'Should public education be gender free?' in Lynda Stone (ed.), *The Education Feminism Reader*. New York: Routledge, 1994.

Kohli, Wendy (Summer 2000) 'Educational theory in the eighties: diversity and divergence,' *Educational Theory*, 50 (3): 339–357.

Laird, Susan (Winter 1998) 'Women and gender in John Dewey's philosophy of education,' *Educational Theory*, 38 (1): 111–129.

Lane, Ann (1990) *To Herland and Beyond: The Life and Work of Charlotte Perkins Gilman*. New York: Penguin Group.

Langton, Rae (2000) 'Feminism in epistemology: exclusion and objectification,' in Miranda Fricker and Jennifer Hornsby (eds), *The Cambridge Companion to Feminism in Philosophy*. Cambridge: Cambridge University Press.

Leach, Mary (1991) 'Mothers of in(ter)vention: women's writing in philosophy of education,' *Educational Theory*, 41 (3): 287–300.

Leach, Mary and Davies, Bronwyn (1990) 'Crossing boundaries: educational thought and gender equity,' *Educational Theory*, 40 (3): 321–332.

Lemert, Charles and Bhan, Esme (eds) (1998) *The Voice of Anna Julia Cooper*. Lanham, Maryland: Rowman and Littlefield.

Lerner, Gerda (1979) *The Majority Finds Its Past. Placing Women in History*. Oxford: Oxford University Press.

Li, Huey-li (2007) 'Ecofeminism as a pedagogical project: women, nature, and education,'*Educational Theory*, 57 (3): 351–368.

Lorde, Audre (1984) *Sister Outsider*. Berkeley: Crossing Press.

Martin, J.R. (1984) 'Bringing women into educational thought,' *Educational Theory*, 34 (4): 341–353.

Martin, J.R. (1985) *Reclaiming a Conversation*. New Haven, CT: Yale University Press.

Martin, J.R. (1995) *The Schoolhome*. Cambridge, MA: Harvard University Press.

Nicholson, Linda (1980) 'Women and schooling,' *Educational Theory*, 30 (3): 225–233.

Noddings, Nel (1984) *Caring: A Feminine Approach to Ethics and Moral Education*. Berkeley: University of California Press.

Orner, Mimi, Miller, Janet L. and Ellsworth, Liz (1996) 'Excessive moments and educational discourses that try to contain them,' *Educational Theory*, 46 (1): 71–91.

Pagano, Jo Anne (1988) 'Teaching women,' *Educational Theory*, 38 (3): 321–339.

Poston, Carol (ed.) (1988) *'Mary Wollstonecraft,' A Vindication of the Rights of Woman: An Authoritative Text, Backgrounds, The Wollstonecraft Debate, Criticism*. New York: W.W. Norton.

Stone, Lynda (ed.) (1994) *The Education Feminism Reader*. New York: Routledge.

Thayer-Bacon, Barbara (2003) *Relational (e)pistemologies*. New York: Peter Lang.

Thompson, Audrey (1998) 'Not the color purple: black feminist lessons for educational caring,' *Harvard Educational Review*, 68 (4): 522–555.

Thompson, Audrey and Gitlin, Andrew (1995) 'Creating spaces for reconstructing knowledge in feminist pedagogy,' *Educational Theory*, 45 (2): 125–150.

12

Education and the Catholic Tradition

Kevin Williams

The religious response to life is a disposition composed of beliefs, convictions, attitudes and feelings concerning the human person and her or his destiny. Religion provides a way of apprehending the world that informs the whole life of believers and provides the spring of moral commitments to act in ways that are consistent with realizing this ultimate destiny. The destiny or end to which the Christian faith looks forward, as St Peter writes in *The First Letter*, is 'the salvation of . . . souls' (Peter 1: 3–9). Thus, woven into the stuff of how we conceive of human life and its purposes, an established religion such as Roman Catholicism has obvious implications for how the aims of education are to be conceived.

Unsurprisingly, there exists a long tradition of reflection on philosophy of education from a Catholic perspective and this philosophy finds authoritative expression in Vatican documents. These documents, now available in a collected volume (Franchi, 2007), have been the subject of analysis, especially by the contemporary educational philosopher Terry McLaughlin (1996), and continue to be drawn upon by other philosophers of education (see, for example, Pring, 2007, p. 518). Religious orders have provided an important source of insight into Catholic education, most famously in the work of St Ignatius and also in the writings of St Jean-Baptiste de la Salle and others. Many distinguished thinkers, including St Augustine, St Thomas Aquinas, Cardinal Newman, G.K. Chesterton and Jacques Maritain, have offered the fruits of their reflections on the subject. The second half of the twentieth century has seen more radical perspectives on education deriving from the Catholic tradition in the work of Ivan Illich and Paulo Freire. In the context of mainstream philosophy of education, Catholic thinking on education has been explored and developed by such philosophers as John Haldane, the late Terry McLaughlin, Richard Pring and David Carr. The references used in this chapter are evidence of a rich seam of insightful work that is philosophically rigorous and which offers the astringency required to take readers beyond what Terry McLaughlin (2002, p. 130, 1996, p. 138) often referred to as Catholic 'edu-babble' – that is, platitudinous, aspirational rhetoric. Interesting too are explorations of the pedagogic practice of Jesus Christ from a philosophical perspective by Pádraig Hogan (1995, pp. 53–59) and Connie Leean Seraphine (2005, pp. 20–24).

One of the features of the writings of major thinkers such as St Augustine, St Thomas Aquinas, Cardinal Newman, and Jacques Maritain is their comprehensiveness of compass when they write about education. For example, readers of the work of St Augustine are given access to reflections of rigour, originality and extraordinary pedagogic sensitivity. Underlying his vision of education is his famous expression of the purposes of all human striving at the start of his *Confessions*, 'our hearts are restless until they rest in Thee'. But the central figure in Catholic philosophy is, of course, St Thomas Aquinas. He addresses education directly only in one short treatise, but his greatest work, the *Summa Theologica*, has been described as 'an educational document of the highest importance' (Lawson, quoted in Beck, 1971, p. 113). This is because the *Summa* provides 'the blueprint for perfect human living' (Beck, 1971, p. 117) and offers a comprehensive philosophy of life and its purpose. According to St Thomas, this purpose is the achievement of happiness and this is understood as 'the attainment of complete truth by the intelligence and supreme good by the will' (Beck, 1971, p. 117). Thomism as a complete comprehensive philosophy of education was reformulated in an idiom suitable for the twentieth century by the French philosopher Jacques Maritain in his *Education at the Crosswords*, a work that received little notice outside of Catholic circles. Robert Dearden (see Carr et al., 1995, pp. 162–163) has expressed surprise at this neglect and four British philosophers undertook the challenge of making Maritain's thought available to an English-speaking world in a major essay published in 1995 (Carr et al., 1995).

As these authors note, what Maritain is offering, in the tradition of St Thomas, is a complete Catholic philosophy of education based on the central underpinnings in Catholic thought – commitments to metaphysical realism, the existence of the soul, natural law theory as a basis for the moral life and a theory of the common good as a basis for social living. This chapter does not purport to provide a defence of the truth of Catholicism or of the fundamental philosophical underpinnings of Catholic beliefs. There is a huge literature on these topics and in the present context it is not appropriate to address them. To draw on a distinction made by Carr et al. (1995, p. 163), much of the chapter addresses what might be described as a theory of Catholic education rather than a Catholic philosophy of education in the sense of a defence of the Catholic positions on the great philosophical questions. In other words, the chapter endeavours to offer an account of education from a Catholic point of view.

Having clarified the remit of this chapter, it may be helpful to provide a brief outline of the argument presented. The first section considers the purpose of education from a Catholic perspective. This is followed by an account of the pedagogical spirit of a Catholic education and some reflections on the related notion of ethos. The main part of the chapter explores what might be a Catholic attitude towards educational content and reviews the role of religious education within the curriculum. The final section of the chapter criticizes the drift of Catholic education away from its essential aims towards socio-political crusading.

THE HEART OF THE MATTER

In the Western tradition, both in the monastic foundations of early Christian Ireland and in the cathedral schools of medieval Europe, the pursuit of learning and praise of God went together. The commitment to spread the Word of God was conceived as an inseparable aspect of the Church's mission. This has always meant that serious intellectual endeavour has a very high profile within the Catholic tradition. In this tradition the principal aim of learning is the pursuit of truth and that of teaching is to transmit this truth. Accordingly, the aims of education are clear-cut, although this is not to claim that all Catholics have precisely the same priorities. But to count as being Catholic, the purposes of education must be based on a conviction of possessing the truth about the ultimate purpose of life and endeavouring to pass this on to young people. The truth claims underlying a Catholic philosophy of education are unambiguous (see Beck, 1971 and Carr, 1999a). In a lucid statement of Neo-Thomism in education, George Beck makes this point well. Faith, he explains 'is an intellectual assent to a proposition whose truth is accepted on the authority of God' (Beck, 1971, p. 124). This faith is based on propositions that are accepted as true – that God exists, that Jesus is the son of God, that there is life after death and that the way human beings live this life has repercussions for all eternity. The period spent on this earth is 'a spring-board into eternity' (Beck, 1971, p. 124) and it is upon these truths that a 'whole philosophy of education is constructed' (Beck, 1971, p. 124). The purpose of education is 'to fit men and women for life, and the purpose of this life, so we hold, is to fit them for eternity' (Beck, 1971, p. 125). Accordingly, the Catholic vision of human life as articulated by St Thomas and Maritain offers 'ideals of perfection' in terms of which educators are enabled 'to evaluate human development' (Carr et al., 1995, p. 168).

One feature of this vision of life is that of necessity it goes 'beyond utility',[47] beyond what, in his poem 'The World Is Too Much with Us', Wordsworth describes as 'getting and spending'. Representing what G. K. Chesterton calls 'truth in a state of transmission' (Chesterton, 2004, p. 192), education very explicitly points young people to the essential values and purposes of human life and introduces them to a quality of life that lies beyond the mere fact of living.[48] For this reason mission statements about the aims of Catholic education that fail to extend beyond platitudes about developing 'the whole person' or 'rounded persons' say little that anyone could possibly disagree with. If, however, we try to unpack the term 'rounded persons', believers and non-believers will be found to differ greatly in what they are prepared to count as 'rounded'. The problem is not so much with the aspiration but rather with how the human development implied is to be interpreted. After all, who would be against the development of persons who are 'rounded' at least in the metaphorical sense?

It is much wiser to accept that a Catholic philosophy of education derives from a commitment to truth and is based on a substantial, thick or comprehensive conception of the purpose of human life rather than the procedural, thin, limited or restricted theories that underpin public schooling in liberal democracies. The Catholic vision is not incompatible with the promotion of democratic citizenship but its conception of the good does not command universal acceptance. It is more honest to acknowledge this than to pretend that Catholicism can be all things to all persons.

At the outset therefore it is important to foreground what is essential in the Catholic vision of life and learning. The impulse behind this vision is well captured in the words of David Carr: it involves 'an active search for knowledge of the way, the truth and the life of the very highest potential consequences for the salvation of the human soul' (Carr, 1999a, p. 185).

PEDAGOGICAL SPIRIT

The Catholic tradition as reformulated by Jacques Maritain affirms the 'essentially Thomistic case for personal wholeness as the key goal of education' (Carr et al., 1995, p. 170). Education is integrative and concerns the whole person and it is also lifelong. One feature of this wholeness is a broad intellectual grasp of the world. For American author, Mary McCarthy, a Catholic education involved the absorption of a perspective on world history and ideas before even the end of primary school. The 'indelible' effect of this process was 'like learning a language early' (McCarthy, 1967, p. 25). The Catholic perspective, she acknowledges, was, indeed, biased but its advantage from the learners' point of view was that it was not 'dry or dead' and that it brought history alive 'by the violent partisanship' that informed it (McCarthy, 1967, p. 25). Another effect of this partisanship was to introduce a coherence into the students' conception of history. This partisanship endowed education with a sense of perspective that served as a 'magnet' (McCarthy, 1967, p. 25) that gathered information together into a single conceptual framework.[49]

McCarthy's account is an intellectual elaboration of the attitude of Germaine Greer, who writes: 'I am still a Catholic, I just don't believe in God . . . . I don't want to escape from it. I'm very glad to be Catholic' (Bennett and Forgan, 2003, pp. 103–104). An interesting image of the integrative and lifelong dimension of

Catholicism is offered by television journalist Anne Robinson in a reminiscence on her convent education. 'Catholicism', she writes, 'is not a religion, it's a nationality. I think that we are always, always, Catholics' (Bennett and Forgan, 2003, p. 171). Her former school principal may not consider that she is a Catholic but, writes Robinson, 'I know I'm a Catholic. If I bang my toe, I will suddenly say 'Jesus, Mary and Joseph'!' (Bennett and Forgan, 2003, p. 171–172). Robinson's image suggests that a religious identity can be very pervasive and that the effects of a religious upbringing may not be readily discarded. A nice irony in the use of the nationality metaphor with regard to Catholicism is that the faith is completely international in its mission and compass. For a Catholic, as Marina Warner puts it, 'you belong to the world in an interesting way' a way that tends 'to transcend local nationalism' (Bennett and Forgan, 2003, p. 196). Poet Paul Durcan communicates the compass of a Catholic upbringing very memorably: 'Irish Christianity was the mother tongue of my soul and it remains the mother tongue of my soul in spite of the institution of the Irish Roman Catholic Church' (Durcan, 2003, p. 121). The long shadow cast by a Catholic identity is reflected in the findings of a survey published in 2007 that revealed half of the French people questioned declared themselves to be Catholic but just over half of this number affirmed a belief in God (*Le Monde des Religions*, 2007, p. 26).

ETHOS

As Catholic schools claim to teach truth and aspire to educate and form the whole person, the issue of ethos is central to a theory of Catholic education. In a penetrating philosophical attempt to disclose the 'educative importance of ethos', Terry McLaughlin (2005) has noted that the concept is complex and that it has tended to be treated rather superficially in educational discourse. An understanding of its significance has been hindered through its association with bland utterances in mission statements – a blandness that is not uncommon in Catholic statements. For this reason it is important to be clear, rigorous and circumspect in using the term. What then is ethos? Every social organization, political party, hospital, sports body or school has its own culture or ethos in the sense of a dominant, pervading spirit or character. When people speak of school spirit, they are referring to an important aspect of the culture or ethos of a school. The still fashionable term 'hidden curriculum' also captures some of what is meant by this ethos or culture. Although rarely to the fore of the consciousness of teachers and pupils, the culture or ethos of a school is often perceptible to visitors. Sometimes it is suggested in the prominence given to symbols – to symbols of religious practice or to other symbols – of patriotism/nationalism, of sporting, artistic and academic endeavour, of civic and community involvement. Though impalpable, ethos is nonetheless something real. When most of what we have learned at school has dropped into the deep well of human forgetfulness, a sense of the ethos of the school we attended remains part of our consciousness. This is not surprising as the ethos of a school touches the quality of our lives and can constitute an important element in the fabric of our very identity.

What is distinctive of the ethos that characterizes a Catholic education is that, as a matter of policy, it aims to foster in young people a commitment to the message of the Gospel and this is reinforced within educational institutions. One expression of this is the structuring of the school year around liturgy. For example, in his autobiography, author/teacher Bryan MacMahon explains that 'the turning year is meaningless if not viewed through the focused lens of Christianity' (MacMahon, 1992, p. 100). Catholic feast-days punctuated the rhythm of school life. For example, the first of February, St Brigid's Day, Ash Wednesday, St. Patrick's Day, Easter, Halloween and Christmas all brought their own colour and excitement. Listening to stories and legends, weaving crosses, receiving ashes, designing cards, singing hymns and other songs, participating in school plays were among the activities that for children marked these moments in the year. Christmas traditions introduced a special magic and delight and illuminated the dark days of winter (MacMahon, 1992, pp. 106–107).

Ethos also connects with the quality of concern for learners. The holism that is a feature of the ethos of a Catholic education extends beyond the cultivation of a comprehensive intellectual perspective on life. It also embraces concern for the overall welfare of pupils, although, as shall be noted later in this chapter, it is misguided to assume that this concern is the monopoly of Catholic institutions. Yet the spirit of commitment to the total welfare of pupils is striking, especially in the case of religious orders. As novelist Maeve Binchy put it: 'One thing nuns have, that other teachers do not, is their wonderful devotion to duty … . We were their life and it was that devotion to duty, I think, which made them so memorable' (Bennett and Forgan, 2003, p. 34). Germaine Greer voices a similar view: 'The nuns made sure that we were taken care of all the time. There was always somebody there' (Bennett and Forgan, 2003, p. 104). Greer considers that in convent schools 'children are looked after in a more comprehensive way' because the nuns 'have a commitment that goes beyond wages' (Bennett and Forgan, 2003, p. 105). As Sister Evelyn, principal of the Marist convent in London, writes in the volume from which all of these the quotations are taken: 'I want them to believe too, that we don't really forget them when we close the doors, we think of them' (Bennett and Forgan, 2003, p. 205).

As Catholics believe they possess the truth about human life and its purposes, this has implications for the approach to the curriculum, although this not does not mean that the approach to the transmission of knowledge is partisan and proselytizing.

THE CONTENT OF EDUCATION

Religious belief itself is, of course, rooted in a rich cultural context and the study of the great sacred texts contributes to the cultivation of general cultural literacy.

Besides alerting us to the action of God in human life, the Jewish and Christian scriptures are great repositories of the Western cultural heritage. The Old and New Testaments are part of the literary and moral capital of this heritage. But there are two other dimensions to the place of religion within a theory of Catholic education. The first is the role of religious subject matter and the second is a Catholic perspective on the general content of education.

Religious subject matter

Awareness of the religious face of knowledge is not a concern peculiar to Catholic education. The profile of religious content across the school curriculum also arises in those jurisdictions (especially in France and in the USA) that exclude religion from public education. In France, recent years have seen the Ministry of Education introduce a mandatory requirement to teach, in the sense of providing information about, religion (what they call *le fait religieux*) where it arises across the curriculum (see Williams, 2007). In the USA, the absence of religion from the curriculum of public schools gives rise to a problem from the point of view of respect for the principles governing a liberal education (see DeGirolami, 2008 and Strike, 2007). This is because serious attention to religious issues, at a very minimum in their cross-curricular manifestations, is necessary if education is to count as being liberal both in the sense of being open to different world-views and also in the sense of being genuinely comprehensive.

As religion is an integral part of culture, it can find many different forms of expression within the school curriculum (see Carr, 2007). For Bryan MacMahon, religion is a 'cultural treasure-house' and he perceives the Catholic Church 'not alone as vehicle for my faith but as a fruitful source of my culture' (MacMahon, 1992, pp. 100–101). The Christian heritage is central to so many of the achievements of Western culture. Religious faith has inspired many great works of art – of painting, sculpture, music and literature. The famous lines by Joyce Kilmer – 'I think that I shall never see/a poem lovely as a tree. Poems are made by fools like me/But only God can make a tree' express a sense of reverent wonder at the bounty of God's creation. Mary McCarthy has written of the profile of religious, indeed, theological concerns in understanding poetry. When adult readers have to study some theology in order to read the English metaphysical poets, it is 'like being taught the Bible as Great Literature in a college humanities course; it does not stick to the ribs' (McCarthy, 1967, p. 24). She claims that most American students 'have no other recourse than to take these vitamin injections to make good the cultural deficiency' (McCarthy, 1967, p. 24). The potency of a religious education is strikingly communicated in the image of 'sticking to the ribs'. By contrast, the image of taking 'vitamins injections to make good cultural deficiency' vividly conveys the consequence of excluding the study of religion from schools. Teaching young people to respond to such poems as John Milton's 'Paradise Lost', 'The Collar' by George Herbert, 'Batter my heart three-person'd God' by John Donne or 'God's Grandeur' by Gerard Manley Hopkins means teaching them to enter more deeply into both their cultural and religious heritage. Due to the significant reciprocity between general cultural literacy and religious literacy, education in religion is then a matter of general public concern rather than an issue that involves religious believers alone.

A Catholic attitude to educational content

One important characteristic of this attitude to much of the knowledge that makes up the curriculum is its non-instrumental and non-utilitarian orientation. This does not imply a denial of a connection between educational content and practical living but in the Catholic tradition knowledge is not primarily conceived as serving as a means to something else, particularly to getting on in the world. As noted earlier, religious faith is woven into the stuff of how we conceive of human life and its purposes, and so shapes significantly the culture that is incorporated into the school's curriculum. Christianity is not simply the placing of an icing of additional, religious values on a neutral cake of culture. It is not that there is a Christian mathematics, science, geography or history but rather that Christians conceive of these and of other areas of the curriculum as the response of the human mind to different aspects of God's creation. Obviously with regard to personal, social and health education and relationships and sexuality education there exists a peculiarly Christian vision of human physical, psychological and spiritual well-being that will inform the approach taken to these areas.

This vision also pervades other areas of knowledge and the curriculum. From both a secular and religious perspective, creation is quite properly a source of awe, respect and reverence. Indeed, concern with humankind's responsibility for creation and an aspiration to communicate this to the young people are shared by many irrespective of religious belief. From a Catholic point of view, science is not conceived as an instrument of control but rather as a vehicle through which young people can experience awe, reverence respect and wonder at the world. This attitude is diametrically opposed to the perception on the part of some education policy-makers of the scientific and technological domains as expressions of humankind's interest in control and mastery over the environment. Science can be conceived as a route to developing an enhanced respect for, and love of, the world *via* the promotion of receptivity and responsiveness to its physical manifestations (see Walsh, 1993, p. 103). In this perspective, Walsh quotes from Einstein:

> A finely tempered nature longs to escape from his noisy cramped surroundings into the silence of the high mountains where the eye ranges freely through the still pure air and fondly traces out the restful contours apparently built for eternity ... . The state of mind which enables a man [sic] to do work of this kind is akin to that of the religious worshipper or lover. (quoted in Walsh, 1993, p. 103)

The teaching of practical subjects can also acquire a religious dimension. This derives from the Christian understanding of human action as participation in the creative activity of God – an understanding that is rooted in the great monastic, notably Benedictine, tradition of Christendom whose monasteries have always been places of labour as well as of learning. Where the teaching of practical subjects is animated by such a view, this teaching involves *pari passu* communicating an aspect of the religious response to the world.

What is most enriching in Catholic education is the connection with a world 'beyond utility' (McCarthy, 1967, p. 26) and with a quality of life that lies beyond the mere fact of living. This is not to claim that such a respect for these educational purposes is exclusive to a Catholic philosophy but rather that in such a philosophy these purposes are seriously honoured. What might be said to characterize Catholic thinking is the promotion of attentiveness to what one is learning and also a concern that students should enter into the spirit of learning or that they should learn in the right spirit or with the right disposition. Entering into the spirit of an activity and pursuing it for morally and educationally appropriate reasons are linked. Fostering this attitude to learning is an essential feature of a Catholic philosophy of teaching.

Religious education

From the foregoing it must be clear that the Catholic dimension of teaching is not 'localised' (Davis, 1999, p. 216) in religious education. But this aspect of the curriculum is especially important. The primary purpose of religious education coincides with that of Catholic education: it is to enable young people to grow in awareness of, and sensitivity to, the transcendent action of God in their lives. The teaching of religion can accommodate the study of religious beliefs in the form of sociology of religion but this must not be confused with denominationally specific religious education of a catechetical character. There is nothing epistemically suspect about the basis for catechesis, an activity so dear to the practical and theoretical concerns of St Augustine. There are two extremes to avoid here. One is the French view that religion belongs in the world of beliefs and the rest of knowledge is securely based on facts (see Williams, 2007, pp. 685–686). The other extreme is to state that every claim to knowledge is an act of faith no different from that of the religious believer. Catholic theology is based on philosophical, historical and literary knowledge. The propositions that are central to the faith – that God exists and that there is life after death – lend themselves to philosophical enquiry. The study of the scripture, both Old and New Testaments, draws on the tools of historical and literary scholarship. The notion of serious study in pursuit of truth is very important in the Catholic tradition and both St Thomas and Cardinal Newman valued very highly the cultivation of the intellect. The emphasis on the use of reason is totally at odds with any attempt to impose the version of predatory Catholicism described by Charlotte Brontë in *The Professor*. Brontë writes of the soul becoming 'warped' and 'conjured by Romish wizard-craft' and of young people being constrained to surrender 'independence of thought and action into the hands of some despotic confessor' (Brontë, 1989, p. 131). By contrast, Catholic catechesis, which might be described as theology in a state of transmission, is rooted in reason.

Accordingly, though Catholic religious education derives from a conviction of holding the truth and wishing to communicate this to the young generation, the tradition precludes any attempt at indoctrination. There is nothing inherently indoctrinatory about direct religious education of a catechetical character and nothing illiberal in affirming the particular need for, and value of, catechesis as long as this is conducted with respect for the principles of openness. Respect for liberal principles does not preclude initiating children into a specific religion. It is hard to see how we can actually teach religion in a serious sense without such initiation, any more than we can teach sport without actually teaching children to play a specific game or activity, or teach languages without teaching a particular language. George Santayana (1954) puts this point well: 'The attempt to speak without speaking any particular language is not more hopeless than the attempt to have a religion that shall be no religion in particular' (Santayana, 1954, p. 43). It is questionable whether it is realistic to expect that a programme of religious education that is not denominationally specific can initiate young people into the lived and living experience of a religious tradition.

Religious education from a faith perspective, where conducted with tact and honesty, is also perfectly compatible with respect for diversity. Given that there exists no view from nowhere, the basis for 'genuine open and mutually respectful dialogue with other faiths' is, as David Carr argues with some metaphorical force, most appropriately 'nurtured in the soil of proper intellectual engagement with the grammar of some particular faith' (Carr, 1999b, p. 454). In any case, religious believers and secularists do well not to underestimate the robust resistance of young people to the proselytizing designs of adults. Opponents of formative education *in* religion seriously exaggerate the susceptibility of young people to indoctrination in this area. In *Portrait of the Artist as a Young Man*, James Joyce (1991) gives powerful imaginative expression to the human capacity to resist the catechetical designs of adults. Stephen Dedalus, like Joyce himself, turns away from the Catholic faith that he found in so many respects appealing and which was urged so insistently upon him.

Reflection on the education of the fictional Stephen provides an interesting insight into Catholic religious and moral pedagogy. Stephen is engaged in both an intellectual initiation into the faith as well as an initiation into a religious way of life. This process is consistent with the Catholic tradition in both religious and moral education because it affirms both the need to set down roots in religious practice as well as the need to exercise reason in the pursuit of religious truth. As Jacques Maritain has noted in respect of moral education (see Carr et al., 1995), this is less a matter of direct teaching than of 'fostering in circumstances and conditions of positive pre-rational affection' those sentiments and dispositions without which 'the explicit rules of morality cannot be expected to secure much of a hold on the human heart' (Carr et al., 1995, p. 173). The provision of moral reasons needs to be 'firmly rooted in the soil of more fundamental pre-rational bonds of positive human association' (Carr et al., 1995, p. 173). On this account, reasoning is 'integral' to, rather than 'foundational' of, the moral life. Moral well-being and the notion of justice informing the common good are 'founded less on abstract laws or principles and more in particular forms of life and sentiment in relation to which formal ethical rules are not so much constitutive as regulatory' (Carr et al., 1995, p. 175).

This account of Catholic moral pedagogy has everything to recommend it but there are aspects of the Catholic tradition that require more critical scrutiny and these are the subject of the final section.

CALLING 'THINGS BY THEIR RIGHT NAMES': TELEOLOGICAL DRIFT WITHIN THE CATHOLIC TRADITION

First it is necessary to note that Christianity, like many religions, does engender a communal identity that promotes mutual support. Christianity also imposes a commitment to assist others, especially the less well off, beyond the borders of the Christian community. For this reason it is a very potent form of civic bonding. As the tremendous work done by Church agencies in the developing world shows, the 'imagined community' in Christian thought extends beyond religious and national boundaries. There are, after all, three principal Christian virtues – faith, hope and charity – and charity is the greatest of the three. The affirmation of compassionate outreach is thus an integral part of a theory of Catholic education. Yet it is important not to overemphasize this aspect of the Catholic educational project.

In recent years some Catholic thinking about education has suffered what might be called teleological drift, i.e., a movement away from its primary purpose and a serious attenuation of this purpose in the interests of aspirational aims relating to 'social justice'. Writing about Catholic education, it is important to remember Cardinal Newman's advice to 'call things by their right names' and not to 'confuse together ideas which are essentially different' (Newman, 1901, p. 144). Commitment to the welfare of victims of poverty can turn into agenda-driven consciousness-raising. Things should be called by their right names: education is one thing and agitprop is something else. In any case, questions have to be raised about any pedagogy with proselytizing intent. Benign motives do not warrant proselytism in the classroom. Moreover, there is always a danger in this work of rationalism, that is, of proposing ideals of universal benevolence and generosity that have little purchase in daily living. It is easy to be generous with the money of other people. If advocacy of the redistribution of wealth is to go beyond aspirational rhetoric, it needs to be grounded in an understanding of how the world of economics works. Catholics who pronounce very attractive ideas about justice would need to be able to explain how these mesh with the taxation system.

This political crusading is often linked to exclusivist moral and civic claims that are sometimes made about the theory of Catholic education. Many positive values are neither peculiar to, nor the monopoly of, Catholic education. A sense that education is not merely a matter of academic success and even a concern for the disadvantaged may be part of the Catholic vision of education, but these values and commitments must not be represented as if they defined the character of Catholic educational institutions. The former conviction should be a feature of any properly educational institution and a commitment to the disadvantaged is not the monopoly of Catholic schools, some of which are indeed conspicuously elitist. Catholic theorists should ask whether there is a difference between a Catholic school and a humane, secular school deeply committed to the welfare of the pupils. One of the most passionate statements of a teacher's commitment to his pupils is to be found in Albert Camus' (1995) posthumous volume *The First Man*. This commitment is voiced both by the fictionalized teacher in this very autobiographical novel (Camus, 1995, pp. 106–137) and also by the letter from Camus' actual teacher that is included as an appendix. This teacher was as committed to his pupils as he was antipathetic to the Catholic Church.[49]

A distinction must be made between a secular view of education that is supported by a conviction that the world is material and ultimately susceptible to scientific measurement and the view that education is about the accumulation of material goods. Philosophical materialism does not commit its proponent to a crudely consumerist view of education. For this reason, crusading slogans about Catholic education as adversarial in respect of the 'consumer orientation' of education today are simply tiresome. For example, the back cover of a well-known volume on Catholic schools (McLaughlin et al., 1996) includes the following sentence: 'Whilst state schools are increasingly dominated by the values of the market place, Catholic schools appear to offer an alternative, more humane vision of schooling'. This kind of claim implies that a Catholic education has a monopoly regarding the promotion of civic and moral virtue and implies that Catholic schools alone are genuinely concerned with the welfare of others. This arrogant claim represents the kind of hubris condemned in the parable of the Pharisee and the publican. The arrogance of proponents of this view of Catholic education is little different from that authoritarian self-righteousness that informed some traditional versions of the Catholic educational mission. An account of a Catholic philosophy of education does not need moralizing indictments of a contemporary 'ethic of individual consumption' or about an 'individualist, competitive, acquisitive culture' that appear to find that the human beings have become dramatically more selfish and greedy over the generations. A reading of the gospels will show that selfishness and greed are not at all new features of human psychology.

In brief, therefore, much that is affirmed in respect of the moral and civic aims of a Catholic education is consistent with the remit of any educational institution. A theory of Catholic education, however, needs to focus on what is unique to the Catholic view of human life. Central to this view of life and of the world is a substantial conception of truth and virtue and of the purpose of life. This purpose is to participate in divine life for all eternity and this is the ultimate end of all human striving.[50]

NOTES

47 This phase comes from Mary McCarthy (1967, p. 26).

48 Here I have slightly adapted a sentence from A.N. Whitehead (1926, p. 80).

49 From a philosophical perspective, Alastair MacIntyre (2001) makes similar points about the unifying value of a Catholic religious vision.

50 This text has benefited from the observations of John Murray, Will Murphy, Caitríona Williams, Patrick Williams and, most of all, David Carr, although responsibility for any deficiencies in style or argument in the chapter is entirely my own.

FURTHER READING

The collection *Catholic Education Inside Out, Outside,* edited by James C. Conroy (1999) contains some very valuable essays as does the volume edited by McLaughlin, O'Keefe, and O'Keeffe (1996) *The Contemporary Catholic School: Context, Identity and Diversity.* Many of the Vatican documents on education are now available in a volume edited by Franchi (2007) *An Anthology of Catholic Teaching on Education.* For a single general text on the subject readers should consult *Catholic Education: Distinctive and Inclusive,* by John Sullivan (Dordrecht, Springer, 2001). The work of the late T.H. McLaughlin is an excellent source of philosophical insight on Catholic philosophy of education. One of his most searching and detailed essays on the subject is 'A catholic perspective on education' (McLaughlin, 2002) (see references above). The posthumous volume *Liberalism, Education and Schooling: Essays by T.H. McLaughlin* (Thorverton, Exeter and Charlottesville, VA: Imprint Academic, 2008), edited by David Carr, John Haldane and Richard Pring, contains some of his finest essays. One of his essays on Catholic education is reprinted but the character of a Catholic philosophy of education also arises as part of his consideration of general themes, particularly in the chapter on teacher example.

REFERENCES

Beck, George Andrew (1971) Aims in education: neo-Thomism. In T.H.B. Hollins (ed.), *Aims in Education: The Philosophic Approach.* Manchester: Manchester University Press, pp. 109–132.

Bennett, Jackie and Forgan, Rosemary (eds) (2003) *Convent Girls.* London: Virago Press.

Brontë, Charlotte (1989) *The Professor.* London: Penguin.

Camus, Albert (1995) *The First Man.* London: Hamish Hamilton.

Carr, David (1999a) Catholic faith and religious truth. In James C. Conroy (ed.), *Catholic Education Inside Out, Outside In.* Dublin: Veritas, pp. 163–187.

Carr, David (1999b) Spiritual language and the ethics of redemption: a reply to Jim Mackenzie, *Journal of Philosophy of Education* 33 (3): 415–461.

Carr, David (2007) 'Religious education, religious literacy and common schooling: a philosophy and history of skewed reflection', *Journal of Philosophy of Education* 41 (1): 659–673.

Carr, David, Haldane, John, McLaughlin, Terence and Pring, Richard (1995) Return to the crossroads: Maritain fifty years on, *British Journal of Educational Studies* 43 (2): 162–178.

Chesterton, Gilbert (2004) *What's Wrong with the World.* Kessinger Publishing (1st edn., 1910).

Davis, Robert A. (1999) Can there be a catholic curriculum? In James C. Conroy (ed.), *Catholic Education Inside Out, Outside In.* Dublin: Veritas, pp. 207–229.

DeGirolami, Marc O. (2008) The problem of religious learning. *Boston College Law Review* 49 (5): 1212–1275.

Durcan, Paul (2003) *Paul Durcan's Diary.* Dublin: New Island.

Franchi, Leonardo (ed.) (2007) *An Anthology of Catholic Teaching on Education*. London: Scepter.

Hogan, Pádraig (1995) *The Custody and Courtship of Experience: Western Philosophy in Philosophical Perspective*. Dublin: The Columba Press.

Joyce, James (1991) *Portrait of the Artist as a Young Man*. New York: Penguin Group (Signet Classic).

Le Monde des Religions (2007) Dossier: La France est-elle encore catholique? Sondage: Les catholiques à la loupe. *Le Monde des Religions* 21 (janvier/février): 23–28.

McCarthy, Mary (1967) *Memories of a Catholic Girlhood*. Harmondsworth, London: Penguin.

MacIntyre, A. C. (2001) Catholic universities: dangers, hopes, choices. In Robert E. Sullivan (ed.), *Higher Learning and Catholic Traditions*, Notre Dame, IN: Notre Dame University Press.

MacMahon, Bryan (1992) *The Master*. Dublin: Poolbeg.

McLaughlin, Terence H. (1996) The distinctiveness of catholic education. In Terence McLaughlin et al. (eds), *The Contemporary Catholic School: Context, Identity and Diversity*. London: The Falmer Press, pp. 136–154.

McLaughlin, Terence H. (2002) A catholic perspective on education, *Journal of Education and Christian Belief* 6 (2): 121–134.

McLaughlin, Terence H. (2005) The educative importance of ethos, *British Journal of Educational Studies* 53: 306–325.

McLaughlin, Terence, O'Keefe, Joseph, S.J. and O'Keeffe, Bernadette (eds) (1996) *The Contemporary Catholic School: Context, Identity and Diversity*. London: The Falmer Press.

Newman, John Henry (1901) *The Idea of a University: Defined and Illustrated*. London: Longman, Green and Co.

Pring, Richard (2007) The common school, *Journal of Philosophy of Education* 41 (4): 503–522.

Santayana, George (1954) My philosophy of religion. In D.J. Bronstein and H.M. Schulweis (eds), *Approaches to the Philosophy of Religion*. Manchester, NH: Ayer Company Publishers, pp. 41–49.

Seraphine, Connie Leean (2005) Jesus of Nazareth 4BCE–AD29. In Joy A. Palmer (ed.), *Fifty Major Thinkers on Education: From Confucius to Dewey*. London: Routledge, pp. 20–24.

Strike, Kenneth A (2007) Common schools and uncommon conversation: education, religious speech and public spaces, *Journal of Philosophy of Education* 41 (4): 693–708.

Walsh, P.D (1993) *Education and Meaning: Philosophy in Practice*. London: Cassell.

Whitehead, A.N. (1926) *Religion in the Making*. Cambridge: Cambridge University Press.

Williams, Kevin (2007) Religious worldviews and the common school: the French dilemma, *Journal of Philosophy of Education* 41 (4): 675–692.

13

Gazetteer of
Educational Thinkers

Compiled by Robert Manery

ADLER, MORTIMER (1902–2001)

An American philosopher who wrote about moral philosophy, the intellect, religion, politics, and education. Adler argued for a liberal education that fostered an individual's intellectual and moral development. His model of education called for the study of the great ideas and the great books of Western civilization.

Selected bibliography

Adler, Mortimer and Mayer, Milton (1958) *The revolution in education*. Chicago: University of Chicago Press.

Adler, Mortimer (1961) *Great ideas from the great books*. New York: Washington Square Press.

Adler, Mortimer (1977) *Reforming education: The schooling of a people and their education beyond schooling*. (Geraldine Van Doren, Ed.). Boulder, CO: Westview Press.

Adler, Mortimer (1982) *The Paideia proposal: An educational manifesto*. New York: Macmillan.

ARISTOTLE (384–322 BC)

A Greek philosopher and student of Plato. Aristotle's writings range over a diverse number of fields. The famous beginning of his *Metaphysics* – 'All men by nature desire to know' – offers a rationale for education. People naturally desire to understand their world and therefore an education should provide them with understanding. However, the *Nicomachean Ethics* suggests a further aim of education: the development of the virtuous person. In this work, Aristotle argues that the purpose of human life is 'eudaimonia' (conventionally, but not altogether happily, translated as 'happiness'), which is conceived as living the good life and involves a striving for inner excellence. Virtue, therefore, is necessary for the good life. One's education should guide a person in this striving for virtue.

Selected bibliography

Nicomachean Ethics.
Metaphysics.
Politics.

ARNOLD, MATTHEW (1822–1888)

A British poet and literary critic, as well as an Inspector of Schools for the British government from 1851 to 1886. Arnold argued for a liberal education that exposed all students to the values and qualities that culture had to offer ('the best that is thought and known'). According to Arnold, the study of culture (which included not just art and literature but also science, philosophy, history and religion) would give society a commonality of experience and lead individuals to strive towards the ideal of human perfection as represented in these works.

Selected bibliography

Arnold, Matthew (1869) *Culture and anarchy.* London: Smith, Elder and Company.
Arnold, Matthew (1973) *Matthew Arnold on education.* (Gillian Sutherland, Ed.). Harmondsworth: Penguin Education.

AUGUSTINE (354–430)

St Augustine was an early Church Father who was greatly influenced by the writings of Plato. In *De Magistro*, Augustine advanced his theory of illumination. He argued that new knowledge is a result of illumination of things our minds were created to perceive rather than a remembrance from past lives as Plato had posited. The teacher is incapable of teaching anything to another person. All the teacher can do is to place the student in a situation that will allow for illumination. According to Augustine, God is the source of all truth and the Platonic Ideal Forms are God's laws that are expressed through natural laws.

Selected bibliography

De Magistro (389).
Confessions (398).
City of God (426).

BACON, FRANCIS (1561–1626)

Philosopher and parliamentarian, Francis Bacon was a proponent of the scientific method. He sought to repudiate humanist traditions and argued for a new general theory of natural philosophy in which he advocated a unified structure to the branches of knowledge. Bacon argued that human society must be perfected through an expansion of knowledge through scientific discovery. It is through an integration of society and science rather than through the book learning of the humanists that society will progress.

Selected bibliography

Bacon, Francis (1985) *The essayes or counsels, civill and morall,* (Michael Kiernan, Ed.). Oxford: Clarendon Press.
Bacon, Francis (1994) *Novum organum; with other parts of the great instauration.* (Peter Urbach and John Gibson, Trans. and Eds.) Chicago: Open Court.
Bacon, Francis (2000) *The advancement of learning,* (Michael Kiernan, Ed.). Oxford: Clarendon Press.

BANTOCK, G.H (1914–2003)

A British 'educationalist' who preferred to style himself thus, although his work was primarily of a historical and philosophical nature. A student of F.R. Leavis, Bantock had a particular interest in the educational views of T.S. Eliot. He was a defender of the grammar school in the face of comprehensivisation, and a critic of much 'progressive' educational theory. Bantock was an advocate of the importance of the humanities in education, believing in particular that not enough emphasis was being placed on history and literature in this scientific age. He was also concerned about the poverty of modern popular culture in this industrial age, as distinct from the folk culture of earlier times.

Selected bibliography

Bantock, G.H. (1952) *Freedom and authority.* London: Faber and Faber.
Bantock, G.H. (1963) *Education in an industrial society.* London: Faber.
Bantock, G.H. (1968) *Culture, industrialization and education.* London: Routledge.
Bantock, G.H. (1980) *Studies in the history of educational theory. Volumes 1: Artifice and Nature, 1350–1765.* London: George Allen and Unwin.
Bantock, G.H. (1984) *Studies in the history of educational theory. Volume 2: The Minds and the Masses, 1760–1980.* London: George Allen and Unwin.

BARZUN, JACQUES (1907–)

An American (French born) historian of ideas and culture with an encyclopedic knowledge of crime and mystery fiction, and a passion for the music of Hector Berlioz. For many years Barzun (with Lionel Trilling) ran the Great Books course at Columbia University. An advocate of liberal education, and, while by no means disdainful of popular culture, a champion of high culture.

Selected bibliography

Barzun, Jacques (1945) *Teacher in America*. Boston: Little, Brown.
Barzun, Jacques (1959) *The house of intellect*. New York: Harper Perennial.
Barzun, Jacques (2002) *A Jacques Barzun reader: A selection from his works*. New York: Harper Collins.

BERNSTEIN, BASIL (1924–2000)

A British sociologist whose best-known, and most controversial, work involved a theory of coding systems. This theory examined linguistic practices and differentiated between elaborated codes (associated with middle class practitioners) and restricted codes (associated with lower class practitioners). According to this theory, lower class students faced barriers to scholastic success because the linguistic code employed by the educational system was the elaborated code of the middle class.

Selected bibliography

Bernstein, Basil (1971, 1973, 1975, 1990) *Class, codes and control*. 4 volumes. London: Routledge and Kegan Paul,
Bernstein, Basil (1975) *Class and pedagogies: Visible and invisible*. Paris: Organisation for Economic Cooperation and Development.
Bernstein, Basil (1996) *Pedagogy, Symbolic control, and identity: Theory, research, and critique*. London: Taylor and Francis.
Brandis, Walter and Bernstein, Basil (1974) *Selection and control: Teacher's ratings of children in the infant school*. London: Routledge and Kegan Paul.

BINET, ALFRED (1857–1911)

A French psychologist who was influential in the development of intelligence tests. He developed the concept of 'mental age' and, along with Théodore Simon, developed the Binet–Simon test to measure intelligence in children. Cognitive ability was measured in relation to chronological age to give the child's mental age.

Selected bibliography

Binet, Alfred and Simon, Théodore (1973) *The development of intelligence in children: The Binet–Simon scale*. (Elizabeth S. Kite, Trans.). New York: Arno Press.

BLOOM, BENJAMIN (1913–1999)

An educational psychologist who categorized educational objectives into what has become widely known as 'Bloom's taxonomy.' This taxonomy posited six levels, which progressed from lower-level cognitive processes to higher-level processes in the following manner: knowledge, comprehension, application, analysis, synthesis and evaluation. Bloom also developed a theory of 'mastery learning' which held that 90% of students could master basic concepts and skills if given sufficient time.

Selected bibliography

Bloom, Benjamin (1964) *Stability and change in human characteristics.* New York: John Wiley and Sons.
Bloom, Benjamin (1980) *All our children learning: A primer for parents, teachers and other educators.* New York: McGraw-Hill.
Bloom, Benjamin, et al. (1956) *Taxonomy of educational objectives: The classification of educational goals.* New York: David McKay and Co.
Bloom, Benjamin, Hastings, J.T. and Madaus, G. (1971) *Handbook on formative and summative evaluation of student learning.* New York: McGraw-Hill.

BRUNER, JEROME S. (1915–)

An American psychologist who has had considerable influence applying psychological concepts to educational practice. Bruner came to prominence in the United States for his work with the National Academy of Sciences and the National Science Foundation conference following in the wake of the educational crisis caused by the successful launch of the Sputnik satellite. Bruner and his colleagues argued that education was not simply a matter of learning facts, but in developing understandings of how the different disciplines operated. Furthermore, Bruner argued that learning should not be conceived solely as an individual activity, but that students construct knowledge as a community.

Selected bibliography

Bruner, Jerome S. (1960) *The process of education.* Cambridge, MA: Harvard University Press.
Bruner, Jerome S. (1966) *Toward a theory of instruction.* Cambridge, MA: Belknap Press of Harvard University Press.
Bruner, Jerome S. (1996) *The culture of education.* Cambridge, MA: Harvard University Press.

COMENIUS, JAN AMOS (1592–1670)

A Czech educator who advocated pansophism. He attempted to construct a universal knowledge, which comprised a synthesis of theology and philosophy. In addition to pansophism, Comenius proposed a universal education for boys and girls, rich and poor, and articulated the educational principles that children should be taught what interests them, that learning should not be coerced, and that play was an essential element of learning. He also recognized that children develop through stages and that these stages should be used as a guide to pedagogical practice.

Following these principles, Comenius pioneered the use of picture books for educational purposes with the publication of *Orbis Sensualium Pictus* (1658).

Selected bibliography

Janua linguarum reserata (The Gate of Languages Unlocked), 1631.
Didactica Magna (The Great Didactic), 1657.
Opera Didactica Omnia (Writing on All Learning), 1657.
Orbis Sensualium Pictus (The Visible World in Pictures), 1658.

DURKHEIM, ÉMILE (1858–1917)

A pioneering figure in the sociology of education. Durkheim saw education as a socializing process; education prepares the young for life in adult society. Durkheim was a proponent of a liberal humanism that advocated that the goal of education was to enable an individual to become autonomous within society while at the same time functioning within and contributing to society. Additionally, Durkheim held that moral education was of prime importance and he advanced arguments for a secular morality within education.

Selected bibliography

Durkheim, Émile (1956) *Education and sociology.* (Sherwood D. Fox, Trans.). Glencoe, IL.: Free Press.
Durkheim, Émile (1961) *Moral education: A study in the theory and application of the sociology of education.* (Everett K. Wilson and Herman Schnurer, Trans.). New York: Free Press of Glencoe.
Durkheim, Émile (1977) *The evolution of educational thought: Lectures on the formation and development of secondary education in France.* (Peter Collins, Trans.). London: Routledge and Kegan Paul.
Durkheim, Émile (1979) *Durkheim, essays on morals and education.* (W.S.F. Pickering, Ed.). (H.L. Sutcliffe, Trans.). London: Routledge and Kegan Paul.

EISNER, ELLIOT (1933–)

An American educationalist whose chief influence has been in the area of art education. Eisner argued that education must involve the development of artistic modes of thinking (imagination, intuition). Furthermore, he argued that art education must involve not only the production of art but also an understanding of aesthetic concerns, historical developments, and critical analysis. His advocacy of this form of art education led to the development of the Discipline-Based Art Education (DBAE) movement.

Selected bibliography

Eisner, Elliot (1972) *Educating artistic vision.* New York: Macmillan.
Eisner, Elliot (1982) *Cognition and curriculum: A basis for deciding what to teach.* London: Longman.
Eisner, Elliot (1985) *The educational imagination: On the design and evaluation of school programs.* New York: Macmillan.

Eisner, Elliot (1987) *The role of discipline-based art education in America's schools.* Los Angeles: The Getty Center for Education in the Arts.
Eisner, Elliot (2002) *The arts and the creation of mind.* New Haven: Yale University Press.

ERASMUS, DESIDERIUS (1466–1536)

A Dutch humanist and theologian. In his writings on education, Erasmus recognized the importance of early childhood development and the role of parents in instilling good habits in the child. He advocated 'gentle instruction' and saw the aim of education as the cultivation of wisdom, integrity, self-restraint, kindness and tolerance.

Selected bibliography

Encomium Moriae (The Praise of Folly), 1509.
De Ratione Studii (On the Right Method of Instruction), 1511.
Institutio principis Christiani (On the Education of a Christian Prince), 1515.
De Pueris Statim ac Liberaliter Instituendis, 1529.

FREIRE, PAULO (1921–1997)

A Brazilian educator who worked primarily in adult education. He argued for a transformational education and provided the foundation for the critical pedagogy movement. The aim of education is, according to Freire, the development of a consciousness, *conscientization*, about one's situation in the world in order to transform it. Freire advocated a methodology that emphasized dialogue and conceived of the teacher as a facilitator rather than as an authority transmitting knowledge. His critique of what he termed 'the banking concept of education', which involved a conception of the student as an empty vessel to be filled with the knowledge chosen by the teacher, has become a central concept in progressive education.

Selected bibliography

Freire, Paulo (1970) *Pedagogy of the oppressed.* (M.B. Ramos, Trans.). New York: Seabury Press.
Freire, Paulo (1970) *Cultural action for freedom.* Cambridge, MA: Harvard Educational Review Monograph Series, No. 1.
Freire, Paulo (1973) *Education for critical consciousness.* New York: Seabury Press.
Freire, Paulo (1985) *The politics of education: Culture, power, and liberation.* (D. Macedo, Trans.). South Hadley, Mass.: Bergin and Garvey.
Freire, Paulo (1994) *Pedagogy of hope: Reliving pedagogy of the oppressed.* (R.R. Barr, Trans.). New York: Continuum.
Freire, Paulo (1997) *Pedagogy of the heart.* (D. Macedo and A. Oliviera. Trans.). New York: Continuum.
Freire, Paulo (1998) *Teachers as cultural workers: Letters to those who dare teach.* (D. Macedo, D. Koike, and A. Oliveira. Trans.). Boulder, Colorado: Westview Press.

FREUD, SIGMUND (1856–1939)

The eminent Austrian psychologist's contributions are far too numerous to outline here. He was the founder of psychoanalysis and his theories of the unconscious had many repercussions for how children were viewed. In particular, his theories regarding the importance of childhood events in shaping an individual's personality suggested that one's early life was a critical period in a person's life and needed to handled with special care in order to minimize the potential for later disorders caused by childhood trauma.

Selected bibliography

Freud, Sigmund (1950) *The interpretation of dreams.* (A.A. Brill, Trans.). New York: Modern Library.
Freud, Sigmund (1962) *The ego and the id.* (Joan Riviere, Trans.). (James Strachey, Ed.). New York: W.W. Norton.
Freud, Sigmund (1965) *The psychopathology of everyday life.* (Alan Tyson, Trans.). (James Strachey, Ed.). New York: Norton.
Freud, Sigmund (1966) *The complete introductory lectures on psychoanalysis.* (James Strachey, Trans. and Ed.). New York: W.W. Norton.
Freud, Sigmund (1977) *Case histories I: 'Dora' and 'Little Hans.'* (Alix Strachey and James Strachey, Trans.). (James Strachey, Ed.). Harmondsworth: Penguin Books.

FROEBEL, FRIEDRICH WILHELM (1782–1852)

Froebel is often called the Father of Kindergarten. He was greatly influenced by the work of Pestalozzi. However, Froebel's thought was founded upon a conception of divine unity. According to Froebel, divine thought was expressed through God's works and actions manifest in the natural world. This divine expression was a model for human behaviour which also should express a unity of expression in concrete works. Froebel saw human development as the unfolding of each individual's creative potential in harmony with divine law. The purpose of education was to foster and support this development. To this end, Froebel developed a programme for children that was designed to allow children to gain insight into the universal unity of their world. Froebel created a series of educational materials, called gifts (fixed form toys or 'Froebel blocks') and occupations (malleable material) whose use revealed the unity of reality through what Froebel called the Forms of Beauty (creations that represent the principles of beauty such as symmetry, proportion, rhythm and balance), the Forms of Life (representations of things from a child's life), and the Forms of Knowledge (representations of mathematical concepts).

Selected bibliography

Froebel, Friedrich Wilhelm (1886) *The education of man.* (J. Jarvis, Trans.). New York: A. Lovell.
Froebel, Friedrich Wilhelm (1900) *Pedagogics of the kindergarten.* (J. Jarvis, Trans.). New York: D. Appleton.

FRYE, NORTHROP (1912–1991)

A Canadian professor of literature, author of the influential *Anatomy of Criticism*, which is seen by many as the first systematic theory of literary criticism. He argued that the study of literary criticism trained the imagination.

Selected bibliography

Frye, Northrop (1957) *The anatomy of criticism*. Princeton, NJ: Princeton University Press.
Frye, Northrop (1963) *The educated imagination*. Toronto: Canadian Broadcasting Corporation.
Frye, Northrop (1988) *On education*. Toronto: Fitzhenry and Whiteside.

GARDNER, HOWARD (1943–)

An American educationalist whose theory of multiple intelligences has been extraordinarily influential. According to this theory, people employ a variety of cognitive abilities (intelligences) to make sense of their experience. Gardner identified eight intelligences: linguistic, logical-mathematical, spatial, musical, bodily-kinesthetic, interpersonal, intrapersonal and naturalist. The educational significance of this work lies in the suggestion that people learn in different ways and that instruction should address these different intelligences.

Selected bibliography

Gardner, Howard (1985) *Frames of mind: The theory of multiple intelligences*. New York: Basic Books.
Gardner, Howard (1991) *The unschooled mind: How children think and how schools should teach*. New York: Basic Books.
Gardner, Howard (1993) *Multiple intelligences: The theory in practice*. New York: Basic Books.
Gardner, Howard (2006) *Multiple intelligences: New horizons*. New York: Basic Books.

GREENE, MAXINE (1917–)

An American philosopher of education whose work offers a critique of instrumental values in education (including those embraced in teacher education) and champions an aesthetic approach to education. She views the goals of education as the development of a critical mind aware of the events and forces shaping society in order to bring about social change. She has argued passionately for the role of literature and the arts in developing critical awareness, and in offering encounters to a range of human experiences not normally available to the individual.

Selected bibliography

Greene, Maxine (1965) *The public school and the private vision: A search for America in education and literature*. New York: Random House.

Greene, Maxine (1973) *Teacher as stranger: Educational philosophy for the modern age.* Belmont, Calif.: Wadsworth.
Greene, Maxine (1988) *The dialectic of freedom.* New York: Teachers College Press.
Greene, Maxine (1995) *Releasing the imagination: Essays on education, the arts, and social change.* San Francisco: Jossey-Bass Publishers.

HERBART, JOHANN FRIEDRICH (1776–1841)

A nineteenth century German philosopher whose influence in the realm of education was not fully felt until after his death. Herbart argued that education must be for its own sake and that the focus of education was the student's individuality. He made a distinction between individuality (a person's possible interests) and moral character, both of which were important educational concerns. Herbart advanced the idea that psychological processes of learning should inform instructional methods and he devised a theory of motivation which stated that learning should build upon an individual's interests. He also formulated a five-step method of teaching based upon the idea that new lessons should be associated with the student's prior knowledge. His ideas greatly influenced teacher training in the latter part of the nineteenth century.

Selected bibliography

Über die ästhetische Darstellung der Welt als das Hauptgeschäft der Erziehung (On the aesthetic representation of the world as the main concern of education), 1804.
Allgemeine Pädagogik aus dem Zweck der Erziehung abgeleitet (General pedagogy deduced from the aim of education), 1806.
Umriss von pädagogischen Vorlesungen (Outlines of pedagogical lectures),1835.

HIRSCH, E.D. (1928–)

An American professor of English who held the view that the author's intention must be the ultimate determinant of meaning. Hirsch believed that reading comprehension was importantly dependent on contextual knowledge, which led him to the view that it was a lack of cultural literacy rather than poor decoding skills that was the main problem in education. However, his *Dictionary of Cultural Literacy* raises the thorny question of what the criteria for selecting important cultural reference points should be.

Selected bibliography

Hirsch, E.D (1996) *The schools we need and why we don't have them.* New York: Doubleday.
Hirsch, E.D (1987) *Cultural literacy: what every American needs to know.* Boston, MA. Houghton Mifflin Company.
Hirsch, E.D., with Kett, Joseph and Trefil, James (1993) *A dictionary of cultural literacy.* Boston, MA. Houghton Mifflin Company.

HIRST, P.H. (1927–)

A British philosopher of education whose 'forms of knowledge' thesis was an influential contribution to the concept of liberal education. Hirst argued for an epistemological basis for education, arguing that distinct forms of knowledge could be identified and that an understanding of these forms was essential for education conceived as the development of the rational mind.

Selected bibliography

Hirst, P.H. (1974) *Knowledge and the curriculum: A collection of philosophical papers.* London: Routledge.

Hirst, P.H. (1974) *Moral education in a secular society.* London: Hodder and Stoughton and National Children's Home.

Hirst, P.H. (1993) Education, knowledge and practices. In Robin Barrow and Patricia White (Eds), *Beyond liberal education: Essays in honour of Paul H. Hirst.* London: Routledge, pp. 184–199.

Hirst, P.H. and Peters, R.S. (1970) *The logic of education.* London: Routledge.

ILLICH, IVAN (1926–2002)

An Austrian philosopher, historian, and social critic. He is known in educational circles primarily for his critique of the school system and his advocacy of deschooling. Illich saw educational institutions as possessing the same oppressive power structures as other institutions and called for an alternative informal, self-directed form of education.

Selected bibliography

Illich, Ivan (1971) *Deschooling society.* New York: Harper and Row.

Illich, Ivan (1973) *Tools for conviviality.* New York: Harper and Row.

ISAACS, SUSAN (1885–1948)

Susan Isaacs was a British educator who espoused a form of progressive education situated within psychoanalytic ideas. She believed that learning required freedom, but, influenced by the work of Melanie Klein, argued that children who experienced too much freedom often fell victim to guilt about their overly aggressive urges. Therefore, a balance between freedom and restrictions had to be found in order for the child to learn to express her instincts in socially acceptable ways.

Selected bibliography

Isaacs, Susan (1930) *The intellectual growth in young children.* London: Routledge.

Isaacs, Susan (1933) *Social development in young children.* London: Routledge.

Isaacs, Susan (1935) *Psychological aspects of child development.* London: Evans.
Isaacs, Susan (1948) *Childhood and after.* London: Routledge and Kegan Paul.

ISOCRATES (436–338 BC)

A Greek philosopher, not to be confused with Socrates, whose teachers included Protagoras, Gorgias, and Socrates. Isocrates was a teacher of rhetoric and oration who founded his own highly successful school in 392 BC. Education, according to Isocrates, should prepare individuals with the practical skills needed to succeed in life. In Athens, this meant learning oratorical skills in order to participate in political and economic life. However, Isocrates did not favour the approach of the Sophists, who claimed that anyone could be taught these skills. For Isocrates, there were three components necessary to their development: natural ability, practice, and training, with training being the least important. He also held that speaking well entailed being a good person, though he did not believe that morality could be taught. Only a good person could speak convincingly of the noble values that constituted great oration.

Selected bibliography

Alcidamas (against the Sophists).
Antidosis (an exchange).

JENSEN, ARTHUR (1923–)

An American professor of psychology. Jensen believed that heredity or nature, rather than nurture, was the crucial determinant in personal and intellectual development. His research led to the controversial conclusion that while the ability to perform lower-level mental exercises (what he termed Level 1 learning) is more or less equally distributed across races, the ability to perform more complex, higher-order mental operations (Level 2 learning) was to be found to a significantly high degree more often among white and Asian-Americans than among African- and Mexican-Americans.

Selected bibliography

Jensen, Arthur (1973) *Genetics and education.* New York: Harper and Row.

KANT, IMMANUEL (1724–1804)

A German philosopher whose work in metaphysics, epistemology, moral philosophy, aesthetics, philosophy of religion, and political philosophy still influences thought in these areas. Kant did not write specifically about education but his work in other areas, especially in epistemology and moral philosophy, has greatly influenced educational thought. He did also comment on education in many works. He held that the goal of education was to enable an individual to think autonomously in order to become capable of genuine moral acts: i.e., acts done from a perspective of rational awareness rather than mere habit or blind conformity. Educational instruction had the task of balancing the student's freedom with his responsibilities while fostering independent rational thought necessary for the autonomous individual.

Selected bibliography

Kritik der reinen Vernunft (Critique of Pure Reason), 1781.
Grundlegung zur Metaphysik der Sitten (Groundwork of the Metaphysics of Morals), 1785.
Kritik der praktischen Vernunft (Critique of Practical Reason), 1788.
Kritik der Urteilskraft (Critique of Judgment), 1790.

KILPATRICK, WILLIAM HEARD (1871–1965)

An American educator, and student and friend of John Dewey. Kilpatrick was also influenced by the ideas of Friedrich Froebel. Generally classified as a 'progressive' educator along with, e.g., Homer Lane and A.S. Neill, he was also a developmentalist.

Selected bibliography

Kilpatrick, William Heard (1918) The project method. *Teachers College Record* 19 (September), 319–334.
Kilpatrick, William Heard (1929) *Education for a changing civilisation.* New York: Macmillan.

KOHLBERG, LAWRENCE (1927–1987)

An American psychologist whose work applied Piagetian development theory to describe the stages of moral development in children and adults. Kohlberg's theory described six stages that progressed from a simplistic avoidance-of-punishment type of reasoning to the final complex stage where an individual reasons from moral principles. Unlike the Piagetian model, an individual does not necessarily progress through all the stages, with the final stage being attained only by relatively few. Kohlberg also developed a conception of schools as 'just communities' where students would participate in decisions about their school community, thereby gaining experience in making moral judgements about situations that arose in the school.

Selected bibliography

Kohlberg, Lawrence (1981) *Essays on moral development.* San Francisco: Harper and Row.
Kohlberg, Lawrence, Levine, Charles and Hewer, Alexandra (1981) *Moral stages: A current formulation and a response to critics.* Basel: Karger.
Power, F. Clark, Higgins, Ann and Kohlberg, Lawrence (1989) *Lawrence Kohlberg's approach to moral education.* New York: Columbia University Press.

LANE, HOMER (1875–1925)

An American educationalist whose work as Superintendent of the Little Commonwealth school community in Dorset, England helped develop his conception of a democratic education, free from coercion. He also advocated a constructivist approach to education which espoused the value of personal freedom and natural curiosity over traditional methods of instruction involving the transmission of knowledge. His work greatly influenced A.S. Neill, who founded Summerhill School.

Selected bibliography

Lane, Homer (1928) *Talks to parents and teachers.* London: Allen and Unwin, 1928.

JOHN LOCKE (1632–1704)

Locke is best known for his political theories, but he also made significant contributions to educational theory. He believed that the human mind was a *tabula rasa* or blank slate, that was susceptible to external influences. Therefore, the environment in which a child was raised was vitally important to his development in that childhood was a period of habit formation which shaped the self. Locke held that the main goals of education are moral training, followed by the learning of correct social skills, the development of wisdom, and lastly the acquisition of useful knowledge.

Selected bibliography

An Essay Concerning Human Understanding (1690).
Some Thoughts Concerning Education (1693).
Of the Conduct of the Understanding (1706).

MANNHEIM, KARL (1893–1947)

A Hungarian sociologist who was a pioneer in the sociology of knowledge. Mannheim argued that knowledge was shaped by social, cultural, and economic forces, and that an individual's knowledge depends upon his or her position within society. However, he was wary of relativism, recognizing it as self-refuting (positing a truth while at the same time denying the existence of truth). Thus, he developed an alternative concept of relationism, which held only that *some* knowledge is true only in a particular time and place.

Selected bibliography

Mannheim, Karl (1936) *Ideology and utopia: An introduction to the sociology of knowledge.* London: Kegan Paul, Trench, Trubner and Co.
Mannheim, Karl (1959) *Essays on the sociology of knowledge.* (Paul Kecskemeti, Ed.). London: Routledge and Paul.
Mannheim, Karl and Stewart, W.A.C. (1962) *An introduction to the sociology of education.* London: Routledge and Kegan Paul.

MARX, KARL (1818–1883)

Marx is best known for his writings on political theory which offered a critique of capitalist society and called for a communist revolution. His critique of capitalist society, however, holds salient implications for education. In such a society, Marx argued, people are reduced to commodities. Society values the function an individual performs and seeks to mould individuals into the roles required by the economic forces which shape society, and indeed, history. Marx decried this situation as one that limits an individual's experience and profoundly alienates him from the world, from his community, and from himself. What is required to liberate people from this oppressive situation is an education that promotes a dialectical view of history and society and thus allows for its possible transformation.

Selected bibliography

Marx, Karl (1906) *Capital: a critique of political economy.* (Samuel Moore and Edward Aveling, Trans.). (Friedrich Engels, Ed.). Chicago: Charles H. Kerr and Company.
Marx, Karl and Engels, Friedrich (1959) *Basic writings on politics and philosophy.* (Lewis S. Feuer, Ed.). Garden City, New York: Doubleday.
Marx, Karl and Engels, Friedrich (1965) *The Communist manifesto.* (Samuel Moore, Trans.). (Joseph Katz, Ed.). New York: Washington Square Press.

MEAD, GEORGE HERBERT (1863–1931)

An American sociologist. Mead was a founding member of the pragmatic school of philosophy along with Charles Peirce and William James. He argued that mind and self are developed within a social context, through the process of communication by signs. Thus, education should take place in a community setting, involving engagement with others through play, games and social rituals.

Selected bibliography

Mead, George Herbert (1934) *Mind, self and society.* Chicago: University of Chicago Press.

MILL, JOHN STUART (1806–1873)

An English philosopher who was an early advocate of utilitarianism as well as empiricism. Mill held that all knowledge must be tested against experience and denied that humans had intuitive knowledge. He also subscribed to the utilitarian dictum that the morally correct course of action pursued the greatest good for the greatest number of people. He argued for a principle of liberty that he saw as stemming from utilitarianism. People must be free to pursue their own happiness. In the realm of education, Mill called for a compulsory universal education with equal access for women. He held that religious views should not be taught in schools since the truth of religious claims cannot be empirically determined. The goal of education, according to Mill, was to train the mind for the rigorous pursuit of knowledge along empiricist lines and to impart the moral understanding that one's individual happiness is a correlative of the happiness of others.

Selected bibliography

Mill, J.S (1971) *John Stuart Mill on education.* (Francis W. Garforth, Ed.). New York: Teachers College Press, Columbia University.
Mill, J.S (2003) *Utilitarianism; and on liberty: including Mill's 'Essay on Bentham' and selections from the writings of Jeremy Bentham and John Austin,* 2nd edn. (Mary Warnock, Ed.). Oxford: Blackwell.

MILTON, JOHN (1608–1674)

The seventeenth-century British poet John Milton published a small pamphlet, *Of Education,* critiquing the medieval education system of the trivium and quadrivium and proposed a humanist curriculum that encompassed a wider ranger of subjects albeit with a concentration on literature. The purpose of this curriculum was to impart an education that would prepare a person for his role in society.

Selected bibliography

Of Education (1644).

MONTESSORI, MARIA (1870–1952)

Montessori was an Italian doctor (the first woman to graduate from medical school in Italy) who turned her thought to education after her experiences working with children in a mental asylum. Her educational thought followed in the child-centred tradition of Rousseau, Pestalozzi and Froebel. She developed the Montessori Method, which consists of designing learning activities that demonstrate different concepts. The child is free to use each activity as she wishes, but does not move to the next activity until the desired concept has been learned. The role of the teacher is one of observer and facilitator rather than instructor, though the teacher demonstrates the proper use of each activity prior to a child's engagement with it and is responsible for designing learning environments for the students.

Selected bibliography

Montessori, Maria (1964) *The Montessori method*. (Anne E. George, Trans.). New York: Schocken Books.
Montessori, Maria (1967) *The discovery of the child*. (M. Joseph Costelloe, Trans.). Notre Dame, IN: Fides Publishers.
Montessori, Maria (1967) *The absorbent mind*. (Claude A. Claremont, Trans.). New York: Holt, Rinehart and Winston.
Montessori, Maria (1969) *The secret of childhood*. (M. Joseph Costelloe, Trans.). New York: Ballantine Books.

NEILL, A.S. (1883–1973)

The British educationalist who founded Summerhill School. Neill advocated a form of education that allowed students to participate in setting school policies, and to decide if and when to participate in studies. Neill argued that providing a non-coercive environment where students could experience personal freedom took precedence over all other educational concerns.

Selected bibliography

Neill, A.S (1960) *Summerhill: a radical approach to child rearing*. New York: Hart.
Neill, A.S (1966) *Freedom-not license!* New York: Hart.

NEWMAN, JOHN HENRY (1801–1890)

A Catholic priest and educator who was a central figure of the 'Oxford Movement' which sought to re-establish the Catholic roots of the Church of England and constituted a reaction against liberalism. At this time Newman was an Anglican priest but his views became increasingly critical of Anglicanism and he became a convert to Catholicism. He went to Dublin to become rector of the Catholic University of Ireland, where he wrote *The Idea of a University*. Newman argued that the university should foster a liberal education, which emphasized a breadth of knowledge as well as depth within an individual's chosen field. He was critical of universities which emphasized their credential-granting role over their role in the production and dissemination of knowledge. However, he also felt that a liberal education did not provide an adequate moral education; therefore, the Church should have an active role in guiding the university.

Selected bibliography

Newman, John Henry (1890) *Apologia pro vita sua: Being a history of his religious opinions.* London: Longmans, Green, and Co.
Newman, John Henry (1959) *The idea of a university.* Garden City, New York: Image Books.
Newman, John Henry (1965) *On the scope and nature of university education.* London: Dent; New York: Dutton.

OAKESHOTT, MICHAEL (1901–1992)

A British philosopher and political theorist who argued against what he termed rationalism, described as the codification and organization of human practices towards a set of social goals. Oakeshott viewed rationalism as an impoverished view of humanity and instead posited an unruly multiplicity of human practices and modes of living which require constant engagement and negotiation. These practices and modes of living derive from traditional practices and tacit knowledge, and are not, therefore, merely anarchic. In terms of education, Oakeshott championed a liberal education, understood as an initiation into the intellectual and moral traditions, but in a manner of detachment that allows for an engagement with (including a rethinking of) these traditions.

Selected bibliography

Oakeshott, Michael (1933) *Experience and its modes.* Cambridge: University Press.
Oakeshott, Michael (1975) *On human conduct.* Oxford: Clarendon Press.
Oakeshott, Michael (1989) *The voice of liberal learning: Michael Oakeshott on education* (Timothy Fuller, Ed.). New Haven, CN: Yale University Press.

OWEN, ROBERT (1771–1858)

A Welsh utopian socialist who believed that education was the key to the transformation of society. He proposed a communitarian model wherein the whole community must take responsibility for the fostering of a nurturing environment for children. The goal of education was to promote an ethical system based upon communitarian ideals. Owen saw the family unit as a potential hindrance to these ideals and therefore proposed infant schools, which children would enter at the earliest possible age in order to be free of any harmful familial influence. In 1825, he established a community, New Harmony, in Indiana that was to serve as a model community that would foster widespread social reform. However, the community dissolved by 1829 due to constant quarreling among its leaders.

Selected bibliography

Owen, Robert (1963) *A new view of society and other writings*. London: J.M. Dent and Sons; New York: E.P. Dutton and Co.
Owen, Robert (1969) *Robert Owen on education: Selections*. (Harold Silver, Ed.). Cambridge: Cambridge University Press.

PESTALOZZI, JOHANN HEINRICH (1746–1827)

The Swiss educator Pestalozzi developed a theory of education from his work with orphans. He posited that the purpose of education was to develop an individual's moral character. This goal was best achieved, according to Pestalozzi, by creating an emotionally secure learning environment. He based his ideas upon what he saw as natural laws. A number of axioms were formulated based upon these natural laws. His concept of *Anschauung* expressed the foundational idea that instruction should be based upon sense-perception, intuition and concept-formation. Pestalozzian education advocates that learning should be based upon sense perceptions and should proceed from the concrete, simple and familiar towards the more complex, abstract and unfamiliar. The purpose of this instruction was to harmonize an individual's mental, physical and moral powers.

Selected bibliography

Lienhard und Gertrud (1781).
How Gertrude Teaches Her Children (1801).

PIAGET, JEAN (1896–1980)

A Swiss psychologist who studied child development. Piaget's highly influential formulation of the stages of childhood development described four stages of cognition through which a child progresses, gradually acquiring greater adeptness with abstract concepts and reasoning. This theory has had great implications for education, since it posits that children of a certain age are incapable of certain types of reasoning or of understanding certain abstract concepts.

Selected bibliography

Inhelder, Bärbel and Piaget, Jean (1958) *The growth of logical thinking from childhood to adolescence; an essay on the construction of formal operational structures*. (Anne Parsons and Stanley Milgram, Trans.). New York: Basic Books.
Inhelder, Bärbel and Piaget, Jean (1964) *Early growth of logic in the child; classification and seriation*. London: Routledge and Paul.
Piaget, Jean (1960) *The child's conception of the world*. London: Routledge and Kegan Paul.
Piaget, Jean (1965) *The moral judgement of the child*. (Marjorie Gabain, Trans.). New York: Free Press.
Piaget, Jean (1970) *Science of education and the psychology of the child*. (Derek Coltman, Trans.). New York: Orion Press.

Piaget, Jean (1973) *To understand is to invent: The future of education.* (George Roberts and Ann Roberts, Trans.). New York: Grossman Publishers.

QUINTILIAN (35–100)

A Roman rhetorician who was granted the first Chair of Rhetoric by the Emperor Vespasian. Quintilian was primarily a teacher of rhetoric and, in his *Institutio oratoria*, formulated an education system designed to educate orators. Quintilian recognized that students developed cognitive abilities in stages and thus designed his system to correspond with these stages. Until the age of 7, the student was to be taught good habits and correct speech. From 7 to 14, the student was to learn reading and languages; however, Quintilian argued that students at this age learned primarily from the senses and that instructional activities should be designed to take account of this. From the age of 14 to 17, the student was to attend grammar school where he would be instructed in Latin and Greek, music, geometry, astronomy and gymnastic. After grammar school, the student's studies would concentrate on rhetoric and the speaking skills necessary to the orator. Additionally, the student would be instructed in poetry, drama, prose, history, law and philosophy. Quintilian's conception of the educated person was that of the orator, who is characterized by his skill at speaking, his broad range of knowledge, and his good moral character.

Selected bibliography

Institutio oratoria (94).

REID, LOUIS ARNAUD (1895–1986)

A British art educator and philosopher. Reid argued that education tends to neglect the feelings and emotions, and that this could be remedied through art.

Selected bibliography

Reid, Louis Arnaud (1962) *Philosophy and education.* London: Heinemann.
Reid, Louis Arnaud (1986) *Ways of understanding and education.* London: Heinemann.

RUSSELL, BERTRAND (1872–1970)

A British philosopher whose work ranged from mathematics to logic, linguistics, political theory, history and education. In his writings on education, he argued that the first concern must be to identify the goals of education which are necessarily linked to the ends of human life. Russell maintained a positivist view that humankind required constant exposure to new ideas. Free and open inquiry was, therefore, the goal of education. He rejected traditional instructional methods as

detrimental to the fostering of open inquiry and the love of the pursuit of knowledge. Philosophy, according to Russell, might play an important role in that it
involves an imaginative engagement with the world and fosters a love of knowledge and a curiosity about the world. In 1927, Russell and his wife Dora founded
the Beacon Hill School in West Sussex. The school was run according to democratic ideals that emphasized cooperation and students' freedom.

Selected bibliography

Russell, Bertrand (1926) *On education, especially in early childhood.* London: George Allen and Unwin.
Russell, Bertrand (1932) *Education and the social order.* London: George Allen and Unwin.
Russell, Bertrand (1948) *Human knowledge: Its scope and limits.* London: George Allen and Unwin.
Russell, Bertrand (1961) *The basic writings of Bertrand Russell.* (R.E. Egner and L.E. Denonn, Eds.).
    London: George Allen and Unwin.

SCHEFFLER, ISRAEL (1923–)

An American philosopher of education. He practiced an analytic approach to the
philosophy of education and argued for the necessity of a rigorous analysis of
educational concepts. Scheffler conceived of education as a fundamentally moral
activity in that education involves changing the student's perspective, but in a way
that requires respect of the student's judgement. Education, at its core, is concerned
with rationality and reason; the teacher's role is to enable students to gain a greater
understanding of rationality and logical reasoning. Additionally, Scheffler argued
that philosophy of education should not be divorced from philosophy in general.

Selected bibliography

Scheffler, Israel (1960) *The language of education.* Springfield, Ill: Thomas.
Scheffler, Israel (1965) *Conditions of knowledge: An introduction to epistemology and education.*
    Chicago: Scott, Foresman, and Co.
Scheffler, Israel (1973) *Reason and teaching.* Indianapolis: Bobbs-Mereill.
Scheffler, Israel (1985) *Of human potential: An essay in the philosophy of education.* Boston: Routledge
    and Kegan Paul.

SKINNER, BURRHUS FREDERIC (1904–1990)

An American psychologist who pioneered research into behaviour psychology.
He developed a theory which saw all human behaviours as determined by
responses to stimuli. Behaviours could be conditioned through reinforcement
and punishment of the behaviour. In educational terms, Skinner's theory meant
that classroom behaviour could be managed through the use of reinforcement
and punishment. More significantly, Skinner suggested that operant conditioning
could effectively be utilized in teaching. He developed a theory of programmed
learning which sought to correct what he saw as the improper use of reinforcements

in the classroom. Skinner invented teaching machines that would present the material to be learned in a carefully programmed manner and which would reinforce proper responses according to the guidelines he developed in his research into reinforcement techniques.

Selected bibliography

Skinner, B.F (1948) *Walden Two*. New York: Macmillan.
Skinner, B.F (1953) *Science and human behavior*. New York: Macmillan.
Skinner, B.F (1968) *The technology of teaching*. New York: Appleton-Century-Crofts.
Skinner, B.F (1971) *Beyond freedom and dignity*. New York: Knopf.

SPENCER, HERBERT (1820–1903)

An English philosopher who embraced science and especially evolution and extended these interests into the areas of philosophy, politics, ethics, sociology and education. In his essay 'What Knowledge is of Most Worth?' Spencer forcefully answered that science provided the necessary knowledge to perform what he categorized as the necessary activities that support human life. The humanities were unnecessary and inefficient. Spencer also rejected traditional instruction in favour of a form of discovery learning. He outlined seven principles which argued that children should be induced to discover knowledge rather than be told facts, and that the interests of the child, rather than the educator's reasoning, should govern a curriculum. Additionally, lessons should proceed from the simple to the complex, the concrete to the abstract, and from the empirical to the rational. Like later advocates of child-centred learning, Spencer argued that education should encourage the process of self-development by facilitating an educational programme based upon children's interests and needs.

Selected bibliography

Spencer, Herbert (1896) *Education: intellectual, moral, and physical*. New York: D. Appleton and Company.
Spencer, Herbert (1901) *Essays: scientific, political, and speculative*. London: Williams and Norgate.
Spencer, Herbert (1928) *Essays on education etc*. London: Dent.

STEINER, RUDOLF (1861–1925)

Rudolf Steiner was the Austrian philosopher and educator who founded Anthroposophy and Waldorf education. Anthroposophy is based upon the assumption that through special training and the development of the moral imagination, intuition and technique, a person could perceive the spiritual world and explore it in a fashion similar to the scientific method's inquiry into the material world. Steiner developed Waldorf education to provide the education and training required to develop the creative and moral skills necessary to perceive the spiritual world. Waldorf education emphasizes individual freedom, creativity, and moral development. Early childhood education is focused upon sense-perception and experience. The next stage (from age 7 to 14) is focused upon the imagination and creativity. From the age of 14, education becomes focused upon abstract thinking, ethical reasoning, and the assumption of social responsibility.

Selected bibliography

Steiner, Rudolf (1972) *A modern art of education: Fourteen lectures given in Ilkley, Yorkshire, 5–17 August, 1923*. London: Rudolf Steiner Press.

Steiner, Rudolf (1973) *Theosophy; an introduction to the supersensible knowledge of the world and the destination of man*. London: Rudolf Steiner Press.

Steiner, Rudolf (1976) *Practical advice to teachers: Fourteen lectures given at the foundation of the Waldorf School, Stuttgart, from 21 August to 5 September 1919*, 2nd edn (Johanna Collis, Trans.). London: Rudolf Steiner Press.

VYGOTSKY, LEV SEMYONOVICH (1896–1934)

The Russian psychologist contributed many concepts important to developmental and cognitive psychology as well as education. Vygotsky developed a theory of cognition as developing within a historically situated culture. The development of a child is understood as the acquisition of the cognitive tools which are necessary to become functionally integrated into one's particular culture and society. Vygotsky also contributed the concept of the Zone of Proximal Development which identifies the difference between what a child can accomplish on her own and what that child can accomplish with the guidance of an adult or a more capable peer. This concept recognizes that there is a limit to the degree to which a child can perform beyond her capabilities. It also recognizes the social aspect of cognitive development since the child learns by mimicking a more accomplished practitioner. Another important Vygotskian concept is inner speech, which involves the internalization of symbols learned through social interaction. This process of internalization regulates the individual's behaviour to facilitate the individual's integration into society.

Selected bibliography

Vygotsky, Lev Semyonovich (1971) *The psychology of art*. Cambridge, MA: MT Press.

Vygotsky, Lev Semyonovich (1978) *Mind in society: the development of higher psychological processes*. (Michael Cole, et al., Ed). Cambridge, MA: Harvard University Press.

Vygotsky, Lev Semyonovich (1986) *Thought and language*. rev. edn (Alex Kozulin, Trans. and Ed). Cambridge, MA: MIT Press.

Vygotsky, Lev Semyonovich (1987) *The collected works of L.S. Vygotsky*. (Robert W. Rieber and Aaron S. Carton, Eds). (Norris Minick, Trans.). New York: Plenum Press.

WARNOCK, MARY (1924–)

British philosopher and educationalist. Mary Warnock is best known in academic circles for her work on moral philosophy and existentialism. But she has also been Headmistress of Oxford High School for Girls and Mistress of Girton College, Cambridge, Chair of national committees of inquiry (including an inquiry into Educational Special Needs), and author of various books on education. In *Schools of Thought*, she has analysed the complex relationship between political, moral and educational criteria and argues that the central question in educational theory is what the curriculum content should be.

Selected bibliography

Warnock, Mary (1960) *Ethics since 1900*. Oxford: Oxford University Press.
Warnock, Mary (1970) *Existentialism*. Oxford: Oxford University Press.
Warnock, Mary (1977) *Schools of thought*. London: Faber.

WHITEHEAD, ALFRED NORTH (1861–1947)

A British mathematician and philosopher noted for his conception of process philosophy. Process philosophy views reality as being in a constant state of change. Those things that we experience as concrete and unchanging are merely the current manifestation of the object in flux. Whitehead termed this manifestation an occasion of experience; each occasion of experience is influenced by all previous occasions and influences all future occasions. His view of metaphysics profoundly influenced his educational thought. Since all things are in a state of change, knowledge itself cannot be unchanging. However, Whitehead argued that although the universe was in a constant state of change, this process was influenced by a universal force so that change was subject to a discernible pattern. The educated person was someone who actively used her mind to grasp this pattern. Whitehead claimed that education followed a rhythm and that learners progressed through three stages of learning: the romantic stage, the stage of precision and the stage of generalization. The romantic stage involves an interest in the new, the stage of precision involves a desire for exactness and the systematization of factual knowledge, while the third stage involves the apprehension of principles.

Selected bibliography

Whitehead, Alfred North (1957) *The aims of education: and other essays*. New York: Macmillan.
Whitehead, Alfred North (1960) *Process and reality: An essay in cosmology*. New York: Harper.

WILSON, JOHN (1928–2003)

A British philosopher of education whose chief influence was in the area of moral education. Wilson argued that a clear conception of what it means to be moral was necessarily prior to any investigation into moral education.

Selected bibliography

Wilson, John (1969) *Moral education and the curriculum: A guide for teachers and research workers.* Oxford: Pergamon Press.

Wilson, John (1973) *The assessment of morality.* Windsor, England: NFER.

Wilson, John (1985) *What philosophy can do.* Basingstoke: Macmillan.

Wilson, John, Williams, Norman and Sugarman, Barry (1967) *Introduction to moral education.* Baltimore: Penguin.

Philosophy of Education and Educational Practice

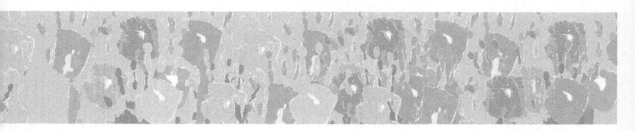

14

The Professional Status of Teaching

Timothy Reagan

The professional status of teaching is a much-debated topic. This is understandable since the extent to which classroom teachers are 'professionals' has important implications for a variety of issues, among them pay, social status, control of one's own working conditions, and so on. At the same time, though, much of the debate has been less a debate per se than a series of polemics. The problem, from a philosophical and conceptual perspective, is that we lack clarity about what it means to be a 'professional.' More than half a century ago, the American historian Carl Becker observed:

> Now, when I meet a word with which I am entirely unfamiliar, I find it a good plan to look it up in the dictionary and find out what someone thinks it means. But when I have frequently to use words with which everyone is perfectly familiar – words like 'cause' and 'liberty' and 'progress' and 'government' – when I have to use words of this sort which everyone knows perfectly well, the wise thing to do is to take a week off and think about them. (1955: 328)

This is very much the case with the terms 'professional' and 'professionalism,' especially as they apply in the educational domain. In this chapter, we will explore the notion of 'professionalism' as it relates to the occupation of teaching. The chapter is divided into four parts: the first deals with the contemporary debate and discourse about professionalism; the second with professionalism as a social construct; the third with the actual case for teacher professionalism; and the last with a discussion of alternative ways in which teacher professionalism might be usefully and productively conceptualized.

CURRENT PERSPECTIVES ON 'TEACHER PROFESSIONALISM'

The current literature that addresses issues of 'teacher professionalism' is fairly extensive, and on the surface also diverse. In actuality, though, the extent to which it is really diverse is quite debatable. Insiders (i.e., educators and their advocates) tend to assert that teachers are indeed 'professionals,' fully engaged in professional practice and entitled to the benefits that should (but generally do not, in their case) accrue to professionals (such as physicians, lawyers, architects, engineers, and so on). Outsiders have been more skeptical, in part because of honest misunderstandings of what classroom teachers really do need to know and be able to do, and in part because of all too accurate understandings of elements of teaching as an occupation, and of teacher education as occupational preparation (see Koerner, 1963; Kramer, 1991; Labaree, 2004). Underlying both sets of arguments, though, is the lack of a clear and coherent definition of what we really mean by 'professionalism.' As Tomas Englund argues, the phrase 'teaching as a profession' 'has no unequivocal meaning, and the conceptual meaning of profession is a void, being no more than a "buzzword"' (1993: 1). This lack of clarity has had significant impact on the reform of education, as Richardson and Placier have noted: 'Teacher professionalism motivated a number of recent reforms, the outcomes of which are disputable because different versions of the supposedly same reform and multiple, conflicting definitions of "professionalism" as an outcome conflict' (2001: 929).

There is, nevertheless, a body of literature that deals with questions of 'teacher professionalism' that requires examination here. What we are exploring at this point might best be termed the 'dominant discourses of teacher professionalism.' The discourses of 'teacher professionalism,' of course, are not static in nature. In fact, these discourses have evolved and developed dramatically over the past half-century, although many of the core assumptions upon which they rest have remained fairly constant, as we shall see. It is also important to note here that we are concerned principally with 'professionalism' rather than with 'professionalization': the former 'refers to the internal works of a profession and the concern of a profession's members to do the best possible job for their clients' while the latter 'refers to external criteria such as status, salary, specialization, and control' (Noddings, 2001: 102).

Initial work on the nature of 'professionalism' in general in the 1950s, largely conducted by sociologists, focused on identifying the specific criteria that might be utilized in identifying a 'profession' and, more significantly, in distinguishing 'professions' from (mere) 'occupations.' Millerson (1964), for example, suggested that the characteristics that distinguished 'professions' from other kinds of work included:

- the use of skills based on theoretical knowledge;
- education in these skills;
- examinations to ensure competence in these skills;

- a code of professional conduct oriented toward the 'public good'; and
- a (powerful) professional organization.

Such a model is very useful in explanatory and descriptive terms. It helps us to understand why medicine and law, for instance, have traditionally been considered 'professions' and why teaching has not been so considered. It is problematic, though, if used (as it has been) to try to promote 'teacher professionalism,' since it assumes that the same path must be followed to gain professional status regardless of whether that path makes particularly good sense or is particularly relevant to the occupation at hand.

This early descriptive model of 'professionalism' was not replaced, but rather supplemented, by more normative models in the 1980s and 1990s. Shulman, for instance, has suggested that there are 'six commonplaces' that are common to all professions:

- *Service to society*, implying an ethical and moral commitment to clients.
- *A body of scholarly knowledge* that forms the basis of the entitlement to practice.
- *Engagement in practical action*; hence the need to enact knowledge in practice.
- *Uncertainty* caused by the different needs of clients and the non-routine nature of problems; hence the need to develop judgment in applying knowledge.
- *The importance of experience* in developing practice; hence the need to learn by reflecting on one's practice and its outcomes.
- *The development of a professional community* that aggregates and shares knowledge and develops professional standards. (1998: 516)

This model of 'teacher professionalism' is useful in that it is inward-looking, and focuses on both the individual teacher and the members of the profession as a whole engaging in what many scholars have called critical reflective practice. The core idea here is that teaching cannot be thought of in solely technicist terms, but rather can be understood only as an intellectual – and a critical intellectual – undertaking (see Giroux, 1988).

Another useful example of this development can be seen in the US Department of Education's National Center for Education Statistics' study, *Teacher Professionalization and Teacher Commitment: A Multilevel Analysis,* in which five broad areas are used to define 'teacher professionalism':

- credentials;
- induction;
- professional development;
- authority; and
- compensation (1997: vii).

Here, we see a number of educational, political and economic factors used to determine the extent to which teaching can be reasonably considered to be a 'profession.' The criterion of 'credentials' refers not simply to the legal credentialing process in the state (although it does, of course, include that), but even more to the education of the teacher, both in terms of subject matter knowledge and with respect to pedagogical knowledge. These two aspects of the education of the classroom teacher are, in turn, supplemented by the induction process. This process is comparable to the residency and internship experiences of medical students, and includes (but is not limited to) the student teaching experience. Of late, induction in many states has gone beyond initial licensure, and includes a multi-year initial school-based induction experience. Ongoing professional development for practicing teachers ensures that professional knowledge remains up to date, and again parallels the model provided by the medical profession. The criterion of 'authority' is concerned with both the collective role of teachers in the school, district and profession, and with the individual role of the teacher, especially at the classroom and school levels. Finally, 'compensation' is concerned with ensuring that teachers are paid at a level appropriate to their preparation.

Such a view of 'teacher professionalism' is not unique to the United States; in fact, it is fairly common throughout the contemporary Anglophone world. For instance, in England the 1998 Green Paper, *Teachers: Meeting the Challenge of Change*, articulated the Government's view of what the contemporary 'teaching profession' needed in the following manner:

- to have high expectations of themselves and of all pupils;
- to accept accountability;
- to take personal and collective responsibility for improving their skills and subject knowledge;
- to seek to base decisions on evidence of what works in schools in the UK and internationally;
- to work in partnership with other staff in schools;
- to welcome the contribution that parents, business and others outside a school can make to its success; and
- to anticipate change and promote initiative.

In essence, although the earlier descriptive models of 'professionalism' have been supplemented by normative ones in the case of 'teacher professionalism' in recent years, both continue to play substantive roles in the definitions, and definitional debates, about 'teacher professionalism.'

'PROFESSIONALISM' AS A SOCIAL CONSTRUCT

A great deal of the discussion and debate about 'teacher professionalism,' as we have seen, presupposes that one can talk about 'professionalism' in a generic manner. In other words, what counts as a 'profession' (and, of course, what does *not* count as a profession) is a matter of certain criteria that are fundamentally unchanging and context-free. Such a view, while common, is nevertheless simply untrue. As Thomas Popkewitz has noted, 'The term profession is a socially constructed word which changes in relationship to the social conditions in which people use it. Further the word has no fixed definition or some universal idea irrespective of time or place' (1994: 2).

Typical discourse about 'teacher professionalism' is provided by the Holmes Group. In *Tomorrow's Teachers*, the Holmes Group asserts that, 'the established professions have, over time, developed a body of specialized knowledge, codified and transmitted through professional education and clinical practice. Their claim to professional status rests on this' (1986: 63). The problem with such a view is that it is simply ahistorical, and is based on a misunderstanding of the rise of other 'professions.' In fact, used as a noun, the term 'profession' dates back roughly to the sixteenth century and denoted those occupations of university-educated men. Indeed, we still occasionally come across the phrase 'the learned professions' in this regard.

Fundamentally, as Eliot Friedson noted in his book *Professional Powers*, professions 'addressed each other and members of the ruling elite who shared some of their knowledge and belief in its virtues. They did not address the common people or the common, specialized trades. So it is in our time' (1986: 3). When discussing 'professions' and 'professionalism,' in short, we are in fact discussing social status determined by a wide variety of factors having little if anything to do with the innate nature of the occupation. It is, of course, precisely because of this that some educators and teachers may wish to be considered to be 'professionals.'

At the same time, it should be noted that there are challenges to such conceptions of 'teacher professionalism.' In the early 1990s, for instance, the Australian Teachers Union sought to define and advocate for what they termed 'democratic professionalism':

> democratic professionalism does not seek to mystify professional work, nor to unreasonably restrict access to that work; it facilitates the participation in decision making by students, parents and others and seeks to develop a broader understanding in the community of education and how it operates. As professionals, teachers must be responsible and accountable for that which is under their control, both individually and collectively . . . (quoted in Preston, 1996: 192)

What is most interesting is this passage, it seems to me, is not what it says, but rather, how far it is from what might be considered to be the 'dominant discourses of teacher professionalism' that we discussed earlier (see also Sachs, 1999).

THE CRITERIA FOR 'TEACHER PROFESSIONALISM'

In this section of the chapter, I want to reexamine the extent to which there is really a compelling case for considering teachers as 'professionals.' As we have seen, there have been a number of different, and different kinds of, efforts to articulate what might be considered to be the sufficient conditions for an occupation to be considered a 'profession.' Although each is useful in its own context, the fact that the meaning of the term 'profession' is, as has been suggested, ultimately a socially constructed one, leaves us in a somewhat difficult position. The debate about whether teaching does or does not constitute a 'profession' is simply not resolvable on the basis of any particular empirical evidence, nor can it be settled based on any particular set of logical arguments. It is a political matter, in fact. That said, while identifying the criteria for sufficiency may not then be possible, there are nevertheless criteria that would, based on the existing literature in the field, seem to be necessary conditions with respect to the question of whether teaching, at this particular point in time and in our own particular setting, can be deemed to constitute a 'profession.' These, I think, could be safely said to include:

- a subject matter knowledge base;
- a knowledge base with respect to pedagogical knowledge;
- a practical and experiential knowledge base, grounded in classroom practice;
- both personal and collective authority with respect to issues of curriculum, assessment, and other policy and decision-making matters;
- control of entry to the profession;
- a meaningful 'career ladder' once one has been admitted to the profession;
- a code of ethics for the profession that is enforced by members of the profession; and
- a commitment to ongoing personal and professional development (see Norlander-Case et al., 1999; Reagan et al., 2000).

At this point, I want to explore these necessary conditions to see if they really do function as promised to distinguish teaching as a truly 'professional' activity.

The first criterion identified as a possible necessary condition for teaching as a 'profession' is that the teacher should have a solid subject matter knowledge base. This is probably among the least debated claims about what teachers need to know; virtually everyone appears to agree that one needs familiarity with a subject in order to teach it. And yet, this is itself problematic in the 'real world' of contemporary public schooling. The requirement in the *No Child Left Behind* legislation for 'highly qualified' teachers – a phrase defined by examination-demonstrated subject matter competence – is one, albeit problematic, manner in which such competence might be determined. The fairly common practice, in some school districts, of teachers teaching 'out of certification area' is also illustrative of this challenge. There is a further concern here, though, that is less discussed, and that is whether an undergraduate degree in a particular subject ensures sufficient subject matter knowledge for teachers. Even with the rise of subject area examinations for future teachers, this largely remains an assumption rather than a demonstrated reality. As for the case of elementary level teachers, the situation is even more problematic, given the breadth of knowledge that is required for effective classroom teaching. In short, although issues of the quality of future teacher subject area knowledge are often laid at the door of schools and colleges of education, the real problem may be in the actual liberal arts and sciences programs that students complete.

The second criterion that might be considered as a possible necessary condition for teaching to constitute a 'profession' is that of the teacher's familiarity with an identified and articulated knowledge base in terms of pedagogical knowledge. It is with this pedagogical knowledge base, and the provision of appropriate clinical opportunities, that schools and colleges of education are primarily concerned. Much has been written with respect to this pedagogical knowledge base, but it remains a controversial topic. The basic problem here is that while elements of this pedagogical knowledge base may indeed be useful, it is far from clear that they are themselves actually necessary conditions for effective teaching. Nor, in spite of our efforts to demonstrate otherwise, is it clear that *explicit* pedagogical preparation is either *necessary* for effective classroom teaching or that it actually ensures or improves student learning. While many of us have concerns about both alternative certification programs and programs such as 'Teach for America,' which place individuals who are, by traditional standards, minimally prepared in pedagogical terms, into classrooms, the outcomes of such efforts are not all that different from the outcomes of traditional teacher education programs. Some studies have suggested positive outcomes from the use of 'Teach for America' teachers (see Decker et al., 2004; Zeyu et al., 2008), while other studies have been more critical of the outcomes of such teachers (see Darling-Hammond et al., 2005). Certainly such programs do sometimes result in poor teachers being placed in classrooms – but they also sometimes result in placing good teachers in classrooms. The same is true for other approaches to preparing classroom teachers.

There is a further concern to be raised with respect to the pedagogical knowledge base, and that has to do with the extent to which much of it is really academically defensible. To be sure, much of the content taught in schools and colleges of education is immensely useful for the practitioner (see, for example, Darling-Hammond and Bransford, 2005). Lesson and unit planning, classroom management strategies, professional ethics, assessment theory and practice, the appropriate use of educational technology, meeting the needs of exceptional students, and so on, all are valuable topics to which future teachers should be exposed. At the same time, though, there is much that is taught as scientifically sound 'fact' that is simply not so. I have, for instance, argued elsewhere that much of contemporary learning theory, as taught typically in educational psychology courses, is not so much psychology as it is metaphorical discourse on learning and the learning process (see Reagan, 2006). This may seem to be a trivial semantic difference, but I do not believe it to be. There is a significant difference between a metaphor for understanding how a particular student constructs reality, and for a scientific theory about the matter. In education in general, and with respect to understanding 'learning' in particular, we are not really at the point where we have anything close to a 'scientific' model or theory to speak of. Claims to the contrary are not merely wrong-headed, but perhaps dangerous. I am thinking here of such popular fads as 'multiple intelligences' (see Gardner, 2006a, 2006b) or, even more, the discourse on 'brain-based' teaching and learning in particular (see, for instance, Jensen, 2005; Sylwester, 1995). There is no question that the study of the human brain has made phenomenal progress in the past decade, nor that we now know much more about the workings of the brain than we once did (see Solso, 1997; Carter, 1998; Obler and Gjerlow, 1999; Thagard, 2005; Purves et al., 2007). We do not, though, know yet what the practical implications of such knowledge are for the learning process, nor are we anywhere near a point at which we might be able legitimately to claim to be ready to utilize 'brain-based' teaching and learning strategies (whatever they might be) in the classroom. To suggest otherwise is to misrepresent what is known – and it is claims of this type that have historically been those which have resulted in criticisms of educators for jumping on the most recent fad to come around.

Finally, there is an additional problem with respect to pedagogical knowledge, and that is how one might go about measuring or assessing it. To be sure, there are now national and state examinations of pedagogical knowledge, but it is by no means certain that what they measure is really pedagogical knowledge at all – nor that what is measured (whatever it is) is actually related in any meaningful way to the ability to teach effectively in a classroom, let alone to actual *classroom practice*. To the extent to which this is true, such examinations really are little more than unnecessary hurdles for potential teachers, as indeed some critics have argued are schools and colleges of education themselves. As Clifford and Guthrie have noted,

> Some would say that neither university schools of education nor the public schools to which they are conceptually and historically linked have a future in the twenty-first century. First, it is argued, education schools have no *content*: the academic departments 'own' the only substantial knowledge which future teachers require. Second, education schools have no *function* except that of keeping bright people from teaching . . . (1988: 323)

In spite of the fact that this is a remarkably popular view, it is one that does not in fact seem credible in the context of 'real world' public education. Although one can indeed make a case for alternative certification programs and programs such as 'Teach for America,' even these efforts include pedagogical training, albeit less than many of us might think appropriate. The fact is that pedagogical knowledge, whatever its limits, does seem to be useful in teaching in the public schools. If one has doubts about this, consider the range of quality of instruction in universities, where one assumes that faculty members are indeed subject matter experts. Many of these experts, we all know, are at best weak teachers, and in a public school setting would be disasters. Knowing one's content, in short, really is not enough.

Related to, though distinct from, the criterion of the pedagogical knowledge base is the third criterion, that of the experiential knowledge base. This refers to the clinical components of teacher preparation, as well as to the tacit knowledge that the experienced classroom teacher possesses. It is clear that the clinical component of teacher preparation plays a crucial role in the process by which educators are prepared, and recent efforts in some states to extend the initial induction period into and even past the first year of actual teaching is an indication of how potentially effective such efforts can be. It is, perhaps, also with respect to the clinical component of teacher preparation that 'teaching as a profession' comes closest to 'medicine as a profession.' It is also important to note that, regardless of the extent to which one decides that teaching is indeed a 'profession,' the experiential and clinical component of teacher preparation plays an essential role in teacher preparation.

The fourth criterion that we have identified as a possible necessary condition for teaching to constitute a 'profession' is that of both personal and collective authority with respect to professional issues. In the case of teaching, such issues would include most notably those of curriculum and assessment. This raises some interesting questions for us, since while historically these were matters that were addressed at the classroom, school and district levels, and only to a minor degree at the state level, we are now witnessing increasing policy-making at the federal level, and at the state levels, in these areas. To a significant degree, much of the historical freedom of the teacher, especially in districts and schools identified as 'low-performing,' has been lost. We are seeing more and more examples of 'scripted instruction,' the curriculum is being increasingly narrowed, and curricular options are being eliminated. Further, in terms of assessment, we are relying increasing on state-level assessment systems that in turn drive curricular and assessment policy at the school and district levels. In short, in terms of this fourth criterion, what seems to be taking place is that we are moving away from evidence of teacher 'professionalism' rather than toward it. As Geoff Whitty has observed in the UK setting, the 'golden age' of teacher autonomy has moved to one in which teachers at best 'steer at a distance' (2006: 3–4). To some extent, of course, most if not all 'professions' in the United States are undergoing similar developments, though nowhere is the change more apparent or significant, I would suggest, than in the case of teaching.

Control of entry to the profession, the fifth criterion, is one of the criteria that has often been used historically to distinguish occupations from 'professions.' The issue here is the extent to which the 'profession' is in fact self-monitoring in terms of who is allowed entry to the profession. In the cases of law and medicine, for example, although external bodies play key roles in the process by which an individual is licensed, so too does the profession itself, both collectively and through individuals (see, for example, Ludmerer, 1985; Mallon, 2007). Although entry to the teaching profession is indeed restricted, more so now than in the past, the restrictions are not for the most part determined by the profession itself. Rather, they are legislative and regulatory restrictions, devised and monitored by state departments of education, generally with minimal input from the profession itself.

The sixth criterion that might be used in determining whether an occupation is in fact a 'profession' is the extent to which there is available, within the occupation, some sort of meaningful 'career ladder' or 'career path' for practitioners. This is an interesting criterion, since it has been much discussed in educational circles as one of the problems in the profession. Although I do not believe that the presence of such a 'career path' is a bad thing – in fact, it is a very good thing, for a variety of reasons – it is not clear that this is a component of the other 'professions' to which educators typically aspire. Although one can, in law, seek to become a partner, other than adding new specialty areas, there is really no equivalent in the practice of medicine. Pediatrics is pediatrics, and once approved to practice as a pediatrician, apart from ongoing professional development requirements (which also exist for teachers), there is really no 'career ladder' to speak of. One could, of course, become a medical administrator, but then a classroom teacher can become a principal. So, where does this leave us? It leaves us, I think, with something of a 'straw man' argument with respect to what are necessary criteria for an occupation to be considered a 'profession.' It is desirable, but not necessary.

The seventh criterion that we have identified here as a possible necessary condition for teaching to be considered a 'profession' is that of a code of ethics for the profession that is enforced by members of the profession. On the one hand, this is a relatively straightforward and easy matter. The National Education Association (NEA) has such a 'Code of Ethics of the Education Profession,' adopted by the NEA Representative Assembly in 1975 (see Strike and Soltis, 1992: xiii–xv), and many states have their own professional code of ethics for teachers as well. The problematic component of this criterion has to do with enforcement. In terms of state professional codes of ethics, it is largely the task of the state department of education to enforce the code, normally through legal and certification sanctions. The NEA's 'Code of Ethics of the Education Profession' does not have a procedure associated with enforcement, and so its force is solely rhetorical and voluntary. This is by no means unique; although there are clear sanctions involved in the practice of both law and medicine for ethical violations, there are also commonly voiced doubts about the extent to which these sanctions are actually applied to members of the profession.

The eighth and last criterion that has been suggested here is that of a commitment to ongoing professional development. Although not unique to 'professions,' such a commitment is clearly a characteristic of them, especially in contemporary settings. In the case of teachers, such professional development is largely (though not exclusively) devoted to what we have called the pedagogical knowledge base. This is interesting, because it tells us something about what practicing classroom teachers, and practicing administrators, believe to be most useful and relevant with respect to improving classroom practice. Although there may be identifiable (and even identified) gaps in teachers' subject matter knowledge, issues with respect to the involvement of teachers in policy and decision-making, ethical issues in the classroom and the school, and so on, it is primarily with the 'how' of teaching that professional development is sought and provided. Apart from anything else, this ought to raise concerns for us about claims related to the lack of usefulness of the pedagogical knowledge base. Clearly, once again, simply knowing one's subject is not enough.

ALTERNATIVE APPROACHES TO CONCEPTUALIZING TEACHING

The discussion thus far in this chapter has focused on the contemporary concept of 'profession' and the question of whether teachers can, indeed, be considered to be 'professionals.' I would like now to turn us back a bit to the related concept of 'professionalism.' It is with the notion of 'professionalism' that the normative, value-derived nature of the concept of 'profession' is perhaps most clear. We generally do not speak so much of 'professionalism' as we do of 'unprofessional-ism,' which is itself an interesting point. In other words, we utilize the concepts of 'professional' and 'professionalism' not so much to produce a positive synthe-sis of appropriate beliefs, behaviors, and dispositions, but rather to produce lists of the reverse – that is, of beliefs, behaviors and dispositions which are not acceptable for educators. What we are really concerned with here, it seems to me, is what Thomas Green once called the 'conscience of craft':

> There is such a thing as the conscience of craft. We see it whenever the expert or the novice in any craft adopts the standards of that craft as his or her own. In other words, it is displayed whenever we become judge in our own case, saying that our performance is good or bad, skillful, fitting, or the like. (1985: 4)

To talk about teaching as a 'craft' is perhaps somewhat anachronistic to the ear, but it is nevertheless a valuable and accurate perspective in many ways. More to the point, the concept of 'conscience of craft,' which the novice is expected to be in the process of acquiring and the master craftsperson is assumed to have internalized, is a very powerful one if we are concerned with defining 'teacher professionalism' – one that merits, at the very least, our serious reflection.

CONCLUDING THOUGHTS

The question of whether teaching is in fact a 'profession' has been the focus of this chapter. We have noted that the concepts of 'profession' and 'professionalism' are not static ones, but are rather socially constructed and thus changing over time. Thus, there is not, and could not be, any permanent or 'objective' list of criteria by which one could determine whether teaching is or is not a 'profession.' All the same, we can, at least in the contemporary context, make a reasonable effort to begin to ask the question, 'Should teaching in the United States today be considered to be a profession?' In order to answer this question, we have identified and examined a number of criteria that one might argue constitute necessary conditions for an occupation to constitute a 'profession' in today's world. The result of this effort is ambiguous: in some ways, teaching clearly meets reasonable standards for being considered a 'profession,' while in others it is certainly in the process of becoming a 'profession,' and in still others, it seems at present to be moving away from 'professional' status. There is really no easy answer, then, to the question of whether teaching is a 'profession.' This does not, however, mean that teachers are not obligated to behave in what would be considered a 'professional' fashion. Furthermore, we have seen that using a different set of concepts and terminology, Thomas Green has provided us with a valuable and worthwhile alternative to the discussion of 'teacher professionalism': that of 'teacher as master craftsman.' Although the language of this concept may strike some as outdated, and while it may not meet our political goals particularly well, as a description – both empirically and normatively – of teaching, it has the potential to be exceptionally powerful, both with new and with experienced teachers.

REFERENCES

Becker, Carl (1955) 'What are historical facts?', *Western Political Quarterly,* 7: 327–340.

Carter, Rita (1998) *Mapping the Mind.* Berkeley, CA: University of California Press.

Clifford, Geraldine and Guthrie, James (1988) *Ed School: A Brief for Professional Education.* Chicago: University of Chicago Press.

Darling-Hammond, Linda and Bransford, John (Eds) (2005) *Preparing Teachers for a Changing World: What Teachers Should Learn and Be Able to Do.* San Francisco: Jossey-Bass.

Darling-Hammond, Linda, Holtzman, Deborah, Gatlin, Su Jin and Vasquez Helig, Julian (2005) *Does Teacher Preparation Matter? Evidence about Teacher Certification, Teach for America, and Teacher Effectiveness.* Stanford, CA: Stanford University. Downloadable at: http://www.srnleawds.org/data/pdfs/certification.pdf.

Decker, Paul, Mayer, Daniel and Glazerman, Steven (2004) *The Effects of Teach for America on Students: Findings from a National Evaluation.* Princeton, NJ: Mathematica Policy Research. Downloadable at: http://www.mathematica-mpr.com/publications/PDFs/teach.pdf.

Department for Education and Skills (1998) *Teachers: Meeting the Challenge of Change.* (Green Paper.). London: Author.

Englund, Tomas (1993) 'Are professional teachers a good thing?', paper presented at the Professional Actions and Cultures of Teaching Conference, London, Ontario.

Friedson, Eliot (1986) *Professional Powers: A Study of the Institutionalization of Formal Knowledge.* Chicago: University of Chicago Press.

Gardner, Howard (2006a) *Five Minds for the Future.* Cambridge, MA: Harvard Business School Publishing.

Gardner, Howard (2006b). *Multiple Intelligences: New Horizons in Theory and Practice.* New York: Basic Books.

Giroux, Henry (1988) *Teachers as Intellectuals: Toward a Critical Pedagogy of Learning.* Westport, CT: Greenwood.

Green, Thomas (1985) 'The formation of conscience in an age of technology', *American Journal of Education,* 94(1): 1–32.

Holmes Group (1986) *Tomorrow's Teachers: A Report of the Holmes Group.* East Lansing, MI: Author.

Jensen, Eric (2005) *Teaching with the Brain in Mind,* rev. 2nd edn. Alexandria, VA: Association for Supervision and Curriculum Development.

Koerner, James (1963) *The Miseducation of American Teachers.* Baltimore: Penguin Books.

Kramer, Rita (1991) *Ed School Follies: The Miseducation of America's Teachers.* New York: Simon and Schuster.

Labaree, David (2004) *The Trouble with Ed Schools.* New Haven: Yale University Press.

Ludmerer, Kenneth (1985) *Learning to Heal: The Development of American Medical Education.* New York: Basic Books.

Mallon, William (2007) 'Medical school expansion: Déjà vu all over again?', *Academic Medicine,* 82(12): 1121–1125.

Millerson, G. (1964) *The Qualifying Association.* London: Routledge and Kegan Paul.

National Center for Education Statistics (1997) *Teacher Professionalization and Teacher Commitment: A Multilevel Analysis.* Washington, DC: US Department of Education, Office of Educational Research and Improvement.

Noddings, Nel (2001) 'The caring teacher', in Virginia Richardson (ed.), *Handbook of Research on Teaching*, 4th edn. Washington, DC: American Educational Research Association, pp. 99–105.

Norlander-Case, Kay, Reagan, Timothy and Case, Charles (1999) *The Professional Teacher: The Preparation and Nurturance of the Reflective Practitioner.* San Francisco: Jossey-Bass.

Obler, Loraine, and Gjerlow, Kris (1999) *Language and the Brain.* Cambridge: Cambridge University Press.

Popkewitz, Thomas (1994) 'Professionalization in teaching and teacher education: Some notes on its history, ideology and potential', *Teaching and Education,* 10: 1–14.

Preston, B (1996) 'Award restructuring: A catalyst in the evolution of teacher Professionalism', in T. Seddon (ed.), *Pay, Professionalism and Politics.* Melbourne: Australian Council for Educational Research.

Purves, Dale, Augustine, George, Fitzpatrick, David, et al. (eds) (2007) *Neuroscience,* rev. 2nd edn. Sunderland, MA: Sinauer Associates.

Reagan, Timothy (2006) 'Learning theories as metaphorical discouse: Reflections on second language learning and constructivist epistemology', *Semiotica,* 161: 291–308.

Reagan, Timothy, Case, Charles and Brubacher, John (2000) *Becoming a Reflective Educator: How to Build a Culture of Inquiry in the Schools,* 2nd edn. Thousand Oaks, CA: Corwin Press.

Richardson, Virginia and Placier, Peggy (2001) 'Teacher change', in Virginia Richardson (ed.), *Handbook of Research on Teaching*, 4th edn. Washington, DC: American Educational Research Association, pp. 905–947.

Sachs, Judyth (1999) 'Teacher professional identity: Competing discourses, competing Identities', paper presented at the Australian Association of Research in Education Conference, Melbourne.

Shulman, Lee (1998) 'Theory, practice, and the education of professionals', *The Elementary School Journal,* 98 (5): 511–526.

Solso, Robert (ed.) (1997) *Mind and Brain Sciences in the 21st Century.* Cambridge, MA: MIT Press.

Strike, Kenneth and Soltis, Jonas (1992) *The Ethics of Teaching,* 2nd edn. New York: Teachers College Press.

Sylwester, R. (1995) *A Celebration of Neurons: An Educator's Guide to the Human Brain.* Alexandria, VA: Association for Supervision and Curriculum Development.

Thagard, Paul (2005) *Mind: An Introduction to Cognitive Science.* Cambridge, MA: MIT Press.

Whitty, Geoff (2006) 'Teacher Professionalism in a New Era', paper presented at the First General Teaching Council for Northern Ireland Annual Lecture.

Zeyu Xu, Hannaway, Jane and Taylor, Colin (2008) *Making a Difference? The Effect of Teach for America on Student Performance in High School.* Working Paper 17.

The Urban Institute, Center for Analysis of Longitudinal Data in Educational Research. Downloadable at: http://www.urban.org/url.cfm?ID=411642.

15

Teaching and Pedagogy

David T. Hansen and
Megan J. Laverty

It is no light task to educate our children aright. (Erasmus)

APPROACHES TO TEACHING

To teach is to be a felt presence as well as reverberating influence in the life of another person. Teaching occurs in countless settings: a parent helping a child learn to ride a bicycle; a news writer penning an editorial; a president speaking to his or her fellow citizens; a dance instructor choreographing a student's steps; or a friend showing another how to fish. In some circumstances people acquire knowledge without the benefit of explicit or intentional teaching; consider how people learn their native language or how to respond to a death in the family. Nonetheless, the activities of teaching – explaining, demonstrating, correcting, and the like – saturate human life. It is possible to work towards an understanding of teaching by examining a broad tableau of human affairs and distilling out their shared educational elements.

A more direct approach is to address the work of people explicitly recognized as teachers. One can ponder historical exemplars such as the Buddha, Christ, Confucius, and Socrates, as well as fictional teachers such as Dumbledore in the *Harry Potter* series and Lucy Winter in May Sarton's *The Small Room*. The lesson from these figures is that to be able to teach is one of humanity's highest ideals. The teacher is someone who strives for wisdom. What the teacher learns through such striving extends beyond the living of her or his own life to the counsel of other people. It may be difficult to reconcile these exemplars with what passes for teaching in familiar, everyday experience: offering swimming lessons, instruction on how to use a computer, or training in a scientific laboratory. As Erasmus remarks, 'It is easier to outline the ideal schoolmaster than to find him in reality' (Erasmus, 1964: 209). However, historical exemplars merit a place in the study of teaching. In metaphorical terms they embody the ideals educators aspire to fulfill. They provide enduring images of both the value and difficulty of teaching.

Most people called teachers work in institutions organized for the education of children, adolescents, and adults. Each year the teacher welcomes new students into his or her classroom. Martin Buber (2002) remarks that 'year by year the world, such as it is, is sent in the form of a school class to meet him [the teacher] on his life's way as his destiny; and in this destiny lies the very meaning of his life's work' (2002: 134). It is in the context of his or her life's work that the teacher assumes responsibility for deciding upon curriculum and scheduling, attending meetings, arranging the classroom, instructing students, identifying different learning styles and difficulties, monitoring social interactions, and offering students opportunities for leadership and service. Consequently, to become a teacher is to choose to participate in a particular constellation of social settings, interactions, and concerns which will dominate one's pedagogical life for as long as it endures.

Teaching in formal institutions constitutes a job or occupation which individuals discharge in a professional capacity. But the work is also formative: teachers undergo a process of becoming. Put another way, a person chooses to become a teacher but does not choose whether to be influenced by the experience of teaching. For better or for worse, that influence is as certain as the rising sun. Concerted and ongoing engagement in the activities of teaching shapes the human being in the role.

Educational researchers deploy analytical tools from the social sciences in order to study and, they hope, improve teaching (including the pedagogy of teacher education). A large industry has grown up around the observation and evaluation of teachers. It approaches teaching as an empirically observable set of actions that teachers undertake in order to educate students. Scholars examine these actions to identify associations (and, ideally, causal connections) between particular instructional acts and student learning. In some cases educational researchers treat teachers as beings who, like themselves, both shape and are shaped by what they do. They attend to the persons in the role of teacher. In other cases researchers concern themselves with acts and activities. They are concerned with the role and its possible effects rather than with persons and their experience.

Philosophers of education also examine teaching. Like their colleagues in the social sciences, they hope that their efforts will make a difference. The difference may be in improving the work. Alternatively, it may reside in better elucidating the nature and purposes of teaching, or in better supporting the hopes of teachers, or in transforming how people conceive the work. Philosophers of education articulate and criticize conceptions of teaching. These conceptions vary widely: some are descriptive and taxonomic, others are normative. The conceptions emanate from society, from field-based and quantitative research, and from fellow philosophers of education. Some philosophers of education derive their concept of teaching from conceptions of knowing or acting. Others borrow theories from fields like art and politics to elucidate the nature of teaching and its existential import. Here again a veritable industry has emerged. Scholars look at teaching through the lens of numerous fields and aspects of philosophy – including aesthetics, critical theory, dialogue, ethics, existentialism, feminism, hermeneutics, and phenomenology, to name only a few.

These scholars aspire to do justice to teaching's uniqueness as a human undertaking. They take seriously its ever-present difficulties as well as its unfathomable promise, even as they acknowledge the ordinary, everyday aspects of the work. Scholars have sought to identify and articulate teaching's paradoxical dimensions. For example, teachers are authorities and yet they strive, at their best, to fuel student freedom and autonomy. Teaching often leads to frustration, failure, and disappointment, and yet those very experiences can trigger moments of delight, beauty, and joy. Teaching in a serious vein forces the teacher to confront her or his limitations – but therein resides the possibility for improvement and fulfillment. Philosophical inquiries create a portrait of teaching's complexity and significance. They also point to moments of mystery and ineffability in the work, with regards to how human influence 'happens,' that may be as old as teaching itself.

Our purpose in this chapter is to characterize some central questions and concerns about teaching that scholarship has raised. We organize such questions and concerns under the following two headings:

1   Humanization, or how philosophical research can illuminate teaching's formative human role.
2   Teacher growth, or how philosophical analysis can show why teaching involves a continual process of learning and renewal.

HUMANIZATION

Human life would be static if not desiccated without teachers. It would carry on, no doubt, just as it did for millennia before the emergence of culture and civilization. If the latter terms mean anything beyond honorifics, they signal the value of movement, growth, and cultivation. They disclose the meaning of ascension: to become educated is to rise to meet the challenges of life and to realize one's capacities as fully as possible. Education is not pulling oneself up by the bootstraps, although it does include, at various junctures, a self-generative gesture.

Education entails taking the hand of more experienced persons willing to assist one to take the next step up. It also means taking in hand books, art objects, scientific equipment, and other materials that can bring individuals into human culture and position them to contribute to it.

Teachers' hands can also help people persevere under the pressure of difficult if not unjust conditions. Consider those who taught newly freed slaves in the American South how to read, write, numerate, and more. Though their efforts may seem puny in comparison with the forces of post-Civil War oppression, they were vital in cultivating a commitment to education that outlasted those forces and that flourishes today. Consider life in Nazi concentration camps and in Soviet gulags, and in less harrowing if also unjust situations such as the internment camps set up by Britain for Afrikaaner families during the Boer War and by the United States for Japanese-Americans during World War II. People under these terrible and often horrifying conditions continued to teach one another everything from writing to music to philosophy. The mere act of teaching signifies that 'meaninglessness, however hard pressed you are by it, cannot be the real truth' (Buber, 2002: 116). Many individuals and organizations today focus on the vital role of teachers in war-torn, strife-ridden regions of the world even as other organizations attend to economic and political concerns. Teaching can be a humanizing force that works against the most formidable powers of dehumanization.

Teachers humanize by cultivating students' humanity: their capacities to think, feel, communicate, explore, analyze, manipulate objects, and the like. They also humanize by contributing to their students' humanity. They bring to their lives not only what they know but also their ways of holding and making use of that knowledge. In short, to teach is to give, but it is also to criticize and challenge. Experienced teachers know that real learning often entails tension, anxiety, moments of uncertainty, and the disconfirmation of expectations. They know that what succeeds with a particular student, in a particular situation, may fail in a different context. The art of teaching is understanding how and when to make use of the science of teaching. 'What works' – that is, what research indicates is efficacious in practice – is never self-justifying in education.

That we enlist a conception of humanization to describe teaching should not be interpreted to mean that we have a notion of the human that we attribute to teaching. Quite the contrary. Our point is that it is always possible to learn about what it means to be human from teaching and teachers. Although we all have aspirations, teaching reveals the contours – the character, quality, and direction – of our next step up. It helps show the way. Teachers assist students in discovering the true object of their desire: they help students perceive and realize what they want to become.

Nor do we intend to imply that students arrive at the door of the school as beings less than or not quite human. To become human is not a matter of undergoing a probationary period, despite the bureaucratic imperatives of institutions that can make people feel that way. As John Dewey posed the issue, all humans – young and old alike – reside on the same plane with respect to growth.

The differences between them are matters of degree rather than of kind. Just as the child has much to learn to be able to function as an adult, so the adult has much to learn to retain the sensitivity and freshness of the child (Dewey, 1985: 48, 55).

An important asymmetry abides at the heart of teaching. Teachers assume responsibility for creating, directing, and coordinating educative influences that occur more naturally elsewhere in human community and life. Moreover, as suggested above, students look to teachers to fulfill the promise of their station by satisfying their expectations for guidance, insight, and inspiration. This expectation is particularly clear in the case of the very young, but it is also present (albeit less overt and more discriminating) in adolescents. Memoirs are filled with descriptions of memorable teachers who, in making a difference, made 'all the difference.'

Memorable teachers humanize by revealing to students the unfathomable capacity and creativity of people. They show students how meaningful human life can be if a person inhabits it as fully as he or she can. They respond to a call to try to exemplify humanity – to try to represent what is best about people. In so doing, memorable teachers dignify themselves and students. They convey worth not as a variable price but as an intrinsic, priceless condition. They do not call attention to themselves but to life itself, to the powers of mind, heart, and spirit. To borrow a trope from Simone Weil (1970: 147), to understand the humanizing influence of a memorable teacher entails looking not at the torch itself but at what the torch illuminates. Many young men and women doubtless aspire to teach in order to be memorable to at least a few of their students, just as they themselves had memorable teachers.

Teaching humanizes because it brings people together to share new ideas, events, texts, activities, and relationships. Teaching helps generate formative experience, such as the absorption of new knowledge, the development of deeper powers of thought and analysis, and the enrichment of capacities to perceive and appreciate. The experience humanizes because it also helps strengthen a sense of reality. Iris Murdoch (1970) illuminates the values in cultivating this sense (for background discussion see Laverty):

> If I am learning, for instance, Russian, I am confronted by an authoritative structure which commands my respect. The task is difficult and the goal is distant and perhaps never entirely attainable. My work is a progressive revelation of something which exists independently of me. Attention is rewarded by knowledge of reality. Love of Russian leads me away from myself towards something alien to me, something which my consciousness cannot take over, swallow up, deny or make unreal. The honesty and humility required of the student – not to pretend to know what one does not know – is the preparation for the honesty and humility of the scholar who does not even feel tempted to suppress the fact which damns his theory. (2007: 89)

This honesty and humility mirrors that of the parent, the policewoman, the lawyer, the politician, the grocer, the mailman, indeed of every person as they recognize the reality of facts (like Russian grammar) and of other people.

Teaching humanizes by cultivating the capacities of attentiveness and responsiveness to reality. This truth is the teacher's own trajectory, too. Teaching humanizes teachers to the extent that they open themselves to its own humanizing impulses. This openness is not simple or straightforward to maintain. It entails continuous teacher education, which is the topic of the next section.

THE TEACHER'S ONGOING EDUCATION

The importance of teaching combined with its demanding complexity has given rise to numerous conceptions of the work. Today's would-be teachers encounter theories such as constructivist, culturally responsive, democratic, and experiential pedagogy in their preparation programs. Such theories are sometimes linked to broad conceptions of education: civic, liberal, moral, multicultural, and others. Part of becoming a successful teacher, it seems, is learning how to hold these various conceptions in judicious ways – rather than being held by them.

We pose the matter this way because philosophers of education, as a community of inquiry, have made clear the incompleteness of every conception of teaching on the table today. Each defensible conception can be said to emphasize a particular aspect of the educational process: intellectual, moral, aesthetic, cultural or political. Alone, none of them encapsulates the whole of teaching and learning. The scholarly community's philosophical critique of educational theory complements the community of teachers' practical critique. New teachers who yearn to do the right thing quickly grasp the truth in Tzvetan Todorov's remark (1996: 161) that while theory is valuable for the study of social reality it can never take the place of that reality. When the teacher faces a student, she or he faces a distinctive individual, not a shifting intersection point of various theoretical and taxonomic categories. Those categories may derive from studies of subject matter or of social justice. They may reflect theories of human and societal development. Even if it were possible to fuse the best of all these theories into a coherent outlook, the resulting amalgam could never substitute for the teacher's living, responsive judgment.

Good teachers enlist many models and conceptions of teaching in order to perform the work effectively. John Dewey and Paulo Freire notwithstanding, sometimes teachers do seek to 'fill' the student with knowledge. At certain moments such cramming is invaluable in order to ascend to another plane of learning. At other moments teachers facilitate intellectual and emotional movement in order to encourage students to take the lead in determining what to study. There are moments when teachers choose to confront their students about such negative attitudes as laziness and disregard, gambling that the conflict will lead to greater student resolve and improved teacher–student relations. At still other moments teachers strive to care: to comfort, to calm, to encourage, to support, and to console.

A unifying aspect of these otherwise disparate postures is that they reveal how learning transmutes character. The teacher who steadily learns from and about the work becomes, in time, a learnèd being. As such, the teacher demonstrates through his or her presence the meaning and possibilities of education. The teacher shows why being educated encompasses more than the recitation of facts, the acquisition of knowledge, and the utilization of skills, indispensable as all of those aspects may be. Rather, to be educated, to be learnèd, means to take an interest 'in learning from all the contacts of life' and to welcome the resulting need for 'continuous readjustment' (Dewey, 1985: 370). The teacher exemplifies such an interest by learning from students' words and deeds how best to educate them. The teacher learns from mundane (to an outsider) classroom incidents as well as from more dramatic interactions, difficulties, and successes. As a human being the teacher reverberates with a commitment to meaning-making and thereby exercises a centrifugal force upon students, drawing them into richer and richer possibilities.

To learn 'steadily' gives rise to a concept that will frame the remainder of this chapter. That concept is steadfastness, and it includes a range of sub-concepts such as maturity, humility, fidelity, and naiveté. Like all taxonomic strategies ours does not provide a 'final' rendering or model of teaching. We think the concept steadfastness mirrors much though not all that philosophers of education have argued about the work. The concept also points to additional questions and topics worthy of further examination. Finally, it represents an attempt to sustain such inquiry. To recall an image sketched previously, the concept may assist scholars and teachers to find efficacious ways of holding theories and possible explanations of teaching rather than being held by them.

PEDAGOGICAL STEADFASTNESS

When is teaching? The question highlights how difficult it can be to *perceive* teaching. Does teaching happen whenever the teacher addresses students, or only when he or she says particular things in particular ways? Does it happen only when the teacher is face-to-face with students, or can it be 'preactive' (Jackson, 1968) – that is, does teaching also encompass the teacher's preparations undertaken at home or in the morning before school begins? Does teaching only happen when learning takes place? Or does teaching include the countless undertakings, both planned and spontaneous, that may lead up to or facilitate learning?

Posing such questions yields the following conclusion: teachers are wise to act as if all that they do with regards to students, subject matter, setting, and the like can become a part of teaching. To cultivate this orientation requires steadfastness – a steady, ever-deepening, ever-widening way of looking, thinking, contemplating, and deciding. The quality of steadfastness has not received much attention in the philosophical and educational literature and it is rarely mentioned as a virtue. Perhaps this is because steadfastness is often associated with the military image of soldiers who stand firm and do not give ground in battle. They overcome their fear and endure often terrible trials so that they may achieve their goal.

Teaching is not war, even if embattled educators may sometimes feel like warriors struggling against societal indifference, or even hostility, toward their profession. Nevertheless, it is worthwhile reflecting on the image of the soldier. Together, soldiers share the burden of protecting a nation's interests. Soldiers contract to act on behalf of their nation, irrespective of who they must coordinate with, and ignorant of what this will entail. Honoring the commitment to serve one's nation requires soldiers to follow orders (even disagreeable ones) and occasionally risk punishment by challenging senior officers. It is similarly the case with teaching. Together, teachers share the burden of educating a community's youth. Teachers take responsibility for educating young people without being fully aware of who they will work with and what their work will involve. Teachers cannot know in advance how subjects will be added or dropped to school curriculum; how teaching technologies will change; what new educational policies will be implemented regarding matters of assessment; and how children will change. Yet, to teach is to remain steadfastly committed to both teaching and the community whom one teaches for.

This condition is not insignificant because it presents its own unique set of challenges. Sometimes, it requires teachers to survive a period of misguided administration by finding ways to 'soften' educational policy. Sometimes, it means working with school leaders, board members, and colleagues who hold differing views of education. At other times it involves retraining and professional development. Sometimes a teacher will conform and at other times feel compelled to speak out. While the teacher sets and accomplishes numerous goals for herself, relative to her changing situation, like the soldier her ultimate goal is bestowed on her by the community in which she serves. Unlike the soldier, however, she honors the community even as she seeks to enlighten it about the substance of education and what is best for its young people.

Within the classroom, teaching necessitates the quality of steadfastness. Teachers must stand firm in their commitment to educate each child who enters their sphere of influence, even though each day is an unknown quantity and there are many hurdles and disappointments to overcome. Steadfast teachers resist the temptation to abuse their position of authority and power in the classroom. They try not to succumb to their own insecurities; they try not to favor some students over others; and they try to fairly assess each student's strengths and weaknesses. Steadfast teachers deploy the authority and power in the role to promote values such as learning and goodness. They encourage students to talk about the meaning of what they are doing and to listen to one another. They provide students opportunities to work cooperatively and to avoid mocking, striking or stealing from one another. They conduct themselves as principled authorities even if they sometimes fall short (as do all persons) of the principles of justice.

This posture of steadfastness does not mean teachers must be dogmatic, inflexible or unyielding. On the contrary, their steadfastness enables them to be adaptive, experimental, and inventive. They are like the reed that sways in the wind, altering its direction with that of the wind and dipping deeply or shallowly in response to change, meantime all the while remaining rooted in the soil. The term 'steadfast' derives from the Old English *stedefæst* which combines *stede* (fixed) and *fæst* (fast). Steadfastness denotes constancy and resoluteness. Through thought, deliberation, careful study, and consultation with trusted colleagues and significant others, the teacher learns to bounce back from the regrets and failures endemic to the work.

Steadfastness is not blind doggedness. It does not shield the teacher from the unpredictability, ever-varying intensity, and shifting emotions in the educational process. 'Reality, from moment to moment, is always new; and this complete, this perennial newness, is the world' (Comte-Sponville, 2001: 7). Change is the one constant to the practice of teaching: changing subject matter, changing classroom dynamics, and changes within teachers and students themselves. The teacher remains steadfast not toward students per se but toward the endeavor of *educating* each student as best as time, resources, and circumstances permit. It is this educational promise that brings teacher and student together in the first place. The teacher retains a steady gaze on the educational project despite endless distractions, which range from the temptation to cynicism and jadedness in the face of societal obstacles to education, to taking the easy way out when confronted with the challenging aspects of the work.

Pedagogical steadfastness does not emerge de novo. No teacher 'decides' to be steadfast, nor determines its contours unilaterally. The way that teachers come into an understanding of the work is similar to the way that people come into an understanding of love, parenting, and friendship. While such phenomena are universal, each person's experience and understanding of them is individualized. People learn the meaning and reality of these concepts – teaching, love, parenting, and friendship – within the particularities of their personal histories and relationships. An individual's thinking about teaching is informed by his or her life experiences, which include those in the classroom. At the same time, his or her experience of teaching is informed by how he or she understands it. While educators may initially derive their understanding of teaching from cultural and discursive cues, they develop it in the context of their own life-worlds with their distinctive forms, undertakings, and contingencies.

The circularity here is inescapable but not vicious. A dynamic understanding of teaching does not require teachers to try to escape it. Teaching is a concept that is 'infinitely to be learned' and that constitutes an 'ideal end-point' (Murdoch, 1970: 29). As such it marks a place where no teacher ever arrives but toward which they can steadily move. A teacher sometimes finds that the question of what to do in the here and now involves not just a consideration of 'what works' but of 'who' he or she has become as a teacher. New realizations about student learning, about the depths of subject matter, about the complexities of assessment, and the like, can lead teachers to reconstruct their outlooks toward the work as a whole rather than merely toward a single dimension of it. The teacher who is alert to the vicissitudes of educational work, and steadfast in engaging them, time and again finds her- or himself abandoning previous understandings and assumptions. The teacher takes on new theories, strategies, maxims, and precepts.

Thus, teaching is an activity that can be continuously refined and perfected. As Epictetus counseled two thousand years ago, 'You, even if you are not yet Socrates, ought to live as someone wanting to be Socrates' (1983: 29, #51). The endless perfectibility of teaching is a necessary and not contingent feature of the work. To teach is to be always underway in learning how to become a better teacher. 'To try to get it right means one has not yet, after all, gotten it right' (Hansen, 2001: 189). The process is not straightforward or linear. It is recursive, circular, and multi-directional. It involves making new discoveries, returning to insights previously overlooked, and renewing old commitments. It requires that teachers trust that they can become better teachers by teaching. In Dorothy Emmet's words, teaching is 'a venture reinforced through following it rather than one whose correctness can be demonstrated at the start' (1979: 141).

Teachers often have to operate on the basis of faith, understood as persevering without evidence that it is worthwhile to do so. For long periods of time it may seem that students are not learning, that the teacher's pedagogy is inadequate, and that the defeats are greater than the gains. And yet, serious-minded teachers persist. They do not turn to counterfeits of teaching: indoctrination, sophistry, propaganda, or self-indulgence. Rather, their experience teaches them that patience, flexibility, self-criticism, and discipline constitute pedagogical steadfastness. Throughout this ever-evolving process, an abiding faith in the value of steadfastness remains an underlying condition of their work. Teachers who regulate their conduct in the light of such faith improve and become better as educators. They learn to weather periods of uncertainty, ambiguity, confusion, and doubt, and to stay the course.

These facts help account for why experienced educators distinguish between mature and novice teachers. The concept maturity connotes a developmental and normative process. When one thinks of fruit, one imagines increasing fullness, richness, and ripeness. Those outcomes are natural and they are also esteemed, prized, and preferred. They are better than their alternatives. In likeness, a mature, seasoned teacher is typically better than a novice – better, for example, in bringing together students, subject matter, and settings in ways that can be substantive and satisfying. But unlike fruit, which ripens through natural processes, the teacher's maturity comes through steadfastness. It emerges through the influence of teaching on the teacher's own sensibility and outlook. It finds expression in the increasingly sophisticated ways in which the teacher assesses student learning as well as his or her methods. It is not simply a matter of age or number of years in the classroom. A person with but 2 or 3 years of experience can be more mature than a person with 20. Maturity is an ever-evolving outcome of how the teacher responds and learns. Unlike fruit, which must linger on the vine, teachers can take steps to cultivate their own deepening maturity.

Teachers who work with children know that they can be mysterious and perplexing to adults. Although everyone has been a child, the transition into adulthood irrevocably transforms the relationship that adults have with childhood. They can no longer perceive or recall it straightforwardly. But teachers of children are brought vibrantly into that distant world – literally, every second they spend in the classroom. Moreover, such teachers spend more time with children than do any other groups of adults. They are the community's only group of adults who spend regular and extended time with a range of children. Jean-Jacques Rousseau urged the educators of his day to pay attention to children – 'for most assuredly you do not know them at all' (1979, p. 34). Teachers of children are in a unique position to observe, register, and contemplate the evolving behaviors and interactions of children over the course of 1 or more years. Teachers are well-placed to be students of students: to come to know them in the regular, familiar environment of the school, classroom, and playground. This unrivaled experience enables teachers to educate the world about the nature of children: about their distinctive ways of seeing, sensing, and relating, and about the very character of childhood. Teachers can help the wider community to better interpret and relate to children as it strives to understand, protect, and educate them. Earlier we wrote that a mature teacher fuses self-criticism, faith in educational progress, and steadfastness. A mature culture understands that its very health and continuity depend upon educating, supporting, and listening to its teachers.

These points do not imply that teachers can come to know everything about children that is pertinent to their growth and flourishing. Steadfast teachers remain ever-underway in this learning process. Their relationship with students mirrors that with subject matter: there is always more to learn, to understand, and to appreciate. These facts conjure the need for self-honesty and a measure of humility. They also call to mind the values in what Dewey called a cultivated naiveté (1988: 40), by which he meant learning to retain as best as possible receptivity to fresh impressions, ideas, and emotions. In this light it bears emphasizing once more that the teacher's steadfastness is not like that of a gate shut fast to the world. Rather it implies firmness and suppleness, steadiness and lightness, seriousness and a sense of pleasure in the work of educating.

CONCLUSION

To teach is to accept a responsibility that stretches back for generations. Teaching connects the practitioner with those who toiled in the past as well as with peers working today. To teach is to find oneself in a community with other teachers. It is to realize that part of the fundamental nature of the work is to examine its nature continuously. In all of these ways, to teach means participating in a tradition whose roots reach back to Confucius, Socrates, and other memorable teachers. These facts do not imply that teachers must agree with or even like one another. Anyone who spends time with teachers knows they can be as contentious and disputatious about the meaning of good practice as any group of dedicated politicians, nurses, or social workers. But teachers share kindred goals and concerns. They are custodians and creators of things that matter. They work in the present for the sake of humanity's future.

One of the greatest challenges in teaching is to survive misconceptions of teaching. We use the verb 'survive' because such misconceptions cannot be overcome in any final sense. Some regard the teacher as a trained technician carrying out the dictates of policy-makers. Some treat the teacher as an economic resource, fabricating 'human capital.' Others regard the teacher as an instrument of political and cultural change. Still others assume that the teacher's charge is merely to conserve extant custom, knowledge, and belief. As a community of inquiry, philosophers of education have challenged these and other conceptions of teaching. They have shown how the activity of teaching is as rich and unfathomable as human life itself, namely because teaching humanizes in countless, substantive ways. They have addressed what it means for the teacher to be steadfast in confronting problems and in engaging opportunities. They have shed light on the perennial difficulties and joys of teaching.

Put another way, philosophers of education have challenged misconceptions of the work by demonstrating why teaching is an endlessly provocative human endeavor. They ask questions such as: When is teaching? Is teaching an activity, an experience, or a form of relation? Is teaching defined by its intentions or by its outcomes? Is teaching a mode of caring for others or a mode of training them? Is teaching the enactment of occupational skills or of a way of life? Is teaching a functional or purposive undertaking? Does it serve socialization and/or does it serve education understood as something other than socialization? What does it mean to grow and improve as a teacher? Why do many teachers attest to its aesthetic, moral, and spiritual dimensions rather than solely to its academic and intellectual aspects? By posing such questions, and by working toward better responses to them, philosophers of education in concert with teachers keep the practice of teaching dynamic and responsive.

We thank Stephanie Burdick-Shepherd, Jeff Frank, Daniel Hendrickson, and Mark Jonas for their excellent bibliographic assistance and for their insightful comments on the philosophy and practice of teaching.

ACKNOWLEDGMENT

We thank Stephanie Burdick-Shepherd, Jeff Frank, Daniel Hendrickson, and Mark Jonas for their excellent bibliographic assistance and for their insightful comments on the philosophy and practice of teaching.

REFERENCES

Buber, M. (2002) *Between Man and Man*. London and New York: Routledge.
Comte-Sponville, A. (2001) *A Small Treatise on the Great Virtues*. New York: Metropolitan Books.

Dewey, J. (1985) *John Dewey. The Middle Works 1899–1924: Vol. 9, Democracy and Education 1916*, in J.A. Boydston (ed.). Carbondale: Southern Illinois University Press.

Dewey, J. (1988) *John Dewey. The Later Works 1925–1953: Vol. 1, Experience and Nature*, in J.A. Boydston (ed.). Carbondale: Southern Illinois University Press. Original work published 1925.

Emmet, D. (1979) *Function, Purpose, and Powers*. London: Macmillan.

Epictetus (1983) *Handbook of Epictetus*, trans. N. White. Indianapolis: Hackett.

Erasmus (1964) *Desiderius Erasmus: Concerning the Aim and Method of Education*, W.H. Woodward (ed.). New York: Bureau of Publications, Teachers College, Columbia University.

Hansen, D.T. (2001) *Exploring the Moral Heart of Teaching: Toward a Teacher's Creed*. New York: Teachers College Press.

Jackson, P.W. (1968) *Life in Classrooms*. New York: Holt, Rinehart, and Winston.

Laverty, M. (2007) *Iris Murdoch's Ethics: A Consideration of her Romantic Vision*. London: Continuum.

Murdoch, I. (1970) *The Sovereignty of Good*. London: Routledge.

Rousseau, J.-J. (1979) *Émile or On Education*, trans. A. Bloom. New York: Basic Books.

Todorov, T. (1996) *Facing the Extreme: Moral Life in the Concentration Camps*, trans. A. Denner and A. Pollak. New York: Henry Holt.

Weil, S. (1970) *First and Last Notebooks*, ed. R. Rhees. London: Oxford University Press.

16

The Wider Ethical Dimensions of Education and Teaching

Hugh Sockett

Variously attributed to Benjamin Disraeli and John Dewey, the sentiment that what the good parent wants for his or her child, so the nation must want for all its children, embodies the complex principle in a democratic society that the conduct and quality of education is profoundly necessary to its survival. Education and teaching are thus set within a broad multi-dimensional social framework that includes parental responsibilities, the character and conduct of institutions, and cultural mores. These are three of the wider ethical dimensions of teaching and education addressed in this chapter, though some topics raised here should be examined through the named chapters in other parts of this handbook.

First, children are brought up by more or less responsible parents, and live in increasingly divergent kinds of family groups. Who should have what responsibilities is increasingly problematic and, if parents are neither consumers nor clients, how is their relationship to the providing schools to be characterized? Secondly, the shape, conduct and character of institutions dedicated to education and teaching invites questions about the qualities of people working in them as administrators or teachers. Finally, the conflict between popular culture, high culture and educational goals creates value tensions which most teachers face daily, although cultural mores shaped by dynamic individualist materialism also influence the attitudes that employers and parents have to all educational institutions.

SCHOOLS, PARENTS AND CHOICE

In the mid twentieth century, *in loco parentis* was gradually replaced by due process as the framework defining the responsibility for the child held by the school and the teacher. The character of the relationships between state, school and family has not been clarified by this shift. Indeed, there are at least four views of the relationship to replace the parental model, each of which could be subject to contract and due process. Is it one of moral partnership, parental control, consumer–provider, or service to clients? 'It is a fact too seldom remembered,' writes Jane Roland Martin (1992) 'that school and home are partners in the education of the young' (1992: 6). Martin's advocacy of such a moral partnership is not reflected in a view of parents as consumers, where schools compete in the 'market' as providers of services (Robenstine, 2001). Nor is it a partnership if the rights of parents are seen as the trump card, as, for example, when Holmes (1998) proposes area public schools directed by elected parent councils and distributed programs of choice accessible (at least nominally if not geographically possible) by all. Nor is it Martin's partnership if parents (and their children) are seen as the clients of teachers-as-social-workers where each child is a 'case' justified by the need for social justice. Although sex education, religious education (see Ch. 30) and book censorship are sometimes battlegrounds between parents and schools, the political topic that throws most light on the school/teacher–parent relationship is parental choice of school.

Both facts and ideology have contributed to the significance of the debate about choice. First, conservative and neo-liberal advocates have followed Freidman in advocating an ideological privatization of education, deploring the power of the unions, but the argument is also a market-based response to deplorable conditions in inner cities in most Western societies that undermine liberal principles of equality of opportunity for all. Secondly, liberal responses insist ideologically that social justice can only be achieved in a public system which they have defended, arguing that its admitted weaknesses are being corrected, that unions protect teacher quality, and that choice systems lack proper public accountability and invite the participation of the unqualified with a profit motive. Education, they claim, is a social good too precious to be left to the market.

Forgotten in this brouhaha has been the historical place of choice in the schools of Western culture. The 1994 Education Act in England and Wales specifically gave parents the right to send their children to denominational schools, provided the churches supplied the buildings and paid 5% of the running costs, the state supplying 95%: similarly in the Netherlands. In the USA, many religious groups, notably the Catholic Church and the Jewish community, established schools that were privately funded, but had charitable status, thereby receiving a considerable public subsidy. Of course, private schools of varying types and educational ideologies have always been available to the wealthy (with a few deserving children getting scholarships). Those with the means usually consider the quality of schools and their catchment areas as they buy homes. Parental choice, in one form or another, has been a common feature of private parental actions and public policy on education since mass education began.

However, 'there's an intensity, even zealousness in the debate on school choice that smothers thoughtful discourse,' wrote Ernest Boyer in 1992 (Carnegie Foundation), some 47 years after Milton Friedman (1955/1962) first argued that in a democratic society government (in a generic sense) should *provide* for the schools, but it need not *run* them. From this position he elaborated the idea of school vouchers, which seemed to many to presage the break-up of the public system and the introduction of market forces. That intensity has not abated. Boyer at least agree that children ought to be compelled to go to school, without which presumption the debate has little point. Leonard Krimerman (1978), however, argued that as schools did not treat children as ends in themselves, the burden is on those who supported compulsory education to defend both the idea and its practice against a view that education should be voluntary – which, if enacted, would presumably entail choice of schools.

Nevertheless, debates on parental choice within a compulsory public system focus on the notion of there being a *public* policy whereby parents or guardians choose public schools for their children, which challenges the view that government (in a generic sense) should assign children to their schools. It may be assumed that either policy is in the children's interests, but trying to evaluate one against the other may not only be empirically weak, but the criteria of evaluation are themselves contestable. Harry Brighouse (2000), for example, notes that there is little convincing empirical evidence that such a policy is in children's interests in the sense that they profit educationally from it, but the criteria of measured success, say, through test scores, miss the moral values that, it can be claimed, are a feature of choosing. Issues of choice, it seems, could not simply be settled by data.

Compulsory education or not, the argument about choice is anchored in a very ancient kind of debate: Is education for the individual good or for civic purposes? Is it for positional or public goods? Market ideologues place overriding importance on efficiency and effectiveness arising through competition and consumer choice. However distasteful such a view is to civic-minded liberals who loathe the commodification of education, modern democratic societies are predominantly meritocratic and education is a positional good (Hirsch 1977). Education, on Martin Hollis' (1982) account, has a special complexity in that its exchange value for individuals depends on its relative position within the competitive and hierarchical structure of a modern society. This analysis is matched by much political, educational and parental rhetoric. Young people are primarily encouraged to stay on at school for their own economic benefit, not to pursue some public good. Classrooms are replete with exhortations to get better Advanced Placement grades, International Baccalaureates, A Levels and so on to get to college to compete in a knowledge-driven labor market. Education buys status and career expectations. To try to correct this individualist emphasis, there has been a burgeoning of interest in many kinds of civic values education or citizenship education at all levels, especially in the USA in undergraduate education.

With respect to parental choice, however, David Ferrero (2004) supports the view that education is inevitably a positional good: approaches to the school–parent relationship (excluding that of moral partnership), he argues, have in common:

> A conception of school that stresses the individual and private benefits of education over common public ones. Schools provide, families consume. And consumers have rights not obligations. The (social) justice model breaks somewhat from this pattern by focusing on the public good of equal opportunity, but it too tends to focus on what the public owes poor children via its schools without much regard for what children might owe in terms of future public commitments or even effort toward their own learning. When reform advocates refer to poor, minority, or disabled children as 'under-*served*', or place the onus for student motivation primarily on teachers, they subtly reinforce this tendency by characterizing students as passive social service recipients rather than as active participants in their own education. (p. 289)

Brighouse (2000), in his book *School Choice and Social Justice*, argues that the liberal position demands that education is a matter of social justice not of enlightened or naked self-interest. Children are 'vulnerable wards' and government must support their interests in becoming autonomous through education. This demands that the public or positional good for the parent is tempered, even secondary to that of justice. Social justice should thus determine educational provision and also, in some way, characterize the school–parent relationship, which might yield limited forms of choice.

There are, however, important arguments for choice that are also connected to democratic values. First a democratic society must provide educational space for parents whose values are at odds with liberal society's norms (see Galston, 1999, quoted in Ferrero 2004). This should be within the system if possible, although the egregious manipulation of such dissent has been displayed by fundamentalist Mormons who use their 'public' schools to provide a curriculum of indoctrination into the cult (Jessop and Palmer, 2007). Secondly, there is widespread agreement that raising a family is one of life's potentially enriching experiences, creating bonds of affection that have unique roots. Family cohesion may also be of significant utilitarian value for a society. For, as writers from Tocqueville (1835) to Putnam (2002) have pointed out, most associations in civil society, family included, promote public goods through networks, norms and trust: schools can stand at the center of these networks, were the idea of partnership more visible. Schooling of children is both civically and individually desirable. Indeed, as societies and schools become more diverse, it is the more critical for social cohesion how schools and parents relate to each other.

Much more extensive and thorough than this brief section is Ferrero's review of recent literature. He remarks that

> . . . in Anglo-American philosophical circles a sizeable literature has emerged over the last few years that has attempted to make respectable again talk of civic virtue, robust citizen

education and the common good, which nonetheless concludes that some form of school choice may actually be a *requirement* of a fair and robustly public-minded system of schooling. (2004: 288)

His excellent essay should be a starting point for any scholar moved to go beyond squabbling about market forces.

THE CHARACTER AND CONDUCT OF INSTITUTIONS

Schools that parents might choose if they had the opportunity are more varied than might be supposed. For educational institutions have designs of two types, e.g. organizational forms such as school, college, or university on the one hand *and* academic forms, e.g. disciplines, fields, subjects on the other. Organizational forms are made individual to the particular institution: Berkeley, West Point, the Sorbonne and Oxford, for example, are each universities, but with differing designs. That idiosyncracy is captured in the institution's ethos where the professional conduct of the role-players express the traditions, conventions, rules and regulations which embody the institution's values (see MacIntyre, 1984). The design type raises few philosophical issues of itself: rather it is the values and principles embedded in such designs that are of philosophical interest. For A.S. Neill (1970) the design of Summerhill (where it was believed that students had little or no formal curriculum) was based in a child-centerd view of the damage that adult authority could do to children (see Chs 7 and 33, and especially an important discussion of that school in Stronach and Piper, 2008). The traditional grammar school, and its variations across the Western world, embodied the paramountcy of knowledge, a view of innate capacities (see Chs 26, 27 and 29), and a belief in elites. The comprehensive high school, and perhaps the common school, has historically had aims of social justice, articulated by Horace Mann (Cremin, 1957) in the nineteenth century and Richard Pring (2007) in the twenty-first century. The design of schools for exceptionally talented youngsters, for instance in the Yehudi Menuhin School near London, is rooted in the belief that such talent manifests itself early and should be nurtured in institutions devoted to it (Renshaw, 1980). Military schools, such as Randolph-Macon College in the USA, are the embodiment of a belief in the virtue of disciplined upbringing, very dissimilar from the discipline of 'muscular Christianity' manifest in the British public school tradition since Thomas Arnold. The traditional Catholic or Jewish school (see Chs 8 and 37) embodies the view that religion is a pervasive part of life, implying that secular institutions are not designed to celebrate this commitment. Pakistani madrasses can carry their religious ideological commitment to the point of revolution (Ahmad, 2006). Many variations are possible: Kohlberg's view of moral development inspired the Just Community School – often a school within a school, as at Brookline High School, just as Froebel's thought inspired the kindergarten of the nineteenth century.

Academic institutional forms such as disciplines, subjects and fields embody distinctive values and modes of enquiry, rooted in epistemological concerns (see Blackmore, 2001 for a postmodern critique.) In History (Dray, 1989, 1995), Literature (Lamarque, 2008), Science (Okaha, 2002), Religion (Hick, 1989) and Social Sciences (Hollis, 1994), these central concerns are dealt with in terms of 'the philosophy of' the discipline. Debate about and within disciplines is profound and widespread. To take one example: How do values enter scientific research? Phillips and Burbules argue that the only values relevant to the scientist are the 'cognitive' values, internal to science, like 'pursuit of truth, openness to counter-evidence ... honesty ... in reporting results' (2004: 55). These values, they claim, are not moral or ethical values. An alternative perspective is offered by Williams (2003, Ch. 6) who argues that the scientist's obligations are to other people as members of the community of science where, if people do not pursue the truth, the activity loses its point: but they also have an obligation to the world of moral agents who are affected by their practices, rather than to some abstraction called scientific methodology or science which can be sinned against. Moreover, if such scientists are viewed solely in their institutional roles, it would be necessary to posit a logical, phenomenological and moral difference between that role and the 'individual' (person or citizen) who inhabits it. That allows the Nazi doctor Mengele to claim he was a scientist and the actors in the Manhattan Project to be merely upbraided for their confusion. Controversy of this and many other kinds rages around disciplines and fields in terms of their power, their epistemology, and even their moral significance, and each controversy has different levels of application to education and teaching.

The matters of moral interest to the philosopher of education then concern the conduct of role-players working in both types of institution: i.e. as an administrator or teacher engaged in teaching X. Examples of misconduct by individuals in each institution, respectively, include sexual exploitation of the young in the organizational and plagiarism in the academic type (Posner, 2007). Yet, if it is correct to say identified values define the institution, either organizational or academic, institutions are obliged to ascertain whether the rhetoric matches the reality. The focus for accountability, institutional self-study or accreditation, therefore, would not be solely on 'goals achieved,' but would include the conduct of role-players in what Davis and White (2001) call an audited self-review.

First, all such inquiry demands both empirical and philosophical study. As Oser puts it: 'Effectiveness may moderate morality and morality may moderate effectiveness. But effectiveness can also enhance morality, and morality can enhance effectiveness.' (Oser, 1994: 64) Without sophisticated data, informed by philosophical work on values and principles, institutional reports would be shallow. In macro terms an agenda might include: What is common about the common school? Do grammar schools manifest the open-mindedness necessary to the pursuit of knowledge and truth? What does Catholic school practice show about the question whether an educational institutional can be a 'family'?

Do schools with a narrow focus (e.g. on music or discipline) promote elitism, and does that matter?

Secondly, the discipline of philosophy of education has its own contentions, which go beyond whether institutional self-reporting can avoid being a mixed empirical–philosophical study. For example, first, what is the discipline's scope? Jane Roland Martin records the exclusionary tendencies of philosophy of education, in which the topic of women's education was regarded as 'out-of-bounds' (Waks, 2008: 127), raising the question what else might be ruled out. Moreover, is the philosopher of education's role spectatorial or participatory? Should the exercise of the role eschew practical recommendations, preserving one's opinions for one's role as a citizen? Or should recommendations derived from worked-out principles be central to the role? (See Moses, 1992; see also Chs 3 and 4.)

Thirdly, how does philosophy of education connect to its institutional home, the university? There appear to be some real instances of, if not corrupt, certainly undesirable attitudes and actions within the institutions. Dennis Phillips (2008) mentions that his authorship of a major report brought attacks from people who accused him of saying things that were nowhere to be found in the report he chaired (Martin, 2008, in Waks, 2008: 127). Michael Peters (2008) explains how his appointment to a chair was derailed on ideological grounds (they didn't like Foucault) (Waks, 2008: 156). Robin Barrow (2008) writes of an institution which 'if not actually corrupt, (was) at any rate self-serving, inefficient, incompetent and above all anti-intellectual' (Waks, 2008: 35). Gary Fenstermacher has recalled the turbulence of his period as a Dean, with deceit and betrayal its major features (Fenstermacher, 1994). The agenda on institutions for philosophers of education could open up a more inquisitorial stance on whether the values and purposes of the institutions are indeed being practiced.

Needed are conceptual tools to facilitate such inquiry. Emmett (1966) and Hansen (1995) more recently have explored the territory of rules, roles and relationships, where the relation between the individual person and his or her work in a role is examined. One useful conceptual framework for such exploration is the complex notion of integrity. Stephen Carter (1996) offers a Kantian view of the concept that can be used to describe how a person handles the role within which he works. David Norton (1990), on the other hand, gives an Aristotelian account that is focused on the personal conduct of one's life of which one's institutional role is a part. Both offer suggestive frameworks for further study of institutions, using the concept of integrity as the working tool.

Carter writes that integrity 'requires three steps: (1) discerning what is right and what is wrong; (2) acting on what you have discerned even at personal cost, and (3) saying openly that you are acting on your understanding of right from wrong' (1996: 7). For him, the person of integrity is morally reflective, steadfast in action, and unashamed of doing what is right. Carter's emphasis is on discernment, and he allows that there are differences between people on what might be right or wrong. He links the integrity of the individual to other admirable virtues: commitment, forthrightness, steadfastness, compassion, the ability to compromise and consistency. The person of integrity is not merely honest, however, and integrity should not be equated with honesty.

Norton suggests that moral integrity has a three-dimensional meaning: namely, (1) the 'integration of separable aspects of the self' – notably faculties, desires, interests, roles, life-shaping choices; (2) 'wholeness as completeness' by which integrity can be distinguished, for example, from fanaticism, and (3) 'a deeper kind of honesty', to be found in self-knowledge, the foundation of all virtues, so that the purpose of democratic politics and educational institutions becomes one of enhancing the quality of life of human beings through 'the acquisition by human beings of moral virtues, where virtues are understood as dispositions of character' (1990: 81). This is not restricted to those being taught, but to all with roles in educational institutions.

The question 'How does the individual deal with conflicts of personal belief and the demands of public practice?' may therefore be approached through the concept of integrity. This question is particularly acute, as institutions are most often bureaucracies. For all role-players in the modern institution, bureaucratic management is problematic,

> . . . because moral choices are inextricably linked to personal fates, bureaucracy erodes internal and even external standards of morality not only in matters of individual success and failure but in all the issues that managers face in their daily work. Bureaucracy makes its own internal rules and social context the principal moral gauges for action. (Jackall, 1988: 192)

Nowhere is this clearer than in the impact of assessment on teaching, on the way in which pay-for-performance teaching shapes the teaching role toward learning product and away from the kind of personal development Norton describes.

Finally, the moral issues have to be named. Do lies and secrets function as institutional norms (Bok, 1989, 1999; Williams, 2003)? What should judgments about the moral ethos of institution look like in accreditation systems (Davis and White, 2001)? Is cheating by students an institutional or an individual failure? Does intellectual bias (see the Michael Peters/Jane Roland Martin examples above) represent a form of academic freedom (see Menand, 1998)? How far are secrets in governance justifiable? To what extent do teachers get a strong match between the moral values they espouse in their work and those they espouse in their lives? Have the bureaucratic and interpersonal pressures of grading supplanted honest judgment? Do teachers, especially in schools, teach to the textbook provided for them as a bureaucratic solution to moral and political argument? Indeed, do teachers care about the truth (Brandon, 1987)? Finally, are teachers or professors driven to make moral choices about students because decisions are, like corporate bureaucrats, 'linked to personal fates' rather than to a student's moral welfare?

These questions point to matters at the heart of the character and conduct of educational institutions where wider ethical and moral concerns surface.

EDUCATION AND POPULAR CULTURE

The conflict between popular culture and educational goals creates value tensions which most teachers face daily, although cultural mores are also shaped by a dynamic individualist materialism that influences the attitudes that employers and parents have to all educational institutions. There are therefore two primary ways in which the relation between popular culture and education may be viewed. First, there are the largely twentieth century debates on high-brow and low-brow culture, with its influence on selection and tracking in education, the content of the university curriculum and the disdain by the high priests of high culture for the democratic impulse and for popular taste. Secondly, there is the clash of what may be called school values (for example, community, lack of explicit competition) with the reality of behavioral norms in a capitalist, especially neo-liberal society (for example, individual, competitive) which explore further some of the topics in Section 1.

The development of mass education in the USA in the mid-late nineteenth century coincided with the disappearance of Shakespeare from the popular culture of most Americans. Levine's (1988) study of the emergence of cultural hierarchy in America suggests that Shakespeare as popular drama across the developing nation was stolen, as it were, by high-brow culture and turned into a boring school subject for the masses. Though not a school subject, the same is true of opera: and the anger at the theft is illustrated, in Levine's account, by the final scenes of *A Night at the Opera* where 'Take Me Back to the Ballgame' is inserted into the overture to *Il Trovatore* with Groucho striding down the aisle shouting 'Peanuts! Peanuts!' (1988: 235). More recently, the movie *Amadeus* too contrasts neatly the high-brow attitudes of the Court with the low-brow audiences Mozart wanted to attract. Yet, he needed the Court's patronage: no art floats free of the marketplace and its eclectic demands. The recent British movie *Shakespeare in Love*, too, seems sensitive to the historical context of Shakespeare's life (see also Ackroyd, 2006). A history of popular culture can inform philosophical debate about education, and especially teaching.

The initial difficulty in talk of popular culture is what it means. This is especially complex when, as Susan Sontag (1987, quoted by Levine, 1988: 244–245) explained, there is a 'new sensibility' which is 'defiantly pluralistic.' By that, she meant that artists and intellectuals are no longer trapped in high-culture discourse, but are creating new standards through adventures in what would have been thought of as popular culture, and, of course, the other way round. Yehudi Menuhin plays the fiddle with Stéphane Grappelli; Paul McCartney writes an oratorio. Gingell and Brandon (2000), in an excellent, authoritative and exhaustive advocacy of high culture as educational content, begin with Matthew Arnold defining culture as 'the best intellectual and artistic beliefs and practices of a given group of people or society' (Arnold, 1869/1932; Gingell and Brandon, 2000: 418). Frequently, definitions of high culture start as a contrast with popular culture. What emerges is the view that, since high culture can by definition be appreciated only by the few, those that are appreciated by the many cannot be works of high cultural value (Gingell and Brandon, 2000: 463).

Defining the qualities of high culture thus would define what popular culture is (that is, everything else). In Britain, Arnold (1869:1932), T.S. Eliot (1948), F.R. and Q.D. Leavis and Geoffrey Bantock (1965, 1967), successively, were its strongest exponents, with Alasdair MacIntyre, Roger Scruton and Anthony O'Hear as contemporary advocates. Eliot (1948) regards the culture of a people as the incarnation of its religion. The Leavises dwell on what they called the 'felt life,' i.e. the kind of experience that 'great' poets and painters have; but their critical work is frequently censorious, stemming from a view that high culture demands moral seriousness which F.R. Leavis found lacking in Science and the work of C.P. Snow. For Q.D. Leavis, quoted in Gingell and Brandon (2000: 462), reading magazines and going to the cinema prevent the emergence of cultural development and establish non-intellectual habits. Bantock was writing at a time when the grammar school in Britain was seen as being under threat from the development of comprehensive high school education. Yet he implicitly supports the 1944 White Paper's view that a selective system could produce 'parity of esteem,' with those not destined for an education in high culture an education suitable for the 'folk.' His references (Bantock, 1965) are to a folk culture (for example, handicrafts) that children might be taught, a culture that was disappearing, whereas a contemporary view of popular culture would see it as based in music, sport and entertainment through the medium of television.

For Americans, the most vociferous protagonist of high culture was Allan Bloom (1988). A liberal education, he argues, means that students seek to investigate the question 'What is man?' 'in relation to his highest aspirations as opposed to his low and common needs' (Bloom, 1988: 21). Levine's critique is apposite. Like earlier high-culture proponents, Bloom holds that 'only the minority can fruitfully investigate and discuss the nature of the cultural authority which the majority needs to accept'(Bloom, 1988: 252). Bloom develops, in Leavisian style, a censorious attack on the curriculum of the contemporary university that he believes has turned the disciplines into an anarchic chaos. With much more balance, the ideal of high culture can be embraced by some as the necessary educational curriculum for all children (see Ravitch, 1996). A different and original view on the problem is offered by E.D. Hirsch Jr (1988) who seeks to reform the curriculum by the criterion of what he calls 'cultural literacy' – what every American needs to know (for an excellent critical discussion, see Beehler, 1991). His famous list, which can constantly be changed and thus is not susceptible to arguments against the canon, includes Shakespeare and swing, Wordsworth and Mae West.

But Ravitch and Hirsch are not arguing for high culture from an argument about the debasing effects of popular culture (though some of their supporters may), or to support elitist education. Rather, they assert its importance against what they see as the trivialization of the school curriculum, its anti-intellectualism, and the poverty of teacher education as a barrier to an effective school curriculum as they define it, a sentiment also expressed by George Steiner (1987). Such arguments about liberal education curricula are meat and drink to philosophers of education. Finally, the relationship between a discipline and the subject-matter curriculum which bears its name (e.g. Science, or, History) is critical in determining what is taught in schools, epistemiological problems, particularly in science (Deng, 2007), a problem which Hirsch – from the assumption of cultural literacy – does not entertain.

Hirsch's stance is thus in accord with Gingell and Brandon's defence of high culture that calls for pluralism. High culture is not defined by a static canon of great works of the past, but rooted in a recognition of the dynamic development of all aspects of culture in a democratic society (e.g. cinema), diminishing but not dissolving the distinction between high brow and low brow. But what are the pieces of culture in this sense that are avowedly popular? Gingell and Brandon suggest music, admirably discussed historically by Huttunen (2008), a justification for music education (Westerlund, 2008), and Packalen (2008) on 'Music, emotions and truth.' Sport, like fashion, is manifestly a major part of popular culture, and Barrow (1993) has argued for its utilitarian uses, although that contrasts with the popular culture rationale of the delights of watching and critiquing physical skill in sport, seeing the expressions of character therein, and forging identities and loyalties with teams. The cinema and television entertainment, like sport, attracts viewers of every intellectual level. In educational terms, certainly in the USA, most school students get musical opportunities and compulsory Physical Education, and there is competition for access to most team sports.

Discussion of the school curriculum is outside the confines of this chapter. Suffice it to say that there is so to speak a default curriculum (Literature, History, Science, and Math) packaged in different ways, sometimes with Art, Music and Sport, depending on the country. Though it retains vestiges of high culture, the school subjects often lack in their teaching the challenges and the excitement of the disciplines, being frequently reduced to testable material. Hirsch has developed a Core Knowledge Series for young children, but two curriculum examples illustrate that pedagogical problems from a discipline base can be overcome. In the teaching of Shakespeare, Rex Gibson (see Gibson 1988) has edited editions of the plays that provide sparkling original material for schools because they are profoundly focused on the works being *plays*, not *verse* for textual analysis. In the teaching of History, Rosenzweig and his co-authors developed a multi-media 'book' *Who Built America?* (Rosenzweig et al., 1993) which has spawned a major national center (http://www.chnm.,gmu.edu) spearheading innovations in the teaching and learning of history, putting up front online primary materials of all kinds for students in schools. Both of these are of philosophical importance as they embody in practice the view that disciplinary origins and methodologies can be harnessed in classrooms. The teaching of mathematics, of course, remains a battleground of content, clashing developmental perspectives and intrinsic vs instrumental views of its worth.

IS THERE A CLASH OF VALUES?

Popular culture is usually linked only to pursuits for the vast majority that are active or passive leisure time activities. Yet the mores and norms of everyday life, i.e. work rather than leisure, are also a profound element of the culture of a people, embedded in attitudes, conventions and, in some cases, in laws. In that sense they are popular and differ from society to society. These attitudes, laws and conventions are embedded in what James Davison Hunter calls 'public' as distinct from 'private' culture:

> The very essence of the activity taking place in both realms – what makes public and private culture possible – is 'discourse' or conversation, the interaction of different voices, opinions, and perspectives. Yet, while public and private culture are similar in constitutions, they are different in their functions – one orders private life: the other orders public life. (1991: 53 ff.)

Public culture not only embraces laws and conventions but also national identity, as 'shared notions of civic virtue and the common ideals of the public good' (1991: 55) become the mores or norms against which actions are evaluated and judged. (See also the work of Jurgen Habermas (Goode, 2005; Calhoun, 1993) on the 'public sphere'.) The work of public culture can be influenced by private culture, as when a personal interest or aspiration is taken into the public realm. The public culture can however be inaccessible, dominated as it is by elites using vocabularies not understood by the average Joe. Or, more significantly in American political culture, faith – a primary element in many private cultures – has reasserted itself in the public culture.

On Hunter's account, the public schools are expected to express and be vehicles for the transmission of the public culture. First, they will often be the vehicles through which private interests seek to invade the public culture: see Judge Jones III's brilliant judgment on Creationism in Science teaching in the case of the Dover School Board (www.pamd.uscourts.gov/kitzmiller/kitzmiller_342.pdf). The norms of school conduct can differ, often considerably, from the norms of the actual culture, rather than the idealized notion of the public culture, children bring with them into school.

Of course the complex issues of faith and religion and the public schools are bound to national and social contexts: for example, American society formally excludes the teaching of religion, yet it is a nation where a considerable majority hold religious beliefs and practice them. In Britain, where religious education is compulsory, practicing religion is very much the habit of a minority. This conflict over faith often spills over into matters of sex education, the censorship of books, and the rights of children and parents. Other private culture demands may be seen to include the claims of different sorts of minority communities of interest: for example, how children dress, provision for children with disabilities, and how provision is made for 'queer' children. On this account, public culture is not to be confused with popular culture, though they may overlap: for example, in the question of supporting, enhancing or ignoring patriotism.

The second issue is the extent to which the actual values embedded in public and private practices clash or are in sync with those in the school. Cheating is one example: 'Joe is a student at a top college in the Northeast who admits to cheating regularly. Like all of the college students who spoke to Primetime, he wanted his identity obscured. In Joe's view, he's just doing *what the rest of the world does*' (my italics) (ABC News, 2008), that is, pursuing his self-interest with little regard for the impact on himself or others, the pursuit of positional goods at any cost. Another is competition, addressed by Gingell and Brandon (2000: 475–81). While competition within organizations is critical for the ambitious, academic competition is discouraged, if disguised in schooling. Nor is this a trivial matter. In an excellent book, former *Washington Post* deputy editor Meg Greenfield (2001) suggested that the only way to understand political behavior in Washington DC was to view it as high school. From that viewpoint, norms of political behavior are 'taught' at school, providing a very strong argument for the inculcation of civic virtue in children and making strong demands on them to promote their sense of obligation to society.

CONCLUSION

Each of these topics has made reference to civil society. Perhaps the most important challenge to contemporary schooling is how it fosters and contributes to civic virtues and to civil society in general. Philosophers might continue the kinds of pragmatic thinking about school choice by working through how to create moral partnerships with parents to which other kinds of relationships can be inimical. They might turn a more carefully judgmental eye on their institutions, especially as universities increasingly resemble corporations. Finally, they must continue to address what, in civil society, are promoted as the goods of popular culture and how they might be connected to the aims of education and human flourishing.

REFERENCES

ABC News (2008) 'A cheating crisis in America's schools.' April 29, 2008. http://abcnews.go.com/primetime/story?id=132376andpage=1

Ackroyd, Peter (2006) *Shakespeare: The Biography*. London: Anchor Books.

Ahmad, Tufail (2008) The Role of Pakistan's Madrassas. http://www.ocnus.net/artman2/publish/International_3/The_Role_of_Pakistans_Madrassas.shtml.

Arnold, Matthew (1869:1932) *Culture and Anarchy*. Cambridge: Cambridge University Press.

Bantock, Geoffrey, H. (1965) *Education and Values*. London: Faber.

Bantock, Geoffrey H. (1967) *Education Culture and the Emotions*. London: Faber.

Barrow, Robin (1993) *Language, Intelligence and Thought*. Aldershot: Edward Elgar Publishing.

Barrow, Robin (2008) 'Or what's a heaven for?', in L. Waks, *Leaders in Philosophy of Education: Intellectual Self-Portraits*. Rotterdam: Sense Publishers, pp. 27–39.

Beehler, Rodger (1991) 'Grading the "Cultural Literacy" Project', *Studies in Philosophy and Education*, 10 (4): 315–335.

Bellamy, Richard (2008). *Citizenship: A Very Short Introduction*. Oxford : Oxford University Press. (Comprehensive introductory study with an excellent Further Reading section that comprehensively covers the field.)

Blackmore, Jill (2001) 'Universities in crisis? Knowledge economies, emancipatory pedagogies, and the critical intellectual', in *Educational Theory*, 51 (3): 353–373.

Bloom, Allan (1988) *The Closing of the American Mind*. New York: Simon and Schuster.

Bok, Sisella (1989) *Secrets: On the Ethics of Concealment and Revelation*. New York: Vintage Books.

Bok, Sisella (1999) *Lying: Moral Choice in Public and Private Life*. New York: Vintage Books.

Boyer, Ernest (1992) *School Choice: A Special Report*. New York: Carnegie Foundation for the Advancement of Teaching.

Brandon, E.P. (1987) *Do Teachers Care about the Truth?* London: Allen and Unwin.

Brighouse, H. (2000) *School Choice and Social Justice*. Oxford: Oxford University Press.

Calhoun, Craig (1993) *Habermas and the Public Sphere*. Boston, MIT Press.

Carter, Stephen (1996) *Integrity*. New York: Basic Books.

Cremin, Laurence A. (1957) *The Republic and the School: Horace Mann on the Education of the Free Man*. New York: Teachers College Press.

Davis, Andrew and White, John (2001) 'Accountability and school inspection: in defence of audited self-review', *Journal of Philosophy of Education*, 35 (4).

Deng, Zongyi (2007) 'Knowing the subject-matter of a secondary school science subject', *Journal of Curriculum Studies*, 39 (5): 503–537.

Dray, William H. (1989) *On History and Philosophers of History*. New York: E. J. Brill.

Dray, William H. (1995) *History as Re-Enactment: R.G. Collingwood's Idea of History*. Oxford: Clarendon Press.

Eliot, T.S. (1948) *Notes towards a Definition of Culture*. London: Faber.

Emmett, D. (1966) *Rules, Roles and Relations*. London: Macmillan.

Emmett, D. (1998) *Outward Forms, Inner Springs: A Study in Social and Religious Philosophy*. London: Palgrave Macmillan.

Fenstermacher, Gary D. (1994) 'From Camelot to Chechnya: the journey of an education dean', in Bowen, Larry S. (eds), *The Wizards of Odds: Leadership Journeys of Education Deans*. Washington, DC: American Association of Colleges for Teacher Education, pp. 37–49.

Ferrero, David (2004) 'Fresh perspectives on school choice', in *Journal of Philosophy of Education*, 38 (2): 287–297.

Friedman, Milton (1962) 'The role of government in education,' in *Capitalism and Freedom*. Chicago: The University of Chicago Press, pp. 85–102.

Galston William (1999) *Liberal Purposes: Goods, Virtues, and Diversity in the Liberal State*. Cambridge Studies in Philosophy and Public Policy. Cambridge: Cambridge University Press.

Gibson, Rex (1998) *Teaching Shakespeare: A Handbook for Teachers*. Cambridge School Shakespeare. Cambridge: Cambridge University Press.

Gingell, J. and Brandon, E.P. (2000) 'In defence of high culture', *Journal of Philosophy of Education* 34 (3) Special Issue, pp. 401–525.

Goode, Luke (2005) *Jurgen Habermas: Democracy and the Public Sphere*. Ann Arbor, MI: Pluto Press.

Greenfield, Meg (2001). *Washington*. New York: Perseus – Public Affairs.

Hansen, David T. (1995) *The Call to Teach*. New York: Teachers College Press.

Hick, John H. (1989) *Philosophy of Religion*, 4th edn. Foundations of Philosophy Series. New York: Prentice-Hall.

Hirsch, E.D., Jr (1988) *Cultural Literacy: What Every American Needs to Know*. New York: Vintage Books.

Hirsch, Fred. (1977) *The Limits to Social Growth.* London: Routledge and Kegan Paul.

Hollis, Martin (1982) 'Education as a positional good', *Journal of Philosophy of Education,* 16 (2): 235–244.

Hollis, Martin (1994) *Philosophy of the Social Sciences: An Introduction.* Cambridge: Cambridge University Press.

Holmes, Mark (1998) *The Reformation of Canada's Schools: Breaking the Barriers to Parental Choice.* Montreal: McGill University Press.

Hunter, James D. (1991) *Culture Wars: The Struggle to Define America.* New York: Basic Books.

Huttunen, Matti (2008) 'The historical justification of music', *Philosophy of Music Education Review,* 16 (1): 3–19.

Jackall, Robert (1988) *Moral Mazes: The World of Corporate Managers.* Oxford: Oxford University Press.

Jessop, C. and Palmer, L. (2007) *Escape.* New York: Visionary Classics.

Krimerman, Leonard I. (1978) 'Compulsory education: a moral critique' in Strike, Kenneth D. and Egan, Kieran (eds), *Ethics and Educational Policy.* London: Routledge and Kegan Paul.

Lamarque, Peter (2008) *Philosophy of Literature.* Foundation of the Philosophy of the Arts Series. Oxford: Blackwell.

Levine, Lawrence W. (1988) *Highbrow/Lowbrow: The Emergence of Cultural Hierarchy in America.* Cambridge, MA: Harvard University Press.

MacIntyre, Alasdair (1984) *After Virtue,* 2nd edn. Notre Dame, IN: University of Notre Dame Press.

Martin, Jane R. (1992) *The Schoolhome: Rethinking Schools for Changing Families.* Cambridge, MA: Harvard University Press.

Martin, Jane R. (2008) 'It's not on the list', in L.Waks (ed.), *Leaders in Philosophy of Education: Intellectual Self-Portraits.* Rotterdam: Sense Publishers, pp. 125–135.

Menand, Louis (ed.) (1998) *The Future of Academic Freedom.* Chicago: University of Chicago Press.

Moses, Michele S. (1992) The heart of the matter: philosophy and educational research', *Review of Research in Education,* 26: 1–23.

Neill, A. S. (1970) *Summerhill: A Radical Approach to Education.* Harmondsworth: Penguin Books.

Norton, David (1990) *Democracy and Moral Development: A Politics of Virtue.* Berkeley, CA: University of California Press.

Okaha, Samir (2002) *Philosophy of Science: A Very Short Introduction.* Oxford: Oxford University Press.

Oser, Fritz (1994) 'Moral perspectives on teaching', in Darling-Hammond, L. (ed.), *Review of Research in Education.* Washington DC: AERA, pp. 57–129.

Packalen, Elina (2008) 'Music, emotions and truth', *Philosophy of Music Education Review,* 16 (1): 41–59.

Peters, Michael (2008) 'Academic self-knowledge and self-deception: a brief excerpt from a personal history of prejudice', in L. Waks, *Leaders in Philosophy of Education: Intellectual Self-Portraits.* Rotterdam: Sense Publishers, pp. 145–159.

Phillips, Dennis C. (2008) 'The Development of a disillusionist', in L. Waks (ed.), *Leaders in Philosophy of Education: Intellectual Self-Portraits.* Rotterdam: Sense Publishers, pp. 173–185.

Phillips, Dennis C. and Burbules, Nicholas C. (2004) *Postpositivism and Educational Research.* Philosophy, Theory and Educational Research Series. New York: Rowman and Littlefield.

Posner, Richard A. (2007) *The Little Book of Plagiarism.* New York: Pantheon Books.

Pring, Richard A. (2007) 'The common school', *Journal of Philosophy of Education,* 41 (4): 503–523.

Putnam, Robert (2002) *Democracies in Flux: The Evolution of Social Capital in Contemporary Society.* Oxford: Oxford University Press.

Ravitch, Diane (1996) *Left Back: A Century of Failed School Reforms.* New York: Simon and Schuster.

Renshaw, Peter (1980) 'The place of special schooling in the education of gifted children', in R. Povey (ed.), *Educating the Gifted Child.* London: Harper and Row, pp. 53–63.

Robenstine, C. (2001) 'Public schooling, the market metaphor, and parental choice', *The Educational Forum,* 65 (3): 234–243.

Rosenzweig, Roy (co-author) (1993) *Who Built America?* (http://www.chnm.,gmu.edu)

Sontag, Susan (1987) 'One culture and the new sensibility', *New York Times*, 31 December, 1987.

Steiner, George (1987) 'Little-read schoolhouse', *The New Yorker,* LXIII (June 1, 1987): 106–110.

Stronach, Ian and Piper, Heather (2008) 'Can liberal education make a comeback? The case of 'Relational touch at Summerhill School', *American Educational Research Journal*, 45 (1) March: 6–38.

Waks, Leonard (ed.) (2008) *Leaders in Philosophy of Education: Intellectual Self-Portraits*. Rotterdam: Sense Publishers.

Westerlund, H (2008) 'Justifying music education: a view from the here-and-now value experience', *Philosophy of Music Education Review*, 16 (1): 79–95.

Williams, Bernard A.O. (2003) *Truth and Truthfulness*. Princeton: Princeton University Press.

17

Moral and Citizenship Education

J. Mark Halstead

INTRODUCTION

This chapter does not aim to provide a comprehensive survey either of the key thinkers within moral and citizenship education or of the major teaching strategies that have emerged in liberal societies in recent times. These topics will be touched on only when they emerge in the more general discussions of key themes. Still less does it aim to provide an overview of different conceptualizations of moral and citizenship education within different cultures and societies, important though this topic is. Rather, it seeks to explore the coherence of the enterprise of moral education itself in the current social and political climate and provide an overview of some of the more general philosophical questions that have been raised about it. The focus is more on moral education than on citizenship, though one of the important issues is the extent to which the two subjects overlap in the values they promote. Other issues include whether schools should transmit values at all, how far moral education is an exercise in rationality, what the goals of citizenship and moral education are, and whether moral education is about giving children the right answers to moral questions, or about giving them the tools they need to exercise their own moral judgement, or about helping them to become virtuous people.

LINKING MORAL AND CITIZENSHIP EDUCATION

The precise relationship between moral education and citizenship education is a complex one that has generated considerable debate (Haydon, 2000; Halstead, 2006). It is true on the one hand that the two subjects have much in common. They both contribute to the development of children's personal, social and cultural identity and they both seek to develop their understanding of the shared values and approved norms of behaviour in the broader society. Values such as equal opportunities, democracy, tolerance, fair competition, human rights and the rule of law are woven into the fabric of citizenship just as much as they are into moral education. The realization that moral virtues and civic virtues are not unconnected and that citizens have moral as well as civic obligations seems to have led to a gradual merging of moral education with citizenship in the last few years, at least in the minds of some politicians and academics. Moral education in any case has had to adapt to rapid social change (in family life, work patterns, cultural diversity, media power, the rise of 'terrorism', anti-social behaviour, and so on), and some of these have been linked with a growing disillusionment among young people with current political processes. A strong emphasis on moral responsibility is now part of the British government's political and civic agenda. Citizenship, we are told, helps pupils to become,

> thoughtful and responsible citizens who are aware of their duties and rights. It promotes their spiritual, moral, social and cultural development, making them more self-confident and responsible both in and beyond the classroom. It encourages pupils to play a helpful part in the life of their schools, neighbourhoods, communities and the wider world. (Qualifications and Curriculum Authority, 1999: 183)

On the other hand, it has been argued that if moral education is to be subsumed under citizenship in the future this will result in a very impoverished form of moral education. Morality is a broad concept which would be distorted if taught only or mainly through citizenship (Halstead, 2006). If they are to become morally mature, young people need to learn qualities of character like love, kindness and generosity that rarely if ever feature in the citizenship curriculum. Moral education also provides the main principles and skills needed if young people are to be able to respond critically to the values underpinning citizenship itself. The two subjects also need to be kept separate, it is argued, because citizenship *can* be conceived as a value-free activity primarily concerned with producing politically literate individuals (cf. Beck, 1998: 108), whereas moral education can never be value-free since it combines information about moral values with the skills of moral decision-making and the motivation to act morally.

There are in fact two main ways of conceiving citizenship education (cf. McLaughlin, 1992). In its narrow sense, it aims to produce informed citizens who know enough to operate effectively in society, whereas in the broader sense its aim is to create active citizens who share a commitment to certain public values and practices such as moral and social responsibility and community involvement.

On the former view, the task of citizenship is a cognitive one, of extending children's understanding of social and political ideas, institutions and issues. Citizenship thus becomes a subject with its own body of knowledge, understanding and skills; for example, students learn about what they are entitled to from public agencies, about the structure of local and national government, the legal system, health care, economics and international relations, and about legislation in the fields of equal opportunities, race relations, community cohesion and human rights. On the latter view, however, citizenship must include the development of values, dispositions, skills, aptitudes, loyalties and commitments in addition to knowledge and concepts (Advisory Group on Citizenship, 1998: 11–13; 44–45). Without a range of shared public values, including a sense of public responsibility, an ability to see beyond one's own interests, and a willingness to identify with the broader political community (Miller, 2000: 28–9), a democratic society would lack coherence and stability. White (1996) argues that democracy is distinguished by its values – justice, freedom and respect for personal autonomy – more than by specific institutions and procedures, but that for democracy to work citizens need to be *disposed* to use their knowledge and skills democratically. If education is to prepare students for citizenship, she argues that it must help them to acquire the civic virtues or dispositions that citizens require for democratic institutions to flourish (cf. McLaughlin and Halstead, 1999: 146–55). These include concern for the common good, belief in human dignity and equality, a proclivity to act responsibly, the practice of tolerance, courage, openness, civility, respect for the rule of law, commitment to equal opportunities, concern for human rights, and so on (Advisory Group on Citizenship, 1998: 44–5).

This broader view of citizenship overlaps significantly with moral education (cf. Beck, 1998, Ch. 4). Crick argues that 'any teaching of citizenship not based on moral values and reasoning would either be mechanical and boring, or even dangerous' (1998: 19). The fact that there is a relationship between citizenship and moral education is not seriously questioned, though the nature and limits of this relationship are open to debate. Torney-Purta claims that 'both moral education and civic education are sub-categories within the larger category of values education' (1996), whereas Crick describes 'PSE, moral education or whatever we call education specifically for values' as 'necessary but not sufficient conditions for good citizenship' (1998: 19).

AIMS OF MORAL EDUCATION

Insofar as citizenship is concerned with the public values of society, it clearly overlaps with moral education – but the latter is just as concerned with private virtues or qualities of character as it is with public values (for a fuller discussion of the distinction between private and public values, see McLaughlin, 1995: 26–7). In fact, statements about the aims of moral education normally focus more on the private than the public, and are often expressed in simple terms – to help children to know right from wrong, to teach children to be good, or to get children to behave morally. But these simple aims mask a great deal of complexity (Wringe, 2006). Are 'right' and 'wrong' relative or absolute terms? What does it mean to 'be good' (cf. Straughan, 1988)? Is the requirement 'to behave morally' satisfied if children have been trained to follow moral rules, even if they do not understand the reasons why – or must they do the right thing for the right reasons? Is morality a matter of conforming to certain externally imposed rules, or a matter of autonomous decision-making, learning how to apply moral principles to particular situations, or a matter of being a certain kind of person?

In view of these complexities, a number of writers on moral education have argued that we can only gain a proper understanding of what is involved in moral education by clarifying the end product, the 'morally educated person' (Wilson, 1973: 21–5). In other words, what sort of qualities, attributes, skills, abilities, knowledge and understanding does a person need in order to be considered morally educated? In this section the aims of moral education are discussed in terms of three characteristics of the 'morally educated person': being informed, being committed to acting morally, and being critically reflective. It goes without saying that such education starts in families, may be reinforced in faith and other communities, and continues through life; schools at best are only one among several influences on moral development.

To produce informed moral agents

This aim may be achieved at three different levels. The first is initiating children into a specific moral tradition. This may be a formal (often religious) tradition, or an informal, family-based one (cf. Harris, 1989, Ch. 2). Internalizing the tradition is important, because moral learning cannot develop in a vacuum. There is research evidence to suggest that this happens anyway, whether or not it is conscious or planned by adults, and family rituals, relationships and interactions familiarize children with a generally informal moral tradition from an early age (Dunn, 1987). Schools may extend this initiation through *character education*, an approach to moral education that emphasizes the direct teaching of key virtues through a range of classroom and extra-curricular activities (Lickona, 1991; for a critique of character education, see McLaughlin and Halstead, 1999). From an educational point of view some such initiation may be necessary so that children can learn what it is to behave morally.

The second level, however, according to Wilson and others, is neither the progressive refinement of family-based or faith-based morality to ensure that it conforms with the expectations of the broader society, nor habituation of this virtuous behaviour through repeated opportunities to practise it until it becomes second nature (cf. Straughan, 1982: 221–2). Indeed, Wilson argues that moral education does not involve passing on specific content at all to students in the form of 'right answers' to moral questions (1996: 90). What is ultimately important in moral education, he says, is understanding principles and procedures, and if this is done properly 'the content will look after itself' (Hare, 1979: 104). The second stage on Wilson's view thus consists of developing what Wilson calls the 'equipment' students need to make good (that is, rational) moral decisions (Wilson, 1990: 128). This 'equipment' consists roughly of the following:

- understanding of relevant concepts such as the nature of virtues or the concept of a moral issue
- identification of the rules or principles which individuals believe they ought to follow in their behaviour
- awareness of other people's (and one's own) feelings and the ability to identify with others and show concern for them
- knowledge of surrounding circumstances and factual knowledge relevant to any given moral situation
- practical wisdom in dealing with people and in moral decision-making (Wilson, 1996: 85–92; cf McLaughlin and Halstead, 2000).

These components of the morally educated person are derived from a consideration of what it means to think and act morally and what is necessarily implied by this. Lickona (1991: 56–61) also puts a strong emphasis on the links between understanding and moral feelings (including conscience, self-esteem, empathy, loving the good, self-control and humility).

The third level is the more academic study of morality, including ethical theories such as utilitarianism and deontology (see below), and the skill of applying these to practical moral issues and dilemmas. Other areas of academic study include psychological theories of moral development, the relation of morality to religion and to the law, and links with spirituality and the emotions.

To produce committed, active moral agents

Most teachers would agree that the aim of developing moral understanding is insufficient in itself: unless it leads to moral action, it has not achieved its purpose. In fact, moral action is both a means of moral education and an outcome of it. Family, school and local community provide important contexts where the normal interaction with others carries many opportunities for moral learning. However, the link between moral understanding and moral action is not always a straightforward one. Commitment to a set of rules or moral principles (by accepting the universalizing nature of concepts like 'good' or 'right') does not guarantee that a person will always live up to these principles in practice – though many people do continue to behave morally when it is easier not to do so. To live up to the principles involves both motivation and strength of will (Straughan, 1982). Wilson's view is that moral motivation is a matter of encouraging students to take seriously the entire form of life or thought that we call morality, to appreciate it for its own sake and to want to become a part of it (Wilson and Cowell, 1987: 35). It has nothing to do with getting pupils to act on 'right answers' because certain kinds of moral behaviour 'pays off' (1987: 34). One of the goals of moral education therefore is to ensure that students have the moral courage to do what they know and feel is right.

To produce autonomous, critically reflective moral agents

It would clearly be a mistake simply to present students with a range of alternative moral views and leave them free to select whichever took their fancy. Teachers have to steer a path between on the one hand implying that there are no right answers in matters of morality and that it is all a matter of taste, and on the other trying to impose right answers on students. To deny the possibility of 'right answers' would overlook the considerable difficulties with moral relativism (cf. Wilson, 1990, Ch. 3), but to serve up the right answers to students on a plate would be unacceptable, as already stated, because they need to reach these answers by the autonomous exercise of their own reason via the appropriate procedures. The ultimate aim of moral education is to create independent, critically reflective, moral reasoners. This involves (*inter alia*) learning the proper use of language, so that students can think and discuss moral issues clearly and rationally and be enabled to approach any moral issue without prejudice, fantasy or other irrational feelings.

The skill of critical reflection may be developed initially through reflection on practice and moral action. Reflection involves asking, for example, whether I should have done this, what else I could have done, why that would have been better, and what others thought of my action. As will be noted later, a similar kind of reflection lies at the heart of Kohlberg's approach to moral education, with its emphasis on the development of moral reasoning through the discussion of moral dilemmas (Colby and Kohlberg, 1987). Moral imagination is an important part of reflection, helping a person to enter into the world-views of others and see how actions and decisions will affect them, and to envisage possibilities that are outside the scope of one's present experience (Harris, 1989: 72–4; Kekes, 1999). The topic of critical reflection brings us back to the links between citizenship and moral education, for it is the key skill needed in dealing with moral issues in citizenship, such as whether there is a moral duty to vote, and whether one should obey an unjust law.

TEACHING AND THE TRANSMISSION OF MORAL AND CIVIC VALUES

Though learning about citizenship and morality, and about values more generally, begins in early childhood and goes on throughout life, teachers are uniquely placed to influence these processes by providing opportunities for discussion, reflection and increasing understanding. The school has three distinct (and perhaps not always compatible) roles to play in values development. The first is that as a public institution it should reflect and uphold the civic values on which the society of which it is a part is based. This does not mean that it should present these values uncritically, for developing critical understanding is central to the mission of all schools. But the school has the responsibility to ensure that the influence it exerts is balanced, partly at least because it represents the official view of society. The school's influence may thus help to counterbalance any extreme opinions and values which the student has picked up elsewhere. The second role is to fill in gaps in students' knowledge and understanding of moral values and of the importance of behaving in harmony with them. Sometimes the gaps in children's knowledge may be substantial ones, and the school has to engage in a programme of character education in order to help children to learn about and internalize core moral values such as honesty, kindness, respect, responsibility, perseverance, compassion, self-discipline and generosity. Of course, judgements about the moral values children need to learn are themselves value judgements, though these are usually based on a broad consensus within society. The third role of the school, and perhaps the most important, is to help students to choose a rational path through the variety of influences that impinge on their developing values. The voice of the school enters the students' consciousness alongside all the other influences (such as the home, peers, the media, the local community and so on) which together form the raw material from which the individual student constructs his or her own civic and moral values; but students need help with sifting, evaluating, synthesizing, appraising and judging the different influences on their values development, and schools are well placed to develop these essential skills. Students may make sense of civic and moral values in different ways, but this need not be a problem from a liberal perspective so long as their decisions are the outcome of rational reflection rather than indoctrination and so long as the public interest is not harmed.

The role of the teacher in both citizenship and moral education therefore involves the transmission of values, at least to younger children (both directly through teaching and indirectly through moral example), as well as (ideally) the encouragement of critical reflection and personal autonomy. The aim of the transmission of values is not to promote unquestioning national or other commitments, for example, or to create a compliant workforce, but to give children a moral start in life, a basis for living together, an opportunity to become habituated into moral behaviour and a set of ideas on which they can in due course sharpen their critical teeth as they move nearer to moral autonomy. Some teachers, however, may initially feel uncomfortable with any notion of transmitting or instilling values (cf. Halstead and Taylor, 2000: 170; Passy, 2003), for several reasons. First, they may want to avoid giving offence, and are aware that the values of the school may not be the values of the home. Secondly, they may believe that values are an individual's private concern and that the imposition of values on anyone is wrong in principle. This belief is the main justification for the *values clarification* approach to moral education in the USA (Simon et al., 1972) and the teacher neutrality approach associated with the School Council Humanities Project in the UK (Schools Council, 1971). Both of these still appear to underpin many texts and materials currently in use in schools, though they have been criticized for being rooted in a spurious relativism, for failing to recognize that it is possible to make mistakes in matters of value (Kilpatrick, 1992, Ch. 4) and for being self-contradictory in that they involve a clear commitment to the value of not imposing values. Thirdly, teachers may claim that there is such a diversity of values in contemporary society on the part of those with a legitimate interest in what goes on in schools that it is impossible to find consensus on any particular framework. On further reflection, however, most teachers recognize that if they are to uphold the essential shared values of society and fill in the gaps in children's moral development, this involves more than just reflection and discussion and implies that learning values (and not just learning *about* values) must be considered an essential part of any programme of citizenship or moral education. All of this has significant implication for teacher education.

MORAL RULES, LIBERAL VALUES AND RATIONAL MORALITY

As already noted, for many people moral education is centrally about helping children to know their moral duties, rights and responsibilities, to understand right and wrong and to be able to decide what to do when facing a moral dilemma. An Aristotelian answer to the question 'How should I behave?' would be to exercise good sense and do what a virtuous person would do. But for many people, this answer does not provide sufficient guidance to children and young people who lack the wisdom and experience to make mature judgements; so teachers try to provide them with a framework of rules that act as guides to moral behaviour. But what rules are appropriate and where do they come from? In their reliance on rules, do teachers sometimes encourage obedience and conformity rather than critical thinking and autonomous decision-making? At what age can children distinguish organizational rules from moral ones? The complexity of classroom realities must not be ignored, but it may be helpful to distinguish three steps in children's growth towards moral maturity and autonomy: the acceptance of externally imposed rules, then internally imposed rules and finally rationally determined rules.

Externally imposed rules, as mediated through teachers, may originate from different sources:

- From religion. Some young people rely on religion for moral guidance, and it is true that many religions provide rules to live by (such as the Ten Commandments, the shariah or the Golden Rule). However, the moral rules of religions are not in agreement over every particular, they may not inspire the respect of young people who have no religious faith, and it is clear in any case that morality can stand alone, without the support of religion.
- From law. A growing number of young people in the West appear to be taking their perspective on right and wrong from the law, on the assumption that if something is not illegal it is not immoral either. But the relationship between the law and morality is a controversial and complex one (see Hart, 1963; Devlin, 1965), and it is far from clear that it is the role of the law in the West to uphold moral values.

- From socialization. Children are often expected to conform to the norms of the local community or the dominant social class, and to internalize the rules that parents and older community members agree on or simply take for granted.

The problem teachers face with the notion of externally imposed rules is that the different sources generate different sets of rules that can't all be right in an absolute sense. So can moral education in schools be based on an objective framework of universal moral rules at all? Moral absolutists believe that there are such rules, though they may be difficult to identify. Moral relativists argue that different moral systems may be equally valid within their own context (Harman and Jarvis-Thomson, 1996). Against absolutism, it is claimed that moral values clearly change over time; slavery, which is morally abhorrent to us, was once widely accepted. Against relativism, it is claimed that it is clearly inappropriate to say that actions like torturing children may be acceptable in some cultural contexts. There are two possible routes out of this impasse. One is the subjective route, which leads one to say something like, 'I don't know whether or not these rules have universal validity, but I know they're right for me'. The other is the rational route, which leads one to say, 'I don't believe we can ever attain absolute certainty in moral matters, but we need to ensure that our moral judgements are as rational as possible'. On this view, the best moral rules are those that are rationally determined. Both subjectivism and rationalism are commonly found within school-based moral education.

The notion of internally imposed rules is thus linked to subjectivism, which itself covers a range of views. Some people ('emotivists') claim that the basis of moral obligation is to be found in radical personal feelings of approval or disapproval. Hume (1739/2000), for example, argues that moral statements like 'Murder is wrong' are simply a way of reporting one's feeling of disapproval of murder, though he does accept that the similarity of our feelings makes it possible in practice to organize society in line with what makes people happy. Ayer (1936) extends Hume's ideas by arguing that moral statements are simply expressions of happiness or disgust, and that moral debate is futile and meaningless. Others have suggested that we intuit certain moral principles and base our moral judgements on them (Moore, 1903); or that individuals base their moral judgements on the core moral principle of love, asking in any given circumstances what love requires them to do (Halstead, 2005); or that it is the fact that an action is based on a personal code of values that makes it moral. Interestingly, a version of moral subjectivism has underpinned numerous official statements about citizenship and moral education in England. The curriculum guidance document *Education for Citizenship* states that 'pupils should be helped to develop a personal moral code' (National Curriculum Council, 1990: 4) and the discussion document *Spiritual and Moral Development* says that morally educated school leavers should be able to 'articulate their own attitudes and values' (School Curriculum and Assessment Authority, 1995: 6). The similarity between this approach and values clarification is worth noting.

The notion of rationally determined rules involves the application of rationally justifiable moral principles to specific moral situations. The emphasis on rational justification and moral principle locates this way of understanding moral rules within a framework of liberal values and once again (since citizenship as conceived in the West is also based on liberal values) draws attention to the links between moral education and citizenship. On the basis of the three core liberal values of individual liberty, equal rights and consistent rationality, a liberal worldview can be constructed that prioritizes such principles as personal autonomy, state neutrality with regard to religion and other definitive conceptions of the good, individual tolerance and respect, equality of opportunity and the just resolution of conflict (Halstead, 1996). From these values and principles it is possible to construct liberal theories of politics (based on democracy, pluralism and social justice), law (based on human rights and an acceptance of the rule of law), economics (based on the free market economy, fair competition and the freedom to hold private property) and education (based on critical openness, the avoidance of indoctrination and the development of personal autonomy). All of these enter into the subject of citizenship as it is currently conceived in the West, as do many of the debates within liberalism, such as whether the right to freedom of expression should take priority over the right to protection against harm or offence; whether private morals can ever be enforced through the criminal law; whether secularism discriminates against religious believers; how to balance civil liberties and state intervention; whether goods should be distributed as a reward for initiative and merit, or in response to welfare needs; and whether free enterprise takes priority over the redistribution of wealth through progressive taxation.

However, liberalism is just as much concerned with morality as it is with politics and economics. At a personal level, certain forms of human behaviour based on the three core liberal values are essential from a liberal perspective. These include telling the truth, keeping promises, treating others justly, respecting oneself and others, avoiding harm to others, being in control of one's own life and body, tolerating diversity, exercising responsibility, supporting the rational resolution of conflict and accepting constraints on one's own actions in order to protect the interests of others. Morality on this view is seen as a set of norms or rules for behaviour that are rationally justifiable through their connection with core liberal values. Morally educated citizens are those who have thought through and internalized these norms.

Beyond that, liberalism provides the basis for a number of ethical theories. The major division in liberal moral theory comes between those like Bentham (1799/1948) and Mill (1863/1970) who believe that *good* is of prior importance and who therefore judge the morality of actions and decisions in terms of their consequences, and those like Kant (1785/1948) who believe that *right* is of prior importance and who therefore judge the morality of actions and decisions by the extent to which they conform to a sense of moral duty. The dominant view in the former category is utilitarianism, which maintains that the justice of institutional and individual action may be measured by its capacity to promote the greatest happiness of the greatest number. Some utilitarians believe that it is possible to construct a system of rules on the basis of the collective experience of happiness or pain in a whole society (Smart and Williams, 1973). According to the dominant view in the latter category, deontology, the compulsory rules (or 'categorical imperatives') which underpin our sense of moral duty can be discovered rationally by the universalizability principle: one should only do something if one is prepared for everyone else to do it as well. Kant also stresses the importance of moral imagination: the capacity to imagine oneself on the receiving end of one's own moral decisions. Deontology is linked to a range of different ethical theories. These include intuitionism (which involves the attempt to fit a set of unrelated low-level maxims of conduct together into a consistent whole, and thus may be considered the nearest philosophically respectable approximation to 'common sense'), and distributive justice (which itself may be understood in different ways, from simply giving people equality of opportunity at one extreme to meeting the needs of the least advantaged first at the other). John Rawls, for example, argues that a just and humane society could best be determined by a group of equal, rational and self-interested individuals making their choice behind a veil of ignorance about their own place in that society; he believed that this situation would generate an appropriate balance between individual freedom on the one hand and justice for the least privileged members of society on the other, because everyone would want some protection against a possible future life of poverty (Rawls, 1971). Liberal moral theories such as these may be seen as an alternative to religious morality, with rules of conduct based on rational principles rather than on prescriptions deriving from religious authority or revelation (though in practice there may be a significant overlap between religious and liberal moral rules).

This all paves the way to the *moral reasoning* approach to moral education, which is rooted in liberal values, particularly the value of rationality. 'Moral reasoning' sees morality as centrally concerned with making critical moral judgements and justifying moral decisions, rather than simply following conventional morals, social expectations or habituated moral behaviour. Following on from Piaget's theoretical research into the development of moral reasoning (Piaget, 1932), Lawrence Kohlberg carried out a longitudinal study of male adolescents and concluded that development in moral reasoning across all cultures progresses through a series of socio-moral perspectives, elaborated in three levels (pre-conventional, conventional and post-conventional) and six stages (Kohlberg, 1968, 1984). The stages are characterized by the nature of the moral reasoning people use, not by the content of the moral judgement they make. Thus at stage one, the fear of punishment provides the main motivation for good behaviour, while at stage two, there is an emphasis on the satisfaction of one's own needs and the continuing acceptance of moral authority. By stage three concern for the welfare of others, particularly one's friends, is the key factor; while stage four sees the emergence of a sense of duty combined with a stronger respect for law and belief in the maintenance of social order. Stage five puts more emphasis on human rights and social contracts, and on the pursuit of the welfare of society in general. The influence of Kant is seen again in the final stage, which emphasizes the universalizability of moral judgements and the importance of moral autonomy. Moral development is thus understood as making progressively more rational moral judgements. Justice is the most central element in moral reasoning. Kohlberg developed the Moral Judgement Interview to assess the stage of an individual's moral development, based on his or her reasoning about how to respond to a hypothetical moral dilemma (such as whether or not Heinz should steal an overpriced drug to save his dying wife). Since no stage can be skipped in individuals' growth towards moral maturity, moral education in Kohlberg's view consists of encouraging people to move to the next stage of moral development, again through discussion of moral dilemmas. The criticism that Kohlberg put too much emphasis on the discussion of hypothetical rather than real-life moral dilemmas may be countered by his experimentation with the establishment of just community schools (that is, small alternative schools within public high schools designed to promote a democratic ethos) which give students practical experience of moral decision-making and pro-social behaviour (Higgins, 1991). The big advantages of Kohlberg's approach are that it is non-authoritarian, it does not side with any particular concept of the good and it facilitates moral autonomy. Moral reasoning continues to play a central role in academic circles in thinking about moral education and Kohlberg himself has been a major influence on subsequent research in both developmental psychology and moral education. Nevertheless, his ideas are far from universally accepted.

SOME CRITIQUES OF RATIONALITY-BASED MORAL EDUCATION

Fundamental challenges to the liberal values that underpin the moral reasoning approach to moral education come in particular from Marxism (cf. Harris, 1979), from existentialism (cf. Cooper, 1999), from radical feminism (cf. Graham, 1994), from various religious world-views, including the Catholic (cf. Arthur, 1994), the evangelical Christian (Pike, 2005) and the Islamic (Halstead, 2004), and from postmodernism (cf. Hutcheon, 2003). To those committed to such world-views, liberalism may be seen as just one more challengeable version of the good. Jean Baudrillard's version of postmodernism, for example, offers a serious challenge to the core liberal value of rationality (1992). Postmodernism has shattered many taken-for-granted 'grand narratives' about shared moral values and universal moral truths. Replacing these 'foundational philosophies' are a moral domain without signposts, a greater plurality of moral beliefs and practices, an increase in moral uncertainty and scepticism, an ironic, almost playful detachment on the part of some moral thinkers, an increase in single-issue moral campaigns and a general increase in tolerance of diversity (cf. Bauman, 1993). MacIntyre (1984) shares many of the postmodernists' misgivings about the way reason has been used by ethical theorists, and sees hope for the future in the moral traditions in the life of communities. Central to the success of local communities are the dispositions or virtues of their members, and so we return to something like the 'virtue theory' of Aristotle, with its emphasis on imitation, habituation and the development of moral sensitivity through guidance and experience rather than training in rational decision-making. The Islamic world-view, on the other hand, is based on values drawn from divine revelation, and produces an approach to moral education which is at odds at several crucial points with liberalism (Halstead, 2007), since the ultimate goal of education is to nurture children in the faith and make them good Muslims rather than turn them into questioning, morally autonomous adults. From a political perspective, it may be argued that the goals of community cohesion and shared values that are at the heart of the liberal citizenship project 'rely on the same desire for social wholeness and identification' (to use Young's words: 2004: 195–9) as do racism and Islamophobia, and may result in the continued alienation and domination of minorities like the Muslims.

Even for those who do not reject the framework of liberal values that underpins much of the thinking about moral and citizenship education in the West, there may be a number of problems with the heavy dependence on rationality that the moral reasoning approach requires. The first is that moral virtues like altruism, which provide a motivation for some people's moral decisions, don't easily fit into a rational framework. Indeed, what is missing from the liberal account of morality is any strong sense of how one should live one's life or what sort of person one should be. An alternative approach to liberalism's rational morality makes the 'virtues' central (Carr and Steutel, 1999). Moral education on this view seeks to develop desirable personal qualities, and to make students into certain kinds of people. Of course, the concept of virtue is itself deeply problematic (Is patriotism a virtue, or humility, or ambition?), and MacIntyre (1984) argues that it is vital to take account of the cultural context and social tradition within which specific understandings and rankings of the virtues have developed. The second problem is the fact that being in a position to work out the right thing to do does not guarantee that it will actually be done; in other words, without moral motivation and will, moral reasoning may have limited benefit. The third is that 'reason' itself may not be a source of moral wisdom but may in fact be morally neutral: it can be used to plan human suffering (as in the Holocaust) just as much as to promote human well-being. Postmodernist thinkers like Foucault (1977) argue that rationality itself has been colonized by the powerful to strengthen their own position and maintain control in society. Fourthly, Gilligan (1982) has argued that Kohlberg's research and its assumptions about justice are based on male thinking and neglect the 'different voice' that is found in female concepts of morality. Some feminists have also criticized the way that citizenship reinforces male dominance (Pateman, 1989: p. 14). For Gilligan, the principle of caring, based on a 'network of relationships', a feeling of connectedness and a sense of responsibility, provides an alternative focus for moral development. Noddings argues that it is the job of the school to 'encourage the growth of competent, caring, loving and lovable people' (1992: xiv), and moral education programmes with 'caring' as their unifying theme are becoming more widespread in the USA (Beck & Newman, 1996).

The relationship between virtue, character and 'caring' on the one hand and moral reasoning, cognition and judgement on the other is one of enduring complexity. In moral education, the notion of practical rather than theoretical reasoning is central, as captured in the Aristotelian concept of *phronesis* (practical wisdom, as opposed to *sophia*, theoretical understanding and wisdom) which unites virtue and character to appropriate forms of reasoning in an intimate way. Aristotle insists that 'it is not possible to be fully good without having practical wisdom, nor practically wise without having excellence of character' (1962: 1144b). Practical wisdom in this sense requires not only appropriate knowledge of moral principles but also skills of discernment and sensitivity to particular situations and individuals. Perhaps more than anything else, the best moral education strives to combine the two.

REFERENCES

Advisory Group on Citizenship (1998) *Education for Citizenship and the Teaching of Democracy in Schools: final report of the advisory group on citizenship.* London: QCA.

Aristotle (1962) *Nichomachean Ethics.* Tr. M. Oswald. Indianapolis, IN: Liberal Arts Press.

Arthur, J. (1994) 'The ambiguities of Catholic schooling', *Westminster Studies in Education,* 17: 65–77.

Ayer, A.J. (1936) *Language, Truth and Logic.* London: Gollancz.

Baudrillard, J. (1992) *The Transparency of Evil.* London: Verso.

Bauman, Z. (1993) *Post-modern Ethics.* Oxford: Blackwell.

Beck, J. (1998) *Morality and Citizenship in Education.* London: Cassell.

Beck, L.G. and Newman, R.L. (1996) 'Caring in one urban high school: thoughts on the interplay among race, class and gender', in D. Eaker-Rich and J. Van Galen (eds), *Caring in an Unjust World: Negotiating Borders and Barriers in Schools.* Albany, NY: State University of New York Press.

Bentham, J. (1799/1948) *Introduction to Principles of Morals and Legislation.* New York: Hafner.

Carr, D. and Steutel, J. (eds) (1999) *Virtue Ethics and Moral Education,* London: Routledge.

Colby, A. and Kohlberg, L. (1987) *The Measurement of Moral Judgement, Volume 1: Theoretical Foundations and Research Validation.* Cambridge: Cambridge University Press.

Cooper, D.E. (1999) *Existentialism: a Reconstruction.* Oxford: Blackwell.

Crick, B. (1998) 'Values education for democracy and citizenship', in D. Christie, H. Maitles and J. Halliday (eds), *Values Education for Democracy and Citizenship.* Aberdeen: Gordon Cook Foundation.

Devlin, P. (1965) *The Enforcement of Morals.* Oxford: Oxford University Press.

Dunn, J. (1987) 'The beginnings of moral understanding: development in the second year', in J. Kagan and S. Lamb (eds), *The Emergence of Morality in Young Children.* London: University of Chicago Press.

Foucault, M. (1977) *Discipline and Punish.* London: Allen Lane.

Gilligan, C. (1982) *In a Different Voice: Psychological Theory and Women's Moral Development.* Cambridge, MA: Harvard University Press.

Graham, G. (1994) 'Liberal vs radical feminism revisited', *Journal of Applied Philosophy,* 11 (2): 155–170.

Halstead, J.M. (1996) 'Liberal values and liberal education', in J.M. Halstead and M.J. Taylor (eds), *Values in Education and Education in Values.* London: Falmer Press.

Halstead, J.M. (2004) 'An Islamic concept of education', *Comparative Education,* 40 (4): 517–529.

Halstead, J.M. (2005) 'Teaching about love', *British Journal of Educational Studies*, 53 (3): 290–305.

Halstead, J.M. (2006) 'Does Citizenship Education make moral education redundant?' in L. Lo, J. Lee and R. Cheng (eds), *Values Education for Citizens in the New Century*. Hong Kong: Hong Kong Institute for Educational Research.

Halstead, J.M. (ed.) (2007) *Islamic Values and Moral Education: a Special Issue of the Journal of Moral Education*, 36 (3).

Halstead, J.M. and Taylor, M.J. (2000) 'Learning and teaching about values: a review of recent research', *Cambridge Journal of Education*, 30 (2): 169–202.

Hare, R.M. (1979) 'A rejoinder', in D.B. Cochrane, C.M. Hamm and A.C. Kazepides (eds), *The Domain of Moral Education*. New York and Toronto, ON: Paulist Press and OISE Press, pp. 115–119.

Harman, G. and Jarvis-Thomson, J. (1996) *Moral Relativism and Moral Objectivity*. Oxford: Blackwell.

Harris, K. (1979) *Education and Knowledge*. London: Routledge and Kegoa Paul.

Harris, P.L. (1989) *Children and Emotion. The Development of Psychological Understanding*. Oxford: Basil Blackwell.

Hart, H.L.A. (1963) *Law, Liberty and Morality*. Oxford: Oxford University Press.

Haydon, G. (2000) 'The moral agenda of Citizenship Education', in R. Gardner (ed.), *Citizenship and Education*. London: Kogan Page.

Higgins, A. (1991) 'The just community approach to moral education: evolution of the idea and recent findings', in W.M. Kurtines and J.L. Gewirtz (eds), *Handbook of Moral Behavior and Development*, Vol. 3, pp. 111–141.

Hume, D (1739/2000) *A Treatise of Human Nature*. Oxford: Oxford University Press.

Hutcheon, L. (2003) *The Politics of Postmodernism*. London: Routledge.

Kant, I. (1785/1948) *The Moral Law*. London: Hutchinson.

Kekes, J. (1999) 'Pluralism, moral imagination and moral education', in J.M. Halstead and T.H. McLaughlin (eds), *Education in Morality*. London: Routledge.

Kilpatrick, W. (1992) *Why Johnny Can't Tell Right from Wrong: Moral Illiteracy and the Case for Character Education*. New York: Simon and Schuster.

Kohlberg, L. (1968) 'Stage and sequence: the cognitive-developmental approach to socialization', in D. Goslin (ed.), *Handbook of Socialization*. New York: Rand-McNally.

Kohlberg, L. (1984) *Essays on Moral Development. Volume 2: The Psychology of Moral Development*. San Francisco: Harper and Row.

Lickona, T. (1991) *Educating for Character: How our Schools can Teach Respect and Responsibility*. New York: Bantam.

MacIntyre, A. (1984) *After Virtue: A Study in Moral Theory*. London: Duckworth.

McLaughlin, T.H. (1992) 'Citizenship, diversity and education: a philosophical perspective', *Journal of Moral Education*, 21 (3): 235–250.

McLaughlin, T.H. (1995) 'Public values, private values and educational responsibility', in E. Pybus and T.H. McLaughlin (eds), *Values, Education and Responsibility*. St Andrews: University of St Andrews Centre for Philosophy and Public Affairs.

McLaughlin, T.H. and Halstead, J.M. (1999) 'Education in character and virtue', in J.M. Halstead and T.H. McLaughlin (eds), *Education in Morality*. London: Routledge.

McLaughlin, T.H and Halstead, J.M. (2000) 'John Wilson on moral education', *Journal of Moral Education*, 29 (3): 247–268.

Mill, J.S. (1863/1970) *Utilitarianism*. London: Everyman.

Miller, D. (2000) 'Citizenship: what does it mean and why is it important?', in N. Pearce and J. Hallgarten (eds), *Tomorrow's Citizens: Critical Debates in Citizenship and Education*. London: Institute for Public Policy Research.

Moore, G.E. (1903) *Principia Ethica*. Cambridge: Cambridge University Press.

National Curriculum Council (1990) *Education for Citizenship*. Curriculum Guidance 8. York: NCC.

Noddings, N. (1992) *The Challenge to Care in Schools: an Alternative Approach to Education*. New York: Teachers College Press.

Passy, R. A. (2003) 'Children and family values: a critical appraisal of "family" in schools'. Unpublished PhD thesis, University of Plymouth.

Pateman, C. (1989) 'Feminist critiques of the public/private dichotomy', in C. Pateman (ed.), *The Disorder of Women: Democracy, Feminism and Political Theory*. Cambridge: Polity Press.

Piaget, J. (1932) *The Moral Judgement of the Child*. London: Kegan Paul.

Pike, M.A. (2005) 'A challenge to Christian schooling in a liberal democracy', *Journal of Research on Christian Education*, 13 (2): 149–166.

Qualifications and Curriculum Authority (1999) *The National Curriculum: a Handbook for Secondary Teachers in England – Key Stages 3 and 4*. London: QCA.

Rawls, J. (1971) *A Theory of Justice*. Cambridge, MA: Harvard University Press.

School Curriculum and Assessment Authority (1995) *Spiritual and Moral Development*. SCAA Discussion Papers: No. 3. London: SCAA.

Schools Council (1971) *The Schools Council/Nuffield Foundation Humanities Curriculum Project*. London: Methuen.

Simon, S.B., Howe, L.W. and Kirschenbaum, H. (1972) *Values Clarification: A Handbook of Practical Strategies for Teachers and Students*. New York: Hart.

Smart, J.C.C. and Williams, B. (1973) *Utilitarianism: For and Against*. Cambridge: Cambridge University Press.

Straughan, R. (1982) *I Ought to But ... A Philosophical Approach to the Problem of Weakness of Will in Education*. Windsor: NFER-Nelson.

Straughan, R. (1988) *Can We Teach Children to Be Good? Basic Issues in Moral, Personal and Social Education*. Milton Keynes: Open University Press.

Torney-Purta, J. (1996) 'The Connections of Values Education and Civic Education. The IEA Civic Education Study in Twenty Countries', paper presented at the Journal of Moral Education Conference, University College of St Martin, Lancaster.

White, P. (1996) *Civic Virtues and Public Schooling: Educating Citizens for a Democratic Society*. New York: Teachers College Press.

Wilson, J. (1973) *A Teacher's Guide to Moral Education*. London: Geoffrey Chapman.

Wilson, J. (1990) *A New Introduction to Moral Education*. London: Cassell.

Wilson, J. (1996) 'First steps in moral education', *Journal of Moral Education*, 25: 85–91.

Wilson, J. and Cowell, B. (1987) 'Method, content and motivation in moral education', *Journal of Moral Education*, 16: 31–36.

Wringe, C. (2006) *Moral Education: Beyond the Teaching of Right and Wrong*. Dordrecht: Springer.

Young, I.M. (2004) 'The ideal of community and the politics of difference', in C. Farrelly (ed.), *Contemporary Political Theory: A Reader*. London: Sage, pp.195–204.

18

Indoctrination

Richard Bailey

INTRODUCTION

The term 'indoctrination' has, generally speaking, strong pejorative associations in current educational discourse. It is often contrasted with educational ideals like autonomy, open-mindedness and critical thinking, and is considered either morally objectionable or a necessary evil that ought to be restricted to highly specific contexts. Indoctrination is usually positioned as the antithesis of the sort of educational practices considered appropriate for a modern, liberal, democratic society.[51] A wide range of subjects and practices have been tarred with the brush of indoctrination. In most cases, the term is used in a rather non-specific way, indicating some sense of inappropriate influence. For example, many journalists use the term in a very emotive way, referring to the blatant processes of persuasion associated with totalitarian regimes, or the more subtle forms of thought control practised by religious cults (Winn, 2000). Suicide bombers, it has been claimed, are indoctrinated into ideologies of self-sacrifice and martyrdom, sometimes through religious schools. Elsewhere, educational writers have condemned as indoctrination attempts by teachers or policy-makers to introduce political topics into the school curriculum, such as teaching left-wing politics (Horowitz, 2007), teaching free-market economics (Chomsky, 2003); citizenship education (Flew, 2000); peace studies (Scruton et al., 1985); and women's studies (Patai and Koertge, 2003). Franklin (2004) even uses the word to describe the UK Labour government's practice of packaging educational and other social policies for media presentation and public consumption. Sometimes teachers themselves label their approach indoctrination, such as during a BBC Radio 4 discussion on faith schools:

> Ibrahim Lawson (IL), headteacher of Nottingham Islamia School: The essential purpose of the Islamia school as with all Islamic schools is to inculcate profound religious belief in the children.
>
> Ernie Rea (ER): You use the word 'inculcate': does that mean you are in the business of indoctrination?
>
> IL: I would say so, yes; I mean we are quite unashamed about that really. The reason that parents send their children to our school is that they want them to grow up to be very good Muslims.
>
> ER: Does that mean that Islam is a given and is never challenged?
>
> IL: That's right ... .
>
> Kate Hellman, course manager at Lambeth FE College who specialises in adults with learning difficulties: My beliefs aren't secular, my beliefs are open-minded. My beliefs ... .
>
> IL: Well, that's precisely what Muslims aren't, you see, we aren't open-minded, you don't have a choice, you are either a Muslim or you are not, and it's a very serious decision to take.
>
> ('Beyond Belief' on faith schools – 10 March 2003 – BBC Radio 4)[52]

One of the common lines of criticism of indoctrinatory teaching is that it contravenes two of the principal ideals of education, at least in modern, liberal societies: autonomy and open-mindedness. Autonomy (see elsewhere in this handbook for more on this topic) leads people 'to make and act on well-informed and well-thought out judgements about how to live their own lives' (Brighouse, 2006, p. 14). Thiessen (1993, pp. 118–19) offers a set of criteria of autonomy that reflect, to some extent, the views of many liberal, analytical philosophers of education, such as Peters (1972) and Scheffler (1989):

- Freedom – whether this is understood in terms of the absence of constraints to *do* what one wants to do, or simply to *think* what one wants.
- Independence or authenticity – which refers to the ability to accept and make rules for oneself.
- Self-control – as autonomous people are not led solely by their passions, but are able to order their desires and aims according to some life plan.
- Rational reflection – as autonomous people subject their actions and beliefs to reflection and criticism.
- Competence – which means that once autonomous people have reached their decisions through rational means they are able to carry them through to completion.

The incompatibility of these ingredients with indoctrination is not difficult to see. In fact, one way of framing the concept of indoctrination is as a form of teaching that interferes with or completely prevents the development of young people's autonomy.

'Open-minded-ness' suggests a willingness to challenge or revise one's beliefs in certain circumstances. Barrow and Woods (2006, p. 73) state their position boldly: 'The most obvious hallmark of the indoctrinated person is that he has a particular viewpoint and he will not seriously open his mind to the possibility that that viewpoint is mistaken. The indoctrinated man has a closed mind'. The argument here is that by producing acceptance of one set of beliefs as true, and consequently rejecting rival views as false, religious teaching closes young people's minds. A problem with indoctrination according to this view is that these sorts of viewpoints act as 'stoppers' that control, limit and channel thought, disavow alternative beliefs, and frustrate critical thinking (Kazepides, 1994, p. 406).

Clearly the ideals of autonomy and open-mindedness are closely linked. Indeed, many argue that the real value of open-mindedness is as a condition of autonomy. The ideal of autonomy promoted within the liberal tradition argues that people should be free to make decisions about their own lives and to act according to their own preferences. Open-mindedness is important, therefore, because it helps generate a critical attitude to the various ideas with which people are routinely exposed in society, and especially in schools. This implies that belief change ought not be based simply on whim or a new form of enforcement, but on a reasoned judgement that the earlier belief was in some way mistaken, or at least less defensible than a latter belief: 'essentially, the open minded person is one who is willing to form an opinion, or revise it, in the light of evidence and argument' (Hare, 1985, p. 16). Open-mindedness allows people to be more self-reliant by examining beliefs for themselves, and, to some extent, make them their own: 'In general terms we might say that the degree to which an individual becomes personally autonomous is closely related to the degree to which he or she becomes open-minded' (Bramall, 2000, p. 203).

TWO PROBLEMS OF INDOCTRINATION

According to Macmillan (1983, p. 370):

> The problem of indoctrination is this: in a modern democratic society, the desired goal of education is that each student develop a set of beliefs that are rationally grounded and open to change when challenged by better-grounded beliefs. In order to develop such students, however, it would seem that they must acquire a belief in rational methods of knowing which must lie beyond challenge, i.e. held in a manner inconsistent with its own content. Thus students must be indoctrinated in order not to be indoctrinated: a pedagogical dilemma or paradox. (Macmillan, 1983, p. 370)

This is a revealing statement as it articulates one of the central themes in recent discussions of indoctrination: namely, that young people need to develop and subscribe to beliefs that are of a certain character or derived through specific means. Macmillan's paradox lies in the apparent dilemma faced by teachers who seek to teach rationally grounded beliefs through non-rational methods. This is not a logical paradox, but rather is a pedagogical paradox (Garrison, 1986; Tan, 2008), since it involves the normative considerations of teachers who find indoctrination objectionable. It would not be a paradox for teachers like the headteacher quoted earlier for whom indoctrination is an acceptable approach, as they would not sanction against the non-rational inculcation of beliefs.

This extends Wittgenstein's argument (1969) that some truths are asserted to young people (especially young children) without explanation. Wittgenstein called this 'training' (as opposed to 'teaching'), by which he meant training in a particular way of seeing ('Weltbild': literally world-picture), or a set of cultural values. This way of seeing provides the 'inherited background against which I distinguish true and false' (Wittgenstein, 1969, p. 94). Propositions describing this way of seeing are inherited before one knows what one is knowing, and before one can doubt it: 'We are taught, or we absorb, the systems within which we raise doubts, make inquiries, draw conclusions. We grow into a framework. We don't question it. We accept it trustingly. But this acceptance is not a consequence of reflection. We do not *decide* to accept framework propositions' (Malcolm, 1992, p. 95).[53] Macmillan interprets this for education as follows: 'Insofar as a set of fundamental convictions is necessary for an individual to enter into any language game, and insofar as these are achieved without rational weighing of grounds, then the mode of teaching comes very close to what recent commentators consider indoctrination' (Macmillan, 1983, p. 370). A paradox arises, he says, when a teacher rejects indoctrination as inadmissible.

Is this really a paradox? It has already been accepted that it is not a logical paradox, as the difficulty does not arise from the process of reasoning. It is neither viciously circular, nor does it lead to infinite regress. Is it, then, necessarily caused by normative considerations of what is and what is not an appropriate teaching method (Garrison, 1986)? In order to address this question properly it is necessary to gain a clearer understanding of the ways in which indoctrination might be demarcated from other teaching approaches, and this will be considered in the next section of this chapter. At this point, however, it is sufficient to acknowledge the potential force of this line of argument, as if it holds it would seem to undermine the moral authority of teaching within the liberal, democratic tradition.

Before moving onto the question of criteria of demarcation for indoctrination, it is necessary to consider a second proposed 'problem': namely, the relationship between indoctrination and doctrines. For example, Peters (1966, p. 41) states that 'whatever else indoctrination may mean it obviously has something to do with doctrines'. Others (such as Flew, 1972 and Snook, 1972b) go on to claim that whenever one is teaching doctrines there is a high likelihood that indoctrination is taking place. At first glance, this might seem to be simply a special case of the preceding discussion, since doctrines can be interpreted as a specific form of belief. However, it seems nonsensical to equate doctrines simply with beliefs, as some dictionary definitions do: we do not talk about 'the doctrine that eight pints equal one gallon, or the doctrine that two twos are four' (Barrow and Woods, 2006). The terms of the debate and the context in which it takes place are often significantly different: in much of the philosophical literature, doctrines are implicitly equated with religious doctrines, or at least, it is the case that religious beliefs and religious instruction are often presented as the paradigm cases of doctrines and indoctrination.

Interestingly, while philosophers of education have gone to great lengths to define indoctrination, relatively little has been written about the concept of a doctrine. Thiessen (1994, pp. 377–380) reviews the different meanings of doctrines offered by philosophers, such as false beliefs, beliefs with insufficient or no evidence, beliefs with ambiguous evidence, unfalsifiable beliefs and beliefs held incorrigibly. He points out, correctly, that some of these proposed characteristics contradict each other, such as false beliefs and unfalsifiable (since to admit a belief as false necessarily requires one to accept that it is falsifiable). Thiessen (1994, pp. 391–392) goes on to offer his own conceptual analysis of doctrines. First, he argues, doctrines refer to the central beliefs, or presuppositions of any belief system. Secondly, doctrines are broad in scope and have wide-ranging implications. Thirdly, doctrines are not verifiable or falsifiable, because (if one is talking about the logical status of statements) they 'are used logically as principles in accordance with which evidence is interpreted, and as such logically could not ever be falsified if they continued to be used in this manner' (1994, p. 392). Finally, doctrines are characterized by their importance. Following on from his account of doctrines, Thiessen (1994, pp. 392–393) makes a bold move: 'It is generally assumed that doctrines are only found in religion, politics and morality, and that the dangers only exist in these areas. I have argued, however, that "doctrines" … are also found in what is usually taken to be a paradigm of non-doctrine, science'. If this position is accepted, it can have one of two outcomes: it either neutralizes the potency of the attack on religious instruction, because indoctrination occurs in all areas of knowledge and belief; or, if one declines to equate science with doctrines, then one is led to abandon the equation of indoctrination with doctrines.

This view of science suffers from a number of difficulties. The first is that Thiessen fails to distinguish properly between descriptive and prescriptive accounts of science, or more specifically between the history and philosophy of science. For example, he writes that

> A review of the history of science would reveal many cases in which false beliefs were adhered to and promulgated … sometimes beliefs are accepted in science which are based on insufficient evidence and even on no evidence at all … there are various presuppositions or first principles underlying science which various authors have recognised as not being susceptible to proof or evidence … science contains beliefs for which the evidence is ambiguous. (1994, pp. 383–384)

To point out the inaccuracies or inadequacies of particular scientific theories at a specific point of time does not undermine the case for a distinctive character for science, nor does it imply conceptual connections with other areas of knowledge in which there have been inaccuracies or inadequacies. A more important criticism is that this account of science may simply be mistaken. A thorough discussion of this issue is beyond this chapter; suffice to say that the position is strongly reminiscent of Kuhn's (1962) historical analysis of science which has received sustained critique since it was first published (e.g. Popper, 1970; Siegel, 1988). Kuhn has been much more influential among social than natural scientists, and presumably this is linked to his emphasis on the sociological and psychological aspects of science (Bailey, 2006). According to many other accounts of science it is misleading to posit a similarity between religious doctrines and scientific explanations, whether the phenomena are called 'beliefs', 'doctrines', or neither. Scientists, in these accounts, are susceptible to subjective factors, but these are not the foci of science. Science concerns itself with linguistically formulated statements and theories that are able to survive precisely the excesses of psychological and sociological interpretation (Miller, 2006). Of course, this short discussion does not settle the matter of the relationship between scientific and religious beliefs. It might, however, raise sufficient doubts about the apparently unproblematic claim that there are doctrines in science, and undermine two possible consequent conclusions: that science indoctrinates; or that the concept of doctrine is too broad to warrant equation with indoctrination.

CRITERIA OF INDOCTRINATION

If it is accepted that education ought to involve only morally acceptable ways of teaching, then most people will conclude that indoctrination is not admissible. However, if some of the arguments discussed above are accepted, it might be conceded as an unavoidable evil that should only be accepted within highly specific contexts. As is apparent, though, the term is used in numerous different ways by different writers, and this has resulted in conflicting accounts of the criteria for demarcating indoctrination.

Philosophers of education have offered a range of interpretations of the conditions necessary or sufficient for indoctrination to take place. The first to be considered here focuses on the *content* of what is taught. As has been seen, many writers on the subject assume that indoctrination is related to a specific type of belief, namely doctrines. Even those philosophers who reject the claim that content is the sufficient condition for indoctrination still maintain that the teaching of doctrines often involves indoctrination (e.g. White, 1972). The problem with doctrines, it has been argued, is that they are not provable, verifiable, or falsifiable (Barrow and Woods, 2006). The discussion of Thiessen's work shows some possible difficulties with this position, but there are others. One problem is that the criticism seems to apply with equal force to almost the whole of the school curriculum. The factual aspects of literature, while important, hardly amount to a worthwhile subject (how might we 'prove' an interpretation of a sonnet?). Much the same could be said for physical education, drama and, indeed, philosophy.

More telling is the charge that the distinction between fact and 'mere opinion' is much less clear-cut than it might appear. In this regard, it is worthwhile considering a cautionary note sounded in different forms by Tan (2008), Mackenzie (2004) and Laura and Leahy (1988). Their concern can usefully be seen in counterpoint to statements like that of Hand (2002, p. 639): 'religious beliefs, since they are not known to be true, cannot be imparted by the presentation of decisive evidence; but to use a form of leverage other than the force of evidence seems to be necessarily indoctrinatory'. Numerous other philosophers follow Hand in relating indoctrination to evidence/reason in this way (e.g. Siegel, 1988; Barrow and Woods, 2006). In fact, the dominant position seems to be what Hepburn (1987) calls the 'basic rational-critical principle' according to which the warrant of a belief is based on the strength of its argument and evidence. Philosophers of science have gone to some lengths to challenge the view that evidence or reason can ever provide proof or certainty in the way implied in Hand's statement (e.g. Popper, 1959; Bartley, 1984), building on fairly well-established discussion within epistemology regarding the inherent fallibility of the senses and reason (Musgrave, 1993). This has led van Inwagen (1991) to conclude that the incessant search for evidence would make everyone agnostics about most philosophical and political questions. This need not follow so long as it is accepted that knowledge does not entail certainty, and that a measure of proof is not necessary to distinguish between better and worse theories, and between currently surviving and dead theories. What does seem to follow, however, is that simple distinctions between different types of content and belief (e.g. rational vs irrational; know-to-be-true vs not-know-to-be-true) ought to be abandoned in favour of a more nuanced and cautious account that acknowledges the inherent fallibility of human knowledge. Of course, it is often (but not always) possible to distinguish between matters of broad consensus and widely contested claims, but the distinction is not strong or easy to articulate, which makes it difficult to accept content as a convincing criterion for demarcating indoctrination.

Discussions of the content of indoctrination also raise questions about the *methods* used to teach it. In Kazepides's words, 'the indoctrinator, because he is inculcating doctrines, must resort to some educationally questionable methods' (cited in Thiessen, 1993, p. 87). It does seem an empirical fact that authoritarian methods have often been used to foster authoritarian beliefs, and presumably this is because the beliefs being promoted do not provide an adequate basis for less authoritarian alternatives. Such methods might include suppressing questions or criticism, forbidding certain topics of discussion, or penalizing dissent. Clearly, some methods of inculcating belief are indefensible, such as brainwashing, drugging, sleep deprivation and subliminal messages (Taylor, 2004). Very few teachers would contemplate the use of such methods. However, subtler methods of indoctrination are possible that might initially appear to be non-authoritative. A charismatic teacher, for example, can rely on rapport with students to promote a misleading impression that certain propositions are unarguable, when they are, in fact, highly contentious, and in doing so, can prevent students from examining the reasons or evidence in favour of them in a voluntary and critical way. Such a teacher might also abuse students' desire to please by rewarding the 'right' answers and punishing, through silence, the 'wrong' answers. This teacher's popularity notwithstanding, he or she can be said to be guilty of indoctrination through failing to give adequate reasons or evidence for the claims being made, or misrepresenting that evidence, and ultimately perverting the teacher–student relationship.

The methods criterion of demarcating indoctrination from other educational practices has been implicitly presumed by many writers on the topic. As Thiessen (1993) notes, even those philosophers (such as Snook, 1972b) who explicitly reject this criterion nevertheless refer to indoctrinatory methods in their analysis. While it may be the case that many descriptive accounts of indoctrination refer to its techniques, method is not a strong candidate as the criteria for indoctrination simply because it is extremely difficult to conceive of methods that are characteristic of indoctrination alone. Many authoritative approaches are used in a variety of illegitimate practices, not just indoctrination: 'The issue is not whether indoctrination is miseducation but what sort of miseducation it is and how it differs from other sorts of miseducation, for example, propaganda' (Kazepides, 1994, p. 400). An account of indoctrination that fails to distinguish it from other practices is of no value.

The third interpretation of the sufficient condition of indoctrination, then, is the *intention* of the teacher. McLaughlin (1984, p. 78) follows this line of argument when he defines indoctrination as the intentional inculcation of unshakeable beliefs, and writes that indoctrination 'constitutes an attempt to restrict in a substantial way the child's eventual ability to function autonomously'. Likewise, Barrow and Woods (2006, p. 70) open their chapter in indoctrination with a description of an imagined school where the whole enterprise is openly committed to nurturing children into the Catholic faith and an unshakeable commitment to the truth of Catholicism. The authors close their account of the school with these words: 'It is difficult to conceive of anyone seriously doubting that these teachers are indoctrinating' (Barrow and Woods, 2006, p. 66). In this regard, there is an important distinction to be drawn between the teachers' *avowed* intentions (what they say they are trying to do) and the *real* intention (what they are, in fact, trying to do). However, this rather presumes that the teachers acknowledge or are aware of their intentions. If these teachers have been educated within an indoctrinatory system, then it is possible that they are no more aware of the actual aims of schooling than their students: the teacher is both a victim and a perpetrator of indoctrination. Leahy (1994) talks about 'unintended indoctrination', by which he refers to teaching that proposes beliefs expressing ideological biases and possibly built into the organizational structure of the school but unrecognized by the teacher, such as sexism, racism or class discrimination. A tight association between indoctrination and intention would, therefore, seem to exclude precisely the types of teaching that the concept of indoctrination was designed to address, and for this reason the intention criterion seems unsustainable.

Finally, there is a fourth proposed criteria for indoctrination, expressed by Scruton et al. (1985, p. 16): 'The most fundamental feature of indoctrination, and the one that most clearly demonstrates its anti-educational character, is its domination by conclusions that are foregone'. This position is different from the content criterion because it is not concerned with the status of the conclusions reached – whether they are justified/proven or not – but with the style by which they have been reached. Another way of phrasing this position is in terms of the *consequences* of indoctrination. According to this perspective, the educational process can be characterized by teaching students how to arrive at conclusions and how to assess them when they are controversial. Indoctrination, then, involves 'a paralysis of intellectual imagination' in which the 'mind becomes closed on those issues which are fundamentally open' (Laura, 1983, p. 45). Closed-mindedness reveals itself in an unwillingness to consider new information and alternative ideas. Therefore, the equation of doctrines with indoctrination is questionable: religious teaching can be characterized by open-mindedness, and science can be indoctrinatory (Bailey, 2006).

Implicit in this account is a prioritizing of the students' ability to judge for themselves the validity of the lessons they are taught. Of course, students learn countless things based on the authority of the teacher, especially during the early stages of schooling. But this does not undermine the argument as a non-indoctrinatory approach would prepare even very young learners to think and act autonomously by equipping them with the intellectual apparatus to deal with reasons and evidence when they are able to do so. Another way of phrasing this position is offered by Thomas Green (1972, p. 37):

> When, in teaching, we are concerned simply to lead another person to a correct answer, but are not correspondingly concerned that they arrive at that answer on the basis of good reasons, then we are indoctrinating; we are engaged in creating a non-evidential style of belief.

Indoctrinated beliefs are impervious to contradictory findings and are, therefore, incapable of amendment by the introduction of evidence or criticism.

The consequences condition is not vulnerable to the criticisms levelled at the other proposed criteria, but it is also not incompatible with them. As Harvey Siegel (1988, p. 81) makes clear, while content, methods and intentions are neither necessary nor sufficient for indoctrination, 'they all tend to promote non-evidential beliefs'. This is the heart of the problem with indoctrination: it fosters a certain style of belief that makes open-mindedness and autonomy unattainable.

THE PERVASIVENESS OF INDOCTRINATION

Philosophers of education have almost universally portrayed indoctrination as a non-educational practice. Indeed, they have gone to some lengths to demarcate education from indoctrination. It is surprising, then, that many of them also believe it is inevitable. Garrison (1986, p. 272) describes indoctrination as 'inevitable' and 'desirable' and even goes as far as to claim that the 'failure to indoctrinate would perhaps be analogous to murder, or at the very least, abortion'. A similar point is made by Green (1972, p. 44), albeit in less emotional tones: 'Indoctrination has a perfectly good and important role to play in education ... and may be useful as a prelude to teaching ... . We need not offer reasons for every belief we think important for children and adults to hold'. Green is arguing here that there are cases in which it is not necessary or possible to teach in an evidential or critical way, and in these instances indoctrination is taking place.

In accepting indoctrination as inescapable, these writers seem to assume that indoctrination involves leading a student to hold a belief that they are unable to justify or defend by reason or evidence. There are countless instances in which students acquire beliefs that they are not able to justify *at that moment*, such as belief about Darwin's theory of evolution by natural selection, or the relevance of mathematical thinking, or the importance of physical health. This predicament is most telling in the case of very young children, since young children are not capable of deliberately choosing to follow the rational course of action or capable of being persuaded rationally. Therefore, non-rational methods are called for. Peters calls this the 'the paradox of moral education':

> What then is the paradox of moral education as I conceive it? It is this: given that it is desirable to develop people who conduct themselves rationally, intelligently, and with a fair degree of spontaneity, the brute facts of child development reveal that at the most formative years of a child's development he is incapable of this form of life and impervious to the proper manner of passing it on. (1966, p. 271)

This argument only holds up if it is accepted that method is the criteria for indoctrination, and there are persuasive arguments against this viewpoint. According to the other proposed criteria of indoctrination – content, intention and consequence – it is entirely reasonable to suggest that young children are *temporarily* unable to comprehend a set of beliefs and practices, yet the content/intention/consequence is fully compatible with educational ideals like autonomy. Accepting that many beliefs are acquired before a student is capable of rationally comprehending them, it is useful to distinguish between two distinct contexts: those in which the lack of reasons or evidence are temporary; and those in which it is a permanent state of affairs. Siegel (1988) argues that facilitating an evidential style of belief means that the students can, in due course, critically evaluate and modify these habits, dispositions and judgements if evidence or reason reveals that they are detrimental to their well-being. He then offers a compromise to those who believe indoctrination to be inevitable by distinguishing between 'good' and 'bad' indoctrination. However, this seems unnecessary. The central issue is not whether or not the students are given reasons or evidence in favour of a belief, but whether or not such reasons or evidence exist. To label any non-evidential teaching as indoctrination robs the term of its normative sense, and blurs the distinction between indoctrination and education.

INDOCTRINATION, AUTONOMY AND OPEN-MINDEDNESS

Snook, who was responsible for two of the most influential books on indoctrination in education (1972a, 1972b) later wrote that:

> For my part, I would not wish to continue the debate on indoctrination though I still believe it to be an important notion. I believe we are as clear about it as we could ever be. We now have to use it in concrete instances to discuss ideas such as evidence, truth, and objectivity and see it as centrally involving a question about the legitimacy of certain kinds of influence on people's minds. The analysis is quite subsidiary to the substantive questions such as 'how, if at all, should religion be taught to the young?' (Snook, 1989, p. 64)

It is up to the reader to decide if Snook is correct on this matter. However, there seems little doubt that indoctrination is a relevant topic in discussions of educational practice. If it is agreed that education should involve only morally defensible ways of teaching, then philosophical questions about educational content, methods, intentions and consequences have significant implications for practice. Some approaches may need to be rejected because they contravene what might reasonably be taken as appropriate for students.

It has been suggested in this chapter that indoctrination can be most usefully characterized in terms of the closed-mindedness and the paralysis of critical thinking and imagination. It is inadmissible because these consequences are incompatible with the principles of open-mindedness and autonomy that are central to education in liberal democracies.

NOTES

51 This has not always been the case: until the second half of the twentieth century indoctrination was understood as no more offensive than concepts like instruction or teaching (Gatchel, 1972). Even today, dictionary definitions generally define indoctrination in a neutral way, emphasizing the transmission of doctrines or beliefs. However, it seems uncontroversial to claim that the term now has a much more negative connotation in both popular and educational usages.

52 The extent to which this perspective is uncharacteristic of Islamic education is discussed by Boyle (2006).

53 There is a parallel between Wittgenstein's 'Weltbild' and liberal philosophers' discussions of 'primary culture' (Ackerman, 1980). For an informed discussion of this concept and how it relates to questions of indoctrination, see McLaughlin (1984).

REFERENCES

Ackerman, A.B. (1980) *Social Justice in a Liberal State.* New Haven, CT: Yale University Press.

Bailey, R.P. (2006) Science, normal science and science education – Thomas Kuhn and education. *Learning for Democracy,* 2, 7–20.

Barrow, R. and Woods, R. (2006) *An Introduction to the Philosophy of Education.* Abingdon: Routledge.

Bartley, W.W. (1984) *The Retreat to Commitment,* 2nd edn. La Salle, IL: Open Court.

Boyle, H. (2006) Memorization and learning in Islamic schools. *Comparative Education Review,* 50, 478–495.

Bramall, S. (2000) Opening up open-mindedness. *Educational Theory*, 50, 201–212.

Brighouse, Harry (2006) *On Education*. London: Routledge.

Chomsky, N. (2003) *Chomsky on Democracy & Education*. London: Routledge.

Flew, A. (1972) Indoctrination and doctrines. In I.A. Snook (ed.), *Concepts of Indoctrination*. London: Routledge and Kegan Paul.

Flew, A. (2000) *Education for Citizenship*. London: Institute of Economic Affairs.

Frankin, R. (2004) Education, education and indoctrination! Packaging politics and the three 'Rs'. *Journal of Educational Policy*, 19, 255–270.

Garrison, W.J. (1986) The paradox of indoctrination: a solution. *Synthese*, 68, 261–273.

Gatchel, R. (1972) The evolution of the idea. In I.A. Snook (ed.), *Concepts of Indoctrination: Philosophical Essays*. London: Routledge and Kegan Paul.

Green, F.T. (1972) Indoctrination and beliefs, In I.A. Snook (ed.), *Concepts of Indoctrination: Philosophical Essays*. London: Routledge and Kegan Paul.

Hand, M. (2002) Religious upbringing reconsidered. *Journal of Philosophy of Education*, 36, 545–557.

Hare, W. (1985) *In Defence of Open-mindedness*. Montreal: McGill-Queen's Press.

Hepburn, R. (1987) Attitudes to evidence and argument in the field of religion. In R. Straughan and J. Wilson (eds), *Philosophers on Education*. Basingstoke: Macmillan.

Horowitz, D. (2007) *Indoctrination U: The Left's War against Academic Freedom*. New York: Encounter.

Kazepides, T. (1994) Indoctrination, doctrines and the foundations of rationality. In J. Astley and L. Francis (eds), *Critical Perspectives on Christian Education*. Leominster: Gracewing, pp. 397–406.

Kuhn, T.S. (1962) *The Structure of Scientific Revolutions*. Chicago, IL: University of Chicago Press.

Laura, R. (1983) To educate or to indoctrinate: that is still the question. *Educational Philosophy and Theory*, 15, 43–55.

Laura, S.R. and Leahy, M. (1988) The fourth dimension of space: a meeting place for science and religion. *Journal of Christian Education*, 91, 5–17.

Leahy, M. (1994) Indoctrination, evangelisation, catechesis and religious education. In J. Astley and L. Francis (eds), *Critical Perspectives on Christian Education*. Leominster: Gracewing.

Mackenzie, J. (2004) Religious upbringing is not as Michael Hand describes. *Journal of Philosophy of Education*, 38, 129–142.

McLaughlin, T.H. (1984) Parental rights and the religious upbringing of children. *Journal of Philosophy of Education*, 18, 75–83.

Macmillan, C.J.B. (1983) *On Certainty* and indoctrination. *Synthese* 56, 363–372.

Malcolm, N. (1992) The groundlessness of belief. In R.D. Geivett and B. Sweetman (eds), *Contemporary Perspectives on Religious Epistemology*. Oxford: Oxford University Press.

Miller, D. (2006) *Out of Error: Further Essays on Critical Rationalism*. Aldershot: Ashgate.

Musgrave, A. (1993) *Common Sense, Science And Scepticism: A Historical Introduction To The Theory Of Knowledge*. Cambridge: Cambridge University Press.

Patai, D. and Koertge, N. (2003) *Professing Feminism: Education and Indoctrination in Women's Studies*. Lanham, MD: Lexington Books.

Peters, R.S. (1966) *Ethics and Education*. London: Allen and Unwin.

Peters, R.S. (1972) Education and the Educated Man. In R.F. Dearden, P.H. Hirst and R.S. Peters (eds), *Education and the Development of Reason*. London: Routledge and Kegan Paul.

Popper, K.R. (1959) *The Logic of Scientific Discovery*. London: Hutchinson.

Popper, K.R. (1970) Normal science and its dangers. In I. Lakatos and A. Musgrave (eds), *Criticism and the Growth of Knowledge*. Cambridge: Cambridge University Press, pp. 51–58.

Scheffler, I. (1989) *Reason and Teaching*, 2nd edn. Indianapolis, IN: Hackett Publishing.

Scruton, R., Ellis-Jones, A. and O'Keefe, D. (1985) *Education and Indoctrination: An Attempt at Definition and a Review of Social and Political Implications*. Harrow: Education Research Centre.

Siegel, H. (1988) *Educating Reason*. New York: Routledge.

Snook, I. (ed.) (1972a) *Concepts of Indoctrination: Philosophical Essays*. London: Routledge and Kegan Paul.

Snook, I. (1972b) *Indoctrination and Education*. London: Routledge and Kegan Paul.

Snook, I. (1989) Contexts and essences: indoctrination revisited. *Educational Philosophy and Theory*, 21, 62–65.

Tan, C. (2008) *Teaching Without Indoctrination: Implications for Values Education*. Rotterdam: Sense.

Taylor, K. (2004) *Brainwashing: The Science of Thought Control*. Oxford: Oxford University Press.

Thiessen, E.J. (1993) *Teaching for Commitment: Liberal education, Indoctrination, and Christian Nurture*. Montreal; McGill University Press.

Thiessen, E.J. (1994) Indoctrination and doctrines. In J. Astley and L. Francis (eds), *Critical Perspectives on Christian Education*. Leominster: Gracewing.

van Inwagen, P. (1999) It is wrong, everywhere, always, and for anyone, to believe anything upon insufficient evidence. In E. Stump and J.M. Murray (eds), *Philosophy of Religion: The Big Questions*. Oxford: Blackwell Publishers.

White, J.P. (1972) Indoctrination and intentions. In I.A. Snook (ed.), *Concepts of Indoctrination*. London: Routledge and Kegan Paul.

Winn, D. (2000) *The Manipulated Mind: Brainwashing, Conditioning and Indoctrination*. Cambridge, MA: Malor Books.

Wittgenstein, L. (1969) *On Certainty*. New York: Harper and Row.

19

Knowledge and Truth[54]

Harvey Siegel

INTRODUCTION: THE RELEVANCE OF EPISTEMOLOGY TO (PHILOSOPHY OF) EDUCATION

Certain general views concerning matters epistemological have often been articulated and defended by philosophers of education, and presupposed by both philosophers and educators. Central among them is the idea that it is possible, and desirable, for people to *know* things, and to engage in and take seriously the fruits of *rational inquiry*, where such inquiry is understood to involve the pursuit of *truth* – concerning the natural world, the human condition, or any other domain about which inquiry is possible. This presumes the legitimacy of talk of truth and falsehood, and of rational belief as belief that is based upon and appropriately related to relevant reasons and evidence. It presumes as well that rational belief is indicative, albeit fallibly, of (probable) truth. The related view concerning education, which relies upon the cogency of these widely presumed epistemological views, is that it is educationally important: first, that students gain knowledge and the ability to engage in rational inquiry; and secondly, that students develop an appreciation of such inquiry, and (insofar as they are able) conduct their believing, judging, and acting accordingly. That is, students should be led, in their education, to value both inquiry and the *justification* that the evidence thereby produced offers to candidate beliefs, judgments, and actions.[55]

I will consider the notions just emphasized – knowledge, truth, justification, and rational inquiry – next, as I develop these widely held epistemological views further; after which I will consider some important recent challenges to them.

THE STANDARD VIEW OF KNOWLEDGE: BELIEF, TRUTH, JUSTIFICATION, AND RATIONAL INQUIRY[56]

Let us begin with *knowledge*. It is uncontroversial, pre-philosophically, that education aims at the imparting of knowledge; students are educated in part so that they may come to *know* things. The familiar parent's question, 'What did you learn in school today, dear?,' is readily interpreted in terms of knowledge, i.e., 'What did you come to know in school today?', and the child's answer equally so: 'I learned/came to know ... .'[57] As has long been recognized, we can distinguish between two sorts of knowledge – propositional knowledge, or knowledge *that*, and procedural knowledge, or knowledge *how*: 'I know *that* the capital of Bulgaria is Sofia, which has many natural springs and has been inhabited by humans for millennia, and that its citizens are presently facing the daunting task of adjusting to Western-style capitalism'; 'I know *how* to factor polynomials, read a topographical map, and ride a bike.' For better or worse, epistemological theorizing in the analytic tradition has centered on propositional knowledge; I follow that tradition here.

How is propositional knowledge to be understood? To ask this question is to ask for a theory of knowledge: What are the necessary and sufficient conditions of knowledge? What conditions must be met in order for some particular knower *S* to know some particular proposition *p*? Since Plato, the standard account of knowledge has been that knowledge is *justified true belief*; these conditions – belief, truth, and justification – being individually necessary, and jointly sufficient, for knowledge. Before enumerating problems with this account, let us briefly consider the reasons which have led philosophers to regard them as *the* conditions of knowledge.

Belief is perhaps the least controversial condition, since it is unclear how a person could know something she did not believe. Suppose you were told by your daughter Mary's teacher that 'Mary knows that the Earth is round, but she does not believe that it is.' Would you think, on the basis of this remark, that Mary *knows* that the earth is round? Could she know it if she didn't believe it? Virtually all philosophical theories of knowledge have answered the last question in the negative, concluding that one can know only what one believes. While I've said nothing about what a belief *is* (a verbal disposition? some other sort of disposition? a psychological state? something else?), it is as universally agreed as anything is in epistemology that belief is a necessary condition of knowledge.[58]

Consider next the *truth* condition. Can a person know something which is false? For example, could I know that the Earth is round, if the Earth were *not* in fact round? Since Plato, most philosophers have regarded it as uncontroversial that these questions must be answered in the negative. If *p* is false, I cannot know that *p*. Of course I can *believe* that *p* even though *p* is false; there is nothing problematic about the idea of a false belief, or even of a justified false belief. Thus I can believe, falsely, that *p* is true, when *p* is false; my false belief that *p* may even be justified, despite being false. But if it is false, I cannot know that *p*. Hence the truth condition.[59]

Finally, consider the *justification* condition. Suppose I believe that there is an as-yet undiscovered species of iguana living in the mango tree in my back yard. Suppose as well that this is true. Suppose, finally, that I have no reason to believe it: I do believe it, but I have (and so can offer) no evidence for the claim. I've made no relevant observations; I have no detailed knowledge of iguanas. I just believe it, and it happens to be true. Do I *know* it? Plato, and the tradition his work spawned, thought not, and considered cases like this one to be cases, not of knowledge, but of 'lucky' true belief. What turns true belief into knowledge is 'an account,' or, in more contemporary language, reasons (evidence) which *justify(ies)* or provide(s) *warrant* for belief. Hence the justification condition.[60]

What is epistemic[61] justification, exactly? What is required of a belief or claim in order that it be justified? There is at present tremendous controversy concerning these questions, which I cannot pursue here.[62] But in general – and especially insofar as this notion is relevant to education – 'justification' is essentially tied to *rational* justification, such that my belief that *p* is justified if and only if I have reasons/evidence which render(s) my belief that *p* is rational. While the two terms 'rational' and 'justified' are not equivalent, they are both *normative* – terms of *epistemic appraisal* – and it is uncontroversial that the primary feature of justification is its normative dimension. Theories of justification seek to explain why beliefs which meet their proposed criteria are *worthy* of belief; why their criteria pick out the worthy beliefs from the infinite range of possible beliefs.

We have already noted the centrality to educational epistemology of the idea that students be brought to an understanding of, respect for, and disposition to engage in rational inquiry, where such inquiry is understood as aiming at *truth*. David Carr, who construes knowledge as 'the grasp of an independent objective order by an epistemic agent who, in his attempts to apprehend it, observes certain rational canons and procedures of disinterested and impartial enquiry' (Carr, 1994: 224) puts the basic idea as follows:

> On any respectable account of knowledge ... the notion of objective truth as a significant goal of human enquiry is simply indispensable if we are to have any confidence that our enquiries may actually get us somewhere by way of an understanding of that which exists beyond the otherwise uncertain contents of our own minds. (Carr, 1994: 225)

How should this notion of 'objective truth' be understood? The natural suggestion is that objective truths are those that *get reality right*, in that sentences are true if and only if what they say corresponds with the way the world actually is. To illustrate with a well-worn example: the sentence 'The cat is on the mat' is true if, and only if, the cat is actually, in fact, on the mat. This so-called *correspondence theory of truth* has been criticized as relying on the rather mysterious notion of 'correspondence.' But the criticism is misplaced, so long as the theory is understood as requiring only a minimal sort of correspondence, captured by Aristotle's dictum that 'To say of what is that it is not, or of what is not that it is, is false; whereas to say of what is that it is, or of what is not that it is not, is true' (Aristotle, *Metaphysics*, Book IV, 6, 1001b). This understanding is sufficient to secure the educational importance of inquiry noted above; it is, moreover, in keeping with more technical recent work in epistemology, metaphysics, and philosophy of language concerning truth.[63] A key feature of the theory is that, according to it, truth is *independent of the beliefs of epistemic agents*: our thinking that something is true does not make it so; what does make it so – its 'truth maker' – is some state of affairs which obtains independently of our thinking that it does.

This conception of truth has come in for serious criticism in recent general philosophy and philosophy of education; we will consider some of these criticisms below. In addition to these criticisms, there are also, as has been noted, important extant controversies concerning the justification condition. There are, furthermore, important controversies concerning the standard, 'justified-true-belief' account of knowledge more generally. Some argue, Plato to the contrary notwithstanding, that justification is not a necessary condition of knowledge. Others point to Gettier cases (Gettier, 1963) – i.e., cases in which persons have justified true beliefs but nevertheless seem not to know – in order to argue that these conditions are not jointly sufficient for knowledge.[64] It must also be acknowledged that further controversies exist about many of the points made thus far, and about many other matters not mentioned. These controversies remain ongoing at present; no immediate resolutions are in sight. This is, I suppose, only to be expected when such fundamental philosophical matters are at issue.

These controversies concerning the analysis of knowledge and its conditions, however, do not automatically or straightforwardly challenge the general view of the relevance of epistemology to education and educational philosophy suggested earlier. Despite them, we seem still within our rights to think it educationally important that students gain knowledge, that they learn how to inquire, that they come to value such inquiry and the rational justification it provides, that such inquiry be conceived as inquiry concerning the truth, and so on. But, are we? To answer this question we must consider some recent challenges to the theses just mentioned.

RECENT CHALLENGES TO (EDUCATIONAL) EPISTEMOLOGY

Code's challenge to 'S-knows-that-p' epistemologies

I begin with a very general critique of the entire approach to epistemology just rehearsed. Lorraine Code criticizes 'S-knows-that-p epistemologies' (1993: 15)[65] on several grounds. In order to appreciate the force of her critique, it is important to keep in mind that Code's critique is of the approach (sketched in the second section of the chapter) that tries to analyze or define the key terms of epistemology – knowledge, truth, belief, justification, rationality, etc. – *generally*, i.e., for all epistemic subjects. The conditions of knowledge, on this view, are what they are, independently of the features/attributes of individual knowers.

This approach abstracts away from the particularities of such individual knowers – who they are, what they believe, what they feel, what assumptions they make or loyalties they hold dear, what culture or historical epoch they live within, what gender, racial, ethnic or class location they occupy, etc. – in order to arrive at a 'universal' epistemology applicable to all knowers. It is this zeal for universality, and rejection (as irrelevant) of particularity, of *whose* knowledge a given bit of knowledge is, that constitutes the focus of Code's critique.

Code's criticism, very briefly, is this. Universal epistemologies attend to only a problematically narrow range of cases (1993: 15) and presuppose illusory and flawed epistemic ideals of 'pure' objectivity and value-neutrality which errone-ously sanction the transcendence of particularity and contingency and treat knowers as essentially equivalent and interchangeable (1993: 16). Because of this, they deny knowers their unique, individual 'subjectivities' and fail to take such subjectivity into account in their analyses of knowledge.[66] Code's overall argument, she summarizes, 'points to the conclusion that necessary and suffi-cient conditions for establishing empirical knowledge claims cannot be found, at least where experientially significant knowledge is at issue' (1993: 39). Thus, the project undertaken by '*S*-knows-that' epistemologies is doomed.

These are fundamental, deep criticisms. While there is much to say about each of Code's points, space allows consideration only of her main claim: that accounts of knowledge must 'take subjectivity into account,' and therefore that general, impersonal accounts of knowledge, in terms of necessary and sufficient condi-tions, are not possible. Code insists on the recognition of the place of subjectivity in knowledge and on its proper analysis Her complaint is that '*S*-knows-that-*p*' epistemologies 'homogenize' knowers: they render crucial differences among knowers invisible, and regard all knowers as essentially equivalent. In particular, these accounts ignore the relevance of *gender* – they problematically presume 'that gender has nothing to do with knowledge, that the mind has no sex, that reason is alike in all men, and man "embraces" woman' (1993: 20). Recognizing that gender intersects with other 'specificities' such as class, race, and ethnicity, Code challenges this 'homogenization' of knowers, and argues that its break-down forces epistemologists to contemplate subjectivity in their analyses of knowledge: 'Homogenizing those differences under a range of standard or typi-cal instances always invites the question, "standard or typical for whom"? Answers to that question must necessarily take subjectivity into account' (1993: 20, note deleted). Consequently, epistemologists must 'pay as much attention to the nature and situation – the location – of *S* as they commonly pay to the content of *p*'; they must 'take subjective factors – factors that pertain to the circum-stances of the subject, *S* – centrally into account in evaluative and justificatory procedures' (1993: 20).

On one reading of it, Code's point is uncontroversial. Epistemologists typically insist that knowledge requires justification, that justification is relative to evi-dence, and that evidence is relative to person, in the sense that different people will have access to different sets of evidence. Just as the non-physicist will lack evidence about technical matters that the physicist has, some people will lack the perceptual and other experience and background knowledge that others have – and will consequently not be in a position to know what others do. Insofar, taking the knower's location into account in determining what she knows is quite standard epistemological fare (Feldman, 1994).

But Code has more in mind than this. Consider two knowers, John and Mary. Both observe a conversation between Mr. Smith, a landlord, and Ms. Brown, a tenant in Smith's apartment building. After observing the conversation, John and Mary discuss it, and discover that they believe quite different things about it. In particular, Mary believes that Smith treated Brown in a sexist manner, while John believes that he did not. Assume that John and Mary have different 'subjectivities' – Mary has been treated as a girl/woman all her life, and has been exposed daily to institutionalized sexism in school, at home, in the media, etc., while John has enjoyed the privileges of patriarchy. Consider now the questions: Does John know that Smith did not behave in a sexist way? Does Mary know that Smith did behave in that way? If Code is right that subjectivity has a central place in knowing and its philosophical analysis, then presumably John and Mary do indeed, or at least might, know different things about the sexist cast of Smith's behavior toward Brown. How can we answer these questions? How can we determine whether or not John and Mary know these things?

I have no desire to resolve these questions about Smith's behavior here. Indeed, it seems clear that the case would have to be filled in in considerably more detail for resolution to be possible. My point, rather, is that once we have taken due note of John's and Mary's subjectivities, answering the questions *still requires an analysis of knowledge*. For example, it seems clear that we cannot simply grant that John and Mary know these things just because their respective subjectivities lead them to believe them. After all, John may himself be sexist, which might call into question his claim to know that Smith is not. Mary's claim to know that Smith's behavior was sexist might be similarly called into question. But to agree that we can't simply grant John and Mary knowledge of Smith on this basis is to hold that 'subjectivity-inspired belief' is not sufficient for knowledge. On the other hand, to grant them knowledge of Smith is to hold that such belief *is* sufficient for knowledge. However we answer the questions about John's and Mary's knowledge, we will be relying upon some analysis of knowledge or other. Code seems, in her insistence on realism and empiricism as 'mitigating' her relativism (1993: 39–41), to be committed to regarding truth as a condition of knowledge. Nothing in her discussion suggests that she would reject the belief condition. I hypothesize that her main diversion from standard 'S-knows-that-p' analyses is her insistence that 'subjectivity' be somehow built into the justification condition. Whether this is right or not, however, the main point is that Code has not escaped the 'S-knows-that-p' tradition. Her challenge to the ideals of pure objectivity and value-neutrality, her insistence that subjectivity be taken into account in determining what knowledge is and who has it, and her recommendation that the sort of knowledge taken as exemplary be expanded, are all consistent with the fact that Code is attempting to develop a conception of knowledge – one which will allow us to determine, for particular S and p, whether S knows that p.

Whatever the other merits of Code's feminist, subjectivity-oriented epistemology might be, then, her critique of 'S-knows-that-p epistemologies' does not succeed; nor does it directly challenge either the epistemological or the educational theses concerning knowledge, truth, justification, and rational inquiry noted above. Let us see how these views fare in the face of criticisms which do directly call them into question.

'Overcoming epistemology': truth, foundationalism, and agency

Charles Taylor (1987) famously urges us to 'overcome epistemology.' However, unlike Code, Taylor has as his target not 'S-knows-that-p epistemology,' but rather the 'correspondence truth'-dependent idea that 'knowledge is to be seen as correct representation of an independent reality' (1987: 466).[67] This, Taylor argues, rests upon an inadequate conception of the *self* as radically disengaged from the natural and social worlds (1987: 471). For selves cannot coherently be seen as so disengaged:

> Even to find out about the world and formulate disinterested pictures, we have to come to grips with it, experiment, set ourselves to observe, control conditions. But in all this, which forms the indispensable basis of theory, we are engaged as agents coping with things ... . [W]e couldn't form disinterested representations any other way (1987: 476).[68]

This point, Taylor suggests, 'undermines' 'the entire epistemological position' (1987: 476), in two ways. First,

> Foundationalism goes, since our representations of things ... are grounded in the way we deal with these things. These dealings are largely inarticulate, and the project of articulating them fully is an essentially incoherent one, just because any articulative project would itself rely on a background or horizon of nonexplicit engagement with the world. (1987: 476–467)[69]

Secondly, and more deeply:

> Foundationalism is undermined, because you can't go on digging under our ordinary representations to uncover further, more basic representations. What you get underlying our representations of the world ... is not further representations but rather a certain grasp of the world that we have as agents in it. This shows the whole epistemological construal of knowledge to be mistaken. It doesn't just consist of inner pictures of outer reality, but grounds in something quite other. And in this 'foundation' the crucial move of the epistemological construal, distinguishing states of the subject – our 'ideas' – from features of the external world, can't be effected. We can draw a neat line between my *picture* of an object and that object, but not between my *dealing* with the object and that object. (1987: 477, emphases in original)

We needn't agree with Taylor here: I can, it seems, perfectly well distinguish, for example, between my *dealing* with the keyboard on which I am now typing, and the keyboard. For example, the latter is made of plastic and is gray, while the former is not; the former is often slow and clumsy, while the latter is not. That I must interact with it to discover its properties or construct a representation of it is quite compatible with the distinction. But the main points to make lie elsewhere.

First, the 'epistemological construal' which Taylor is criticizing is not required by anything said about knowledge, truth, epistemology or education thus far; the positive, standard view advanced in the second section of the chapter does not presuppose that 'underlying our representations of the world' are 'further representations.' On the contrary, the standard view is perfectly compatible with the claim that our representations in some sense depend upon our interaction, as agents, with the world which our representations represent.

Secondly, Taylor's argument suffers from a basic unclarity. When he writes that 'the whole epistemological construal of knowledge' is mistaken because knowledge 'doesn't just consist of inner pictures of outer reality, but grounds in something quite other,' how exactly is '*grounds*' to be understood? As the passage is written, the 'grounds' of knowledge are just what knowledge 'consists of'; [70] but Taylor seems clearly to mean by 'grounds' not what knowledge 'consists in' but rather what our beliefs about and representations of the world are ultimately *caused by* – they are caused, the argument goes, by our dealings with/ in the world. Let us, for the sake of argument, grant Taylor this claim: our knowledge of the world depends (causally) ultimately on our agency in the world. This in no way undermines the standard view that knowledge consists of beliefs which (among other conditions) accurately portray 'an independent reality.' That is, Taylor's being right (if he is) that our gaining knowledge of the world requires our engagement with that world, is completely compatible with the claim that knowledge is the product of successful inquiry, where 'success' is understood in terms of truth.

Thirdly, Taylor's argument against the 'epistemological construal' depends upon the key epistemological notions of the standard view. Taylor is arguing that it is *true* that the 'epistemological construal' fails; that Heidegger's argument shows it to be rationally untenable; that our representations depend in some sense upon our agency; etc. Insofar, Taylor's attempt to 'overcome epistemology' requires something very like the epistemology defended thus far.

Taylor's main thesis is that we must follow Heidegger in recognizing that in the end we are not disengaged subjects, but *agents*, and that our knowledge depends upon this fact. I have argued that Taylor's/Heidegger's argument for this claim fails. But even if it succeeds, it is unclear what follows other than that we must embrace fallibilism – which the targeted epistemological-educational views clearly do. In other words, Taylor's 'overcoming' of epistemology leaves epistemology pretty much as it is. In particular, we are free, Taylor's criticisms to the contrary notwithstanding, to understand knowledge, and truth, in terms of 'correct representation of an independent reality' (1987: 466).

Fallibilism, foundationalism, and the challenge of postmodernism

Finally, in view of the popularity of recent 'postmodern' challenges to it, it will be useful to make some further general observations concerning 'foundationalism' and the several senses in which the educational epistemology advocated here is, and isn't, 'foundationalist.'

Several recent critiques of epistemology have focused on 'foundationalism' and certainty, and have urged that these be abandoned, and that *fallibilism* – the view that none of our beliefs are certain, that we can always be mistaken, and that we ought therefore to have an attitude of modesty and humility toward our epistemic judgments – be embraced. According to fallibilists, our views are far too susceptible to error for us ever to be warranted in arrogantly proclaiming ourselves to 'have' the truth, or to know with certainty.[71] I hope it is clear that such fallibilism is completely in keeping with the epistemological views defended thus far; it is embraced by contemporary epistemologists virtually universally. Despite this embrace, that epistemology is routinely criticized as 'foundationalist.' What exactly is the target of these critiques?

Within mainstream epistemology, 'foundationalism' has a narrow, technical meaning, denoting one possible response to the 'regress problem' concerning epistemic justification.[72] It is not this sense of 'foundationalism' that is at issue. Rather, the object of criticism is a broader notion of foundationalism, helpfully summarized by Wilfred Carr (1995).[73] Carr is concerned to describe (and presumably to endorse) the 'postmodernist challenge' to 'Enlightenment educational values' (1995: 78) and 'the postmodernist critique of Enlightenment philosophical thought' – in particular, the 'theoretical criticisms collectively aimed at dismantling the Enlightenment conceptions of reason and the rational subject' (1995: 79). The main target of postmodernist critique is,

> Kant's 'foundationalist' philosophy – a philosophy designed to show that the Enlightenment concept of the rationally autonomous subject did not simply apply to a particular culture or society but was grounded in *a priori* truths about the 'universal essence' of human nature itself. At the risk of oversimplification, three of the familiar postmodernist strategies used to undermine and discredit this foundationalist philosophy can be rapidly stated. The first is to call into question the Enlightenment's universal, *a priori* and absolutist conception of reason. To its universality, postmodernists counterpose the 'local' determinants of what counts as rational thought and action; to its *a priori* necessity, they counterpose its fallibility and its contingency; and to its absolutism they insist that rationality is always relative to time and place. What, secondly, postmodernism opposes and denies is the Enlightenment idea of a disembodied 'rational autonomous subject'. In opposition to the assumption that the self has at its centre an essential human nature that predates history and is prior to a particular form of social life, postmodernism counterposes the image of the self as 'decentred': a centreless configuration mediated and constituted through the discourses learned and acquired in becoming a participant in a historical culture. ...
>
> Third ... is its critique of the Enlightenment distinction between the 'knowing subject' and an 'objective world' to be known. Against this postmodernism insists that the subject's knowledge of the world is always preinterpreted: it is always situated in a conceptual scheme, part of a text, internal to a tradition outside of which there are only other conceptual schemes, texts and traditions and beyond which it is impossible to stand. It follows from this that knowledge is never 'disinterested' or 'objective' and that the Enlightenment idea of the knowing subject, disengaged from the world, is a myth ... . What postmodernism insists is that there is no realm of 'objective' truths to which science has exclusive access, no privileged position that enables philosophers to transcend the particularities of their own culture and traditions, no Archimedian point which can provide philosophical inquiry with a neutral ahistorical starting point (1995: 79–80).

I beg the reader's indulgence for the length of this quotation; I offer it in order to make clear just how broad this broader sense of 'foundationalism,' against which the postmodernist rebels, actually is. Space does not permit a detailed reaction to the many points Carr makes. But some general comments are in order.

First, Carr does not here defend either these several criticisms of 'Kant's foundationalist philosophy,' or the alternative postmodernist views, but only offers the latter as alternatives to (Kant's) foundationalism, in the form of 'postmodernism denies ... ,' 'postmodernism insists ... ,' and 'postmodernism counterposes ... .' Carr suggests that these 'postmodernist strategies' in fact 'undermine and discredit this foundationalist philosophy,' but it is unclear why we should agree. Carr's discussion does not defend postmodernism, but simply takes it for granted.

Secondly, some of these criticisms of foundationalism, as stated, face huge difficulties, as they appear to presuppose what they want to reject. For example, Carr's postmodernist wants to reject the possibility of objective knowledge, but apparently regards it as an objective fact about the world that a subject's knowledge of that world is always 'preinterpreted,' and that knowledge is therefore never objective. Despite the postmodernist's repudiation of 'universal reason,' she likewise seems to presuppose a 'universal' conception of reason (or rationality or logic), since the non-objective character of knowledge is said to *'follow from'* (emphasis added) the fact that a subject's knowledge is always preinterpreted, where this implication is not relativized or contextualized – it follows, apparently, for us all.[74] Similarly, the postmodernist insistence that there is 'no privileged position that enables philosophers to transcend the particularities of their own culture and traditions' seems itself an attempt to speak from just such a position, since it seems to be making an assertion concerning all philosophers, cultures, and traditions. Equally problematic is the apparently incoherent suggestion that 'rationality is *always relative* to time and place' (emphases added): does the suggestion apply to itself? Either way this question is answered, deep difficulties loom.[75] In short, there appear to be deep internal inconsistencies in the postmodernist position as Carr articulates it.

Thirdly, 'foundationalist philosophy' is specified in such vague and general terms that it would be hard to locate a clear advocate of it in the contemporary literature. For example, even if Kant thought so (which is less than clear), no contemporary philosopher claims that there is 'an essential human nature that predates history and is prior to a particular form of social life,' if that is taken to mean that there might exist actual possessors of human nature outside of history or some particular form of social life, or that there might be a 'disembodied "rational autonomous subject".' Similarly, which contemporary epistemologist regards empirical knowledge as infallible? Which philosopher holds that there is an 'Archimedean point which can provide philosophical inquiry with a neutral ahistorical starting point'? Which philosopher subscribes to the 'myth' that objectivity requires that cognitive agents be 'disengaged from the world'? The contemporary 'foundationalists' that Carr's postmodernists oppose are exceedingly hard to find.

Fourthly, the postmodernist's argument against the possibility of objective knowledge is a strikingly weak one. Which principle of postmodernist logic sanctions the move from 'knowledge ... is always situated in a conceptual scheme, part of a text, internal to a tradition' to 'outside of which there are only other conceptual schemes, texts and traditions'? Does it really follow, as Carr's postmodernist alleges, that because my knowledge of trees, atoms, and people is always situated within my conceptual scheme, that there aren't trees, atoms, and people which exist independently of my scheme? Is it really being alleged that there were no stars before there were people to declare their (the stars') existence in their (the people's) schemes? The postmodernist critique of objective knowledge, and of a reality independent of us and our schemes, is, alas, deeply problematic.

Finally, and most importantly in the present context: this postmodernist critique of 'foundationalist philosophy' fails seriously to challenge the educational epistemology articulated and defended earlier. Some aspects of the critique successfully challenge positions – e.g., that knowers have a 'view from nowhere,' outside of all conceptual schemes – which are not part of that epistemology.[76] Other aspects of the critique simply fail – for example, the criticism of the distinction between the 'knowing subject' and the 'objective world' has been shown to be multiply problematic in this and previous sections. In any case, nothing in the postmodernist case we have been considering suggests that there is anything problematically 'foundationalist' about the views defended here: that it is educationally important that students gain knowledge, and develop the ability to engage in rational inquiry which seeks the truth; and that they develop an appreciation of such rational inquiry, and (insofar as they are able) conduct their believing, judging, and acting accordingly.

CONCLUSION

If my arguments have succeeded, then the challenges to the views of knowledge, truth, justification, and rational enquiry articulated earlier – and by implication, to the place of these views in educational theorizing – have not. The criticisms considered – Code's challenge to 'S-knows-that-p epistemology'; Taylor's challenge to views of knowledge which regard it as representing an independent reality, and which do not recognize that knowers are agents; and Carr's postmodernist's challenge to everything 'modern' – fail to upend either the epistemological position defended above, or the basic ideas that education ought to strive to impart to students knowledge, the ability to engage in rational inquiry, and the disposition to engage in such inquiry and to take seriously its results. These claims are not 'foundationalist' in any pernicious sense. They fully embrace fallibilism, and while they are 'objectivist,' they are unproblematically so, presupposing neither a 'view from nowhere' nor disembodied knowers. I hope my consideration of these criticisms has not been unduly negative, for there is much of value in them, as I hope my discussion has acknowledged. Still, what is right and valuable about them is completely compatible with acknowledging both the epistemological and the educational legitimacy of the epistemically oriented aims and ideals of education articulated above.

ACKNOWLEDGMENT

Thanks to David Carr for helpful editorial advice.

NOTES

54 From 'Knowledge, truth and education', Siegel, H. in D. Carr (ed.), *Education, Knowledge and Truth: Beyond the Postmodern Impasse*. © 1998. Reproduced by permission of Taylor & Francies Books UK.

55 I should note that this cluster of epistemic aims of education skates over recent controversy concerning their relative priority. Robertson (2009) offers an excellent overview.

56 I intend this section to be uncontroversial; it presents information routinely covered in more detail in epistemology textbooks: e.g., Audi (2002), BonJour (2002), and Feldman (2003). Scheffler (1965) remains an important basic discussion of the conditions of knowledge, both in general and as they relate to education.

57 I don't mean to suggest that the two notions are equivalent; they are not. While I may rightly be said to have learned something which is false (e.g., 'in school today, I learned that the atomic number of gold is 55'), I cannot come to know that which is false – I may have *learned*, but cannot be said to *know* that the atomic number of gold is 55, for it isn't. For lucid clarificatory discussion, see Scheffler (1965), Ch. 1.

58 For further discussion of the belief condition see the texts cited in Endnote 2.

59 For an excellent brief guide to extant controversies concerning truth and defense of his 'descriptive-success' version of the correspondence theory, see Goldman (1999, Ch. 2).

60 See, especially, Plato's *Theaetetus*, reprinted in Hamilton and Cairns (1961).

61 As opposed to other sorts of justification, e.g., prudential or moral. I leave 'epistemic' out below, but presuppose it throughout.

62 The literature here is vast. BonJour and Sosa (2003) offers a wide-ranging introduction to the issues.

63 See here Horwich (1990), Schmitt (1995), Alston (1996), and Goldman (1999, Ch. 2), all of which defend conceptions of truth consonant with Aristotle's dictum, and which (I believe) avoid the problems afflicting other, more robust views of 'correspondence.'

64 Gettier's brief paper spawned an enormous literature, and generated a wide range of attempts to adjust or supplement the standard account of knowledge, either by deleting one or more of the original three conditions, by adding some fourth condition, or by some combination of these; thus were born (or came to prominence) defeasibility, causal, explanationist and many other accounts of knowledge.

65 See also Code (1991, 1992). Unless otherwise noted, citations are to Code (1993).

66 Code also claims that these epistemologies presume an indefensible political neutrality, and that the political dimensions of epistemological theorizing need to be much more central to such theorizing (1993: 16, 20, 23, 26; 1992: 138). I have some sympathy for this claim, although I believe that it is in important respects overstated; I regret that I cannot consider it further here.

67 All page references to Taylor are to Taylor (1987).

68 This point seems to conflate disengaged *persons*, on the one hand, and disengaged or disinterested *representations*, on the other. But I will not pursue this worry here.

69 Here too there seems to be an important equivocation: '*grounded*' in the cited passage seems clearly to mean *caused by*. But that our representations of things are caused by our dealings with these things seems irrelevant to the epistemological issue Taylor takes himself to be addressing: namely, the adequacy or justificatory status of our representations. In other words, Taylor's point about agency, even if correct, does not undermine the epistemic status of our representations.

70 This is already a quite charitable reading of the passage, which conflates (a) the grounds of *knowledge* and (b) the grounds of the '*epistemological construal*' of knowledge.

71 Peirce and Popper famously advocated fallibilism; virtually all contemporary epistemologists embrace it to some significant degree. For discussion, see Siegel (1997, Chs 1–2, 8).

72 According to this response, foundational beliefs are those beliefs which are not justified in terms of other beliefs. For discussion, see Siegel (1997: 112–114).

73 All page references in this section are to Carr (1995).

74 For a more detailed response to the postmodernist critique of 'universal reason,' see Siegel (1997, Ch. 10). Carr's critique of universality also presupposes a sharp local/universal dichotomy (see esp. 1995: 81); for arguments against this dichotomy, see Siegel (1997, Ch. 12).

75 For discussion, see Siegel (1987, 2004).

76 For further discussion of the implications of the idea that there is no 'Archimedean point,' no vantage point beyond all schemes, see Siegel (1987, ch. 2); and Siegel (2004).

REFERENCES

Alston, W.P. (1996) *A Realist Conception of Truth*. Ithaca, New York: Cornell University Press.

Audi, R. (2002) *Epistemology: A Contemporary Introduction to the Theory of Knowledge*. New York: Routledge.

BonJour, L. (2002) *Epistemology: Classic Problems and Contemporary Responses*. Lanham: Rowman and Littlefield.

BonJour, L. and E. Sosa (2003) *Epistemic Justification: Internalism vs. Externalism, Foundations vs. Virtues*. Malden: Blackwell.

Carr, D. (1994) 'Knowledge and truth in religious education', *Journal of Philosophy of Education*, 28 (2): 221–238.

Carr, W. (1995): 'Education and democracy: confronting the postmodern challenge', *Journal of Philosophy of Education*, 29 (1): 75–91.

Code, L. (1991) *What Can She Know? Feminist Theory and the Construction of Knowledge*. Ithaca, New York: Cornell University Press.

Code, L. (1992) 'Feminist epistemology', in J. Dancy and E. Sosa (eds), *A Companion to Epistemology*. Oxford: Blackwell Publishers, pp. 138–142.

Code, L. (1993) 'Taking subjectivity into account', in L. Alcoff and E. Potter (eds), *Feminist Epistemologies*. New York: Routledge, pp. 15–48.

Feldman, R. (1994) 'Good arguments', in F.F. Schmitt (ed.), *Socializing Epistemology: The Social Dimensions of Knowledge*. Lanham, Maryland: Rowman and Littlefield Publishers, pp. 159–188.

Feldman, R. (2003) *Epistemology*. Upper Saddle River, New Jersey: Prentice-Hall.

Gettier, E. (1963) 'Is justified true belief knowledge?', *Analysis*, 23: 121–123.

Goldman, A.I. (1999) *Knowledge in a Social World*. Oxford: Oxford University Press.

Hamilton, E. and H. Cairns (eds) (1961) *The Collected Dialogues of Plato*. Princeton: Princeton University Press.

Horwich, P. (1990) *Truth*. Oxford: Basil Blackwell.

Robertson, E. (2009) 'The epistemic aims of education', in H. Siegel (ed.), *The Oxford Handbook of Philosophy of Education*. New York: Oxford University Press.

Scheffler, I. (1965) *Conditions of Knowledge*. Glenview, Illinois: Scott, Foresman and Company.

Schmitt, F.F. (1995) *Truth: A Primer*. Boulder, Colorado: Westview Press.

Siegel, H. (1987) *Relativism Refuted: A Critique of Contemporary Epistemological Relativism*. Dordrecht: D. Reidel Publishing Company.

Siegel, H. (1997) *Rationality Redeemed? Further Dialogues on an Educational Ideal*. New York: Routledge.

Siegel, H. (2004) 'Relativism', in I. Niiniluoto, M. Sintonen and J. Wolenski (eds), *Handbook of Epistemology*. Dordrecht: Kluwer, pp. 747–780.

Taylor, C. (1987) 'Overcoming epistemology', in K. Baynes, J. Bohman and T. McCarthy (eds), *After Philosophy: End or Transformation?* Cambridge, Massachusetts: MIT Press, pp. 464–488.

20

The Value of Knowledge

Brenda Almond

INTRODUCTION

The human brain is superior to any computer. This is true at the present time, and will probably remain so for the indefinite future. Of course, some will dispute this. What about the search engines, they will say. What human brain could carry the information Google can produce at the touch of a mouse? But here lies the virtue of the human brain. It has its own way of dealing with information. It knows from the earliest stage of conscious development how to abstract. It doesn't allow itself to become clogged up with the welter of unneeded or irrelevant information it encounters, but discards most of the information that comes to it from experience via by the senses.

Some educational thinkers in the progressive tradition have taken scepticism about the need to acquire and retain facts far beyond this point. But it would be a mistake to discount the value of readily accessible knowledge in this way. Not everything can be 'looked up' just when needed. Memory is important, and success in most ordinary aspects of living depends on being able to retain background information, including much of what has been read and absorbed from various sources. In the contemporary world, too, all the knowledge associated with practical skills, from building work to advanced science or medicine, together with the mathematical understanding on which many of these depend, needs to be retained by the mind for easy access.

Most educational theory takes its start from these assumptions, grounded as they are in basic ideas about what humans are, what they need, and how they develop, particularly in their capacity to learn and acquire knowledge. The educational challenge is to work out where, on this spectrum, ordinary learning belongs.

Is all knowledge potentially valuable? Or can we distinguish the sort of knowledge that we should value from the kind we either do not need or can consign to external memory banks like our personal computer? And what of that related concept, knowledge of a more subtle kind, to which we give the name wisdom?

KNOWLEDGE OR WISDOM?

In legal circles, a story circulates about a barrister who was interrupted by the judge during his long and tortuous cross-examination of a witness: 'I fail to see how your questioning of this witness is going to make us any the wiser', complained the judge. The barrister replied: 'None the wiser your honour, merely better informed'.

It is not difficult to apply this apocryphal tale to the world of education. Is it the business of the teacher to foster wisdom, or simply knowledge? Is there a difference between being wise and being clever, and do either of these consist simply in having at your fingertips a large body of information? It is certainly easier to plan a curriculum around the idea of imparting knowledge than of cultivating wisdom, and maybe that is not something to complain about. Individual teachers would have to be very confident of their *own* wisdom if they decided their only task was to share that with their students. And even if they were tempted by the prospect, they might hesitate, remembering the example of Socrates, who reflected on these matters in the Athens of the fifth century BCE. Said to be one of the wisest people of his time, Socrates refused to accept that title, saying that his only claim to wisdom was that, unlike other people, while he knew nothing, he *did* know how little he knew, while they were just as ignorant as he was but didn't recognize the fact![77]

But perhaps the position isn't quite as stark as that. To accept that knowledge does not necessarily mean wisdom is not to claim deep metaphysical insight. It may just mean recognizing that, in the kind of education that values wisdom as well as knowledge, there is a role for feeling and sensitivity as well as intellectual judgement, and a place for values as well as facts. It is to say, in other words, that the richer knowledge that deserves to be called wisdom involves a kind of empathy, first with other people, and then with the natural world. It is part of the search for meaning in life – the attempt to find order, plan, purpose and method when faced with the tortuous path of human history and the apparent arbitrariness of the way the world works.

But perhaps more relevant to day-to-day educational preoccupations is the fact that wisdom also connects, in a way that simple straightforward knowledge does not, with the choices people make in their personal lives – especially matters of lifestyle, personal relationships, career choices and goals. This reflects in some ways the distinction the Greek philosopher Aristotle, writing more than two millennia ago, drew between abstract or intellectual wisdom and what he called *practical* wisdom – the kind of ethical knowledge that answers the question,

how to live. This question, and its answer, links to Aristotle's notion of a *telos* –
the ultimate point and purpose of a human life, or indeed the life of any other
living being, that is the fulfilment of their essential nature and the only way to
true happiness. So, for instance, while many people think that a happy life is a life
of material pleasures – winning the lottery on a Saturday night perhaps – Aristotle
is clear that wiser people will prefer the satisfactions of honour, or of respected
participation in public life, while the wisest of all will look to the satisfactions of
philosophy – reflection, reasoning, and the thoughtful pursuit of truth. Aristotle
also saw that the scope for practical wisdom goes beyond the personal life of the
individual, and extends to the broader political and social scene. Indeed, in today's
world it may be easier for us than it was for Aristotle to see that the personal and
the political are interconnected: that the personal choices people make have
implications for the community in which they live. So, because private decisions
often determine public choices, wise private choices make possible a community
life governed by wisdom, while large-scale carelessness in the personal life of
individuals can lead to the disintegration or unravelling of the social fabric.

This leads to some more prosaic questions about the value of different kinds of
knowledge. Whereas wisdom may be the right goal both for individuals and for
society, it cannot in the end be detached from knowledge of a more mundane kind.
For uninformed opinion often leads to poor and unproductive choices, and wisdom
itself is constrained and limited if it lacks the knowledge of facts and skills that
conventional educational practice aims to supply. And if wisdom is to guide day-
to-day decision-making, it will not be enough to know how to access information;
the kind of knowledge that matters may well be knowledge that has been sufficiently confidently acquired that it no longer needs to be looked up in a book or
on the computer – something that applies in most areas of the curriculum, including
science, foreign languages, mathematics, history, geography and so on.

KNOWLEDGE WORLDS: SCIENCE, CULTURE,
AND ABSTRACT REASONING

This idea of a well-stocked mind creates a contrast between knower and known.
It implies that knowledge is something external – something that has an objective
existence, independent of its creators, and has taken on a life of its own. It was
this thought that inspired the philosopher Karl Popper to paint a picture of three
'worlds' of knowledge. The first of these, World 1, is the physical world; the
second, World 2, the world of our conscious experiences. Both of these offer us
only subjective knowledge. For objective knowledge, Popper suggested, we have
to look to a different conception: knowledge that has been, in a sense, sloughed
off by its originators and then become independent of them. It is like a spider's
web – something that is created by and continues to be part of an organism, but
is nevertheless an independent entity. This is Popper's third world – the World 3
of objective knowledge. It is a body of human knowledge that has been, and

continues to be, contributed to across cultures and over generations, and it contains our theories, conjectures and even our guesses. Popper describes it as the logical *contents* of books, libraries and computer memories – 'the logical content of our genetic code' (Popper, 1972: 73). So there is a sense, Popper says, in which World 3 is autonomous, and 'in this world we can make theoretical discoveries in a similar way to that in which we can make geographical discoveries in world 1' (Popper, 1972: 74).

Popper's theory properly belongs in the area of the philosophy of science, but theories of knowledge with an educational focus have historically often had a more humanistic and literary focus, with an emphasis on culture rather than scientific exploration. There is a longstanding view – it goes back to Plato – that education is a matter of initiation into a cultural heritage that is valued both by educators and by those who want to learn from them. But education in this sense is not defined just by the content it seeks to pass on. It also involves a judgement about the worth or value of that content. This is what distinguishes a liberal approach to education from a rote conception of learning. 'Liberal' in this context also means a *broad* education – an education with what is sometimes called a 'broad cognitive perspective'. Traditionally, it includes certain key areas of human knowledge – mathematical, linguistic and literary, ethical, scientific, historical, aesthetic and religious. These are marked out as distinct from each other in two ways: first, because they use a distinctive range of concepts, and secondly, because they have a distinctive way of establishing truth or testing theories. For example, the method by which you go about establishing the truth of a mathematical theorem is quite different from the way you check the truth of a scientific claim and different again from a judgement about a literary work, just as the concepts you must employ in discussing a piece of poetry have little or no overlap with those you need when you enter the laboratory. The long-held assumption is that these diverse areas of study and their related skills combine to provide a worthwhile, well-rounded education, while to lack any of these is to be educationally limited or deprived. This is not only a description of a certain kind of education but also involves a judgement about its worth or value. In the end, though, debate may turn less on the question of its intrinsic value as on a judgement of a more utilitarian kind: What kind of education is likely to be of *use* to the student later in life?

USEFUL VERSUS WORTHWHILE KNOWLEDGE

While educational theorists and politicians may fall out over whether schools should focus on what is intrinsically worthwhile or just pursue what can be shown to be useful, the first thing to notice is that these objectives are not necessarily in conflict. Take, for example, a story in Jean-Jacques Rousseau's fictional account of the education of a boy, Émile, in eighteenth century France. His tutor has tried to interest him in astronomical matters, including an explanation of how you can find your bearings from the sun. Émile interrupts with the demand,

'What's the use of that?' Instead of replying directly, the tutor waits for the next day and then takes Émile for an early morning walk in the forest near Montmorency. He ensures that they both become (apparently) lost and when Émile begins to cry – not least because he is hungry and wants the breakfast they have missed – he reminds Émile of the lesson of the day before. This included how to find north and south by looking at the shadows cast by the sun at midday. Suddenly Émile begins to remember what he heard. It is enough to see them safely home and Émile enthusiastically concludes: 'Astronomy is some use after all!'(Rousseau, 1966: 143–4).

In some ways this is a reprise of an earlier story from the dawn of philosophy, when the first philosopher in the Western tradition, Thales (*c.* 585 BCE), was mocked by his contemporaries for his interest in the stars. His star-gazing was once responsible, it was said, for him falling into a well. However, he managed to recover his reputation by using his astronomical observations to predict that weather conditions were likely to produce a bumper crop of olives. Keeping this to himself for a while, he made a fortune by buying up all the oil presses in the region and obtaining an olive oil monopoly. So both Thales and Rousseau seem to have shown in very different ways and in very different contexts that knowledge that it would be easy to dismiss as 'academic', i.e. of no practical value, can often turn out to be useful in the most direct and everyday sense of the word.

However, can the same be said of more abstract knowledge? Here again, a story from antiquity throws light on the issue. In one of Plato's dialogues, the *Meno*, the philosopher Socrates is seen engaging in what may well be one of the first and most famous of educational experiments (Plato, 1956). What he wanted to show was that knowledge doesn't always come to us from the senses, by observation of the world outside us. Instead, there is, deep within the human brain, knowledge of a different kind. Traditionally and historically, this has been called innate knowledge, but we might prefer to call it simply *latent* knowledge – it is knowledge we have from birth without even being aware of it. Socrates is shown demonstrating this theory by questioning a young boy who has had no mathematical education at all. He asks him the apparently simple question of how to make a square which is twice the size of a square with a 2-foot side (2 metres will do if you prefer a metric version!). Once the boy has grasped why none of the obvious solutions work (such as a 3-foot or a 4-foot side) he is ready to grasp the logic of Pythagoras' famous theorem: that the way to get a double-sized square is to base the new square on the diagonal of the original one. And, as Socrates points out, since the boy himself has seen how to get to that conclusion, he is unlikely to forget it and unlikely, too, to have any doubts about it later. So can abstract knowledge of this sort be dismissed as useless? Hardly. Abstract knowledge of this kind, particularly mathematical knowledge, is fundamental to scientific research of a much more 'applied' kind, which may in the end reach out to human needs in a way that trying to address those needs directly can only do in a much more ineffectual and limited way. Abstract knowledge, then, is in principle no more 'useless' than empirical knowledge.

But, of course, this doesn't mean that education has to be strictly vocational or narrowly technological. On the other hand, it suggests that it shouldn't be entirely child-centred or 'learner-oriented' either. The Socratic approach is a long way from a *laissez-faire* policy on the part of the teacher, and an educational philosophy of pure self-expression risks leaving a void at the centre of a child's development. For while individuals are in the end responsible for what they are and what they become, the structure of knowledge itself imposes constraints that are bound to affect the success of any attempt to follow the learner's own choices exclusively.

KNOWLEDGE AND CULTURAL IDENTITY: THE SCEPTICAL CHALLENGE

But talk of downplaying the role of the learner can strike a deviant note in today's postmodernist world, for it raises questions about what is perhaps the most important current challenge to traditional ideas. These sceptical doubts start from the observation that human beings are in the end organisms that respond to their environment and are at least partly shaped by it. Hence, knowledge must relate in some way to persons, and people are affected by their cultural settings. Indeed, the word 'culture' is often used to evoke the idea of difference and diversity. It has to be accepted, then, that there is a connection between knowledge and cultural identity, and that what people are expected to know may depend on the particular time, place and political system they live. It may also be influenced by the family and the religion into which they have been born, and affect the moral perspective they acquire. The philosopher Alasdair MacIntyre paints a fuller picture

> What I am, therefore, is in key part what I inherit, a specific past that is present to some degree in my present … . I am never able to seek for the good or exercise the virtues only *qua* individual. This is partly because what it is to live the good life concretely varies … . What the good life is for a fifth-century Athenian general will not be the same as what it was for a medieval nun or a seventeenth-century farmer. (MacIntyre, 1981: 204–206)

But is this to say that social context is *all* that matters? Are all our ideas, knowledge and ideologies socially constructed? Or are individuals able to use their unbiased reason to think for themselves? Sceptical doubt about the meaningfulness of the very idea of truth and hence of knowledge is not uncommon. There is a popularly held view that it is not possible to build a single true account of factual or scientific matters from generally agreed 'foundations'. But the liberal view of education, which defines it as initiation into a culture, seems to presuppose a common foundation and a common culture (Peters, 1963, 1966).[78] This poses several problems. To begin with, it is a challenge for multicultural societies. Educational planners meet this difficulty in different ways. Some appear to believe that multiplicity is good in itself. But there is no reason to believe that adding to the stock of cultures children are introduced to will enrich their understanding. Whether the objective is to introduce children to all cultures, or whether it is to create a single new hybrid form for this generation alone, this very process risks turning students into sceptics and relativists. For in placing a large sceptical question mark over the ideal of a common intellectual tradition based on a common reason, it has thrown into doubt the traditional conception of education as a framework for passing on the accumulated knowledge of human beings – in Matthew Arnold's words, 'the best that has been thought and known' (Arnold, 1960: 70).

Many of today's theorists and educators have fallen under the influence of modern philosophical sceptics about knowledge, such as Thomas Kuhn and Paul Feyerabend in the scientific area, and Marx and Marcuse in the area of social science and political theory. This has added to the cultural scepticism generated by consciousness of difference and diversity, an analysis of knowledge as something that is socially imposed – an artificial construct of those who have power in society and wish to exploit others and exercise control over them.[79] This analysis not only deprives the curriculum of a secure foundation, but also throws into doubt the authority of the teacher as a communicator of special knowledge, understanding or insight.

The background to these developments is a deeply entrenched relativism which radically reinterprets the notion of truth. For according to this form of relativism, to accept any claims as true is to submit yourself to the social power of those who put them forward. So ideas, arguments and beliefs become pawns in the power struggles of human beings, while the concept of worthwhile learning becomes simply a matter of who has emerged as top dog in the shifting power struggles of contemporary science, literature and the arts. As a result, many contemporary commentators seem willing to reject the possibility of reaching a common conception of either science or truth, taking their inspiration, perhaps, from philosophers such as Richard Rorty, who described such beliefs as old-fashioned religion – the kind of 'motives which once led us to posit gods' (Rorty, 1985: 10).

But it would be a mistake to take the sceptics' case at face value. Traditional approaches to education were based on following the logical structure of knowledge. This would usually mean adopting a step-by-step approach, in which students work through a sequence of learning levels, starting with the most simple and moving on to the more complex, each of which needs to be grasped and understood in order to progress. The sceptical view takes as its basis the idea that knowledge is something rather more amorphous and flexible than this, and that each of us has our own conception not only of knowledge but also of truth – that each of us makes our *own* truth.

KNOWLEDGE: THE PHILOSOPHICAL ARGUMENT

It seems, then, that whether in general, or simply in relation to education, everything turns on how we judge the status of knowledge and of truth.[80] The educational debate relates closely to what might be called the epistemological debate about knowledge – what it essentially *is*. Although this is an old debate, it has echoes in modern times. A recent example of this was provided by the US politician Donald Rumsfeld, who was widely mocked for a complicated explanation he gave of the difficulty of political policy-making posed by 'known unknowns' and 'unknown unknowns'. In fact, though, more than two millennia ago, Socrates had introduced these concepts in his own discussion of knowledge in the *Theaetetus* (Plato 1969: 845–919).[81] In this dialogue, Socrates puts the baffling question: 'Can the same person know something and also not know that which he knows?' (Plato, 165b).

As a first step to answering such questions, he suggests, we have to abandon the belief that knowledge is something we get directly from the senses, as well as the idea that what each person believes is true for that person. The young Theaetetus, who had begun by suggesting that knowledge consists of the various things you learn in school, is happy to agree that there is such a thing as sound knowledge, and to accept Socrates' claim that this is the knowledge that is valuable in teaching and learning, in the healing professions, and in politics and government, especially in times of crisis (Plato, 1969: 170b).

In a colourful image, Socrates suggests that knowledge can be compared to a collection of birds kept in an aviary – the items of knowledge are securely there, just as the birds are securely held in the aviary, even though the owner of the aviary is not physically holding on to each bird all the time. Our minds are like the aviary, empty at birth, but gradually filling up with items of knowledge as we grow up. We file these nuggets of knowledge away until we need them. Mistakes are possible, of course, because we may mix up our pieces of knowledge, just as the bird owner may pick out the wrong bird without realizing it. This is like someone thinking he knows something that in fact he does not know. The discussion is complex, and the conclusion of Plato's dialogue is fairly indeterminate. Theaetetus is left feeling not at all sure about how to define knowledge, but Socrates assures him that he will be a better person as a result of their debate, simply because he will have the good sense not to imagine he knows what he does not know.

What the discussion has shown, however, is that it is hard to separate the issues of knowledge and truth. Indeed, contemporary philosophers have tended to prefer to conduct the epistemological debate in terms of truth rather than knowledge, but often what they have to say has implications for education. For example, the American philosopher, Hilary Putnam, offers a conception of truth as 'objectivity for us' which could usefully be applied as a possible solution to educational agnosticism. Putnam explains his apparently paradoxical notion in this way:

> Our conceptions of coherence and acceptability are deeply interwoven with our psychology. They depend upon our biology and our culture; they are by no means 'value free'. But they are our conceptions, and are conceptions of something real. They define a kind of objectivity, *objectivity for us,* even if it is not the metaphysical objectivity of the God's Eye view. Objectivity and rationality humanly speaking are what we have; they are better than nothing. (1981: 184).

Despite its possibly relativistic overtones, Putnam's notion of 'objectivity for us' could offer a way forward in the educational debate about how far we may take as established the universality of our culture and our knowledge. For it implicitly accepts the universality of human psychology and biology and, in doing so, it sets limits to the relativity of knowledge, and opens up the possibility of a genuinely common culture based on our common human nature. This could offer something like a life-raft for educators hopeful of rescuing the idea of objective knowledge from the sea of scepticism. It counters the claim that truth is something that belongs in separate compartments – the 'truth' of Western science, the 'truth' of this or that religion, or even the validity of morality – and is a reminder that the 'true' and the 'good' were set up as the objects of learning and research at the dawn of the Western era. It is not unreasonable, then, to want to continue to respect, and possibly interpret, that tradition in a modern context. Putnam, and in a different way Popper, too, offer us the possibility of retaining, if not the idea of absolute truth, at least a belief in the possibility of getting *nearer* to that truth. As Popper puts this: 'It is only the idea of truth which allows us to speak sensibly of mistakes and of rational criticism, and which makes rational discussion possible ... . Thus the very idea of error – and of fallibility – involves the idea of an objective truth as the standard of which we may fall short' (1963). Popper acknowledges that more often than not we fail to find the truth, and do not even know when we have found it, but he insists on retaining the classical idea of absolute or objective truth as a regulative idea.

IN SUM . . .

In this chapter, I have argued that behind rival conceptions of knowledge, and their accompanying rival presumptions about the value of teaching and learning, lies a debate about relativism and rationality that is as old as the tradition of philosophy within which it is embedded. It may be necessary to accept that the principle of the sovereignty of reason – of being prepared to accept the conclusion of rational argument – is in the end simply and necessarily a prior commitment, and not itself the conclusion of an argument. But education is based on this prior commitment and its accompanying belief in truth, openness and toleration. In terms of older educational debates, those who cling to some notion of objectivity, to the idea of an unequal relationship between teacher and taught, and who believe that some claims are better grounded, some skills more worth having than others, belong to a long educational tradition – a tradition which respects and values knowledge. Others, often described as educational progressives, defend a radical form of equality between teacher and taught, based on the idea that all opinions, whether factual or moral, are essentially equal, and that knowledge itself is a shifting concept. This debate is not just of theoretical interest. It has practical importance for education, not only in weighing the value of knowledge itself but also in its ethical and policy implications.

NOTES

77 Wisdom was one of the four cardinal virtues recognized in ancient times. For Plato, virtue and happiness coincide because both are a kind of knowledge – a wise assessment of what is truly in a person's interest.

78 This view is particularly associated with the work of R.S. Peters: See Peters, R.S. *Ethics and Education*. London: Allen and Unwin, 1966. See also, Peters, R.S. *Education as Initiation*. London: Evans, 1963.

79 Michael Young (ed.) in *Knowledge and Control* (London: Macmillan, 1971) argues that those in positions of power will attempt to define what is to be taken as knowledge, to determine how accessible any knowledge should be of different groups and to determine the relationships between knowledge areas and those who have access to them.

80 For a full discussion of these two issues, see Chapter 19 in this volume.

81 In a very complex passage in Plato's *Theaetetus* at 192.

REFERENCES

Arnold, M. (1960) *Culture and Anarchy*. Cambridge: Cambridge University Press. (First published 1869.)

MacIntyre, A. (1981) *After Virtue*. London: Duckworth.

Peters, R.S. (1963) *Education as Initiation*. London: Evans.

Peters, R.S. (1966) *Ethics and Education*. London: Allen and Unwin.

Plato (1956) *Meno*, in *Protagoras and Meno*, Guthrie, W.K.G. (trans.). Harmondsworth: Penguin.

Plato (1969) *Theaetetus*, in *Plato: Collected Dialogues*, E. Hamilton and H. Cairns. (eds). Princeton: Princeton University Press.

Popper, K.R. (1963) *Conjectures and Refutations*. London: Routledge.

Popper, K.R. (1972) *Objective Knowledge: An Evolutionary Approach*. Oxford: Oxford University Press.

Putnam, H. (1981) *Reason, Truth and History*. Cambridge: Cambridge University Press.

Rorty, R. (1985) 'Solidarity or objectivity?', in J. Rajchman and C. West (eds), *Post-analytic Philosophy*. New York: Columbia University Press.

Rousseau, Jean-Jacques (1966) *Émile*. London: Dent.

Young, Michael (1971) (ed.) *Knowledge and Control.* London: Macmillan.

21

Concepts of Mind

Christine McCarthy

INTRODUCTION

The term 'mind' is common enough in educational discourse: we nurture minds, we open them, we hope not to waste them. Yet when we think about the meaning of the term 'mind,' in common usage and in educational discourse, its meaning (or meanings), is surprisingly elusive, so much so that one might wonder if there is any meaning conveyed by the term at all. The casualness of our use of the term 'mind' masks a vast conceptual difficulty, and glosses over a process of philosophical inquiry into the nature of mind that has persisted for thousands of years, and yet seems still to be one of the most difficult and intriguing puzzles in philosophy. I shall assume without arguing for the point that influencing for the better the developing mind of the student is at least one core objective of education, and, indeed, is central to the very concept of education. To set about the educative task in a productive way, it is useful, although perhaps not necessary, to begin with a conception of human mind that is rich and reasonably clear.

The conceptual difficulty regarding 'mind' is particularly odd because mind has come to have not one, two, or three, but a host of contemporary disciplines all dedicated to understanding the nature of the thing (or things) we call mind. We have an embarrassment of riches in the study of mind, and yet understanding remains elusive. And consensus, a shared understanding of the nature of mind, seems quite impossible.

In this chapter I will try to bring out some of the fundamental disagreements about the nature of mind. I will begin by sketching out some of the earlier philosophical work on the nature of mind, establishing several lines of thought and inquiry that to some extent still structure the discourse. There will be major leaps in time along the way, leading to countless omissions. But having set out a few historical beacons, I will pick up the story in contemporary times, setting out for examination the major conceptualizations, puzzles, and conflicts in philosophy of mind today.

This chapter will of course be too short to do justice to its subject. The historical and contemporary literature in philosophy of mind is enormous, too vast to be more than sketched in a single chapter; a mere introduction is all that can be given. I hope it will be enough to spark an interest in further exploration.

EARLY CONCEPTIONS OF MIND

Plato's idealism

A common point of departure in philosophy of mind is the philosophy of Plato, because of his idealist conception of reality, and consequently, of mind. Plato's work is of such influence that it has received a full chapter treatment in this text, so only a brief reprise will be given here. For Plato, the term '*idea*' referred to the immaterial, immutable, eternal and perfect concept-objects that constitute the realm of true being. The idea, or 'form,' of justice, for example, is something that will never deteriorate. Mind, for Plato, is of a fundamentally different 'substance' than the material substance of body. Like idea, or form, mind is immaterial and eternal, and apprehends the eternal forms. This immaterial mind exists before being, in some manner, joined to a material body; it is separable from body, and continues to exist in perfect form, even after the body has disintegrated. Plato's conception is a monism, an 'idealistic monism,' since there is only one true reality, the realm of being, and that is the realm of mind. (See Edwards, 1967, for a thorough explication.)

Aristotle's 'psyche'

The early philosophical conceptions of mind vary widely, and this is nowhere as evident, I think, as in Aristotle's departure from Platonic conception of mind. Aristotle at first accepts, but then abandons, Plato's idealist mind, developing a radically different conception, termed '*psyche*' (or *psuche*) (see Bennett and Hacker, 2003). 'Psyche' is conceived as a certain set of natural capacities or powers of the human being, of which there are several subsets: first, the capacities required to live, which is the nutritive psyche; secondly, the capacities required to be sensitive and responsive to the environment, which is the sensitive psyche; and thirdly, the capacities required to think rationally about self and world, and their interconnection, and to will action accordingly. This last is the rational psyche. Note the biological basis, and the hierarchical relation of the capacities: all organisms must have the first capacity; most (now we would say, all) must have the second as well, in varying degrees of complexity. Many fewer organisms, principally human beings, have the third set of capacities, and again, in varying degrees.

Psyche, usually translated, rather misleadingly, as 'soul,' or 'mind,' is thus inseparable from the living body; it is 'immaterial' only in the sense that it is an indication of the dynamic characteristics of material bodies in action. This is true, however, only of 'passive reason,' the part of the soul which 'becomes' its object in the process of knowing it. Curiously, given his seemingly modern biological turn, Aristotle also allows for an 'active reason' that always actually knows its objects and that is the initiator and necessary condition of the knowing process in the organism; this capacity is universal, and does survive the death of the body, a strong vestige in Aristotle of the Platonic conception of mind.

A necessary condition of thought for Aristotle is imagination – the formation, juxtaposition, and evaluation of images of things. Aristotle's biological conception has an intriguingly modern tone, which will be picked up again, for example, in the work of Dewey, and in contemporary cognitive neuroscience.

Descartes' dualism

Cartesian dualism is the view that there are two fundamentally different substances – material substance and mental substance – i.e., mind and matter (Descartes, 2002). The mind substance (or soul) is necessarily and fundamentally different in kind from matter. To point out a few of the fundamental differences: matter is extended in space, and all the particular attributes of matter derive from this extension. In particular, the material universe, according to Descartes, is one solid interconnected system. Having no voids, any movement of any portion of the system necessarily causes movement throughout the system in a mechanistic manner. In distinct contrast, mind, which is the active thinking substance, is not extended in space, and hence is not subject to the mechanical laws of causality constraining physical matter. Because mind is not extended, there can be infinitely many separate minds.

Human beings are unique in that the material body is connected (in some way) to the immaterial substance that is mind. It is the mind alone that is conscious – without mind, the body is merely a mechanical device, and for example, feels no pain; pain only occurs when the mind becomes conscious of certain sensations of the body, and feels pain. It is the direction of the body by the mind that gives humans free will, and it is the intellectual capacities of the mind that allow for language and reasoning. Mind is separable from the material body to which it is conjoined, as, for example, at the death of the material body.

Descartes's position is a 'substance dualism,' since there are two fundamentally different substances that are, somehow, in interaction. A serious problem is to explain why mind should choose to become associated with matter in the first place; a second problem is to explain the nature of the causal connections between immaterial mind and material body.

A leap in time

In early philosophy of mind, the now separate disciplines of philosophy and psychology were one, in large part because of the distinct absence of any knowledge about the biological workings of the brain, nervous system, and human organism as a whole. In the absence of an empirical science, the best, and only, scholars of the mind were of necessity philosophers. Even by 1890, with William James' publication of *Psychology*, the empirical research-based discipline of psychology was in its infancy. John Dewey, in his early work, 1887, also called *Psychology*, conceived the true method of philosophy to be the 'method of psychology,' the empirically aided search for the laws of the mind. (See, for example, Dewey, 'Science and the Method of Psychology' Ew. 2.12–18). Dewey conceived mind to be the central problem of philosophy; through understanding the nature and workings of mind, we would understand the cosmos. But this philosophic understanding was soon to be considerably aided by empirical work. An early proponent of what would now be termed a biological naturalism, with his philosophy informed by empirical science, was John Dewey.

John Dewey's empirical naturalism

Dewey, in his early period, took an absolute idealist stance, conceiving mind, the soul, the psychical, to be universal and eternal, and ultimately the source of all else; at this early stage, he emphatically rejected materialism, maintaining that the psychical is immanent in the physical. The human being, then, is 'psycho-physical,' a term he continued to use following his later rejection of idealism and turn to naturalistic empiricism (for example, 1958: 254).

In his later work, for example, Dewey, in *Experience and Nature* (1958) conceives mind to be a set of meanings. A meaning is a particular relation, between two things: that is, a thing has meaning when it is a sign of some other thing. Mind emerges when organisms are complex enough that things in the world can be apprehended as significant. Dewey sees this as coincident with the development of language, seeing words (or their mental precursors) as the necessary bearers of significance. Someone, of course, must employ the thing as a sign. There can be no meaning, no mind, without a complex organic entity, capable of treating objects as signs. Note that organic states themselves can be things having significance. Any meaning we construct has cognitive reference, i.e., reference to objective natural events. ' ... all meanings intrinsically have reference to natural events ... the objective reference of meanings is complete; it is a hundred percent affair' (Dewey, 1925: Lw.1.219).

Dewey's interpretation of the nature of mental things anticipates the current biological naturalistic conception. He writes that 'Psychical things are thus themselves realistically conceived; they can be described and identified in biological and physiological terms, in terms (with adequate science) of chemicophysical correspondents' (1925: Mw.3.155).

This is clearly just a sampling of influential early philosophical conceptions of mind. But I want to turn at this point to the contemporary field of philosophy of mind. Through the 1900s, the scientific study of the cognitive activities of animals, from sea slug to human being, advanced dramatically. The questions the various cognitive sciences, broadly conceived, have developed and began to answer, often seem in their detailed focus and specificity to be far removed from the loftier concerns of philosophy of mind. In the last 50 years, our knowledge of the cognitive biology of human beings has exploded; we have an enormous body of knowledge about the gross and fine details of the anatomy, physiology, and dynamics of the human organism, including, most pertinently, our neuroanatomy, neurophysiology, and neurodynamics. And this is only one corner of scientific inquiry. When considering the nature of human mind, we would do well to consider the contributions from paleoanthropology, archeology, genetics, and human evolution, as well as from psychology, sociology, social anthropology, and a whole host of other sciences.

Despite this wealth of new knowledge, the philosophical conceptions of mind developed over thousands of years without benefit of this knowledge continue to influence our 'common sense' understandings of the nature of mind, and hence of the nature of ourselves, and of the social lives and institutions that promote our well-being. Philosophical conceptions of mind, I think it plausible to assert, should be informed by and consistent with the best science of the day, if their conceptions are not to be irrelevant. There is a paradox here – when scientific inquiry was in its infancy, appealing to, and incorporating its most current findings was feasible, but futile. Now that the knowledge is so vastly increased, the potential benefits of appealing to and incorporating the most current findings are immense, but, doing so seems an impossible task. So the question arises: can our current scientific knowledge of ourselves – from psychology, cognitive science, and neurobiology – inform, refine, delimit, and illuminate our philosophical conceptions of the nature of mind?

It might seem that, with the emergence of the contemporary science(s) of the mind, the field of philosophy of mind has been eclipsed, and that all the interesting work on the nature of mind today is coming from the sciences. But philosophy still has its peculiar mode of contribution. Many of the concepts that arose in and structured the early philosophical conceptions of mind are still framing the contemporary conceptions of mind, for philosophers and scientists of the mind, and still permeate our general social conceptions, and still puzzle and have the potential to mislead us. It is up to philosophers to attempt to untangle these conceptual knots. But equally important is the philosopher's role in attempting to synthesize the manifold inputs of science and, in doing so, perhaps to resolve some of the 'eternal questions.' In the next section, contemporary philosophy of mind will be explored, with apologies for the brevity of treatment.

CONCEPTIONS OF MIND: CONTEMPORARY THESES

This section will be organized around fundamental conceptions, theses, issues, and terms, as there are simply too many important philosophers engaged in this discourse to do otherwise. Having said that, certain prominent theorists will be mentioned as exemplars of various positions examined.

The first important distinction is that between 'monism' and 'dualism.' The monist thesis is that there is one and only one sort of 'stuff' that constitutes the cosmos.[82] Everything that is is but a variation in the form of this fundamental constituent. But monists can and do disagree about the nature of the 'one' constituent. Other monists take the fundamental constituent of the cosmos to be matter.

Idealistic monism

The idealistic monist takes the ontological position that the stuff of the cosmos is mind, i.e., that all that exists is mental, rather than material. The mental stuff, mind, is eternal, non-spatial, uncaused, and freely and spontaneously active. While things in our ordinary experience might appear to be material, this is an illusion, and apparently material things are actually mind-dependent, in a radical way – they are in fact mental, and their very existence is dependent on mind. One classical expression of this position is Berkeley's dictum, *esse est percipi,* which means 'to be is to be perceived.' Nothing can be, except as active perceiving mind causes it to be, with the mind of God as the perceiver of last resort, maintaining the stability of the cosmos by perpetual perception (Berkeley, 1982). Idealistic monism is a view that has few adherents in contemporary philosophy of mind. John Foster argues for a Berkeleyan sort of idealism, which he terms phenomenalistic idealism (2004). David Chalmers sketches out such a position, which takes the intrinsic properties of the world to be phenomenal, i.e., experiential, but this he regards as simply an extreme version of his own naturalistic dualism (1996: 155). Some earlier philosophers in this category, for example, C.S. Peirce and Whitehead, have taken the thesis to what seems to be its most consistent form, to a position called panpsychism. The central claim is that mind occurs not only in human beings, not only in living beings, but in everything that can be, including rocks, and subatomic particles. Panpsychists see the cosmos as an infinite realm of mental life. The difficulty lies in explaining why so many of the putative mental things persistently act, freely, in ways that are consistent with the 'mechanistic' attributes of material things, apparently obeying by choice the laws of physics, and seeming to be immersed in complex networks of causation (see Edwards, 1967: 22–31).

Physicalism; materialism

Physicalism is the predominant view in contemporary philosophy of mind today, as it is considered, at least by its many proponents, to be the only view compatible with contemporary science. Its most extreme version, materialism, is the view that the cosmos consist of one type of stuff, holding that nothing exists except things of a physical, material nature. Interactions in the material realm are all subject to the relevant physical laws, and all apparent 'mental' states or events are either illusory or reducible to material things.

What, then, is the materialist to make of the many ordinary references we make to minds and to mental things, such as thoughts, beliefs, ideas, hopes, and the like?

There are several ways that a materialistic monist may answer. The simplest route is to hold that talk of mental objects is akin to talk of the sun 'setting' in the west as it travels around the earth. Because there are no mental things, we should stop talking about them, and seek more accurate discourse.

A group of philosophers, the eliminative materialists, adopt just this view. They hold that all the propositions concerning our (alleged) mental states and events are elements in a fatally flawed theory, a 'folk theory' of human behavior. The folk theory in question employs the common psychological terms, and posits the existence of such things as beliefs, desires, feelings, intentions, motivations, etc., in short, all the things that we commonly use to explain human behavior. This folk theory seems to its adherents (i.e., to most people) to be true and basic common sense, but, they are wrong. Eliminative materialists believe it will be fruitless to try to bring the mentalistic concepts of folk theory into line with the materialist concepts of the future correct neuroscientific (and materialist) theory about organic cognition. Instead we should (gradually) eliminate references to beliefs, feelings, desires, etc., while working toward a well-grounded scientific, biological, and neurophysiologically based theory of human behavior. Patricia Churchland, author of *Neurophilosophy*, is a principal proponent of this position (1989).

Bennett and Hacker (2003) reject the eliminitivist approach, arguing, first, that our ordinary psychological concepts and language do not constitute a 'theory' at all, and secondly, that our ordinary vocabulary both describes human behavior as it is observed to be, and is expressive, and hence constitutive of human behavior.

Reductive materialism

There is another way to deal with the persistent talk of mental entities. One can attempt what the eliminitivists believe impossible, and try to show that the terms in the mentalistic folk theory can in fact be understood as, and explained by, the terms and inter-relations of the better materialist theory yet to come. This approach accepts that the phenomena we currently call 'mental' do occur, that there are such things as beliefs, hopes, and fears, and that we need not eliminate reference to them. It is simply that such things, once elements of mentalistic folk theory, can be better understood in terms of the new materialist theory. In this sense, the terms and relations of the older theory are 'reduced to,' i.e., linked up with, the terms and relations of a newer theory. This would be a *theoretical reduction*.

There is another type of reduction that might be attempted: an *explanatory reduction*. Taking this tack, we would continue to use the mental terms for certain phenomena, but would explain those phenomena by reference to the underlying physical/biological events that give rise to them.

Mind–brain identity theory

A third type of reduction is an *ontological reduction*, which occurs when the entities of one sort, e.g., mental things and processes, are shown to be identical with entities of another sort, e.g., brain states and processes. This move leads to what is called, unsurprisingly, a 'mind–brain identity theory.' The identity in question is sometimes understood as a 'type–type' identity theory, meaning that certain *types* of mental states, e.g., being in pain, are identical to certain *types* of dynamic brain states. More commonly, the identity claimed is a 'token–token' identity, meaning that every particular instance (token) of a mental state is identical with some corresponding particular instance (token) of a brain state.

Thomas Polger, in *Natural Minds* (2004), argues for a mind–brain identity theory, of the 'type–type' variety. In Polger's conception of mind, consciousness is paramount; indeed, it is the necessary and sufficient condition of mind. Polger is a strong advocate for a mind–brain identity theory, but my reference to his work here illustrates the difficulty of categorizing philosophers, for Polger does not take his version of identity theory to constitute a reduction of mind to brain.

Before moving on, we should return to the position of 'non-reductive materialism,' which is often termed 'physicalism.' This is the view that the entities of physics and the laws of their relation are basic, and structure the cosmos. But, at higher levels of organization, new relations and new entities emerge. The entities at the higher level would not be what they are were the underlying physics to change, but the laws of physics are not sufficient to explain the dynamics of the new systems. So, for example, an 'economy' is a real thing, a complex system, but it would not do much good to try to describe it using only the entities and laws of physics. The same may be true of mind and mental relations. Jaegwon Kim (2005) provides an excellent introduction to the thesis, in *Physicalism, or Something Near Enough*.

Contemporary dualism

One can avoid all the reductive and causal difficulties, of course, simply by allowing for the existence of two different sorts of things – mind and matter. The early dualism, Descartes' conception of two fundamentally different substances, is still a live possibility today, although as noted, the majority of philosophers of mind today accept some form of physicalism. Contemporary dualists generally are not 'substance dualists,' but take a less radical position, holding simply that mind and mental events differ in certain important ways from ordinary physical things and events, and their differences justify a conceptual distinction.

Such a view is that the cosmos is unified, and is basically physical, but that certain highly complex physical things have both physical and non-physical, i.e., mental, properties. This is 'property dualism.' The mental properties are said to 'emerge' from complex physical dynamic systems, such as the brain of an organism, for example. The mental properties are a new sort of property, but it is not uncommon at all for new properties to emerge from complex arrangements of physical systems.

David Chalmers (1996) is a proponent of one form of contemporary dualism, which he terms a naturalistic dualism. Chalmers focuses on consciousness as the principal phenomenon, and mystery, confronting philosophers of mind. Whereas he accepts that consciousness is 'natural,' and that it arises from physical/biological events, he denies that consciousness can be fully explained by physical/biological science. He argues that like the rest of the natural world, consciousness must be governed by law-like relations, but holds that these laws of consciousness need not be the same as the laws of the physical world. He argues that all attempts at reduction of the mental to the physical must fail, that the mental is truly something 'extra' and beyond the constraints of the physical world. This is why the occurrence of consciousness is such a mystery.

The puzzles about the relations of the fundamentally different domains of the mental and the material are still alive, as well. If mind, which is outside of the constraints of physics, can have effects on the material world – for example, on the biological matter of the brain – how does this mental causation happen? If mental causation cannot occur, how can a material entity, such as a person, escape from mechanistic causation, and experience freedom, free will, spontaneous action? If mental causation does happen, it must be that the matter so affected has, momentarily at least, ceased to conform to the laws of physics, e.g., the law of the conservation of energy. This is no small matter!

Interactionism

Interactionist theories attempt to resolve these issues. Some interactionists claim to find an opening for mental causation in the 'indeterminism' of quantum theory. Ulrich Mohrhoff (1999), for example, examines the arguments for a quantum solution in 'The Physics of Interactionism'; he concludes that quantum indeterminism cannot be the source of mental causation, but goes on to argue that mind can modify electromagnetic interactions among physical particles, and in this way mind can affect matter. Jaegwon Kim (2002) also addresses the problem(s) of mental causation succinctly.

We can escape all the difficulties of mental causation by turning to an alternative position.

Epiphenomenalism

In this view, the occurrence of mental events is caused, in every instance, by physical events, but mental events are causally inefficacious, i.e., incapable of having any causal effect on physical events. This one-way causal connection explains the presumed correlation of mental with physical events and, simultaneously, eliminates the problem of presumed mental causation – there is no such thing, and apparent instances of mental causation are illusory.

Yet, how do we explain the claim that physical events, occurring in the material realm, can cause changes in the spontaneously active, free and non-spatial mental realm? It is easy to think of putative examples of physical to mental causation:

a serious physical injury to the body might bring on a profound mental depression. But, assuming, as we are, that mental and physical realms are fundamentally different, in the most basic respects, how can such a physical–mental causation occur? Perhaps the most common answer is 'supervenience.' Mental events 'supervene' on physical/biological events; i.e., mental events are causally affected, in law-like ways, by physical events occurring, for example, in the brain. Once all the physical facts are fixed, or, in philosophical terms, 'determined,' the biological facts are also fixed, determined, and so, in turn, are the mental facts (see Kim, 1993).

At this point, I will turn to a brief explication of several prominent general theories of the nature of mind, which in some cases are sharply disparate, in other cases related, and sometimes overlapping.

Representational theories

A representational theory of mind holds that there are indeed mental states, and that these are representational. But a representational mental state is simply a physical object that has acquired a semantic content, i.e., has acquired meaning. Each mental state, then, is a symbol. A mental state acquires its semantic content by virtue of a causal relation with some other physical thing in the world. Each mental representation has causal powers, being able to influence the development of more complex mental states, leading ultimately to overt behavior. The relations among various mental states and actions are law-like. Because 'intentional laws' can be discovered, mental interactions can be empirically investigated, and are squarely in the natural world.

Mental representations are the primitive bearers of intentional content; their meaning is carried along into formal language, when, and if, linguistic abilities develop in a species. Thinking, which is the computational processing of mental representations consistent with their semantic content and causal relations, is prior to overt cultural situated linguistic practices. Thought can thus occur without language in this sense. There is however, a 'language of thought,' in the sense that thought is systematic and productive. An infinite number of thoughts can be created by combining simpler elements, in systematic ways. The causal effect of a mental representation is considered to be due to its local syntax, i.e., to the internal, essential, syntactic structure of that particular mental representation. For example, because of its syntactic structure, a thought such as 'P and Q are both occurring' causes one to infer that P is occurring. Fred Dretske (1995) is a proponent of a representationalist view, holding that to understand the mind it is necessary to understand the biological processes of representation that occur in the brain/organism.

The modularity of mind thesis

Jerry Fodor holds a representational theory of mind, and in much of his work argues in favor of a computational theory of mind. Fodor (1989) has argued for the 'modularity of the mind,' and he distinguishes sharply between 'local' mental processes and 'global.' Local mental processes are those that occur in 'informationally encapsulated' mental modules (note: these are *not* spatially encapsulated). Each mental module is a cognitive processing mechanism, a computational system that incorporates and operates on innate information that is usable by the organism only in that system (even though it may actually be relevant to tasks occurring in separate modules).

Fodor points to a difficulty: logically, 'global' causal effects must be able to occur, arising from the syntactic structure of the local mental representation *in the context of* the surrounding representations. This non-local surrounding set of representations could conceivably be the entirety of one's belief system. And here is the problem: a computer is quite capable of dealing effectively with local considerations, to reach truth-preserving conclusions. However, it cannot effectively deal with global considerations, with an exhaustive search of the entire belief system, checking for all relevant global effects, prior to any inference. This inability, Fodor concludes, accounts for the failure of artifical intelligence efforts to produce satisfactory simulations of what the human mind can easily do.

Fodor makes clear his current position, in *The Mind Doesn't Work That Way* (2000), that the modular, innate processes adequate to deal with the logically local cannot constitute the whole story about how the mind works, and he rejects the 'massive modularity' account of the mind. Unfortunately, the processes by which the human mind is able to deal with logically 'global' considerations are not well understood, Fodor states.

Functionalist theories of mind

Functionalism is the view that a 'mental state' is best understood as a particular set of causal relations occurring among elements in a complex system. To understand what belief X is, one would search for the causal relations that belief X has, both to other mental states and to biological, behavioral, or cultural states.

Functionalist theories have, as a key element, the thesis of 'multiple realizability.' The complex system in question need not be human, or even biological. If the causal relations that constitute belief X in a human being were to occur in some other complex system of causal relations, belief X would be occurring in that system. The very same belief, or an entire belief system, could conceivably be instantiated in any sort of material, just as long as the causal relations constituting the belief or belief system could be put into effect. This thesis is what grounds 'computer functionalism,' or 'strong artificial intelligence,' theories.

Functionalism had its earliest statement in 1967, in the work of Hilary Putnam; Polger (2004) analyzes the many varieties of functionalism, and critiques them strongly. Polger considers functionalism to be both the 'received view' in philosophy of mind today, and the principal competitor to his own identity theory, described above. For a compelling critique of functionalism, see Hilary Putnam's *Representation and Reality* (1991).

Computational theories of mind

In this view, the mind works like a computer, performing formal logical operations on thoughts, which are syntactically structured, just like sentences in a language. The form of every complex thought is a function of the form of the simpler component thoughts that give rise to it. Because of this, a mechanical device, i.e., a computer, is an adequate model of the workings of the human mind.

For the mind to work like a computer, the mind must be conceived as 'massively modular,' i.e., a whole mind is a vast hierarchical arrangement of numerous smaller, smaller, and still smaller autonomous processors, reaching eventually to the molecular level, and beyond. Each module performs its own set of operations on the input it receives. Eventually, the outputs of the computational modules are (in some way) integrated, so that a global understanding is ultimately reached.

Both the architecture and the computational activity of the mental modules are considered to be in large part genetically determined, honed by evolutionary processes to perform their functions adequately. Much of the machinery of the modular mind, and hence many of our mental capacities, e.g., perception, language, reasoning, emotion, etc., are innate and species-specific.

Biological naturalism

In this view, mind and consciousness are considered to be natural phenomena occurring only in complex biological organisms. Mental things and events are simply higher-level macro phenomena that emerge from lower-level biological phenomena. The mental phenomena are caused by the micro physical/biological processes occurring in the brain, and can be causally reduced to, i.e., explained in terms of, the underlying physiological processes.

John Searle is a proponent of a version of biological naturalism. Searle's view (1983, 2004) is that mind, consciousness, and mental processes, though causally reducible to the physical, are not *ontologically* reducible to the physical, because mental phenomena differ in fundamental ways from things and events of the physical sort. Mental states and events are subjective, i.e., they exist only when experienced, they are private, and they have a certain qualitative feel to them. Despite having this different ontological status, Searle considers mind and mental states to be features of certain biological systems, and to be causally efficacious in those biological systems.

Searle holds that mental states can be unconscious, and that at any given moment the vast majority of them are. However, our understandings of mental states are derived solely from our conscious experiences of them. Consciousness itself is a natural, evolved feature of certain complex biological organisms (including non-human organisms), and Searle takes it to be the key element in the study of mind. To understand mind, both the functional role of consciousness and its production by neurophysiological processes must be understood.

For biologically focused studies as to what, exactly, some of those biological bases of mind might be, see, for example, Stanislas Dehaene's *The Cognitive Neuroscience of Consciousness* (2001), or Evan Thompson's *Mind in Life: Biology, Phenomenology, and the Sciences of the Mind* (2007), among many other possibilities.

Cognition and emotion

Israel Scheffler argued against the common conceptual splitting of cognition from emotion; this split leads to an education which is split into 'unfeeling knowledge and mindless arousal' (1977: 3). Emotions serve cognition in several ways. First, there are the 'rational passions': the love of truth that drives one to seek truth, to respect reasoned arguments, and to abhor distortion, evasion, and deception of all sorts. There are also the perceptive feelings, emotional responses to the world that guide our perceptions. There are emotions that support our imagining of novel, creative ideas through which to understand the world. And there are specifically cognitive emotions, that arise in response to cognitive activity: for example, the joy of verification, when one's theoretical expectations are fulfilled, or the experience of surprise, when they are not. It is the experience of surprise that, provided one is receptive to it, allows one to learn from experience.

In contemporary naturalistic theories of the mind, the significance of the emotions in cognition is again central. Antonio Damasio, in *Descartes' Error* (1994), set out an accessible account of the role of emotional systems in the brain in the process of cognition, the 'somatic-marker' hypothesis. A bodily state (a somatic state) that is emotionally laden with a positive or negative valence is generated automatically, in connection with images or ideas of certain situations, of the past, present or the future. These somatic states, which we might call 'gut feelings,' are associated with (i.e., 'mark') each option in a cognitive process, highlight certain options, and may even lead us to immediately reject or pursue the various options. The somatic markers, which result from emotional valences attached to our past experiences, are necessary to supplement, and shorten, a supposed logical, cost–benefit analysis sort of 'reasoning process,' which by itself may never reach a conclusion, due to the complexity of the practical problem, or the lack of information or time.

Jesse Prinz (2004) takes emotions to be central to all thinking, and chides cognitive science for omission of emotion from theories of the mind He considers emotions to be 'embodied appraisals' which have 'valence markers,' either positive or negative. Physiologically, emotions are perceptions of the occurrent bodily changes that enable incipient actions; as such, they are simple, meaningful, and 'feelable' wholes. Emotions are meaningful because emotion involves the use of the bodily state to represent the organism–environment relationship; e.g., fear represents danger. In this sense Prinz holds that emotions are, conceptually, thoughts.

CONCLUSION

There is much that remains unsaid. I can only point the interested reader toward a few more of the many additional lines of inquiry. The first is the field of neuroscience itself – it is a hard dictum that Dewey set out, that one's philosophical conceptions must be based on the best science of the day, but it is clear that the philosophical understanding of the organic life of the organism in its dynamic interaction with the physical and social environment requires of us today a serious attempt at understanding the brain. One might begin with Paul Churchland's *The Engine of Reason, the Seat of the Soul* (1995) for a basic primer on the brain. John Pinel's *A Colorful Introduction to the Anatomy of the Human Brain* (1998) is very helpful and a lot of fun.

We haven't examined 'consciousness' at any great length, breadth or depth. A place to start might be David Rosenthal's *Consciousness and Mind* (2005), or Antti Revonsuo's *Inner Presence: Consciousness as a Biological Phenomenon* (2006). Then there is the very puzzling matter of 'intentionality,' a central concept in philosophy of mind. How can anything, mental or physical, be 'about' something else? One might be interested in the 'origins' of mind, developmentally – Jean Matter Mandler's *The Foundation of Mind: Origins of Conceptual Thought* (2004) might be useful. Or, for an evolutionary approach to the nature of mind, there is Geary's *The Origin of Mind: Evolution of Brain, Cognition, and General Intelligence*.

The nature of language and its role in thought, the nature of creative thought, of imagination and play, of images in the mind, of visual thinking, of representation ... each could have a chapter of its own. For the time being, though, perhaps this is enough of a beginning.

NOTE

82 I use the term 'cosmos' here, in the way the term 'world' is often used, simply to refer to 'everything that is.'

REFERENCES

Bennett, M.R. and Hacker, P.M.S. (2003) *Philosophical Foundations of Neuroscience*. Malden, MA: Blackwell.

Berkeley, George (1982) *A Treatise Concerning the Principles of Human Knowledge*. Indianapolis, IN: Hackett Publishing Company. (Originally published in 1710.)

Chalmers, David J. (1996) *The Conscious Mind: In Search of a Fundamental Theory*. Oxford: Oxford University Press.

Churchland, Patricia S. (1989) *Neurophilosophy: Toward a Unified Science of the Mind-Brain*. Cambridge, MA: MIT Press.

Churchland, Paul (1995) *The Engine of Reason, the Seat of the Soul: A Philosophical Journey into the Brain*. Cambridge, MA: MIT Press.

Damasio, Antonio (1994) *Descartes' Error: Emotion, Reason, and the Human Brain*. Harper Collins.

Dehaene, Stanislas (2001) *The Cognitive Neuroscience of Consciousness*. Cambridge, MA: MIT Press.

Descartes, Rene (2002) 'Meditations on first Philosophy (II and VI)', in David J. Chalmers (ed.), *Philosophy of Mind: Classical and Contemporary Readings*. Oxford: Oxford University Press, pp. 10–21.

Dewey, John (XXXX) 'Science and the method of psychology,' in *The Collected Works of John Dewey. The Electronic Version. The Early Works: 1882–1898*, Ew. 2.12–18.

Dewey, John (XXXX) 'The realism of pragmatism', in *The Collected Works of John Dewey. The Electronic Version. The Middle Works: Essays 1903–1906*, Mw.3.155, J.A. Boydston (ed.). Carbondale: Southern Illinois University Press.

Dewey, John (1925) 'Experience and nature' in *The Collected Works of John Dewey. The Electronic Version. The Later Works 1925–1953*, Lw.1.219, J.A. Boydston (ed.). Carbondale: Southern Illinois University Press.

Dewey, John (1958) *Experience and Nature*. New York: Dover Publications. (Republication of 2nd edn, 1929.)

Dretske, John (1997) *Naturalizing the Mind*. Cambridge, MA: The MIT Press.

Edwards, Paul (ed.) (1967) 'Plato', in *The Encyclopedia of Philosophy, Vol. 5*, pp. 314–333.

Edwards, Paul (ed.) (1967) 'Panpsychism,' in *The Encyclopedia of Philosophy, Vol. 6*, pp. 22–31.

Fodor, Jerry A. (1989) *Modularity of Mind: An Essay on Faculty Psychology*. Cambridge, MA: MIT Press.

Fodor, Jerry A. (2001) *The Mind Doesn't Work That Way: The Scope and Limits of Computational Psychology*. Cambridge, MA: MIT Press.

Foster, John (2004) 'The succinct case for idealism', in John Heil (ed.), *Philosophy of Mind: a Guide and Anthology*. Oxford: Oxford University Press.

Kim, Jaegwon (1993) *Supervenience and Mind: Selected Philosophical Essays*. Cambridge: Cambridge University Press.

Kim, Jaegwon (2002) 'The many problems of mental causation', in David Chalmers, *Philosophy of Mind: Classical and Contemporary Readings*. Oxford: Oxford University Press.

Kim, Jaegwon (2005) *Physicalism, on Something Near Enough*. Princeton: Princeton University Press.

Libet, Benjamin, Freeman, Anthony and Sutherland, Keith (eds) (1999) *The Volitional Brain: Towards a Neuroscience of Free Will*. Imprint Academic Journal of Consciousness Studies, 6, No. (8–9).

Mandler, Jean Matter (2004) *The Foundation of mind: Origins of Conceptual Thought*. Oxford: Oxford University Press.

Mohrhoff, Ulrich (1999) 'The physics of interactionism' in Benjamin, Libet, Anthony, Freeman, and Keith, Sutherland (eds), *The Volitional Brain: Towards a Neuroscience of Free Will*. Imprint Academic: Journal of Consciousness Studies, 6, No. (8–9).

Pinel, John P.J. (1998) *A Colorful Introduction to the Anatomy of the Human Brain*. Boston: Allyn and Bacon.

Polger, Thomas W. (2004) *Natural Minds*. Cambridge, MA: MIT Press.

Prinz, Jesse J. (2004) *Gut Reactions: A Perceptual Theory of Emotion*. Oxford: Oxford University Press.

Putnam, Hilary (1991) *Representation and Reality*. Cambridge, MA: MIT Press.

Revonsuo, Antti (2006) *Inner Presence: Consciousness as a Biological Phenomenon*. Cambridge, MA: MIT Press.

Rosenthal, David (2005) *Consciousness and Mind*. Oxford: Clarendon Press.

Scheffler, Israel (1977) *In Praise of the Cognitive Emotions*. New York: Routledge.

Searle, John (1983) *Intentionality: An Essay in the Philosophy of Mind*. Cambridge: Cambridge University Press.

Searle, John (2004) *Mind: A Brief Introduction*. Oxford: Oxford University Press.

Thompson, Evan (2007) *Mind in Life: Biology, Phenomenology, and the Sciences of the Mind*. Cambridge, MA: Harvard University Press.

22

Learning

Andrew Davis

INTRODUCTION

When we think about learning we tend to use sets of interconnected metaphors. In this chapter I explore a number of philosophical issues that are raised by the most influential of these metaphors.[83]

One cluster of metaphors contrasts transmission and construction. The transmission account runs as follows: When I learn some history I 'take in' an item of knowledge. After I learn that the Battle of Hastings occurred in 1066 there is a fact 'in' my head that was not there previously. The teacher may have *transmitted* this fact to me. This thought in turn is associated with more metaphors. The learner is an empty rucksack to be 'filled' with knowledge, or even an empty vessel into which knowledge is to be poured. (The Maths educator Hilary Shuard once commented in a famous TV documentary that children had proved to be 'very leaky vessels'.)

Over recent decades educational thinking about learning has been strongly influenced by images opposed to transmission; these featured *construction* and *invention*. Learners cannot have knowledge inserted into their minds. They construct their knowledge. Many contemporary versions of constructivism emphasize the role of the social world. Constructivists drawing on the Piagetian tradition are often characterized as individualist, whereas *social constructivists* owe their inspiration to Vygotsky. The social approach denies that learners are left to their own devices when constructing knowledge. Vygotsky claims that learners have functions in an embryonic state which will be realized if they work alongside learners and/or adults with a greater mastery of the subject matter concerned (Vygotsky, 1978).

A second cluster of metaphors are associated with the classic psychological idea of *transfer*. A primary school child acquires the ability to use full stops in the context of school English lessons. She then (we can always hope …), she transfers this ability to a range of contexts outside school, and eventually to innumerable circumstances she encounters as an adult. The thought here is that she *carries* the skill with her from school to real-life situations. Or again, a student acquires her information about the Battle of Hastings in the history lesson. Once she is in possession of it, she can 'take' her knowledge to a very different context, such as participating in a quiz, or perhaps many years later when visiting that part of the English coastline she might talk to her child about the Norman Conquest and mention the said battle.

It is as though the skill or item of knowledge is likened to a physical asset such as blood group or height, physical traits which individuals can certainly take with them from one situation to another. A crucially linked additional metaphorical ingredient here introduces the notion of 'distance' to the transfer process. Sue learns to tell the time at school, and is successful at home too – the situations concerned are quite similar and hence only 'near transfer' is needed. Jones learns to ride his own bike, and when on holiday in Spain is able to take advantage of some cycling activities there even though he has left his own machine at home. Again we have 'near transfer', on the grounds that the cycling abilities he needs in Spain will be very close to those he acquired at home – even with some minor differences between the Spanish bikes and his own.

Thus on one account 'near transfer' is about someone succeeding in taking their capacity from the context in which they acquired it to one which is very similar. An alternative account of near transfer talks of a performance in a new situation being better than it otherwise would have been as it closely resembles a performance of which they already have mastery. It is often difficult to distinguish clearly between these two versions of 'near transfer'.

QUESTIONS ABOUT THE TRANSFER METAPHOR

The history of psychology is bedevilled with research evidence both about surprising transfer failure and success. However, if we attempted to deny transfer we would be committed to a manifestly absurd position. In terms of the metaphor, without transfer learning cannot take place. If I learn something, then this is supposed to affect what I know and can do in situations other than the one in which I learned it. If not, there is no such thing as learning.

Some authorities, both from empirical disciplines such as psychology (there is an extensive literature: see e.g. Beach, 1999, and Packer, 2001), and those writing from a philosophical perspective feel that there are serious conceptual problems linked to the transfer metaphor. Here I explore some of the philosophical issues.

The first problem relates to *what* it is that is supposed to transfer. In the examples outlined above there are phrases purporting to refer to items of knowledge, or abilities, capacities or skills. We may well play around with a phrase such as 'the fact that the Battle of Hastings took place in 1066'. Superficially this resembles expressions such as 'the brown dog that lives next door' and 'the copy of *Anna Karenina* on the top shelf in my sitting room'. There is a strong tendency to think that all these phrases function in the same kind of way: that is, to *refer* to something specific, whether a dog, a book or a fact. We all know that 'facts' are not in the same category as physical objects, but nevertheless we are still tempted to conceive of them as specific items which are distinct from each other, just as a particular dog is distinct from a particular book. This perspective is certainly needed to buttress the transfer metaphor. Dogs and books can be transported or transferred, and so can facts, at least on the account under consideration. 'Facts' are abstract in comparison with dogs and books but they are still discrete, according to this way of thinking. Jones can carry a certain fact with him from one situation to another without bringing other facts along, just as he could take *Anna Karenina* on holiday without also packing *Tom Jones*.

'Discrete' is a difficult idea to unpack in the context of abstract ideas. It connotes the thought that a fact can be *separated* from others, and indeed that it can be separated from the environment of the individual who is in possession of it. But does either kind of separation make sense in the context of facts?

To address this question we need to make some initial inroads into the construction metaphor, although the main discussion of this is reserved for the following section. Piaget is one of the intellectual ancestors of constructivism. 'To understand is to discover, or reconstruct by rediscovery ...' (Piaget 1973). How, asks Piaget, do children progress from one knowledge state to another? He invoked two ideas to capture what takes place: *assimilation* and *accommodation*. A child assimilating new knowledge fits it into existing ways of thinking, concepts or structures. A child knows about hammers. She encounters a wooden mallet, and decides this is a hammer. The mallet is assimilated into her current way of thinking about hammers. Actually, it may not behave like other hammers according to her, since she may discover that the nail goes into the mallet rather than into the wall.

In the process of accommodation an individual's existing ways of thinking, concepts or structures must be modified to cope with the fresh knowledge. For instance, Parveen understands numbers to 100. She appreciates their function for basic counting and at least something of how they relate to each other. For instance, it is evident to her that if 5 is 2 more than 3, then 3 must be 2 less than 5. When we need more than one digit to represent a number she grasps the function of each digit. Hence 52 is seen as five tens and two more units, and so forth.

She now follows a programme of activities about fractions. She divides wholes into equal parts (the 'cake model' of fractions) and splits sets or groups into equal subsets to find fractions of them – 12 is carved up into two equal parts to find half of it, and so on. She reaches a point where she learns that fractions themselves are numbers between the whole numbers and can be represented on the number line.

This transforms her previous conception of numbers. She can now use numbers to represent *quantities* in addition to counting with them. To sum up, Parveen's existing knowledge has *accommodated* the new knowledge about fractions. (This account of accommodation is adapted from Davis, 1994: 10–11.)

The Piagetian story in effect offers us a powerful interpretation of knowledge possessed *with at least some degree of understanding*. In the picture of the child's mind as an empty rucksack being filled with facts we entertain the possibility that knowledge can be 'in' her mind without being understood. In contrast, learning that has been assimilated by an individual, and to which an individual's existing knowledge has accommodated, is learning that has become linked in many ways to the learner's existing stock of knowledge.

Admittedly, in the attempts to reveal the flaws in a metaphor we are employing *other* metaphors – the idea of a 'link' is no exception. Before offering a few observations about 'links' it should be made clear that the use of metaphor per se cannot be open to objection. Talk about the mind and psychological processes is saturated with metaphor. If we try to avoid it we just end up using other metaphors. Typical phrases include 'sharp intelligence', 'deep sadness', 'cold personality' and 'drained of all emotion'. Such language is not the monopoly of the layman. Psychology has plenty – e.g. 'fluid ability', 'fuzzy concept', 'cognitive map', 'problem space' and many others. So there is nothing wrong with metaphor: we are exploring what some feel are the flaws in *specific* metaphors associated with learning.

Many types of 'link' between content can feature in an individual's stock of knowledge. That the Battle of Hastings took place in 1066 *excludes* the possibility that it occurred in 1166, *includes* the idea that fighting was involved, *implies* some system for numbering the years, *as a matter of fact* featured Normans confronting Anglo-Saxons and so forth. One of the difficulties in speaking in this way is that it may once again raise the spectre of individual items which could be joined together in some way in an individual's mind. The deeper point here is that there is no such thing as a discrete item of content, a 'bit' of content which is separable from other content (see Davis, 1998, for much more discussion of these ideas).

Informed by an appreciation of the holistic character of knowledge we can begin to see some of the problems with the transfer metaphor, at least as it might be applied to *an individual knowledge item*. 'Bits' of knowledge lack a standalone identity. Knowledge content is partly a function of its links with other knowledge content owned by the individual concerned. When someone 'moves' from one context to another then, or so it might be thought, the whole of their knowledge could be transferred from the first situation to the second. However, in a new situation the individual will acquire new knowledge. This will impact on the resident knowledge and subtly transform it. This must be the case if the person concerned is going to apply aspects of their existing knowledge to the new situation. In a sense the old knowledge will no longer be present – at least not in its original guise. In one literal-minded construal of 'transfer', at least, the old knowledge *cannot* be transferred.

A second aspect of the problematic character of the transfer metaphor relates to the assumption that learning can be 'in' an individual in any sense which implies that it is separable from the individual's environment. According to a rival tradition known as 'situated cognition', learners are involved in a 'community of practice'. The community shares various beliefs and behaviour patterns which learners, as apprentices, gradually acquire. On this perspective, learning should not be seen as something done by an atomistic individual agent, but rather something distributed across many participants (Lave and Wenger, 1991).

It is not always easy to extract clear and simple meanings from writers in the situated cognition camp. An example from a related philosophical perspective may help. Wittgenstein, and his follower Peter Winch (1958), held that social phenomena could be understood by appealing to the ideas of *rule governed activity* and *language games*. Individuals inhabit a social and cultural environment structured by innumerable rules or conventions which give meaning to most of behaviour and certainly to language. When someone marks an X in pencil on a piece of paper in certain circumstances this counts as voting. By way of background much is needed, including the existence of a range of democratic institutions. These are made up of many complex conventions, associated patterns of behaviour, beliefs and intentions sustained by the members of the society concerned. Suppose Jones knows that his wife has voted. What 'makes it true' that Jones has this knowledge evidently involves at least something about Jones himself and also about an action that his wife has taken. But it is a great deal more. It is also a matter of the convention-governed practices outlined above. Jones's state of knowing is a complex state of affairs which extends 'outside his head' into the social and cultural environment in which he and his wife are embedded.

So if learning or coming to know cannot appropriately be characterized as something exclusively pertaining to an individual, the transfer metaphor is in serious trouble. It relied on a picture of an individual carrying something with them, which implied that the 'something' was separable from their environment.

The situated cognition tradition has been criticized for adopting an unnecessarily extreme position. Its proponents have been accused of claiming that 'all knowledge is specific to the situation in which the task is performed and that more general knowledge cannot and will not transfer to real-world situations' (Anderson et al., 1996: 6). The corollary of this extreme position would be that transfer does not occur. Such a position is, of course untenable.

Some researchers not only oppose the alleged transfer limitations implied by the situated cognition tradition but also argue that educators can meet context limitations head on. In his paper tellingly entitled 'Situated cognition and how to overcome it', Carl Bereiter (1997) observes that 'in order to work effectively with knowledge objects, people have to master the practices of nonsituated cognition ...'. Again, philosophers influenced by the Wittgenstein/Winch tradition will question the very possibility of 'nonsituated cognition'. Their doubts will not be empirical, but rather amount to the thought that *there could not be such a thing in principle*.

I turn now to the idea of 'distance', 'near' and 'far' in the transfer figure. When I note that Pluto is far from the sun and that Mercury is near, I am contemplating states of affairs that are independent of my thinking, and indeed of anyone else's. The planets' distances would be what they are even had no humans ever existed to discover them. Of course, the *names* of the planets reflect human decisions, but this does not affect the point. Now the idea of 'distance' in transfer is linked to degrees of similarity: it may be an instance of near transfer if Jane, having added two bricks and three bricks together to make five, succeeds in adding two cakes and three cakes to get five in total. We judge that the cake situation is very similar indeed to the brick context, and hence that the transfer has only a short distance to travel. The analogy with spatial distances might hold good if similarity in the context of human activity were independent of human thinking and decisions. But it is not. Two people voting in a general election write 'X' on a piece of paper. In virtue of a complex set of human practices, the two actions are similar: they both are instances of voting. They may differ in other ways, of course. The physical dimensions of one 'X' is most unlikely to be exactly like that of the second. The chemical constituents of the pigments that make up each X may well vary. And so on.

Suppose that all the social practices and conventions in respect of which thoughts and actions are similar or dissimilar were explicit and stable. Imagine also that they were the same across social groups, societies and cultures. Then judgements about near and far transfer would be robust over time, contexts, times and cultures. However, the opposite is true. Many of the unimaginably complex set of practices and conventions which inform similarity judgements are not explicit. They vary from one society to another, and even within a particular society. Although some will endure, others will be ephemeral. It follows from all this that there is no simple and unquestionable route to verdicts about the 'distance' between a learning context and a situation to which the learning might transfer.

A closely related point can be pursued if we conceptualize that which is supposed to transfer as an ability, capacity or skill rather than as a 'bit' of knowledge. We have already noted our propensity to be misled by the syntactical similarity between phrases such as 'the table' and 'the fact that the Battle of Hastings took place in 1066'. Similar issues are provoked by expressions such as 'the ability to solve problems', 'punctuation skills', 'spatial ability' and the like. Surely people can acquire such psychological traits and retain them over time, or so we may think. However, I have argued that we need to be aware that no amount of talk can conjure such entities into existence and that in many cases it is wholly unclear what it would be for them to exist (see e.g. Davis 1988, 1998, 2005). To select and summarize just one strand of the relevant arguments, the idea of an ability invariably involves a *kind of action*. These may be types of behaviour, such as kicking a ball, or they could feature some mental activity – for instance, imagining how the house will look when it is finished. Often both observable and 'inner' elements will be combined.

Some directly observable actions may be categorized independently of the social contexts in which they are performed. These are generally *physical movements* of various kinds – waving my hand, bending my knee, shaking my head or closing my eyes. A hand waving is a hand waving whatever the cultural context. It may also fall into other action categories too – such as waving goodbye – but whether this is the case *does* depend on prevailing social practices and conventions. For the transfer metaphor to make sense, it needs action classifications to be social context-independent. It is only in this way that we can begin to get some kind of grip on the idea of a context-independent ability. If the nature of the action depends conceptually at least in part on the context in which it is performed, it makes no sense to think of a 'something' that the actor can transfer from one situation to another.

THE CONSTRUCTION METAPHOR

According to this fashionable perspective, learners are portrayed as agents who construct or build up their own learning. Teachers join in with this metaphor, so to speak, by providing *scaffolding* for their students to build up their knowledge (Wood et al., 1976). Some philosophers feel that the image of construction has been more successful in what it sought to oppose than in terms of the light it has shed on the process of learning. Denis Phillips holds that constructivism has 'become akin to a secular religion' with many sects (Phillips, 1995). As we will see shortly, some of its more extreme interpretations have played into the hands of its enemies.

The *transmission* analogy, referred to at the beginning of the chapter, seems to leave room for the possibility that knowledge could be put into a learner regardless of the learner's cognitive state at the time. Now arguably this is actually possible, at least if we are not too fussy about what we count as 'learning' and as 'knowledge'. On the traditional account of what it is to know, for example, that the Battle of Hastings took place in 1066 (see, for example, Ayer, 1956: 31–35), it must be true that the battle occurred on the said date, I must *believe* that it took place at this time, and I must be *justified* in believing this. This apparently allows for my teacher to transmit such a fact to me. My justification for believing her could be the following: that she has told me things on many previous occasions and I have found her to be reliable. Hence it could be reasonable for me to take it from her on this occasion.

Things are not quite as simple as this, however, even if we put on one side the question of how I found out that she was reliable. On the transmission model just outlined, the teacher might tell me that 'the mome raths outgrabe' (Carroll, 1872). On the grounds that she has proved a trusted authority, I might be inclined to accept that she has told me something true (on the assumption, of course that I am ignorant of children's literature classics). However, I would have absolutely no idea what she was attempting to convey, and hence I could scarcely be described as having acquired knowledge. This, of course, is an extreme case, since the sentence concerned means nothing and hence *in principle* cannot be understood. Consider, instead, a teacher informing a 9 year-old student of Einstein's claim that gravity is the curvature of time-space. A clever child might have some vague ideas about this, but again, she could hardly be said to have come to know something as a result of the teacher's 'transmission'. Her problem is that her current knowledge is not of an appropriate kind to 'accommodate' the Einstein material. Links cannot be made. It is true that *in principle* the material could be understood. However, the child's epistemic state with respect to this is similar to that achieved when confronting the excerpt from Carroll's jabberwocky. The child would not know anything as a result of the teacher's transmission.

A troublesome theme in the history of constructivism is the thought that if we *invent* or *construct* knowledge then that is exactly what we end up with – merely our invention. Constructivism is pitted against the thought that learning involves discovering aspects of an *independent reality*. A famous, or infamous, radical constructivist, Ernst von Glasersfeld, is often quoted as claiming that 'the results of our cognitive efforts have the purpose of helping us cope in the world of experience, rather than the traditional goal of furnishing an "objective" representation of a world that might "exist" apart from us and our experience' (1991: xiv–xv).

Radical constructivism has sometimes set itself up as the sane alternative to a naïve correspondence theory of truth and a crude empiricist foundationalist account of knowledge. The latter ideas in broad outline are that sense experience directly informs us of the nature of an independent reality, and our claims about this reality, if true, are true in so far as they mirror the features of that reality. As sketched here, few if any thinkers ever held such views. The putative constructivist alternative arguably involves a very familiar self-refuting relativism. Von Glasersfeld and his followers presumably want us to take his claims about the status of our constructed knowledge very seriously. Yet on his own account, these claims are 'merely' constructed, and fail to achieve an 'objective' representation of how things are with our knowledge. Understood in this spirit, he would seem to have undermined his own credentials.

From the construction metaphor to infinite regresses and the 'paradox of learning'. Pushing the construction metaphor further than it can go produces an infinite regress. The student constructs her knowledge from … what? The answer has to be knowledge she already possesses. Was that knowledge itself constructed? Either it was, so we continue the regress; or it was not, in which case we are confronted with the possibility of knowledge which is *not* constructed. If this is possible, does this not undermine the very power of the construction metaphor? If a student can know something which she has not constructed, could it not be argued that this lets the possibility of transmission back in? At what point is construction deemed essential for learning? Why?

These kinds of regresses have long been explored by philosophers of education, and indeed some trace them back to Plato's *Meno*. Hamlyn investigates the thought that 'the acquisition of knowledge implies already existing knowledge ... . Where does that ultimately come from?' (1978: 89).

Atkinson (1982) discusses a similar regress, though not explicitly in connection with the construction metaphor. Both Hamlyn and Atkinson are well aware of the errors inherent in thinking of the acquisition of knowledge as 'an all or nothing event like coming to possess a piece of property' (Atkinson, 1982: 70), and talk of the slow process of coming to master interconnected concepts. Both writers deny that appealing to innate ideas could halt the regress, since the latter could not amount to knowledge. For knowledge, we are told, requires the existence of interpersonal standards and social communication. Hamlyn and Atkinson argue that the way out of the regress is to appreciate that the earliest elements from which knowledge is constructed are not themselves instances of knowledge, but rather reactions which learners have in common with all of us. Atkinson appeals to Wittgenstein's ideas about patterns of agreement in how we perceive and react to the world. This is a matter of sharing forms of life, or inhabiting a common background, to employ John Searle's phrase.

Luntley (2008) explores a related problem that he casts in terms of concept acquisition, though the ideas of *construction* and of interconnected content do not figure in his discussion. The paradox of learning (which he attributes to Jerry Fodor) is that the 'learning process presupposes the ability to entertain the very concept whose learning is supposed to be explained' (2008: 2). Fodor in one place expresses the point thus:

> There literally isn't such a thing as the notion of learning a conceptual system richer than the one that one already has; we simply have no idea of what it would be like to get from a conceptually impoverished to a conceptually richer system by anything like a process of learning. (Fodor, 1980: 148–149)

As so often in philosophy, there is an important purpose in exploring such a paradox. Needless to say it is not to show that something is impossible when we all know perfectly well to the contrary. In this particular case, for instance, no one is trying to 'prove' that learning cannot take place. Working out how to avoid the paradox promises to deepen our understanding of learning itself and of any flaws in our thinking that feed the paradox. Bereiter is inclined to take Fodor seriously, and urges us to contemplate the possibility that 'in making learning out to be a much simpler process than it is, educators have overlooked important factors in the promotion of learning' (Bereiter, 1985: 202).

Again, one obvious escape route from the problem is to postulate some kind of innate knowledge. Luntley sidesteps this possibility by appealing to the notion of *'purposeful activity'*.

On his account, individuals can experience 'affective' states and can deal with them so as to become as 'comfortable' as possible: people have some kind of basic and 'pervasive thrust' to 'set their lives in order'. Human beings have this from the very beginning of their lives. This 'ordering of one's life' can involve activities prior to the formation of any concepts even though there are later, conceptually sophisticated stages. From the earliest times individuals have expectations which, when frustrated, render aspects of reality 'salient' for them. Behaviour can take account of such elements of reality even when they cannot yet be conceptualized. This allows the formation of habits and for the possibility of matching others' behavioural patterns before concepts are formed. In this way, Luntley feels that the regress can be halted. His account is general, and necessarily avoids content-specific psychological attitudes and intentions, for these would involve the very concepts that we must not presuppose. It apparently involves an *empirical* claim about all young human beings. There are affinities between his proposals and Atkinson's thoughts about halting the regress by appealing to aspects of our 'forms of life'.

ACTIVE LEARNING

Part of the motivation for the construction metaphor in the first place was the vision of *active* learners constructing knowledge as opposed to a passive student absorbing knowledge from the teacher. The notion of 'activity' and the active learner have been central to child-centred education at least since the time of Dewey. However, it has a troubled history in the long-standing campaign to oppose transmission and the idea of the passive learner. Bonnett denies a link between *self expression* in the classroom and a room 'full of noise and blustering "busyness"' (1994: 111). Whether individuals can best build or construct during their learning while physically active is an empirical question, and cannot be settled merely by appealing to the metaphor. Even the idea of physical activity is unclear. Must activity involve the whole body, or will just part of it do? Can the activities vary or could the same physical movements be repeated?

Without empirical evidence to the contrary, why deny the possibility that students sat still listening to a teacher or lecturer can be engaged in constructing learning? So it might be *mental activity* that is the key, but again we cannot arrive at a verdict without being clearer about the nature of the proposal. If I decide to summon up the same mental image repeatedly for some reason, I might be said to be mentally active, at least after a fashion. Intuitively, however, this is not the kind of mental activity valued by the constructivist. Is the use of imagination required? The constructivist who assented to this would not be out of the woods, since *imagining* seems to cover a number of importantly different mental activities. Repeatedly summoning up the same mental images might count as using the imagination, but perhaps the constructivist wants something more creative or 'inventive'.

Supporters of the idea of active learning might protest that we are being too severe, and argue that at least it rules out *passivity* even if it is not immediately clear what it rules in. They might appeal to the ancient idea of emotions as *passions* – that is to say, as psychological episodes that happen to people rather than being chosen by them. Thus I see a lion and experience fear, or someone vandalizing my car and feel anger. I do not (apparently) choose these emotions. In commonsense thinking, at least, psychological events that happen to us are to be contrasted with *reasoning* which is something we do, something active (see Price, 2005: 2). Psychological events that happen to us may be thought of as not really part of us.

Bakhurst (2008) casts doubt on the differential valuing of active and passive learning in his application of some of John McDowell's ideas to education. On McDowell's view, to have a mind, and in particular to be a thinker, is 'to be at home in the space of reasons'. Children are born in a kind of animal state, and through enculturation or *Bildung* they learn to be able to operate with concepts and a conception of the world rather than merely to respond to biological stimuli. McDowell draws from Wilfred Sellars the thesis that we do not experience and *then* apply concepts. That would be the 'Myth of the Given'. McDowell insists that experiences have conceptual content from the start. 'In experience one takes in, for instance sees, *that things are thus and so*' (McDowell, 1994: 9).

So events that just happen to us can have conceptual content and hence can 'exercise a rational constraint on judgment' (Bakhurst, 2008: 9). Bakhurst proceeds to argue that even within the sphere of reasoning itself there can be elements of passivity. Points can 'occur' to me without being the result of active deliberation. He suggests persuasively that understanding itself is or can be significantly passive:

> Suppose you are struggling with a philosophical problem. Frustrated, you decide to sleep on it. In the morning, you awake and the solution comes to you. In such cases, we cannot say the answer comes unbidden, since one certainly has bid (even begged) it come. Yet the reception of the answer is passive. (2008: 10)

Vygotsky's views about the formation of reason imply, on Bakhurst's view, that the young child cannot be 'represented as actively constructing its conception of the world, since she lacks the wherewithal to do so' (Bakhurst, 2008: 21). If we find Bakhurst convincing we have to abandon the exclusive grip that many educators have seen between 'active' learning (viz., learning that *is not passive)* and the development of understanding.

AFFECTIVE STATES AND LEARNING

The emphasis on activity does not simply stem from empirical convictions about the link between active involvement and the development of understanding. It also appeals to the intuition that motivated students learn better than their unmotivated peers and that the 'active' learner is more likely to be motivated than the passive student. 'Motivation' is, of course, a very broad idea in this connection but covers a variety of what psychologists call 'affective' states.

Could Luntley's proposal for stopping the learning regress be characterized as a claim to the effect that individuals 'know how to learn', and thus be related to the perennial favourite of child-centred educators, learning how to learn? Now Luntley's suggestions focus on affective states, yet it might be thought that if there *is* such a thing as knowing how to learn it is some kind of *cognitive* capacity.

However, Christopher Winch (2009) doubts whether a cognitive account of learning how to learn is available. On his view the very idea of a general ability to learn, apparently implied by the possibility of learning how to learn, is difficult to grasp. He examines whether characterizing learning as forming and testing hypotheses could form the basis of a cognitive account of learning how to learn. He concludes that not all learning is covered by such an account and that in any case aspects of the particular subject knowledge concerned make a difference to the character of the learning involved. He also dismisses the idea that learning how to learn relates to the ability to consider relevant factors when reaching verdicts or decisions. That is a mark of all mature rational persons, even those who are not 'good' at learning. He feels that reading and numeracy are 'specific transferable abilities' and that they will turn out to be highly significant in any defensible account of learning how to learn. Yet he is pessimistic about current achievement levels in reading and numeracy and so in his search for an account of learning how to learn he looks to the *affective* domain. Before we follow this line of thought further we should note that questions might be asked about the status and nature of reading ability and of numeracy. Are these expressions merely shorthand for a host of more specific abilities? What *kinds* of actions might such specific abilities implicate? What, if anything, binds these specific abilities together? To what extent, if at all, can they be characterized in culture-independent ways?

Turning now to Winch's focus on affective states: he denies that we have a general desire to learn, an assumption made by Rousseau and others. He thinks, however, that we can *acquire* this desire to learn. He emphasizes the importance of confidence, independence or autonomy in learning and the so-called 'petty virtues' of 'patience, persistence, diligence, attention to detail, the ability not to be too discouraged by initial failure ... .' (Winch, 2009).

He believes that his favoured virtues are 'transferable'. They certainly need to be, if they are to play the key role he identifies for them. He makes it clear that transferability in this connection includes the claim that they can be practised in a variety of contexts and that they can be acquired through the provision of a broad curriculum offering music, sport and other activities or content 'likely to assist in the development of such virtues' (Winch, 2009).

I suspect that most educators would agree that if students can acquire confidence through success in an activity or subject that motivates them then this will affect their performance and achievements in other areas, even those which they were previously finding challenging and in no way motivating. Nevertheless, conceptual questions about the *identity* of Winch's virtues across learning contexts might parallel those raised earlier in connection with cognitive abilities and could prove difficult to answer. However, it is beyond the scope of this chapter to pursue them further.

NOTE

83 I am indebted to some of the writings of Paul Hager for insights into the importance of key metaphors relating to learning. See, for example, Hager P. and Halliday J. (2006) *Recovering Informal Learning: Wisdom, Judgement and Community*. Dordrecht: Springer, Chapter 5.

REFERENCES

Anderson, John R., Reder, Lynne M. and Simon, Herbert A. (1996) 'Situated learning and education', *Educational Researcher*, 25 (4): 5–11.

Atkinson, Christine (1982) 'Beginning to learn', *Journal of Philosophy of Education*, 16 (1): 69–75.

Ayer, Alfred J. (1956) *The Problem of Knowledge*. London: Penguin, pp. 31–35.

Bakhurst, David (2008) 'Life in the space of reasons: mood, music, education, and the philosophy of John McDowell', paper presented at the Philosophy of Education Society of Great Britain Annual Conference: available at http://www.philosophy-of-education.org/conferences/pdfs/David_Bakhurst.pdf

Beach, K. (1999) 'Consequential transitions: a sociocultural expedition beyond transfer in education', *Review of Research in Education*, 24: 101–139.

Bereiter, Carl (1985) 'Toward a solution of the learning paradox', *Review of Educational Research*, 55 (2): 201–226.

Bereiter, Carl (1997) 'Situated cognition and how to overcome it', in David Kirshner and James A. Whitson (eds), *Situated Cognition: Social, Semiotic, and Psychological Perspectives*. Hillsdale, NJ: Erlbaum, pp. 281–300.

Bonnett, Michael (1994) *Children's Thinking*. London: Cassell.

Carroll, Lewis (1872) *Through the Looking-Glass and What Alice Found There*. London: Macmillan.

Davis, A. (1988) 'Ability and learning', *Journal of Philosophy of Education*, 22 (1): 45–55.

Davis, A. (1994) 'Constructivism', in Andrew Davis and Deirdre Pettitt (eds), *Developing Understanding in Primary Mathematics*. London: Falmer.

Davis, A. (1998) *The Limits of Educational Assessment*. Oxford: Blackwell.

Davis, A. (2005) 'Social externalism and the ontology of competence', *Philosophical Explorations*, 8 (3): 297–308.

Fodor, J. (1980) in Massimo Piatelli-Palmerini (ed.), *Language and Learning*. Cambridge, MA: Harvard University Press, pp. 143–149.

Hamlyn, David (1978) *Experience and the Growth of Understanding*. London: Routledge and Kegan Paul.

Lave, J. and Wenger, E. (1991) *Situated Learning: Legitimate Peripheral Participation*. Cambridge: Cambridge University Press.

Luntley, M. (2008) 'Conceptual development and the paradox of learning', *Journal of Philosophy of Education*, 42 (1): 1–14.

McDowell, J (1994) *Mind and World*. Cambridge, MA: Harvard University Press.

Packer, M. (2001) 'The problem of transfer, and the sociocultural critique of schooling', *Journal of the Learning Sciences*, 10 (4): 493–514.

Phillips, D. (1995) 'The good, the bad, and the ugly: the many faces of constructivism', *Educational Researcher*, 24 (7): 5–12.

Piaget, Jean (1973) *To Understand is to Invent*. New York: Grossman.

Price, Carol (2005) *Emotion*. Milton Keynes: Open University.

von Glasersfeld, E. (1991) 'Introduction', in E. von Glaserfeld (eds), *Radical Constructivism in Mathematics Education*. Dordrecht: Kluwer Academic Press, pp. xiii–xx.

Vygotsky, L. (1978). 'Interaction between learning and development', in *Mind in Society*, M. Cole (trans.). Cambridge, MA: Harvard University Press, pp. 79–91.

Winch, Peter (1958) *The Idea of a Social Science and Its Relation to Philosophy*. London: Routledge and Kegan Paul.

Winch, C. (2009) 'Learning how to learn: a critique', in Ruth Cigman and Andrew Davis (eds), *The New Philosophies of Learning*. Oxford: Wiley-Blackwell.

Wood, D., Bruner, J. and Ross, G. (1976) 'The role of tutoring in problem solving', *Journal of Child Psychology and Psychiatry*, 17 (2): 89–100.

23

Motivation and Learning

Frederick S. Ellett, Jr. and
David P. Erickson

INTRODUCTION

Motivating students to learn is among the highest of teaching arts. Yet what is motivation? And how might student motivation be related to learning? These questions are connected with many general interests pursued by philosophers, psychologists, and educators. In 'The challenge of folk psychology,' we consider basic philosophical accounts of the relationship between motivation and action. In 'Motivation and affective characteristics,' we consider important *general* views held by educators on the relationship between motivation and learning. In 'Motivation and learning: key concepts,' we consider influential *specific* views held by educators on the relationship between motivation and learning.

MOTIVATION AND ACTION

What is it for a person to be *motivated* to perform an action? For philosopher William Alston (1967), typical cases of motivation include doing something: to keep a promise; in order to get revenge; because it is the polite thing to do, etc. The phrases 'doing something for a purpose,' 'acting to realize an end or achieve a goal,' or 'doing something in order to do so-and-so' have all been found useful in characterizing the typical cases. Alston prefers the phrase 'doing something (A) in order to bring about so-and-so' because it can nicely cover the typical cases. It can also cover the case where a person goes to a meeting because he is obligated to do so, but in which the person's going (now) to the meeting is fulfill-ing (now) those obligations. In such a case, the person's doing A does not lead to something later in time.

It is important to understand the next step which is typically made. To what sorts of facts are we relating the action, A, if we ask why the person did A? Alston (1967: 400) argues that we may get a clue by noticing that the following are [logically] *equivalent*:

(1) He got up early in order to get some yard work done.
(2) He got up early because he wanted to get some yard work done.

Alston goes on to consider some other answers which might conceivably be given to the question 'Why did Jones get up early this morning?' Here are three:

(3) He has always been an early riser.
(4) He was very nervous and couldn't stay still.
(5) He had a violent argument with his wife and got up in a fit of anger.

In Alston's view, the answer given in (3) is a 'habit explanation' while those answers given in (4) and (5) are 'agitation explanations.' Thus, for Alston, there are *three* kinds of answers to the more general question, 'Why did person P do action A?' These are (a) motivational, (b) habit (or character), and (c) agitation explanations. Consider the following cases of 'motivational' explanations.

(6) P did A out of a sense of duty to Q.
(7) P did A out of a sense of gratitude to Q.
(8) P did A because he had promised Q he would.
(9) P did A because Q had asked him to.
(10) P did A because he was afraid of the consequences of not doing it.
(11) P did A because he couldn't stand to stay in that place another minute.

Alton argues that in cases (6) through (11) the statement *implies* that a certain desire (or a certain kind of occurrent desire, a 'want') gave rise to the action A.

Alston is very careful to point out that he is using the widest sense of 'want,' which can and often does stand in contrast to the normal and narrow sense of 'want.' For example, it might be the case that a person P goes to visit her aunt because she has an obligation to do so, and so she has a desire, in the widest sense, to do her duty. But it is possible that, in the narrow sense of want, she wants neither to make the long drive nor to spend much time with her aunt.

Are wants and beliefs necessary for motivation explanations?

But just what is a want, in Alston's wide sense? Alston considers the case in which he has a desire to plant some shrubs as a screen for a wire fence in his backyard. Suppose that, in order to satisfy this desire, one morning Alston drives out to Frank's Nursery, selects some shrubs, brings them home and plants them. Alston (1967: 402) argues that it is surely *not* the case that any particular conscious state – be it a felt urge to get *x*, an idea of *x* as pleasant, or whatever – is present during all the time the want (to plant some shrubs) is in existence and/or operative. Thus, Alston argues against 'phenomenological' accounts which construe a 'want' (in the wide sense) as a concrete and directly accessible 'entity.' Alston (1967: 408) also argues against attempts to define desire in terms of hedonic pleasure. A prominent motivational theorist in psychology observes that '[a]n axiom of virtually all theories of motivation is that the organisms strive to increase pleasure and to decrease pain' (Weiner, 1992b: 356). But Alston's philosophical arguments provide strong reasons for thinking such psychological theories need serious modification.

The view which links motivational explanations and wants in the wide sense has been maintained, extended, and defended by A. Goldman (1970) and D. Davidson (1980a). But Lawrence Davis (1979: 6–9) plausibly argues that the only way to defend the necessity of desire for action would require stretching the meaning word 'want' – even in its widest sense – to the point where it has no useful content. Davis holds that people sometimes do their duty *just* from a sense of duty. When asked 'Why did the person P do A?,' the person can reply 'out of my sense of duty' (or 'out of my commitment to duty'). The fact that the person P has this sense (or this commitment) helps explain why the person did A; neither a want nor a desire is necessary. Davis argues that there are several species of motivational explanations that need to be carefully distinguished.

In light of Davis's concern, it is surprising, perhaps, that the moral philosopher John Kekes (1995: 75–76) argues that 'desire' is to be understood in an even wider sense. For Kekes, the object of desire may be literally anything, whether significant or not, the intensity of desire may be strong or weak, its duration long term, or fleeting. It may be conscious, or not. 'Understood in this way, then, "desire" includes wishes, whims, wants, [felt] needs, aspirations, efforts, inclinations, and so forth ...' (Kekes, 1995: 75–76).

Thus, Kekes uses the term 'desire' to cover not merely motivation explanations but also character and impulse explanations. Let us call this the *radically wide* sense of the term. Kekes tries to show that it is in a person's interest to have (more) control over such desires. Kekes is not just interested in providing a unitary account of all those 'states' which influence what people do; rather, he is arguing that persons have the capacity to control such a wide variety of desires.

It has now become a fairly widespread convention to use the term 'desire' in Alston's sense rather than that of Kekes. But we shall see that some educators do use Kekes' radically wide sense. Perhaps we can accept Lawrence Davis's point, using these terms while remembering that they are 'placeholders' for a set of states that are extremely diverse.

Alston rejects the 'phenomenological view,' denying that the term 'want' refers to some simple, inner state, similar to a color sensation or a pain sensation. How, then, should we analyze what a want is? Alston considers whether a particular want can be given a 'dispositional analysis.' A dispositional analysis takes the form of a conditional: 'If a person P *wants* to do A, and also has features C1 and C2 and ..., then P will do A.' An adequate analysis would explicate the features

C1, C2, etc., which make the conditional true. Consider again the case in which Alston wants to plant some shrubs as a screen. In the analysis, it becomes clear that '… there are a number of factors which, if present, would prevent the performance of the action, however keen the desire' (Alston, 1967: 403). Here is a sample set of 'factors' from Alston:

I do not know about Frank's Nursery;
I do not believe that there are appropriate shrubs at Frank's Nursery;
I am ill disposed to Frank's Nursery;
I have a stronger desire which I am using the time to satisfy… .

Two important points can be drawn from these examples. First, an adequate analysis of a want must make some use of the terms 'knowledge,' 'belief,' 'perception,' and so on. There have been two lines of thought about the relation of motivation to knowledge, belief, etc. First, some early thinkers, e.g., Socrates, held that if a person knows what the good thing to do is, then the person will do that thing. But most philosophers, from Aristotle onward, hold that a person's knowing (or believing) that an action is good does not guarantee the person will do it. Aristotle held that a person could even knowingly do evil! For such philosophers, a good education is one that brings a person's desires to align with doing what is good.

The second line holds that for almost all desires which a person has, the action the person performs is, at least implicitly, taken to be an action which will satisfy the desire. As Black (1972) puts it, an action is judged to be reasonable (or not) insofar as the action satisfies our desires (or ends). The action a person performs will depend, then, on what the person believes about what the options are and about how likely it is that the options will be successful. We add a 'Davis' word of caution here: 'belief,' like 'desire,' must be used in the widest possible sense if it is to cover all the cases. (So, one risks, again, stretching the meaning of the term so that it has no useful content.')

There is a second important lesson to be drawn from Alston's set of factors. An adequate analysis of a want must make mention of the many other desires a person has. The action a person performs depends on the total set of desires, and on how each desire is related to the others. An adequate dispositional analysis will thus be very complicated, and perhaps unmanageably so.

So, if the phenomenological view fails, and if an adequate dispositional analysis is too complex to be achieved, how can we explain people's actions in terms of their desires and beliefs (in the wide sense)? For, despite the problems, we seem to be on the right track in thinking that motivation has something to do with desire-related and belief-related states, however they are ultimately to be understood.

Want and belief explanations as singular causal explanations

In the early 1960s, Donald Davidson published 'Actions, reasons, and causes,' a paper which had enormous influence on philosophical thought. In this paper,

Davidson (1980a) argues that people do indeed try to explain a person's action in terms of the person's wants and beliefs and that they are generally successful. This explanation of an action is a special kind of causal explanation, viz., a singular causal explanation, a causal explanation that cites no universal laws. Davidson tries to show, moreover, that at the level of persons (and cultures), there are no universal laws to be found and cited! (see Davidson, 1980a, 1980b, 1980c, 1980d). Davidson also argues that a person's *having reasons* could be part of an adequate causal explanation; he rejects the views of such thinkers as Anscombe (1958), Melden (1961), and Peters (1958), who held that a person's having a reason for doing action A *could not* be part of A's causal explanation (see also Donnellan, 1967). L. Davis (1979: 102–105) argues against C. Taylor's (1964) claim that teleological (goal-linked) explanations cannot be causal.

As shown in the Alston shrub case, to identify (to individuate) a person's want and a person's belief requires that we get rather specific about the content of that person's want and belief. We will need to understand many of the concepts, desires, and beliefs that the person has. Since the *contents* of the desire and of the belief are given in propositional form, the factors that explain a person's doing A have been called *propositional attitudes*. Desires and beliefs typically are directed toward an object (or have an object); this is to say that desires and beliefs are *intentional* attitudes. Intentional attitudes have another property: they are typically *intensional*. (To give an example of one mark of the intensional, consider Lois Lane, who wants to marry Superman. It does not follow that she wants to marry Clark Kent, even though Clark Kent is Superman, because Lois does not *believe* they are one and the same. (For more discussion, see Rosenberg, 1995: Ch. 2.)

The challenge of folk psychology

Fodor, in 1975, set out an apparently growing consensus among philosophers and cognitive scientists: that cognitive science ought to be committed to *intentional realism*. This is the doctrine that propositional attitudes are contentful and causally efficacious states instantiated in neural systems (see Greenwood, 1991a: 'Introduction'). The seeming agreement did not last long. A group of critics, led by P.M. Churchland (1984), P.S. Churchland (1986), and S. Stich (1983), argued that such want-belief explanations have no place in a legitimate science, and that contentful propositional attitudes have no place in science. These critics called the practice of giving want-belief explanations, and attributing propositional attitudes to persons, 'folk psychology.' For these critics, 'folk psychology' had a very negative connotation, even though they conceded that its practices may well be indispensable in everyday life. But, because want-belief explanations and propositional attitudes would not *reduce* to terms in a physicalistic framework, because of their intentional and intensional properties, they had to be *eliminated* from science.

Soon many philosophers and psychologists joined in responding to the 'eliminativists.' The defenders of folk psychology argued that folk psychology has a legitimate role to play in the social sciences and that the social sciences are legitimate sciences. The want-belief conceptual template, despite its limited predictive value, is still regarded as central to the singular causal explanations of folk psychology.

For more on these philosophical issues, the interested reader should see the Greenwood (1991b) collection, which presents key arguments for and against folk psychology. One should also see J. Margolis (1987), who vigorously argues in favor of folk psychology, and A. Rosenberg (1995), who is still troubled by its explanations. In a recent work (1996), Stich reconsiders and revises his earlier views (1983). It will be useful to compare the views of H. Putnam (1999), who argues that we understand the various uses of cause by mastering the explanatory practices, with the views of J. Kim (2006), who advances a 'physicalism or something near enough.' Educator Jerome Bruner (1990, 1997) defends the role of folk psychology in education.

MOTIVATION AND AFFECTIVE CHARACTERISTICS

Our focus here is primarily on two books which have been very influential in education: L.W. Anderson and S.F. Bourke's *Assessing Affective Characteristics in the Schools* (2000), and J. Brophy's *Motivating Students to Learn* (2004). Anderson and Bourke's (2000) text is widely cited by educators as a good source for reliably and validly assessing students' 'affective characteristics.' We agree with Anderson and Bourke that the affective characteristics of students are educationally important, because affective characteristics can be both a motivational *means* to educational outcomes (2000: 8–11), and a part of the educational *outcomes* themselves (2000: 11–15). But, to be reliable and valid, these assessments must be built upon a sound general account of affective characteristics. We will argue that Anderson and Bourke's work lacks such an account.

In many ways Jere Brophy (1987, 2004) provides a careful, thoughtful, and balanced review of the literature on the motivation. Still, we argue that this work too has some serious limitations.

Anderson and Bourke (2000) and Brophy (2004) both build upon the taxonomies of educational objectives developed by Bloom (1956) for the 'cognitive' domain and by Krathwohl et al. (1964) for the 'affective' domain. In the original Bloom (1956) work, the cognitive domain consists of 'knowledge' (as the ability to recall) and five, higher order skills (or processes). In the revised version, Anderson et al. (2001), there are two kinds of remembering and the five, higher-order skills (or processes). What should be recognized is that *belief* belongs to (fits into) neither the 1956 nor the 2001 taxonomies! In 1964 Krathwohl sets out the taxonomy for 'affective' domain. Although *belief* is not mentioned, it perhaps fits into domain as a kind of 'acceptance.' And though Krathwohl explicitly places values (and valuing) in this taxonomy, most educators place feelings, emotions, and attitudes into the affective domain.

How, then, do Anderson and Bourke (2000) conceive affective characteristics? First, they set out the general criteria (2000: 4):

> ... affective characteristics can be thought of as feelings and emotions that are characteristic of people, that is, qualities that represent people's typical ways of feeling or expressing emotion.

Then, additionally, (2000: 4–6):

> [t]hree more specific criteria must be met by all affective characteristics: intensity, direction and target ... . *Intensity* refers to the degree or strength of the feelings ... . *Direction* is concerned with the positive or negative orientation of feelings ... . *Target* refers to the object, activity or idea toward which the feeling is directed.

Comparing Anderson and Bourke's analysis of emotion to that provided by the philosopher George Pitcher (1972) reveals serious shortcomings in the former. Both analyses do take emotions to be intentional. (Beliefs and wants are intentional, too.) But Pitcher begins by drawing a distinction between occurrent and dispositional emotions (1972: 223–224). More important is the fact that Pitcher then draws out three other, key features of emotions. First, for a person to have an emotion, he or she must have some factual belief (or some kind of factual knowledge). Pitcher uses the term 'apprehension' (or 'misapprehension') for such beliefs. Secondly, Pitcher notes that different emotion-situations have differing characteristics, ranging from 'modes of behavior and inclinations to behave ... through wants or desires, up to beliefs ... that something is, or would be, good or bad' (1972: 225). Pitcher uses the term 'evaluation' to refer to this broad range of characteristics, evaluations which may be either positive and negative. Thus, emotions are not only intentional but also they include 'apprehensions' and 'evaluations.' The features revealed by Pitcher's analysis explain how changing a person's beliefs can change the person's emotional state. These features also help explain the third, key feature of emotions: emotions can be appraised as reasonable (or unreasonable).

How, then, do Anderson and Bourke see the relationship between affective characteristics and *motivation*? A passage which nicely summarizes their view comes early (2000: 2–3):

> ... Messick (1979) linked noncognitive [i.e., affective] characteristics with motivation. 'Since a motive is any impulse, emotion, or desire that impels one to action, almost all ... noncognitive variables ... qualify as motivational to some degree' (1979: 285). Among affective characteristics empirically linked with motivation are locus of control and interest (Messick, 1979), expectancies for success and the value of academic success (Berndt and Miller, 1990), and a sense of school belongingness (Goodenow and Grady, 1993).

Notice that Messick's definition of a motive is not very helpful. If 'impel' just means 'motivate,' then the definition is circular. If 'impel' really means impel, then the definition seems to focus on drives and compulsions to the exclusion of attractions.

The passage shows that Anderson and Bourke allow 'locus of control' (which is a kind of student *belief* about what (primarily) caused the learning outcomes) and 'expectancies for success' (which is another kind of *belief*) as motives. Later on (2000: 34), they include 'self-efficacy,' and they adopt B. Weiner's (1992a) definition of self-efficacy as 'a person's belief in his or her capability of performing a behavior [action] to reach a goal.' Since Anderson and Bourke have claimed that the affective domain is comprised of feelings and emotions, one could expect them be aware of the oddity of counting 'belief' as a feeling or emotion. They do say they will include only those 'beliefs that have emotional components' (2000: 2, footnote 2). But we do not think it is plausible to see most cases of 'locus of control' and 'self-efficacy' as involving emotional components.

Anderson and Bourke set out only eight 'affective characteristics': attitudes, values, academic self-esteem, locus of control, self-efficacy, interest, educational aspirations, and anxiety. (We will come back to 'value.') Motivation itself is not included in the set of specific characteristics, because, they state, to do so would be 'somewhat redundant' (2000: 39).

In their analysis, Anderson and Bourke begin by claiming that many studies have confirmed the affect–motivation link. It seems that studies have shown that many teachers think that their properly motivated students were those who 'believed that school was important (value), loved school and loved learning (attitude), and had high educational aspirations (value)' (2000: 166).

Anderson and Bourke (2000: 32) follow Getzels' (1966) definition of *value*, holding that values are *beliefs* about what *ought* to be desired, as opposed to what the person actually desires. And they follow Getzels in holding that such beliefs 'influence or guide behavior.' But several concerns arise. First, even if we want to allow such a belief – a Getzels' value – to count as an affective characteristic, how can we not allow 'what a person actually desires' to count as one too? Secondly, even if we define 'value' in this manner, where is the link to feelings and emotions which Anderson and Bourke have promised? If value is so central to motivation, why bring in feelings and emotions? Thirdly, perhaps Getzels and Anderson and Bourke hold the Socratic view that believing one ought to do A actually 'influences' (leads) one to do it. But, for example, many think the Socratic view is false. Finally, is it plausible that the teachers are attributing no other beliefs to their students?

Anderson and Bourke next consider the *expectancy-value* theory of motivation (2000: 166):

> One of the most widely accepted theories of motivation, the *expectancy-value* theory (Feather, 1982), asserts the affect-motivation connection. In simplest terms, the theory asserts that the amount of time and effort people will spend on a task (i.e., their degree of motivation) is a product of two factors. The first is the extent to which they *expect to be able to perform the task successfully* if they apply themselves; the second is the extent to which they *value participation* in the task itself or they *value the benefits or rewards* that successful completion will bring to them.

There are several problems here. First, Feather's formulation uses the term 'expectation,' which is best seen as just a variant on the term 'belief' (belief taken in the widest sense). Feather's formulation does use the term 'extent,' and hence can deal with all those cases where people act on the *less than certain* belief that their actions will be successful.

A second, more serious problem: What does Feather mean by the term *value*? Anderson and Bourke owe us an account here, for they have already used Getzels's definition of 'value' and made it but one of the eight kinds of affective characteristics. So, they cannot now use Getzels' definition to characterize the entire set (range) of affective characteristics. And, whatever Feather means by 'value,' Anderson and Bourke owe us some account of how 'value' refers to feelings and emotions. Brophy (2004: 18), whose earlier work (1987) is cited by Anderson and Bourke, warns the reader that the use of 'value' in the Feather formulation 'should not be confused with the noun *values*, meaning ethical principles or ideals.' For Brophy, the word *value* is used 'as a verb meaning to appreciate or see worth in.' We do not think it is plausible for Feather and Brophy to claim that people *can never* act on a desire which conflicts with what they appreciate and see as worthwhile. And we are not convinced that any use of the term 'value' will do the job, unless one gives it the widest possible sense, which nearly strips all meaning from it: Here is the Davis (1979) concern again. We recommend using the term 'value' in the radically wide sense that includes character traits and impulses.

Thirdly, the most complex claim: Feather's formulation claims that the 'degree of motivation' *is the product* of the two factors, expectation and value. In macro-economics such a formula is actually stated and used: the 'maximizing expected utility' maxim. But this formula makes such strong (idealized) assumptions about the agents that the maxim *does not apply* to everyday people. (Economists have long since given up on measuring 'cardinal utility;' they now use 'preferences.') At any rate, the formula explains macro-level regularities at best; it does not explain the particular actions of specific persons (see Blackburn, 1998: Chs 5 and 6; Rosenberg, 1995: Ch. 3).

Anderson and Bourke might have anticipated our concern – they admit (2000: vii) that their earlier book (1981) assumed that affective assessment instruments yield *interval* measures; the revised text acknowledges the *ordinal* nature of the data. Brophy (2004: 18) also argues that the degree of motivation is 'viewed as a product rather than the sum of the expectancy and value factors because it is assumed that no effort at all will be invested if one factor is missing entirely.' We agree with all of these researchers that one of the features of a value (want) is that it comes in degrees, say, weak, mild, and strong. (The same holds for expectations (beliefs) and emotions.) But these facts about the nature of values (and expectations or beliefs) do not imply that a quantitative *ratio* (or an *interval*) scale exists for 'measuring' these features. If there is no ratio (or an interval) scale, then the product is not defined. It has been given no meaning.

Folk psychology, however, need not make such strong quantitative assumptions; it can deal quite nicely with *ordinal* scales. (see Stevens, 1960, for brief and clear definitions of ordinal, interval, and ratio scales.) Suppose that one has an ordinal scale for 'values' with three levels (very low, middle, high) and that one also has an ordinal scale for 'expectations' with three levels (very low, middle, high). These two scales give rise to a (partial) ordering where judgment is still required. It can be shown that 'very low – very low' will be ranked far below all other combinations. Does it follow one would never perform a 'high – very low' ranked act? No. For this might be the highest ranked of the actions available! (see Black, 1972). The basic rationale of this kind of *rubric* assessment has now become standard for *cognitive* states as well (see Arter and McTighe's *Scoring Rubrics in the Classroom, 2001*).

Educators, including teachers, need to understand what motivates students and why students act as they do. Anderson and Bourke's 'official' explication of *affective* characteristics limits these to feelings and emotions. But Anderson and Bourke's analysis in fact incorporates Getzels values and several different kinds of beliefs. We are not opposed to this extension. Indeed, in our judgment the two concepts have not been extended far enough. For the 'want (value)' term, we believe the following (at least) should be included: a student's sense of moral justice, sense of legal duty, a sense of moral duty, a sense of prudence, compassion, concern, respect, courage, trust, and friendship. And we also recommend that 'negative' ones be included: self-deception, repressed desires, narrow selfish interest, jealousy, hatred, and prejudice. (And let us not forget about students and their 'passive, hedonic pleasures': smoking, drinking, doing drugs, and having sex.)

The interest in the nature of affective characteristics stems from educators' interest in student motivation. Anderson and Bourke do take some good steps, bringing in several kinds of belief: Getzels value, locus of control, and self-efficacy. But they make no mention at all of student beliefs about the 'extrinsic value' of what one has learned. Popham (2003), a leading educator, mentions attitudes, interests, and values but makes no mention of (the equally important) beliefs. Stiggins (2005) mentions attitudes, interests, and values; yet he also mentions self-efficacy. But neither mentions student beliefs about the 'extrinsic value' of what one has learned.

Where are we then? We are still left with the central features of folk psychology. At the center of folk psychology is the want–belief (value-expectation) conceptual template. The want–belief conceptual template is used primarily for explaining the particular action (A) of a specific person, although it has a rather limited value as a tool for prediction. And, although many begin their inquiry with a person's *wants* (or desires), knowledge of that person's *beliefs* will also be required to explain why the person did action A. In this general approach to motivation, 'belief' is typically a factual (empirical) belief which need not and normally does not involve any feelings. Thirdly, to try to get the template to cover as many (kinds of) actions as possible, one needs to use the terms 'want' and 'belief' in the widest possible senses.

Let us draw out some features of our discussion. Theories of motivation are explanatory theories of why a person performs an *action*. In educational settings, theories of motivation will directly apply to the activities which students perform: taking notes, doing problem sets, doing homework, reading articles, writing papers, performing skills, practicing, and so on. Although these activities are often called learning activities, these activities are the means whereby (if all goes well) students will learn (that is, come to acquire various beliefs and attitudes, master certain skills, and so on). Suppose a teacher wants the students to learn how to solve quadratic equations, and so sets up a suitable learning activity. If all goes well, the students will have (a) learned how to solve such equations, and (b) will have come to value this part of mathematics. There are thus three 'objects' which need to be distinguished: the learning activity and the two student learnings ('mastery of the skill' and 'valuing of the subject matter').

MOTIVATION AND LEARNING: KEY CONCEPTS

Here we will explicate several specific concepts which play a key role in the way educators think about motivating students to learn. Three important concepts are 'extrinsic motivation,' 'intrinsic motivation,' and 'freedom.'

Let us start by reconsidering the case of Alston's desire to plant some shrubs as a screen for a wire fence, and his going to Frank's Nursery and buying some. To say that Alston desires the shrubs as a screen is to say that Alston has an *extrinsic desire* for the shrubs; to have an *extrinsic desire* for the shrubs is to be *extrinsically motivated* (towards the shrubs). Alston may also have another desire (in the wide sense), for, say, blue spruce shrubs, which he finds to be beautiful. On most accounts of aesthetic judgment, to say that the shrubs are beautiful is to say that they are intrinsically valuable. In this case, then, Alston has an *intrinsic desire* for the shrubs and is *intrinsically motivated* toward them. Alston could, of course, have both intrinsic and extrinsic desires. In the Western tradition, a rational person can order a set of desires into intrinsic desires and extrinsic desires. Indeed, it has been argued that, for the extrinsic desires to be justifiable, they must serve as means to satisfying intrinsic desires.

These distinctions readily apply to educational settings. A student could have an intrinsic desire for a learning activity, or not; a student could have an extrinsic desire for a learning activity, or not.

But, in the mid 1970s, a group of 'intrinsic motivation theorists' became quite prominent in education (at least in Canada and the USA). (see Brophy, 1987, 2004; Weiner, 1992a, 1992b; and Woolfolk, 1998). This group held that, as a matter of fact, the *best* way to get students to learn is to get students to have intrinsic desires for all three learning objects: the learning activity and the two student learnings ('mastery of the skill' and 'commitment to valuing the subject matter'). Furthermore, the group held that allowing a student to have extrinsic desires for any of these objects would seriously, if not totally, undermine the student's intrinsic desires. Therefore, the group recommended that teachers should get their students to have intrinsic desires for all three objects and strongly discourage their having extrinsic desires for them – as if the two types of desire could never be conjoined, or separately offer good reasons for mastering a subject or skill. Finally, intrinsic motivation theorists gave intrinsic desire a hedonistic reading: to intrinsically desire an object is to find the object enjoyable or pleasurable. Weiner (1992b: 356) considers it an axiom of virtually all theories of motivation that organisms strive to increase pleasure and to decrease pain! Anderson and Bourke (2000: 166) quote Brophy (1987): 'Intrinsic motivation usually refers to the affective aspects of motivation – the liking or enjoyment of an activity' (1987: 41). For almost three decades intrinsic motivation theory influenced many of the approaches to teaching in which the activities (and outcomes) were designed to be hedonistically fun and enjoyable.

Anita Woolfolk (1998), who produced an educational psychology textbook widely used in teacher education, has a conception of 'intrinsic motivation' which is related to, but different from, that of Anderson, Bourke, and Brophy. Woolfolk advises teachers to help students see the *value* of the learning task and offers three definitions of 'value' (pp. 413, 428–430, Glossary 1, 6, 12). For Woolfolk, 'intrinsic (or interest) value' is simply the *enjoyment* one gets from doing the activity itself. As she puts it, some people just *like* the experience of learning. In contrast, an activity has 'utility (or instrumental) value' when it helps the student achieve some short-term or long-term goal. Woolfolk also defines 'attainment value' as the importance to the student of doing the task well. Woolfolk, however, is again identifying 'intrinsic value' with 'hedonistic pleasure.' We are opposed to this narrow and restricted, hedonistic definition of 'value.' For a critical review of Woolfolk's views, see Ellett and Ericson, 2002, which relies upon the concept of 'social practice with its internal and external goods,' as developed originally by MacIntyre (1984) and extended by Kekes (1989). See also Tom Green (1999).

The early intrinsic motivation theorists based their recommendations on some strong empirical claims about how best to motivate students, and conceived 'intrinsic motivation' in terms of hedonistic pleasure. Two things led to this theory's demise. First, research started to show that if students were to *believe* that learning something is likely to yield long-term, important benefits for themselves, they would probably be strongly motivated to learn (see Brophy, 2004). That is, if students were to believe that learning X has great *extrinsic value* for them, then they would form a strong, extrinsic desire to learn X. In Ericson and Ellett (2002), we argue that if students see themselves as rational agents who are concerned to find and make good lives for themselves, and if they *believe* that learning something has (comparatively high) *extrinsic value* for them, then they are likely to try to learn it. (We also argue that students should become aware of the need to find and make a conception of a good life for themselves. But they should realize that nothing guarantees they will be able to carry it out. See our comments on Kekes below.)

The second reason for the demise of the original 'intrinsic motivation' group's influence was that some of the leading thinkers of the group (for example, Deci and Ryan, 2000) revised their position in major ways (see Brophy, 2004; Woolfolk, 1998). The newer work has tried to conceptualize 'intrinsic motivation' in terms of freedom (or autonomy). Instead of focusing on hedonistic 'intrinsic desires,' these contemporary theorists focus on issues of control and therefore on an 'internal' state, viz., self-determination. The core idea is this: a student will be more motivated to do A when the student has freely chosen to do it rather than when the student is forced by someone to do A.

Deci and Ryan (2000) and Woolfolk (1998) seem to hold that a student's choice is free when no outside person influences the choice. Several problems arise: first, outside influences (constraints) come in various degrees; secondly, a student's acting out of self-deception, false consciousness, or strong addiction will not count as a free action; thirdly, most agents have a conception of the good life, which will itself be opposed to acting on some of one's own desires. The difficulty is that when one is *so overcome* that one acts against one's reasonable view of what one should do (or be), most people would *not* regard it as plausible to call such actions *free*, or self-determined! Finally, suppose a student has developed a reasonable conception of a good life, and has come to see learning statistics (say) as extrinsically very important. That student will likely see learning statistics as a *necessary* means to carrying out his or her conception. Would it make sense to say the student is free not to choose to study statistics? But the student sees it as a necessary means! In this approach a person's conception of a good life plays a key role.

Kekes' account of self-control links it to our ability to evaluate and control *our desires*. A corresponding educational goal, consequently, would be for students to learn how *to get more control over their desires*. Kekes (1995) argues that we are in control of actions insofar as we *identify* (by reasoned evaluation) with the desires that motivate the actions: see also Frankfurt (1971) and Dworkin (1988). The goal is not to achieve *total control*, but rather to *increase the control* one already has.

There are social–political implications of this view. For Kekes (1989, 1995, 2002), reasonable humans seek to live a good life (and avoid evil). A good society will help provide basic conditions needed for living a good life. It will foster basic decency and help maintain an adequate variety and number of social practices (local traditions), so individuals may acquire the internal and external goods best suited to their own 'good life.' In a pluralistic society, high school students will vary greatly in their conceptions of the good life. To 'motivate a student' adequately, a teacher will have to understand the student's conception of good life. For the student, the conception of the good life is the relevant standard for judging actions and learning outcomes.

The new intrinsic motivation theorists are right to be concerned about the relationship between freedom (autonomy) and motivation. If the explanation of what a person does has a form of causal explanation, then it must be asked whether this is compatible with the person's acting freely. There has been considerable work on this issue: see Alston (1967), Goldman (1970), Davis (1979), and Kekes (1995). For helpful works on freedom (or autonomy), see Dearden (1972), Kekes (1995), and Levinson (1999). Finally, an expanded version of this chapter is available from the authors.

REFERENCES

Alston, W.P. (1967) 'Motives and motivation', in P. Edwards (ed.), *The Encyclopedia of Philosophy*. New York: Macmillan, Vol. 5, pp. 399–409.

Anderson, L.W. and Bourke, S.F. (2000) *Assessing Affective Characteristics in the Schools*, 2nd edn. Mahwah, NJ: Lawrence Erlbaum Associates, Publishers.

Anderson, L.W., Krathwohl, D.R. and Bloom, B.S. (2001) *A Taxonomy for Learning, Teaching, and Assessing: A Revision of Bloom's Taxonomy of Educational Objectives*. New York: Longman.

Anscombe, G.E.M. (1958) *Intention*. Ithaca: Cornell University Press.

Arter, J. and McTighe, J. (2001) *Scoring Rubrics in the Classroom*. Thousand Oaks, CA: Corwin Press.

Black, M. (1972) 'Reasonableness', in R.F., Dearden, P.H. Hirst, and R.S. Peters, (eds), *Reason: Part 2 of Education and the Development of Reason*. London: Routledge and Kegan Paul, pp. 44–57.

Blackburn, S. (1998) *Ruling Passions: A Theory of Practical Reasoning*. Oxford: Clarendon Press.

Bloom, Benjamin S. (ed.) (1956). *Taxonomy of Educational Objectives – the Classification of Educational Goals – HandbookI: the Cognitive Domain*. New York: David McKay Company.

Brophy, J. (1987) 'Synthesis of research on strategies for motivating students to learn', *Educational Leadership*, 45 (2): 40–48.

Brophy, J. (2004) *Motivating Students to Learn*, 2nd edn. Mahwah, NJ: Lawrence Erlbaum Associates, Publishers.

Bruner, J. (1990) *Acts of Meaning*. Cambridge, MA: Harvard University Press.

Bruner, J. (1997) *The Culture of Education*. Cambridge, MA: Harvard University Press.

Churchland, P.M. (1984) *Matter and Consciousness*. Cambridge, MA: MIT Press.

Churchland, P.S. (1986) *Neurophilosophy: Towards a Unified Science of Mind-Brain*. Cambridge, MA: MIT Press.

Davidson, D. (1980a) 'Actions, reasons and causes', in D., Davidson, *Essays on Actions and Events*. Oxford: Clarendon Press, pp. 3–20.

Davidson, D. (1980b) 'Agency', in D., Davidson, *Essays on Actions and Events*. Oxford: Clarendon Press, pp. 43–63.

Davidson, D. (1980c) 'Causal relations', in D., Davidson, *Essays on Actions and Events*. Oxford: Clarendon Press, pp. 149–162.

Davidson, D. (1980d) 'Mental events', in D., Davidson, *Essays on Actions and Events*. Oxford: Clarendon Press, pp. 207–224.

Davis, L.H. (1979) *Theory of Action*. Englewood Cliffs, NJ: Prentice-Hall.

Dearden, R.F. (1972) 'Autonomy', in R.F., Dearden, P.H. Hirst, and R.S. Peters, (eds), *Education and Reason: Part 3 of Education and the Development of Reason*. London: Routledge and Kegan Paul, pp. 58–75.

Deci, E.L. and Ryan, R. (2000) 'The "what" and "how" of goal pursuits: Human needs and the self-determination of behavior', *Psychological Inquiry*, 11: 227–268.

Donnellan, K.S. (1967) 'Reasons and causes', in P. Edwards, (ed.), *The Encyclopedia of Philosophy*. New York: Macmillan, Vol. 7, pp. 85–88.

Dworkin, G. (1988) *The Theory and Practice of Autonomy*. Cambridge: Cambridge University Press.

Ellett, F.S., Jr. and Ericson, D.P. (2002) 'Misleading the students: Conceptual difficulties in Woolfolk's account of motivation', *The Philosophy of Education 2002*. Normal, IL: The Philosophy of Education Society.

Ericson, D.P. and Ellett, F.S., Jr. (2002) 'The question of the student in educational reform', *Educational Policy Analysis Archives*, July 2, 2002, EPAA, Vol. 10, No. 1 (http:/epaa.asu.edu/epaa/v10n1).

Fodor, J.A. (1975) *The Language of Thought*. Cambridge, MA: MIT Press.

Frankfort, H.G. (1971) 'Freedom of the will and the concept of a person', *Journal of Philosophy*, LXVIII, 5–20.

Goldman, A.I. (1970) *A Theory of Human Action*. Princeton, NJ: Princeton University Press.

Green, T.F. (1999) *Voices: The Educational Formation of Character*. Notre Dame, IN: University of Notre Dame Press.

Greenwood, J.D. (1991a) 'Introduction: Folk psychology and scientific psychology', in J.D. Greenwood, *The Future of Folk Psychology*. Cambridge: Cambridge University Press, pp. 1–21.

Greenwood, J.D. (1991b). *The Future of Folk Psychology*. Cambridge: Cambridge University Press.

Kekes, J. (1989) 'The Eudaimonistic conception of good lives', *Moral Tradition and Individuality*. Princeton, NJ: Princeton University Press, pp. 16–30.

Kekes, J. (1995) 'Judgment and control', *Moral Wisdom and Good Lives*. Ithaca, NY: Cornell University Press, pp. 73–83.

Kekes, J. (2002) 'Dominant attitudes', *The Art of Life*. Ithaca, NY: Cornell University Press, pp. 177–204.

Kim, J. (2006). *Philosophy of Mind*. Cambridge, MA: Westview Press.

Krathwohl, D.R., Bloom, B.S. and Mosia, B.B. (1964). *Taxonomy of educational objectives – the Classification of Educational Goals – Handbook II: the Affective Domain*. New York: David McKay Company.

Levinson, M. (1999) 'Autonomy and the foundations of contemporary liberalism', in *Levinson, The Demands of Liberal Education*. Oxford: Oxford University Press, pp. 9–35.

MacIntyre, A. (1984) *After Virtue*, 2nd edn. Notre Dame, IN: University of Notre Dame Press.

Margolis, J. (1987). *Science without Unity: Reconciling the Human and Natural Sciences*. Oxford: Basil Blackwell.

Melden, A.I. (1961) *Free Action*. London: Routledge and Kegan Paul.

Messick, S.J. (1979) 'Potential uses of non-cognitive measurement in education', *Journal of Educational Psychology*, 71: 281–292.

Peters, R.S. (1958) *The Concept of Motivation*. London: Routledge and Kegan Paul.

Pitcher, G. (1972) 'Emotion', in R.F., Dearden, P.H., Hirst, and R.S. Peters, (eds), *Reason: Part 2 of Education and the Development of Reason*. London: Routledge and Kegan Paul, pp. 218–238.

Popham, W.J. (2003) 'The value of affective assessment', *Test Better, Teach Better*. Alexandria, VA: Association for Supervision and Curriculum Development, pp. 106–121.

Putnam, H. (1999) 'First afterword: Causation and explanation', *The Threefold Cord: Mind, Body and World*. New York: Columbia University Press, pp. 137–150.

Rosenberg, A. (1995) *Philosophy of Social Science*. Boulder, CO: Westview Press.

Stevens, S.S. (1960) 'On the theory of scales of measurement', in A. Danto (ed.), *Philosophy of Science*. New York: World Publishing. pp. 141–149.

Stich, S.P. (1983) *From Folk Psychology to Cognitive Science: The Case against Belief*. Cambridge, MA: MIT Press.

Stich, S.P. (1996) 'What is folk psychology?', in S.P. Stich, *Deconstructing the Mind*. Oxford: Oxford University Press, pp. 115–135.

Stiggins, R.J. (2005) 'Assessing dispositions', in R.J. Stiggins, *Student-Involved Assessment for Learning*, 4th edn. Upper Saddle River, N.J.: Pearson, pp. 199–224.

Taylor, C. (1964) *The Explanation of Behaviour*. London: Routledge and Kegan Paul.

Weiner, B. (1992a) 'Motivation', in M. Alkin (ed.), *The Encyclopedia of Educational Research*, 4th edn. New York: Macmillan, pp. 860–865.

Weiner, B. (1992b) *Human Motivation: Metaphors, Theories, and Research*. Newbury Park, CA: SAGE.

Woolfolk, A.E. (1998) *Educational Psychology*, 7th edn. Boston, MA: Allyn and Bacon.

24

Transferable Skills

Stephen Johnson

King Ptolemy asked Euclid for an easy way to learn geometry. Euclid replied, 'Sire, there is no royal road to geometry'. The king sought entry into the mysteries of geometry without having to expend a great deal of time and effort on complicated and confusing content. Today the same desire to avoid subject-specific content is pervasive throughout education and the answer is thought to be transferability. Transferable skills, such as problem solving, critical thinking and learning to learn, hold out the prospect of avoiding 'the need to delve into vast subject matters' (Scriven, 1990, p. 3). Such transferability offers the huge educational bonus of being able to, for example, solve problems in many or every domain without the chore of the detailed learning of specific content; it offers general admission at a massive discount. Such claims may, however, prove to be bogus – perhaps separate, domain-specific entrance fees are required.

In a minimal and trivial sense, all abilities and skills are transferable in so far as they can be repeated in relevantly similar circumstances; this being a criterion of possessing an ability at all. We may refer to such skills as portable. Transferable skills could simply be portable skills that occur in many contexts – word processing, for example. If, however, transferability is taken to imply the existence of generic skills that are not tied to any specific content or domain, then their existence is far more debatable.

As all skills can be repeated, to designate certain skills as specifically transferable seems to imply that they are transferable in some special sense. I am prompted to this view by Grice's notion of 'conversational implicature' (see, for example, Grice, 1975, pp. 41–58) where certain conversational 'maxims' govern what is normally implied by speakers. For instance, as all men are mortal, to say of a man that he is going to die implies something particular about his death, such as its imminence.

If there were a subset of skills that were transferable in a special way, what might constitute such specialness? It might be that these skills transfer to quite different physical settings, or that they transfer to different domains of knowledge, or that they transfer spontaneously or at least with little effort, or that they facilitate the transfer of other skills.

In education the problem of transfer mainly concerns whether or not knowledge or skills acquired in one situation can be applied in other situations. Arguably this question is educationally of pre-eminent importance. In fact, Hare sees transfer as being a condition for any learning taking place at all, for he writes that, 'To learn to do anything is never to learn to do an individual act; it is always to learn to do acts of a certain kind in a certain kind of situation' (Hare, 1952, p. 60). Dearden makes a related observation when he writes that, 'Unless someone is able to recognize "same again" or is able to repeat a performance on another appropriate occasion we would, barring special circumstance, decline to say that, he had learned' (Dearden, 1984, p. 71). Not only is it argued that there is a close relationship between transfer and learning but also some, Thorndike (1914) for example, would deny that there is any distinction between transfer and learning; a more recent example of this view is Butterfield et al., who have declared that there is 'no principled difference between learning and transfer' (1993, p. 194). It could be argued, then, that if there is no transfer there is no learning.

Thus, learning to do something is to be able to transfer it. This depends, however, on there being an appropriate similarity between contexts. The main problem is that the notion of context is enigmatic at two levels: (a) Is the context similar and if it is in what does that similarity consist? (b) Does the agent perceive the context to be relevantly similar and if so why? Nelson Goodman, writing of the elusive nature of the notion of similarity, says: 'Whether two actions are instances of the same behaviour depends upon how we take them' (1970, p. 22). In other words, judgements about the sameness of human performances require a 'theory' in the sense of being in need of some interpretation or explanation. Wittgenstein says that a student has been taught to understand when he can independently continue with a sequence or procedure, 'If he succeeds he exclaims: "Now I can go on!"' (Wittgenstein, 1958, p. 59). Wittgenstein's point about being able to continue with a sequence or procedure requires the application of a particular rule. But, as Kripke explains, after, for example, the sequence 2, 4, 6, 8, ... 'an indefinite number of rules ... are compatible with any such finite initial segment', so he concludes that there is no such thing as 'the unique appropriate next number' (Kripke, 1993, p. 18). Any interpretation will need to include the beliefs and intentions of the agent, as well as the social settings. In some social settings, for example, the correct continuation of the sequence 2, 4, 6, 8, is 'who do we appreciate'! As Lave and Wenger have observed, activities and tasks 'do not exist in isolation; they are part of a broader system of relations in which they have meaning. These systems of relations arise out of and are reproduced and developed within social communities' (1991, p. 53). As may be appreciated from this, the difficulties these issues raise for the transfer of skills become particularly acute for skills claiming to enjoy general transferability to all, or most, contexts.

It is the specialness of these skills that raises high expectations, but also creates the sort of doubts expressed by many researchers. Perkins, for example, after examining a number of studies of transferable cognitive skills, observed that there was no support for the existence of such skills, and stated: 'It is easy to extend this list of negatives and "don't knows", but I have no firm positives to add' (1985, p. 348). Singley and Anderson, after scrutinizing 10 research studies that had failed to discover any general transfer of cognitive skills, summarized their findings: 'Besides this spate of negative evidence, there has been no positive evidence of general transfer' and conclude, 'unfortunately the evidence for the existence of general transfer is not good' (1989, p. 25). Later, Singley concluded that, 'nearly a century of psychology has generated a depressing lack of evidence for the notion of general transfer' (1995, p. 69).

Despite doubts such as these, it would be difficult to exaggerate the influence and appeal that the notion of transferable skills has had, and continues to have, on education and training in the UK. In the youth training schemes of the 1980s and 1990s, transferable skills were seen as the solution to pressing economic, social and educational problems. As Kemp and Seagraves observe, 'The need for a flexible, adaptable workforce ... has focused attention on the development of transferable skills' (1995, p. 315). Such skills are now considered important at every phase of education. For instance, the Dearing Report on 16–19 education, emphasized transferable skills (see Dearing, 1996, pp. 3, 6, 46, 55). In addition, the National Curriculum for England and Wales for 2000 onwards contains critical thinking, information processing, creative thinking and reasoning, all presumed to be generally transferable. Also, from the mid 1990s, there has been a growing emphasis on transferable skills in higher education (see, for example, Assiter's book *Transferable Skills in Higher Education*, 1995). The influence of these skills extends into the burgeoning area of management training. In his book *Outdoor Development for Managers*, Banks (1993) claims that among the skills that can be learned on outdoor courses and readily transferred to the office or the boardroom are: 'leadership, teamwork, ... problem-solving, managing change, and coping with stress' (p. 27).

Despite transferable skills being prominent throughout education and training, definitions are rare. Furthermore, when definitions are found they are less than helpful. The Skills Portal for Oxford University researchers defines a 'transferable skill' as 'an ability learnt in one context, which can be applied in another'(Oxford University, 2008). But what is to constitute a changed context? Would a change of location suffice? As well as 'context', meaning 'location' or 'setting', it can also refer to domain, subject or field of knowledge. Whatever the meaning of context, the definition does nothing to indicate that such skills are special in any way.

If we now turn to a definition from the University of Warwick, we find 'transferable skills' are defined as those 'used across a wide range of jobs' (University of Warwick, 2008). One problem with this definition is that 'job' could mean either 'occupation' or 'task'. If 'job' is used in the occupational sense, then exactly the same action, typing for example, could be repeated in a number of jobs. So, the definition fails to establish a special subclass of skills. In the light of these difficulties, perhaps 'job' is being used in the sense of 'task'. A task, however, is often defined by the skill that is being deployed, and vice versa. Furthermore, occupations are also often defined by the skills deployed.

Putting these difficulties to one side, the part of the definition that may distinguish transferable skills from skills *tout court* is that transferable skills are said to be used in 'a *wide range* of jobs'. Even so, on this formulation, transferable skills are only skills that can be used in many situations and transferable to the relevantly similar. So, although this may constitute a subclass of skills, it still appears quotidian and inadequate to the task of revolutionizing education and training, and solving the nation's social and economic problems. Nor does portability coupled with generality raise problems concerning the nature and mechanisms of transferable skills. They would hardly lead to the accusation that such skills rest 'on untested assumptions' (Evans et al., 1987, p. 58) or that there is 'no real agreement about the nature and mechanisms of their transfer' (Fay, 1988, p. 31).

Fortunately, some comments accompanying the definitions are more interesting. Annett, for example, asks, 'Are some skills more "transferable" than others in the sense that they can be identified as occurring in a large number of contexts but in a relatively context-independent form?' (Annett, 1989, p. 4). Disappointingly, this question remains unanswered, and there is nothing to indicate what might constitute such context-independence. A similarly tantalizing comment occurs on the Oxford University Skills Portal where students are told that transferable skills 'can be a welcome addition to the knowledge-based skills specific to your subject'. Likewise, Adams (2004) stresses the difference between 'subject specific outcomes … and generic (sometimes called key transferable skills) outcomes that relate to any and all disciplines'. These three comments do point towards transferable skills that transcend domains. Perhaps purported examples of transferable skills will provide more enlightenment.

The first difficulty encountered when setting out to consider examples of transferable skills is that of *embarras de choix*: transferability appears to be a necessary condition for any ability to be included on a list of educational or training skills. All of the following have appeared on lists of transferable skills produced by universities, government reports or employers' organizations: logical thinking, foresight, goal setting, typing, loyalty, flexibility, motivation, honesty (Pratzner, 1978); problem-solving, adaptability, self-confidence, coping with uncertainty, decision-making (University of Warwick, 1996); sequencing, classifying, comparing, distinguishing fact from opinion, hypothesizing, generating new ideas, being systematic (McGuinness, 1999); team work, initiative, problem-solving, loyalty, honesty, motivation (Gibb, 2004, p. 11); planning, motivation, team-working, stress management, clarity of thought, assertiveness, managing change, writing (Oxford University, 2008); communication, application of number, information technology, problem-solving, working with others, improving own learning (DCSF, 2008); leadership, influencing, motivation, enthusiasm, self-awareness, flexibility (University of Warwick, 2008).

It is difficult to know what to make of such a farrago of skills, abilities, disposi-tions, virtues and attitudes. The only thing these 'skills' have in common, or so I would suggest, is that they are, or could be, the outcome of learning that employers consider to be desirable in an employee: an employers' wish list.

The allure of transferable skills persists in the face of strong doubts, such as those expressed by Wilson in a report to the Scottish Executive, who stated: 'Transference beyond the specific context remains problematic' (2000, p. 38). But far from such doubts reducing enthusiasm for transferable skills, faith in them goes from strength to strength.

What accounts for this faith? Anderson suggests that, 'One reason why general transfer keeps rising from the grave is that it is such an attractive proposition for psychologists and educators alike' (1993, p. 25). It has become, as White says, 'the educational policy-makers' magic key' (2002, p. 106). Wishful thinking is indeed a powerful force; as Julius Caesar said, 'men willingly believe that for which they wish' (*libenter homines id quod volunt credunt*). Certainly, vast edu-cational profit would flow from being able to teach students to solve problems, be creative, think well, learn how to learn, etc., without these being tied to specific content. Such skills are thought simply too good *not* to be true.

Another factor in the allure of content-free skills is the present disparagement of subject knowledge. An early example is afforded by Husen, who writes:

> In a changing society the school cannot provide an intellectual fare of specific items of knowledge for lifelong use. The shift that has to take place in the content of teaching is one from emphasis primarily on specific items of knowledge which may soon become obsolete, to one with emphasis on the intellectual skills that are applicable to a broad and largely unforeseen repertoire of tasks and situations (1979, p. 153).

Hence, an attraction of transferable skills is that they are thought to be of per-manent value, immune to obsolescence. So, whereas transferable skills are seen as active and useful, subject knowledge is portrayed as being inert bits of infor-mation that will rapidly become obsolete. This view is exemplified by Professor Sir Graham Hills, Vice Chancellor of Strathclyde University, who tells us that skill 'can, in stark contrast to knowledge, be the bringer of great wealth' (1989, p. 15). In a later article, Hills tells us 'heads crammed with knowledge are no longer as desirable as they once were. Such is the power of data bases and infor-mation networks that knowledge is instantly accessible at the press of a button' (*The Guardian* 18/9/90). These remarks presuppose there can be knowledge without assessment or judgement; such a passivity-grounded view of proposi-tional knowledge is common among supporters of transferable skills (see, e.g., Higgins and Baumfield, 1998, p. 396). This view is clearly in keeping with the information-processing model of the mind, which will be considered later, where knowledge is seen as inert data that have to be manipulated.

Another reason for belief in transferable skills is simply that they are ubiquitous in the language of education and training. As Cooper explains, 'The most effective means for winning a contested concept is not rhetoric or blarney but constant repetition, constant association of a word with the content, policy or whatever one favours or disfavours' (1983, p. 44). Repetition can be more effective than the strength of reason, in the same way as dripping water hollows out a stone, not by strength, but by constantly falling: *Gutta cavat lapidem non vi, sed saepe cadendo.*

Such persistent use could also prompt, albeit tacitly, a presuppositional argument: transferable skills must surely exist as they feature prominently in innumerable Government reports and the like. This is on a par with Chief Justice Hale's remark in 1676: 'There must be such things as witches, since there are laws against witches, and it is not conceivable that laws should be made against that that does not exist'.

There are other errors and fallacies at work here. A common error in this area, as may be seen in the previous lists, is that of confusing a disposition, personality trait or virtue with a skill. Central to being 'honest' or 'systematic' (see above) is being disposed to act in certain ways, but one may have a skill without being inclined to exercise it. It makes good sense to say that I have the skill of being able to swim, but choose never to exercise it; however, to say I have the skill of honesty, but choose never to exercise it sounds very odd.

Philosophers have long realized that common linguistic usage may lead us into the ontological error of assuming the existence of non-existent entities or properties, or at least of ascribing to them an inaccurate ontological status. Anselm of Canterbury, for example, observed that 'many things are said to *be* something or other according to the form of the spoken expression, which in fact are *not* anything: we just speak about them as we do really existing things' (cited in Henry, 1984, p. 12). I will now concentrate on four, often interconnected, conceptual errors prevalent in discussions about transferable skills.

REIFICATION

The error of reification (or the fallacy of misplaced concreteness, as Whitehead called it) is the act of wrongly treating X as if it were a *thing*. There might, however, be nothing wrong with treating many things as things, but it is important to treat them as the right sorts of things. One example of this error, particularly relevant to this present inquiry, is moving from the properly adverbial or adjectival to the improperly substantive. It is often assumed that if X can do Y skilfully, there must be a skill of Ying and that X has it. For example, because it is meaningful to talk of someone who thinks well as being a skilful thinker, we are tempted to believe that there is a 'skill' to be identified, isolated and trained for. Thus, there is in effect a jump from talk of performing an action well or successfully to the existence of some specific, discrete skill or skills possessed by and exercised by the performer, the very name of which is given, or at least suggested, in the description of the successful performance. This can have the unfortunate consequence of classing as skills activities and attributes that are ill suited to such a description, which may in turn lead to faulty pedagogy. A stark example of this error may be found in de Bono's claim: 'Manifestly thinking is a skill in as much as thinking can be performed skilfully' (de Bono, 1978, p. 45).

ESSENTIALISM

Essentialists in this area believe that just as a magnet has the power to attract iron filings because of some underlying structure, so the ability to solve problems or to think critically is explicable in terms of underlying structures of the mind or brain. Hence, Norris writes:

> To say that someone has critical thinking ability is to make a claim about a mental power which that person possesses. Mental powers, in turn, arise from mental structures and processes in the same way that physical powers (magnetism is an example) arise from internal structures and processes of physical objects'. (Norris, 1990, p. 68)

But transferring this idea from inorganic substances to human intellectual abilities can have unfortunate results. It may lead to motivation, beliefs, desires and context being ignored. Furthermore, general labels such as 'problem-solving' or 'critical thinking' gain a spurious unity and precision. Finally, this idea makes it difficult to explain how someone with the mental power of problem-solving could ever fail to solve a problem; in the same way as it would be difficult to explain why a magnet failed to attract iron filings.

NAMING FALLACY

This is committed by supposing the existence of a general skill X, from the existence of a general label or category, X. In other words, because we have a general name which can be correctly applied to a range of activities, then it is assumed that there must be a general skill corresponding to that general name. For instance, because there is the general label 'problem-solving', it is assumed that because it is possible to speak of 'problem-solving', then there must be a general skill of problem-solving. However, from the fact that there exist conditions for the correct application of concepts such as 'good judgement', or 'accuracy', it cannot be inferred that there are such general activities, or corresponding psychological abilities, such that we could coherently claim to be able to teach a person good judgement or accuracy skills in themselves.

GENERALIZING FALLACY

This error consists in putting a task competence under the heading of a wider, perhaps an extremely wide, task descriptor and assuming that if a person has mastered the task competence then, *ipso facto*, she can do whatever falls under the wider descriptor. So, if a person has mastered a task competence X, say that of knowing how to use a tin opener, and X falls under a broader and more general heading Y, say of using a device for opening things or even using a tool, then the person can do whatever falls under Y, that is, the person can use any device that opens things or even can use all tools. This fallacy involves at least two errors. First, there is the naming fallacy, which, as we have seen, assumes that because a general category of activities can be named then there exists a corresponding skill. Secondly, it is assumed that to master one or a few skills that fall within this general category means that one simply has the general skill and all it encompasses. Such reasoning, if not corrected, can be seen to justify a move from the original task competence into situations that are relevantly, even extravagantly, dissimilar. This fallacious move helps account for the crucial role transferable skills play in youth training and pre-vocational education; for training in such skills would fit trainees for an incredibly wide range of tasks and occupations.

PSYCHOLOGICAL THEORIES

One reason for transfer being of interest to psychologists is the supposed connection between transfer and intelligence. Annett tells us that ''Intelligence' is the name used for the most general form of cognitive ability' (1989, p. 5). He goes on to say that,

> The ability to profit from experience and intelligence has often, therefore, been taken as virtually synonymous with transfer. Individuals who can readily transfer the benefits of experience in one situation to another, apparently different, situation are generally deemed to be intelligent ... . The concept of transfer and transferable skills is, therefore, closely linked with the idea of general intelligence (1989, p. 8).

For psychologists, then, intelligence may simply be the ability to transfer what has been learned in one situation to another situation. Is there any theoretical support for general transferability from psychology? I will examine three theories.

Faculty psychology

This is the theory that 'the mind is divided up into separate inherent powers or faculties' (Gregory, 1987, p. 253). Aristotle can be seen as the progenitor of faculty psychology with his five great faculties (*De Anima*, 432b). But was Aristotle guilty of an error of reification: did he talk about processes in substantive terms? That this is a real danger may be illustrated by a brief examination of the word 'faculty'. Cicero introduced the term 'facultas' for the Greek word for power.

'Facultas' was a form of 'facilitas', which meant the facility to do something or the potential for something happening. In time however it changed, first from a propensity to an active, causal force, and thence, fallaciously, to a substantive property. The way in which reification has infected the transmission of Aristotle's work is well illustrated by the fact that he used 'remembering', 'willing', etc., as names of his classes. However, when his works were translated into Latin, these became 'faculty of remembering,' 'faculty of willing,' etc.

Aquinas developed Aristotle's faculty theory. The rational faculty, for instance, he divided into *intellectus*, the active intelligence which carries out abstraction, and *ratio*, the receptive intelligence which deals with judgement and reasoning. It was upon Aquinas's model that later faculty psychology developed. It was first formulated as a clear and explicit doctrine by Wolff in 1734. He held that the mind comprised separate and distinct faculties, which he compared to bodily organs. Tetens, one of Wolff's followers, proposed three major groups of faculties: cognitive, affective and conative. This was the tripartite model that was adopted by Kant.

Further support for faculty psychology came from Reid in his book *Essays on the Intellectual Powers of Man* (1785). He believed that the mind could be described by a finite number of faculties or powers of the mind, and drew up a list of 24: for example, 'judgement', 'conception' and 'memory'.

The main fault with this theory is assuming that for each of a whole range of mentalistic verbs there exists a particular faculty, a particular part of a person's mind, which is exercised whenever a sentence involving the verb can be applied to that person. Yet surely the fact that I doubt (wonder, speculate, conjecture, ...), does not mean I am exercising my faculty of doubting (wondering, speculating, conjecturing ...).

Faculty psychology, despite seemingly devastating criticism (see, for example, James, 1890; Dewey, 1916), has proved to be remarkably resilient. One of the places in which this doctrine has found refuge is, I would suggest, in the area of transferable skills. As Annett concedes, there are similarities between the 'faculties' of the eighteenth century and present-day transferable skills; he writes that 'reasoning might refer either to a "faculty" or to a skill' (Annett, 1989, p. 6). Support for the theory's continued existence and influence also comes from Barrow, who talks of 'an unheeding commitment to the tenets of faculty psychology' as one of the 'erroneous beliefs that are part and parcel of the way we talk and think about education, that directly or indirectly lead to untenable or false claims about how we should teach and organise school curricula' (Barrow, 1990, p. 22).

It is the theory of faculty psychology that helps to underpin notions of general powers of the mind and the existence of transferable skills, such as, observation, judgement, imagination, critical thinking and creativity. This leads to the view that someone can think critically, solve problems or be imaginative *simpliciter*, regardless of context. Proponents of this theory believe that transferable skills are based on an underlying faculty to be developed.

Identical elements

The second theory may be called the identical elements theory. This maintains that in order for learned responses to be transferred there have to be identical stimulus–response elements between the two situations. This reveals a certain naivety with regard to the notion of 'identity'. As I have stressed, even the less rigorous notion of 'similarity' can be elusive. The difficulties, for example, of stereotyping mathematical ability on the basis of the similarity of mathematical operations has been well illustrated by Ruthven (1988, pp. 243–253), and Davis (1996, pp. 5–8 and pp. 16–17) has shown that there are serious problems in claiming that apparently very closely related subtraction problems are sufficiently similar to afford confident predictions about transfer.

In the USA a generation of curriculum planners adopted the identical elements approach. Bobbitt, the leading exponent of this method, explained that there are three steps in constructing a curriculum: (1) divide life into major activities, (2) analyse these activities into specific skills and (3) make these skills your behavioural objectives (see Bobbitt, 1926, p. 9).

It is this theory, I suggest, that provides a theoretical base for transferable core skills, because these notions are frequently founded on the supposed existence of a set of elementary components that underlie many other skills. Core skills, for example, were 'intended to identify *common*, essential and *transferable elements* of tasks' (Evans et al., 1987, p. 67, emphasis added). These components, or atoms of behaviour, it is claimed, once learned, can be strung together to form many different skills. Here transfer is the result of the prior acquisition of component skills. For, as the University of Surrey research team on the Core Skills Project puts it: 'Transfer of skills can, it is believed, be promoted by identifying the fundamental common elements of most tasks' (Evans et al., 1987, p. 14).

Information processing

The final theory of learning transfer emanates from cognitive psychology. This theory views the brain as a digital computer, an information processor that has three sets of components: input, output and control. It is argued that it is the control strategy that is important in transfer. This approach is prominent in a number of educational programmes that aim to teach general thinking skills, e.g., Instrumental Enrichment: a contents-free cognitive intervention programme (Feuerstein et al., 1980).

Goal-setting is often considered to be a good example of this approach, and McGuinness has 'setting up goals' as a transferable skill (McGuinness, 1999, p. 5). But what general plan could control all goal-setting? In the absence of guidance we could speculate: goals should be as clear and specific as possible; never choose goals that are impossible except where pursuing the impossible itself is a goal; a goal is impossible if the means are impossible; before selecting goals decide on your priorities; select goals which, if achieved, would best satisfy your priorities. Such principles are, of course, vacuous. This highlights a pervasive and intractable problem for transferable skills and for the information processing model of transfer in particular: as the generality and abstract nature of the principles increase, their usefulness and effectiveness decrease.

Feuerstein's work, although probably the best-known thinking skills programme worldwide, is a victim of this problem. In a 2-year study, that McGuinness called 'an immaculately conducted UK evaluation', Blagg 'reported no significant improvement in intellectual performance' (McGuinness, 1999, p. 9). Blagg attributed this to 'the abstract nature of the programme' (Wilson, 2000, p. 38).

The information-processing approach also raises the question of what in turn controls the control strategy and thus opens up the prospect of infinite regress. As Ryle notes: 'If we had to plan what to think before thinking it we would never think at all, because this planning would itself need to be thought about, which would need planning, which would itself need ... and so on' (Ryle, 1949, p. 31).

Finally, there is a question of the status of the control strategies. Are they created techniques or heuristics like, for instance, a mnemonic, or are they processes that go on in the brain? Sternberg writes that the 'status of these classification schemes is not entirely clear at the present time' (Sternberg, 1982, p. 7). However, in his own work Sternberg claims to have discovered a number of general processes that are involved in cognition. But I would contend that Sternberg did not so much discover these processes as postulate them on the basis of what he thought was involved in solving a problem. The danger is that of assuming that processes are going on in us by reading back from a product of some sort to the idea that certain mental processes must have occurred – an example of faulty thinking if ever there was one.

All three theories of transfer may encourage people to accept as correct the generalizing fallacy, discussed earlier. Faculty psychology proposes that because a number of activities fall under one broad faculty heading, e.g. 'creativity', then there is some transfer between creativity on a football pitch and creativity in the physics laboratory. The identical elements theory has a proclivity to classify tasks on the basis of a very wide common element. In practice this has led to such absurd claims as that those who can use kitchen knives have acquired the wider transferable skill of 'cutting with one blade' (FEU, 1982, p. 72). Beware of brain surgeons who trained as lumberjacks! Finally, the information processing model proposes that there is a general strategy that can be used to facilitate the solving of a chess problem, show people the way out of difficulties in personal relationships, diagnose an electrical fault or help sort out a difficult passage in Hegel. All of which shows that being in the grip of a theory can keep reality away.

PROBLEMS WITH TRANSFERABLE SKILLS

In spite of the current popularity of the notion of transferable skills, there is a respectable and long-established philosophical tradition which fiercely opposes the idea of such generality. We may begin with Plato's attack on the Sophists and their transferable skill of rhetoric. Gorgias, for instance, argues that subject knowledge is not necessary for success (*Gorgias*, 456). Plato, however, maintains that if one wishes to speak or think intelligently, then detailed knowledge of the subject is essential (*Phaedrus*, 262). In turn, Aristotle argues against Plato's view that in all particular instances of something being good there must be a single good present (*Nicomachean Ethics*, 1095a28). Aristotle maintains that there are different goods depending on different domains of knowledge; as he says, if there were a universal good present in all cases of things being good 'there would be one science of all good things' (op. cit., 1096a19). Dearden puts the point succinctly: 'the good general is not possessed of the same abilities as the good doctor, and he is different again from the good gymnast' (Dearden, 1984, p. 78).

Ryle (1972) is also unequivocally context-specific and insistent that there are vast differences between the different disciplines and domains of knowledge. He observes that:

> A first-rate mathematician and a first-rate literary critic might share the one intellectual virtue of arguing impeccably, while their other intellectual virtues could be so disparate that neither could cope even puerilely with the problems of the other. (p. 191)

Elsewhere, Ryle refers to lessons in general thinking as a 'ridiculous suggestion' (1979, p. 65).

In a similar vein, Powell (1968) argues that epithets such as 'careful', 'vigilant', and 'thorough' are without meaning until the details of their context and application have been filled in and, thus, 'it follows from this that they will be field-dependent and of low generality'. He goes on to argue that:

> There is no such animal as 'Careful Man'; there are simply men who do particular things in particular ways and it is always necessary to specify these in some detail before we can understand what is meant by careful surgery or careful driving. (p. 45)

The context-bound character of abilities is also endorsed by Phillips Griffiths (1965), who notes that because a subject requires 'imagination, wisdom and intelligence ... it would be a mistake to think that these qualities are *generally* developed by any activity requiring them. In pursuing history or physics or philosophy ... one becomes better at history, physics or philosophy', but this 'does not mean becoming a more intelligent boxer ... or a more imaginative ... joke-teller, or a wiser father' (p. 205).

In support of Phillips Griffiths, there is considerable evidence that even experts can go astray if they wander a little way from their area of expertise. Consider the case of the famous historian E.H. Carr, who was taken to task by Isaiah Berlin in the following manner:

> His short way with the problem of individual freedom and responsibility ... is a warning to us all of what may happen to those who, no matter how learned and perspicacious, venture into regions too distant from our own (cited in Mehta, 1965, p. 107).

When it comes to transferable thinking skills, McPeck (1981, 1990) has been a robust and cogent critic. He points out that critical thinking demands different things in different domains and that general thinking skills are, to all intents and purposes, a waste of time; a matter of transmitting hollow, truistic prescriptions that are of little or no help in dealing with the informationally demanding problems that confront us in everyday and academic life. This position is supported by White (2002), who agrees that 'each major discipline of thought ... has its own forms of reasoning' and that 'to aim at improving thinking in general is a logical nonsense'. (p. 105).

Somewhat surprisingly, powerful evidence against general thinking skills comes from the study of artificial intelligence and its search for general rules of thought. Hunt (1989) points out that research workers in artificial intelligence 'have found from bitter experience that there are no domain-independent inferential rules which could be used to construct a general intelligence' (p. 23). Hunt also stresses that in each domain there is a need for 'an enormous background of knowledge and judgement specific to that domain' (p. 26). Furthermore, it may well be that thinking expertly within a domain does not consist of possessing even domain-specific rules, but consists in acquiring a vast repertoire of knowledge of typical cases and in being able to recognize a current situation as being similar to those cases. There is certainly much research to support the view that expert reasoning is not a formal matter but that what is important is familiarity with detailed, domain-specific knowledge (see, e.g. Chi et al., 1988; Tennant, 1991). There is also evidence that when people tackle issues formally the results can be disastrous. Plato's 'ideal state' is the kind of thing I have in mind.

That it is desirable that people should think imaginatively, creatively, critically and be able to solve problems is not in dispute, but can these be taught as general skills? Of the differences between those who espouse transferable skills and those who question them the most profound concern the nature and value of knowledge. A shibboleth here is the attitude towards content. Is it inconvenient, and largely unnecessary, time-consuming clutter? Or do we tend more towards Blake and 'the holiness of the minute particular'?

CONCLUSION

This chapter has indicated that there are no cheap and easy short cuts in education and that content is not an inconvenience, but an essential component of education. In fact, I would suggest that, together with the learner and the teacher, content forms the educational trinity. Whitehead is surely right when he says that, 'education is the patient process of the mastery of detail' (1959, p. 10). Detail is to be celebrated rather that bemoaned. For, as Nabokov (1972) puts it:

In art as in science there is no delight without the detail ... . All 'general ideas' (so easily acquired, so profitably resold) must necessarily remain but worn out passports allowing their bearers shortcuts from one area of ignorance to another.

We began with Euclid declaring that there is no royal road to geometry. Whitehead correctly extends this by stating that there is 'no royal road to learning through an airy path of brilliant generalisations' (Whitehead, 1959). Transferable skills, far from being royal roads or short cuts, are educational cul-de-sacs.

REFERENCES

Adam, S. (2004) *Using Learning Outcomes*. Report for United Kingdom Bologna Seminar 1–2 July, Heriot-Watt University (Edinburgh Conference Centre), Edinburgh.

Anderson, J.R. (1993) *Rules of the Mind*. Hillsdale, NJ: Lawrence Erlbaum Associates.

Annett, J. (1989) *Training in Transferable Skills*. Sheffield: Training Agency.

Aristotle *De Anima* (1952) trans. Smith, J.A. Oxford: Clarendon Press.

Aristotle (1987) *Ethics*, trans. Thomson, J.A.K. London: Penguin.

Assiter, A. (1995) *Transferable Skills in Higher Education*. London: Kogan Page.

Banks, J. (1993) *Outdoor Development for Managers*. London: Gower.

Barrow, R. (1990) *Understanding Skills*. Ontario: The Althouse Press.

Butterfield, E.C., Slocum, T.A., Nelson, G.N. (1993) Cognitive and behavioral analyses of teaching and transfer: Are they different?, in Dettermon, D. and Sternberg, R. (eds), *Transfer on Trial: Intelligence, Cognition, and Instruction*. Norword, NJ: Ablex.

Bobbitt, F. (1926) *How to Make a Curriculum*. Boston: Houghton Mifflin.

Chi, M., Glaser, R. and Farr, N. (1988) *The Nature of Expertise*. Hillsdale, NJ: Lawrence Erlbaum Associates.

Cooper, D.E. (1983) *Authenticity and Learning*. London: Routledge and Kegan Paul.

Davis, A. (1996) Assessment, accountability and transfer. Unpublished paper given at Cambridge Philosophy of Education Society.

DCSF (2008) *Key Skills*: Department for Children, Schools and Families, www.dcsf.gov.uk/keyskills (accessed 29 May 2008)

Dearden, R.F. (1984) *Theory and Practice in Education*. London: Routledge and Kegan Paul.

Dearing, R. (1996) *Review of Qualifications for 16–19 year olds*. Hayes, School Curriculum and Assessment Authority.

de Bono, E. (1978) *Teaching Thinking*. Harmondsworth, Penguin.

Dewey, J. (1916) *Education and Democracy*. London: Macmillan.

Evans, K., Brown, A. and Oates, T. (1987) *Developing Work-Based Learning: An Evaluative Review of the YTS Core Skills Project*. University of Surrey/Manpower Services Commission.

Fay, P. (1988) Stalling between fools: contradictions in the structure and processes of YTS. *Journal of Further and Higher Education*, 12, 2, 23–50.

FEU (1982) *Basic Skills*. London: Further Education Unit.

Feuerstein, R., Rand, Y., Hoffman, M. and Miller, R. (1980) *Instrumental Enrichment*. Baltimore: University Park Press.

Gibb, J. (ed.) (2004) *Generic Skills in Vocational Education and Training*. Summary of Australian Chamber of Commerce and Industry/Business Council of Australia's employability skills. Adelaide: National Centre for Vocational Education Research.

Goodman, N. (1970) Seven strictures on similarity, in Foster, L. and Swanson, J. (eds), *Experience and Theory*. London: Duckworth, pp. 19–29.

Gregory, R.L. (ed.) (1987) *The Oxford Companion to the Mind*. Oxford: Oxford University Press.

Grice, H.P. (1975) Logic and conversation, in Cole, P. and Morgan, J.L. (eds), *Speech Acts*. New York: Academic Press, pp. 41–58.

Hare, R.M. (1952) *The Language of Morals*. Oxford: Clarendon Press.

Henry, D.P. (1984) *That Most Subtle Question*. Manchester: Manchester University Press.

Higgins, S. and Baumfield, V. (1998) A defence of teaching general thinking skills. *Journal of Philosophy of Education*, 32 (3): 391–398.

Hills, G., (1989) Put your money on the doers. London, *Times Educational Supplement*, 20/1/89.

Hills, G. (1990) The pursuit of judgement, *The Guardian*, 18/9/90.

Hunt, G.M.K. (1989) Skills, facts and artificial intelligence, in M.J. Coles and W.D. Robinson (eds), *Critical Thinking: A Survey of Programmes in Education*. Bristol: The Bristol Press, pp. 23–29.

Husen, T. (1979) *The School in Question*. Oxford: Oxford University Press.

James, W. (1890) *Principles of Psychology*. New York: Henry Holt.

Kemp, I.J. and Seagraves, L. (1995) Transferable skills: can higher education deliver? *Studies in Higher Education*, 20, 3, 315–328.

Kripke, S.A., (1993) *Wittgenstein on Rules and Private Language*. Oxford: Blackwell.

Lave, J. and Wenger, E. (1991) *Situated Learning: Legitimate Peripheral Participation*. New York: Cambridge University Press.

McGuinness, C. (1999) *From Thinking Skills to Thinking Classrooms*. DfEE Research Brief No. 115.

McPeck, J.E. (1981) *Critical Thinking and Education*. Oxford: Martin Robertson.

McPeck, J.E. (1990) *Teaching Critical Thinking*. New York: Routledge.

Mehta, V. (1965) *Fly and the Fly-Bottle*. Harmondsworth: Penguin.

Nabokov, V. (1972) *Eugene Onegin: A Novel in Verse, by Alexander Pushkin*. London: Routledge.

Norris, S.P. (1990) Thinking about critical thinking: philosophers can't go it alone, in McPeck J.E. (ed.), *Teaching Critical Thinking*. New York: Routledge, pp. 67–74.

Oxford University (2008) Skills Portal for Oxford University, www.skillsportal.ox.ac.uk (accessed 20 May 2008).

Perkins, D.N. (1985) General cognitive skills: why not?, in Segal, J., Chipman, S. and Glaser, R. (eds), *Thinking and Learning Skills, Vol. 2, Research and Open Questions*. Hillsdale, NY: Lawrence Erlbaum Associates, pp. 339–363.

Phillips Griffiths, A. (1965) A deduction of universities, in Archambault R.D. (ed.), *Philosophical Analysis and Education*. London: Routledge and Kegan Paul, pp. 187–207.

Plato (1960) *Gorgias*, trans. Hamilton, W. Harmondsworth: Penguin.

Plato (1953) *Phaedrus*, trans. Fowler, H.N. London: William Heinemann.

Powell, J.P. (1968) On learning to be original, witty, flexible, resourceful, etc. *Proceedings of the Philosophy of Education Society of Great Britain*, Vol. 2, pp. 43–49.

Pratzner, F.C. (1978) *Occupational Adaptability and Transferable Skills*. National Centre for Research in Vocational Education, Ohio State University.

Reid, T. (1785) *Essays on the Intellectual Powers of Man*. Edinburgh: Bell and Bradfute.

Ruthven, K. (1987) Ability stereotyping in mathematics. *Educational Studies in Mathematics*, 18, 243–253.

Ryle, G. (1949) *The Concept of Mind*. London: Hutchinson.

Ryle, G. (1972) A rational animal, in: Dearden, R.F. Hirst P.H. and Peters R.S. (eds), *Education and the Development of Reason*. London: Routledge and Kegan Paul.

Ryle, G. (1979) *On Thinking*. Oxford: Basil Blackwell.

Scriven, M. (1990) Foreword, in McPeck, J.E., *Teaching Critical Thinking*. New York: Routledge.

Singley, M.K. (1995) Promoting transfer through model tracing, in Keough, A. Lupart J.J. and Marini A. (eds), *Teaching for Transfer*. Hillsdale, NJ: Lawrence Erlbaum Associates.

Singley, M.K. and Anderson, J.R. (1989) *The Transfer of Cognitive Skill*. Cambridge, MA: Harvard University Press.

Sternberg, R.J. (ed.) (1982) *Handbook of Human Intelligence*. Cambridge: Cambridge University Press.

Tennant, M. (1991) Expertise as a dimension of adult development, *New Education*, 13 (1), 49–55.

Thorndike, E.L. (1914) *The Psychology of Learning*. New York: Teachers' College.

University of Warwick (1996) Wallis, M., Personal Transferable Skills: what are employers looking for? *Forum*, University of Warwick, 3, p. 3.

University of Warwick (2008) Warwick University Careers Service, www2.warwick.ac.uk/services/careers (accessed 21 May 2008).

White, J. (2002) *The Child's Mind*. London: Routledge/Falmer.

Whitehead, A.N. (1959) *The Aims of Education – and Other Essays*. London: Ernest Benn.

Wilson, V. (2000) *Can Thinking Skills Be Taught?* Edinburgh: Scottish Council for Research in Education.

Wittgenstein, L. (1958) *Philosophical Investigations*. Oxford: Basil Blackwell.

25

Educational Assessment

John Halliday

INTRODUCTION

According to the electronic data base ERIC, accessed 9.9.08, there were 26,339 publications on the topic of assessment in education during the last 10 years. Of these 10,411 were articles in refereed journals and 3179 were books. Five English language journals are specifically concerned with educational assessment at the levels of practice, theory and policy. Such statistics indicate that the topic is of considerable interest and highly developed. Certain common distinctions have emerged in the course of this development and these are outlined and discussed at the beginning of the chapter. From the discussion three topical debates in the philosophy of educational assessment are reviewed, with reference to the work of Andrew Davis (1995, 1998, 1999, 2006) and his critics Christopher Winch and John Gingell (1996, 2000, 2004) and Randall Curren (2004, 2006). The chapter concludes by offering a critical review of issues that might become central to the philosophy of educational assessment in the future.

FORMATIVE AND SUMMATIVE, FORMAL AND INFORMAL

Informal assessment may be seen as part of learning. Its results are not necessarily recorded or noted. It would not be possible to know whether and the extent to which learning is taking place without informal assessment. When such assessment takes place in a formal context, such as in a school or college, it is sometimes termed formative. Formative assessment takes place throughout a course of study, whereas summative assessment takes place at the end. There are instances where the results of formative assessment can be combined to produce a summative statement of what has been learned, as will be explained later in the chapter. The key definitional points are that it is the timing of the assessment that determines whether the adjective 'formative' or 'summative' best applies. It is the context within which the assessment takes place that determines whether the adjective 'formal' or 'informal' best applies. Formal summative assessment is sometimes termed 'high stakes testing' (Curren, 2006; Davis, 2006) when the consequences of failing the assessment are severe.

INTERNAL AND EXTERNAL

When learning takes place as part of a course of study, formal assessment may be carried out internally by the institution or teacher that sponsors the course of study or externally by some other agency such as an examination board. It may be claimed that the main advantage of internal assessment is that the teacher or student's own institution is in the best position to judge how well the student has learnt. That is because the members of that institution know the student sufficiently well to be able to interpret the student's change in behaviour appropriately. The main advantage of external assessment is that it is likely to be more objective in the sense that the assessor has no personal knowledge of the student or direct interest in the result.

VALIDITY AND RELIABILITY

Assessment is valid when it assesses what it is supposed to assess. Assessment is reliable when it consistently produces the same results irrespective of extraneous factors such as when the learner took the assessment, with whom and in what settings. Ideally, assessments would be both perfectly reliable and valid. However, it is generally accepted that there is a trade-off between these two factors (Davis, 1998: 124). For example, a written examination taken in the same examination room under standard conditions of quietness, time allowed, seating arrangements and so on is more likely to be reliable than observations of performance made in variable contexts. On the other hand, a written examination always assesses to some extent the learner's ability to write under tightly controlled conditions. Through such writing, the learner's ability or knowledge in some area of knowledge or skill is typically inferred. That assessment may not be particularly valid because it is a test of writing as well as a test of knowing or skilful behaviour. Indeed, in the worst cases, the assessment may largely be a test of writing and coping with stressful conditions rather than a test of knowledge or skill in a real and normally variable context.

Formal assessment purports to state something general about the attributes of learners on the basis of particular performances. Such statements typically take the form of certificates. For certificates to have validity it is necessary to be able to infer from satisfactory performance on a discrete number of occasions that future satisfactory performance is likely. A certificate based on observation of actual practical performances may seem more valid than a certificate based on a written examination that asks for a description of a practical performance. That is not necessarily correct, however, because the problem of inferring something general from particularities applies. Moreover, as Davis (1999: 11) points out, the particularities need to be similar subspecies of what is claimed generally. The determination of sameness or similarity depends upon purposes and interests, which may vary depending on who is interested and for what purpose. Whereas reliability in assessment depends upon the minimization of variability in tasks set, validity in assessment depends upon the opposite. Hermeneutics is central to a proper understanding of the relationship between validity and reliability.

Other than in cases where something relatively trivial is being assessed, such as whether someone can define a concept correctly, assessors are likely to interpret candidates' performances in varying ways. Davis (1995: 5) introduces the notion of rich knowledge to indicate that knowledge is interconnected and many layered. We may imagine someone being able to define a concept without having any understanding or rich knowledge of it. For example, it would be possible for someone to state the main formula pertaining to Einstein's special theory of relativity correctly without any rich knowledge of the theory. Rich knowledge of the theory involves knowledge of physics in general and especially Newtonian mechanics. In turn, physics involves knowledge of mathematics and so on. To know Einstein's theory in a rich sense is to be able to relate it to a wide variety of concepts, some of which feature in differing subject areas. To assess such knowledge depends upon this relational ability too. According to Davis (2006: 11), 'Close agreement between assessors can only be obtained by a tight marking scheme and/or a very prescriptive set of exemplar responses'. Such schemes and exemplars cannot cover the possible relations of rich knowledge. Therefore, for Davis, assessment of rich knowledge will be insufficiently reliable for any significant consequence to be based on it.

For rich knowledge to be assessed, marking criteria must be open to interpretation and exemplar responses should be widespread. That is because the assessment of rich knowledge requires learners to respond to tasks and problems in ways that they could not have foreseen. Otherwise the assessment is bound to be little other than an elaborate test of memory. Drawing on Searle (1995), Davis (2006: 12) concedes that where assessors do share more by way of a common understanding of the subject area, then reliability is more likely. As Curren (2006: 26) puts it, 'Adequate consistency of judgment could arise from the common educational background shared by subject matter experts'. An important point of disagreement between Curren and Davis appears to rest on what would constitute an adequate level of reliability. Both agree that validity in assessment requires performance, the details of which are unknown before the performance itself. For Davis the requirement for validity in the assessment of rich knowledge means that reliability can never be high enough to justify summative assessment where the stakes of success or failure are high.

Davis (2006: 13) acknowledges that psychometricians accept 0.8 inter assessor reliability as adequate but considers that even this level would be 'nothing like high enough to justify the effects of high stakes testing'. Curren (2006: 27) points out, however, that it is far too simplistic to claim that 0.8 would not be good enough for high stakes testing. The justice of high stakes testing is of concern to Davis and his critics whether or not there are high levels of reliability. As Curren points out, however, considerations of justice go beyond the reach of philosophical analysis in abstraction from the ethics of evidence and risk management. Some students and institutions whose performance is judged by the assessment results of its students may indeed be unfairly disadvantaged because reliability cannot be 100% for the assessment of any significant or 'rich' ability or understanding. According to Curren (2006: 27), everyone could potentially be disadvantaged if high stakes testing was given up altogether. For example, societies generally prefer the rich knowledge of medical students to be assessed, albeit imperfectly, than not to attempt to assess such knowledge at all.

There are risks involved both in assessing and not assessing. There is always the suspicion that institutions might seek to maximize the success rates of their students in order to raise their own performance levels if external summative assessment is not involved. There are trade-offs between reliability and validity. Internal assessment may seem more reliable than external assessment but, as Curren (2006: 27) points out, rather than abandon external assessment altogether one could simply reduce the threshold on which the risk is based. So, for example, societies could adjust the threshold of evidence necessary to make an adverse judgement against an individual or institution rather than abandon the whole attempt externally to assess rich knowledge.

NORM AND CRITERION REFERENCING

The fact that formal external assessment tends to be repeated year on year for different cohorts of learners taking roughly the same course of study prompts the question: How well has the learner done compared to what? Two answers come readily to mind. The first response is to compare performance with a written statement that sets out what the learner should be able to do or have learnt as a result of the course of study: this is called criterion-referenced assessment. The second response is to compare the performance with the average or norm of all those taking the same assessment: this is called norm referencing.

The results of norm-referenced assessments tend to have higher status than their criterion-referenced counterparts because, by definition, norm referencing produces winners and losers in the form of those who do better than the norm and those who do worse. Typically, learners will be graded. By selective adjustment of the grades awarded and selective movement of the pass mark, relatively stable numbers of winners and losers can be produced year on year. In a competitive environment in which the results of assessments are used to select, significant positional advantage can be gained by being certified to have performed better than competitors. However, there are difficulties in trying to ensure that those selective adjustments and movements are made in a way that is fair to those who might just be part of a very able cohort. There is also the difficulty in setting assessment tasks that are sufficiently predictable to enable candidates to prepare properly for them and sufficiently unpredictable to test ability rather than memory of standard answers.

The performance of other learners should be irrelevant to criterion-referenced assessment. In its simplest form, if the learner is required to define x as y, then there is not much an assessor can do other than ask the learner to define x as y. Similarly, if the learner is required to do something under certain conditions, then there is no room to make the assessment anything other than the requirement actually to do it under those conditions. For more complex assessments, of understanding for example, the assessor might attempt to break down the constituents of understanding into apparently simple criteria in order to try to make the assessment transparent. Such atomization does not avoid the hermeneutic problem however, not only because even the simplest statements require some degree of interpretation but also because the atomization itself can be called into question.

The distinction between norm and criterion referencing is not as straightforward as it might seem. In the case of norm referencing, it is important to have some idea of the criteria upon which grades will be based and the way a performance is marked, otherwise the assessment may have no validity. In the case of criterion referencing, the criteria must be written in such a way that respects both what an average performance might be and the interpretative capabilities of an average student, which is why some forms of criterion-referenced assessment include further criteria to define what a merit or performance of distinction might be (Johnson, 2008).

AREAS OF CONTROVERSY

The hermeneutic problem of judging the extent to which a performance or series of performances matches a statement or series of statements purporting to describe someone or some group's ability is common to all forms of assessment. A great deal of debate is concerned with this problem. A further source of debate concerns precisely what is being assessed or certified to have been assessed. This in turn depends upon what is being learned and how the learning is theorized. A third source of debate concerns the relative merits of the uses to which the results of assessment can be put. Should assessment primarily aid learning, serve as a means of making schools and other educational institutions accountable for the money they spend or serve as a means of selection? Each debate will be outlined below, along with a historical account of the way that values in assessment have recently shifted in the UK and elsewhere.

DEBATE 1 – THE PROBLEM OF INTERPRETATION

The debate concerning interpretation arises at at least three levels. The first level concerns the way the student interprets the assessment task. The second level concerns the way that the student's answer is interpreted by the assessor. The third level concerns the way that the results of the student's assessment are interpreted by those who use the results of assessment. At all levels the distinction between subjectivity and objectivity is relevant and it is worth examining what this distinction entails. It might be claimed that since assessment is so dependent upon interpretation its results must be subjective. It might also be claimed that a requirement for justice requires that the results should be free from the prejudices of the interpreters and objective.

Prejudice need not be regarded negatively and to be always working against objectivity. Rather, prejudice may be regarded as the enabling of objectivity. It is argued (Halliday, 1996) that an ideal of objectivity based on the model of the physical sciences leads to confusion. Such a model leads to the idea that an ideal performance in assessment may be described in advance of the actual performance and be used as a sort of ruler or standard against which the actual performance is judged. A commonsense notion of measurement supports this idea. Common sense leads us astray here if we try to adapt this idea to try to assess learning.

An ideal performance is not a physical object. If there is such a thing as an ideal performance, then that performance is only judged ideal within a social context that has a tradition of comparing performances of certain types. It is not possible to describe such comparisons in ways that avoid the interpretative prejudices of those who have an interest in the measurement and who carry on the tradition. Gadamer (1975) seeks to show how the Enlightenment deformed the use of the word 'prejudice' so that it now seems to function only in a pejorative way. Instead of an ideal of objectivity as something free from prejudice, Gadamer acknowledges the essential temporality and prejudicial nature of all interpretation. For Gadamer, interpretation is necessarily a temporal event in which a text or performance is mediated by an interpreter's expectations, which must be based on the prejudices of a tradition within which the interpreter stands. Instead of there being one final objective interpretation, interpretation consists of a series of mediations or 'fusions of horizons' between prejudices. The concept of a fusion of horizons indicates that the horizons of the interpreter change in the course of interpretation. This makes it appear as if all judgements must be subjective.

According to Rorty (1980: 334), however, 'objective' can mean corresponding to a pre-existing reality and it can mean 'characterising the view that would be agreed upon as a result of argument undeflected by irrelevant considerations'. In the context of assessment, the former meaning is inappropriate for the reasons set out above. According to the latter meaning, 'subjective' indicates that someone is bringing in considerations which others think beside the point, such as whether someone is liked. What we need according to Rorty, who follows Gadamer, is to get used to the idea that all interpretations are judgements of value but that does not make all judgements subjective. It can be and is argued that some values are preferable to others. So it can be and is argued that some actual performances are superior to others and that some people are more able to judge such superiority than others.

At the first level, there are the prejudicial backgrounds of students who attempt to interpret the assessment task and the backgrounds of those who set the task. At the second level, the backgrounds of the markers too are relevant. Finally, the results of the assessment may be interpreted by the students themselves as an indicator of their ability, by their teachers keen to know how well they are doing or by those with an interest in selecting them for future study, employment or whatever. All this does not mean that the results of the assessment or the process itself are entirely subjective, invalid, unreliable and of little use to those with an interest in how good a student is at something. What it does mean is that there are good reasons to try to ensure that students, assessors, interpreters and others with an interest have an opportunity to test their prejudices through continuing dialogue with others and that there is acceptance that some others do have superior insight knowledge and judgement in particular areas of learning. Without the latter requirement, there would indeed be a potentially irresolvable debate about whose judgement is to be preferred, as if assessment comes down to a matter of taste or personal preference. Taken together, both requirements indicate the importance of shared understandings of the way areas of learning are distinguished and of systems of assessment that enable authoritative mastery of each area to be recognized.

Assessment for learning

Following the influential research of Black and Wiliam (1998a, 1998b), it is now widely accepted that formal summative assessments are less helpful to most learners than formative assessment. The phrase 'assessment for learning' (James 1998 and see http://www.qca.org.uk/qca_4334.aspx) captures this acceptance. Various projects take this phrase as part of their title. Such projects are based on the view that learners themselves and/or their teachers are in the best position to assess how well learning is taking place. Recognition of the hermeneutic problem appears to support such a view, and there have been moves to formalize formative assessment so that its results can be externally recognized in a summative way. Such recognition would seem to be most useful where it includes the widest possible comparison of students and most credible where people accept the authority of those who have carried out the assessment.

A wide comparison of students is not easily enabled, however. The logic of teaching is to avoid making individual adverse comparisons. Indeed, teachers may well be tempted to overstate the abilities of their students, whereas assessors should not be so tempted. Moreover, even though there is some evidence to suggest that teachers are good at making comparisons of ability within a group (Gipps, 1994), they are not so good at making comparisons between groups for the obvious reason that they have no direct experience of groups other than the ones they themselves have taught.

Criterion referencing and the competence revolution

Criterion referencing appears to offer a way of objectivizing teachers' judgements so that formative assessments can be combined into a summative statement of ability to serve the interests of the assessment for learning movement. However, criteria may need further criteria for their application and, potentially, criterion referencing may lead to an infinitely long set of criteria as more and more qualifications are added to a statement of performance. Criterion referencing of desirable values is especially problematic. For example, we may wonder about the number of occasions on which someone has to be honest before they meet the criterion of honesty. We may wonder if there is not something dishonest about trying to be honest on say ten occasions as if the eleventh did not matter.

In the case of practical knowledge, it seems that accomplished practice cannot consist of a fixed number of performances of particular tasks. Instead, accomplished practice involves the ability to go on one's own to complete new tasks in unforeseen contexts in ways that meet with the approval of people similarly engaged. Practical knowledge cannot be made fully explicit. We only need to think of the difference between the 'do it yourself' attempt to hammer a nail and the accomplished joiner performing the same task. In the former case, the attempt seems awkward, the wrist is held stiff, the nail does not go in at a right angle and the head of the nail may not be buried in the wood. In the latter case, the performance seems effortless. It is not difficult to think of many other examples where it is not easy to specify the differences in the way that a task is completed, but we are aware of the differences none the less. In the case of theoretical knowledge there is a difference between the repetition of words as if those words had been memorized by rote and fluent articulation in response to unforeseen questions, which indicates a deeper understanding.

Supporters of criterion-referenced assessment often cite the driving test as a good example of the superiority of criterion-referenced assessment. They attempt to generalize from this example. The generalization is misleading, however. That is because the context within which driving takes place is so familiar to most of us that we do in a real sense belong to a community with a tradition of motoring. As a result of this membership, we interpret and reinterpret criteria for successful driving regularly as we observe behaviour on the roads. Moreover, the examiners form a relatively coherent group with opportunities for regular dialogue.

As a result of all these considerations, the criteria for successful performance in the driving test are well-understood, relatively uncontentious and accepted.

Criterion referencing has been developed worldwide for vocational areas of learning in an attempt to certify workplace competence (Hyland, 1994). The notion of competence is broken down into 'elements of competence' that are supposed to be 'evidenced' in terms of behavioural criteria and range statements. There is a large gap, however, between the normal ascription of the term 'competent' to someone and a completed checklist of prescribed behavioural criteria. At the first level of interpretation, the learner cannot yet have a full grasp of what the social practice she is learning entails, for otherwise she would not be a learner. Criteria that the novice understands are not the same as criteria an accomplished practitioner would use if such use is necessary at all for accomplished practice. A large part of learning consists in coming to understand what accomplished practice involves. Criterion referencing such practice in a way the learner understands is likely to distort or at least risks trivializing the learning for reasons concerned partly with connectedness that were discussed earlier.

This debate about the problem of interpretation suggests that assessment may best be viewed as a social practice (Delandshire, 2001). Assessment is not free of power relations that could distort the certification of someone's ability in unjust and unfounded ways. Assessment should include considerations of justice, the ethics of evidence and acceptable levels of tolerance in applying results, as was argued above. It should be based on other social practices that form traditionally established areas of learning for there to be a possibility of objective judgements. It has been argued that the competence revolution, assessment for learning and other attempts to produce summative statements of internal formative assessment fail to deal adequately with the problem of interpretation (Hyland, 1994; Halliday, 1996). These types of assessment are criticized too on the basis of the behaviourism that underpins them.

DEBATE 2: THEORIES OF LEARNING – WHAT IS BEING ASSESSED?

Criterion referencing suggests that the extent to which behaviour matches a statement of desirable behaviour is what is being assessed. Some of the debate between Davis and his critics suggests that changes in mental states are being assessed. Davis (1998: 78) argues that it is an illusion to imagine that human behaviour can be interpreted in such a way that the nature of individual mental states can be determined. As Curren (2006: 19) points out, however, either Davis's sceptical arguments undermine the whole enterprise of interpreting human behaviour or they undermine nothing. Since behaviour is interpreted in this way, then, for Davis's critics, the sceptical argument about assessment fails.

The influence of psychological constructivism may be seen in Davis's work. Davis (1998) argues that for high stakes testing, mental states would need to be similar to physical states such as magnetism. If a metal is magnetic, then it will be disposed to behave in certain predictable ways and at any time those ways may be tested. Similarly, Davis argues, if a pupil has a belief, then she will be disposed to behave in certain predictable ways and at any time those ways can be tested. Beliefs are not like physical states, however. Rather, the manifestation of a belief can emerge through unpredictable connections with other beliefs. For this reason 'fine grained judgements about the contents of other minds' (Davis 2006: 3) are not possible. It is not possible to posit a stable internal state, ontologically separable from other states involved in propositional attitudes. Hence, for Davis, high stakes testing of what might be in pupils' minds is not possible. For Curren (2004, 2006), this argument is mistaken. First it is not clear what a mental state might be without some neurophysiological data. There is no such data available to date and good reason to suppose that such data may not be forthcoming. The Wittgensteinian argument that it is not possible to distinguish between using a word correctly and knowing its meaning (Malcolm, 1972: 58) cuts through any idea that someone could have an identifiable mental state which gave meaning to the belief she thought that state represented.

Social constructivism, and in particular situated cognition, may provide a better basis for a proper understanding of the meaning and purposes of assessment. Within these theories, areas of learning are considered to be practices that have become established over time through social construction. Novices are inducted into the practice under the guidance of experienced practitioners who are able informally to assess when novices are coming to understand and act according to the social norms of the practice (Lave and Wenger, 1991). It is commonly assumed that each practice consists of some combination of acquiring theoretical knowledge, practical knowledge and dispositions to act for the good: sometimes these three types are simplified as knowledge, skills and attitudes. Learners should know that certain things are true, know how to do certain things and have certain values. Rarely, however, if at all, do learners exercise their ability in one type. Rather, any significant task involves some combination of all three and it is often not possible to distinguish precisely which type is being exercised.

It might be argued that the influence of psychological constructivism has led to the dominance of practices with a strong theoretical component such as mathematics, english, geography and history. It can also be argued, however, that such dominance has arisen because theoretical knowledge is most easily and economically assessed. For the assessment of theoretical knowledge, tools of pen and paper are commonly involved, whereas, for other practices, other tools are involved. In the interests of reliability, assessment of theoretical knowledge may be preferred, even though practices with a strong theoretical component can be viewed practically as an ability to write, reason, argue and talk in certain socially approved ways.

Hirst's (1974) forms of knowledge thesis mapped seven theoretical practices that were thought to be most worthwhile to learn. In his 1993 publication Hirst acknowledges that this thesis was mistaken and that practical knowledge has primacy over its theoretical counterpart. He sees theoretical knowledge as 'developments within the contexts of practice ... and generalisations concerning successful and unsuccessful practices rather than disinterested truths' (Hirst, 1993: 193). In other words, appropriate use of terms such as 'know' and 'knowledge' is part and parcel of many social practices and not essential determinants of those practices. In his 1999 publication, Hirst explains this a little further:

> It is my contention that, holding to the central importance of propositional knowledge for a good life, education has for far too long been mistakenly dominated by the content and character of academic theoretical disciplines. For the good of us all we must now begin to see the good life and the aims of education in terms of rational social practices by which alone we can find the satisfaction and fulfilment which constitute our good, individually and collectively. (Hirst, 1999: 132)

In contrast to the idea of learning as acquisition of knowledge, skills and attitudes, learning for social constructivists consists of participation in established practices within an evolving continuously renewed set of relations. Those relations enable the recognition of authority. Since assessment depends upon the recognition of authority, then it seems that for social constructivists only established practices can enable just and valid forms of assessment. That is not to say that those practices are fixed. Debate within and between them enables their development. Nevertheless, it seems some distinctions between practices are necessary to preserve a sense of objectivity in assessment. That is why some critics have condemned movements such as learning to learn and other context-free skills literature that has come to the fore (Johnson, 1998) on the back of the assessment for learning movement. For example, abstractions such as critical thinking or problem-solving that are not related to an established practice are particularly difficult to assess with any degree of validity or reliability according to the arguments advanced in this chapter.

DEBATE 3: THE PURPOSES OF ASSESSMENT

Not everyone is convinced by the 'practice turn' (Chaiklin and Lave, 1993) to learning theory. Nor are they convinced by the assessment for learning movement (Winch and Gingell, 1996, 2004). A dominant purpose of assessment remains selection and positional advantage as a result of selection. For reasons advanced above, assessment for selection tends to privilege theoretical knowledge. It is the possibility of assessing rich cognitive achievement that Davis challenges and that challenge matters because the purported assessment of rich cognitive achievement is most often used for high stakes testing. For Davis (1998: 143):

> It is not possible for a common language to be used to characterise rich cognitive achievements by pupils in such a way that their attainments may be reported on in a wider arena and intelligible comparisons made.

A supporter, John White (1999: 203) puts it this way:

> To make judgements about pupils' achievements at this deeper level (of rich knowledge) one has to know something of the particular conceptual schemes and beliefs with which they are operating and of what logical and epistemological connections they make between different parts of this mental structure. Since individuals are bound to differ in these ways, assessors will have to have a good understanding of how particular learners operate.

Again for Davis (1998: 17):

> Rich or proper knowledge lacks the definitive and specific character which would be required if its presence were to be detectable by standard educational devices.

It seems obvious to White and Davis that internal assessment is better than external assessment for assessing rich cognitive achievement. According to Winch and Gingell (2000), however, there are many criteria for successful practice that include significant cognitive achievement. Such criteria are widely understood. For example:

> Pupils be given opportunities to use and apply mathematics in practical tasks in real life problems. (Winch and Gingell, 2000: 688)

For them, there is nothing particularly problematic about interpreting such a criterion. Working out simple arithmetic in a shop, calculating floor areas for a carpet fitter, working out tax returns, and so on, are examples. It is not necessary to know learners personally to see whether they can meet this criterion. Similarly, it is not necessary to know a leading literary critic personally in order to be able to recognize that his work is at the cutting edge of research. So it is simply wrong to suppose that

> We should trust those who have the most personal knowledge of pupils in assessing their educational progress. (Winch and Gingell, 2000: 693)

Although these people may be trusted to have pupils' well-being at heart, they may not have either the knowledge or the disinterest necessary to be able to tell them that their understanding of something is not as deep as might be hoped. It troubles Winch and Gingell that, by overstating the hermeneutic problem, Davis and White provide philosophical support for the wilder variants of the assessment for learning and content-free skills movements. They are also concerned that Davis and White are providing tacit support for educational initiatives that are introduced without any real idea of what would constitute success in them. Finally they argue,

> Progression and selection in education form the basis of procedures that are accepted because whatever their imperfections they are assumed to be the best way of ensuring procedural justice. By undermining the very possibility of objective external assessment of learning, Davis and White also undermine the very possibility of publicly funded education in which institutions can be held to account through publicly available results of external forms of assessment in which people can have confidence. (Winch and Gingell 2000: 694)

Procedural justice requires educational assessment to be objective in the sense that it is free from irrelevant considerations. An inappropriate notion of objectivity taken from the physical sciences should not lead to the view that it is only on the basis of personal acquaintance that assessment can be reliably and validly carried out. It is possible to make judgements about someone's ability even though not everyone is an expert to the same degree. There are sufficient shared practices for us to be able to communicate with one another and recognize both the degree of difficulty involved in tasks with which we might not be very familiar and the authority of those who are expert.

IMPLICATIONS

The present situation, where external examinations tend to be limited to paper and pencil tests and internal assessment limited to the more practical subjects, has unfortunate implications. Areas of learning that are externally assessed will continue to have more status than their internally assessed counterparts. Insofar as academic means theoretical knowledge tested by written examination and vocational means practical tested by observation by the students' own teacher, academic qualifications are likely to continue to have more status. This is not good for the proper recognition of skill at work in all those practical areas of life that are so important to the proper functioning of society.

Moreover, even those external examinations that include some moderated elements of internal assessment are likely to have less status than those forms of assessment that are completely summative and external. Most recently, some popular universities have announced that they are going to select students on the basis of their own supplementary assessments rather than trust the results of examinations that include elements of internal assessment. Commercial organizations have been doing the same for some time. Put simply, whenever positions are in short supply assessment is used as a means of selection and if public assessments do not grade with sufficient discrimination then private forms of assessment will emerge. The real difficulty with this prospect is that public schools and public examinations are bound together. Private schools are not so bound and have the freedom to offer whatever assessments they want. More wealthy parents can pay to secure positional advantage for their children. The less wealthy cannot. However able the children of the latter might be, less wealthy parents may not have the opportunity even to compete with their more privileged counterparts in what could effectively become privately sponsored examinations.

Thus, the implications of conceptual confusion in assessment are severe for considerations of justice as fairness. In this chapter it has been argued that a mistaken conceptualization of objectivity, coupled with a failure to distinguish properly between the logics of teaching and assessment, may have led to the situation when some practices essential to the proper function of society are insufficiently valued. Conversely, performance in other practices may become increasingly assessed through highly selective private examinations to which many do not even have entry. Assessment is for learning, but it is also for selection and accountability:

> No assessment can be perfect … this is not a reason for dispensing altogether with summative assessment. It is an argument for taking it seriously, designing and administering carefully and for keeping it under review. (Winch and Gingell 2004: 73)

REFERENCES

Black, P.J. and Wiliam, D. (1998a) Assessment and classroom learning, *Assessment in Education: Principles, Policy and Practice*, 5 (1): 7–74.

Black, P.J. and Wiliam, D. (1998b) *Inside the Black Box: Raising Standards through Classroom Assessment*. London: King's College. Also published (2006) by NFER Nelson, London (online summary available at www.pdkintl.org/kappan/kbla9810.htm)

Chaiklin, S. and Lave, J. (eds) (1993) *Understanding Practice: Perspectives on Activity and Context*. Cambridge: Cambridge University Press.

Curren, R. (2004) Educational measurement and knowledge of other minds, *Theory and Research in Education*, 2 (3): 235–253.

Curren, R. (2006) Connected learning and the foundations of psychometrics: a rejoinder, *Journal of Philosophy of Education*, 40 (1): 17–29.

Davis, A. (1995) Criterion referenced assessment and the development of knowledge and understanding, *Journal of Philosophy of Education*, 29 (1): 3–23.

Davis, A. (1998) *The Limits of Educational Assessment*. Oxford: Blackwell.

Davis, A. (1999) *Educational Assessment: A Critique of Current Policy*. London: Philosophy of Education Society of Great Britain.

Davis, A. (2006) High stakes testing and the structure of the mind: a reply to Randall Curren, *Journal of Philosophy of Education*, 40 (1):1–16.

Delandshire, G. (2001) Implicit theories, unexamined assumptions and the status quo of educational assessment, *Assessment in Education*, 8 (2): 113–133.

Gadamer, H.G. (1975) *Truth and Method*. London: Sheed and Ward.

Gingell, J. and Winch, C. (2000) Curiouser and curiouser: Davis, White and Assessment, *Journal of philosophy of education*, 34 (4): 687–697.

Gipps, C.V. (1994) *Beyond Testing: Towards a Theory of Educational Assessment*. London: Falmer.

Halliday, J.S. (1996) *Back to Good Teaching: Diversity within Tradition*. London: Cassell.

Hirst, P.H. (1974) *Knowledge and the Curriculum*. London: Routledge and Kegan Paul.

Hirst, P.H. (1993) Education, knowledge and practices, in R. Barrow and P. White (eds), *Essays in Honour of Paul Hirst*. London: Routledge and Kegan Paul.

Hirst, P.H. (1999) The nature of educational aims, in R. Marples (ed.), *The Aims of Education*. London: Routledge, pp. 124–132.

Hyland, T. (1994) *Competence, Education and NVQs*. London: Cassell.

James, M. (1998) *Using Assessment for School Improvement*. Oxford: Heinemann.

Johnson, M. (2008) Grading in competency based qualification – is it desirable and how might it affect validity?, *Journal of Further and Higher Education*, 32 (2): 175–184.

Johnson, S. (1998) Skills, Socrates and the Sophists: learning from history, *British Journal of Educational Studies*, 46 (2): 201–213.

Lave, J. and Wenger, E. (1991) *Situated Learning: Legitimate Peripheral Participation*. Cambridge: Cambridge University Press.

Malcolm, N. (1972) *Problems of Mind: Descartes to Wittgenstein*. London: Allen and Unwin.

Rorty, R. (1980) *Philosophy and the Mirror of Nature*. Oxford: Blackwell.

Searle, J. (1995) *The Construction of Social Reality.* London, Penguin.

White, J.P. (1999) Thinking about assessment, *Journal of Philosophy of Education,* 33 (2): 201–212.

Winch, C. and Gingell, J. (1996) Educational assessment: a reply to Andrew Davis, *Journal of Philosophy of Education,* 30 (3): 377–389.

Winch, C. and Gingell, J. (2000) Curiouser and curiouser: Davis, White and Assessment, *Journal of Philosophy of Education,* 34 (4): 697–709.

Winch, C. and Gingell, J. (2004) *Philosophy and Educational Policy. A Critical Introduction.* London: Routledge Falmer.

26

Inclusion and Diversity

Penny Enslin and Nicki Hedge

INTRODUCTION: CONCEPTS IN TENSION

Diversity and inclusion emerged in the later decades of the twentieth century as two central preoccupations of political and educational theory in liberal democracies. Social movements pressed for recognition of many forms of diversity: ability, class, culture, ethnicity, gender, language, nationality, race, religion and sexual orientation. If diversity is 'the great issue of our time' (Macedo, 2000: 1), inclusion is commonly regarded in public discourse and policy as a key solution to the injustices suffered by groups excluded from the mainstream of society. These injustices have taken the form of misrecognition of the traditions, cultures, preferences and material needs of the excluded, as well as their needs for access to and inclusion in educational provision. So it is widely agreed that education should recognize diversity and thereby be inclusive. But, as we will show, from here the issues become less straightforward. Key concepts in philosophy of education, while compelling at face value, are usually contested and often problematically in tension with one another. If we talk of inclusion, into what are we talking of including those who have been excluded? Are all kinds of inclusion just and desirable? What if respecting some forms of diversity simply results in new forms of exclusion?

Concepts of inclusion and diversity have been the focus of some of the most consistently fraught normative issues in education, implicated in wider concepts like equity, fairness and justice. In the analysis that follows we will explore the complexity that surrounds inclusion and diversity in education, through discussion of two related issues: multicultural and inclusive education, in the broader theo-retical context of multiculturalism and inclusion. Our review of the issues will attend to the potential pitfalls of 'internal exclusion' (Young, 2000) as well as to concerns about threats to inclusion from universalization and normalization in response to diversity. It will incorporate recent work from two competing theo-retical traditions – liberal and poststructuralist – suggesting that both contribute valuable perspectives to our understanding of the problems at stake in addressing the imperatives of inclusion and diversity in education.

Recognizing diversity appropriately in relation to differences has led to commendable efforts to provide education that is inclusive, stressing common citizenship and entitlements, and a shared education system. But while in some instances the compatibility of inclusion and diversity seems relatively clear, what it means to 'include' as a response to exclusions based on diversity is far from straightforward. Some failures to acknowledge diversity have encouraged resis-tance to inclusion, prompting separatist responses by blacks and women, who have sometimes seen voluntary exclusion as a more viable way of achieving social justice. In education as we will see shortly, this may take the form of for-mally admitting previously excluded groups, for example those with disabilities or from marginalized ethnic or religious groups, but maintaining practices that exclude them, resulting in what Iris Marion Young (2000) calls internal exclusion, as against the external exclusion they suffered previously. Exemplifying instances when some separation might serve equality better, Anne Phillips (2007: 36) notes that 'some have argued that girls will get more attention from their teachers or more opportunity to specialise in scientific subjects if they are taught in single-sex schools' and Afro-Caribbean pupils might enjoy better educational opportunities in separate classes.

Despite such contrary cases, policies aimed at including diverse groups have commonly set out to create shared institutions and values. This has prompted some to warn against tendencies attributed to mainstream liberalism's approach to diver-sity as 'an assimilationist ideal that espouses treating everyone equally according to the same "neutral" principles, rules and standards' (Herr, 2008: 39). But such a stance tends to ignore the variety of approaches to diversity within contemporary liberalism. Whereas liberal feminism is often criticized for failing to value diver-sity, it has brought to our attention ways in which the defence of diversity as the right of communities to follow their own traditions in the treatment of girls and women can result in perpetuating their subordination (see Okin, 1999) and creat-ing complex patterns of exclusion. Although supposed inclusion in a community whose practices receive recognition might look inclusive of its individual female members, and inclusive of that community within a larger political community, its girls and women may be internally excluded from decision-making and, as a result, externally excluded from educational opportunities available in the wider society. This critical perspective on accommodating certain kinds of diversity brings us to the first of our two major themes in diversity and inclusion: multicultural education.

MULTICULTURALISM AND MULTICULTURAL EDUCATION

Why has multiculturalism emerged as one of the predominant approaches to diversity? There are three basic premises of multiculturalism according to Dominic McGoldrick (2005). The first of these, the permanent ethnic diversity of states, reflects the negative deployment of multiculturalism to manage cultural diversity resulting from migration. Secondly, technological advances have made states and their citizens more connected and interdependent, identities are simultaneously local and global and our understanding of cultures and groups 'even more amorphous and contingent' (p. 30). Finally, with the rise in its legal and political status has come a more positive understanding of multiculturalism that values diversity and the traditions and values of other cultures.

Multicultural societies continue, however, to face unprecedented challenges, with Bhikhu Parekh (2000: 343) observing that they must find ways to reconcile the equally legitimate demands of unity and diversity, seek political unity that does not depend on cultural conformity, become inclusive without assimilation, cultivate a common sense of belonging that respects legitimate cultural differences, and prize plural cultural identities as well as shared citizenship. Arguing the benefits of diversity to multicultural societies, Parekh includes amongst these: access to different cultures, which expands one's horizons; the freedom to step outside one's culture and to see beyond its contingency; opportunities for dialogue between different traditions; and an enhanced sensitivity to the diversity within our own culture.

'Multiculturalism' is a strongly contested and controversial concept that has shifted in use across time and place, with Blum (2001) observing that it is more salient in the USA than the concept of anti-racism in the UK. For McGoldrick (2005: 36), although multiculturalism had become the dominant discourse by the start of the new millennium, it is regarded by some as 'supporting illiberal cultures, particularly those that do not have at least a formal premise of gender equality' (see also Okin, 1999). He points to Will Kymlicka as one of 'the most influential contributors' to theories of multiculturalism. Observing that most countries are now culturally diverse and that approaches to minority rights in the liberal tradition have varied considerably, Kymlicka's approach to this diversity is 'grounded in a commitment to freedom of choice and (one form of) personal autonomy' (Kymlicka, 1995: 7). Liberalism, he argues, is both consistent with and requires us to take cultural membership seriously. Most of us have a strong attachment to our own culture and 'individual choice is dependent on the presence of a societal culture, defined by language and history' (p. 8). Minority rights that are consistent with respecting individual freedom actually promote freedom. Arguing the intimate connection between culture and freedom, Kymlicka defends what he calls a societal culture, one 'which provides its members with meaningful ways of life across the full range of human activities' (p. 76), through institutions like the media, government and, significantly, schools.

Freedom to choose the good life, led from the inside, as a defining feature of liberalism will, following Kymlicka, require resources to examine and question beliefs in relation to other alternatives. Traditional liberal freedoms of expression and association make such judgements possible – as does education that enables individuals to learn about other ways of life and to make informed choices.

For meaningful individual choice to be possible, individuals need access to information, the capacity to reflectively evaluate it, freedom of expression and association and access to a societal culture. Group-differentiated measures that secure and promote this access may, therefore, have a legitimate role to play in a liberal theory of justice (Kymlicka, 1995: 84). Acknowledging people's deep attachments to their own cultures, Kymlicka notes that it may sometimes be necessary to question and even to revise understandings 'of the good and our fundamental commitments' pointing to a liberal education to provide both 'cultural access and the means for revision of beliefs and values' (pp. 92–93).

Qualifying his endorsement of rights for national minorities and ethnic groups, Kymlicka notes that some group demands will exceed the bounds of acceptability, arguing that, 'Liberal democracies can accommodate and embrace many forms of cultural diversity, but not all' (p. 152). Internal restrictions on political and civil freedoms cannot be justified in a liberal theory of minority rights and individuals should have the right to revise their community's traditional practices (p. 152). Furthermore, Kymlicka suggests that liberals should aim to support those trying to liberalize their culture from within and to liberalize 'non-liberal nations', not to dissolve them (p. 94). Moreover, minority rights should prevent domination by one group over others; no group should be allowed to oppress its members and there should be freedom and equality both between and within groups. How, then, might such views be realized in multicultural education?

The United States' National Association for Multicultural Education (NAME, 2003) states that 'Multicultural education is a philosophical concept built on the ideals of freedom, justice, equality, equity, and human dignity', as a process that 'helps students develop a positive self-concept by providing knowledge about the histories, cultures, and contributions of diverse groups' while preparing all to work towards structural equality by providing 'the knowledge, dispositions, and skills for the redistribution of power and income among diverse groups'. For NAME, a multicultural curriculum must directly address issues of 'racism, sexism, classism, linguicism, ablism, ageism, heterosexism, religious intolerance, and xenophobia'. Few might fault such ideals, yet Nieto and Bode's (2007: 44) claim that multiculturalism not only accepts but also affirms pluralism points to potentially more contentious issues, raising once again the legitimacy of all forms of diversity.

Whereas implementation of multiculturalism has taken varying forms, the idea of the common school brings the central tension between inclusion and diversity into focus. Questioning the compatibility of these two concepts, Meira Levinson (2007: 639) concludes that common schooling and multicultural education are 'fraught with conceptual and practical predicaments that challenge each enterprise independently as well as in relation to one another'. Acknowledging that the ultimate value of their shared goals is not in question, she claims that the very diversity of students in an inclusive common school will result in multiple challenges, not least with respect to the development and implementation of culturally relevant curricula and pedagogies (p. 632). Despite the appeal of bringing diverse individuals together to get 'used to' each other, Levinson cautions that instead of fostering mutual tolerance and respect common schools may worsen tensions and misunderstandings. Such schools may fail to pay adequate attention to less obvious forms of diversity, with students and teachers being cast as 'race (or culture) representatives' of groups, thereby essentializing these groups and the individuals who belong to them. Similarly, alleging that a tendency to overstate the degree of value divergence within groups can lead to the kinds of stereotyping that multiculturalism sets out to counter, Anne Phillips' (2007) recent defence of 'multiculturalism without culture' urges us to problematize culture, recognizing that people differ not only in ways that reflect their culture but also in gender, class and as individuals.

Arguing for comparable criticality, Stephen Macedo (2000: 6) has cautioned against embracing diversity in ways that distract from the need to promote citizenship and a shared civic life, suggesting that 'diversity and difference, like all good or potentially good ideas, can be taken to an extreme or grasped in the wrong way' (p. 10). Advocating a tough-minded version of liberalism that diverges from Kymlicka's as resting not on diversity 'but on shared political commitments weighty enough to override competing values' (p. 146), Macedo points to the limitations of diversity in a liberal democracy. He argues that the intolerant should be tolerated only in so far as they do not threaten free institutions, proposing that 'we need not bend over backward to make life easy for them' (p. 147).

This reconsideration of multiculturalism, which could be reflected in approaches to culture in education, would not be complete without attention to the insights of poststructuralist writers. Acknowledging that poststructuralist ideas might initially seem at odds with concerns for educational inequalities and exclusions, Deborah Youdell (2006) asserts that they derive from a 'recognition that existing structural understandings of the world, whether these focus on economic, social, ideological, or linguistic structures, do not offer all the tools that we need' (p. 34). Accordingly, she recommends Judith Butler's work for insights into educational inequalities and exclusions persist.

For Butler (1996: 52), the task set by cultural difference is to better articulate universality 'through a difficult labour of translation'. She charges that 'What is named as universal is the parochial property of dominant culture', claiming that 'universalizability' is indissociable from imperial expansion' (Butler, 2000: 15). Arguing that because abstract universalism cuts individuals off from personal qualities that they may or may not share with others, Butler contends that it is probably impossible to 'establish universality as transcendent of cultural norms' (pp. 17–20). On that view she would likely reject a prioritization of inclusion over diversity, say on grounds of gender inequality, if embedded in cultural/religious belief. On a universalist's approach, the dispossessed and under-represented will fail to 'rise to the level of the recognizably human within its terms' (p. 23).

Accordingly, she criticizes Nussbaum and Okin for their claims about the conditions and rights of women, suggesting these fail both to afford due regard to the prevailing norms in local cultures and to address the task of 'cultural translation' (p. 35). Butler argues that such efforts ignore issues posed by local cultures exemplified by the way in which feminism 'works in full complicity with US colonial aims in imposing its norms of civility through an effacement and a decimation of local Second and Third world cultures' (p. 35). She acknowledges that translation alone can become 'the instrument through which dominant values are transposed into the language of the subordinated' (p. 35) but maintains that has 'counter-colonialist possibility' if it can be made to expose the limits of the dominant language (p. 37).

Whereas universality presents significant issues Butler indicates that were it to be framed in an insistence that 'the "not yet" is proper to an understanding of the universal itself' and were one to regard the universal as a 'non-place' (p. 39), then this might allow us to acknowledge a necessary sense of 'not-knowing'. Asking such questions on inclusion and diversity we would not, following Butler, seek to answer them so much as 'to permit them an opening ... that sustains questions and shows how unknowing any democracy must be about its future' (p. 41). As we turn now to a consideration of educational inclusion we shall, in that respect, voice questions to summarize and provoke political discourse.

INCLUSION AND INCLUSIVE EDUCATION

If to 'be included' means to be homogenized into a status quo reproducing injustice then it will fail to meet either Butler's poststructuralist (2000) call for translation and contingency or Martha Nussbaum's modified liberal (2006) insistence on dignity for all. Seeking to avoid such homogenization, Linda Graham and Roger Slee (2008: 278) endeavour to 'jettison the rhetorical inertia of instrumentalist gestures towards inclusion ... by making visible and deconstructing the centre from which all exclusions derive'. Noting the term inclusion implies a 'bringing in', they are concerned that it 'discursively privileges notions of the pre-existing by seeking to include the Other into a prefabricated, naturalised space' (p. 278). This would establish a margin and centre, privileging 'universal categories and a romanticized, universalised subject' (Lather, 2003: 260 cited in Graham and Slee). Observing that the centre is, anyway, 'but a barren and fictional place' (p. 279), Graham and Slee prefer to regard inclusion as 'already-begun', asking if replacing it with 'inclusive' might less likely lead to the foreclosure inclusion implies. Accordingly, they refer to inclusion 'under erasure' or 'crossed out', as a term that is *there* but is not to be relied upon or taken for granted, not to be used as if it is universally understood but left open to convey the political message that it continues to be under critique.

Rather than reifying inclusion and diversity as unquestionably desirable, we would, following Graham and Slee, 'challenge the centred-ness implicit in tokenistic attempts to "include" ... that characterise instrumental accommodations for alterity within an otherwise mainstream education system' (p. 279). Asking what we might do to disrupt the construction of a centre from which exclusion derives, they worry that an answer will deploy Stiker's (1999: xi) 'normative circuitry ... based on a notion of 'disability [and difference] as an alien or exceptional condition'.

Arguably, 'normative circuitry' will not necessarily regard disability and difference as either alien or exceptional. Rather, it might follow Nussbaum's (2006: 210) view that progress would mean acknowledging there is no such thing as a 'normal child': 'instead there are children, with varying capabilities and varying impediments, all of whom need individualized attention as their capabilities are developed'. That position is not apparently at odds with Graham and Slee's (2008: 280) need to denaturalize 'normalcy' in order to 'arrive at a ground-zero point', banishing 'idealisations of centre' and making 'redundant the very language of special and regular'. Proposing that human variation is omnipresent, that many human beings are 'atypically disabled', that people vary considerably, including at different points in their life span, and that such diversity must be both recognized and attended to in any search for global justice, Nussbaum's (2006: 88) modified universalist stance appears not so far removed from Graham and Slee's (2008) approach to inclusion.

Regardless of differing theoretical starting points, in order to avoid assimilation or integration, it is useful to follow Graham and Slee's (2008) call for inclusion to move beyond current, limited notions and models. They would have us ensure that individual differences are not objectivized (p. 280), thereby avoiding 'the production of normative domains as comparative grids of intelligibility that are not only constitutive of exteriority but protective of the centre from which they emanate' (p. 282). They assert that normative discourses will necessarily be 'comprised of valorising and affirming statements of the desirable and the normal subject' versus a discourse of deficits that 'demarcate the abnormal object' (p. 282). They claim that as these two competing discourses pressurize each other they result in a 'normative centre' that locates those not deemed 'normal' on the margins, as 'Other'. Arguably this would hold only if narrow understandings of 'normal' and 'other' pertained. If that were the case, then integrationist ideals attempting to ignore diversity, especially in the name of inclusion, would likely exacerbate exclusion. Integration, warns Ratcliffe (2000: 171), may be the 'penultimate step en route to assimilation' if it is used to accommodate outsiders, those on the margins, as a means of maintaining social control by those in power. Against that background, we extend a consideration of inclusion and inclusive education to issues of diversity beyond those focussed on impairment and disability.

Warning of the possible dangers of an overly narrow focus and highlighting the contradiction of seeing the 'the struggle for inclusion' only in relation to particular groups, Felicity Armstrong (2003: 3) cautions against failing to make connections between wider issues of diversity including those occasioned by ethnic, political, class, race and gender struggles. In the discussion that follows we shall, accordingly, note broad trends in policies attending to diversity alongside those largely focussed on disability and impairment. That said, it is salutary that key debates in educational inclusion continue to focus on [dis]ability, on integration and inclusion, inclusive and special education. In this context, integration tends to highlight 'special' needs, difficulties requiring 'special' measures, with inclusion more focused on rights and the acknowledgement that difference is normal. Accordingly, Miles (2000) contends that definitions of inclusive education should use the Salamanca Statement and Framework for Action (UNESCO, 1994) to emphasize respect for difference and diversity.

Following UNESCO (2004), inclusive education relates to the learning needs of *all*, especially those 'vulnerable to marginalization and exclusion', treating all with respect and providing 'opportunities to learn together'. Reminding us that the debate on 'ordinary' versus 'special' classrooms has been ongoing since society started to question segregation and work towards equality and integration, UNESCO's (2004) Inclusive Education website encourages us to look briefly to history. Similarly, Dyson (2001, p. 24) recommends recourse to the past to offer insights into the dilemmas and contradictions encountered today while acknowledging 'a dearth of historical studies' in the field. Alert to this, we will outline some of the key historical turns in policy in order to sketch shifts in the interpretations and meanings of inclusion and diversity, starting from an understanding that for thousands of years 'physical and mental differences have been ascribed special meaning' resonating with the '… stigma, negative attitudes and stereotypes' often persisting today (Rieser, 2008: 13).

Until the mid twentieth century, segregated special provision reflected a model of philanthropy often referred to as a 'charity' approach or model for those deemed unable to benefit from regular schooling (see Borsay, 2002; Reiser, 2008). With the expansion of public schooling, learners in the UK deemed 'ineducable' continued to remain outside mainstream education, labelled 'educationally subnormal' rather than, as previously, 'educable defective' (Education Act, 1944 and Tomlinson, 1982: 50). Eleven categories of disability were made official, signifying 'new refinements in the decanting of children' to special schools (Armstrong, 2003: 64). In North America, public schools were never designed for every child and especially not for 'those designated "insane" or "feebleminded" and they are still not attended by every child', suggests Bernadette Baker (2002: 699–700). Not until the late 1950s did questions of institutionalization and segregation emerge, and at this point policy shifted, with more concerted moves to include children in regular schools against a backdrop of 'normalisation' (Kisangi, 1999: 4–5 citing Wolfensberger, 1972). Linking normalization with integration, Joseph Kisangi notes that this was education designed to ensure conformity to a predetermined norm of behaviour (p. 5).

Between the 1950s and 1970s, increased scientific knowledge, alongside 'official humanitarian and medical discourses', resulted in burgeoning special education until a shift in focus following the 'radicalization' of the 1960s (Armstrong, 2003: 68), from whence there was some move from difference to commonality (Dyson, 2001). Special education, including specialist schooling for those still deemed unable to benefit from regular schooling and the placement of children with 'special needs' in schools where possible, had far from run its course.

At this time, with an increase in Commonwealth immigration in the UK, assimilation was an underlying trend here and in many Western democracies. This resulted in diversity policies aimed at bringing ethnic and immigrant groups into the dominant mainstream culture, with education charged to remedy cultural and linguistic deficits. Whereas moves to equal opportunities and 'tolerance' of cultural differences appeared in Britain in the 1960s, a deficit model still prevailed (Maylor et al., 2005: 61). Not only were young people from different cultures and backgrounds deemed different from and in need of assimilation into the majority culture but also, in common with children labelled physically or mentally 'different', they were regarded as problematic and in need of special measures.

The next watershed commonly referred to in the history of special education and its increasing shift to mainstreaming is the Warnock Report (DES) of 1978. Retaining the language and provision of 'special education', education authorities were to broaden the concept of special education to include learning difficulties and 'emotional or behavioural disorders' and to focus on a child's individual needs 'as distinct from his disability' (para. 3.42). With the ensuing introduction of Statements of Special Educational Needs (Education Act, 1981), the 1980s then became 'boom years for special education provision' (Potts, 1995: 398).

Whereas inclusive education was focussing on the recognition of children's needs, diversity policies in the 1970s and 1980s drew on multiculturalism to realize a more positive recognition of diversity, although this been criticized for its homogenizing tendencies (Maylor et al., 2005: 61). In 1985, the Swann Report (DES, 1985) marked another significant shift, with its emphasis on education for all. Asserting that the key issue now was not how to educate ethnic minority children but how to best educate *all* children in a UK society now acknowledged to be multiracial and multicultural, there was a concerted effort to change behaviour and attitudes. The Swann Report introduced the language of pluralism, noting this was now a marked feature of British life, and sought to combat racism and stereotyping by promoting and embedding multicultural understanding in schools. However, with the introduction of the National Curriculum to England's schools in 1988, Uvanney Maylor et al. (2005: 61) submit that young people were then, once again, to be educated without much attention to their cultural and racial identities in order to protect 'British identity'.

The 1990s saw a range of legislative and policy changes affecting inclusion and diversity in the UK, with an increasing emphasis on anti-discrimination and rights. Whereas the protection of disabled people was now enshrined in law, the presumption of mainstreaming, i.e. educating young people in regular not special schools, was explicit (Education Act, 1996). However, such mainstreaming remained limited and pertained only if three key conditions were met: young people would be educated in ordinary schools only if their special educational needs could be met; only if their presence in the school would not interfere with other children's learning; and only if their education would be compatible with efficient resource use. Full inclusion remained a long way off, although, in 1997, the 'Excellence for all Children' Green Paper (DfEE, 1997) was hailed by the Labour Government as a key move towards inclusion. Despite the rhetoric, Derrick Armstrong (2005) maintains that it would be misleading to look to 1997 as a turning point. Rather, with the Government's focus on human capital, it represented 'the recreation of the special educational industry under the banner of "inclusion"' (p. 136). For many advocates of inclusion any form of segregation within or across schools remains part of the medical model of disability rooted in a deficit, child-as-problem model that continues to fail children and society and certainly fails to uphold the moral rights of young people (Kenworthy and Whittaker, 2000).

The Parekh Report (2000) on the future of multi-ethnic Britain represented a departure from goals of assimilation and integration. Basing its recommendations on three central concepts – cohesion, equality and difference – the report asserted that while people should be treated equally, this should be with due regard to difference. Racial injustice and associated social exclusion were to be attacked and existing social inclusion programmes were to have an explicit focus on race equality and cultural diversity. Overall, the report sought to promote a pluralistic culture of human rights that supplanted exclusion, tokenism and paternalism with mutual recognition, collegiality and equality. In a similar vein, the rights model of education was arguably helping to shift inclusive education from a medical, integrationist model towards greater inclusion for all. The UK's Special Educational Needs and Disability Act 2001 (SENDA) attacked discrimination on the grounds of disability, while in the United States, the Individuals with Disabilities Education Act (IDEA, 2004 formerly the Education for All Handicapped Children Act) insisted all young people receive a Free Appropriate Public Education (FAPE) to prepare them for further education, employment and independent living. Avowing '... a shared commitment to help all children learn to high standards set for all', IDEA (2004) stresses the goal of 'free appropriate public education in the least restrictive environment'. Full inclusion, however, still seemed bound by conditions, not least around understandings of and loopholes in the concept of the 'least restrictive environment' and, although the discourse of IDEA steers clear of terms such as inclusion, the issues are not dissimilar to those in the UK and beyond. Whereas inclusion may be apparently high on policy agendas, its realization remains elusive, as the example below indicates.

Following the presumption of mainstreaming in Scotland, the 2004 'Education (Additional Support for Learning) (Scotland) Act ensures that 'additional support needs' should be met for learners at any stage. Intuitively, this looks more inclusive than a model focussed on the pathologized 'special' needs of some children marked as 'other'. Inclusive education, thus framed, apparently goes beyond a 'bringing in' of learners hitherto excluded from 'normal' schools to a more systemic reorganization attending to a wide diversity of needs that can change over time and apply to any and all young people. Potentially this could meet Slee's (1999: 127) requirement of the 'cultural reconstruction' needed if inclusive education is to move beyond assimilation. A recent evaluation, however, reveals that there is evidence of continuing and widespread support for specialist provision, albeit within a policy climate of inclusion. Pointing to 'some of the most vulnerable children and young people with SEBD [severe emotional and behavioural difficulties]', Head and Pirrie (2007: 95) maintain a number of such children are 'demonstrably unable to face the challenges presented by mainstream schools' in research that highlights the perception of inadequate experience, training, facilities and resources to support such children in Scotland's regular schools.

Conceivably, we are currently witnessing a 'backlash against inclusion – not against its fundamental values, but against its insistence on unconditional universality' (Cigman, 2007: 272). Ruth Cigman maintains that for any children failing to flourish in mainstream schools, we are failing 'to accord respect to all, in favour of the spurious notion of inclusion' (p. 792). For her, the inclusion debate must prompt the recognition that decent societies are those whose institutions avoid humiliating people. She claims that 'moderates' will follow the 'universalist's' inclusion without exceptions maxim only in so far as they accept 'mainstream schools are incompatible with an adequate education for some children' (p. 776). Criticizing the homogenizing tendencies of universalists seeking full inclusion, she favours, instead, the moderates' 'distinguishing tendency' more focussed on individual needs and differences (p. 783). Drawing on Warnock's (2005) controversial statements on the dangers of exclusion within inclusion, Cigman concludes that strong inclusion fails to promote respect for those children unsuited to an ordinary school.

Although such a view resonates with Graham and Slee's (2008: 278) contention that 'to include is not necessarily to be inclusive', Cigman's stance differs in significant respects, striking at the heart of tensions between integration and inclusion as she questions what is normal and typical. For her, diversity apparently trumps inclusion if some prefer not to be included or if their carers choose not to include them. Nussbaum's (2006) capabilities approach insists that just as all individuals have the right to a threshold level of human capabilities, then they also have 'the right not to use them' (p. 185). Might we argue then that as all individuals have the right to quality education that is free from exclusion, that all children must 'be seen as legitimate claimants at the educational table' (Slee, 2006: 117), that they also have the right to exclude themselves from that if they or their guardians wish? Nussbaum (2006) contends that children with mental disabilities 'need the support required to be freely choosing adults, each in his or her own way' (p. 220). Simultaneously, her emphasis on individuality and freedom for all implies she might endorse an approach affording a choice between special and inclusive schooling but would do so only if adaptive preferences did not come into play. Any choices between regular or special schools would need to be equally enabling of human flourishing, allowing all to attain their maximum possible potential. Whereas education continues to be financially constrained, recourse to what is more familiar and already funded, that is to specialist provision rather than full inclusion, may well offer the more desirable option.

Asking what would constitute just educational provision for students with disabilities and special educational needs, Lorella Terzi (2007: 758) draws on Nussbaum's capabilities approach and 'liberal egalitarianism' to offer a response. Raising issues of fair distribution, she notes that the competing demands of those with and without disabilities could be dealt with in the capability approach through its provision of 'additional requirements ... as requirements of justice' (p. 766). That view accords, of course, with Nussbaum's (2006) argument against any notion of devising a differential set of capabilities for the disabled, not least because it is reasonable to insist that the central capabilities are important for all citizens and thus worth any additional expenditures that may have to accrue to those with particular needs (p. 190).

With the recent merger of the UK's Commissions on Racial Equality, Disability Rights and Equal Opportunities, inclusion and diversity have the opportunity to come together and render Armstrong's (2003: 3) 'struggle for inclusion' less disconnected than hitherto. Expressing cautious optimism on that merger, Robin Richardson (2007) notes that in order to reduce inequalities, wherever they are located on the equalities agenda, much more is required. Resonating with Graham and Slee's concerns to confront understandings of inclusion, he contends that to challenge the view of a weak, resourceless 'Other', we need 'to share resources with the Other, empower the Other, and (it follows) disempower ourselves' (p. 7).

Although nomenclature and policies have changed, the challenge of ensuring that inclusion does not result in new forms of exclusion remains. Often intended to promote social cohesion and active participation, Maylor et al. (2005: 63) question if today's citizenship education can meet the needs of all learners. Countering that the assimilationist interpretations of the 1960s and 1970s have been challenged by the 'ethnic revitalization movements', initiated in the United States but reverberating globally, James Banks (2008: 58) points to Kymlicka and Young for theories of minority rights and differentiated citizenship, respectively. Contending that diversity is now both 'recognised and sanctioned' in Western democracies, he acknowledges that it remains a contested concept, arguing the need for a transformed citizenship education that can realize the goal of a 'delicate balance of diversity and unity' (p. 59). Such an aspiration is reflected in a move, particularly in Europe, to replace multicultural education with 'intercultural education'. Observing that multiple terms – multicultural, transcultural and intercultural – have frequently been used interchangeably, Jagdish Gundara and Agostino Portera (2008) remind us to ask if such terms are used to connote similar or different concepts, approaches and practices. Although advocating intercultural education as the most appropriate response to today's global context,

Portera (2008) acknowledges that simply renaming a concept will not necessarily ameliorate the challenges it poses and alludes to the continuing need for vigilance with respect to the overemphasis on difference, stereotyping and continuing marginalization that inclusion would seek to disrupt.

At the start of this section we asked if to 'be included' means to be homogenized into a status quo reproducing old injustices in new ways. The historical overview here indicates shifts in policy and increased attention to inclusion and diversity as key concepts for the twenty-first century and we might venture that some progress has been made. There has been some de-centring to view inclusion not as an activity that will reproduce inequalities and 'otherness' but as an ongoing, always incomplete process that disrupts an inequitable, unjust status quo. However, on a global scale more thoroughgoing attention to material inequalities and the need for a redistribution of resources ought to supplant what could arguably be seen as attention to educational exclusion and diversity that have overemphasisized the recognition of difference per se (see Enslin and Tjiattas, 2009). As processes of globalization continue, increased diversity is paralleled by trends towards cultural homogeneity regarded by some as a new form of cultural imperialism (Merryfield and Duty, 2008: 83). Additionally, with more than 90% of children with disabilities in developing countries not attending schools, child labour and maltreatment resulting in mental illness and physical and psychological disabilities, and inappropriately designed curricula continuing to cause segregation and exclusion (UNESCO, 2006), it is clear that inclusion is 'a road to travel rather than a destination' (Mittler, 2003).

DIVERSITY AND INCLUSION: BEYOND MULTICULTURALISM AND INCLUSIVE EDUCATION?

Our exploration of diversity and inclusion and attempts to address these principles in education has demonstrated that these two concepts are highly problematic, regardless of the theoretical orientation we might adopt – liberal or poststructural. This prompts the question: Are the notions of inclusion and diversity, for all the attention they have received, so problematic that they simply cannot do the work expected of them? Approaches to diversity and inclusion have both been shown to be vulnerable to tendencies that threaten to undermine the very objectives of the policies that pursue them, resulting in further and ongoing exclusion, internal and external, whatever their intentions. However, we propose that despite the pitfalls pointed to by both liberal and poststructuralist approaches – the ever-present danger of excluding by homogenizing assimilation or normalizing – both theoretical positions hold out the conceptual and theoretical tools to addresses failures to recognize diversities of different kinds.

Liberalism offers an articulation of a wider set of normative principles that need to be applied in pursuit of inclusion that meets the demands of justice for the individual as well as for groups. Poststructuralism challenges us to rearticulate, to reconceptualize understandings of inclusion and diversity in ways that insist inclusion must be de-centred, that it should be thought of more as an ongoing struggle than an end game. Whereas any consideration of inclusion will 'expose deeply politicized tensions and differences relating to democracy, school reform and social justice' (Leo and Barton 2006: 171), the two approaches outlined here offer complimentary insights that might, together, enable a differently considered process of inclusion. That process deserves consideration if it offers a discursive, political, policy and practical space from which to reconcile diversity and inclusion as two key drivers in a just educational future.

REFERENCES

Armstrong, Derrick (2005) 'Reinventing 'inclusion': new Labour and the cultural politics of special education', *Oxford Review of Education*, 31(1): 135–151.

Armstrong, Felicity (2003) *Spaced Out: Policy, Difference and the Challenge of Inclusive Education*. Dordecht, the Netherlands: Kluwer Academic Publishers.

Baker, Bernadette (2002) 'The hunt for disability: the new eugenics and the normalization of school children', *Teachers College Record*, 104(4): 663–703.

Banks, James A. (2008) 'Diversity and citizenship education in global times', in James Arthur, Ian Davies and Carole Hahn (eds), *Education for Citizenship and Democracy*. London: SAGE, pp. 57–70.

Blum, Lawrence (2001) 'Recognition and multiculturalism in education', *Journal of Philosophy of Education*, 35(4): 539–559.

Borsay, Anne (2002) 'History, power and identity', in Colin Barnes, Mike Oliver and Len Barton (eds), *Disability Studies Today*. Cambridge: Polity Press, pp. 98–119.

Butler, Judith (1996) 'Universality in culture', in Joshua Cohen (ed.), *For Love of Country: Debating the Limits of Patriotism*. Boston: Beacon Press, pp. 45–52.

Butler, Judith (2000) 'Restaging the universal: hegemony and the limits of formalism', in Judith Butler, Ernesto Laclau and Slavoj Zizek (eds), *Contingency, Hegemony, Universality: Contemporary Dialogues on the Left*. London and New York: Verso, pp. 11–43.

Cigman, Ruth (2007) 'A question of universality: inclusive education and the principle of respect', *Journal of Philosophy of Education*, 41(4): 775–793.

Department for Education and Employment (DfEE) (1997) *Excellence for All Children Meeting Special Educational Needs*, Cm 3785, http://www.dcsf.gov.uk/consultations/downloadableDocs/45_1.pdf

Department of Education and Science (DES) (1978) *Special Educational Needs, Report of the Committee of Enquiry into the Education of Handicapped Children and Young People*. Cmnd. 7212. London: Her Majesty's Stationery Office (The Warnock Report).

Department of Education and Science (DES) (1985) *Education for All: Report of the Committee of Inquiry into the Education of Children from Ethnic Minority Groups*. Cmnd. 9453. London: Her Majesty's Stationery Office (The Swann Report).

Disability Discrimination Act (1995) (c. 50). London: Her Majesty's Stationery Office, at http://www.opsi.gov.uk/acts/acts1995/ukpga_19950050_en_1

Dyson, Alan (2001) 'Special needs in the twenty-first century: where we've been and where we're going', *British Journal of Special Education*, 28(1): 24–29.

Education Act (1944) (c. 31 7_and_8_Geo_6) London: Her Majesty's Stationery Office, with Revised Statute from The UK Statute Law Database at http://www.opsi.gov.uk/RevisedStatutes/Acts/ukpga/1944/cukpga_19440031_en_1

Education Act (1981) (c. 60) London: Her Majesty's Stationery Office, with Revised Statute from The UK Statute Law Database at http://www.opsi.gov.uk/RevisedStatutes/Acts/ukpga/1981/cukpga_19810060_en_1

Education Act (1996) (c. 56) London: Her Majesty's Stationery Office, at http://www.opsi.gov.uk/ACTS/acts1996/ukpga_19960056_en_1

Education (Additional Support for Learning) (Scotland) Act (2004) (asp 4) at http://www.opsi.gov.uk/legislation/scotland/acts2004/asp_20040004_en_1

Enslin, Penny and Tjiattas, Mary (2009) 'Philosophy of education and the gigantic affront of universalism', *Journal of Philosophy of Education*, 43(1): 1–17.

Graham, Linda J. and Slee, Roger (2008) 'An illusory interiority: interrogating the discourse/s of inclusion', *Educational Philosophy and Theory*, 40(2): 277–293.

Gundara, Jagdish and Portera, Agostino (2008) 'Theoretical reflections on intercultural education', *Intercultural Education*, 19(6): 463–468.

Head, George and Pirrie, Anne (2007) 'The place of special education within a policy climate of inclusion', *Journal of Research in Special Educational Needs*, 7(2): 90–96.

Herr, Ranjoo S. (2008) 'Politics of difference and nationalism: on Iris Young's global vision', *Hypatia*, 23(3): 39–59.

IDEA (2004) 'Building the legacy', United States Department of Education, at http://idea.ed.gov/.

Kenworthy, John and Whittaker, Joe (2000) 'Anything to declare? The struggle for inclusive education and children's rights', *Disability and Society*, 15(2): 219–231.

Kisanji, Joseph (1999) 'Historical and theoretical basis of inclusive education', keynote address for the Workshop on Inclusive Education in Namibia: The Challenge for Teacher Education, Rossing Foundation, Khomasdal, Windhoek, Namibia, 24–25 March, www.eenet.org.uk/theory_practice/hist_theorectic.doc.

Kymlicka, Will (1995) *Multicultural Citizenship: A Liberal Theory of Minority Rights*. Oxford: Oxford University Press.

Lather, Patti (2003) 'Applied Derrida: (mis)reading the work of mourning in educational research', *Educational Philosophy and Theory*, 35(3): 257–270.

Leo, Elizabeth and Barton, Len (2006) 'Inclusion, diversity and leadership: perspectives, possibilities and contradictions', *Educational Management Administration and Leadership*, 34(2): 167–180.

Levinson, Meira (2007) 'Common schools and multicultural education', *Journal of Philosophy of Education*, 41(4): 625–642.

Macedo, Stephen (2000) *Diversity and Distrust: Civic Education in a Multicultural Democracy*. Cambridge, MA: Harvard University Press.

McGoldrick, Dominic (2005) 'Multiculturalism and its discontents', *Human Rights Law Review*, 5(1): 27–56.

Maylor, Uvanney, Ross, A. and Hutchings, M. (2005) 'National policy and practitioner practice in the UK, in A. Ross (ed.), *Teaching Citizenship*. London: CiCe, pp. 59–66, http://cice.londonmet.ac.uk/pdf/2005–59.pdf

Merryfield, Merry M. with Duty, Lisa (2008) 'Globalization', in James Arthur, Ian Davies and Carole Hahn (eds), *Education for Citizenship and Democracy*. London: SAGE, pp. 80–91.

Miles, Susie (2000) 'Enabling inclusive education: challenges and dilemmas', paper presented at A Symposium on Development Policy: Children with Disabilities and the Convention on the Rights of the Child, Gustav Stresemann Institute, Bonn, Germany, October 27–29, http://www.eenet.org.uk/theory_practice/bonn_2.shtml.

Mittler, Peter (2003) 'Building bridges between special and mainstream services', http://www.eenet.org.uk/theory_practice/build_bridges.shtml.

National Association for Multicultural Education (NAME) at http://www.nameorg.org/aboutname.html with 'Definition of Multicultural Education' (2003) at http://www.nameorg.org/aboutname.html#define

Nieto, S. and Bode, P. (2007) *Affirming Diversity: The Sociopolitical Context of Multicultural Education*. Boston: Allyn and Bacon.

Nussbaum, Martha, C. (2006) *Frontiers of Justice: Disability, Nationality, Species Membership*. Cambridge, MA: Belknap Press of Harvard University Press.

Okin Susan M. (1999) 'Is multiculturalism bad for women?' in Joshua Cohen, Matthew Howard and Martha C. Nussbaum (eds), *Is Multiculturalism Bad for Women?* Princeton, NJ: Princeton University Press, pp. 9–24.

Parekh Report (2000) *A Commission to Examine the State of Multi-ethnic Britain.* London: Profile Books Ltd. and see http://www.new-diaspora.com/CultureandIdentity/2-Parekh%20Report%202000.html

Parekh, Bhikhu (2000) *Rethinking Multiculturalism: Cultural Diversity and Political Theory.* Basingstoke: Macmillan Press/Palgrave.

Phillips, Anne (2007) *Multiculturalism Without Culture.* Princeton, NJ: Princeton University Press.

Portera, Agostino (2008) 'Intercultural education in Europe: epistemological and semantic aspects', *Intercultural Education*, 19(6): 481–491.

Potts, Patricia (1995) 'What's the use of history? Understanding educational provision for disabled students and those who experience difficulties in learning', *British Journal of Educational Studies*, 43(4): 398–411.

Ratcliffe, Peter (2000) 'Is the assertion of minority identity compatible with the idea of a socially inclusive society?' in Peter Askonas and Angus Stewart (eds), *Social Inclusion: Possibilities and Tensions.* New York: Palgrave, pp. 169–185.

Richardson, Robin (2007) 'Getting them together – the equalities agenda in education, autumn 2007 and beyond', *Race, Equality and Teaching*, 26(1): 6–12, http://www.insted.co.uk/equalities-article.pdf.

Rieser, Richard (2008) *Implementing Inclusive Education: A Commonwealth Guide to Implementing Article 24 of the UN Convention on the Rights of People with Disabilities*, the Commonwealth Secretariat.

SENDA (Special Educational Needs and Disability Act) (2001) (c. 10) London: Her Majesty's Stationery Office, at http://www.opsi.gov.uk/ACTS/acts2001/ukpga_20010010_en_1

Slee, Roger (1999) 'Special education and human rights in Australia: how do we know about disablement, and what does it mean for educators?', in Felicity Armstrong and Len Barton (eds), *Disability, Human Rights and Education: Cross-Cultural Perspectives.* Buckingham: Open University Press, pp. 119–131.

Slee, Roger (2006) 'Limits to and possibilities for educational reform', *International Journal of Inclusive Education*, 10(2–3): 109–119.

Stiker, H. J. (1999) *A History of Disability.* Michigan: University of Michigan Press.

Terzi, Lorella (2007) 'Capability and educational equality: the just distribution of resources to students with disabilities and special educational needs', *Journal of Philosophy of Education*, 41(4): 757–773.

Tomlinson, Sally (1982) *The Sociology of Special Education.* London: Routledge and Kegan Paul.

UNESCO (1994) The Salamanca Statement and Framework for Action on Special Needs Education, adopted by the World Conference on Special Needs Education: Access and Quality, Salamanca, Spain, 7–10 June, 1994, at http://www.unesco.org/education/pdf/SALAMA_E.PDF

UNESCO (2004) Education: Inclusive Education at http://portal.unesco.org/education/en/ev.php-URL_ID=11891andURL_DO=DO_TOPICandURL_SECTION=201.html

UNESCO (2006) Education: Inclusive Education – Our Challenge at http://portal.unesco.org/education/en/ev.php-URL_ID=18542andURL_DO=DO_PRINTPAGEandURL_SECTION=201.html

Warnock, Mary (2005) *Special Educational Needs: A New Look.* London: Philosophy of Education Society of Great Britain.

Wolfensberger, Wolf (1972) *Normalization: The Principle of Normalization in Human Services.* Toronto: National Institute on Mental Retardation.

Youdell, Deborah (2006) 'Diversity, inequality, and a post-structural politics for education', *Discourse: Studies in the Cultural Politics of Education*, 27(1): 33–42.

Young, Iris Marion (2000) *Inclusion and Democracy.* Oxford: Oxford University Press.

27

Equality and Justice

Claudia Ruitenberg and
Daniel Vokey

INTRODUCTION

In *Whose Justice? Which Rationality?*, Alasdair MacIntyre (1988) shows how
rival philosophical traditions articulate radically incompatible conceptions of
justice corresponding to their competing theories of *practical rationality*:

> Some conceptions of justice make the concept of desert central, while others deny it any
> relevance at all. Some conceptions appeal to inalienable human rights, others to some notion
> of social contract, and others again to a standard of utility. Moreover, the rival theories of
> justice which embody these rival conceptions also give expression to disagreements about
> the relationship of justice to other human goods, *about the kind of equality which justice
> requires*, about the range of transactions and persons to which considerations of justice are
> relevant, and about whether or not a knowledge of justice is possible without a knowledge
> of God's law. (p. 1, italics added)

As MacIntyre observes, throughout history the concept of *justice* has been
related to the concept of *equality* in many different ways. Not surprisingly, then,
ideas about what forms of education are just and promote justice have, likewise,
varied.

Perhaps the best-known articulation of this relation between equality and
justice, and one that continues to inspire many of our social institutions today, is
Aristotle's principle that people should be treated equally in the respects in which
they are equal, and unequally in the respects in which they are unequal: 'that the
unequal should be given to equals, and the unlike to those who are like, is contrary to nature, and nothing which is contrary to nature is good' (*Politics*, Jowett,
trans., VII. 356 p. 157). In the case of educational assessment, for example, this

principle dictates 'that all students being examined who are members of the same or equivalent school class and who demonstrate equal knowledge, learning achievement or whatever is defined as the object of assessment and grading get equal grades' (Kodelja, 2005, p. 67).

Aristotle's discussion of equality highlights a difficulty that still troubles discussions of equality and justice in education today: 'equality' can be interpreted both as likeness or sameness, and as equivalence. In the first case, difference is opposed to equality, whereas in the second, it is not difference in and of itself that poses the problem, but rather hierarchical relations of inferiority and superiority. 'We are all equal' can thus be taken to mean, 'We are all the same' as well as, 'We may be the same or we may be different but none of us is superior to anyone else'.

In this article we discuss four conceptions of justice, how equality or inequality play a role in these conceptions, and how they have informed ideas about the distribution of educational 'goods' and about education's relation to a just society, more generally. The first is Plato's conception of what we will call *justice as harmony*. This conception of justice legitimates – and even requires – unequal educational opportunities. The second is Kant's conception of what we will call *justice as equality*. Under this conception, equal treatment is paramount, even if such equal treatment leads to quite unequal outcomes. The third conception is what we call *justice as equity*, and this, we believe, is the dominant conception of justice informing public education today. Based on the work of political philosopher John Rawls we discuss ideas about equal opportunity and unequal treatment in education. The fourth conception of justice we will discuss is *justice as difference*. To expose this demanding and, to many, less familiar conception of justice, we turn to the work of the French philosophers Emmanuel Levinas and Jacques Derrida. Finally, we raise two challenges to discourses of equality and justice posed by contemporary scholars. The first is a challenge by French philosopher Jacques Rancière about the assumption of inequality, which keeps social equality an elusive goal. The second is a challenge to the anthropocentrism of all the conceptions of justice we have discussed, in which new ideas about the (in)equality of human and other living beings generates new theories of justice and new conceptions of the forms of education that promote it.

JUSTICE AS HARMONY

In *The Republic* Plato recounts a dialogue between Socrates and several interlocutors (most notably Thrasymachus) about the concept of justice. Socrates, in his rhetorically clever way, asks whether Thrasymachus agrees 'to define a thing's function in general as the work for which that thing is the only instrument or the best one' (*The Republic*, Cornford, trans., I, sec 352). The idea that every object and every person has its, her, or his own 'excellence' or *arete* is a central component of Socratic ontology. A second important component of this ontology is the idea that persons are not self-sufficient, and need to live with others in a community. Socrates concludes that, if people are born with different talents and need to cohabit in a community with others who have different talents, the community in which they live will be strongest if all fulfill that role for which they have the most natural talent. It would be irresponsible for someone to take on an occupation for which she or he has little innate predisposition, thus weakening the community as a whole.

> You remember how, when we first began to establish our commonwealth and several times since, we have laid down, as a universal principle, that everyone ought to perform the one function in the community for which his nature best suited him. Well, I believe that that principle, or some form of it, is justice. (*The Republic*, Cornford, trans., IV, sec 432).

Of course, if each member of the community should perform the one function in the community for which her or his natural talents have best suited her or him, education should support rather than counteract these natural talents. Education that enhances justice as defined by Socrates, then, should not the same for everyone, but rather targeted to enhance people's natural talents.

In education thus conceived, the first task is to recognize a child's talents and predispositions, and determine whether the child should receive training to be a Guardian (in other translations called 'Auxiliary,' a kind of soldier), and perhaps be selected, later on, to be a Ruler, or whether the child should be a farmer, merchant or craftsman. The second task is to design an education fit for Rulers. This education, Socrates postulates, should prepare Rulers to contemplate the absolute truths and values such as goodness and beauty, so that they can make their worldly decisions based on them. Note that in Socrates' conception of justice through inequality, people are considered unequal both in the sense that they are dissimilar – they have different talents – as well as in the sense that these talents are not valued equally. It is clear that the Rulers are not just different from but also superior to the farmers and craftsmen (and never mind the slaves!).

The idea that people are unequally endowed with natural talents, and that such inequality justifies a differentiated education, has influenced education for centuries. As Graham Haydon (1998) notes, the question 'how far is there to be a common curriculum and a common approach to delivering it, and how far are there to be differences at the level of communities, schools or individuals' has proven persistent (pp. 5–6). Although designers of curricula and education systems today are perhaps less likely to be driven by absolute truth than by economic efficiency, the idea that a society as a whole becomes stronger if it fosters excellence in areas ranging from scientific discovery to athletic achievement is still quite prevalent. For example, one can easily recognize in the ideas of the political scientist Leo Strauss, which have been quite influential on neoconservative educational policies in the United States and elsewhere, Plato's ideas about virtue and excellence, and the need not to occupy oneself with what one happens to enjoy but rather with 'studying with the proper care the great books which the greatest minds have left behind' (Strauss, 1968, p. 3, as cited in York, 2008, p. 69).

Strauss rejects the idea that education is the great social equalizer, and proposes, in terms that underscore that not all will achieve the virtue that equips them to rule a society, 'Liberal education is the ladder by which we try to ascend from mass democracy to democracy as originally meant. Liberal education is the necessary endeavour to found an aristocracy within democratic mass society' (Strauss, 1968, p. 10, as cited in York, 2008, p. 73). Although Strauss recognizes, as does Plato, that 'there is no reason to think that the common man and the gentleman are unequal, except by an accident of birth', the fact of the matter remains that only the 'gentleman' (Strauss' term for someone who has received a liberal education) is properly equipped to rule a society in the best interest of all (York, 2008, pp. 73–74).

In Plato's and Strauss' ideas about inequality, the well-being of the community as a whole – of course, based on particular ideas about what that communal well-being looks like – overrides the individual's freedom to choose an education and career path. This is a pragmatic, utilitarian idea: neither Plato nor Strauss asks whether the 'accident of birth' poses an injustice to the individual that requires redress; what matters is fostering the excellence of society as a whole, and this end justifies the unequal treatment that individuals receive through a differentiated educational system. In the next section, we will see how Kant proposes quite a different perspective on the treatment of individual persons as means to social ends.

JUSTICE AS EQUALITY

The Prussian Enlightenment philosopher Immanuel Kant (1724–1804) is well known for developing a universalist deontological (duty-based) moral theory grounded in reason. In *Groundwork for the Metaphysics of Morals* (1785) Kant argued for the following universal moral law, which he called a 'categorical imperative': 'Act only on that maxim whereby you can at the same time will that it become a universal law' (IV, 421). He then derived two other formulations of the categorical imperative from the first. Justice is achieved when people act in accordance with the categorical imperative, and this imperative holds equally for all human beings, as all human beings are, first and foremost, *rational* beings and the categorical imperative is a rational principle. In this way, the categorical imperative indicates that all human beings have equal moral worth as moral agents. In other words: although human beings are not the same, they are equally deserving of respect as rational beings as well as equally responsible for using their reason.

American philosopher Harvey Siegel (1988) makes use of Kant's ideas to defend the teaching of critical thinking to all children. After positing that critical thinking is an educational ideal we *ought to* aspire to (p. 48), one of the reasons he provides to justify this claim is that, if we accept the Kantian principle that all persons deserve to be treated with respect, then students deserve to have their demand for reasons and explanations honoured, to be dealt with honestly, and to have their independent judgment confronted (p. 56). In other words, because all students are, fundamentally, rational beings, treating them respectfully requires treating them as rational beings who deserve to have their critical questions answered and, in turn, to be questioned critically by their teachers.

Another American philosopher, Harry Brighouse (2006), also argues along Kantian lines that all children should be offered an education designed to facilitate their development into autonomous persons. Brighouse argues that it is never acceptable to prevent the child from developing herself or himself as a moral agent. The child, although not yet a full moral agent and in need of protection, is not the parents' property, and the right of the child to grow up to be a rational moral agent, capable of making independent decisions based on a full a range of information as can be had, is inalienable. In line with the second formulation of Kant's categorical imperative, that people should always be treated as ends in themselves and never as means to an end only, the discomfort of parents with rational decisions that their children reach or appear to be reaching is never sufficient reason for them to deny their children the opportunity to learn to form independent judgments (p. 20).

One important idea that flows from Kant's basic assumption that human beings are rational actors is the retributive principle of 'just desert'. Since justice requires that human beings are treated as people who have acted rationally, human beings can be said to deserve both the positive and negative consequences of their actions, including punishments. Polish philosopher Zdenko Kodelja (2005) explains that, while it might appear that this principle does not apply to school children who, it is generally agreed, are not yet fully rational and thus not yet fully responsible for their actions, older high school children should be considered mature enough to bear the consequences of their actions. He advocates an approach in which children are progressively treated as rational persons and thus also progressively held responsible for their actions. This is a way of showing the student respect as a rational person who has made her or his own decisions:

> Freedom and rationality pertain to persons. Accordingly, when an offender is recognized because he has committed an offence, he is being recognized as a person, and respect is shown to that which is distinctively human in him, that which gives him the dignity that sets him apart from all other beings – his freedom and rationality. (Primoratz, 1997, p. 79, as cited in Kodelja, 2005, p. 77)

JUSTICE AS EQUITY

The big difference between justice as equality in the sense of equal treatment and justice as equity is that the latter focuses on equality of educational *opportunity*. This idea is more egalitarian; that is, it has as an explicit purpose – the reduction of social inequality. Authors who focus on equity seek not to overcome or reduce all inequalities, but to redress specifically those inequalities they consider unjust because they are outside the sphere of control of the subject bearing them.

For example, if two students in the same school and class take the same test, but one student has studied diligently for the test while the other has not, the expected differential outcome in their grades appears to be a justifiable inequality. Treating the students unequally, for example, by allowing one but not the other to redo the test in an attempt to improve the grade, would, then, be unfair. However, if it turns out that the student who has studied diligently has her own room in which she can study quietly, and does not have an after-school job, while the student who has not studied shares his room with two younger siblings for whom he is expected to care after school, the inequality appears less justifiable. The two students in this example may be said not to have the same opportunity to succeed, and under the conception of justice as equity it is justifiable to treat the students unequally to improve the equality of their opportunity.

Likely, the best-known proponent of the idea of justice as equity is American political philosopher John Rawls. In his influential *A Theory of Justice* (1971) he proposes the following two principles of justice:

1 Each person is to have an equal right to the most extensive total system of basic liberties compatible with a similar system of liberty for all.
2 Social and economic inequalities are to be arranged so that they are both: (a) to the greatest benefit of the least advantaged ... and (b) attached to office and positions open to all under conditions of fair equality of opportunity. (p. 266)

Rawls introduces the hypothetical device of the 'veil of ignorance' to argue that the principles of justice he has asserted are those that would be developed by any unbiased rational agent. If all designers of the social contract saw the world through a 'veil of ignorance' that made them unaware of any unearned advantage or disadvantage they held – because of gender, class, ethnicity, or other factors – their natural rational self-interestedness would lead them to design a social contract that protected and benefited the least well-off; after all, they themselves might be the least well-off! In other words: the 'veil of ignorance' is a metaphor that expresses the idea that the 'contingencies of the social world' should not affect the agreement reached about the principles of political justice (Rawls, 1993, p. 23).

Rawls affirms Kant's principle of just desert, allowing people to reap the differential fruits of differential labour, but also wishes to compensate for the injustice of undeserved disadvantage. He addresses the latter by elaborating on the 'principle of redress', which is implicit in the principles of justice he has laid out:

The principle holds that in order to treat all persons equally, to provide genuine equality of opportunity, society must give more attention to those with fewer native assets and to those born into the less favourable positions. The idea is to redress the bias of contingencies in the direction of equality. (Rawls, 1971, p. 86)

The principle of redress is the central principle in what are known as 'affirmative action' programmes in educational institutions and elsewhere. Affirmative action programmes seek in a variety of ways to redress the undeserved disadvantages typically suffered by women and minorities. In some places, a certain number or percentage of openings are reserved for members of groups that have suffered from undeserved social disadvantage because of racism, sexism, homophobia and other forms of discrimination. In other places, applicants are asked to identify whether they are members of groups that have suffered from undeserved social disadvantage, and this affects the criteria with which the application file is reviewed. The rationale is that applications submitted by members of socially advantaged and members of socially disadvantaged groups should not be evaluated with the same criteria, because the historical record of marginalization has negatively affected the opportunities of current members of this group to produce the same quality of application as members of groups who have historically had social privilege. The unequal treatment is justified as a form of redress or compensation for the long-lasting effects of unjustifiable unequal treatment in the past. The South African scholar Berte van Wyk (2006), for example, argues 'that equity and redress, through affirmative action, are needed, because past inequities will not disappear of their own accord; they must be actively dismantled' (p. 187).

Advocates of justice as equality often challenge the arguments and policies based upon justice as equity. Kodelja (2005) analyzes the lowering of assessment criteria for students from groups that have suffered from undeserved social disadvantage from both a utilitarian and Kantian perspective. He concludes that this practice is unjustifiable because,

> Past wrongs done to disadvantaged students cannot be either rectified or settled by actuating a new form of injustice, regardless of the fact that schools must fight for social justice and tend both the vocational and personal needs of all students equally well ... . (p. 71)

In this context it is significant that, in his discussion of the principle of redress, Rawls (1971) does not discuss affirmative action in the form of quotas or differential criteria described above. He limits himself to the comment that 'in pursuit of this principle greater resources might be spent on the education of the less rather than the more intelligent, at least over a certain time of life, say the earlier years of school' (p. 86).

The principle of redress offers a critique of Strauss' pragmatic view mentioned earlier, that although 'there is no reason to think that the common man and the gentleman are unequal, except by an accident of birth', the fact of the matter remains that only the 'gentleman' is properly equipped to rule a society in the best interest of all (York, 2008, pp. 73–74). Rather than accept the social reality that people of different backgrounds are unequally prepared for important leadership tasks, proponents of justice as equity would argue that this unjust social reality ought to be changed and that, in the meantime, those who bear unearned disadvantage should be offered additional opportunities.

JUSTICE AS DIFFERENCE

In the preceding three conceptions of justice, ideas about justice have been based on ontological assumptions. For Plato, for example, the idea that justice requires the harmonious relations between the different parts of society all doing what they do best is based on the belief that we are social beings and that we are differently talented. For Kant, the idea that justice requires the consistent application of an imperative is based on the ontological belief that humans are rational beings, and that the ethical imperative can be arrived at by rational thought.

However, do ideas about justice need to be based on ontological assumptions? The Lithuanian-French Jewish philosopher Emmanuel Levinas did not think so, and proposed to reverse the usual order of philosophical thinking: ethics, he argued, precedes ontology. According to Levinas, in other words, we cannot think about what it means *to be* without thinking about what it means *to be ethically bound by our relations with others*. Levinas (1985) maintains that the question of what makes one fully human – of what it means to *be* human – can only be answered ethically: 'I am I in the sole measure that I am responsible, a non-interchangeable I' (p. 101).

Ethics, for Levinas, is the response to a singular 'other', who calls me into responsibility and who remains ungraspably 'other' to me. The heading of this section, 'Justice as difference', is somewhat deceptive in this regard because the otherness of the other is not just any difference, but rather absolute alterity:

> Alterity is not at all the fact that there is a difference, that facing me there is someone who has a different nose than mine, different colour eyes, another character. It is not difference, but alterity. ... It is the beginning of transcendence. You are not transcendent by virtue of a different trait. (Levinas, in Levinas et al., 1988, p. 170)

An ethical relation with the other thus requires respecting her or his absolute alterity. This perspective radically changes the relation between ethics and equality: if ethics requires heeding the call of a singular other, then equality, which is incommensurable with singularity, cannot be an ethical principle. Levinas acknowledges, however, that an ethical relation can only be a relation of one singular person with another singular person. In most everyday situations – and certainly most educational situations – we find ourselves in relation with and called upon by more than one singular other. Such situations require us to move from ethics to politics, from the ethical principles of charity and love to the political principle of justice:

> I don't live in a world in which there is but one single [other]; there is always a third party in the world: he or she is also my other, my neighbour. Hence, it is important to me to know which of the two takes precedence. ... Must not human beings, who are incomparable, be compared? Thus justice, here, takes precedence over the taking upon oneself of the fate of the other. (Levinas, 1983/2001, pp. 165–166)

We are, according to Levinas, caught in a double bind of obligations: the obligation to respond to one singular other, but also to respond to a second other. Ethically speaking, the two others cannot be considered equal, but, politically speaking, I am *equally responsible* to both. Justice requires me to compare individuals to whom, ethically, any comparison does unpardonable violence.

The point of Levinas's views for education is not to despair about the ethical imperfection of educational situations, which typically require relations with more than one other, and thus justice and comparison. Rather, it is to remember that justice is necessary but secondary, that 'it is always ... from the responsibility for the other, that justice appears' and that 'love must always watch over justice' (pp. 166, 169). In situations where more than one student clamours for attention, in which more than one assignment awaits a response, teachers have no choice but to use principles of equality and justice – as long as they remember that, in the end, they are doing so in response and responsibility to persons who are singular others.

Jacques Derrida has been influenced by Levinas but, rather than follow Levinas's (later) view of ethics and justice as incommensurable but complementary, Derrida reclaims the concept of justice for ethics.[84] 'Justice is ... the experience of the other as other, the fact that I let the other be other, which presupposes a gift without restitution, without reappropriation, and without jurisdiction' (Derrida, 1993/2002, p. 105). Taking Derrida's cue, justice has no relation to equality; equality is a consideration in policies, laws and regulations – necessary, just as Levinas considers politics necessary, but ultimately inadequate for doing justice to the other. Gert Biesta (2001) analyzes the predicament this poses for educators: 'We could argue that the only way to do justice to the other, the other whom we dare to educate, is by leaving the other completely alone' (p. 51). However, 'this neglect (which would not even count as a border-case of education)' could not do justice to the student as other because it would ignore rather than receive her or him (p. 51). Tetsuya Takahashi (2008) acknowledges that the educational demands of Derridean justice are impossible, and at the same time he posits them as absolute: 'education that affirms the existence of children unconditionally, education that ... pardons children's faults unconditionally and education that receives the arrival of children with unconditional hospitality'. Such education is impossible but, to paraphrase Derrida's (1993/2002) words, an education that does not maintain a reference to the principles of unconditional affirmation and hospitality is an education that loses its reference to justice (p. 101).

THE ASSUMPTION OF INEQUALITY

Most educational scholars concerned with social justice today believe that education should contribute to greater equality between groups whose actual social inequality they consider unjustifiable. The inequality between men's and women's salaries for similar jobs, the unequal social valorization of reproductive and productive tasks, and the legal inequalities between same-sex and opposite-sex partnerships are examples of such inequalities. The French post-Marxist philosopher Jacques Rancière shares the belief in the justice of equality, but believes most arguments for it are wrongheaded. He contends that arguments that proceed from the assumption that people are unequal but, given the right interventions, can become equal, will forever postpone the achievement of equality:

> Equality is not a goal that governments and societies could succeed in reaching. To pose equality as a goal is to hand it over to the pedagogues of progress, who widen endlessly the distance they promise they will abolish. Equality is a presupposition, an initial axiom – or it is nothing. (Rancière, 2002, p. 223)

What Rancière means by his claim that equality ought to be an axiom is that the assumption that people are unequal is one of the strongest forces keeping people unequal. He aims to reverse the reasoning by hypothesizing that people are equal, and seeking to verify this hypothesis:

> What if equality, instead, were to provide the point of departure? What would it mean to make equality a presupposition rather than a goal, a practice rather than a reward situated firmly in some distant future so as to all the better explain its present infeasibility? (Ross, 1991, p. xix).

It should be pointed out that by 'equality' Rancière is not referring to material equality in income, housing conditions, and so on, as it is easy to establish that such inequalities exist. What interests him is an ontological equality or what he calls 'equality of intelligence'. As Ruitenberg (2008) has written elsewhere, in *The Ignorant Schoolmaster* Rancière (1987/1991) provides an account of the experiences of nineteenth century teacher Joseph Jacotot, who realized by chance that the assumption of equal intelligence worked as a self-fulfilling prophecy. By understanding that teacher and student are unequal in will but equal in intelligence, Jacotot was able to use his will to direct his Flemish students to use their intelligence to learn French by themselves, by studying a bilingual text.

One of Rancière's main scholarly disagreements has been with Pierre Bourdieu, whose work on the social reproduction of inequality in schooling has been influential in educational theory and policy. Rancière (1983/2003) mockingly refers to Bourdieu as a 'sociologist-king' – to parallel Plato's philosopher-king – who establishes his own superiority over and over again by explaining to the 'common people' how to interpret their unequal conditions properly and how to emancipate themselves. Rancière insists that the 'common people' do not need emancipatory pedagogues to overcome their inequality, as they already demonstrate their fundamental intellectual equality in many ways. It is up to the pedagogues to learn to recognize this equality.

JUSTICE, EQUALITY, AND THE NON-HUMAN WORLD

> A condition of environmental justice exists when environmental risks and hazards and investments and benefits are equally distributed without direct or indirect discrimination at all jurisdictional levels and when access to environmental investments, benefits, and natural resources are equally distributed; and when access to information, participation in decision making, and access to justice in environment-related matters are enjoyed by all. (Central and Eastern European Workshop on Environmental Justice, Budapest, 2003)

Environmental justice and related terms such as *environmental racism* and *ecological justice* refer broadly to how environmental goods and harms are distributed locally, nationally, and/or globally – and temporally as well, when the interests of future generations are taken into account. Those advocating one or another conception of environmental justice point to evidence that members of marginalized social groups suffer a disproportionate share of environmental harms, reflecting the intersection of multiple forms of oppression based upon nationality, race, class, gender, age, sexuality, and ability (Nelson, 1990; O'Sullivan, 1999, pp. 133–176). However, contemporary theorists of environmental justice disagree on whether or not non-human living beings should be seen to have moral status; and, if so, what *kind* of moral status should be acknowledged and how far that recognition should be extended. This dispute is not new: objections to anthropocentrism have been part of the modern environmental movement since the publication of Rachel Carson's *Silent Spring* (Fox, 1990, pp. 1–8). As Brian Baxter (2005) observes, however, there are still those whose objections to ecologically unsustainable practices are argued exclusively with reference to the negative consequences for *Homo sapiens*: 'Apparently it is only the possible losses to actual and future human beings, whether aesthetic, cultural, scientific, medical, economic, recreational and so forth, that count' (p. 1).

Advocates of environmental justice cite a variety of reasons – some empirical, some logical, and some moral – for believing anthropocentrism to be an unjustifiable prejudice (Fox, 1990, esp. pp. 13–19). Often, there is a link between the meta-ethical basis of the argument presented and both *the kind of moral standing* that is granted to non-human living beings, and *the categories of non-human beings* to which moral standing is extended. For example, Peter Singer (1989) has argued that, because the moral characteristic humans and non-humans share is the capacity to experience pleasure and pain, all sentient beings should participate equally in the utilitarian calculus of the greatest good. Therefore (for example), it is wrong to inflict severe suffering and death on non-human animals for the pleasure that human animals derive from access to cheap meat. Against Singer, Brian Baxter (2005) extends a liberal, more deontological 'justice as impartiality' position to argue that non-sentient living beings should also be understood to qualify for moral standing, on the grounds that having 'welfare interests' is the relevant characteristic we all share: 'all living creatures have a general interest in flourishing after their kind by developing their specific capacities' (p. 52). However, Baxter also argues that, when there is competition for scarce resources, it is just to assign unequal moral status to different groups of living creatures according to their greater or lesser capacities when compared to human moral agents. A third meta-ethical orientation is represented by authors and activists such as Arne Naess (1990) and Vandana Shiva (2005), whose calls for environmental justice appeal to the moral intuition that all living beings have intrinsic value, which puts humans and non-humans on a more equal footing as interconnected parts of the same community of life. Indeed, in some variations on this theme, humans lose their privileged place on top of the moral hierarchy:

> The position of the human subject is decentred, and the ecosystemic webs of life – the watersheds themselves – become sites invested with the highest moral value. The decentred subject is thus repositioned within a complex mosaic of mutual relationships among all living beings inhabiting a shared place. (Devon Peña, 1998, p. 49, as cited in Brandt, 2004, p. 98)

Conceptions of environmental justice have profound implications for identifying, not so much *how* educational goods should be equitably distributed, as *what* the content of those educational goods should be. From the view that humans have a duty to ensure that the rights of non-humans to existence and a fair share of environmental resources are protected (Shiva, 2005, p. 9), it follows that civic education must provide whatever knowledge and dispositions are needed to discharge these responsibilities competently (Baxter, 2005, pp. 83, 141, 156). Broadly speaking, the causes of environmental injustice are diagnosed as some combination of misguided moral motivation and inadequate ecological understanding, and so the educational remedies prescribed attend both to *why* and *how* we should assume responsibility for the rights of non-human living beings. This leaves plenty of room for substantive disagreement on what particular forms of education are essential for competent environmental citizenship arising from differences among the accounts of how and why environmental inequities persist. Those who locate the sources of not only environmental but also political, cultural, and economic injustices in deep structures of personal, social, and/or spiritual alienation seek forms of education that will inspire radical shifts in personal consciousness, social relations, and/or spiritual experience (Eisler, 1990; Orr, 2004; O'Sullivan, 1999). Many of these authors contest the idea that education's role is limited to compensating for larger social inequalities through redistribution of educational goods, and instead affirm that education is a site where the transformation of unjust social structures can be initiated. In programmes inspired by this view, students learn to question and critique the justifications for existing inequalities – whether between genders, ethnic groups, social classes, nations, or species – and to imagine and work towards a more just social order.

CONCLUSION

And so this chapter ends where it began, observing how the relationships between equality and justice on the one hand and education that is fair and promotes justice on the other are understood differently according to the distinct constellations of implicit assumptions, explicit beliefs, normative commitments, and practical priorities that characterize rival philosophical traditions. That educational initiatives to promote justice must locate local concerns within global horizons leaves us with the question 'How should those committed to a particular conception of justice pursue their cause in social and political contexts character-ized by radical disagreement?'

NOTE

84 This is in line with Levinas's earlier work *Totality and Infinity* (1961/1969), in which he writes, 'the relation with the other – that is to say, justice' (p. 89).

REFERENCES

Baxter, B. (2005) *A Theory of Ecological Justice*. London: Routledge.

Biesta, G.J.J. (2001) 'Preparing for the incalcuable'; deconstruction, justice, and the question of educa-tion, in G.J.J. Biesta and D. Egéa-Kuehne (eds), *Derrida & Education*. New York: Routledge, pp. 32–54.

Brandt, C.B. (2004) A thirst for justice in the arid southwest: the role of epistemology and place in higher education, *Educational Studies*, 36(1), 93–107.

Brighouse, H. (2006) *On Education*. New York: Routledge.

Derrida, J. (2002) The deconstruction of actuality (E. Rottenberg, trans.), *Negotiations: Interventions and Interviews 1971–2001*. Stanford, CA: Stanford University Press, pp. 85–116. (Original work published 1993.)

Eisler, R. (1990) The Gaia tradition and the partnership future: an ecofeminist manifesto, in I. Diamond and G.F. Orenstein (eds), *Reweaving the World: The Emergence of Ecofeminism*. San Francisco: Sierra Club Books, pp. 23–34.

Fox, W. (1990) *Toward a Transpersonal Ecology: Developing New Foundations for Environmentalism*. Boston: Shambhala Publications.

Haydon, G. (1998) Between the common and the differentiated: reflections on the work of the School Curriculum and Assessment Authority on values education, *Curriculum Journal*, 9(1), 5–21.

Kodelja, Z. (2005) Justice in education: two examples, *Metodicki Ogledi*, 12, 67–79.

Levinas, E. (1969) *Totality and Infinity* (A. Lingis, trans.). Pittsburgh, PA: Duquesne University Press. (Original work published 1961.)

Levinas, E. (1985) *Ethics and Infinity* (R. Cohen, trans.). Pittsburgh, PA: Duquesne University Press.

Levinas, E. (2001) Philosophy, justice, and love (M.B. Smith, trans.), in J. Robbins (ed.), *Is it Righteous To Be? Interview with Emmanuel Levinas*. Stanford, CA: Standard University Press. (Original work published in 1983.)

Levinas, E., Wright, T., Hughes, P. and Ainley, A. (1988) The paradox of morality: an interview with Emmanuel Levinas (A. Benjamin and T. Wright, trans.), in R. Bernasconi and D. Wood (eds), *The Provocation of Levinas: Rethinking the Other*. New York: Routledge, pp. 168–180.

MacIntyre, A. (1988) *Whose Justice? Which Rationality?* Notre Dame, IN: University of Notre Dame Press.

Naess, A. (1990) *Ecology, Community, and Lifestyle: Outline of an Ecosophy* (David Rothenberg, trans.). Cambridge: Cambridge University Press.

Nelson, L. (1990) The place of women in polluted places, in I. Diamond and G. F. Orenstein (eds), *Reweaving the World: The Emergence of Ecofeminism*. San Francisco: Sierra Club Books, pp. 173–188.

Orr, D. (2004) *Earth in Mind: On Education, Environment, and the Human Prospect,* 10th anniversary edn. Washington: Island Press.

O'Sullivan, E. (1999) *Transformative Learning: Educational Vision for the 21st Century*. Toronto: University of Toronto Press.

Rancière, J. (1991) *The ignorant Schoolmaster: Five Lessons in Intellectual Emancipation* (K. Ross, trans.). Stanford, CA: Stanford University Press. (Original work published 1987.)

Rancière, J. (2002) Afterword. *The philosopher and his Poor* (A. Parker, C. Oster and J. Drury, trans.). Durham, NC: Duke University Press.

Rancière, J. (2003) *The Philosopher and His Poor* (J. Drury, C. Oster and A. Parker, trans.). Durham, NC: Duke University Press. (Original words published in 1983.)

Rawls, J. (1971) *A theory of Justice.* Cambridge, MA: Harvard University Press.

Rawls, J. (1993) *Political Liberalism.* New York: Columbia University Press.

Ross, K. (1991) Introduction, in J. Rancière, *The ignorant Schoolmaster: Five Lessons in Intellectual Emancipation* (K. Ross, trans.). Stanford, CA: Stanford University Press.

Ruitenberg, C.W. (2008) What if democracy really matters? *Journal of Educational Controversy,* 3(1). Available online from http://www.wce.wwu.edu/Resources/CEP/eJournal/v003n001/a005.shtml

Siegel, H. (1988) *Educating Reason: Rationality, Critical Thinking, and Education.* New York: Routledge.

Shiva, V (2005) *Earth Democracy: Justice, Sustainability, and Peace.* Cambridge, MA: South End Press.

Singer, P. (1989) All animals are equal, in T. Regan and P. Singer (eds.), *Animal Rights and Human Obligations.* New Jersey: Prentice-Hall, pp. 148–162.

Takahashi, T. (2008) *On the Unconditional: Thinking of Education in Japan.* Paper presented at the 11th Biennial Conference of the International Network of Philosophers of Education, Kyoto, Japan.

Van Wyk, B. (2006) Exploring constitutive meanings of educational transformation in South Africa, *Interchange,* 37(3), 181–199.

York, J.G. (2008) Neoconservatism and Leo Strauss: the place of a liberal education, *Critical Studies in Education,* 49(1), 67–80.

28

Individual and Community Aims in Education

John P. Portelli and Francine Menashy

INTRODUCTION

The aim of this chapter is to identify the historical roots and qualities of two major and conflicting views regarding the controversial issue of aims in education: the individual and community stances. Before focusing on the educational aspects, including references to particular proponents of each, we offer some general background and the philosophical roots to the position. Given the long history of this dispute, it is impossible to offer very detailed accounts and argue for all the specific interpretations of the authors alluded to. However, where possible, we have provided direct quotes from the authors or references to secondary accounts so the reader will be able at her leisure to pursue the topic in greater depth. Although we believe that a natural account is not possible, we have attempted, however, to offer a fair account of each view. Following this, we offer a bird's eye view of the major criticisms and problems identified with each stance. The chapter ends with a suggestion regarding the possibility of an alternative position that goes beyond either of these views while acknowledging the realities of both the individual and the community.

INDIVIDUAL AIMS IN EDUCATION

Individualism

In order to adequately provide an examination of individual aims in education, we must first look to its philosophical foundation in individualism. Rooted in liberalism, individualism places the individual person at the centre of all analyses (Peters and Marshall, 1996). The concept has several descriptions, but for the study of educational aims, building on Watt (1989), the following six points will suffice:

1   Individuals are ends in themselves and have ultimate, intrinsic value.
2   Individuals hold primacy in human relationships; the social is secondary, for social institutions exist only for the benefit of the individual.
3   Individual rights are universal and inherent (natural) in contrast to group rights and responsibilities.
4   Individual autonomy needs to be preserved and protected by restricting the social or collective influence or control in various areas (economic, religious, etc.); hence, the belief that the uniqueness of individuals and their interests take precedence over group or collective perspectives.
5   Individual responsibility is valued over social responsibility.
6   Human beings are essentially competitive and aim to protect self-interest rather than altruistic or 'fraternal'.

As Triandis summarizes, individualism is a construct characterized by the individual defining himself or herself as independent, while subjugating most aims to personal goals (2001). Although a broad and varied concept, individualism, at its core, privileges individual human beings, while analyses of actions surrounding and benefits to wider society are considered secondary.

Instances of placing the individual at the core of analyses and action can be rooted in early Greek philosophy and in some Christian scriptures.[85] However, the eighteenth century and the Enlightenment are generally seen as the beginning of a true individualist movement in philosophy. Certain thinkers from this 'age of reason' stand out as prominent individualists. For instance, Adam Smith's economic theory posits that society functions at its best when all parties act to serve their own individual interests. Through a conception of human nature where human beings are motivated most by self-interest, competitiveness and ambition, Smith argues that government control over economic activity must be limited, and that the 'invisible hand' of the market will create stability and prosperity. Therefore, although proposing that self-interest does indeed serve wider society, it is the individual that is at the centre of Smith's philosophy (Triandis, 2001; Smith, 2003; Watt, 1989).

Kant's theory of morality also proposes the primacy of the individual. He argues that we ought to treat all individuals 'as ends in themselves' not as means to some other ends, for all humans are rational, independent beings (Kant, 1993/1785, p. 37). His categorical imperative, which posits that our moral actions as individuals must be universalizable, implies that humans are autonomous beings and that moral action is a result of each individual's rational behaviour. This is an individualist position, for each person is essentially capable of acting in accordance with his or her own reason, and therefore we determine our own actions (Kant, 1992/1785).

A third major Enlightenment thinker who relies heavily on individualism is the romantic Jean-Jacques Rousseau, who argues for individual freedom and autonomy as would be found in the 'state of nature'. Rousseau is critical of any restraint on human freedom, and believes in a 'social contract', into which a human being enters freely and individually agrees to follow, as opposed to coercion under the law. And so, Rousseau's political philosophy rests on the primacy of the individual, placing 'him' at the centre of society (Rousseau, 1987/1762). Rousseau's educational philosophy, which will be discussed later in this chapter, exemplifies his political theory.

John Stuart Mill's nineteenth century liberal political theory emphasizes individual liberty. His philosophy can be cited as a major force behind individualism, and notably he was an early defender of freedom of speech and open discourse, regardless of the views expressed. He argues that power over others, by government or otherwise, should only be exercised if it is to keep others from being harmed. Beyond this '[i]n the part which merely concerns himself, his independence is, of right, absolute. Over himself, over his own body and mind, the individual is sovereign' (Mill, 1991, p. 14). And Mill's dictum became a motto for the liberal tradition.

The twentieth century saw several theorists influenced by individualism and, in particular, the form of individualism found in Smith's economic philosophy. These include Freidrich Hayek (1994) and Milton Friedman (Friedman, 1990; Friedman & Friedman, 2002) who both argue against government intervention in individuals' lives and tie this to support of free-market capitalism. According to Giroux (2004),

[a]s a public pedagogy and political ideology, the neoliberalism of Friedrich Hayek and Milton Friedman is far more ruthless than the classic liberal economic theory developed by Adam Smith and David Riccardo in the eighteenth and nineteenth centuries. Neoliberalism has become the current conservative revolution because it harkens back to a period to American history that supported the sovereignty of the market over the sovereignty of the democratic state and the common good. (pp. 12–13)

As mentioned earlier, and as can be seen in this brief overview, individualism is rooted in social and political liberalism, which essentially places individual rights and freedoms as paramount. Whereas usually the liberal philosophical position on individualism is seen as a logical extension of the 'Enlightenment project', one also needs to note the influence of romanticism (as for example exhibited in Rousseau). The romantic element was influential in the development of individualism in education in the twentieth century. And, as will be argued later, many of the major critiques of individual aims in education can also be viewed as criticisms of both liberal philosophy's and romanticism's influence on educational theory.

Individualism and aims in education

The concept of individualism has been taken up in various ways by several philosophers of education. This chapter will briefly outline some crucial arguments made in support of an individualist focus in education, demonstrating how the concept has been adopted to differing degrees by some major theorists. The most notable of these are Rousseau, A.S. Neill, Ivan Illich, John Holt, Carl Rogers, P.S. Wilson and R.S. Peters. To some extent John Dewey can also be defined as an individualist, but, as will be shown, he also argued for community aims in education. The major common characteristic among these philosophers is that they all theorized about education under the framework of individualism, and view individual aims in education as paramount to other educational objectives.

Rousseau's 1792 treatise *Émile, or, On Education,* presents a fictional account of the ideal education of a young child – Émile – into adulthood, one that would enable the child to live as a moral adult in his corrupt contemporary society. Rousseau begins by outlining the early education of the boy, including physical development and emotional growth. Written from the perspective of the child's tutor, *Émile* exemplifies Rousseau's belief that society acts to corrupt human beings, who are, by nature, essentially good. He then proposes a moral education that focuses on an individual student, educated alone, so that his education can be based on his individual aptitudes, preferences and experiences. Émile 's education can be argued to be an early form of 'experiential' education, where a student learns not via books and direct instruction, nor in an institution, but through self-discovery and personal interest (Rousseau, 1979/1782).[86]

A.S. Neill, best known for establishing the 'Summerhill School', critiques most schools for suppressing individual nature and thereby the happiness of the child. As an alternative, Summerhill allows children the freedom of optional attendance to classes and to participate democratically in determining rules of the school. Teachers are meant to simply facilitate learning, for according to Neill: '... a child is innately wise and realistic. If left to himself [sic] without adult suggestion of any kind, he will develop as far as he is capable of developing' (Neill, 1997, p. 369). Neill's philosophy stresses the individual nature of the student and his or her freedom to choose how and when to learn. The influence of romanticism in Neill is obvious and perhaps the strongest of those who promoted individualism in education in the twentieth century.

The concern with individualism is also reflected in the work of Ivan Illich, best known for his educational philosophy of 'deschooling'. Illich argues that schooling as an institution either directly or indirectly teaches or a 'hidden curriculum' where:

> Students learn that education is valuable when it is acquired in the school through a graded process of consumption; that the degree of success the individual will enjoy in society depends on the amount of learning he consumes; and that learning about the world is more valuable than learning from the world. (Illich, 1981, p. 95)

In this, Illich is critical of school for disabling the freedom of individual students and hindering their access to the wider world from which they can truly learn. Illich advocates the establishment of an entirely new form of education, where students are free from coercion – an education that is based on 'conviviality' (Illich, 1981).

John Holt provides a similar critique of schools. He argues that schools are 'serving the purpose of someone other than the learner' (Holt, 1981, p. 6). He also supports deschooling, where he rejects educational resources, for they 'limit access to what is already known' (p. 7). Holt argues that students ought to be free to choose what and how they learn, and accuses the educational system as 'getting large numbers of people to learn what other people have decided will be good for them' (p. 6). However, he does have a conception of the 'community' in his educational philosophy, for it is outside the institution of schooling – in the community – that he believes students ought to learn: 'We need to think of a community, and a community of communities, in which it will be much easier for people to share what they know, or to get their questions asked and their curiosity satisfied' (p. 9). Despite this mention of community, however, Holt must first be considered an individualist in educational philosophy: he promotes the individual freedom of the student and how he or she learns, for it is considered unethical to impose an education determined by others. Carl Rogers also advocates for individual aims in education. In his *Freedom to Learn*, he accuses schools as imparting a 'meaningless' curriculum, which 'does not involve feelings or personal meanings; it has no relevance for the whole person' (1983, p. 19). Instead he advocates the 'whole-person learning' (p. 20) and 'significant, meaningful, experiential learning' (p. 19). However, unlike Illich and Holt, Rogers does not reject outright the institution of schooling. He believes that these aims can be achieved within the current system.

P.S. Wilson and R.S. Peters, two influential philosophers of education in the 1960s, defend the interests of the individual by focusing on the notion of 'intrinsic value'. However, their arguments, which are based on child-centred education (in the case of Wilson) and the nature of knowledge within the liberal education tradition (in the case of Peters) take different forms. In his provocative article 'In defence of bingo', Wilson (1967), following the romantic tradition, strongly distinguishes between education and schooling, and insists that education does not involve imposition or 'socially approved conditioning' (p. 113). Wilson believes that education ought to be intrinsically valuable, rather than extrinsically valuable, for example, a purely instrumental education, or a process which efficiently attempts to meet 'objective needs' and, for him, such a concept makes sense only in terms of 'what interests someone'. Hence Wilson (1971) concludes that an educational process ought to identify those goals students find interesting (and hence for him valuable) and help them see the significance of these goals. Peters, too, strongly links education to intrinsic value. But his conception of intrinsic value contrasts with that of Wilson, since for Peters something is intrinsically worthwhile because it possesses certain unique characteristics which necessarily relate it to some ultimate value. Based on this conception of intrinsic worth, Peters (1966, 1973) concludes that certain subjects (for example, philosophy, literature, mathematics and history) are intrinsically worthwhile and hence assist the individual to free himself or herself from the limitations of narrow usefulness.

Finally, John Dewey can be described as an individualist, in some respects, due to his focus on individual development and child-centred learning. He does not reject the institution of schooling, but instead feels that the interests of the students are central to the learning process: ' ... the value of recognizing the dynamic place of interest in an educative development is that it leads to considering individual children in their specific capabilities, needs, and preferences' (Dewey, 1997, p. 130). However, despite this focus on the individual student, Dewey also argues for community aims in education. Dewey's case for promoting a compatibility between community and individual aims will be discussed in more detail later in this chapter.

In this, most individualists in the history of philosophy of education are concerned with the individual freedom of the student, and critique the institution of school for neglecting the student's uniqueness and imposing a rigid curriculum on him or her. However, most of the theories presented thus far have been conceived by some as being radical, potentially rejecting educational institutions overall and positing a re-conceptualizing of the structure of schooling. Other contemporary educators also promote individualism in education, but stress that schooling ought to offer private benefits rather than gear toward benefiting the wider society, within the accepted institutional structure. This view presents schooling as meant to instil knowledge and skills that an individual can utilize to better enable him or her to work and live a self-sufficient life. To generalize, a more moderate individualist might view education at the primary level as meant to provide young children with basic skills, in line with the individual child's aptitudes and interests, in various subject areas that prepare them to operate safely and more independently in the world. These skills are then to be built upon in secondary school, along with knowledge in a wide range of subjects with the primary aim of providing practical skills, geared to the students' interests, which can be used in his or her future. Higher education, be it university level or technical training, can allow the student to specify his or her knowledge and thus develop a repertoire of more advanced skills, specific to the student, that can be used when he or she seeks employment. And, of course, most aspects of the spectrum of education can offer enjoyment and fulfilment while contributing to the student's development. This simple description provides a less radical illustration of an individualistic view on the aims of education, and one that is likely more familiar to the contemporary reader. A student studies to better him or herself, and schools are meant to contribute to the individual's development, while respecting his or her uniqueness, and to prepare that person for life outside the educational arena. The overarching and paramount aim of education is to serve the needs of the individual, but these are determined by Ministries of Education and interpreted by School Boards – in contrast to the needs determined by the students themselves or by the interests *of* the students (rather than what is *in* the interest of the student).

Therefore, a less radical philosophy of education for the individual generally argues that ' ... schooling has tended to suppress the individual. It has acted to promote uniformity and collectivism and has distracted the individual from the human challenge of achieving self-definition, self-expression, self-realization ... ' (Griffin and Nash, 1990, p. 2). Taking to heart liberal notions of individual freedom, schools should encourage competition between individual students and prepare students to live independent lives in society, respecting their uniqueness and distinct capabilities. A less radical view of individualism in education may support the traditional schooling structure, but asks how, within the institution, students can be granted a degree of freedom, along with 'independence, autonomy, self-reliance, initiative' – all towards the end of respecting the individual student and best strengthening his or her own learning process and outcomes (Hargreaves, 1980, p. 193).

COMMUNITY AIMS IN EDUCATION

Communitarianism and community

Arguments forwarding community aims in education are arguably rooted in the sociological and political theory of communitarianism. Communitarianism contrasts liberal political theory and its associated individualism. Political and social aims are thereby focused not on the individual, but the collective, or community. It is argued by communitarians that a focus on individual freedom and giving primacy to individual goals subjugates values held critical at a community level. Such twentieth century philosophers as Charles Taylor (1991) and Alasdair MacIntyre (1981) present critiques of liberalism while promoting communitarian theory.

Theories of communitarianism obviously embody specific concepts of community. However, there is no single definition for the term community. Historically, the concept can be traced back to the Greek *polis* and Christian scriptures. It was also found to be present in political philosophies of the Renaissance and Enlightenment, as well as in nineteenth century German philosophy, such as Hegel (Peters and Marshall, 1996). It then became prominently used by communitarians of the twentieth century mentioned earlier. Marx also utilized a specific concept of community in his work.

Community has been argued to be a vague and ambiguous concept embodying both a descriptive as well as normative element. Plant, Lesser and Taylor-Gooby provide the following description, denoting the varied meanings of the concept:

> Conventionally the term is used to refer to locality; interest group; a system of solidarity; a group with a sense of mutual significance; a group characterized by moral agreement, shared beliefs, shared authority, or ethnic integrity; a group marked by historical continuity and shared traditions; a group in which members meet in some kind of total fashion as opposed to meeting as members of certain roles, functions or occupational groups; and, finally, occupational, functional or partial communities. (Plant et al., 1980, p. 207)

As Peters and Marshall argue, 'community ... is an essentially contested and contestable concept with a cluster of complex descriptive meanings ranging from "locality" and "interest group" to "shared belief, authority and traditions" ' (1996, p. 22). Nash denotes certain community-based 'principles as core values, context-embeddedness, and tradition' (Griffin and Nash, 1990, p. 10).

Based on and building on the work of such authors, in our discussion of community aims in education, when we refer to community we mean either of the following:

- a group with a common aim supported by a set of values notwithstanding differences among members
- community as society at large.

Aims in education: community perspectives

Several educationalists have focused on community in education in terms of schooling by a community or developing the school into a democratic community or a community of inquiry (Goodman, 1992; Sharp, 2001). Our focus here, however, is to discuss education *for* the community, or community *aims* in education rather than the role of community in schooling or school as a community.

Generally speaking, in current educational practice, there are two broad conceptions of community aims: the first group of community aims we term 'social justice' aims in education; the second is 'economic' or 'utilitarian' aims in education. Both these concepts can be depicted as community aims, but they embody very different senses of both community and education.

Education for community in order to gain greater social justice in society has been advocated by several educational philosophers, most notably those considered 'critical pedagogues'. As described by Nash,

Communitarians emphasize that educators should be truly radical, progressive, and enlightened. Educators should get students to examine critically the ideals, the assumptions, the taken-for-granted habits and routines of the individualistic imperative in this culture. In part, this means that we need to explore the media's distortions of both individualism and communitarian loyalties. This also entails a cautious, non-doctrinaire, non-ideological dialectical conversation, one that reflects on the tensions between reason and experience, the individual and the community, tradition and social change, and human perfectibility and human frailty. (Griffin and Nash, 1990, p. 12)

Community education aiming at social justice then endeavours to change society via education. Education in this sense is transformative, and moves beyond the simple instilling of knowledge to encouraging students to critically examine their lives and communities. Education has wide social repercussions, and if students are not explicitly taught to examine certain assumptions – such that might be racist, sexist, homophobic, etc. – schooling will only reproduce injustices.

Several educational philosophers and theoreticians have advocated this position, including John Dewey (to some extent), George S. Counts, Paulo Freire, Bowles and Gintis, and various critical pedagogues, such as Maxine Greene, Antonia Darder, Henry Giroux, Peter McLaren, Roger Dale, Peter Mayo and Carmel Borg.[87]

John Dewey's 'progressive' education, whilst focusing on individual development, also posits the importance of community and societal aims in education. He provides the following description of community:

> Men [sic] live in a community in virtue of things which they have in common ... . What they must have in common in order to form a community or society are aims, beliefs, aspirations, knowledge – a common understanding – like-mindedness ... . (Dewey, 1997, p. 4).

He goes on to argue that a community can only continue to exist via communication of this common knowledge, which occurs through education. Therefore, education is crucial for the perpetuation of the society, or community, in which one operates. He states:

> Persons do not become a society by living in physical proximity ... . Individuals do not even compose a social group because they all work for a common end ... . If, however, they were all cognizant of the common end and all interested in it so that they regulated their specific activity in view of it, then they would for a community. But this would involve communication ... . Consensus demands communication. (pp. 4–5)

He then adds that 'all communication ... is educative' (p. 5). Therefore, Dewey posits that education, in the form of communication, is critical for the establishment and continued existence of a community. Community or society[88] for Dewey also involves an element of social justice, for its existence allows for a 'better future society' and 'the school is its chief agency for the accomplishment of this end' (p. 20).[89]

George S. Counts, a follower of Dewey, who focuses on the social aspect of education, is concerned about (1) an overemphasis on capitalism that diminished the role of democracy, and (2) the overemphasis on individualism by 'progressive education' since 'it constitutes too narrow a conception of meaning of education; it brings into the picture but one-half of the landscape'. (Counts, 1932, p. 6). Contrary to romantics in education and some progressive educators, he holds that human beings are not born free and they are not good by nature, and hence his emphasis on the formative role of education. Focusing on the moral aspect of education since he believes that 'building a good society is to a very large degree an educational process' (1932, p. 15), he argues that inevitably education cannot be neutral and that it necessarily involves some element of 'imposition' or influence.[90] Rather than leaving such a formative role of education to the hidden curriculum, he believes teachers should be conscious, of this role and make sure that they use it to improve society. According to Counts, to do so we need to formulate 'a theory of social welfare' (1932, p. 7) and 'plan for social reconstruction' (p. 27), and in the educational realm he proposes that schools 'establish an organic relation with the community' (p. 9). More explicitly and strongly he concludes: 'Until school and society are bound together by common purposes the program of education will lack both meaning and vitality' (1932, p. 17).

The political nature and social justice aims of education are very explicit in Paulo Freire. He stresses the transformative aim of education and critiques 'banking education', whereby students are perceived as simply receptacles of facts.

For Freire, education is a component of a process toward 'conscientization', which is his 'perennial phrase for critical self-consciousness' (Aronowitz, 1998, p. 18; Freire, 1998, 2003). Within banking education, conscientization is not possible, for the passive student does not have room to be critical of his or her own thoughts, nor those of others. A facet of conscientization is recognition of one's own conditioning, or an understanding that we are influenced by dominant discourses and must consciously strive to be critical of them (Freire, 2003). Freire is concerned that schools are rarely recognized as sites for social or political change, and instead are seen as politically neutral arenas for the production of a workforce (Freire, 1998). In contrast, a 'pedagogy of the oppressed' or 'pedagogy of the heart' or 'pedagogy of freedom' or 'pedagogy of indignation' or 'pedagogy of the unfinished' recognizes the inherently political nature of education, identifies and criticizes systemic inequities and, by focusing on human agency and courage, critical democracy, 'a universal human ethic' and hopes proposes an alternative vision of schooling that goes beyond excessive individualism as it recognizes the important relation between schooling and society. Such a vision of education, which conceives of an intricate relationship between the 'word' and the 'world', practice and theory, the formal curriculum and the substantive issues arising from the daily lives of people, teaching and learning, and subjectivity and objectivity, aims to bring about social transformation based on 'the ethics of human solidarity' (Freire, 1998, p. 116).

Building on the work of Freire, those scholars in the field of critical pedagogy, which include the likes of Henry Giroux, Peter McLaren, Stanley Aronowitz and Maxine Greene, share a common undertaking in being 'not only seriously committed to the ideal and practice of social justice within schools, but to the transformation of those structures and conditions within society that functioned to thwart the democratic participation of all people' (Darder et al., 2003, p. 2). In this, critical pedagogy emphasizes social justice-based, community aims in education. Giroux further argues for schooling for social justice, and ties education closely to his vision of community. He states: ' ... there is a dire need to develop pedagogical practices ... that bring teachers, parents, and students together around new and more emancipatory visions of community ...' (Giroux, 1988, p. 152). He contends that teachers must provide students with 'a relational or contextual understanding of how the knowledge they acquire in the classroom can be used to influence and transform the public sphere ...' by 'linking classroom experiences to the wider community' (Giroux, 1988, p. 201). For Giroux, not only is a school a community itself but also, in it, students are to be educated towards transforming the wider community. Other critical pedagogues, such as Peter McLaren and Stanley Aronowitz, argue similarly for a transformative aim, to change the wider community, in educative practice (Aronowitz and Giroux, 1985; McLaren, 1998). Critical pedagogues in general connect the transformative aim of education with that of *social* justice. As Kohli (2006) notes, it is crucial to distinguish the conception of social justice utilized by critical and feminist pedagogues from the mainstream liberal notion of social justice as based on the work of, for example, John Rawls, who assumes a liberal-capitalist worldview. In contrast, critical pedagogues and other anti-oppressive educators (including socialists, Marxists, neo-Marxists, feminists and Afro-centric scholars) have argued for the broadening of the conception of social justice based on an alternative conception of the good life. As Kohli (2006) concludes: 'Broadening the concept of social justice to include multi-cultural meanings, identities and differential power/privilege, affects our understandings of politics and political change. It also affects how we need to educate others about justice and injustice' (p. 100).

The second conception of education for the community is what we term the 'utilitarian' or 'economic' conception of education, where students are taught in order to best contribute to their community, or society, in economic terms.[91] Those who advocate this position argue that education is for the economic development of a nation, and students are presented as 'human capital'. It is argued that a well-educated workforce is critical for a country's economic growth and competitiveness, and so schooling ought to be designed with this aim. Curriculum content is then geared towards creating a profitable and efficient workforce.

Adam Smith posited an early utilitarian argument for education. Smith argues that capitalist society must be separated into classes, where a lower class is responsible for manual labour, primarily on assembly lines, putting into practice ideas and inventions of those produced by the higher class. This 'division of labour' is essential for efficient production of materials (Smith, 2003). As a result, Smith describes two tiers of schooling, one for the 'inferior ranks' and another for the higher classes, each instructing different curricula. The lower classes are only meant to have 'the most essential parts of education', including only basic skills in mathematics, science and language (Smith, 2003, p. 990).

It is this division of schooling which in turn perpetuates and supports the division of labour. One class is taught basic skills that enable them to effectively work on assembly lines, while the higher classes are taught more abstract and 'higher level' skills to prepare them to work as professionals. In this, education is designed with economic aims in mind. Smith's argument set the groundwork for views of education as a major contributor to economic development and capitalist society.

Much later, human capital theory of the twentieth century acted as proof that education is critical for economic development. The theory argues that the knowledge of a populace is a strong determinant of a country's economic growth. As argued by such scholars as Schultz (1989), schooling is a major means by which a nation can increase its human capital. Therefore, education is considered a determinant of economic growth. By inculcating not only basic skills but also knowledge that can be utilized by a workforce, schools act to increase production via providing an educated population. Such economists as Milton Friedman (2002) have argued for education as a means to increase human capital, advocating a view of education that contributes to the community, yet purely in an economic sense.

Possibly more importantly, this view has been adopted by many national governments and multilateral institutions, and has thus altered education programmes throughout the world with this economic, utilitarian aim in mind. For instance, the World Bank – the largest single donor to education programmes in the developing world – has adopted a policy surrounding 'Education for the knowledge economy', which 'refers to World Bank assistance aimed at helping developing countries equip themselves with the highly skilled and flexible human capital needed to compete effectively in today's dynamic global markets' (World Bank, 2008). The World Bank thus defends a notion of education for human capital, in assisting the wider national community in an economic sense.

Several developed nations have also promoted the concept of education towards human capital. These include the United States, United Kingdom, Canada and New Zealand, and have been labelled 'efficiency' or 'effectiveness' movements, where schooling is, first and foremost, aimed at creating a workforce which in turn will strengthen a nation's economy (Peters and Marshall, 1996; Taylor, 2001; Wrigley, 2003). Therefore, these education policies with a wider societal aim of expanding human capital, extend across both the developing and developed world.

In a nutshell there are two major contrasting aspects on community aims in education: one that strives for greater social justice, the other for economic development. In each case, however, and for different reasons, proponents of both aspects have issues with an individualist perspective and the way they respond to it leads to the different foci and ideological stances.

CRITICAL PERSPECTIVES ON INDIVIDUAL AND COMMUNITY AIMS OF EDUCATION

Now that we have identified the characteristics of the two positions regarding the individual and community aims in education as well as the degrees and varieties in each case, we will briefly focus on some of the major criticisms that have been raised with regard to each position.

Those who advocate for community aims in education generally do not lay critique on individual aims of education. In this, those on the side of community aims probably also believe that an individualistic component to education is not only acceptable but also crucial. It is *excessive* individualism, which is gained at a cost to certain community aims, that is most critiqued. From the education for social justice perspective, individualism and communitarianism in education are considered compatible insofar as individualism does not necessitate a neglect of other aims. For instance, an individualistic education can foster in the student a respect for other individuals, to view them as unique human beings worthy of tolerance and kindness. Individualism can then potentially contribute to social justice (Griffin and Nash, 1990; Hargreaves, 1980).

However, community aims in education, and in particular for social justice, are arguably hindered as a result of an excessive promotion of individualism in education. According to Hargreaves,

> ... the fallacy of educational individualism, namely the belief among teachers that if every individual is encouraged to grow and develop in the appropriate way, if the school can generate autonomous, self-reliant and self-realized individuals, then society can be left with confidence to take care of itself. (1980, p. 194)

An individualistic education then risks subjugating societal aims (Counts, 1932; Peters and Marshall, 1993, 1996; Portelli, 2001).

Moreover, assuming the primacy of the individual, essentially places that individual above others. In an educational setting, this may translate for the student into his or her own development as being more important than those of fellow peers. The focus on the self risks that the 'individual is almost idolized in isolation from the rest of the universe, as if the individual exists in and of himself or herself' (Portelli, 2001, p. 287).

This emphasis on the individual, as Portelli describes, 'generates the illusion that the school ... is distinct from, and impermeable to, the influences of other institutions, and once we fix the problems in school the rest will take care of itself' (2001, p. 288). The individualist perspective is then critiqued for both neglecting and simplifying the problems facing wider society (Counts, 1932; Goodman, 1992). Advocates of individual aims in education, Portelli continues, support 'the illusion that equality can be achieved or is taken seriously as long as we give the same opportunity to all' (2001, p. 288). This view ignores the multitude of societal and systemic factors that contribute to inequality and it conflates equality with equity. In this sense, what counts as 'natural' and 'normal' is in fact very biased and based solely on certain individual, liberal values. Such simplistic conceptions though, as Walkerdine (1983) has argued, need to be problematized and questioned rather than taken for granted and considered to be neutral, and hence, not assumed to be influenced by for example the categories of gender, race and social class (Delpit, 1988).

From the utilitarian, or economic perspective, a focus on the individual risks sacrificing wider society in terms of economic growth and competitiveness on a larger scale. However, this stance is more in line with an individualist position than the social justice argument. If an individual works hard and succeeds, even to purely further his or her own goals, he or she will likely contribute to the wider economy and society. This ambition may be instilled via an education that focuses on the individual. Therefore, an education for the individual may in fact contribute to human capital. However, it is more likely that an advocate for this view would press for an education that explicitly teaches skills that can be put in place to further the 'knowledge economy' as opposed to the individual's development.

Proponents of social justice aims in education have laid strong critiques on the exclusivity of economic aims in education, arguing that equality and other social justice-based goals of education are subjugated in favour of economic aims. These scholars, such as Freire (1998), Apple (1999, 2001, 2006), Dei and Karumanchery (2001), Hyslop-Margison and Sears (2006), and Hatcher (2007), critique the 'ethic of the market'. The criticism of such a neoliberal approach based on market economy is based on the ethical problem of turning students into mere objects that blindly consume and 'democracy is turned into consumption practices' (Apple, 1999, p. 10). While neoliberals claim that consumer choice will guarantee democracy, Apple (1999) notes that '[t]here is increasing empirical evidence that the development of "quasi-markets" in education has led to the exacerbation of existing social divisions surrounding class and race' (p. 10).

As argued by advocates of individualism, community aims in education neglect the uniqueness of the individual student and suppress his or her individuality. In this sense, education can be viewed as unethical for it obstructs the individual's right to grow and develop in whatever way is most appropriate for the student. An education rooted in communitarianism can be viewed as coercive, potentially authoritarian, and therefore unjust. It is this position that has fuelled many of the arguments made by 'free school' advocates. Students ought not to be forced to be 'one of the herd' for the benefit of wider society, even if it strengthens the economy or increases social justice. In both the education for social justice and for human capital senses, students are treated in an instrumentalist fashion, as a means to some other end (Griffin and Nash, 1990; Peters and Marshall, 1993).[92]

There are then several critiques levied against both sides of this debate. And it should be noted that many of the major tenets of each perspective have arisen out of critiques made of the other position. For instance, a contemporary individualist might posit that education neglects a student's uniqueness due to instruction that aims to teach for the wider community. At the same time, a communitarian may attribute a lack in the teaching of social justice to an overemphasis on individuality in education.

CONCLUDING REMARKS: GOING BEYOND INDIVIDUALISM AND COMMUNITARIANISM?

Traditionally, the two major positions of individualism and communitarianism in education have been popularly conceived as being irreconcilable since their basic assumptions and beliefs are deemed to be incompatible. In other words, the common discourse both in theoretical and professional circles is that either one favours individualism at the cost of communitarianism, or one favours communitarianism at the cost of individualism. We would argue that while one has to recognize the substantive differences in these positions, it would be beneficial not to essentialize or stereotype each of these stances. Neither would it be helpful to create a compromise between the two, for example, by considering some qualities of one stance and some from the other and somehow weaving them together to create a middle of the road position that would be suitable to both. In our view, a healthier position would be to address the realities of both individualism and communitarianism and address the issues that arise from a qualitatively different position that would go *beyond* either. Our position builds on aspects of both Dewey's and Freire's work as well as the work of some contemporary political theorists like Chantal Mouffe.

In *School and Society* (1900/1974), while commenting on the connection between schools and social progress, Dewey notes:

> All that society has accomplished for itself is put, through the agency of the school, at the disposal of its future members. All its better thoughts of itself it hopes to realize through the new possibilities thus opened to its future self. Here individualism and socialism are at one. Only by being true to the full growth of all the individuals who make it up, can society by any chance be true to itself. (p. 7)

In this classic quote, Dewey seems to be both critiquing the rigid dichotomy between individualism and society, and the rugged individualism (in contrast to the socially responsible individual), and also at the same time encouraging us to focus on the *relationship* between the two such that in a sense they become one. As Philip H. Phenix (1964) remarks: 'The proper question is not whether we shall choose to be individual or social, but what shall be the quality of the individual-social complex' (p. 46). And in the same vein as Dewey, in the Preface to the *Pedagogy of the Oppressed* (1971), Freire cautions us:

> ... the radical is never a subjectivist. For him the subjective aspect exists only in relation to the objective aspect (the concrete reality which is the object of his analysis). Subjectivity and objectivity thus join in a dialectical unity producing knowledge in solidarity with action, and vice versa. (p. 22)

The focus again is on the relationship between subjectivity and objectivity, the individual condition and the social condition.

The crucial and difficult question that the dialectically relational position has to face is the one that liberalism claims to solve by focusing on individual rights and procedural values (e.g. open-mindedness, impartiality, non-repression and non-discrimination, etc.): What do we do when the individual and social realms conflict? How do we resolve this tension? Our suggestion of a qualitatively different perspective implies that rather than resolving these tensions in the abstract or eliminating the conflict by favouring individualism over communitarianism or vice versa, we would be better off if we analyse the tensions in concrete, deal with them in a non-antagonistic manner and occasionally allow for different yet possibly equally plausible positions to flourish at the same time (i.e. go beyond the consensual model of democracy). This suggestion would also entail that we radicalize the liberal values. Hence, for example, rather than focusing on equality, we need to focus on equity, rather than expecting that procedures can always be rational and lead to a rational resolution, we need to focus on specific issues of identities. Mouffe (1993), while distinguishing between 'liberal democracy' and 'liberal democratic capitalism', argues: 'A healthy democratic process calls for a vibrant clash of political positions and an open conflict of interests. If such is missing, it can too easily be replaced by a confrontation between non-negotiable moral values and essentialist identities' (p. 6). Mouffe's focus once again is on the relational aspect referred to earlier. Her suggestion, which we believe will contribute to the qualitatively different position regarding the relationship between the individual and society, is to focus on an agonistic rather than antagonistic form. She concludes:

> While antagonism is a we/they relation in which the two sides are enemies who do not share any common ground, agonism is a we/they relation where the conflicting parties, although acknowledging that there is no rational solution to their conflict, nevertheless recognize the legitimacy of their opponents. They are 'adversaries' not enemies. This means that, while in conflict, they see themselves as belonging to the same political association, as sharing a common symbolic space within which the conflict takes place. We could say that the task of democracy is to transform anatagonism into agonism. (Mouffe, 2005, p. 20)

Such a procedural *and* substantive way of being in the world defies both the liberal, neutralized individualism as well as the standardized, consensual communitarianism.

With regard to education, such a dialectically relational stance would have several implications. At a general level, for example, educational discourse in the field would have to go beyond the simplistic 'pendulum swings' metaphor whereby, as the popular saying goes, 'what goes around, comes around'. It is very commonly held among practicing educators (including policy-makers) that the emphasis on either individualism or the community is simply a matter of taste and the popularity of either varies from era to era, depending on what is trendy.[93] At a more specific level, for example, the issue of whether or not we should be dealing with controversial issues and how we should be dealing with such issues, would need to go beyond the simplistic stance that we should not do things that 'offend' other people. Hence, it is commonly and too hastily concluded, if parents do not wish their child to deal with certain controversial issues in schools, that individual views should hold or, alternatively, parents have to abide by what the majority happen to accept. Again, the position suggested in this concluding section would entail that we engage in serious discussions, even passionate ones, recognizing that disagreements do not necessarily amount to an offence. Our position is consistent with a more substantive notion of democratic education that distinguishes between the private and individual domains, as well as the communitarian and consensual domains. A more substantive democracy accepts the inevitability of both individual and communitarian aspects in education without accepting the primacy of the private and the consensual.

NOTES

85 Although Christian scriptures also support a communitarian perspective. Yet some 'Christian philosophers', for example St. Augustine, emphasize the importance of the individual in learning. See his dialogue *On the Teacher*.

86 Rousseau also offers an account of an ideal education of a female student – Sophie – which bears little resemblance to that of Émile. Sophie's education is primarily meant to create a good wife for Émile, to make her an adequate homemaker and mother.

87 While some do not explicitly state that they advocate education with a community aim, we believe their work can indeed be viewed as such.

88 For Dewey, the terms 'community' and 'society' seem to be interchangeable.

89 However, despite Dewey's arguments for the importance of education for a community, as mentioned earlier, he does have an equally charged argument in favour of education for individual development. The compatibility of these two aims will be discussed later in this chapter.

90 For Counts not all kind of imposition amounts to indoctrination.

91 This conception of education is, in fact, that of which most critical pedagogues are most critical, and some would even argue that it is not a community aim, but instead is more an individualist position – these critiques will be presented later in this chapter.

92 This critique, which questions the ethical grounding of a communitarian view, is rooted in liberal political theory and, more specifically, libertarianism.

93 For example, the 1950s focused on a return to the basics, the 1960s advocated child-centred education, the 1970s emphasized education for employment and vocational education, the 1980s heralded whole language, and the 1990s re-emphasized standardization, excellence and accountability.

REFERENCES

Apple, M. (1999) Freire, neo-liberalism and education, *Discourse: Studies in the Cultural Politics of Education*, 20(1), 5–20.

Apple, M. (2001) Comparing neo-liberal projects and inequality in education, *Comparative Education*, 37(4), 409–423.

Apple, M. (2006) Understanding and interrupting neoliberalism and neoconservatism in education, *Pedagogies: An International Journal*, 1(1), 21–26.

Aronowitz, S. (1998) Introduction, in *Pedagogy of freedom: Ethics, democracy, and Civic Courage*. Lanham: Rowman and Littlefield Publishers, Inc.

Aronowitz, S. and Giroux, H.A. (1985) *Education Under Seige: The Conservative, Liberal, and Radical Debate over Schooling*. Massachusetts: Bergin and Garvey Publishers, Inc.

Counts, G.S. (1932/1969) *Dare the School Build a New Social Order?* New York: Arno Press and the New York Times.

Darder, A., Baltodano, M. and Torres, R. D. (2003) Critical pedagogy: an introduction, in A. Darder, M. Baltodano and R.D. Torres (eds), *The Critical Pedagogy Reader*. New York: Routledge Falmer, pp. 1–21.

Dei, G. and Karumanchery, L. (2001) School reform in Ontario: the 'Marketization of Education' and the resulting silence on equity, in J.P. Portelli and R.P. Solomon (eds), *The Erosion of Democracy*. Calgary, AB: Detselig, pp. 189–215.

Delpit, L. (1988) The silenced dialogue: pedagogy and power in educating other people's children, *Harvard Educational Review*, 58(3), 280–299.

Dewey, J. (1900/1974) *School and Society*, Chicago: University of Chicago Press.

Dewey, J. (1997; originally published 1916) *Democracy and Education: An Introduction to the Philosophy of Education*. New York: The Free Press.

Freire, P. (1998) *Pedagogy of Freedom: Ethics, Democracy, and Civic Courage*. Lanham: Rowman and Littlefield Publishers, Inc.

Freire, P. (1970/2003) *Pedagogy of the Oppressed*. New York: Continuum.

Friedman, M. (2002) *Capitalism and Freedom*. Chicago: University of Chicago Press.

Friedman, M. and Friedman, R. (1990) *Free to Choose: A Personal Statement*. San Diego, CA: Harcourt.

Giroux, H.A. (1988) *Schooling and the Struggle for Public Life: Critical Pedagogy in the Modern Age*. Minneapolis: University of Minnesota Press.

Giroux, H.A. (2004) The terror neoliberalism: rethinking the significance of cultural politics, *College Literature*, 32(1), 1–19.

Goodman, J. (1992) *Elementary Schooling for Critical Democracy*. New York: SUNY Press.

Griffin, R.S. and Nash, R.J. (1990) Individualism, community, and education: an exchange of views, *Educational Theory*, 40(1), 1–18.

Hayek, F. (1994) *The Road to Serfdom*. Chicago: University of Chicago Press.

Hargreaves, D.H. (1980) A sociological critique of individualism in education, *British Journal of Educational Studies*, 28(3), 187–198.

Hatcher, R. (2007) 'Yes, but how do we get there?' Alternative visions and the problem of strategy, *Journal of Critical Education and Policy Studies*, 5(2).

Holt, J. (1981; originally published 1973) A letter, in J.M. Rich (ed.), *Innovations in Education: Reformers and Their Critics*. Boston: Allyn and Bacon, Inc., pp. 6–8.

Hyslop-Margison, E.J. and Sears, A.M. (2006) *Neo-Liberalism, Globalization and Human Capital Learning: Reclaiming Education for Democratic Citizenship*. Dordrecht, the Netherlands: Springer.

Illich, I. (1971/1981) The alternative to schooling, in J.M. Rich (ed.), *Innovations in Education: Reformers and Their Critics*. Boston: Allyn and Bacon, Inc., pp. 94–103.

Kant, I. (1993/1785) *Grounding for the Metaphysics of Morals*. Cambridge: Hackett Publishing Company, Inc.

Kohli, W. (2006) What is social justice education? in W. Hare and J.P. Portelli (eds), *Key Questions for Educators*. Halifax, NS: Ephil Books, pp. 98–101.

McIntyre, A. (1981) *After Virtue*. Notre Dame, IN: University of Notre Dame Press.

McLaren, P. (1998) *Life in Schools: An Introduction to Critical Pedagogy in the Foundations of Education*. New York: Longman.

Mill, J.S. (1863/1991) *On Liberty and Other Essays*. Oxford: Oxford University Press.

Mouffe, C. (1993) *The Return of the Political*. London: Verso.

Mouffe, C. (2005) *On the Political*. London: Routledge.

Neill, A.S. (1960/1997) Summerhill, in S.M. Cahn (ed.), *Classic and Contemporary Readings in the Philosophy of Education*. New York: McGraw-Hill.

Peters, R.S. (1966) *Ethics and Education*. London: Allen and Unwin.

Peters, R.S. (ed.) (1973) *The Philosophy of Education*. London: Oxford University Press.

Peters, M. and Marshall, J. (1993) Beyond the philosophy of the subject: liberalism, education and the critique of individualism, *Educational Philosophy and Theory*, 25(1), 19–39.

Peters, M. and Marshall, J. (1996) *Individualism and Community: Education and Social Policy in the Postmodern Condition*. London: The Falmer Press.

Phenix, P (1964) *Realms of Meaning: A Philosophy of the Curriculum for General Education*. New York: McGraw-Hill.

Plant, R., Lesser, H. and Taylor-Gooby, P. (1980) *Political Philosophy and Social Welfare: Essays on the Normative Basis of Welfare Provision*. London: Routledge and Kegan Paul.

Portelli, P. (2001). Democracy in education: beyond the conservative or progressivist stances, in W. Hare and J.P. Portelli (eds), *Philosophy of Education: Introductory Readings,* 3rd edn. Calgary: Detselig Enterprises Ltd, pp. 279–294.

Rogers, C. (1983). *Freedom to Learn for the 1980s*. Columbus: Charles E. Merrel Publishing Company.

Rousseau, J. (1979/1782) *Émile , or on Education*. New York: Basic Books.

Rousseau, J. (1987/1762) *On the Social Contract*. Cambridge: Hackett Publishing Company.

Schultz, T.W. (1989) Investing in people: schooling in low income countries, *Economics of Education Review,* 8(3), 219–223.

Sharp, A.M. (2001) The community of inquiry: education for democracy, in W. Hare and J.P. Portelli (eds), *Philosophy of Education: Introductory Readings,* 3rd edn. Calgary, AB: Detselig, pp. 295–305.

Smith, A. (2003, originally published 1776). *The Wealth of Nations*. New York: Bantam.

Taylor, A. (2001) Education, business, and the 'knowledge economy', in J. Portelli and R.P. Solomon (eds.), *The Erosion of Democracy in Education: Critique to Possibilities*. Calgary: Detselig.

Taylor, C. (1991) *The Malaise of Modernity*. Toronto: Anansi Press.

Triandis, H.C. (2001) Individualism and collectivism, in D. Matsumoto (ed.), *The Handbook of Culture and Psychology*. Oxford: Oxford University Press, pp. 35–50.

Walkerdine, V. (1983) It's only natural: rethinking child-centred pedagogy, in A. Wolpe and J. Donald (eds), *Is There Anyone Here from Education?* London: Pluto.

Watt, J. (1989) *Individualism and Educational Theory.* Dordrecht: Kluwer Academic Publishers.

Wilson, P.S. (1967) In defence of bingo, *British Journal of Educational Studies*, 15(1), 5–27.

Wilson, P.S. (1971) *Interest and Discipline in Education.* London: Routledge and Kegan Paul.

World Bank. (2008) Education for the knowledge economy. Retrieved March 2008 from: http://www.worldbank.org/education.eke.asp

Wrigley, T. (2003) Is 'school-effectiveness' anti-democratic?, *British Journal of Educational Studies*, 51(2), 89–112.

29

Art and Aesthetics in Education

Constantin Koopman

INTRODUCTION

Ever since Plato (2005) stated that the divine encompasses beauty, truth, and goodness, the realm of aesthetics has been associated with those of knowledge and morality.[94] Nevertheless, aesthetics has received much less attention than its two companions in philosophy and educational theory. During the last two decades, hardly any book has appeared dealing with aesthetic education in its full scope. Occasional papers by philosophers of education mainly deal with the connection between moral education and aesthetic education. On the other hand, authors on philosophical aesthetics demonstrate little interest in education issues. The typical contribution to the *Journal of Aesthetic Education* discusses an aesthetic issue as such, addressing implications for education only in a short, obligatory concluding section.

By contrast, educators from specific art disciplines (music in particular) have shown increasing interest for philosophical issues in recent times. Because many of these authors have a background as teachers, they focus on issues relating to art education in the school. They tend to write only about their own discipline – music, visual art, literature, etc. – and their discussions easily cross the border between philosophical questions and issues relating to practical pedagogy, learning theory, and psychology.

In this chapter, I review the present state of aesthetic education.[95] I start by discussing definitions of art and the aesthetic. In the following section I discuss various conceptions of art education that have emerged in the past. In the final section, I consider some current issues in art education, and I end by giving some clues to approach the changed situation.

DEFINING ART AND THE AESTHETIC

'Art' and 'the aesthetic' are often used interchangeably in aesthetic discourse. The realm of aesthetics is equated with art, while art is seen as centring around aesthetic appreciation. Yet the aesthetic and art are by no means coextensive. Phenomena of nature and all kinds of artefacts that do not pretend to be art can be approached from an aesthetic point of view. 'Aesthetic' does not pick out a certain kind of object. Rather it denotes two things: (1) a certain property, feature or aspect of things (e.g., beauty or grace), and (2) a certain kind of attitude, perception, or experience (Levinson, 2003: 3). By contrast, the arts primarily involve a certain kind of practice, activity or object. Art can be studied not only from an aesthetic standpoint but also from a range of perspectives, including the social, political, religious, didactic, and economic ones.

How could this equation of 'the aesthetic' and 'art' come about? Art is generally seen as the realm that offers the most varied and richest opportunities for encountering aesthetic properties and having aesthetic experiences (Levinson, 2003: 4). For this reason, reflection on art education has almost exclusively focused on education in the arts. But how can 'art' and the 'aesthetic' be defined?

Art

Until the 1950s definitions of art were based on some purported essence. From Antiquity to the eighteenth century art has been defined in terms of *imitation*. Art was understood as the imitation of nature. Modern versions of the theory use the more precise concept of representation instead of imitation. Works of painting, sculpture, literature, drama, and film do indeed often imitate or represent all kinds of phenomena. It is also clear, however, that many artworks do not appear to imitate or represent anything at all – for instance non-figurative art, music or functionalist buildings. It could further be doubted whether imitation is the sole or main function of imitative art. Moreover, the concept of imitation is unclear: Does it denote merely representation of external phenomena or also of inner states of mind?

The *expression* theory of art, which emerged in the eighteenth century but was particularly influential in the nineteenth century, more clearly specifies what art is about: emotions. But while expression catches the most salient aspect of a significant class of artworks, including many ones not aimed at representing external reality, expression is neither a necessary nor a sufficient feature of art: there are plenty of artworks that are emotionally neutral, while not every expressive phenomenon can count as an artwork.

The *formalist* theory defines art in terms of form. Developed by the music critic Eduard Hanslick as early as 1854, formalism became particularly influential when the art critic Clive Bell (1914) defined art as significant form. Although most artworks do indeed seem to be the result of a careful process of structuring and balancing, definitions of art in terms of form have been rejected no less than definitions based on imitation and expression. How are we going to specify the necessary and sufficient conditions for *artistic* form as opposed to the non-artistic form of ordinary objects?

While such theories of art fail to define a common core of all art, they remain important in that they provide major criteria for interpreting and assessing artworks. Surely, the interest and value of most artworks lies in their form, expressive content or representation, or in a combination of these aspects. The same goes for alternative theories of art focusing on play (Schiller, 1795/1967), symbol systems (Goodman, 1976), problem solving, and aesthetic experience (Beardsley, 1982). They point out additional sources of artistic value.

Stephen Davies (1991) calls definitions that try to identify some intrinsic property shared by all artworks functionalist. Functionalist definitions attempt to define artworks according to the specific point or purpose they serve. By contrast, procedural definitions of art pick out artworks by a specific kind of procedure followed in creating them. George Dickie's institutional theory of art presents the best-known definition of this kind: 'A work of art is an artifact of a kind created to be presented to an artworld public' (Dickie, 1992: 112). Dickie admits that his definition is circular: art is defined in terms of the artworld, which in turn is defined in terms of art and the artist.

A final option is to define art historically, rather than functionally or procedurally. Jerrold Levinson (1990: 38–39) defines an artwork as 'a thing that has been seriously intended for regard-as-a-work-of-art – i.e., regard in any way pre-existing artworks are or were correctly regarded'. This definition emphasizes that how we approach art always in some way builds on how we understand artworks we encountered in the past. The problems of this definition include the issue of whether the artist's intention determines whether something is a work of art, and how to distinguish correct ways of regarding artworks from incorrect ones (Davies, 1991: 172–173).

Dickie's institutional and Levinson's historical definitions do not directly point to substantial values in art, as the imitation, expression, formalist, play, and symbol theories do. Nonetheless, they also direct our attention to important dimensions that should be addressed in art education: the social and historical contexts in which artistic practices take place.

The aesthetic

The concept of the aesthetic has been discussed much less than the concept of art. 'Aesthetic' derives from the Greek word 'aisthesis', which denotes sensuous engagement with some external object. Wolfgang Welsch (1997: 8–15) points out that the aesthetic has two sides, a subjective one and an objective one. One the one hand, we have *sensation*, which has the nature of feeling and is particularly related to pleasure; on the other hand, there is *perception*, which is directed to the features of the object and is cognitive in nature. Aesthetic *pleasure* transcends the level of pleasures related to our direct vital needs, such as the pleasure of a cold drink on a warm summer day. Aesthetic pleasure is a reflexive pleasure, one which judges its objects not as necessary or useful, but as beautiful, harmonic, sublime or superior. On the cognitive side, the side of perception, 'aesthetic' refers to the relations between the elements of the object. Here the concepts of *form* and *proportion* come to the fore. *Beauty* relates to the perfecting form of the sensuous (Welsch, 1997: 13).

In this way, Welsch demonstrates how the key concepts of aesthetic discourse – sensation, perception, feeling, pleasure, form, proportion – arise from the basic notion of the aesthetic as the sensuous. Welsch's approach is to uncover the web of relationships between these key concepts. This appears to be more fruitful than trying to define necessary and sufficient conditions for the aesthetic, because it is doubtful that such definitions can be found.

Even the concept of beauty appears to be unfit to delineate the aesthetic realm. The sublime and the picturesque are traditional categories of the aesthetic, while in the twentieth century even categories like the ugly, the repulsive, and the disgusting have come to be seen as possible dimensions. On the other hand, it can be doubted whether such alternative categories really challenge the central position of beauty within the aesthetic realm. Typically, it is by appreciating examples of beauty that one gains a sense of the aesthetic. I doubt that individuals might come to know what 'aesthetic' means by merely encountering instances of the ugly, the repulsive or even the sublime. Thus, while the aesthetic realm is not confined by the beautiful, beauty may be the most important concept. It is not surprising, then, that dictionaries in all Western languages connect the aesthetic with beauty.

The concepts of the aesthetic attitude and aesthetic experience have been put forward to elucidate the special nature of the aesthetic realm. They have met with scepticism in Anglo-American aesthetics, however. Philosophers have denied that a specific kind of attitude or perception is necessary to relate properly to aesthetic phenomena (Hospers, 1982: 350–353.) Likewise, the concept of aesthetic experience, widely used in artistic discourse, has come under attack. It has been doubted that what is called aesthetic experience has a phenomenally distinctive character that could be distinguished from other kinds of rewarding experiences. Noël Carroll (1999: 202–203) defends a minimal definition that is formal rather than phenomenal; aesthetic experience comprises the detection of aesthetic properties and the appreciation of design.

In contrast to such reductions of aesthetic experience to little or nothing, theorists of art education have employed aesthetic experience as a key concept in the second half of the past century, interpreting it in a much more generous way.

In the United Kingdom, Michael Ross (1982, 1984, 1985) and Peter Abbs (1987) were among the main proponents of 'the aesthetic imperative'; in the United States, Ralph Smith and Bennett Reimer (1989) played a key role in promoting art education as the education of aesthetic experience. Ralph Smith (discussed in Muelder Eaton and Moore, 2002: 15) characterizes aesthetic experience as something essentially gratifying, that is, rewarding our attention in a rich expansive variety of ways. Aesthetic experience has both an emotive aspect (a propensity for delight or despair) and a formative aspect (its generation of a creative reaction to familiar things). It has also cognitive value in that it invites us to deploy our skills in interpreting and reinterpreting the world.

CONCEPTIONS OF ART EDUCATION

In the past decades, art education has often been defined as the cultivation of aesthetic experience as a rich and unified kind of experience. Alternative conceptions of art education have been proposed, focusing on different aspects of engagement in the arts: feeling, cognition, and ethos.

Art education as education of feeling and emotion

From the 1960s to about 1980 the view of art as self-expression was influential in formal education. The arts were seen as a particularly apt means by which children could learn to express their emotions. Finding an adequate expression of one's emotion was seen as more important than acquiring artistic technique. Although this view has had considerable impact on primary and secondary education, theorists of art education strongly opposed it. Reimer (1989: 44) argues that artistic creation can never be a matter of spontaneously expressing one's emotions. The creation of an expressive artwork requires, in addition to intense involvement, a 'working out' process. This process involves controlled thought rather than emotional discharge.

Reimer dismisses art education as self-expression, but he does argue that the arts can educate feeling. Following Suzanne Langer, he conceptualizes feeling as a dynamic and organic process: 'at every moment our feelings are in motion, developing, changing, waxing and waning, gathering energy to a peak, then fading to quietude' (Reimer, 1989: 45–47). Language can point at these feeling processes, but it cannot be used to explore and clarify the complexities in a phenomenological sense. This, exploring and clarifying feelings, is precisely what the arts can do. Instead of 'conceptualizing about' feeling, they give us an 'experience of' feeling (Reimer, 1989: 50–52). Whereas in our everyday life feelings occur in a haphazard way, artworks explore and shape our feeling processes in systematic ways. The deeper the sense of feeling captured, the better a work of art is. In this way, art allows us to discover and appreciate the richness and profundity of human feeling.

Reimer develops a phenomenological account, dealing with the dynamic processes of feeling we live through when experiencing art. By contrast, Ronald Hepburn (1998) and David Best (1985, 1989) take a more cognitive approach, focusing on the concept of emotion. Emotions have objects: I have fear of x (e.g., my exam), I am delighted about z (Hepburn, 1998: 171–172). These two authors stress the rationality of emotion: emotions can be adequate or inadequate, justified or unjustified. Thus, they can be educated.

Best (1989: 83) argues that feeling in the arts depends on reason rather than being opposed to it: 'in learning to understand the art form one is *ipso facto* extending the range of feelings it is possible to have'. Hepburn (1998: 173–177) discusses the various ways in which the arts can educate emotion. First, engaging in art, especially literary art, leads to the *enlargement* of our emotional experience. By developing language in which richer content can be conveyed, the author of literature enables us have a much wider range of emotion and perception. Secondly, literature develops the precision of emotion and thus transcends the emotional cliché and blurred emotional experiences of everyday life. '[T]he resources of literature make it possible for a reader to experience quite precise emotional responses to complexes normally beyond his powers to hold together in perception or imagination, and about which he therefore tends to have confused and anxious emotions' (1998: 173). Thirdly, in going beyond the emotion-clichés, art also enhances one's personal freedom. Aesthetic education can introduce pupils to countless alternative possibilities for feeling. By coming to understand our feelings and urges better, we can gain better control of them. Fourthly, besides enlarging and clarifying our emotions and allowing increased control over them, art also has the power of revivifying emotion. Art is an antidote to the numbing effect of emotional habits. Finally, education of emotion through art helps us to understand other people's behaviour and to manage our relations with them.

Art education as cognitive growth

Art has been seen as enhancing various cognitive functions, ranging from perception to knowledge, insight, and wisdom.

Percipience

Harold Osborne (discussed in Smith, 1989: 35–38) argued that the pre-eminent function of the arts is to stimulate and expand direct perception – 'percipience'. When engaging in art, we guide our attention over a limited sensory field so that the field's properties come into focus according to their own inherent intensities and the particular ways they are structured. Percipience is synoptic perception of the artwork's fusion of subject and form. It is unusually vivid, full, and complete. Such perception differs from other cognitive modes like ordinary seeing, conceptual analysis, and problem-solving, and therefore it should be deliberately cultivated. While Osborne concedes that percipience can occur in many areas of human life, he argues that only works of fine art and their counterparts in nature are capable of developing percipience to the fullest.

Symbol system

Nelson Goodman has conceived art as a symbol system rather than as a phenomenon of direct perception. He argues that there are five 'symptoms' of aesthetic symbols (Goodman, 1976; cf. Smith, 1989: 93–94).

1 Syntactic density (density of structure): the finest difference in certain respects (e.g., colour, movement, sound) constitutes a difference between artistic symbols.
2 Semantic density (density of meaning): symbols are used to denote the finest differences of meaning. Thus, art usually employs the most subtle differences in syntax to convey the most subtle nuances of meaning.
3 Relative repleteness: many aspects of the art symbol are significant; artworks are full of meaning.
4 Multiple and complex reference: a still life refers to the depicted objects themselves (flowers, fruits), but may also point to wealth, transience, vanity, the skill of the artist, etc.
5 Exemplification: artworks select particular qualities (e.g., beauty, elegance) and refer to them in an emphatic way. Often artworks express emotional qualities like sadness, happiness or confidence. Because artworks cannot be literally sad, happy or confident, Goodman calls artistic expressiveness metaphorical exemplification.

In sum, artworks are fine-grained, complex, and explicit symbols, which, according to Goodman, contribute to our understanding of the world. They allow us to see things we did not see before and thus to see the world in a fresh way.

Knowledge and insight

Knowledge is typically held to be the privilege of science, which provides us with true statements based on sound evidence. Such a view of knowledge has led theorists like John Hospers (1982: 233–270) to be sceptical about truths conveyed by the arts. However, Carroll (2003: 371–382) sums up and combats three epistemic arguments against art as serving educational purposes in relation to knowledge. First, the banality argument states that artworks teach knowledge of a trivial sort. Carroll replies that quite frequently truisms are forgotten, ignored, or even suppressed. The banality argument disregards the importance in education of enlightening persons by reminding them of what they already know and its relevance (Carroll, 2003: 378). The second argument against the epistemic relevance of art is that it cannot communicate knowledge in the strict sense of the word because it doesn't provide justified belief. Art may involve beliefs but it doesn't supply the evidential warrant for these. Thirdly, art is denied the status of knowledge because it lacks the kinds of argumentation and analysis that are required to justify knowledge claims. Carroll counters the second and the third arguments by arguing that authentic communication does not necessarily depend on justified propositions. Works of art, especially narrative ones, often function like philosophical thought experiments. Such experiments deal with conceptual knowledge rather than empirical evidence, exploring new conceptual possibilities and challenging universal claims about the nature of art and humanity. For instance, Warhol's 'Brillo box' functions as a counterwork, questioning traditional theories of art. Or a film might lead us to reassess the strong distinctions we make between friends and foes. Moreover, art allows us to gain not only conceptual knowledge but also other sorts of knowledge. We may gain insight into psychology by exploring the character types portrayed in novels, films, and plays. Art can also illuminate and stimulate reflection on various sections of society (Carroll, 2003: 380).

Art as education of the ethos

Art as education of the ethos is the oldest of the three conceptions discussed here. In Plato's *Republic* (2003: 67–99), Socrates argues that aesthetic education is essential to a well-balanced and harmonious education as a whole. Engagement in the arts can contribute to the educand's truthfulness and virtuous behaviour. Plato holds that most literature, poetry, and drama of his time presents false views and weak characters and therefore he puts a ban on them. Music is an even more powerful force. While music employing the Dorian and Phrygian modes ennobles and strengthens the character of young men, music in the Ionian and Lydian modes is to be banned because it promotes weakness and licentiousness. Another well-known moralist in art education is Leo Tolstoy. In *What is Art* (1898), he rejects almost all classics of art – including, for example, the works of Sophocles, Shakespeare, Michelangelo, and Beethoven – because they appeal only to the elite and fail to do what art should do: educate common people by instilling solidarity and charity.

One century earlier the German poet and philosopher Friedrich Schiller (1795/2000) defended a different view of aesthetic education. He took aesthetics to be mediating between the 'drive to form' (*Formtrieb*) and the 'drive to matter' (*Stofftrieb*). The drive to form represents the rational and ethical requirements of human life: truth and duty. The drive to matter refers to our sensuous engagement in the material world. According to Schiller, human beings oscillate between these two extremes: at one time they are too much caught up with material concerns, while at the other time there are caged by the rigid constraints of duty and law. Art can bridge the gap by combining form and matter, reason and sensuousness. Art succeeds in doing this through a third drive, the drive to play (*Spieltrieb*), which combines the sensuous aspect of the material realm with the rational constraints of form.

Following Plato, Schiller, and Tolstoy, Herbert Read (1958) argues that art should be the basis of education. True moral discipline can never be imposed from without by adults; it is the natural outcome of children's group activities centring on aesthetic play.

Whereas Schiller tried to connect the realms of aesthetics and ethics through the concept of play, recent authors have emphasized cognitive enquiry and affective sensibility. Taking up Anthony O'Hear's position that art can play a central role in value enquiry, John White (1998: 191–193) argues that the ethical realm comprises more than duty and obligation. He takes it to cover all aspects of how people are to live their lives, including their commitments, enthusiasm, and attachments to persons and communities. In aesthetic engagement we dwell in feelings and desires crucially related to such aspects of ethical life and hence the arts contribute to ethical contemplation. In a similar way, David Carr (2005: 149–150) construes moral education as initiation into the attitudes and values of civilized sensibility rather than as socialization into conventional codes of conduct. Such education involves two aspects that are covered par excellence by the great artistic and literary traditions: (1) moral evaluation, i.e., exploring and assessing the consequences for well-being, flourishing of character, and choice as grounded in the motives, passions, and desires of human agents; (2) developing the qualities of affect presupposed by moral sensibility. Carr (2003) indicates that such exploration of human nature comprises the spiritual as well as the moral dimensions.

In summary, we see that, while the three conceptions of art education can be considered separately, they may also be bound together in a comprehensive view. Engagement in art extends our capacities for feeling, our capacities of discriminative perception of sensuous form and symbols, as well as our insight into psychological and social constellations. These capacities also enable us to probe deeper into the moral and spiritual issues addressed in the arts. Such a comprehensive view remains problematic, however, for non-representational arts like music and abstract painting. Lacking reference to lifelike situations, they do not seem to allow for exploration into psychological, moral or spiritual issues. Yet it appears that experiences in these arts can be as profound and existential as those we have in literature, drama, film, and non-abstract visual art. How to explain this value of non-representational art remains one of the big questions in aesthetics.

ISSUES IN ART EDUCATION

Justification

The legitimization of art as a subject in general education has received much attention, both in philosophy of education and empirical studies. The reason for this is the constant pressure from educational administrators and policy-makers who want to reduce time spent on the arts in favour of academic subjects like reading and mathematics. Defenders of art education have pointed at the intrinsic value and the extrinsic (or instrumental) value of art education. Regarding the latter, theorists have tried to justify art education on the ground that it promotes non-artistic values. All kinds of benefits have been claimed, including improved abilities in reading, mathematics, spatial thinking, social behaviour, emotional balance, and self-esteem. The results of research into such 'outcomes' of art education are not conclusive, however. Surveys (e.g., Winner and Hetland, 2000) indicate that at best very moderate effects may exist. It appears, then, that art education is not an efficient way to further such outcomes. One additional hour of reading is likely to enhance reading skills better than many hours of art education. Moreover, arguments depending on extrinsic effects legitimize only those art activities that make a significant contribution to the effects at hand. They do not lead to a justification of art education that is well-balanced from an artistic point of view. Arguments pointing to art's capacity to enhance and deepen psychological, moral, and spiritual insight are more promising. Art provides a unique way of exploring these realms and doing so is only possible by engaging in artworks in a truly aesthetic way.

Other authors have emphasized the intrinsic value of art experience. The value of artworks cannot be reduced to the capacity they offer to explore psychological, moral, and spiritual issues; in fact, many artworks have no such capacity whatsoever. Eventually, the value of art resides in our total engagement in receiving, creating or performing an art work. Great art goes beyond the mundane: as an intense, even existential experience, it constitutes a major way of life fulfilment (Koopman, 2005).

Creation versus reception; praxis versus formal knowledge

A special characteristic of the arts, as opposed to other subjects in education, is that it allows several modes of engagement: receptive, creative, and reflective. With performance arts like music, dance, and drama, the creative mode can be divided between into creating new works, recreating (performing) existing works, and the combination of both – improvization. Should education emphasize the productive or the receptive side of the arts?

Educational philosophers like Redfern (1986: 68–77, 93–96) and White (1992: 27–33) favour a focus on artistic reception for a number of reasons: (1) artistic creation can only thrive on the basis of sufficient receptive experience, so we have to start with the latter; (2) creative talent is scarce, so that many pupils will fail to develop their artistic sensibility and skills in production-based education; (3) the capacity to respond far outruns the capacity to create and perform major artworks; (4) through reception we are able to acquaint ourselves with a much larger range of art forms, styles, and works. These authors admit that making art may help children to get to know the arts from the inside, but they hold that such a route is neither necessary nor sufficient.

Educators with a background in specific art disciplines (e.g., Bowman, 2005; Elliott, 1995) often have a preference for artistic creation. They point to the higher intensity in terms of presence, vividness, and physical involvement. Making art contributes to personal growth much more than artistic reception; performing music, dance or drama together (tuning-in to each other) also assists to social development. Furthermore, it is held that, besides developing artistic sensibility more profoundly, artistic creation yields a special kind of procedural knowledge not available through reception.

Theorists of liberal education (Peters, 1966: 33–34; Hirst, 1974: 152) have emphasized the distinction between education as the acquisition of formal knowledge and training as the acquisition of skills. From this perspective, education in the arts yields a specific kind of knowledge to be derived from critical engagement in works of great art. In contrast, Elliott (1995: 49–60) argues that art is a praxis centring on procedural knowledge. To make music is not merely a matter of applying and strengthening skills but rather a matter of complex forms of thinking-in-action. Musical knowledge as a unique form of knowledge is developed by such thinking-in-action rather than by verbal reflection on musical works. According to such a view, music and the other arts are best learned through actively engaging in making art rather than through the reception of artworks. Whereas traditional philosophical perspectives tend to focus on the form and the content of artworks, the 'praxial' philosophy proposes a broader view, including the aspects of performance and interpretation, the standards and traditions of practice, as well as the cultural and ideological setting (Elliott,1995: 199).

A debate about the primacy of creation or reception in the arts can only be fruitful if distinctions are made between the various art forms. It is perhaps not surprising that music, dance, and drama have always exploited their special characteristic: performance. Performance can combine the intensity and creative element of direct engagement within the arts with the use of great artworks created by others. Alternatively, one can well understand that reading great works of literature has always played a much larger role in education than, for instance, listening to classical works of music: the verbal arts are a crucial way of transmitting key ideas and values. Again, with art forms like architecture or large-scale installations we are very much tied to reception, because we lack the means to realize them by ourselves. On the other hand, computer software is available now that has greatly extended opportunities to design architecture, create videos, compose music, etc.

New challenges: pluralism, relativism, overexposure

During the last decades, the social reality in which art education takes place has changed dramatically. From an orderly cultural landscape with a clear hierarchy between high and popular art, we have moved to a bewildering pluralism. An enormous range of traditional, popular, ethnic, and intercultural styles are available. Boundaries between traditional art forms as well as between art and amusement have been obliterated by multimedia performance and crossovers. How can art educators do justice to the wild variety of artistic forms and styles? Can the traditional boundaries between art forms like literature, visual art, drama, and music be maintained or should we move to comprehensive forms of aesthetic education?

Within the climate of artistic plurality, relativism has come to take a dominant position. Today, many people find it hard to accept that some styles and traditions of art should be more worthy of cultivation than others. The traditional focus on high art in art education comes under pressure. The canons of classical artworks of the West have been criticized by feminists, African-Americans and sociologists for consolidating the hegemony of white upper-class males. In this way, the canon as a universal instrument for educating humanity has been reinterpreted as an instrument of power that secures the hegemony of a particular segment of society.

While traditional art educators focus on particular types of artworks, art and the aesthetic are omnipresent in our daily lives. Through technological development and commercialization, art has become a commodity that is available anywhere any time. Even when we do not choose to engage in art, we are bombarded by visual and aural stimuli. The quality of aesthetic stimuli in our environment is often dubious, and overexposure can lead to what Welsch calls 'anaesthesia' (1997: 25–27), insensitivity to such stimuli. How can aesthetic education build on children's everyday aesthetic experiences? Can it still maintain and strengthen their aesthetic sensitivity?

EPILOGUE: SOME LEADS

Suitably connecting educational practices with the new aesthetic realities appears to be the most challenging task of aesthetic education today. Philosophers of education have largely neglected the issues of pluralism, relativism, and overexposure so far. Whereas artistic canons seem to be further removed from young people's experience than ever before, the works of Shakespeare, Beethoven, and Rembrandt are often still the philosopher's unquestioned points of reference. Art educators tend to focus on their specific disciplines and are unable to give sufficient attention to new art forms transcending the boundaries of such disciplines. Moreover, artistic activities in schools largely revolve around activities tailored to the constraints of the classroom and the limited technical proficiency of the pupils, resulting in practices of 'school art' that have little to do with the current situation in the art world.

On the other hand, alternative forms of artistic learning occur at all kinds of places: community art is being developed in community centres, literary skills are cultivated through peer critique on Internet forums, youngsters support each other in mastering the newest styles of dance and music in their private places, while museums, theatre companies, and orchestras have become much more active in organizing educational arrangements at their own venues. Shouldn't we acknowledge that instances of aesthetic and artistic growth are bound to occur in manifold contexts, serving a wide range of goals and functions? And, given this fact, is it still feasible to formulate a comprehensive conception of aesthetic education with precisely articulated goals and effective paths leading to these?

However, *laissez faire* is not an adequate educational response to the current state of affairs. The scattered opportunities for aesthetic learning do not warrant a well-balanced result, nor does every child have access to a wide range of options for aesthetic education. The need for general and formal education in the aesthetic and the arts will continue to exist. Even when defining a comprehensive conception is neither possible nor desirable, we may articulate some conditions such an education would have to satisfy.

First, aesthetic education should strive to include all major areas. It should not be restricted to the art forms that have been traditionally favoured – literature, music, painting/drawing – but also include dance, film, installations, and other multimedia artforms.

Secondly, a well-balanced aesthetic education requires that a variety of modalities be covered: direct engagement with artistic materials; reception and performance of a wide range of artworks; knowledge of the properties of artworks and their context; and aesthetic judgement. There is a developmental sequence in these modalities, as developmental research suggests (Parsons, 1987; Swanwick, 1988). At first, the artistic materials are to be explored. Then, children acquaint themselves with the representational, expressive, and formal dimensions of art through reception, performance, and creation. Propositional knowledge follows direct artistic engagement, clarifying it, generalizing it, and putting it into context. Judgement, in turn, can mature only on the basis of the triad of knowledge *of* (acquaintance with art), knowledge *how* (knowing how to engage in art), and knowledge *that* (propositional knowledge).

Thirdly, much weight is to be given to critical engagement in the two senses of acute discrimination and accurate judgement. Acute perception counters the threat of 'anaesthesia', the numbing effect of overexposure to superficial aesthetic stimuli. By refining our perception skills we become sensitive to new dimensions of artistic meaning and expand our opportunities to have authentic and profound artistic experiences. Critical judgement will help educands to find their way in the world of omnipresent aesthetic stimuli. Visual culture, music, and multimedia art often serve manipulative purposes such as influencing consumer behaviour and forging exclusive group identities. Art is one of the most effective ways of influencing our sense of identity and our behaviour because it not only operates at the cognitive but also at the emotional and somatic level. Because art can be so powerful in modelling our identities, direct artistic engagement should be complemented by critical reflection and judgement.

Critical appreciation and judgement are also important, of course, in developing one's own taste and preferences. In a world of artistic plurality where the possibility of universal standards of good art is questioned, autonomous judgement is an important asset. This leads to a fourth point: the central role of the individual in aesthetic education. As the idea of a singular and orderly artworld into which educands are to be initiated dwindles, enhancing individuals' ability to make their own choices and discoveries becomes a major goal of education.

Fifthly, the role of art educators changes. They cannot pretend that their knowledge covers everything that matters in the world of art. Besides transferring aesthetic and artistic knowledge, they increasingly function as mediators, to guiding the pupils to the loci where they can find the knowledge they need. In addition to a shift from transferring to mediating, there will also be a shift from content to process. The point of the educational undertaking will not so much be to teach a predetermined body of artistic knowledge and competences as to assist children in discovering, appropriating, and expanding their artistic world. On the other hand, educators cannot and should not be neutral functionaries. Their principal task continues to be to inspire their pupils and to foster a love for art and the aesthetic in them. Personal preferences become manifest, as educators try to convey their enthusiasm for art to the pupils. This is no problem so long as these preferences do not function as an absolute standard.

Finally, while ample room is to be given to individual preferences, aesthetic educators should also be keen to look for common ground. Although the tendency is towards increased pluralism and even fragmentation, we should not neglect art's potential to bind people together at all levels, from the school and the neighbourhood to the nation and worldwide. Society can only continue to exist if we find ways to prolong and strengthen our shared identities, and aesthetic education can make a significant contribution to this. Canons, as collections of our most treasured artworks, can play a major role here, provided that they are socially inclusive.

In summary, the issues are not new: breadth versus depth, free play versus critical appreciation, reception versus creation, pedagogical guidance versus spontaneous development, autonomy versus collective identity. But the dilemmas now need to be dealt with in a radically changed environment. When investigating the new situation, aesthetic education can take advantage of disciplines such as cultural studies, anthropology, and sociology. While these can help us to develop a wider view of the roles of aesthetic education in society, they also tend to reduce art and the aesthetics to their social and cultural functions. Philosophy of aesthetic education has the task to orient itself to new perspectives of the many meanings, purposes, and uses of the aesthetic, while remaining faithful to its particular approach of aesthetics and aesthetic education as a special area of value.

ACKNOWLEDGEMENT

I want to thank Wouter van Haaften for his valuable comments on earlier versions of this chapter.

NOTES

94 Although the term 'aesthetic' was introduced only in the eighteenth century, the realm designated by this term was, of course, discussed much earlier.

95 I shall deal with general aesthetic education here without discussing professional education at art academies, conservatoires, etc.

REFERENCES

Abbs, P. (1987) *Living Powers: The Arts in Education*. London: Falmer Press.

Beardsley, M.C. (1982) *The Aesthetic Point of View*. Ithaca: Cornell University Press.

Bell, C. (1914/1987) *Art*. London: Chatto and Windus.

Best, D. (1985) *Feeling and Reason in the Arts*. London: Allen and Unwin.

Best, D. (1989) 'Feeling and reason in the arts: the rationality of feeling', in P. Abbs (ed.), *The Symbolic Order: A Contemporary Reader on the Arts Debate*. London: The Falmer Press, pp. 70–85.

Bowman, W. (2005) 'Why musical performance? Views praxial to performative', in D.J. Elliott (ed.), *Praxial Music Education: Reflections and Dialogues*. Oxford: Oxford University Press, pp. 142–164.

Carr, D. (2003) 'Spiritual, moral and heroic virtue: Aristotelian character in the Arthurian and grail narratives', *Journal of Beliefs and Values*, 24: 15–26.

Carr, D. (2005) 'On the contribution of literature and the arts to the education cultivation of moral virtue, feeling and emotion', *Journal of Moral Education*, 34: 137–151.

Carroll, N. (1999) *Philosophy of Art: A Contemporary Introduction*. London and New York: Routledge.

Carroll, N. (2003) 'Aesthetics and the educative powers of art', in R. Curren (ed.), *A Companion to the Philosophy of Education*. Oxford: Blackwell, pp. 365–383.

Davies, S. (1991) *Definitions of Art*. Ithaca: Cornell University Press.

Dickie, G. (1992) 'Definition of "art"', in D. Cooper (ed.), *A Companion to Aesthetics*. Oxford: Blackwell, pp. 109–113.

Elliott, D.J. (1995) *Music Matters: A New Philosophy of Music Education*. New York: Oxford University Press.

Goodman, N. (1976) *Languages of Art: An Approach to a Theory of Symbols*. Indianapolis: Hackett.

Hanslick, E. (1854/1991) *Vom musikalisch-Schönen* [On the Beautiful in Music]. Darmstadt: Wissenschaftliche Buchgesellschaft.

Hepburn, R.W. (1998) 'The arts and the education of feeling and emotion', in P.H. Hirst and P. White (eds), *Philosophy of Education: Major Themes in the Analytic Tradition*, Vol. 4. London: Routledge, pp. 171–185.

Hirst, P.H. (1974) *Knowledge and the Curriculum*. London: Routledge and Kegan Paul.

Hospers, J. (1982) *Understanding the Arts*. Englewood Cliffs, NJ: Prentice Hall.

Koopman, C. (2005) 'Art as fulfilment: on the justification of education in the arts', *Journal of Philosophy of Education*, 39: 85–97.

Levinson, J. (1990) *Music, Art, and Metaphysics*. Ithaca: Cornell University Press.

Levinson, J. (2003) 'Philosophical aesthetics: an overview', in J. Levinson (ed.), *The Oxford Handbook of Aesthetics*. Oxford: Oxford University Press, pp. 3–24.

Muelder Eaton, M. and Moore, R. (2002) 'Aesthetic experiences: its revival and its relevance to aesthetic education', *Journal of Aesthetic Education*, 36 (2): 9–23.

Parsons, M. (1987) *How we Understand Art: A Cognitive Developmental Account of Aesthetic Experience*. Cambridge: Cambridge University Press.

Peters, R.S. (1966) *Ethics and Education*. London: George Allen and Unwin.

Plato (2003) *The Republic* (trans. D. Lee). London: Penguin.

Read, H. (1958) *Education through Art*. London: Faber and Faber.

Redfern, H.B. (1986) *Questions in Aesthetic Education*. London: Allen and Unwin.

Reimer, B. (1989) *A Philosophy of Music Education*, 2nd edn. Englewood Cliffs, NJ: Prentice Hall.

Ross, M. (ed.) (1982) *The Development of Aesthetic Experience*. Oxford: Pergamon Press.

Ross, M. (1984) *The Aesthetic Impulse*. Oxford: Pergamon Press.

Ross, M. (ed.) (1985) *The Aesthetic in Education*. Oxford: Pergamon Press.

Schiller, F. (1795/2000). *Über die ästhetische Erziehung des Menschen in einer Reihe von Briefen* [On the Aesthetic Education of Man in a Series of Letters]. Stuttgart: Reclam.

Smith, R.A. (1989) *The Sense of Art: A Study in Aesthetic Education*. New York: Routledge.

Swanwick, K. (1988) *Music, Mind, and Education*. London: Routledge.

Tolstoy, L. (1898/1995) *What is Art?* (trans. R. Pevear and L. Volokhonsky). London: Penguin.

Welsch, W. (1997) *Undoing Aesthetics.* London: SAGE.

White, J. (1992) *The Arts 5–16: Changing the Agenda.* London: The Tuffnell Press.

White, J. (1998) 'The arts, well-being and education', in P.H. Hirst and P. White (eds), *Philosophy of Education: Major Themes in the Analytic Tradition, Vol. 4, Problems of Educational Content and Practice.* London: Routledge, pp. 186–196.

Winner, E. and Hetland, J. (2000) 'The arts in education: evaluation the evidence for a causal link', *Journal of Aesthetic Education,* 34 (3–4): 3–10.

30

Religious Education

James C. Conroy and
Robert A. Davis

For the ancients, the idea that the processes of education should be concerned with the claims and contents of religious belief was a self-evident truth. Knowledge of the gods, their stories, the various orders of being over which they presided, their laws for human behaviour and the rituals and practices associated with devotion to them were integral elements of learning and teaching for all who received a formal education. Effective understanding of religious doctrines in such cultures was not only regarded as vital to full and successful participation in society but also was frequently seen as essential in securing the eternal destiny of individuals beyond this life – whether that destiny lay in spiritual union with the gods, future incarnations or passage to a higher mode of consciousness. In its fundamental concern with the ultimate meanings and purposes of existence for all of its adherents – and, in some religions, for the cosmos as a whole – religion laid a considerable claim on the practices of education, playing a decisive role in the formation of individuals and in the regulation of the community (Marrou, 1956). Although it would be inaccurate to conclude that these societies offered a 'religious education' as a discrete area of study in anything like the modern sense of that term, it is important to note that the content of learning and teaching included the dedication of considerable resources of time and energy to the reading and recital of sacred texts, the memorization of religious narratives and the application of the religion's core teachings to the conduct of daily life. The classical school curriculum perfected by the Greeks and the Romans included no separate study of religion, but religious texts and ideas permeated the practices of learning and teaching in grammar, rhetoric, music and astronomy, while in the higher academies of learning, theological and metaphysical speculation was seen frequently as the pinnacle of philosophical enquiry (Hadot, 2004).

Christianity inherited from its Roman and Near Eastern cultural matrix the systematic organization of knowledge embedded in the classical curriculum. The expansionist Church brought to this ancient structure in the first few centuries of the Common Era the twin imperatives of evangelization and catechesis, employing the systems of education both to convert those outside the Church (evangelization) and to form the faith, from childhood onwards, of those within it (catechesis). In practice, of course, only a small minority of the population received any substantial formal education, but Christianity articulated a clear understanding of the place of the study of religion within the processes of education at many different levels. For elite sections of society, and for those preparing for a clerical role within the Church, this took the shape of formal, literate instruction in the sacred scriptures, the teachings of the Church, the prayers and rites of divine service and the traditional, edifying narratives of saints' lives and martyrdoms. For the illiterate masses, it assumed the form of instruction and guidance through the various ministries associated with preaching and teaching within the patterns of congregational worship (Markowski, 2008, pp. 136–152).

With the rise of, first, monastic centres of study and then the medieval universities, Christian education in faith differentiated into two distinct but related practices. For the unlettered masses, basic oral instruction in the rudiments of faith was provided (often very inadequately) by parish clergy. Much more advanced forms of theological education were reserved for priestly and monastic elites, for whom an increasingly sophisticated and philosophically complex discipline evolved, leading to the acquisition for the theology of the title 'the Queen of the sciences' – a Christian religious capstone, as it were, on the hallowed edifice of classical university learning. The extent to which medieval universities essentially existed for this kind of study and training in theology is too easily overlooked from a modern perspective. It was not until the early nineteenth century that the prestige of theology – and the preparation of candidates for the ordained Christian ministries – was seriously challenged within European universities by the growth of independent study of the arts, humanities and natural sciences (Bellitto, 2005, pp. 35–50; Vitz, 2005, pp. 20–35).

The late medieval expansion of civic schooling, still regulated by the Church but increasingly funded and administered by secular authorities and associations, witnessed the arrival of the first systematic references to religious instruction as a dedicated subject of study on the school curriculum. A Christian society set upon the steady extension of educational provision to the children of urban and mercantile interests, many of whom were not destined for formal employment by the Church, and incorporated into the inherited classical curriculum identifiable periods of time for careful instruction in faith and the cultivation of detailed knowledge of the sacred scriptures (Mandelbrote, 2003, pp. 19–40; Willemsen, 2008, pp. 167–189). In the turbulent period of the sixteenth and seventeenth century European Reformations, in both Catholic and Protestant communities, the role of formal religious instruction assumed almost overnight a vital significance, as increasingly confessional state and regional authorities sought to enforce uniform instruction in religious orthodoxy as part of the shaping of their political subjects and in opposition to their religious rivals. In Protestant nations, in particular, a renewed interest in the extension of basic literacy to a broader cross-section of society than had previously been the norm followed naturally from the translations of the Bible into vernacular languages. This was accompanied by increased control by Church authorities of religious instruction in schools, leading to the widespread introduction of formal programmes of catechesis for the teaching of the young and for the preparation for their full, adult entry into the Church. Catholic powers soon followed suit, leading to the development across Europe of highly trained networks of religious educators playing a prominent role in the authorized teaching of religious instruction on behalf of Church and State. Indeed, in many European societies in the early modern period, tensions between the powers of Church and State centred precisely on the demands of impatient Church apologists that the State prosecute with greater singlemindedness the active promotion of the teaching of sound doctrine within the expanding schools sector, as broader sections of the population began to receive a basic education (Ehrenpreis, 2006, pp. 39–53; Smith, 1944, pp. 306–313).

The compact of Church and State for the preservation and extension of formal school instruction in religion endured in many Western countries largely untouched for several centuries. In the United Kingdom, for example, even as popular compulsory education entered into a period of large-scale expansion on the eve of the Industrial Revolution, and a greater diversity of subjects began to impinge on the school curriculum, the place of religious instruction in learning and teaching was scrupulously protected by a mix of custom, legislation and ecclesiastical oversight of schools. There were two great national exceptions to this norm, each of which posited a challenge to the place of state-sponsored religious instruction in the education of children. The first was the United States, which, in its achievement of independence from the British Crown in the 1770s, incorporated into its new Constitution a strict separation of Church and State, eschewing the European norm of an 'established' or official national religion and banishing all confessional instruction in a particular faith from schools controlled and administered by the State. In the American model – most of which survives to the present day – while religion might on occasion be studied as part of a general humanities education, formal faith-based religious instruction was seen as the preserve of Churches and religious organizations, which then might sponsor privately-funded religious schools in which a more premeditated programme of religious instruction could be pursued.

The second national alternative was France. In their revolutionary overthrow in 1789–93 of the ancient system of royal and feudal despotism, the authorities of the new French republic sought also to remove the allegedly repressive influence of the Catholic Church from all of the institutions of civil society, including the provision of education. The struggle between the Church and a succession of revolutionary regimes in France was a difficult and protracted one, extending well into the nineteenth century. Nevertheless, as France modernized and the influence of the Church declined, state education in the country became heavily secularized, leading to the emergence of another model where confessional religious instruction had been effectively removed from the institutions of state education.

Events in late eighteenth century France and America reflected the growing influence among certain cultural and political elites of Enlightenment conceptions of education and society. These ideas coincided with, and helped foster, the rise of the modern nation-state with its increased administrative–bureaucratic control of the institutions of popular education. In reaction to the violent and destructive upheavals of the seventeenth century Wars of Religion, moves towards religious toleration in many centres of educated opinion across Europe placed the inherited practices of formal religious instruction under increasingly sceptical scrutiny (Marshall, 2006). This scepticism typically took two forms. First, the complicity of confessional affiliation with sectarian conflict demanded, for thinkers such as Locke and Comenius, that education in religion should equip students to understand (if not necessarily endorse) the worldviews of others in order to secure civil harmony between doctrinally diverse communities (Moseley, 2007, pp. 98–100). This growth in toleration heralded the rise of the idea of the liberal state as a neutral space for the peaceful coexistence of divergent communities of religious practice. Secondly, the more general growth in religious doubt, which is such a hallmark of Enlightenment thought, began to give rise to serious questions about the locus of religion – and religious instruction – in its entirety within systems of education founded upon principles of rationality and autonomy. Anticlerical and sceptical thinkers such as Spinoza and Bayle, laying the foundations of modern philosophical materialism, began to challenge the legitimacy of the study of religion in schools and universities, fearing that even the most restrained and objective engagement with religious revelation risked according credibility to beliefs and values which fell short in the criteria for admission into the canons of rationality (Israel, 2006, pp. 94–115). A view began to emerge from this debate suggesting that there might be some fundamental incompatibility between the pursuit of education and the catechetical promotion within schools of adherence to a specific faith tradition (Israel, 2001, pp. 265–270, 331–342).

With the exception of the United States and France, it is clear that these ideas, despite their philosophical appeal to academic elites, commanded little institutional or political favour. Hence, even as a general intellectual scepticism towards religious belief gained ground in the United Kingdom in the nineteenth century, for example, the grasp of the Christian churches on the character and teaching of religious education in schools remained firm, accompanying the enlargement of state-controlled mass education that continued throughout the industrial period. Certainly, a society that was moving towards greater religious toleration and diversity faced the reality within its expanding educational provision of different – and sometimes even rival – versions of religious education operating in its schools. The nations of the British Isles arrived in the late nineteenth and early twentieth centuries at various forms of accommodation with this experience of religious difference, including partnerships of various degrees of cooperation, with a range of Christian denominations active in the running of schools. The status of formal religious education – of an unarguably Christian character – remained nevertheless central and for the most part compulsory as the numbers of schools began to expand rapidly in response to a growing industrial population. The great Educational Reform Acts of the period 1870–1920 in Britain – introducing far-reaching change into the governance, content and structures of mass education – continued to underline the place of religious education in the school curriculum as Britain entered the modern era, emphasizing its role in the initiation of the young into a still notionally Christian society and underscoring its vital importance to moral development and the maintenance of social coherence (Moran, 2006, pp. 41–51).

Indeed, the perceived importance or this version of religious education to the defining forms of social order and national identity endured into the second half of the twentieth century in the United Kingdom. In 1944 the highly reformist Butler Education Act (so-called after the Secretary of State for Education, Rab Butler) retained the provision of religious education as an important feature of public schooling in England and Wales. The form of religious education, or *instruction*, as it was then still called, was to be regulated by an agreed syllabus of a non-denominational but still decidedly Christian character. Hence, as late as the 1968 Agreed Syllabus for London, *Learning for Life*, the dominant discourse remained unashamedly Christian. While there is some perfunctory mention of other faiths in this important document, these are only considered significant to the extent that they help illuminate 'what it means to be a Christian and to be religiously committed' (ILEA, 1968, p. 9). Thus,

> The immigrant child, just because he hails from another land, may have something to contribute to religious studies in the school … . He may have seen beggars, or have experienced disease with no hospitals … . It is necessary also to have an awareness of the children's [i.e. those of other faiths] feelings, avoiding any expression or choice of subject which might hurt or give offence. Philip sharing the 'good news' with the Ethiopian is a better representation of missionary activity than that of the evangelist 'converting the heathen.' (p. 10)

This substantial quotation is particularly interesting because the statements contained in it were penned on the crest of a radical shift in patterns of migration, social convention and epistemic commitment across the European and Anglophone worlds of the time. Moreover, it was published some 3 years after one of the less trumpeted documents of the Second Vatican Council of the Roman Catholic Church, *Nostra Aetate* (the Declaration on Other Faiths). *Nostra Aetate*, apparently somewhat less grudgingly than *Learning for Life*, describes, for example, Hinduism, as possessing 'limitless riches and insights' (1965). Given the some what unflattering opinion held by many liberals of the Catholic Church then and since, the contrast in tone between the two documents is striking. On the one hand what was perhaps the most progressive education authority in the United Kingdom, with the then proportionally largest multi-faith/cultural population in the country, expresses a surprisingly narrow, sectarian attitude to the non-Christian faiths of others, seeing their insights as essentially an asset in promulgating the Christian Gospel. Here the only question is not the appropriateness or inappropriateness of missionary activity within liberal education, but the sensitivity with which this self-evident good is to be handled. On the other hand, an avowedly conservative religious institution such as the Catholic Church appears, on the face of things, to be much more open to the first principle claims of other faiths and insists that they be treated both graciously and seriously in their own right. What this may suggest is that educational and pedagogical practices have a tendency to lag behind broader epistemological shifts in society more generally and that a major religious institution had more intellectual resources to hand than established educationalists who, it could be argued, needed to take their lead from 'front-line' thinkers in the realities of religious practice and religious difference.

Yet, within a very few years two significant changes had occurred. First, religious education underwent a sudden identity crisis, becoming abruptly much less concerned with 'what it means in every sense to be a Christian and be religiously committed' (ILEA, 1968 p. 9). Secondly, the place of world religions was very rapidly confirmed as of educational value in its own right, becoming central to the religious education curriculum in both primary and secondary schools across Britain. Simultaneously, the established notion that Bible study was to be deemed the chief source of and for national moral improvement was robustly challenged. In turning briefly to analyse some features of a defining policy document from this period – the 1976, *Religious Education: Avon Agreed Syllabus* – we see that it is considerably less concerned than the ILEA syllabus of just a few years previously with ensuring that the concerns and codes of religion and morality are refracted through the lens of the Christian scriptures – and, indeed, with affirming that the purpose of cultivating acquaintance with those scriptures is to mould people as good religious citizens. Instead, 'the principal aim should be to understand the nature of religion and what it would mean to take it seriously ... the pursuit of [this] aim will help pupils to identify for themselves the fundamental questions of human existence' (County of Avon Education Service, 1976, p. 2). The purposes of religious education were shifting away from an introduction to Christian belief and practice as the source and foundation of public morality to the widening of students' religious horizons and the facilitation of their personal spiritual growth. Hence, at some conceptual distance from the ILEA Agreed Syllabus, the Avon Syllabus suggests that 'It should not be the intention of those engaged in Religious Education in schools to require a particular religious commitment of pupils'. (p. 4) Moreover, while Christianity continues to be clearly foregrounded by the Avon materials, acquaintance with other faiths is now deemed as necessary in its own right and students are required to have access to a broader range of material for their studies, including knowledge of at least one major religion other than Christianity. How was it possible that such a dramatic educational shift could take place in less than 8 years?

Let us take the two issues separately – though in truth they are to be seen more appropriately as two expressions or manifestations of the outworking of the same cultural and epistemic forces. The move away from seeing religious education as *nurturing the Christian faith* to regarding it as *a means for personal growth* is part of a general cultural realignment where both religion and much personal morality come to be seen as essentially private experiences in modern plural societies. This move from the public to the private mirrors other trends in late twentieth century liberal democratic culture, notably a tilt towards seeing such civic institutions as marriage and divorce – indeed even the question of religious practice itself – as largely a matter of private disposition rather than public concern. It is not difficult to see how this movement away from the public purposes of religion influences attitudes to those holding beliefs other than Christianity. After all, if *my* religious beliefs and attachments are private, then *yours* also are private; and if they are both private, then *your* beliefs have a claim equivalent to *mine* to be admitted to the curriculum of the school. Coupled with the continuing migration into the United Kingdom of large numbers of committed followers of other world faiths, most notably Islam and Hinduism, this transition from the public to private triggered a remarkable shift in the expectations around religious education as a still compulsory subject on the school curriculum.

While this change in both attitude and practice was in cultural terms very rapid, it would be a mistake not to recognize it as a consequence of a much longer historical narrative to which this essay has referred – reaching back to the Enlightenment, and indeed the Reformation – and a consequence of early modern developments such as the revolution of communication technologies and the coming of print. The rise of the private has its roots in the technology of print, which enables the Bible to reach a mass audience. When the Bible is copied by hand, access has to be restricted as the cost is prohibitive. Scarce access by a largely illiterate population requires intermediaries to translate and interpret the holy texts, but with print access comes the possibility that *I* might read the scriptures for myself and I in turn might be able to make sense of (interpret) them for myself. This ability of the individual to access and make sense of religious texts gradually led to the emergence (or some would argue, *re-emergence*, given its antecedents in Greek philosophy) within Reformation humanism of *reason* as the guide to human understanding and behaviour. No longer would it be necessary to justify readings of texts or interpretations of moral action by exclusive reference to received tradition. Instead careful reasoning would reveal the truth. It is this impulse that is key to shaping the eighteenth century Enlightenment and its emphasis on rationality. Gradually the epistemological shift away from knowing the world through 'given' or pre-ordained categories to knowing it through the application of reason opens up a question about religious texts themselves.

No longer were such texts to be understood even in overtly religious contexts simply as the inerrant or unequivocal word of God, but rather as the product of the interaction between rational minds, texts and belief in a creator God. In other words, the documents were to be regarded as simultaneously divinely inspired *and* humanly communicated and interpreted. This shift in thinking about, and relating to, religion would develop further in the nineteenth and twentieth centuries, culminating in a hermeneutical movement that saw different religions not as competing accounts of objective truth but as competing accounts of *meaning*. It was not, then, that some religions were to be taken as self-evidently true and others not: rather, each religion was seen to offer a unique cultural perspective on the nature of the divine and the various belief-systems arising out of efforts to make sense of the encounter with the divine.

In the 1960s a British Professor of Theology emerged from this intellectual and cultural ferment to become immensely influential in the development of religious education. Having taught theology at Birmingham University, Ninian Smart asked some pointed questions about the relationship between the teacher, who believed in a particular (usually Christian) theological account of the nature and existence of God and God's relationship to creation, and the students, whose religious beliefs and attachments were, Smart noted, increasingly quite divergent from these fideistic assumptions. It was significant enough that the large-scale cultural shifts around sexual freedom, women's rights, new working practices and de-industrialization taking place in Western countries frequently pitted adolescents against adults as protagonists in an ongoing intergenerational struggle over values, beliefs, meaning and lifestyle practices. Added to this, countries such as Britain continued to experience other forms of far-reaching social change, such substantial immigration from former colonies where the dominant religious beliefs were often not Christian. Significant numbers of new migrants came to advanced industrial nations like Britain and America from countries that had very large numbers of adherents of Islam, Sikhism, Hinduism and Buddhism. Here were peoples who could not, like Jewish communities before them, be described or readily domesticated as Abrahamic forerunners of Christianity. How was religious education in the context of compulsory schooling in a formerly quite uniform society to deal with these new minorities? As we have noted above, the Agreed Syllabuses slowly began to change in response to such developments, and, importantly, it was Ninian Smart who was the driving force and 'hands-off' architect of many of the disciplinary changes. Adopting a position of educational agnosticism with regard to any particular collection of beliefs or their related truth claims, Smart set about understanding the structural and organizational similarities between religions, publishing in 1969 the highly influential book, *The Religious Experience of Mankind* (Smart, 1969). In this landmark volume, Smart distinguished six dimensions of religious experience, which, he argued, could be recognized as shaping religious beliefs everywhere, irrespective of culture or geography. These dimensions were *doctrinal, mythological, ethical, ritual, experiential and institutional*. (To these he later added a seventh, *material*.) Integrating these categories into an interpretative or heuristic framework for religious education enabled the scholar to make comparisons and demonstrate that the particular claims of any given religion to absolute or revealed truth were invariably subject to serious doubt. The resultant transition, essentially from theological studies to religious studies in many UK schools, was embraced in religious education because Smart led a major development project that culminated in the release of a number of highly significant publications, including *Working Paper 36* (Schools Council, 1971) and *A Groundplan for the Study of Religion* (Smart, 1977). The aim of these publications was to instantiate and systematize the *phenomenological* study of religion – an approach which relied on the cultivation of two separate but related capacities in both the teacher and the student. The first was the ability of the observer to suspend judgement as to the veracity or verisimilitude of particular religious claims. The second was the ability to use the dimensions identified by Smart as a morphological tool to classify and categorize particular features and practices of religion in an educational setting.

But could teacher and student move as seamlessly to this new way of engaging with religious education as the model assumed? And, in any event, was such a move in any sense theoretically or pedagogically coherent? Could learners simply engage with another's beliefs without bringing to bear their own ontological and epistemological attachments upon them? Such questions have bedevilled religious education, certainly in Anglophone education systems, since Smart began to formulate his thinking. It is therefore worth pausing here to reflect on these three questions. Is it in fact possible to 'bracket out' all my previous attachments, understandings, indeed judgements in the encounter with religious experience? If I have been brought up by my parents or community to believe that the doctrines of *my* particular faith are true, and have come unequivocally to accept this to be the case, can I really look at *your* doctrines and say, 'You may just as well be as right as me'. To suspend or bracket out my own beliefs may work at a superficial level, but is that enough for an authentically educational engagement with religious realities? Surely an educated rationality which is concerned with important foundational *epistemological* (what it is to know the world) and *ontological* (what it is to be) questions cannot simply prescind from asking the related question(s) fundamental to the kinds of attachments and beliefs I may wish to bring into the conversation in the first place.

To see the issue more clearly, let us take an example from a related but different sphere of education – moral education. In recent years the development of citizenship education in a number of countries has received heightened attention because governments and civic polities have become extremely nervous about what they perceive to be declining standards of conduct, behaviour and participation in the public spaces of civil society. In seeking to remedy such circumstances, we generally wish that our students will form unequivocal attachments to certain core moral values such as tolerance, honesty, justice and so on. Here we do not really wish them at any juncture to 'suspend' their belief that in 'our' society adherence to these values matters. We wish them to learn and hold fast to these values so that they will be 'good citizens'. The suspension, or bracketing out, of personal attachment is to be avoided; or, where it might reasonably be admitted, it is to be seen strictly as a pedagogic device for encouraging students in their recognition of the 'obvious absurdity' of rejecting the universalist claims of citizenship. Of course there is a difference between citizenship and religious education. In a liberal political community the claims of citizenship represent a claim on *all* because they are intended to represent those values that are deemed to be held by all in order that the whole community may thrive and prosper. Religious affiliations are self-evidently more particular and partial than this and consequently cannot be accorded the same status as liberal civic values. After all, different religions often make radically different claims about everything from day-to-day practice to ultimate truths. Indeed, it is precisely because religion has at its core attachments and commitments of this peculiar and frequently exclusivist kind that it is all the more difficult to ignore them, putting them in a box as if they were add-ons and optional extras. Perhaps, then, the suspension of belief is therefore not quite as straightforward as its advocates would suggest.

There are two discrete and contrary responses to these difficulties. On the one hand, the secular atheist/humanist might wish to argue that it is precisely because the problems of adjudicating between different religious beliefs are so intractable that religious education should be removed from the curriculum. After all, it is argued, religious systems – with their myriad attendant doctrines and intransigent demands – are no more than expressions of a preference and make nothing that a rational person would consider a 'truth claim'. The curriculum, the liberal humanist might argue, should deal only with those things that are verifiable. Of course, this attitude leads quite easily to the old philosophical position given classic expression in A.J. Ayer's, *Language, Truth and Logic*, which suggested that there were only two kinds of meaningful propositions: those that are tautologies and those that are empirically grounded (Ayer, 1936). As any undergraduate philosophy student now knows only too well, such a formulation instantly precludes large swathes of human thought and intercourse from any claim to be meaningful – or meaningfully present in learning and teaching. Forms of intellectual activity such as historical enquiry or deliberative citizenship are vulnerable to similar accusations of meaninglessness, since historical studies and citizenship studies both contain multiple statements that are certainly not tautological but equally are not verifiable. For example, is the proposition that 'good citizens should always be tolerant of others' differences' genuinely meaningful? It is clearly not the kind of statement that we might verify empirically (though we might count the number of people who agree with it or act as if it were the case), nor is it a tautology. Yet in a liberal democracy we might want to say it is a meaningful injunction placed on citizens so that they can live in relative harmony one with the other. It is a statement of *value*, but as a statement of value it is not self-evidently any less contentious than many religious propositions.

There are a great many people in the United Kingdom, or France or the United States who would disagree profoundly with the demand for both tolerance and toleration. So it is that a great many value statements that are not grounded in a religious worldview nevertheless make their way into the curriculum. It is not clear that religious claims are structurally any different from these.

A quite different response to the same challenge has been articulated by a variety of contemporary scholars of religious education (Barnes, 2009a, 2009b; Conroy and Davis, 2008; Wright, 2008). This response acknowledges that while religious claims are contentious, they are so precisely because they do indeed make attempts at capturing truth. It also points to the reality that adherents of religious traditions routinely conduct their lives in accordance with the tenets grounded in these truth claims, thus constituting a primary focus of educational interest. It then proceeds to argue from these principles that a liberal democracy needs to be open to a range of alternative beliefs and worldviews because these alternatives are manifestations of how the world actually is and how it is inhabited and navigated by countless numbers of people. What this response in effect attempts to do is to highlight nothing less than the existence of two contrasting accounts of liberal democracy, each of which has a bearing on whether or not religious education should be taught in the common school and, if it should, what shape it should then take. On the one hand, there exists liberalism as a form of institutional secularism, which is formally (if not actually) represented at its purest in the US constitutional separation of Church and State discussed above. Here the task of the liberal state is to prohibit all religious attachments from entering the arena. A second, contrasting account of liberal democracy, while agreeing unreservedly that secularism is indeed necessary to the health of an advanced civil democratic polity, interprets secularism and the role of the secular state in a quite different light. For this perspective, the task of the liberal democratic state is to mediate in its institutions between competing claims to both value and truth while itself maintaining a vigilant but scrupulous neutrality between them. In religious education, the second account of liberal democratic education rejects the abandonment of the subject of religious education (RE) and advocates instead the promotion of a variety of different strategies for approaching the study of religion in formal educational settings. The shared character of these various strategies has come to be understood in recent debates within a framework set by the philosophical movement known as critical realism – an account of understanding described by the theologian N.T. Wright as

> A way of describing the process of 'knowing' that acknowledges the *reality of the thing known, as something other than the knower* (hence 'realism'), while fully acknowledging that the only access we have to this reality lies along the spiralling path of *appropriate dialogue or conversation between the knower and the thing known* (hence 'critical'). (Wright, 1992, p. 36)

The genealogy of religious education summarized above gives rise to three classic and testing philosophical dilemmas for the positioning of the discipline within a liberal democratic vision of the curriculum. Critical realist responses seek a way out of all three dilemmas by construing the study of religious education as a locus for their active resolution. The first dilemma has been alluded to at length in this chapter and concerns the compatibility of the claims of religious belief, and the character of religious experience, with the cultivation and application of a critical rationality that is everywhere seen as central to the work of liberal education. If religious education deals with experiences that are either demonstrably delusory or unsusceptible to the procedures of rational enquiry, then its place in the curriculum must be highly doubtful. A critical realist response to this quandary defends a robust account of religious education as a mode of educational reflection unswervingly devoted to the pursuit of truth but prepared to recognize that the understanding of truth is commonly embedded in the social and symbolic practices of actual human communities. Without compromise to its critical integrity, examination of the nature and claims of particular worldviews calls forth from education sincere engagement with the hermeneutical and epistemological dimensions of religious experience, whether these are embodied in doctrinal statements, ritual practices, sacred narratives or principles for the ethical conduct of life. No privilege need be accorded any particular religious formulation by this method, but it nevertheless becomes one of the duties of religious education to extend the repertoire of rational enquiry in order to engage coherently with the manifold ways in which human beings fashion meaning in the patterns of their lives (Hella and Wright, 2009, pp. 53–64).

The second enduring problem for modern religious education concerns the question of autonomy, because the promotion and development of autonomy has been seen since the Enlightenment as one of the primary purposes of a liberal education. Yet many religions look askance on the exercise of personal autonomy, suspicious of its incompatibility with religious belonging and the necessary submission to customary authority, while fearful of its elevation of the individual ego and its appetites above the needs and identity of the community. A key response of contemporary religious education to this issue is to place the concept of autonomy directly at the heart of the RE classroom and its philosophical and theological deliberations; to subject it to the critiques commonly levelled at it by religious tradition and to examine the ways in which it is always inevitably discursively situated against a backdrop of all sorts of rival yet equally legitimate ethical interests interacting with the freedom and the choices of groups and individuals. Indeed, understanding the role played by religious constructions of the self in the formation of secular definitions of autonomy becomes one of the contributions of religious education to the cultural and moral work of the liberal school, serving to strengthen the grounds upon which an enriched, dynamic construction of autonomy can be articulated and defended (Carr, 1996, pp. 159–178).

The third dilemma which contemporary religious education must tackle is the issue of religious pluralism – an area where the challenge to religious education echoes the wider questions associated with living in a multicultural society. The challenge of diversity was one of the motivations of Smart's work and the inclusive liberalism of Smart's approach to religious education endeavoured to meet it in several creative ways. One important approach was to treat specific religious affiliations as local manifestations of a universal phenomenon and to see structural continuities and resemblances that might function as the focus of classroom analysis and enquiry. A second, related approach involved the calculated recoding of religious belief as cultural identity, a strategy that resonated with the wider, secularist assumptions of liberal multiculturalism and its political interpretation of ethnic and confessional particularism. In this approach, the question of doctrinal difference is politely marginalized within religious education in favour of the celebration of the external cultural trappings of diverse faith communities coexisting within the liberal polity. There has always been dissatisfaction with the superficiality of this strategy, exacerbated by its obvious refusal to deal with religious difference in an era when the expression of such difference has become much more salient for liberal democratic societies than the established narratives of secularization and modernization once presumed they would be (Berger, 1999, pp. 1–19). Critical realist methods propose religious education as part of a shared intellectual framework for debate and interaction in a plural society, endorsing the mainstream liberal view that learners from diverse religious and non-religious backgrounds ought to be encouraged to pursue rival versions of the good life in conditions of mutual toleration. Authentic toleration then demands, however, that religious education fully acknowledges divergence of belief and conviction, enabling learners to describe, celebrate, rationalize and defend beliefs, even up to the point of irreconcilability on the basis that it is a morally vital, and educationally defining, end in itself to search for and live by the truth derived from an apprehension of the ultimate order of reality. The reality may be radically independent of any and all attempts to understand it, but any meaningful knowledge of it is entirely reliant on the specific discourses, doctrinal formulations and cultural practices through which it is encountered and interpreted. It is the responsibility of religious education to enable learners to make critically literate and rational judgements about the relationship between the embedded processes of faith through which an informing order of reality might be experienced and the authenticity of the reality disclosed by these processes.

The recent revival of interest within religious education in the critical adjudication of some of the fundamental truth claims of religious belief – and the existential life choices to which they commonly give rise – perhaps restores to the discipline some of the curricular centrality it implicitly enjoyed before the rise of the modern forms of instrumental rationality that were to prove, in the Western world at least, so inimical to the authority of religious faith (Micklethwait and Wooldridge, 2009). Acknowledging this possible realignment implies no necessary endorsement of the fashionable 'post-secular turn' in contemporary philosophy or social theory, still less a longing for any return to pre-Enlightenment irrationalism in the curriculum. It does suggest, however, that successful religious education will now and in the future have to engage earnestly with the grammars of faith, the investments of confessing communities and the challenge of religiously grounded commitments to the styles of reasoning recognized and affirmed by the educated mind.

REFERENCES

Ayer, A.J. (1936) *Language, Truth and Logic*. Harmondsworth: Penguin.
Barnes, L.P. (2009a) An honest appraisal of phenomenological religious education and a final, honest reply to Kevin O'Grady, *British Journal of Religious Education*, 31.1: 69–72.
Barnes, L.P. (2009b) *IMPACT No.17: Religious Education: Taking Religious Difference Seriously*. Philosophy of Education Society of Great Britain.
Bellitto, C.M. (2005) Revisiting ancient practices: priestly training before Trent, in R.B. Begley and J.W. Koterski (eds), *Medieval Education*. New York: Fordham University Press, pp. 35–50.
Berger, P.L. (1999) The desecularization of the world: a global overview, in P. Berger et al (eds), *The Desecularization of the World: Resurgent Religion and World Politics*. Grand Rapids, MI: Eerdmans, pp. 1–19.
Carr, D. (1996) Rival conceptions of spiritual education, *Journal of Philosophy of Education*, 30.2: 157–178.
Conroy, J. and Davis, R.A. (2008) Citizenship, education and the claims of religious literacy, in M.A. Peters et al (eds), *Global Citizenship Education: Philosophy, Theory and Pedagogy*. Rotterdam: Sense Publishers, pp. 187–203.
County of Avon Education Service (1976) *Religious Education: Avon Agreed Syllabus*. Bristol: County of Avon.
Ehrenpreis, S. (2006) Reformed education in early modern europe: a survey, in W. Janse and B. Pitkin (eds), *The Formation of Clerical and Confessional Identities in Early Modern Europe*. Leiden: Brill, pp. 39–53.
Hadot, P. (2004) *What is Ancient Philosophy?*, trans. M. Chase. London: Harvard University Press.
Hella, E. and Wright, A. (2009) Learning 'about' and 'from' religion: phenomenography, the Variation Theory of Learning and religious education in Finland and the UK, *British Journal of Religious Education*, 31.1: 53–64.
Inner London Education Authority (ILEA) (1968) *Learning for Life*. London: ILEA.
Israel, J.I. (2001) *Radical Enlightenment: Philosophy and the Making of Modernity 1650–1750*. Oxford: Oxford University Press.
Israel, J.I. (2006) *Enlightenment Contested: Philosophy, Modernity and the Emancipation of Man 1670–1752*. Oxford: Oxford University Press.
Mandelbrote, S. (2003) The Bible and didactic literature in early modern England, in N. Glaisyer and S. Pennell (eds), *Didactic Literature in England, 1500–1800*. London: Ashgate, pp. 19–40.
Markowski, M. (2008) Teachers in early Christianity, *Journal of Research on Christian Education*, 17.2: 136–152.
Marrou, H-I. (1956) *A History of Education in Antiquity*, trans. G. Lamb. London: Sheed and Ward.
Marshall, J. (2006) *John Locke, Toleration and Early Enlightenment Culture*. Cambridge: Cambridge University Press.
Micklethwait, J. and Wooldridge, A. (2009) *God Is Back: How the Global Revival of Faith Is Changing the World*. London: Penguin.
Moran, G. (2006) Religious education and the nation state, in M. De Souza *et al* (eds), *International Handbook of the Religious, Moral and Spiritual Dimensions in Education*. New York: Springer, pp. 41–51.

Moseley, A. (2007) *John Locke*. London: Continuum.

Nostra Aetate (Declaration on the Relation of the Church to Non-Christian Religions) (1965). http://www.vatican.va/archive/hist_councils/ii_vatican_council/documents/vat-ii_decl_19651028_nostra-aetate_en.html (last accessed 21-05-09).

Schools Council (1971) *Working Paper 36: Religious Education in Secondary Schools*. London: Evans/Methuen.

Smart, N. (1969) *The Religious Experience of Mankind*. Englewood Cliffs, NJ: Prentice Hall.

Smart, N (1977) *A Groundplan for the Study of Religion*. London: Schools Council.

Smith, E.A. (1944) Principles of Reformation education, *Religious Education*, 39.5: 306–313.

Vitz, E.B. (2005) Liturgy as education in the middle ages, in R.B. Begley and J.W. Koterski (eds), *Medieval Education*. New York: Fordham University Press, pp. 20–35.

Willemsen, A. (2008) *Back to the Schoolyard: The Daily Practice of Medieval and Renaissance Education*. Turnhout: Brepols.

Wright, A. (2008) *Critical Religious Education, Multiculturalism and the Pursuit of Truth*. Cardiff: University of Wales Press.

Wright, N.T. (1992) *The New Testament and the People of God*. London: SPCK.

31

Physical Education

Mike McNamee and
Richard Bailey

THE PROBLEM OF PHYSICAL EDUCATION

The majority of scholarship in the field of the philosophy of physical education orbits around a single issue. Reid (1996, p. 8) captured the problem neatly when he writes, 'While "physical" seems to speak of the human body, its nature and functioning (most particularly, in the context of structured forms of movement, physical activities of various sorts, games, gymnastics, and exercises), "education" typically connotes the mind and its development'. This bifurcation is to be understood within the context of the Platonic–Cartesian tradition of Western philosophy, in which a distinction is made between the mind and body, and as usually happens in dualisms one aspect is privileged. Some philosophers even question the appropriateness of the term 'physical education' since, in Barrow's (1982, p. 60) foreboding words, 'physical education instructors are in the interesting position of being only marginally related to education'.[96] To be clear, there is no suggestion here that physical activities do not deserve a place in the school curriculum, merely that they do not warrant the praiseworthy label 'educational'! Pupils' health and fitness, it is often argued, are important and ought to be supported by teachers in one way or another, but this is damning with faint praise as it clearly relegates physical education (or whatever it is decided to call the subject) to second class status in the curriculum.

This, then, is the problem of physical education, and the dominant task of academic writing from within the subject (as well as some supportive outsiders) has been concerned to respond to it. Although our concern here is philosophical, it ought nevertheless to be acknowledged that questioning the status of physical education in the curriculum has occupied (and continues to occupy) scholars from other disciplines and practitioners, too. There have been more declarations, agendas and calls for action in support of physical education than for any other subject area. Ironically then, given these many and varied public pronouncements, advocates have seemingly felt compelled to embrace numerous and transient policy priorities in order to secure physical education's place in schools. At any particular time in the subject's history, it had been claimed that physical education offers an instrumental contribution to children's health and fitness, character development, educational attainment, social skills, attitudes to school, peer acceptance and sporting prowess; it can also help combat obesity, social exclusion, crime and ethnic conflict (Bailey et al., 2009). While the veritable panoply of potential goods it secures keeps alive the interests of governmental policy advisors and makers, it is noteworthy that none of these types of arguments address the central problem identified above. The strategy seems to be that in the absence of a strong argument in favour of physical education, it may yet be important to compile a legion of logically weak ones.

Reid (1996, p. 8) correctly highlighted the route to the only genuinely persuasive solution to the problem: 'We have to show how or whether physical education can be given a legitimate place within the category of recognised educational activities; how it can be accommodated within the school curriculum; how it can be justified in terms of educational goals and values'. It is to these questions that most writers on the philosophy of physical education have addressed themselves and which forms the substance of this chapter.

EDUCATION AND PHYSICAL EDUCATION

Recent writing on the educational status of physical education is largely a continuation of debates begun around the 1960s. Generally speaking, there was a stark difference between philosophical writing on the subject in the USA and the UK. American writers tended to accept the 'schools of thought' conception of philosophy (see Ch. 2), and drew on a wide range of literature such as pragmatism, existentialism and phenomenology (e.g. Zeigler, 1968). However, academic interest in the philosophy of physical education in the USA was relatively short-lived, as theorists embraced its conceptual cousin the philosophy of sport. Led by established mainstream philosophers such as Paul Weiss, this development had at least the virtue of being a discipline in its own right, rather than eking out an existence as a poorly regarded sub-discipline of the philosophy of education. It was thus able to nourish conceptual work on the nature and importance of sports, games and play, following historically significant ancient and modern predecessors from Plato to Huizinga. It could also draw upon substantive normative topics in aesthetics, ethics, philosophical anthropology and political philosophy (Gerber and Morgan, 1979; Morgan and Meier, 1995).

The picture in the UK was different and was bound to the development of analytical philosophy of education. Most philosophers with an interest in the activities of physical education were heavily under the influence of the analytical tradition represented by Peters, Hirst, Dearden and others (see Ch. 9). They were not remarkable in this fact, for most of the philosophical work in education across the British Commonwealth was similarly under its hegemonic influence. For Peters, the many uses of the word 'education' could be reduced to a central case and the philosophical task was to tease out criteria implicit in that case. This led Peters to develop his well-known and sophisticated account of education as the transmission of intrinsically worthwhile activities to learners in order to open the initiates to a vaster and more variegated existence. That same worthwhile knowledge was continuous with the various forms of knowledge that Hirst had delineated by his own set of epistemological criteria. Peters' thesis was summarized thus:

> (i) 'education' implies the transmission of what is worth-while to those who become committed to it; (ii) 'education' must involve knowledge and understanding and some kind of cognitive perspective, which are not inert; (iii) 'education' at least rules out some procedures of transmission, on the grounds that they lack wittingness and voluntariness on the part of the learner (Peters, 1966, p. 45).

The first two criteria are sometimes referred to as the axiological and epistemological conditions (Carr, 1997; Reid, 1997). The third criterion refers to the processes by which such transmission was ethically acceptable.

Some writers on the philosophy of physical education sought to reject Peter's position on the appealing but ultimately unsatisfactory grounds that it incorporated a dualistic philosophical anthropology (Arnold, 1979). This line of attack has recently been resuscitated with greater substance mainly by drawing in phenomenological ideas of embodiment (Thorburn, 2008; Whitehead, 2001). However, as a criticism of Peters it was neither fair nor sustainable. It is certainly true that Peters focused on the development of mind and reason, but it is not accurate to claim that he assumed a crude Cartesian or dual substance theory of human agency. In the wake of the Wittgensteinian and Rylean attacks on the privacy of mind, Peters – even from his earliest writings on the concept of motivation – had a rich conception of mind as an embodied collection of psychological habits, skills, powers and capabilities. Nevertheless, his focus on the development of rational mind betrayed his normative philosophical anthropology that was certainly buttressed by Hirst's account of the forms of knowledge that privileged the propositional over the physical or practical.

Others defended physical education from within the analytical framework. An interesting case in point is that of Carlisle (1969), who suggested that the activities of physical education were best conceived of as aesthetic ones, thus placing them at least within one recognizable form of knowledge in the

Hirstian sense. This proposal proved to be unsuccessful: whereas there are many aspects of physical activities that are conducive to aesthetic enjoyment or praise, it would not be accurate to portray them as intrinsic to the activities themselves (Best, 1978). Physical education therefore was not a form of knowledge. But Hirst's thesis allowed that the educational elements – though not forms in their own right – might combine to form fields of study. Thus, physical-education could be framed as a university subject by combining forms such as mathematics and the physical sciences (i.e. anatomy, biomechanics and physiology) or human sciences (such as sociology and psychology), and so on. Yet it was clear that only forms of knowledge were the proper constituents of education at the level of schooling that was the focus for the key battleground of educational status.

The work of later philosophers such as Barrow (1982) and White (1973) took issue with many key points of the Peters/Hirst account, but their focus remained resolutely on education conceived of as the development of rationally autonomous learners. Even those philosophers sympathetic to physical education's claim to educational status, such as Carr (1997, p. 201), shared this commitment. Despite the fact that Carr recognized and articulated the value of practical as well as theoretical rationality, he undermines any claim that physical education might be better understood in terms of practical knowledge:

> The key idea here is the traditionalist one that certain forms of knowledge and understanding enter into the ecology of human development and formation – not as theories of a scientist or the skills of a golfer, but as the horizon of significance against which we are able to form some coherent picture of how the world is, our place in it and how it is appropriate for us to relate to others. Strictly speaking, it matters not a hoot on the traditionalist picture whether such received wisdom is theoretical or practical or located at some point in between; what matters is that there should be – in the name of education – some substantial initiation into this realm (or these realms) of human significance alongside any training in vocational or domestic or merely recreational skills. This is not to deny any proper normative conception of the latter, or that any pursuit of such skills may involve considerable rational judgement and discrimination; it is rather to insist that the sort of rationality they do exhibit may not and need not have anything much to do with education. Very roughly, one might put the point of the liberal-traditionalist distinction between educational and non-educational knowledge by observing that the former is knowledge which informs rather than merely uses the mind.

Other philosophers have offered a revised account of the relation between the forms of knowledge and physical education (Parry, 1988; Reid, 1996). They argue for a proper recognition of the centrality of practical knowledge embodied in intentional action and meaningful participation in the activities such as swimming, games playing and trampolining. Practical knowledge is demanded by and developed in participation in the constituent activities of physical education, thus satisfying the epistemological criterion of education. But to evaluate this claim requires that a further unpacking of the phrase 'epistemological criterion' – used rather loosely so far – is required.

Peters' remarks on the epistemological criteria of educational activities are subtle and variegated. He argued that the development of knowledge and understanding which is constitutive of education must (1) not be inert but rather inform our operations in the world; and that (2) such knowledge and understanding must be framed in some 'cognitive perspective'. Might it be argued that practical knowledge of physical education activities may come to characterize part of one's way of viewing the world. Is this not what is meant by the phrase an active lifestyle? Here one's knowledge is such that it is not inert but rather tied to action and choices in one's living. And an extension of this recognition might lead one to consider the conceptual obligation regarding cognitive perspective to be satisfied.

It is unlikely that Peters would have agreed with this position; after all, 'sports and games' were his chosen foils when he articulated his conception of educational significance:

> In so far as knowledge is involved in games and pastimes, this is limited to the hived off end of the activity which may be morally indifferent. A man may know a great deal about cricket if he is a devotee of the game; but it would be fanciful to pretend that his concern to find out things is linked with any serious purpose, unless the game is viewed under an aesthetic or moral purpose. Cricket is classed as a game because it's end is morally unimportant. Indeed an end has almost to be invented to make possible the various manifestations of skill …. Curriculum activities, on the other hand, such as science or history, literary appreciation, and poetry are 'serious' in that they illuminate other areas of life and contribute much to the quality of living. They have, secondly, a wide ranging cognitive content which distinguishes them from games. Skills, for instance, do not have a wide ranging cognitive content. There is very little to know about riding bicycles, swimming, or golf. It is largely a matter of knowing how rather than of 'knowing that', of knack rather than of understanding. Furthermore, what there is to know throws little light on much else. (Peters, 1966, pp. 158–159)

Modern defenders of physical education might legitimately respond to those who question the subject's cognitive credentials that their opponents are basing their judgements on an outmoded image of the subject, and that there are, in fact, plenty of examples of propositional knowledge that form the educational substance of physical education lessons. They might, for example, refer to the development of Teaching Games for Understanding (Bunker and Thorpe, 1982), which places considerable emphasis on the development of both propositional and procedural knowledge, and was an explicit response to the limitations of the 'traditional' technique-based methods. Here skills were taught alongside conceptual appreciation for the nature of games in terms of attack and defence in such principles as 'delay', 'depth', 'width', 'penetration', 'possession' and 'space'. Or they could draw attention to the widespread introduction of physical education examinations, in which biomechanics, physiology, psychology and sociology came to assume a significant place. However, the emergence of examinations in physical education does not touch the key question of the educational status of its practical activities; it merely re-labels as sport or physical education what were previously sciences.

This raises the thorny question of how one selects what ranges of practical knowledge are educationally relevant. While one might point to the profoundly complex kinds of practical knowledge required, for example, in playing

Tchaikovsky or flying a plane, as Reid does, they are not exemplars of the range of practical knowledge that has historically been definitive of physical education. Nor can they be used helpfully as analogues in such an argument. There is also a complication in the contrast between the 'serious' forms of knowledge and sports and games that relate to the ease with which children are initiated into cultural practices. 'Serious' educational subjects have easy skills and techniques at their onset, yet these are the first steps in practices of immense rational sophistication in range and depth. Most physical activities do not possess this range and it would be folly to argue that they do (Barrow, 2008). Yet there is more to them than mere knack: a forward roll is a skill, and so is a double twisting back somersault, but compare the range of complexity.

PHYSICAL EDUCATION AND PHYSICAL ACTIVITIES

It was argued by Hirst and Peters (1970) that there was a certain conceptual unity to the forms of knowledge that comprised education that was exhibited by qualities like central concepts and peculiar methodologies. Could a claim of conceptual coherence be maintained for physical education. What might bring together activities as diverse as athletics, dance, and competitive games? Perhaps the breadth of physical education activities is self-defeating, and what is required is a narrower focus.

In the *locus classicus* of analytical Philosophy of Sport, Suits (1978) argued that for an activity to be called a game it must have (i) a pre-lusory goal (i.e. a goal specified prior to the contest such as scoring more goals, jumping the furthest, and so on); (ii) a set of means that limited the ways in which the goal could be legitimately achieved; (iii) rules which define the activity and specify permissible and impermissible means in the achievement of the pre-lusory goal; and (iv) a disposition that the game player must adopt in their attempt to achieve the pre-lusory goal. This disposition to achieve the pre-lusory goal (as opposed to any further goals the sportsperson may individually hold) is called the 'lusory attitude': 'the knowing acceptance of constitutive rules just so the activity made possible by such rules can occur'. Anyone failing to hold such a disposition is simply not playing a game even where they share the same field, or court, or track with others so engaged. Suits maintained that, 'Playing a game is the voluntary attempt to overcome unnecessary obstacles' (Suits, 1978, p. 54). This elegant formulation accedes to Peters' point above that an end has to be invented for games in order for them to exist. That an end has to be invented, however, does not render the activity morally or educationally insignificant. Equally, art has no end beyond itself yet we do not regard it in such derisory terms as have been used in the educational status debate concerning physical education. One area that has traditionally received positive (though too frequently uncritical) attention is the idea of ethical development in and through sport and we shall turn our attention to this topic next.

AXIOLOGY AND PHYSICAL EDUCATION

What Reid (1997) attempted, more generously than other liberal philosophers of education, was to connect the ways in which different kinds of knowledge embody different kinds of value. He set out a fuller list of the sources of value and attempts to relate physical education to them. In addition to arguments about the value of theoretical knowledge, he articulated the following range: intellectual, ethical, aesthetic, economic, hedonic and health. To argue that games playing confers a wide-ranging cognitive perspective on the world seems to go beyond both reason and evidence. A more circumscribed claim regarding theoretical knowledge in physical education may, however, be plausible.

Understanding sports and other forms of physical activities from the appropriate field of theoretical standpoints (anatomy, biology, history, sociology, and so on) illuminates the ways in which those activities can contribute to a worthwhile life. A student can benefit from knowing that steady-state, medium-intensity, exercise over 20 minutes' duration draws significantly upon aerobic rather than anaerobic metabolism and is therefore more appropriate to my maintaining lower levels of body fat. Conversely, the student can come to appreciate that circuit training is more conducive to anaerobic fitness and that by altering her body positions while performing sit-ups she may more specifically target the abdominal muscles and reduce the contribution of the hip flexors. Moreover, this student may begin to appreciate critically the gendered atmosphere of the locker room or the offensiveness engendered by racist or anti-Semitic attitudes in some sports crowds. Despite these benefits, the value arguments for physical education ought not to be erected on *exactly* the same grounds as other curriculum subjects that are palpably different in nature. This inspired Reid's search for a broader range of values.

There is a sense in which Reid brought this axiological problem upon himself because of his conceptualization of physical education. He recognized that no satisfactory account of the subject will flow simply from linguistic analyses of the words 'physical' and 'education'. Rather, such an account must begin from an analysis of the historical practices and traditions that have been prominent in giving shape and form to physical education. The task is, therefore, to elucidate,

> The conceptual features of a set of well-founded educational practices and traditions. What is 'given', from this standpoint, is not some set of axioms or intuitions about the nature of 'physicality' and 'education', but what might rather be called physical education as a form of life, that is the practices and traditions of physical education as they have evolved historically and continue to evolve, in concrete social, cultural and institutional contexts. (Reid, 1996, p. 10)

This seems a persuasive approach, but it is problematic to argue simply that physical education is the sum of its practices and traditions without also offering an account that articulates and brings together the disparate nature of those practices and traditions.

In terms of ethical value, Reid points out the inherent normativity of physical education activities. Here, it must be pointed out, the diversity of what goes under the heading physical education renders generalizations problematic. In sporting games, the moral educational features are written into their very nature (i.e. the regulative rules). As Aspin (1975) noted long before him, where games are taught properly, ethical notions such as equality, fairness, honesty and rule-abiding action necessarily arise. The extent to which these notions are merely caught rather than taught is another matter. Reid made two points that are designed to defuse the arguments of those who deny sports' ethical dimension. Reid wrote:

> The first relates to the discussion earlier on the relations between the constituents of our axiology, which concluded in favour of the priority of ethical values (when competing values are entertained). In the context of games teaching, this reflects the traditional principle that fair play, sportsmanship and respect for one's opponent take precedence over the competitive objectives of winning and avoiding defeat. The second point, likewise, concerns questions of priority. The position adopted in this paper ... is that games and sports are forms of play, aimed essentially at promoting pleasure, enjoyment, excitement, recreation, and the like; their primary value, in short, is hedonic. Winning, from this point of view, is not, as is sometimes supposed, the ultimate goal of competitive games: enjoyment is, and competitive action, structured in highly specific ways by the operation of the norms, rules, codes, conventions and so on of the various particular sports and games, is the way in which the conditions of enjoyment are fulfilled, its possibilities realized. ... Games themselves are, as essentially hedonic activities, fundamentally self-contained and in some sense non-serious ... and this observation gives some weight to the scepticism sometimes expressed about the prospects for extending those ethical principles beyond the boundaries of the game. (Reid, 1997, p. 12)

Reid sought to answer Peters' question regarding the source of (educational) value. However, his response is not persuasive. First, Reid failed to apply his own reasoning to his analysis of the logic of competitive games: viz. their ethical dimension. He posited that where there is conflict between the competitive urge to win, and other, ethical, principles such as fairness and honesty, the latter should prevail. Yet he has already informed the reader that to play games logically entails the observance of such principles. This being the case, there can be no such conflict, for where players are dishonest, or unfair or not rule-abiding (assuming they are breaking the rules, in being dishonest, or violent or disrespectful) they *are ipso* facto not playing the game. This formalist point is commonly discussed under the heading of the 'logical incompatibility thesis' (Fraleigh, 1984). Adherents of the formalist thesis argue that to play a game one must play by the rules and to do otherwise is to be engaged in behaviours that are, by definition, not part of the game (Lehman, 1982).

Secondly, Reid's emphasis on the hedonism appears to equate physical education with competitive games. In fact, numerous empirical studies show that games do take up a large proportion of physical education lessons in many countries, and this has been the case for many years in the UK and the USA. Nevertheless, from a philosophical point of view, it seems clear that if one were to conceptualize or justify physical education solely in terms of sports and games then this would beg questions as to the educational place of the other members of the family of activities that often fall under the heading of physical education. Furthermore, if one were to alter the conception of the physical education it seems clear that one's arguments concerning the types of knowledge entailed therein, the aims, value and educational justification of the subject, ought correspondingly to alter. Reid did not acknowledge this as problematic since he later discusses at length the benefit of health values wrought by a physical education curriculum. The precise picture of physical education Reid wanted to defend is not specified, though the contours are visible: a distaste for theoretical engagement; a predominance of sporting games; and a reductionism to hedonic values. What Reid argued later is for a kind of eclecticism that blurs the emphasis on competitive sporting games. He urged that the full value of physical education is to be found in its manifold contributions to different sorts of value, but that as a matter of logic, on his analysis, their value is essentially hedonic.

A significant difficulty with the hedonic thesis is that it offers no criteria (and hence no logical basis over and above mere preference) against which to evaluate such practices or make subsequent policy decisions (McNamee, 1994). The hedonists' mantra 'it gives me pleasure' and 'I enjoy it' fail to provide any sort of logical answer to a sceptical questioner but stops them from further exploration. Of course, many children and adults who are committed to sports find the exercise of skilful acts deeply satisfying, fulfilling or pleasurable and attribute their value to nothing other than the experience or engagement in the activity. The language in which their accounts of the value of their experiences are often couched is hedonistic in the sense that they refer exclusively to the subjective value of pleasurable feelings. By way of criticism, consider first those activities that are ill-characterized as felt pleasure. For instance, there may be many qualities, goods or values associated with, for instance, outdoor and adventurous activities in the winter time. It may be assumed, however, that fun or pleasure may not commonly be among them. These activities may come to be enjoyable but only after some considerable time and effort and this may only be afforded to a limited number of people who are genetically predisposed to them or who, through training, have come to be committed to them. Secondly, as Parry (1988) noted, the pursuit of pleasure itself does not demarcate any special class of activities except those logically thus defined. The corollary of the hedonic view would entail the justification of whatsoever people found pleasurable simply because they found it pleasurable. And the contents list of such an account could render some fairly unthinkable items for education (Bailey et al., 2008). Thirdly, pleasures differ in quality. The pleasures derived by a 6-year-old child from engaging in simple motor actions are considered inappropriate for 16 year olds who demand something more complex. Essentially, this is the Rawls' (1972, p. 435) Aristotelian Principle:

> Other things equal, human beings enjoy the exercise of their realized capacities (their innate or trained abilities), and this enjoyment increases the more the capacity is realized, or the greater its complexity. The intuitive idea here is that human beings take more pleasure in

doing something the more they become proficient at it, and of two activities they do equally well, they prefer the one calling on a larger and more intricate and subtle discriminations.

Indeed, the values of sports and games may themselves be considered time-related goods (Slote, 1989). No-one would deny that the satisfactions afforded by the successful grasping of timing a boast in squash or spotting a somersault are tremendously rewarding but they might well deny that this is always the case, and that pleasure is the right concept to denote the attendant satisfactions.

Every account of the value presupposes a particular framework and, moreover, a particular philosophical anthropology. Any particular and substantive account of the value of sports and related practices will therefore be related conceptually to an account of a person that is thought desirable for one to become. Sports and related practices thus become seen as one of a family of engineering processes (less deterministically, practices and traditions) that are constitutive of a person's becoming just that: a person of a certain, perhaps athletic, kind.

Each culture has more or less tightly defined horizons that inform and are informed symbiotically by each other. How are such horizons informed by the hedonic thesis? Aristotle observed long ago that one cannot pursue pleasure in isolation: pleasure is derived *through* actions and activities. A similar point was made by Nozick (1974) with his notion of an 'experience machine' that can give an individual a perfect simulation of the experiences desired while floating in a tank hooked up to various psychotropic equipment. Critics of hedonistic axiology object that a life of passivity and simulation is a life not worthy of human agency. They are repelled by the thought of passivity that is characteristic of life in the experience machine. All it has to offer is a simulation of living. This is not the life of a person. *Qua* persons they want to *do* certain things: to achieve the attendant satisfactions of being a successful teacher or pupil, cricketer, or athlete. To *be* such things is to be committed to various activities, roles and relationships that define the sort of persons they are.

These arguments about the inadequacy of educational justification being based upon hedonic lines leave untouched the philosophical questions concerning the nature of value itself and classes of value used to account for physical education. Carr criticized Reid, and Peters before him, for blurring the distinction between intrinsic/instrumental values. They employed the terms 'intrinsic', 'extrinsic', 'inherent' and 'instrumental' to refer to both the value of an activity and the motivational states of a person. It is helpful here to stipulate linguistic usage in the interests of conceptual clarity. It is perhaps less conducive to error to restrict the terms 'intrinsic' and 'extrinsic' to one's motivations or valuing of an activity but reserve the terms 'inherent' and 'instrumental' to refer to the (potential) value of a given thing or activity. For one can be intrinsically motivated to bang one's head against a wall (i.e. where one did it for its own sake and sought no further end), whereas no one would want to maintain that it was an inherently valuable act. On the other hand, it could be argued that while sport is inherently valuable, any particular athlete only values it instrumentally and therefore that their motivations were entirely extrinsic. Much confused debate in physical education has occurred precisely for the want of drawing these distinctions with care. Moreover, as Plato (1974) argued, the highest goods: are mixed goods: those which are inherently valuable *and* valuable as means to further valuable ends Furthermore, the debate could be extended to consider not only the relationality between means and ends but also between particular persons who have particular capacities, abilities, dispositions and potentialities, and those means and ends: the same activity might be inherently valuable but, as a matter of fact, be valued intrinsically by one person, extrinsically by another, both by the same and/or not at all by a third person.

PHYSICAL EDUCATION AND PERSONHOOD

At an analytical level rather than arguing that a particular school subject meets the criteria of cognitive depth and breadth (or the capacity to inform rather than merely use the mind, as Carr put it), acknowledgement must be given of the fact that there are competing conceptions of education. This is not to resort to the subjectivist's or relativist's abandonment of education as an 'essentially contested concept'. Despite the fact that different conceptions of education embody particular evaluative commitments regarding the nature of persons and society, they all share the formal notion that education is the development of persons toward the living of full and valuable lives (Langford, 1984; McNamee, 1992). The next step of an argument regarding educational status or value would be to develop an account of persons and the kinds of things that makes their lives worthwhile over and above Peters' intellectual pursuits. Persons, on the kind of account that has been hinted at in this chapter,[97] are beings who have the capacity to develop, evaluate and live out life plans based on a combination of projects, relationships and commitments.[98] Among this combination of activities are a variety of practices that are valuable by virtue of their internal goods – the inherent satisfactions attendant on the engagement of the range of physical activities that comprise physical education such as the practical knowledge and abilities demanded and reproduced in them. Moreover, these activities can also be valued because of their capacity to secure external goods such as health, wealth, status and so on (which, though valued, are only contingently associated with the activities in particular ways). The activities of physical education are exemplified by a certain range of sporting and other physical activity practices, which can be characterized as mixed goods because they have the capacity to be valued not only for their internal goods but also for the particular manner in which they secure external goods. In attaining these goods, while upholding the best traditions of the social practices that demand and develop them, learners develop a range of instrumental virtues (such as commitment, dedication, discipline, and tenacity) and moral virtues (such as courage, honesty and moderation). In proper pursuit of the excellences of the activities of physical education, learners are enlisted into the traditions of physical cultures that can, therefore, contribute to the living of full and valuable lives (McNamee, 2008). It can be argued that if this does instantiate or confer educational value it is difficult to see what might.

This kind of argument, it might be said, holds true only for those practices recognized as sporting games or athletic activities (and possibly dance too). While the argument is long on initiation into those practices that are partly definitive of a culture and its identity(ies) it is short on the kinds of individualized, health-related activities. Historically, there have been two strands in what is called physical education: sports and health (or in older times hygiene, posture and so forth) (Bailey et al., 2009). It may be that a different type of justificatory argument is required to support each. Perhaps Carr (1997) was right to classify the latter activities – along with life-saving and other 'anomalies' that fall to the task of physical educators – as valuable but not educationally valuable because of their lacking in what can be referred to as cultural significance or cultural capital.[99]

Time and space do not allow a proper comment upon these strands except to note conceptual unity seems a chimera. As Reid (1996) remarked, one must look rather to culture-specific, historical, and political factors that have shaped the professions. Or, as Kirk (2010, p. 11) put it: 'What physical education "means" is embedded in and expressed through the interactions of the participants; the teachers and students, the designers of lessons and programmes, the builders of facilities, and the creators and suppliers of equipment, just to name a few'. Dance is a cultural practice that employs large motor-skilled activity like tennis or football. Some forms of gymnastics require interpretative movements and proceed with music like dance. Sculpting bodies, like training for rugby or netball, often requires highly structured regimes and exercises. But these resemblances are nothing more than that.

If all that one can do is to point out commonalities, then there is little that is philosophically interesting here for anyone attempting a conceptual analysis by necessary and sufficient conditions of linguistic usage. Reid's peroration towards value pluralism should extend so far as to recognize the inherent openness of the concept of physical education: pluralism in activities, pluralism in values. If this is true, then no universal criterion of demarcation can be raised that will help physical education teachers select activities that are available. Instead, they should consider the types and natures of rituals that sports instantiate in the modern world.

NOTES

96 It is surely not insignificant that Barrow labels the section in which this quotation can be found 'Primary and Physical Instruction'.

97 They are developed substantially by McNamee (1992) and revised in the light of the ethics of sports in McNamee (2008).

98 A debt to the writing of Charles Taylor is clearly evident here and is explicitly acknowledged and developed in relation to the emotions by McNamee (2008).

99 Notwithstanding this, Hardy (1991, p.19) cited Sinclair and Henry, who remarked over a century ago that: 'The ability to save lives is the glorious privilege of a swimmer'. As we talk of the importance of physical education in terms of the value of its skilled repertoires, the poignancy of this remark ought not to be lost.

REFERENCES

Arnold, P.J. (1979) *Meaning in Movement: Sport and Physical Education.* London: Heinemann.

Aspin, D. (1975) Ethical aspects of sport and games and physical education, *Journal of Philosophy of Education,* 9 (1), 49–71.

Bailey, R.P., Bloodworth, A. and McNamee, M. (2007) Gender, sport and well-being, in I. Wellard (ed.), *Rethinking Gender and Youth Sport.* London: Routledge.

Bailey, R.P., Armour, K., Kirk, D. et al. (2009) The educational benefits claimed for physical education and school sport: an academic review, *Research Papers in Education,* 24, 1–27.

Barrow, R. (1981) *The Philosophy of Schooling.* Brighton: Wheatsheaf Books.

Barrow, R. (2008) Education and the body: prolegomena, *British Journal of Educational Studies,* 56, 272–285.

Best, D. (1978) *Philosophy and Human Movement.* London: Allen and Unwin.

Bunker, D. and Thorpe, R. (1982) A model for the teaching of games in secondary schools, *Bulletin of Physical Education,* 18, 5–8.

Carlisle, R. The concept of physical education, *Proceedings of the Philosophy Education Society at Great Britain,* 3, 1–11.

Carr, D. (1997) Physical education and values diversity: a response to Andrew Reid, *European Physical Education Review,* 3, 195–205.

Fraleigh, W. (1984) *Right Actions in Sports: Ethics for Contestants.* Champaign, IL: Human Kinetics.

Gerber, E.W. and Morgan, W.J. (1979) *Philosophy and the Body,* 2nd edn. Philadelphia, PA: Lea & Febiger.

Hardy, C. (1991) Swimming history, *Swimming Times,* 68, 3, 18–20.

Hirst, P.H. and Peters, R.S. (1970) *The Logic of Education.* London: Routledge and Kegan Paul.

Kirk, D. (2010) *Physical Education Futures.* London: Routledge.

Langford, G. (1984) *Education, Persons and Society.* London: Macmillan.

Lehman, C. (1982) Can cheaters play the game? *Journal of the Philosophy of Education,* 8, 41–46.

McNamee, M.J. (1992) Physical education and the development of personhood, *Physical Education Review,* 15, 1, 13–28.

McNamee, M.J. (1994) Valuing leisure practices: towards a theoretical framework, *Leisure Studies,* 13, 288–309.

McNamee, M.J. (2008) *Sports, Virtues and Vices: Morality Play.* London: Routledge.

Morgan, W. and Meier, K.V. (1995) *Philosophic Inquiry in Sport.* Champaign, IL: Human Kinetics.

Nozick, R (1974) *Anarchy, State and Utopia.* New York: Basic Books.

Parry, J. (1988) Physical education, justification and the national curriculum, *Physical Education Review,* 11(2), 106–118.

Parry, J. (1998) Reid on knowledge and justification in physical education, *European Physical Education Review,* 4, 70–74.

Peters, R.S. (1966) *Ethics and Education.* London: Allen and Unwin.

Plato (1974) *The Republic* (trans. D. Lee). London: Penguin.

Rawls, J. (1972) *A Theory of Justice.* Oxford: Oxford University Press.

Reid, A. (1996) Knowledge, practice and theory in physical education, *European Physical Education Review,* 2, 94–104.

Reid, A. (1997) Value pluralism and physical education, *European Physical Education Review,* 3, 6–20.

Slote, M. (1989) *Goods and Virtues.* Oxford: Clarendon Press.

Suits, B. (1978) *The Grasshopper: Games, Life and Utopia*. Toronto: University of Toronto.

Thorburn, M. (2007) Articulating a Merpeau–Pontian phenomenology at physical education: the quest for active student engagement and authentic assessment in high-stakes examination awards. *European Physical Education Review*, 14, 263–280.

Whitehead, M. (2001) The concept of physical literacy, *European Journal of Physical Education*, 6, 127–138.

Zeigler, E. (1968) *Problems in the History and Philosophy of Physical Education and Sport*. Englewood Cliffs, NJ: Prentice-Hall.

32

Philosophical Questions about Learning Technologies

Craig A. Cunningham and
Briana L. Allen

INTRODUCTION

In *Experience and Nature*, John Dewey (1925) described philosophy as creating a 'ground-map of the province of criticism' (Dewey, 1925, LW1:308–309), thus providing a useful metaphor for our task in this chapter, which is to discuss the questions that philosophy of education might raise about technology in education. If we want to think critically about such questions, a ground-map can help define the territory of interest; its boundaries, regions, and topography; its climate, resources, and scarcities; and any particular points of interest that should attract our attention.

Our chapter consists of six parts. In the first, we discuss some (1) definitional issues that will help us to know which regions are part of our territory. The next four sections discuss these particular regions: (2) epistemological, questions of knowing; (3) psychological, questions of learning; (4) pedagogical, questions of teaching; and (5) social, questions of associated living. While such categorizations are arbitrary, and the boundaries between them are hazy, they help us to simplify the topography. In a final section (6), we pay particular attention to a transcendent issue: whether new technologies are likely to significantly democratize education and society.

Before we begin, we want to say a few words about our perspective. We think of 'criticism' as careful observation and the use of critical thinking as shining its light especially on conceptions or structures that often remain above criticism, such as power relations, assumptions, and unintended consequences. A critical perspective constantly reflects upon itself, seeking a better and more comprehensive understanding. In addition to being critical, the reflective observer of educational technology should also be a connoisseur. A 'critical connoisseur' doesn't necessarily possess the highest level of technical expertise, but has learned how to appreciate when educational technologies are used well and when their use could be improved, building a collection of best practices to share with others (Eisner 1998; Smith 2005). It is our hope that this chapter will help to cultivate this perspective.

DEFINITIONAL ISSUES

Technology can be defined simply as 'the application of knowledge to meet objectives or to solve problems'. This definition can be deepened by examining the variety of ways that the word 'technology' is used in everyday speech. Technology sometimes refers to an object (such as an interactive whiteboard), sometimes as knowledge (the applied science that makes the touch-screen capability of the interactive whiteboard possible), sometimes as an activity or practice (using the interactive whiteboard in a classroom to support brainstorming or a creative process), and sometimes as a form of volition or cultural 'enframing system' that sees the world in a particular way (for example, the desire to use an interactive whiteboard to involve a group in brainstorming a topic) (Ankiewicz et al., 2006; Franklin, 1999; Heidegger, 1977; Peters, 2003). In each instance, technology involves the application of knowledge to meet human purposes (Hansen, 1997; Warnick, 2004). Thus, *technology is always instrumental; it is always used for some end other than itself.* For this reason, a given technology can never be separated from the uses of that technology, because, by definition, a technology without an application isn't technology at all.

In this chapter, we are interested in the application of knowledge to produce learning, or 'stable, persisting changes in knowledge, skills and behaviour' (Spector 2001, p. 394). On this broad conception, *schooling* itself is an educational technology involving the continuous application of knowledge to make the mass shaping of ideas and behaviours possible and affordable. Furthermore, nearly everything used in schools involves technology. Some examples include pencils, chalkboards, books, podiums, chair-desks, bells, schedules, school buses, school buildings, playgrounds, athletic fields, band rooms, band instruments, coloured chalk, and PA systems. But 'technology' isn't just things; it includes the systems of ideas that legitimate and constrain the uses of those things, such as teacher certification systems, age-segregated classrooms, school architecture, the ways we divide subjects into disciplines, educational standards and performance objectives, testing and other forms of assessment, school districting, pedagogical approaches such as anchored instruction, and many other activities, processes, devices, and frameworks that make schooling possible.

Technologies used in schools can roughly be divided into those that existed before the emergence of computers and those that came afterwards. The former include things like chalkboards, books, and bells; while these *are* technologies, they have shifted into a different category where they are simply referred to as tools or practices. They are established and taken for granted; they have become 'transparent' (Bruce and Hogan, 1998). Newer educational technologies include devices and approaches that are not yet universal in schools and thus demand recognition as technology rather than simply practice. This latter distinction depends, of course, on one's perspective, since tools and techniques that are taken for granted in wealthier suburban or private schools (such as interactive whiteboards) are often considered exotic or a luxury in poorer, urban or rural schools.

Educational technologies can be further specified as 'instructional technologies', which excludes school buses and PA systems because they are more about the infrastructure and management of education. But the word 'instructional' has connotations that are not desirable from our perspective: it assumes that there is an 'instructor' who is using the technology to foster learning, or that the technology itself is 'instructional' (Cronje, 2006), implying that education primarily involves one-way communication, which is not at all obvious (Cremin, 1989; McClintock, 2000). A far better label is 'learning technologies'. A 'learning technology' is a technology that is intentionally used to support learning (McClintock, 2000). Because we believe that the focus of educational professionals should be on student learning, this puts the emphasis where it should be. Many commentators – especially outside the United States – use the designation 'information and communication technology' (ICT), which includes those technologies that are used for gathering, storing, retrieving, processing, analyzing, displaying, and transmitting information. We use ICT to refer to thosetechnologies specifically used for information and communication, but use 'learning technologies' more generally.

EPISTEMOLOGICAL: QUESTIONS OF KNOWING

Epistemological questions concern the nature of knowledge, its categorizations and representations, and ways of evaluating which knowledge is of most worth. These questions bear directly on psychological and pedagogical questions, as we discuss below. Perhaps the most important question from an educational stand-point is: What should be taught? It is to that question we turn first.

Herbert Spencer's question, 'What knowledge is of most worth?' is fundamental to deciding what to teach. This is never simply an empirical question about the cost–benefit of including particular knowledge in the curriculum, but a socio-cultural question about whether particular forms of knowledge are valued by particular interest groups (Martin, 1970). When we prioritize knowledge, we are answering fundamental questions about how we want our children to spend their time, what kind of people we want them to become, and what kind of society we want. These questions should be revisited occasionally, and 'inert ideas' (Whitehead, 1967, p. 1) and obsolete skills culled from the curriculum to make way for potentially more valuable topics. On this consideration, as society adopts new technologies, schools have an obligation to teach students how to use them, not only because they are likely to be useful once a student has left school but also because their utilization in school might enhance the educational process (Britton et al., 2005; Brogden and Couros, 2007; SCANS, 1991). What's more, the adoption of new technologies in society leads to new needs that require alterations to the school curriculum. For example, the advent of the Internet raises issues of child safety, the evaluation of information, and the need for new skill-sets such as how to create and maintain a safe online identity. These topics may have no obvious 'place' within the existing curriculum and yet cannot responsibly be ignored by schools (Hedberg and Brudvik, 2008).

The age-old purpose of schooling – to produce a literate citizenry able to participate in everyday life and the affairs of society – remains as true as ever, but the nature of literacy is changing. Literacy means not simply reading and writing, but is 'the means we use to construct and share meaning, to establish relationships, to gain power, to learn, and to participate in social worlds … . The word literacy then describes that space in which we make meaning in interaction with others' (Bruce 2003, p. 330; see also Burbules, 2000; Hedberg and Brudvik, 2008; Kellner, 2000). Schools must teach not only the basic tools of reading and writing and learning in an information age, including the capacity to interpret and to create images and video and facility with new forms of information such as hypertext and databases, but also the disposition to engage in lifelong learning in collaboration with others.

Even knowledge that is not new may be dramatically transformed when it is processed with, represented by, or encountered through technology. Modern word processing software allows documents to be automatically summarized or shown in an outline form that draws attention to either details or general contours, and fundamentally alters the writing process (Heim, 1987). Spreadsheets allow users to interchange dependent and independent variables through pivot tables or quickly convert a data set into a chart or graph (Jacoby, 2008). Semantic networking or concept-mapping software draws attention to the interrelationships among concepts when outlines are converted to or from bubble charts (Nesbit and Adesope, 2006; Steyers and Tenenbaum, 2005). New tools for creating and processing images and video or building sophisticated animations allow students to demonstrate their learning through slideshows, short films, and complex models, demand new forms of visual literacy in their interpretation, and provide opportunities for multiple forms of intelligence to achieve equal status (Elkins, 2008; Coiro, 2008; Hill, 1997; Robbie and Zeeng, 2008). Relatively new technologies such as virtual reality environments encourage three-dimensional collaborations among multiple participants in different geographic locations that would not be possible otherwise (Calongne, 2008; Hedberg and Brudvik, 2008).

New types of interaction fostered by what is known as Web 2.0 (or the Read/Write Web) encourage users to generate their own content and to remix or 'mash up' the content generated by others, often producing new knowledge (Duffy, 2008; Hedberg and Brudvik, 2008). One example is the emergence of folksonomies, or user-generated sets of 'tags' of content that evolve as users adopt and adapt them to their particular needs. Such tags allow users to connect different resources and ideas together in ways that reflect their own understanding and experience – in a 'bottom-up' classification that challenges traditional categorizations by librarians or subject-matter specialists and allows different users to learn from the information-collecting activities of others (Alexander, 2008). Annotating the information collected by others is a form of 'dialogic literacy', the ability to generate new knowledge through productive and creative collaboration (Bereiter and Scardamalia, 2005; Dwight and Garrison, 2003; Robbie and Zeeng, 2008). Each of these examples offers new ways of representing or accessing knowledge and experience that lead to new forms of literacy which may require a place in the curriculum (Bruce, 2003; Kellner, 2000).

While technologically afforded modes of experiencing and representing knowledge are potentially transformative, new approaches may also result in the loss of knowledge or in knowledge which is less rich, meaningful, or significant. For example, technologically supported simulations may preserve some of the pedagogical qualities of 'real' experience but may leave out less-privileged forms of knowledge such as the emotional, interpersonal, intrapersonal, kinesthetic, and embodied (Bonnett, 2004). One example is the use of tools that allow for so-called 'virtual' dissection of animals, which simulates some of the educational aspects of an actual dissection (Cross and Cross, 2004). While the virtual approach is less expensive, takes less time, can be easily repeated or experienced across time and space, does not harm animals, and is often as effective in terms of measured learning outcomes, students report that the 'reality' aspect of experience with a scalpel, pins, blood, and the 'feel' of actual organs adds tremendously to the significance of the experience (Peat and Taylor, 2004). This raises questions about whether the students' attention is focused on less educationally valuable aspects of the experience or perhaps that the truly significant knowledge and skills are not being assessed (Hansen, 1997).

Another example refers to Oppenheimer's (2003) claim that uses of technology in schools are likely to reduce student empathy which, while not strictly 'knowledge,' has epistemological implications. Oppenheimer's claim is based in part on a body of research (e.g. Funk et al., 2003) that shows that long-term exposure to violent video games reduces children's sensitivity or their capacity to interact in socially acceptable ways. Of particular concern is the intuition that use of computers tends to isolate children from each other or even from their own bodies (Dreyfus, 2001). Yet some educators are using technology specifically to *increase* the empathy of students (Daily and Brennan, 2008). And a recent *New York Times* article on teenage socializing on the Internet quotes Mizuko Ito, lead researcher on the study, 'their participation is giving them the technological skills and literacy they need to succeed in the contemporary world. They're learning how to get along with others, how to manage a public identity, how to create a home page' (Lewin, 2008). These outcomes may not be part of the curriculum or current assessments, but maybe should be.

A second set of epistemological questions raised by new technologies concern how knowledge is acquired. It is to those questions that we now turn.

PSYCHOLOGICAL: QUESTIONS OF LEARNING

Psychology plays a central role in shaping teaching. Of particular importance are theories about the nature of the child and how people learn, which often reflect particular epistemological or metaphysical perspectives and imply preferred approaches to pedagogy (Spector, 2001).

There are two major epistemological perspectives that inform theories of learning (Cronje, 2006): the first is objectivism, also known as realism, which is the view that knowledge is produced by the impact of external reality onto the senses; the second is constructivism, also known as pragmatism, which is the view that knowledge is created though the meaning-making activities of each person's mind. These two perspectives inform two competing schools of thought about how to support learning, which are sometimes seen as incompatible (e.g. Bednar et al., 1992).

The first approach – which we call 'instructionism' – emphasizes *instruction*, sees knowledge as mediated through external reality, and usually favours a direct form of pedagogy with measurable objectives that are fixed in advance of planning curriculum. The archetypal proponent of this camp was Ralph Tyler, followed by Robert Mager (1991), Robert Gagne (1970), and others. Tyler's *Basic Principles of Curriculum and Instruction* (1971)

> ... has all the ingredients characteristic of modern structuralist thinking. These include a firm commitment to decontextualized rationality, progress, theory (or philosophy) as independent of fact, value neutrality, a profound commitment to an external *telos* as the essence of action, and faith in a detached 'method' for arriving at whatever we may consider of value. (Dwight and Garrison 2003, p. 706)

However, the Tyler rationale is not 'value neutral' at all, but may privilege hegemonic norms over individuality and creativity, and stifle democratic education (Dwight and Garrison, 2003, p. 706).

The competing approach – which we call 'constructionism' – has incorporated a constructivist epistemology and favours more open-ended pedagogical approaches such as problem-based learning which embrace pluralistic outcomes. The original exemplar of this approach is John Dewey (1938), followed by David Jonassen (1994) and others.

> For Dewey, ends emerge in the course of agents (e.g., students) striving to coordinate their activities. Students with differing needs, desires, interests, and abilities, may successfully coordinate their activity in entirely different ways. That is why we cannot determine objectives entirely in advance. In the course of inquiry we may learn that the end-in-view with which we began is unobtainable given our abilities, resources, and contextual constraints or that another end may emerge as more worthy. (Dwight and Garrison, 2003, p. 708)

In a variant known as 'social constructionism', additional emphasis is placed on the social context of knowledge construction – including issues of language, motivation, and power (Bijker et al., 1989; Hansen, 1997; Hill, 1997; Howard et al., 2000; Phillips, 1995; Robbie and Zeeng, 2008).

A relatively new approach to learning is an ecological theory of knowing, which prioritizes participation rather than knowledge acquisition (Barab and Roth, 2006). 'From this ecological perspective, learning is a process of becoming prepared to effectively engage dynamic networks in the world in a goal-directed manner' (p. 4); it is 'an ecological, not an individualistic, phenomenon that is distributed and enables the learner to engage in progressively more adaptive individual–environment relations' (p. 8). While we find this approach refreshing and especially like the way that it highlights the importance of student engagement and collaborative groups for solving problems, it has not yet had a significant impact on the field of educational technology.

Instructionism has had the benefit of an emphasis on reusable structures and generalized pedagogical models – thus fitting quite well within industrial organizations strongly influenced by Taylorization and Fordism (Hill, 1997; Kytle, 2004) – and has become the predominant approach to learning technology in corporate, military, and higher education outside colleges of education. Constructionism, on the other hand, is less formalized, and may fit more easily with the humanistic and student-centred dispositions of the prek-12 teachers and professors of teacher education. Constructionism finds support in the National Educational Technology Standards (NETS), where the 'essential conditions' for successful use of technology include a 'Student-Centred Learning' environment, in which ICT is used to 'facilitate engaging approaches to learning' (ISTE, 2007). However, much of prek-12 education remains instructionist.

While instructionism was traditionally combined with a behaviourist theory of learning, and constructionism is often combined with a constructivist theory of learning, more sophisticated adherents to either approach reveal elements of a cognitive theory. Cognitivism offers a sort of 'third option' for learning theory, having incorporated attention to both real objects and their properties and to the internal processing of learners' minds. Cognitivism also has a strong inherent compatibility with learning technology due to its tendency to see the mind in information-processing terms (Alessi and Trollip, 2001; Friesen and

Feenberg, 2007). Cognitivist theories of learning provide support for both
supplantive (teacher-supplied – for example, scaffolding) and generative (learner-
supplied) aspects of learning events (Smith and Ragan, 2004, 2005). While
some radical constructivists and phenomenologists – who highly value the
intuitions about mind that come from reflective individuals – have rejected
cognitivism for its positivism and tendency to reduce all phenomena to what is
observable and measurable, these qualities have made cognitivism highly popular among psychologists, especially those who think of themselves as learning
scientists.

Cronje (2006) helpfully suggests that 'objectivist' and 'constructivist' epistemologies are not diametrically opposed, but should be seen as two axes on a grid,
resulting in four quadrants describing the qualities of learning events. In 'immersion'
learning, learning is opportunistic and has little coordination. In 'construction',
students build on previous knowledge and achieve understanding, but often at
the expense of a great deal of time. In 'injection', teachers take the primary
responsibility for transferring knowledge to students. Finally, in 'integration',
the best elements of instructionism and constructionism are combined, with careful attention to objectives, a developmental pathway of skills and sub-skills along
with appropriate scaffolding, opportunities for constructing understanding when
helpful, and a range of assessments from traditional to portfolio assessment.
Teachers choose which quadrant to emphasize in any particular learning situation, depending on whether the goals involve getting the right answer, following
a specific procedure, understanding a group of complex interrelationships, or
learning how to solve problems in a complex situation. A more sophisticated
version of Cronje's model would also take account of the social context in which
teaching decisions are made, seeing them not just as the application of detached
reason to pedagogical problems but as the results of social negotiation and
agreement (Hansen, 1997).

Thus it seems possible to take the best that objectivism and constructivism
have to offer and combine them with the insights of cognitivism. That seems to
be the strategy of perhaps the most influential statement on learning in the
educational community today: *How People Learn,* produced by the National
Research Council under the direction of John Bransford et al. (1999). They
summarize current research with a list of four principles (that educational
environments should be learner centred, knowledge centred, assessment centred,
and community centred); encourage sensitivity to the particular culture,
language, and learning styles of each learner; emphasize the importance of
metacognition to help learners learn how to learn; stress that both automaticity
and understanding are necessary for learning; suggest greater acceptance
of alternative forms of assessment; and describe important ways to build
community in and outside the classroom. The authors draw particular attention
to the ways that learning technologies can support pedagogical innovations that
are well-supported by current theories of learning, such as learning by doing,
visualization of complex concepts, and access to information and expertise that

would not be otherwise available in schools. Technology, they write, can be used to improve learning in five major ways:

- bringing exciting curricula based on real-world problems into the classroom;
- providing scaffolds and tools to enhance learning;
- giving students and teachers more opportunities for feedback, reflection, and revision;
- building local and global communities that include teachers, administrators, students, parents, practicing scientists, and other interested people; and
- expanding opportunities for teacher learning. (Bransford et al., 1999, p. 195)

It is to these pedagogical implications that we now turn.

PEDAGOGICAL: QUESTIONS OF TEACHING

Pedagogy is the application of knowledge to produce learning. Since teaching and learning are complex – especially when learners are diverse – this requires contextually informed problem-solving on the part of teachers. The proper use of learning technologies to meet objectives and solve problems is one important aspect of effective pedagogy (Brogden and Couros, 2007).

A major pedagogical problem is finding the time in the school curriculum to teach new knowledge, skills, or dispositions. Not only are teachers often relatively unskilled in new technologies (both in terms of their use and in terms of how they are best used for teaching) but also the combination of the traditional school disciplines of language, arts, mathematics, science, and social studies with fairly new areas of content such as physical education, health, character education, and world languages, together with somewhat neglected yet important subjects such as the arts and philosophy, has resulted in a curriculum which is extremely 'full'; and, as with any container with a fixed volume, something must be taken out before something else can be put in. So we must not only ask what to put in, but what to take out.

It is often thought that the best way to introduce technology in schools is to integrate it meaningfully into other subject-matter (Brogden and Couros, 2007). Rather than teaching technology in what is typically called a 'computer class', why not allow students to learn new technologies more deeply while learning other subject-matter, thus 'understanding their application here and now in the circumstances of [their] actual life' (Whitehead, 1967, p. 2). Technology integration offers the prospect of adding technology to the curriculum without taking up too much additional time. The metaphor here might be a container of water, into which is stirred some soluble material such as salt. You can add quite a bit of salt to the container without appreciably increasing the volume of water. Perhaps technology can be like the salt, disappearing into the empty spaces between the subject-matter. This alluring prospect has become the current mantra of educational technology advocates (Roblyer, 2006; Smaldino et al., 2008).

However, integration does not necessarily solve the time problem. Whereas some general technological skills like searching the Internet are relatively easy to learn and can be applied across subject areas,

> Nearly every significant technology for education across the disciplines require an investment of effort on the part of teacher and students to yield the meaningful learning the tools can support … . If we expect teachers to make meaningful use of technology in education, they need time, and they need to know it takes time. (McCrory 2006, p. 157)

So we are back to the question of how to make time or, putting it differently, how to select priorities for learning.

McCrory's use of 'meaningful' is not accidental. Her quote appears in a book that describes 'meaningful' as involving intentionality, content centrality, authentic work, active inquiry, the construction of mental models, and collaborative work (Ashburn, 2006). These criteria can be used to set priorities for the allocation of time in the curriculum, provided that 'meaningfulness' is considered a priority over other criteria such as content coverage or relevance to a job. But these qualities do not simply appear whenever a learning technology is used; they need to be cultivated.

If technology is to be meaningfully integrated into the teaching of subject matter, teachers need to consider the forms and domains of knowledge that might emerge. They are most likely to pay attention to the knowledge that relates to the subject-matter being studied. So, for example, a unit on the architecture of Renaissance theatres will result in knowledge about the Renaissance, theatres, or culture in general. However, if technologies such as Internet searches or architectural modelling software are used, students may also gain knowledge related to the technology itself, such as the important role that keyword selection has in searching a database or the advanced features of a particular piece of modelling software. Students may learn strategies for using technology to access information, such as searching, selecting, mixing, matching, transforming, and creating (Hedberg and Brudvik, 2008). Such knowledge may take the form of value judgements about the relative worth of particular technologies for particular purposes; it may relate to the social consequences of particular technologies; or it may consist of increased capacity to engage in critical thinking, decision-making, or problem-solving (Ankiewicz et al., 2006; Kellner, 2000). Students may gain appreciation for subtle aspects of technological use and design such as the process of 'satisficing' (Simon, 1981), which refers to finding the optimal solution to a problem, rather than a perfect solution, and involves weighing alternatives and making decisions based on predictions of the likely effects (Mishra and Koehler, 2006, p. 1040), or learn adaptability, innovation, exercising responsibility, or organizing information (Brogden and Couros, 2007). Often, these skills are not taught directly, but rather emerge as students participate in a sort of apprenticeship in the use of technology (Dreyfus, 2001; Peters, 2003). To add to this complexity, there may also be outcomes that rest in the undefined area between the subject-matter and technology. For example, students may discover that a particularly useful database of images related to Renaissance theatres exists in the British Museum, or may find that their particular architectural software package allows for expansion packs that include relevant types of presidium arches. These situational forms of knowledge are valuable, but educators have to decide whether to include them in their assessments – paying some attention to the reality that that which is assessed is given more weight than that which is not assessed.

One age-old strategy for helping teachers to adjust their assessments to emphasize new priorities is teacher professional development, despite the money and time it takes to be effective (Ashburn and Floden, 2006; Borthwick and Pierson, 2008; Brogden and Couros, 2007; Howard et al., 2000). Not only must teachers reconsider assessments and acquire technology skills but also they must also be aware of specific technologies that pertain to each area of content, new pedagogical skills and concepts to be mastered, ways of dealing with the unintended consequences of new tools and information sources, and specialized knowledge about teaching with technology, some of which lies in the interactions between technology, content, and pedagogy. A heuristic known as Technological Pedagogical Content Knowledge, or TPACK, represents a conceptual framework for technology in education that illustrates these interactions (AACTE, 2008; Mishra and Koehler, 2006).

> [TPACK] is an understanding that emerges from an interaction of content, pedagogy, and technology knowledge. Underlying truly meaningful and deeply skilled teaching with technology, [TPACK] is different from knowledge of all three concepts individually. [It] is the basis for effective teaching with technology and requires an understanding of the representation of concepts using technologies, pedagogical techniques that use technologies in constructive ways to teach content; knowledge of what makes concepts difficult or easy to learn and how technology can help redress some of the problems that students face; knowledge of students' prior knowledge and theories of epistemology; and knowledge of how technologies can be used to build on existing and to develop new epistemologies or strengthen new ones. (AACTE 2008, pp. 15–16)

TPACK sees education as a complex system with numerous components and loosely defined interrelationships, including human agents with diverse perspectives. The variety and internal complexity of this knowledge domain require that professional development must be interdisciplinary, involving attention to multiple perspectives and factors, including the implications of epistemological assumptions and beliefs about learning (Borthwick and Pierson, 2008; Hansen, 1997). If we want teachers to adopt a more constructionist approach to technology, we need to include opportunities to work on solutions with others, for reflection and peer feedback, and explicit attention to the type of student thinking that might be fostered by particular pedagogical approaches (Howard et al., 2000).

Teachers also need to consider the ways in which students' out-of-school experiences with technology relate to their in-school experiences. This is difficult for some, who simply do not have the same level of facility with computers and who may not understand how immersed in technology the students are in their daily lives. For some teachers, learning *how* to use new tools may present major challenges; for the students, the emphasis may need to be placed on *why* and *when.*

SOCIAL: QUESTIONS OF ASSOCIATED LIVING

In our introductory section, we wrote that schooling is an educational technology. However, the reverse is not true. A majority of education occurs outside of school, and learning technologies are central to out-of-school experiences as well. In fact, some would say that popular technologies such as television have proved to be far more significant than those used in school:

> The electronic environment makes an information level outside the schoolroom that is far higher than the information level inside the schoolroom. In the nineteenth century the knowledge inside the schoolroom was higher than knowledge outside the schoolroom. Today it is reversed. The child knows that in going to school he is in a sense interrupting his education (McLuhan, 1967).

In the 40 years since that was written, the personal computer and Internet have brought an incredibly rich information and communication environment into the home.

> Sweeping changes in the nature, uses, and delivery of information have radically transformed the ecology of education ... and fundamentally altered the circumstances under which schools and colleges carry on their work. The result has been a cacophony of teaching, the effects of which have been at best difficult to determine and even more difficult to assess. (Cremin, 1989, p. 59).

Many teachers today struggle for attention of their students, who have become accustomed to the multimedia overload of Hollywood films, video games, and 'edutainment' and to the rapid self-selection of new content with the pressing of a button or the click of a mouse (Burbules, 2000; Hedberg and Brudvik, 2008).

What's more, the privatized information marketplace afforded by television and the Internet has allowed corporate interests to pursue their own agendas regarding communication technologies, entertainment, and online education. The mostly corporate mass media use all forms of technology to affect the choices of consumers and citizens, and don't usually prioritize democracy or critical thinking. Schools compete with the state-of-the-art visuals, robust backend systems, and well-trained instructional designers hired by these well-financed interests for students' attention. Businesses also seek influence on technology use within the walls of schools. A grand dramatization of this can be seen on the Exhibits Floor at the annual National Educational Computing Conference, where hundreds of companies compete for educational technology dollars.

Schools also reflect business interests, not least in their attempt to deliver the types of workers that corporations demand. Schools adopt curriculum that they believe will prepare students for economic success and often teach kids how to use the corporate tools of choice (Kellner, 2000). Educational technology has largely been created by corporate, military, and higher education institutions interested in training efficiency and market share, and the technologies reflect those interests. Because technology currently has buzz with young people and seems to provide economic viability, the largely corporate proponents of twenty-first century skills in schools have tremendous leverage, indicated by NCATE's (National Council for Accreditation of Teacher Education) recent indication that it will use twenty-first century skills as a criterion in accrediting teacher education (Honawar, 2008).

Merely infusing technology more fully into education will be unlikely to produce graduates who are critical of corporate hegemony and hierarchical power relations, which seems essential for resurgent democracy. Whereas teachers may strive to co-opt technologies for their own goals rather than for corporate goals, pedagogy can only go so far in masking the designed-in biases of the technology. We believe the language of critical connoisseurship could be helpful here, not only in terms of the attitude of educators but also of the students who emerge from the education. A critical stance toward technology is essential if we want our students to resist some of the mindlessness and consumerist behaviour sought by corporate interests. Students must come to appreciate the ways that uses of imagery and associations can be used to manipulate viewers of advertisements and even ostensibly-artistic movies and television shows. Having them produce and critique exhortative pieces of their own can help them appreciate some of the subtle methods that sophisticated producers employ.

As schools shift from using monologic sources of information such as text-books and print encyclopaedias to multiple pluralistic sources on the web, including both 'official' knowledge providers such as governments, museums, and mass-media outlets and also 'unofficial' providers such as wikis and blogs, information evaluation becomes important in schools as well as outside of them (Kellner, 2000). Students need to understand privacy issues as well, coming to know when it may be appropriate to give personal information on web sites or to others (Burbules, 2000) as well as how to protect themselves from phishing and other forms of fraud. Schools also have an obligation – as part of their mission to support equality of opportunity – to address the 'digital divide,' which separates the technology haves and the have-nots and creates an 'information-caste' society (Burbules, 2000). Of particular concern in the late 1990s – and leading to federal 'e-rate' legislation designed to fund technology for schools with large numbers of economically disadvantaged students – the digital divide matters more as technology matters more, both in schools and in society at large, and it may be getting worse in some ways (Vargas, 2007). The divide is not just economic, but between those with technology skills and critical awareness and those without, and it carries consequences that are not just economic, but for the quality of democracy (Kellner, 2000).

Ironically, one widely used 'educational' technology in American schools is the use of Internet filters designed to keep certain information and communication opportunities *out* of the building. Newer technologies favoured by young people – such as role-playing games such as Grand Theft Auto, virtual reality environments such as Second Life, social networking sites such as MySpace, and web sites dealing with issues of student interest – are actually *banned* from schools due to the possibility that students might access information or experiences that could be considered non-educative, miseducative, or even harmful. Even powerful learning technologies such as blogs and wikis, content aggregation sites, and student email accounts are banned in some schools, thought to present the possibility that 'unregulated pollutants' such as 'pornography, hate literature, and inchoate ramblings' (Hope, 2008, p. 103), gambling sites, paedophile attacks in chat rooms, and discussions of drug use, sex, and 'hacking' (Warnick, 2004) will violate student innocence or corrupt their thoughts. Various disciplinary measures, including the denial of access, suspension or expulsion of students, and exclusionary technologies – such as firewalls, filters and activity monitoring software – are utilized by schools to maintain the order or so-called purity of their learning environments. Filters can take the form of 'deny lists' that disallow access to certain identified Internet addresses, keyword filters that prevent pages containing certain words, and even visual content management applications which disallow images containing certain skin colours or textures (Hope, 2008). While such filtering technologies are thought to be moderately effective in keeping out certain kinds of materials, they also inevitably 'overblock', by disallowing access to content that is not objectionable but meets certain criteria. For example, including the word 'breast' in a keyword filter will block pornography but also web sites related to breast cancer, breastplates, and music that soothes. Indeed, many pieces of literature and art contain words and images that might be deemed pornographic by some observers. 'In such instances, the situational, culturally constructed nature of pollution labels and the desire to protect external boundaries from pollution could restrict the educational process, bringing the two principal outcomes of schooling, academic and moral development, into conflict' (Hope, 2008, p. 109) and undermining one of the central factors in school effectiveness: trust (Bryk and Schneider, 2002). Filters also inevitably lead to students expending effort to overcome the barriers, such as learning about proxy servers that allow access to an Internet address that has been blocked. This leads to the conferring of status onto students who are well-versed in such strategies, which, ironically, makes students more likely to try to learn them (Warnick, 2004). Using filters may seem to provide a quick technological fix to the problem of inappropriate content or contact in schools, but it does little to develop critical media literacy among students, or to educate them how to avoid the content or contacts when they are out of school (EFF, 2003; Kellner, 2000).

One of the primary ways that students encounter technology out of school is in games. Of particular interest from a learning technology standpoint are Massive Multiplayer Online Role Playing Games (MMORPGs). While on their face these games promote activities that are quite distinct from the academic and moral mission of schools, the problem-solving skills and lessons about cooperation and leadership that are gained may be more valuable in terms of economic and social life than many of the skills learned in school (Salen, 2008). World of Warcraft, in particular, is constructed in such a way that success in ascending the levels of the game is really only possible by participating in temporary or long-term cross-functional teams capable of cooperating to meet complex objectives. While the 'gaming' aspect of these experiences may turn off many educators – and leads many schools to ban their use – it greatly enhances the motivation and engagement of the participants (Garzotto, 2007). Some researchers are building some of the elements of games into role-playing environments designed to teach science and mathematics (Barab et al., 2005; Harvard GSE, 2008). It remains to be seen whether such simulations will be widely adopted in schools. Again, this probably depends on whether schools will adopt new answers to the question of what knowledge is of most worth.

LEARNING TECHNOLOGIES AND SOCIAL TRANSFORMATION

Unlike science, which sometimes professes to seek value-free 'facts', technology is *never* value-free. Technologies reflect the norms, expectations and socio-cultural milieu of their designers (Hickman, 1990; Westera, 2004). 'Technology uses value judgments as a unique part of the design process ... . Values are evident in decisions on problems addressed, solutions developed, resources utilized, and processes employed' (Hill, 1997; Hutchinson, 1993, p. 94). Feenberg (1996) refers to the built-in evidence of the values of the designer as 'implementation bias', referring to the implementation of the design in a given technology. Consider the differences between the operating systems of Macintosh and PC-compatible computers: there is a greater emphasis on the importance of graphics and music in the Macintosh operating system. These implementations represent the different value systems and audiences of Apple and Microsoft as well as a sort of encoded history of the versions of each system. Substantial differences can also be seen between a corporate product such as Microsoft Office and the primary open-source alternative, StarOffice. The proliferation of open-source software, shareware, and freeware alternatives to corporate software allows educators to choose from among them. But with the grip that corporate providers maintain on learning technology procurement, most schools are unlikely to opt for non-corporate alternatives.

Some believe that new technologies – particularly hypertext as a non-linear, non-hierarchical system for representing knowledge – offer more compatibility than print does with constructionist pedagogy (Dwight and Garrison, 2003; Hill, 1997; McClintock, 2000; Theodore, 2008). Bereiter and Scardamalia (2005) argue that print technologies, which have predominated in schools for the last 400 years, lead to a standardization of content across schools and learners, with information being disseminated from a single source to a mass audience, and organizing knowledge in a linear fashion that encourages 'fractioning' of thought and information into discrete subject areas and grade levels, thus reinforcing what Freire (1970) referred to as 'banking' education. New ICTs, however, offer individualized information access, associative or participatory knowledge creation, and non-hierarchical approaches to organizing learning. Blogs and wikis encourage learners to critique each other's ideas, taking the teacher out of the centre of discussion and encouraging 'a new, more active, critical, and creative reading of texts that deconstruct regimes of power in order to recognize how dominant metanarratives [often] script authoritarian theories of learning' (Alexander, 2008; Dwight and Garrison, 2003, p. 701; Hedberg and Brudvik, 2008). Classrooms may thus be synergistically transformed by new tools that encourage collaborative student inquiry and by the inevitable increase in the number of students who are members of the 'Net Generation' (also referred to as 'digital natives'), with their preexisting understanding of new technologies and embodied experiences of multiliteracies, multimedia, and multiple channels of communication (Duffy, 2008; Hedberg and Brudvik, 2008; Tapscott, 1998).

Some believe that new learning technologies have an intrinsic 'democratizing potential' (Kellner, 2000; Theodore, 2008), perhaps leading toward Dewey's (1907) vision of democratic education:

> Learning has been put into circulation … . Knowledge is no longer an immobile solid; it has been liquefied. It is actively moving in all the currents of society itself. It is easy to see that this revolution, as regards the materials of knowledge, carries with it a marked change in the attitude of the individual … . But all this means a necessary change in the attitude of the school, one of which we are as yet far from realizing the full force. (Dewey, 1907, pp. 40–41)
>
> …The obvious fact is that our social life has undergone a thorough and radical change. If our education is to have any meaning for life, it must pass through an equally complete transformation. This transformation is not something to appear suddenly, to be executed in a day by conscious purpose. It is already in progress. Those modifications of our school system which often appear … to be mere changes of detail, mere improvement within the school mechanism, are in reality signs and evidences of evolution … . It remains but to organize all these factors, to appreciate them in their fullness of meaning, and to put the ideas and ideals involved into complete, uncompromising possession of our school system. To do this means to make each one of our schools an embryonic community life, active with types of occupations that reflect the life of the larger society, and permeated throughout with the spirit of art, history, and science. When the school introduces and trains each child of society into membership within such a little community, saturating him with the spirit of service, and providing him with the instruments of effective self-direction, we shall have the deepest and best guarantee of a larger society which is worthy, lovely, and harmonious. (Dewey, 1907, pp. 43–44)

Dewey's vision is compelling. Yet it is hard to find evidence that schools have become more democratic in the 100 years since he wrote these words. This brings to mind that social changes such as the effects of technology on education are often overestimated in the short run and underestimated in the long run (Bruce, 2003, p. 336). Perhaps the 'long run' in this case is centuries rather than decades.

Is transformation toward Dewey's vision a likely result of greater use of new learning technologies?

In our view, new technologies do not inevitably lead to meaningful learning, constructionism, or any other priority in education. In many cases, they serve instead as substitutes for more traditional ways of doing the same things that have been done before. 'Substitutional approaches are basically instrumental, incremental and long-term focused; they require substantial time and sustained investment' (Westera, 2004, p. 508). Transformational approaches, on the other hand, seek to radically alter learning activities, the structures of classrooms, and even the social role of schools. Often based on a trenchant critique of current conditions, transformational approaches require strenuous advocacy, administrative buy-in, occasional mandates, continuous professional development, large-scale adjustments by many people with multiple roles, and a compelling vision of change (Westera, 2004, p. 508). However, if technology demands are inconsistent with other demands of the workplace, or resources are scarce, transformational change will be stymied. Inevitably, transformationalists will be accused of unfairly evaluating those who resist change, some of whom justify their resistance as maintaining enduring values while others 'grow numb to reform because of the relentless pace of partial solutions, one upon the other' (Kytle, 2004, p. 13). The official curriculum, the limitations of time, the level of student cooperativeness, teachers' desires to fit in and survive the demands of the job, standardized testing and accountability, and so forth constrain teacher choice (Davies, 2003). Transformational approaches often ignore those constraints and the difficulty of changing schools. When you add in the necessity to learn technology skills along with the many variables of technology implementation – including inevitable technical problems, the common lack of timely technical support, the need for software and hardware upgrades, incompatibilities between different versions and systems, veteran teachers who may not have had much experience with computers – transforming pedagogy through technology can seem like a daunting task.

An interesting case study of the effects of new technologies on schooling is the implementation of the programing language Logo in K-12 schools. Logo's developer, Seymour Papert (1980), hoped to use Logo as a powerful – even revolutionary – tool for helping children to think deeply about science and mathematics, tapping into their intuitions as they engaged in experimentation and inquiry. But Agalianos et al. (2006) conclude from their study that institutional and social factors altered Logo from a tool of revolution to a diversion that was widely seen as a children's game. Because schooling is a fundamentally conservative institution (Westera, 2004) wrought with 'viscosities of procedure and habit' (McClintock, 2000), the story is similar with respect to other technologies. While the web offers wide open access to information, in many cases students are using it more or less as a substitute for print encyclopaedias, searching for titbits of information to fill in blanks on worksheets. Even structures such as WebQuests, intentionally designed to raise student activity from information-finding to inquiry, tend to be co-opted by more traditional learning activities (Vidoni and Maddux, 2002).

Yet pure substitution without innovation is impossible. For example, the adoption of print media inexorably changed education from a focus on lecture and oral recitation to a near-fixation with reading (Theodore, 2008). Similarly, substituting traditional journal writing with greater use of blogs will inevitably change the teaching of writing. Interactive whiteboards, even when utilized in a teacher-centred manner like a traditional chalkboard, may offer greater student control of content, support multiple learning styles and forms of representation, and increase the salience of external sources of information (Christensen, 1997). While the web can be used in traditional ways, its hypertextual structure will dilute the effectiveness of such approaches, if only because students will inevitably follow links that catch their interest, some of which will lead them in directions not determined in advance. Of course, 'this unique trailblazing may lead to en masse solipsism' (Dwight and Garrison, 2003, p. 718) or feed directly into the corporate agenda of consumerism that has in many ways taken over the web.

The inherent biases of a technology will often be overshadowed by the rather strong biases and values implicit in classroom contexts (Hansen, 1997; but see McClintock, 2000). Variations in pedagogy may be far more important than the inherent values of the hardware or software in terms of whether a particular use of technology reflects objectivist or constructivist epistemologies, structuralist or poststructuralist metaphysics, or hegemonic or democratic social organization.

However, new technologies may potentially decrease the importance of schools as loci for education. To the extent that technologies enable learning *outside* of schools, controlled by the learners themselves, it will be them and not teachers who construct the learning activities. Traditionally, most learners were likely even outside school to duplicate the pedagogies that they have experienced in schools, thus dramatically limiting the potential for social transformation. However, Dwight and Garrison (2003) cite Pearson's (2002) report of how economically disadvantaged students, when given access to computers outside of a traditional instructional environment 'were able to master the technology without being steered into a confining, teleological curriculum' (Dwight and Garrison, 2003, p. 716) and quickly learned to use the tools for higher-order thinking tasks and felt empowered. One lesson to be learned is that young people rarely need stifling didactic instruction in how to use new technologies, but figure it out on their own with help from their peers. The key issue is whether marginalized students will actually have access to these tools outside of strictly controlled venues. However, digital natives – who learn technology from other users rather than hegemonic systems of curriculum and instruction – may subvert the dominant paradigm in unpredictable ways. What is not clear is where – other than in reconstructed schools – they will gain the motivations and skills necessary to use their skills to support democracy.

REFERENCES

AACTE; American Association of Colleges for Teacher Education (2008) *Handbook of Technological Pedagogical Content Knowledge for Teaching and Teacher Education*. New York: Routledge/Taylor & Francis Group for AACTE.

Agalianos, A., Whitty, G., Noss, R. (2006) 'The social shaping of logo,' *Social Studies of Science*, 36(2): 241–267.

Alessi, S.M. and Trollip, S. (2001) *Multimedia for Learning: Methods and Development*. Boston, Allyn and Bacon.

Alexander, B. (2008) 'Web 2.0 and emergent multiliteracies,' *Theory Into Practice*, 47(2): 150–160.

Ankiewicz, P., de Swardt, E., Vries, M. (2006) 'Some implications of the philosophy of technology for science, technology and society (STS) studies,' *International Journal of Technology and Design Education*, 16(2): 117–141.

Ashburn, E.A. (2006) Attributes of meaningful learning using technology (MLT). In *Meaningful Learning Using Technology*, E.A. Ashburn and R.E. Floden (eds). New York: Teachers College Press, pp. 161–179.

Ashburn, E.A. and Floden, R.E. (2006) *Meaningful Learning Using Technology: What Educators Need to Know and Do*. The TEC series. New York: Teachers College Press.

Barab, S. and Roth, W.-M. (2006) 'Curriculum-based ecosystems: supporting knowing from an ecological perspective,' *Educational Researcher*, 35(5): 3–13.

Barab, S., Thomas, M. Dodge, M. (2005) 'Making learning fun: Quest Atlantis, a game without guns,' *Educational Technology Research and Development*, 53(1): 86–107.

Bednar, A.K., Cunningham, D. Dulfy, TM., Perry, J.P. (1992) Theory into practice: How do we link? In *Constructivism and the Technology of Instruction*, T.M. Duffy and D.H. Jonassen (eds). Hillsdale, NJ: Lawrence Erlbaum Associates, pp. 17–34.

Bereiter, C. and Scardamalia, M. (2005) Technology and literacies: from print literacy to dialogic literacy. In *International handbook of Educational policy*, N. Bascia, A. Cumming, A. Datnow, K. Leithwood and D. Livingstone (eds). Dordrecht: Springer, pp. 749–761.

Bijker, W.E., Hughes, T.P., Pinch, T.J. (eds) (1989) *The Social Construction of Technological Systems: New Directions in the Sociology and History of Technology*. Cambridge, Mass.: MIT Press.

Bonnett, M. (2004) 'Lost in space? education and the concept of nature,' *Studies in Philosophy and Education*, 23(2/3): 117–130.

Borthwick, A. and Pierson, M. (2008) *Transforming Classroom Practice: Professional Development Strategies in Educational Technology*. Eugene, OR: International Society for Technology in Education.

Bransford, J., Brown, A.L., Cocking, R.R. (eds) (1999) *How People Learn: Brain, Mind, Experience, and School*. Washington, DC: National Academy Press.

Britton, E., Long-Cotty, B.D., Levenson, T. (2005) *Bringing Technology Education into K-8 Classrooms: a Guide to Curricular Resources about the Designed World*. Thousand Oaks, CA: Corwin Press.

Brogden, L.M. and Couros, A. (2007) 'Toward a philosophy of technology and education,' *Delta Kappa Gamma Bulletin*, 73(2): 37–42.

Bruce, B.C. (ed.) (2003) *Literacy in the Information Age: Inquiries into Meaning Making with New Technologies*. Newark, Del.: International Reading Association.

Bruce, B.C. and Hogan, M.C. (1998) The disappearance of technology: toward an ecological model of literacy. *In Handbook of Literacy and Technology Transformations in a Post-Typographic world*, D. Reinking, M. McKenna, L. Labbo and R. Kieffer (eds). Hillsdale, NJ: Lawrence Erlbaum Associates, pp. 269–281.

Bryk, A.S. and Schneider, B.L. (2002) Trust in Schools: a Core Resource for Improvement. New York: Russell Sage Foundation.

Burbules, N.C. (2000) 'Why philosophers of education should care about technology issues,' *Philosophy of Education Yearbook*, pp. 37–41.

Calongne, C.M. (2008) 'Educational frontiers: learning in a virtual world,' *Educause Review*, 43(5): 36–38, 40, 42, 44, 46, 48.

Christensen, C.M. (1997) *The Innovator's Dilemma: When New Technologies Cause Great Firms to Fail*. Boston, Mass.: Harvard Business School Press.

Coiro, J. (2008) *Handbook of Research on New Literacies*. New York: Lawrence Erlbaum Associates/ Taylor and Francis Group.

Cremin, L.A. (1989) *Popular Education and its Discontents*. New York: Harper and Row.

Cronje, J. (2006) 'Paradigms regained: toward integrating objectivism and constructivism in instructional design and the learning sciences,' *Educational Technology Research and Development*, 54(4): 387–416.

Cross, T.R. and Cross, V.E. (2004) 'Scalpel or mouse? A statistical comparison of real and virtual frog dissections,' *American Biology Teacher* 66(6): 408.

Daily, S.B. and Brennan, K. (2008) Utilizing technology to support the development of empathy. Poster presented at Interaction Design and Children Conference, May, Chicago, IL: http://web.media.mit. edu/~kbrennan/saywhat.html.

Davies, D. (2003) 'Pragmatism, pedagogy and philosophy. A Model of thought and action in action in primary technology and science teacher education,' *International Journal of Technology and Design Education*, 13(3): 207–221.

Dewey, J. (1907) *The School and Society: Being Three Lectures*. Chicago: The University of Chicago Press.

Dewey, J. (1925) *Experience and Nature*. Chicago: Open Court Pub. Co.

Dewey, J. (1938) *Experience and Education*. New York: Macmillan.

Dreyfus, H.L. (2001) On the Internet. New York: Routledge.

Duffy, P. (2008) 'Engaging the YouTube Google-eyed generation: strategies for using Web 2.0 in teaching and learning,' *Electronic Journal of e-Learning*, 6(2): 119–129.

Dwight, J. and Garrison, J. (2003) 'A manifesto for instructional technology: hyperpedagogy,' *Teachers College Record*, 105(5): 699–728.

Eisner, E.W. (1998) *The Enlightened Eye: Qualitative Inquiry and the Enhancement of Educational Practice*. Upper Saddle River, NJ: Merrill.

Electronic Frontier Foundation (EFF) (2003) 'Internet blocking in public schools: a study on Internet access in educational institutions,' from: http://www.eff.org/Censorship/Censorware/net%5Fblock%5Freport/.

Elkins, J. (2008) *Visual Literacy*. New York: Routledge.

Feenberg, A. (1996) 'Marcuse or Habermas: two critiques of technology,' *Inquiry: an Interdisciplinary Journal of Philosophy and the Social Sciences*, 39(1): 45–70.

Franklin, U.M. (1999) *The real World of Technology*. Toronto, Ont.: Anansi.

Freire, P. (1970) *Pedagogy of the Oppressed*. New York: Herder and Herder.

Friesen, N. and Feenberg, A. (2007) '"ed tech in reverse": Information technologies and the cognitive revolution,' *Educational Philosophy and Theory*, 39(7): 720–736.

Funk, J.B., Buchman, D.D., Jenks J., Bechtolt, H. (2003) 'Playing violent video games, desensitization, and moral evaluation in children,' *Journal of Applied Developmental Psychology*, 24(4): 413–436.

Gagne, R.M. (1970) *The Conditions of Learning*. New York: Holt, Rinehart and Winston.

Garzotto, F. (2007) Investigating the educational effectiveness of multiplayer online games for children. *Interaction Design and Children: Proceedings of the 6th International Conference on Interaction Design and Children*. Aalborg, Denmark.

Hansen, K.-H. (1997) 'Science and technology as social relations towards a philosophy of technology for liberal education,' *International Journal of Technology and Design Education*, 7(1/2): 49–63.

Harvard GSE (2008) *The River City Project: A Multi-User Virtual Environment for Learning Scientific Inquiry and 21st Century Skills*. Website: http://muve.gse.harvard.edu/rivercityproject/index.html.

Hedberg, J.G. and Brudvik, O.C. (2008) 'Supporting dialogic literacy through mashing and modding of places and spaces,' *Theory Into Practice*, 47(2): 138–149.

Heidegger, M. (1977) *The Question Concerning Technology and Other Essays* (William Lovitt, trans.). New York: Harper Torchbooks.

Heim, M. (1987) *Electric Language: a Philosophical Study of Word Processing*. New Haven: Yale University Press.

Hickman, L.A. (1990) *John Dewey's Pragmatic Technology*. Bloomington, IL: Indiana University Press.

Hill, A.M. (1997) 'Reconstructionism in technology education,' *International Journal of Technology and Design Education*, 7(1/2): 121–139.

Honawar, V. (2008) New president hopes to use NCATE as reform lever, *Education Week*, 28(7, October 8): 6.

Hope, A. (2008) 'Internet pollution discourses, exclusionary practices and the "Culture of over-blocking" within UK schools,' *Technology, Pedagogy and Education*, 17(2): 103–113.

Howard, B.C., McGee, S., Schwertz, N., Purcell, S. (2000) 'The experience of constructivism: transforming teacher epistemology,' *Journal of Research on Computing in Education*, 32(4): 455–465.

Hutchinson, J.P. (1993) 'Outlook for the next century and its implication for and impacts on technology education,' *NATO ASI SERIES F COMPUTER AND SYSTEMS SCIENCES* 109: 85.

ISTE (2007) Essential Conditions: necessary conditions to effectively leverage technology for learning. Eugene, OR: International Society for Technology in Education. Available at http://www.iste.org/Content/NavigationMenu/NETS/ForStudents/2007Standards/NETS-S_2007_Essential_Conditions.pdf.

Jacoby, C. (2008) *Simple Spreadsheets for Hard Decisions*. Long Beach, Calif: City Shore Press.

Jonassen, D.H. (1994) 'Thinking technology: toward a constructivist design model,' *Educational Technology*, 34(4): 34–37.

Kellner, D. (2000) 'New technologies/new literacies: reconstructing education for the new millennium,' *Philosophy of Education Yearbook*, pp. 21–36.

Kytle, J. (2004) *To Want to Learn: Insights and Provocations for Engaged Learning*. New York: Palgrave Macmillan.

Lewin, T. (2008) 'Teenagers' internet socializing not a bad thing, *New York Times* November 20, p. A20. Available at http://www.nytimes.com/2008/11/20/us/20internet.html?_r=1andemc=eta1v.

McCrory, R. (2006) Technology and teaching: a new kind of knowledge. In *Meaningful Learning Using Technology*, E.A. Ashburn and R.E. Floden (eds). New York: Teachers College Press, pp. 141–160.

McClintock, R. (2000) *Experience and Innovation: Reflections on Emerging Practice with New Media in Education*. New York: Institute for Learning Technologies. Available at http://www.ilt.columbia.edu/about/ILT_history.pdf; last accessed November 29, 2008.

Mcluhan, M. (1967) *Understanding Media: The Extensions of Man*. London: Sphare Books.

Mager, R.F. (1991) *Preparing Instructional Objectives*. London: Kogan Page.

Martin, J.R. (1970) *Readings in the Philosophy of Education: a Study of Curriculum*. Boston: Allyn and Bacon.

Mishra, P. and Koehler, M.J. (2006) 'Technological pedagogical content knowledge: a framework for teacher knowledge,' *Teachers College Record*, 108(6): 1017–1054.

Nesbit, J.C. and Adesope, O.O. (2006) 'Learning with concept and knowledge maps: a meta-analysis,' *Review of Educational Research*, 76(3): 413–448.

Oppenheimer, T. (2003) *The Flickering Mind: the False Promise of Technology in the Classroom, and How Learning Can Be Saved*. New York: Random House.

Papert, S. (1980) *Mindstorms: Children, Computers, and Powerful Ideas*. New York: Basic Books.

Pearson, T. (2002) 'Falling behind: a technology crisis facing minority students,' *TechTrends*, 46(2): 15–20.

Peat, M. and Taylor, C. (2004) 'Virtual Biology: How well can it replace authentic activities?' *Synergy*, 19: 25–28. Available at http://www.itl.usyd.edu.au/synergy/synergy20.pdf#page=28.

Peters, M.A. (2003) *Technologising Pedagogy: the Internet, Nihilism, and Phenomenology of Learning*. Simile: University of Toronto Press. 3: N.PAG.

Phillips, D.C. (1995) 'The good, the bad, and the ugly: the many faces of constructivism,' *Educational Researcher: a Publication of the American Educational Research Association*, 24(7): 5.

Robbie, D. and Zeeng, L. (2008) 'Engaging student social networks to motivate learning: capturing, analysing and critiquing the visual image,' *International Journal of Learning*, 15(3): 153–160.

Roblyer, M.D. (2006) Integrating Educational Technology into Teaching. Upper Saddle River, NJ: Pearson/Merrill Prentice Hall.

Salen, K. (2008) *The ecology of Games: Connecting Youth, Games, and Learning*. Cambridge, Mass.: MIT Press.

Secretary's Commission on Achieving Necessary Skills (SCANS). (1991) *What Work Requires of Schools: a SCANS Report for America 2000*. Washington, D.C: Secretary's Commission on Achieving Necessary Skills, US Dept. of Labor.

Simon, H.A. (1981) *The Sciences of the Artificial*. Cambridge, Mass.: MIT Press.

Smaldino, S.E., Lowther, D.L., Russell, J.D. (2008) *Instructional Technology and Media for Learning*. Upper Saddle River, NJ: Pearson Merrill Prentice Hall.

Smith, M.K. (2005) 'Elliot W. Eisner, connoisseurship, criticism and the art of education', *The Encyclopaedia of Informal Education*, www.infed.org/thinkers/eisner.htm.

Smith, P.L. and Ragen, T.J. (2004) *Insturctional Design*. Hoboken, NJ: Wikley.

Smith, P.L. and Ragan, T.J. (2005) *Instructional Design*. Hoboken, NJ: J. Wiley and Sons.

Spector, J.M. (2001) 'Philosophical implications for the design of instruction,' *Instructional Science*, 29(4/5): 381–402.

Tapscott, D. (1998) *Growing up Digital: the Rise of the Net Generation*. New York: McGraw-Hill.

Theodore, P.A. (2008) 'Pedagogy unbound: possibilities for education in an age of electronic communication,' *Journal of Philosophy and History of Education*, 58: 177–182.

Tyler, R.W. (1971) *Basic Principles of Curriculum and Instruction*. Chicago: University of Chicago Press.

Vargas (2007) 'Binary America: split in two by a digital divide,' *Washington Post*, July 23, 2007. Website: http://washington.post.com/wp-dyn/context/article/2007/07/22/AR2007072201278.html.

Vidoni, K.L. and Maddux, C.D. (2002) 'WebQuests: Can they be used to improve critical thinking skills in students?' Computers in the Schools, 19: 101–118.

Warnick, B. (2004) 'Technological metaphors and moral education: the Hacker ethic and the computational experience,' *Studies in Philosophy and Education*, 23(4): 265–281.

Westera, W. (2004) 'On strategies of educational innovation: between substitution and transformation,' *Higher Education*, 47(4): 501–517.

Whitehead, A.N. (1967) The Aims of Education, and Other Essays. New York: Free Press.

33

Personal and Social Education

Graham Haydon

INTRODUCTION

In writing a chapter on personal and social education for a handbook intended for an international readership, there is an initial difficulty in specifying just what the chapter is about. There are at least three interconnected aspects to this difficulty.

The first is a matter of terminology. Some terms labelling curriculum subjects would be recognized (or could be uncontroversially translated so as to be recognized) anywhere in the world: 'mathematics' is a clear example. Even terms covering a disputed area of content, such as 'moral education' and 'citizenship education', are widely recognized. The same cannot be assumed for 'personal and social education'.

Secondly, and more substantially, 'personal and social education' is similar to 'moral and citizenship education', though different from 'mathematics', in at least one respect: i.e. it is open to dispute whether what it labels is a curriculum subject at all, as opposed to an aspect of education or a kind of educational aim.

Thirdly, and an additional complication, the area covered by the term 'personal and social education' is, in advance of further specification, very likely to overlap with other areas which are better recognized, including 'moral and citizenship education' and arguably also religious education or spiritual development.

No doubt partly because 'personal and social education' does not name an internationally recognized subject or an undisputed area of educational concern, there is not a large body of philosophical literature focusing on personal and social education explicitly (though there is a great deal of philosophical literature that is relevant, depending on how 'personal and social' is interpreted). This chapter cannot, then, be a definitive map of a well-defined territory. It will be more an exploratory exercise in mapping a territory that has disputed boundaries, though there are one or two (probably overlapping) areas, such as 'health education' and 'sex education', that are generally acknowledged to fall within the territory.

In this exploration I shall sometimes refer to the curriculum area which in England has been widely referred to by teachers since the late 1980s as (initially) 'PSE' (personal and social education) and (later, with the addition of 'health') as 'PSHE'.[100] This is a useful reference point because an area under this name has been recognized in official curriculum policy in England, as it is not in all countries. In 2000 PSHE became part of the National Curriculum for England, albeit a slightly anomalous part, since unlike the other subjects of the English National Curriculum it had no statutory programme, so that the content to be taught was a matter for guidance rather than prescription. Typically, this content would include, but not be exhausted by, sex education, drugs education and careers education – all areas that may be included in the curricula of schools in many parts of the world without necessarily being grouped together. In England the grouping of such concerns into a recognized curriculum area has been supported by a large amount of teaching material and guidance to teachers, a professional association of teachers of PSHE, and many years' experience on the part of teachers and schools. Out of this experience, questions have emerged about, among other issues, how PSHE is related to citizenship education, whether the promotion of moral values has any place in PSHE, and how far the whole area should be dominated by the concerns of health education.

At the time of writing, debate over these questions, and the development of the curriculum area itself, is still ongoing. Even the nomenclature is not fixed. In primary schools, where the same teachers have often been responsible for PSHE and citizenship, the abbreviation 'PSHCE' is sometimes used. For secondary schools, the official curriculum policy has recently been stressing the importance of developing economic and financial awareness in young people; hence, from 2008, the term 'PSHEE' (personal social health and economic education) is beginning to appear. It has also been proposed that PSHE should, like other National Curriculum subjects, have a statutory programme of study; one reason for this proposal is to ensure that sex education – long seen as a concern of PSHE – becomes compulsory throughout the years of schooling.

With so much still in flux, PSHE in England cannot be treated as a guide to the terrain, still less as a model of how personal and social education should be conceived and pursued. The purpose of referring to it here is to illustrate some of the complexities that need to be considered in translating into practical curriculum policy any theoretical conception of what personal and social education is about. A less polite term for 'complexities' would be 'untidiness'; the actual content of PSHE in England seems to have accrued piecemeal without being derived systematically from any coherent underlying rationale.

However, in a philosophical investigation it will be best to start, not with this specific case, but with some much more general questions about how we can reasonably interpret the notion of personal and social education.

THE PERSONAL AND THE SOCIAL IN EDUCATION

There is surely a sense in which all education is undeniably the education of persons. We treat as 'educatees' *only* those living beings, and (slightly more controversially) *all* those living beings whom we recognize as persons or, at the very least, as potential persons. The qualifications in that sentence are intended as acknowledgements that there is some room for discussion about whether the very young (say in the first 2 or 3 years of life) or the severely intellectually disabled are to be seen as educatees. There are genuine issues for debate here, both concerning practice in the fields known as early years education and special needs education, and concerning the conceptualization of education. Most views would have it that human beings must be persons before their education can begin, but some (e.g. Langford, 1985) speak of education as a process of becoming a person. Views of both kinds can agree that education involves the development of qualities that are peculiar to persons. It can also be agreed with little contention that all education is social inasmuch as persons are social beings and the development of the qualities of persons involves initiation into language, practices and ways of interpreting experience that are socially given and shared (notable proponents of this position include Hirst, both 1974 and 1993, and Oakeshott, 1989).

There is a sense, then, in which any education can be counted as both personal and social; learning mathematics, for instance, initiates persons into a particular language in which communication can go on, and this potentially makes a difference to a person's experiences in his or her life. It needs to be asked, then, why – or whether – we should differentiate some particular territory within education as 'personal and social'. Here it should be acknowledged that there is a degree of contingency and arbitrariness in the fact that an area of concern under this label has in fact emerged (and this contingency accounts for the fact already mentioned that it is not necessarily so recognized in all parts of the world or in all educational practices). Nevertheless, a promising way to proceed is by reflecting on the aims that education can, and arguably must, have over and above the learning of traditional curriculum subjects. And if such an account is to have cross-cultural relevance, it should not be too closely rooted in a specific moral or political perspective or specific cultural traditions. I shall suggest below that certain approaches to personal and social education that are currently popular in Britain fail this test.

PREPARATION FOR ADULT LIFE: ONE ASPECT

I suggest the following as an account of *one* aim for formal education that would be widely agreed: that formal education should help children to develop into adults who are able to take a degree of responsibility for their own lives so that they will be neither wholly dependent on nor wholly subservient to others. This is *not* specifically a liberal conception, and is very widely shared across many religious and cultural communities. While there are attitudes and practices within some religious and cultural communities – concerning, for instance, upbringing within religious doctrine or the status of women within marriage – that cause disquiet to liberals, communities maintaining these attitudes and practices do in general want their children to become able to make their way in the world as adults in their own right. Moreover, the world in which their children need to make their way is, for a large and increasing portion of the world's population, a world in which the route to material success generally lies through school learning and the development of competences both technical and social, and in which at the same time there are for most people many possible routes through life rather than one pattern laid down in advance. Within the range of opportunities that the modern world offers, some possibilities will be seen as advantageous to an individual's chances of a good and independent life, others as deleterious. Even though communities may differ to some extent in which possibilities they see as advantageous and which as deleterious, the concern to prepare young people to face and cope with the possibilities can be shared.

Whether by default or with deliberate intent, young people make many choices along the way that may turn out for better or worse. At the level of a slogan, personal and social education can be seen, I suggest, as a preparation for making one's own way through the world. I shall argue below that this conception of personal and social education does *not* imply detachment from any given framework of values; it does not, then, rest on any radical conception of individual autonomy.

THE CONTENT OF PERSONAL AND SOCIAL EDUCATION

With this perspective in place, we can see why certain concerns have tended to have a central place in personal and social education, by considering the kinds of opportunities, challenges and problems that young people are likely to face while finding their way into and through adult life. First, whatever an individual's goals may turn out to be, lack of fitness, ill health and injury can be major obstacles to the achievement of goals. Education can help children and young people to realize the degree to which they can take personal responsibility for their health and for the avoidance of dangers. Relationships with others, whether or not they are not objectively an essential part of every good life (see the discussion of well-being below), are certainly likely to figure importantly in most young people's lives, while popular culture and media reinforce the idea that sexual relationships in particular are central. Sex education for obvious reasons brings together – if it is sex *and relationships* education, as it is often now called – an evaluation of the importance of sexual relationships and an awareness of the potential conse-quences of such relationships. Perhaps less obviously, education about drugs is also partly about social relationships, given that the use of drugs, including alco-hol and tobacco, usually takes place within and may be encouraged by a social context. These examples already illustrate how the personal is also social (whether the personal is also *political*, as the old feminist slogan had it, is a question that would take us into the difficult area of the relationship between personal and social education and citizenship education; I shall say a little about this later).

Two other aspects of education often included in personal and social education – financial awareness and competence, and career choice – continue the interaction of the personal and the social. Both ambitions for material income and security, and decisions about how to manage one's financial resources, happen within a social setting incorporating norms and expectations. Thinking about a choice of career, in addition to the obvious interaction with financial awareness, is partly too a choice of what sort of social environment one wants to be in during one's working life, and whether and how one wants to see oneself as contributing to society.

There are further related areas that could very well be included under personal and social education, even if they are not necessarily included under that rubric in specific school systems. Education for parenthood is one that has often been neglected in schools, though it can very reasonably be seen as an extension of sex and relationships education. Another is how to handle that area of problematic decisions often if misleadingly called the 'work/life balance' (misleadingly because work would be better seen as a part of life rather than distinct from it). If such areas are to be included, exactly what is to be taught, and how much detailed preparation can be done, is a further issue; at the very least there is the possibility of alerting young people to future decisions and potential problems in their lives, something that has not always been done within schooling.

THE IMPORTANCE OF UNDERLYING VALUES

If personal and social education is about preparation for making one's own way through the complexities of opportunities and obstacles in the personal and social aspects of modern life, then it inevitably requires an awareness of values that can underpin choices and life courses taken. Underlying values determine what seems to any individual a good or not a good life; any decision must refer, whether explicitly or implicitly, to some values if it is not to be an arbitrary plumping or drifting. This is not to say that all decisions in life are or ought to be made through a fully articulated process of reasoning. Many paths in life, including some of the most important in relationships and work, may be taken because one option 'feels right' and another does not. This does not mean that no underlying values are operative; it may rather be that a person's feelings reflect or incorporate evaluations that it might be hard to articulate. There is indeed a possibility that following 'intuition' will sometimes involve a more accurate recognition of what really matters to a person than a conscious working out of reasons that may amount to rationalization. On the other hand, it may also be that feelings can blind someone to considerations that ought – even from the point of view of a person's own underlying priorities – to be taken into account. There is no argument here for every decision being made through explicit weighing up of pros and cons but there is an argument for the value of a person's having and at times exercising the capacity to reflect on their underlying values, on what matters to them in their life. Indeed, some such reflective awareness is arguably a necessary condition of our being able to say that a person finds her own way through life.

In discussing personal and social education, then, we cannot neglect the question of the relationship between the educator's aims and the evaluative stances that underlie the thinking and action of the individuals being educated. Is it part of the responsibility of personal and social education to try to ensure that individuals live their lives in the light of certain values rather than others? If so, then there is at least a close affinity between personal and social education and moral education, and on some views the two areas would essentially coincide. Or is it that teachers of personal and social education should be trying to remain neutral as regards any substantive influence on an individual's own values, while doing their best to equip individuals to live their own lives according to the values that matter to them? If the latter, then personal and social education may be seen as not a matter of moral education at all, unless indeed moral education is itself interpreted as a matter of individual values clarification (Simon et al., 1978) rather than substantive influence in one direction rather than another.

As a matter of historical fact that is interesting in this connection, perceptions of the relationship between personal and social education and moral education in England have changed during recent decades. Several philosophical or interdisciplinary books published in England in the 1980s under the heading of personal and social education were essentially concerned with moral education (see Pring, 1984; Straughan, 1982, 1988;[101] Thacker et al., 1987). By the beginning of the twenty-first century, moral education was likely to be seen as aligned with citizenship education (as in Halstead and Pike, 2006) rather than with personal and social education. This change in perceptions can be explained in part by the political fact that citizenship education, which was seen as incorporating a strand of moral and social responsibility (Crick, 1988), had been put high on the policy agenda.

Meanwhile, there were developments within personal and social education that worked towards the removal of an explicit moral content. Social and political concerns about teenage pregnancy, drug abuse and other health-related behaviour led to such issues becoming central to the practice of personal and social education, potentially to the detriment of broader reflection by individuals on how to live their lives (Haydon, 2005). At the same time, the fact that questions about sex and drugs were (rightly) perceived as controversial probably contributed to a reluctance to bring an explicit moral content into PSHE. Added to the reluctance on the part of teachers to appear judgemental about certain sorts of behaviour or certain sorts of relationship, there was an empirically grounded opinion that telling young people that such-and-such behaviour was wrong was likely to be quite ineffective (and possibly even counterproductive) as a way of actually influencing their behaviour. Both factors together no doubt contributed to a certain approach towards value questions arising in personal and social education that has become common within broadly liberal approaches to education.

At this point I step back again from these local and historical reflections, interesting though they are, to return to philosophical analysis of this variety of liberal approach to personal and social education.

THE ETHOS OF INFORMED CHOICE

Within this ethos, there is a conscious attempt not to 'impose' values on the young. The aim rather is that young people should be aware of – or equipped to inform themselves of – the consequences of one life choice or another, and aware also of their own underlying values so that they can assess the desirability or risk of one set of consequences or another in the light of their underlying values. In some cases it may be presumed within this approach that the relevant consequences are wholly or predominantly self-regarding. Such a presumption might be made in the case of career choice: people should be aware of the opportunities and costs that will be involved in aiming at one kind of occupation or another, but the decision is entirely for them to make in the light of their own self-referring goals. A similar presumption may be made, for instance, where the decision is whether or not to use alcohol, tobacco or other drugs: people should know the risks to their own health, but if they knowingly choose to run those risks then there is no basis for condemning their decision as wrong. Actually in both cases – occupation and drug-taking – this presumption that the decisions involved are primarily self-regarding, and not ones to be made in the light of other-regarding moral concerns, could very well be challenged, but the liberal ethos I have in mind does tend – perhaps sometimes inadvertently – to put emphasis on individuals deciding in the light of informed reflection about the consequences for themselves.

What of matters, including sexual relationships, where it is simply not plausible to represent consequences as only self-related? Here the development of the same approach is that if informed choice in the light of what one values is important for one person, then it is important for another as well. So one individual should have respect for the wishes (hopefully informed wishes) of another, and not impose his or her own preferences on the other. Thus what is, in the case of self-regarding actions, a matter of informed choice, becomes where others are involved a matter of informed consent. Such consent must be genuine and not merely apparent; thus, to the capacity for informed decision there has to be added the capacity to put one's own decision into practice. So, for instance, people will need to the capacity (which might once have been conceptualized as strength of will, but is more likely now to be seen as a matter of interpersonal skills) to stand up to pressure from boyfriends, girlfriends or peers, so as not to agree to what they do not really want to agree to.

In one sense such an approach does avoid moralizing while still giving individuals a kind of grounding in living their own lives. It does not say 'You must not do this because it is wrong'; it says 'You must not do this unless you are really sure, from an informed position, that it is what you want to do'. At the same time, it is clear that this is by no means a value-free approach from the point of view of the educator; it is, rather (like the values clarification mentioned above), an approach in which the central value is respect for an individual's freedom to make their own way through life provided the like freedom on the part of others is respected.

Once it is recognized that an ethos stressing informed choice is itself a normative position, there is room for critique of such a position. For one thing, the stress on informed choice may sometimes disguise more instrumental aims. This is perhaps especially true in the field of sex education. From a social policy perspective, the main reason for promoting programmes of sex education in schools is – or so it often appears – an instrumental reason: namely, that sex education is seen as a means for reducing teenage pregnancy, together with incidence of sexually transmitted disease. There is nothing wrong with that as an argument for the importance of sex education, but it should be recognized that it makes the justification of any particular approach to sex education a matter of empirical investigation of consequences. *If* an approach that stresses informed choice is as a matter of fact the most effective in reducing teenage pregnancy (and there is in fact a good deal of evidence supporting this), well and good so far as the policy perspective goes. By the same token, *if* an approach trying to enforce abstinence turned out to be more effective, that is the approach that – by a parallel argument – ought to be adopted.

However, alongside debates that turn – or ought to turn – on empirical questions of effectiveness towards social goals, there are debates that turn on differences in underlying normative, including moral, positions.

THE SCOPE FOR DIVERGENT NORMATIVE APPROACHES TO PERSONAL AND SOCIAL EDUCATION

Here, the stress on informed choice – holding that what individuals do with their own lives is up to them provided they recognize the risks and are prepared to live with and take responsibility for the consequences – is not the only possible position. It is possible for personal and social education to be conducted within a different kind of ethos. This might, for instance, be an ethos in which certain ways of living are considered substantively better than others – and therefore more worthy of choice, even though not always in fact chosen. Or it might (and the two possibilities are not exclusive) be an ethos in which service to others is put above the pursuit of individual well-being (on which see below). An ethos of either of these kinds may – but need not – rest in an underlying religious commitment, as will be the case in certain faith schools.

There is no contradiction in the idea that a personal and social education that is concerned to support individuals in finding their own way through life should take place within a substantive normative ethos. If an apparent contradiction is perceived, this may be because it is thought that any education pursued within a substantive normative ethos is necessarily indoctrinatory. While this is not the place to enter into a discussion of indoctrination (see Ch. 18), to think that a substantive ethos implies indoctrination is to interpret 'ethos' in far too rigid a manner, or 'indoctrination' too loosely (or perhaps both). That a person grows up and is educated within a particular ethos does not mean that she will not be able to endorse or reject that ethos as the one by which she will seek to live. And if she does endorse that ethos as her own, she will still have to make her own life choices within that ethos (for no ethos can be a complete blueprint that determines how she lives her life in every detail). It is not only very common but also very reasonable for parents and educators to want children to be able to make their own decisions in life while at the same time hoping that they will make those decisions within a certain framework of values.

THE IDEA OF WELL-BEING AS PROVIDING ONE FRAMEWORK AMONG OTHERS

Some of the points made above can be illustrated by reference to a notion, with evident links to the ethos of informed choice, that has gained some popularity in recent educational discourse in Britain: namely, that education in general, and personal and social education in particular, should be fundamentally concerned with individual well-being. Such an idea, advocated philosophically by John White (2007) among others, has been written into recent documentation for the English National Curriculum. This is not the place for a detailed examination of the nature of well-being and its place as an educational aim.[102] Leaving aside here the question of whether well-being provides an overarching aim for education, I shall here raise some reasons for doubt about whether the idea of individual well-being can provide a universally acceptable basis for aims more specific to personal and social education.

First, and related to a point made in the context of sex education above, there is room for doubt as to how far the discourse of individual well-being really does express the actual aim of much educational policy, rather than being a rhetorical gloss on priorities that are actually different. Any governmental policy, including that for schooling, will be driven partly by economic aims. Individual well-being – including notably that aspect of it labelled economic well-being in the English National Curriculum – can have an instrumental value in relation to broader economic and social goals. Individual well-being – perhaps on what I shall call below a subjective interpretation – can also be seen as having an instrumental value towards other, perhaps more traditional, educational goals; thus, it is sometimes said that personal well-being helps pupils achieve academic goals (people will learn better if they feel good about themselves and their achievements).

Secondly, there is often an ambiguity in educational discourse over whether the well-being prioritized is short term or long term. Is it of greater importance to ensure that the child in school has a life of well-being now, or that he or she is likely on the whole to have a life of well-being in the long term? There is a long tradition of educational practice suggesting that an aim of long-term good for the person concerned may extract a certain cost in the individual's well-being while in schooling, but it seems often now to be assumed that there is no conflict. To decide on the emphasis between well-being here and now and well-being in the future is already to make a normative decision.

Thirdly, there is an unresolved philosophical debate over the interpretation of well-being: Is it something open to objective measurement, or is it a subjective condition? Roughly, the objective camp considers that there are certain specifiable elements that must be present in a person's life if it is to be a life of well-being, while for the subjective camp well-being is, essentially, the possession of a feeling that life is going well. It can be readily seen that the difference between such accounts could lead to significantly different accounts of what needs to go into an education aims at well-being. At the risk of slight caricature, if it is reckoned, for instance, that a life of well-being *must* include a long-term committed relationship with the opposite sex, a well-paid job, and membership of a particular religious community, there are ways in which the influence of formal education could be employed to make it more likely that persons will achieve such things, or less likely that they will reject them. If, on the other hand, it is reckoned that well-being is essentially a state of mind, there is likely to be an emphasis (as indeed there is in some educational practices) on the achievement of such qualities as confidence, self-esteem and indeed happiness.[103]

Fourthly, and most fundamentally, there is room to question whether individual well-being *is* (properly to be seen as) *the* overarching aim of education. It is hard to deny that education (if it stands in need of justification at all) needs to be justified as in some sense making human lives better. The idea that education aims at 'the good life' is a useful shorthand for this idea. What is more questionable is whether 'the good life' has to be cashed out in terms of individual well-being. Without further argument for a liberal and individualistic perspective, the possibility cannot be excluded of an internally consistent set of educational aims that interprets a good life as a life of service to the community or a life lived in accordance with the tenets of a particular religion. Much that is taught and learned within an education aimed at such a conception of a good life might be consistent with the practices of a liberal education, however, the overarching reason for engaging in education would be different. And where personal and social education in particular is the focus, much content would be the same, because common opportunities and problems can be identified, as can a range of empirically grounded information relevant to those opportunities and problems; however, the significance attached to the opportunities and problems, and hence the use to be made of the factual information, could be different within different value frameworks.

SOME TENTATIVE CONCLUSIONS

What conclusions of practical relevance might be drawn from this philosophical survey of some issues about personal and social education?

One is that the inevitability and necessity of addressing issues about underlying values within both the planning and the practice of personal and social education should be acknowledged. It should not be thought that the kind of liberal approach sketched above somehow avoids controversial questions about values, nor should it be thought that such an approach is the only option. It may be that in the context of a plural society, if there is to be one policy for personal and social education across state-provided common and secular schools, something like this liberal approach will be the most defensible option, but the argument for that will be an argument of a broadly political kind (perhaps part-principled, part-pragmatic) in the context of the society in question (cf. Archard, 2000), rather than a conceptual argument about the necessary features of anything that could count as personal and social education.

Furthermore, whatever approach is adopted within a plural society, it should not try to hide from students the diversity of relevant value positions that are held within the society; indeed, it should ensure that students are aware of this diversity. The main reason for this is that the world in which students are being prepared to make their own way through life *is* a world in which they will encounter such diversity; even if they have full confidence in their own position, whatever it may be, they will at times have to take into account the differing positions of others. Here again, the difficulty can be seen of trying to separate personal and social education from moral education.

Partly because personal and social education has to address issues about values, while at the same time it is not the only curriculum area that has to do this, serious consideration needs to be given in curriculum planning to the relationship between several relevant subjects or possible subjects. If any society were in the process of starting from scratch in its curriculum planning, it would be an open question whether personal and social education as such should be one compartment in the curriculum.

One area with which there might very well be overlap, though the connection is likely to be overlooked within secular schools in a secular society, is religious education. Since a strong religious commitment can make a difference to how a person lives her life in just the kinds of areas on which personal and social education focuses, an argument could be made, though more strongly in faith schools than in secular schools, for a deliberate coordination of some of the concerns of personal and social education with some of the concerns of religious education.

In secular schools within a secular society, as in state schools in England, the more pressing question, already touched on above, is about the relationship between personal and social education and citizenship education. Insofar as citizenship directs attention to the political and policy aspects of issues, it requires a distinctive range of information and a focus of concern more detached from what is desirable or undesirable for a given individual. Thus, thinking as a citizen about, say, government policy on the provision and funding of health care is different from trying to look after one's own health. Yet at the same time, without an appreciation of the significance of health and fitness in a person's life – without in short an appreciation of the value of health – there would be no basis either for personal responsibility or for democratic deliberation. The individuals who are being educated both to take personal responsibility in their own lives and to engage with public affairs as citizens should not be expected to bring two quite separate sets of values – labelled 'personal' and 'public' – to their thinking. While it may be helpful to see personal and social education, and citizenship education, as two curriculum areas, there is a case for using a focus on underlying values as a basis for coordination between the two areas.

NOTES

100 In this chapter the term 'PSHE' will refer specifically to this recognized curriculum area in schools in England; 'personal and social education' will continue to refer to the broader concern, not specific to England, which is the topic of the chapter.

101 Roger Straughan's 1982 book *Can We Teach Children To Be Good?* acquired a reference to personal and social education in its title only in its second edition in 1988.

102 John White has argued that well-being should be the overarching aim of education (in which case, of course, it is not possible to differentiate the role of personal and social education simply by saying that it is the part of education concerned with well-being). Some of the National Curriculum documentation in England contains at least a nod to the idea that all education is a route to individual well-being, but the documentation for the secondary curriculum (the most recent development of the National Curriculum at the time of writing) overwhelmingly uses the notion of well-being directly in the context of PSHE. Indeed, the guidance for secondary PSHE divides the whole area into personal well-being and economic well-being (itself an odd division, as if a person's financial security or otherwise were distinct from, rather than contributing to, their overall personal well-being). See http://curriculum.qca.org.uk/key-stages-3-and-4/subjects/pshe/index.aspx for details: accessed in February 2009.

103 There are extant educational programmes aimed at the promotion of happiness, practised and advocated in Britain by Anthony Seldon of Wellington College among others.

REFERENCES

Archard, D. (2000) *Sex Education* London: Philosophy of Education Society of Great Britain (IMPACT series).

Crick, B (1988) *Education for Citizenship and the Teaching of Democracy in Schools.* London: QCA.

Haydon, G. (2005) *The Importance of PSHE: A Philosophical Perspective on Personal, Social and Health Education.* London: Philosophy of Education Society of Great Britain.

Hirst, P.H. (1974) *Knowledge and the Curriculum.* London: Routledge.

Hirst, P.H. (1993) Education, knowledge and practices, in: R. Barrow and P. White (eds), *Beyond Liberal Education: Essays in Honour of Paul H. Hirst.* London: Routledge.

Langford, G. (1985) *Education, Persons and Society: a Philosophical Enquiry.* London: Macmillan.

Oakeshott, M. (1989) *The Voice of Liberal Learning: Michael Oakeshott on Education.* New Haven, CT: Yale University Press.

Pring, R. (1984) *Personal and Social Education in the Curriculum: Concepts and Content.* London: Hodder & Stoughton.

Simon, B., Howe, L., Kirschenbaum, H. (1978) *Values Clarification.* New York: A & W Publishers.

Straughan, R. (1982) *Can We Teach Children to be Good?* London: Allen and Unwin.

Straughan, R. (1988) *Can We Teach Children to be Good? Basic Issues in Moral, Personal and Social Education.* Milton Keynes: Open University Press.

Thacker, J., Pring, R., and Evans, D. (eds) (1987) *Personal, Social and Moral Education in a Changing World.* Windsor: NFER-Nelson.

White, J. (2007) *What Schools Are For and Why.* London: Philosophy of Education Society of Great Britain (IMPACT series).

34

Education and the Environment

Michael Bonnett

INTRODUCTION

The issue of the environment and its relevance to education has been one of growing interest to philosophers of education over recent years. In particular, since the proposals of *Agenda 21* (UNCED, 1992) through which some 170 signatory nations agreed to incorporate sustainable development into their educational curricula there has been a particular impetus to examine the aspirations and pedagogy of environmental education. But independently of this more recent, global and focussed official attention to environmental issues, education has often engaged with topics that have been considered environmental. There is a long, if sometimes patchy, history of such activities as nature study, outdoor education, urban studies and interest in the functional and aesthetic aspects of the school and its surroundings. While such aspects are not to be dismissed, the current centre of interest largely reflects the emergence of a set of concerns arising from a sense of what has been labelled our environmental 'crisis', or more modestly our environmental 'predicament'. Here the central issue is how humanity should respond to gathering signs of various interrelated forms of environmental degradation such as resource depletion, pollution, rapid species extinction and climate change that are taken to be the result of human activity and to have serious implications for future human well-being.

Before indicating some of the ways in which such concern has been conceptualized and addressed – and the outcomes of ensuing philosophical examination and imagination in relation to them in the educational context – it might be helpful to note some key ways in which the topic of environmental education is both of interest to, and stands to benefit from the attention of, philosophers of education. First, given the perceived seriousness and extent of the environmental degradation alluded to above, it would be hard to argue that education should not make some response. It is difficult to think of a more pressing set of issues that confronts citizens of the early twenty-first century. This being the case, the general goals and pedagogy of environmental education are a proper focus for philosophy of education (see, for example, Chapman, 2007). Secondly, given that there is a need for such philosophical engagement, it becomes important to identify and review the considerable range of perspectives, ideas and debates that inform our understanding of environmental issues and to weigh their significance for education. Many have sought to link environmental education with educational innovation, not infrequently claiming educational implications of a radical kind. Clearly, such claims stand in need of sober evaluation. Thirdly, and following from this, some of the innovative practices recommended by such perspectives require scrutiny both in respect of their consistency with the principles and values that they are taken to express and their repercussions for the broader educational contexts in which they occur. For example, some of the arising views of knowledge as emergent and the need for pedagogy to become radically dialogical do not sit easily within conventional curricula and school organization. This, in turn, raises questions of how such notions relate to learning theory more generally in education and the criteria to be employed for judging the success of environmental education (see, Meyers, 2006). Finally, it rapidly becomes evident that a thorough-going examination of the significance of environmental concern for education invites an engagement with the metaphysical underpinning of education as a whole, thereby promising to disrupt conventional understandings of truth, knowledge and value in this context.

ENVIRONMENT, NATURE AND EDUCATION

In order to understand the issues that are being pursued in relation to the above it will be helpful to delineate some important senses of the key terms of the debate, for none of them is univalent.

The basic sense of the idea of an environment is relational: it refers to that in which something is located or embedded, the surrounding conditions in which it operates or has its being and with which it interacts. At the macro level, for humans, it raises the issue of our place in the world and the quality of our relationship with it. Not inconsistent with this, but intimating of a different focus, David Cooper (1992) has suggested that in the context of environmental education the idea of the environment as 'one's intentional field of significance' is salient. By this he refers to that web of entities and phenomena with which one has an intimate familiarity – the world in which one *lives*. This can be contrasted with the 'global environment' and even one's geographically local environment – with which one might have scant familiarity. This interpretation of environment as 'life-world' clearly contrasts with its interpretation in the natural sciences as essentially a law-governed causal (ecological) system in which any individual is nested and by which it is biophysically sustained. The significance for accounts of environmental education of this distinction between environment understood as an intentional structure and a causal system will be taken up presently. First it is important to note a further interpretation of the idea of environment: as 'place'. On some accounts, this idea appears to straddle the above two interpretations, for 'place' can be understood as composed of both intentional and physical elements and it has been suggested that humans are always already geographical beings because nothing that they do is unplaced (Casey, 1997, p. ix). This, in turn, has been taken to draw attention to the fact that we are embodied beings and the importance of locale to the significance of action, our sense of identity and our sense of responsibility towards the environment.

Not unrelated to these distinctions is another: that drawn between the 'built' and the 'natural' environment. While some attention will be given to the former – particularly in the sense that it can be taken to include our social/political/economic/cultural environment – in a more straightforward 'physical' sense it is probably fair to say that those aforementioned aspects of environmental concern that are currently experienced as most pressing foreground the natural environment. Of course, addressing issues of environmental degradation has extensive implications for the built environment (including an interest in 'ecological design'), but the fundamental locus of attention lies in our attitudes towards and the impact of our behaviour upon the natural environment. In much environmental discourse, nature's economy assumes a certain salience and when we encounter educational talk of learning 'through', 'for' and 'in' the environment, usually the implicit reference is to the natural environment.

But even within this focus it can be important to draw some distinctions. What do we mean by the natural world? Are there not significant differences in the entities that compose it such as to warrant corresponding differences in value and treatment? Here categories such as human, conative, sentient, biotic, or material, and individual, population, species, or ecosystem, can be relevant to particular areas of debate – particularly that concerning whether any non-human entities have intrinsic value or should be considered to be bearers of moral value. This brings us to a topic that has been heavily problematized by some strands of environmental concern: the issue of the meaning of nature and its normative functioning.

The first point to make about the idea of nature is that it has a long history and has many senses (see, for example, Glacken, 1967; Soper, 1995). Whether as for example, Andrew Stables (2001) has claimed, a serious problem for environmental education is that it relies on an idea (nature) that has little cultural or historical stability is a matter of ongoing debate, but concern of this kind has a number of sources and it will be useful to mention some of them here as they can have strong implications for the approach taken to environmental education. In its problematizing of and efforts to disrupt established 'grand narratives' postmodernism has done much to undermine traditional understandings of nature and the natural as foundational by making the point that, as Ulrich Beck puts it, they 'do not grow on trees, but must be constructed' (Beck, 1994, p. 39) and that this is often done in a way that reflects and authenticates certain power relationships. Feminist writers such as Donna Haraway (1991) have been particularly sensitive to the ways in which, for example, natural categories such as 'man' and 'woman' (and we might add 'child') are constructed as part of a political matrix and that emancipation requires their deconstruction. Interpreting nature as a text can lead to a semiotic perspective that deeply problematizes the human–non-human distinction (Stables, 2007). Others have claimed that because of the all-pervasive planetary impact of human activity, nature is 'at an end' (McKibben, 1989) or that in our post-traditionalist culture it has 'dwindled away' and 'no longer exists' (Giddens, 1994). It might be argued that this latter view is lent support by the rarity of references to nature in much contemporary official educational policy, including that which relates to the environment (Bonnett, 2007) and in the frequently disjointed and enervated representations of the natural environment in policy documents (Ross, 2007; Winter, 2007).

The following sample of current senses of nature is indicative of different ways that education with regard to the environment might be interpreted:

- nature as the cosmos in which the individual and humanity as a whole has (or must find) its place;
- nature as the hale, the wholesome – a reference for what is proper or fitting;
- nature as wilderness – the ineluctably other that can both challenge and refresh;
- nature as innate essence, an authoritative source with which a harmony has to be sought.

Each of these senses has its own possibilities of further interpretation – e.g. the cosmos can be variously interpreted as, say, a blind law-governed causal system or divine creation – that in turn would influence pedagogy and give different orientations towards what are two key underlying and interrelated questions that are posed by environmental concern: What would count as a right relationship with nature? Against what criteria should humankind judge its progress/success/ flourishing in relation to nature? Arguably, the answers to such questions that we provide or assume are significant not only for environmental education but also education as a whole.

Yet, contra claims concerning its unstableness, is there no underlying unifying conception of nature? In what could be regarded as a response to this question, Martin Heidegger draws upon what he takes to be a central aspect of the Greek experience of nature expressed in the word 'physis' which speaks of an unaided 'bringing forth'. This idea of the self-emergent or self-arising seems consistent with modern understandings of nature as that which occurs independently of human intention and arguably this lies at the heart of the various senses delineated above, in substantial part lending them whatever weight that they possess

(Bonnett, 2004). This would mean that while, as with all concepts, our concepts of nature are indeed socially produced, it is precisely our understanding of nature that it is *not* socially produced. Rather, nature befalls us. Furthermore, it has been argued that this understanding is deeply embedded in our form of sensibility such that it cannot be regarded as optional in the way that postmodernists such as Rorty (1994) have suggested and that therefore it constitutes a key element in understanding ourselves in the environment (Bonnett, 2004). On this line of argument understanding nature as the self-arising and establishing a right relationship to it become essential aspects of our well-being and form central educational aims – which, of course, is not to exclude careful scrutiny of particular ideas of nature for their ideological or other bias and the ways in which they are used to lend authority to essentially arbitrary forms of discrimination. The experience of nature as self–arising is important in foregrounding otherness and an element of essential mystery in our relationship with the environment, that in turn can disconcert the prevalent humanistic hubris that a number of writers claim to detect. It also raises interesting questions about how we come to know nature.

Aside from the direct focus on various forms of environmental degradation and its consequences, the topic of education and the environment has been expressed in two further significant ways: (a) that direct contact with the natural outdoor environment in some way contributes to the formation of an individual's character; (b) that the natural environment is something to be respected for itself and should be cherished and responded to aesthetically and morally (rather than instrumentally). On the second of these points, David Carr (2004) has argued that engagement with the arts may help students to form an attachment to nature that is essential to them coming to regard it with moral care. Arts such as sculpture can *inter alia* engender an awareness and appreciation of the physical aspects of nature – shapes, colours, textures – and for example through outdoor sculpture, such as that for which Henry Moore is famous, bring out a spiritual dimension of a landscape. Poetry, too, can convey with great immediacy the sensual impact of nature. But also it can be effective in evoking and communicating various aspects of our complex and tensioned relationship with the natural world: its indifference to us; our continuity with it; our alienation from it; and its redemptive power. As Carr points out, the imaginative attention that is poetic contemplation can bring us to experience aspects of nature as *sub specie aeternitatis* and this is a powerful way of (again) allowing a non-ego-centred attachment entry into conscious life, enabling that life itself to be invested with wider moral and spiritual significance. Thereby, our sensibility can be cultivated and refined so as to admit true awareness of intrinsic worth.

THE ISSUE OF SUSTAINABILITY AND AN ENVIRONMENTAL ETHIC

Without doubt the chief form in which environmental concern has gained global currency and purchase in educational debate and policy has been through the vocabulary of 'sustainability' and 'sustainable development'. Yet, notwithstanding its pivotal role in the discussion of environmental issues, the meaning of 'sustainability' seems frequently to have been taken as somehow self-evident and value neutral – almost as though it simply reflected a desire to preserve some readily identifiable underlying natural state of equilibrium. But of course this cannot be the case; clearly there can be divergence over *what* is to be sustained. Prominent candidates include sustaining: economic growth; the 'balance of nature' or an ecosystem; a culture (for example, 'the ability of a community to create a way of life which is an expression of its values and aspirations' (Vandeburg, 1995)); and the capacity to meet human needs (Brundtland Commission, 1987). Such differing foci imply different sets of policy implications, and there is no prima facie reason for supposing that they need be compatible with each other. Indeed it has been pointed out by, for example, Rist (1997), that trading on such ambiguities has enabled the rhetoric of some policy-makers to give the impression that they wish to do one thing (such as sustaining natural ecosystems) while in fact attempting something quite different (such as sustaining conditions for a narrowly defined economic growth).

Similarly, there can be an easy assimilation of ecological sustainability with sustaining *democratic* culture. However, not all find this plausible. William Ophuls (1997, p. 3) claims that 'liberal democracy as we know it ... is doomed by ecological scarcity; we need a completely new political philosophy and set of institutions'. He suggests that certain fundamental 'ecological imperatives' that derive from the laws of nature and the fact that the biosphere, as effectively a closed system, cannot sustain endless economic growth will increasingly determine 'how we run our lives' (pp. 7–8) – in effect defining a conception of the good life to which citizens need to be brought to conform. The authoritarianism implicit in the notion of such imperatives presents a serious challenge to assumptions of a comfortable alliance between democracy and ecological sustainability. (For further discussion of such issues see Bell, 2004; Saward, 1995).

But perhaps the most significant general feature to arise from a discussion of sustainability at this point is the recognition of the value position inherent in the views of all who use the term. Not everything can be sustained and as soon as one clarifies *what* is to be sustained (and at what level and over what spatial and temporal scales), one is involved in a selection that reflects a particular value/cultural position. In its broadest sense this brings us up against one of the great axes of debate in the area of environmental ethics: that of anthropocentrism as against biocentrism: should we give priority to, measure policy in terms of, the satisfaction of (long-term) human needs, or the needs of the biosphere (of which human beings are but one small part)? Generalized talk of 'sustainability' tends to cloak the tension between these positions, allowing a tacit decision to hold sway unquestioned, for generally the foundation for expression of concern for natural systems is inherently anthropocentric in assuming the overriding desirability of sustaining those natural systems that are conducive to *human* flourishing (however that is defined). But, philosophically, not all thinkers believe that this should be accepted as a given. A number wish to champion the worth and 'rights' of non-human nature – either setting human needs strictly on a par with the needs of all other members of the 'great community of life' (Taylor, 1986) or subordinating them to the well-being of the biosphere (Foreman, 1993).

Finally, ideas of sustainability as a policy raise a set of thorny epistemological issues. It has been noted that even so-called stable systems remain predictable for relatively short periods of time and the significance of contingency in the evolution of human–environment relations in particular (for example, what was there to predict that it would be Europe and not India or China that first would develop into modern industrialism? (Simmons, 1995)) – makes far-reaching prediction a hazardous business. But often, as with nuclear power and genetically modified crops, it is precisely far-reaching effects (social, biological, climatic, etc.) that are of such importance in environmental matters. Yet the extreme complexity of the systems relevant to environmental sustainability and the highly imperfect state of our current knowledge of them make the ambition of framing holistic policies, that in principle is entirely appropriate to dealing with systems of organic interrelationship, highly problematic.

Wedding 'development' to sustainability generates yet further problems. Ostensibly 'sustainable development' brings into harmony two politically attractive but potentially conflicting notions: (1) the idea of sustaining that which is valued, but that is currently endangered through depletion, pollution and so forth; and (2) the idea of accommodating ongoing human aspirations to *develop*, i.e. in some sense to have more or better. Its proponents argue that it both makes clear that any moves to address environmental degradation must be made in tandem with legitimate concerns of large sections of humanity to improve their material conditions and it gives a necessary focus on positive action rather than acceding to overweening and sometimes paralyzing gloom at the scale of the problems faced.

But the seductiveness of 'sustainable development' has been matched by a suspicion that it might involve a certain semantic sleight of hand. Take its most influential definition given in the Brundtland Commission Report (1987): 'a development that meets the needs of the present without compromising the needs of future generations to meet their own need'. This definition, officially consolidated into the education systems of the nations signatory to *Agenda 21* (UNCED, 1992) and an orientating idea for much of the debate in this area, not only inexorably reinforces a questionable anthropocentric stance but also, for writers such as Carl Mitchum (1997), it both valorizes an escape from the economy of subsistence as defined by the modern (Western) world and a subtle addiction to management. Yet it may turn out that an economy closer in spirit to subsistence and self-reliance is the only truly sustainable way of life and that such managerialism is highly problematic in continuing to express the kind of arrogant instrumentalism towards nature that some see as a prime contributor to present problems. Vandana Shiva (1992) suggests that in the context of Western market economies 'development' will inevitably become interpreted as economic development in the sense of economic *growth*, and that true sustainability requires that development is not separated from conservation and should reflect the logic of *nature's* economy.

Others are more sanguine about the prospect of marrying sustainability to development. For example, Robin Attfield (1994, pp. 223–233) has argued that developmentalism and environmentalism, properly understood, can be complementary. It is such mutually reinforcing factors as malnutrition, high infant mortality, low levels of literacy and education, relatively high morbidity and low levels of productivity and income per head that both contribute to population growth and ecological problems and offend against the idea of justice.

But notwithstanding this, philosophical examination of Brundtland-type definitions continues to reveal a range of serious unclarities and a problematic underlying moral stance. The criteria for judging humans needs – both present and future – remain unspecified and are likely to be highly contested in a global context of differing cultural, economic and geographical situations. The danger of paternalism on the part of the powerful is large, as is the possibility of its ambiguity allowing it chiefly to serve as a term of political convenience used to mask and/or legitimate vested interests. It seems clear that the notion of sustainable development requires careful explication – and perhaps ultimately stipulative definition – if its use is not to invite confusion and risk betrayal of the motives it was originally intended to express. But perhaps the most fundamental criticism of sustainability articulated in this way is that it exhibits a speciesism and instrumentalism of a pretty high order such that the non-human world is conceived purely as a resource. It has been argued that such stark anthropocentrism is precisely what lies at the root of the current regrettable environmental state of affairs.

Here then we have a further reminder that central to environmental issues is the manner of our consciousness of them and that we need to conceive of sustainability not simply as a policy designed to achieve a certain state of affairs but also as an attitude of mind, a way of relating to nature–environment. The importance of an honest appraisal of our underlying motives towards nature grows in proportion to our increasing power to implement them. Policy stands in need of constant revision in the light of new evidence. Arguably, this can only be properly undertaken if we work from a right frame of mind in terms of basic values, motives and attitudes towards nature. To the extent that this is true, to develop such a frame of mind becomes an important educational concern. It entails addressing the contentious task of identifying the qualities of a flourishing, mutually sustaining, relationship in its lived day-to-day occurrence – in effect an existential sense of human care for the natural world (Postma, 2006, Ch. 3) – that would energize an adequate environmental ethic. In somewhat Heideggerian vein, it has been argued that human consciousness conceived essentially as the place where things show up – 'are let be' – is intrinsically involved in sustainability and that education should be concerned to promote and nurture this by disrupting the metaphysics of mastery that currently runs through so much Western-style culture (Bonnett, 2004, Ch. 9).

In an interesting, if bleak, analysis of late-modern society that is illustrative of the insidiousness of this motive, Ingolfur Bluhdorn (2000) describes the arrival of a 'post-ecologist constellation' that has the following features: seeing nature as a heavily contested social construction; the de-ideologization of eco-politics and the loss of its specific identity through integration into other fields; and the reformulation of ecological issues as economic issues and issues of efficiency. He argues that in such a society unsustainability has become inherent and tacitly accepted such that the central political problem is the management of unsustainability in a way that allows society to reassure itself that it still upholds modernist and ecological ideals. On Bluhdorn's analysis a combination of reflexive redefinition of these ideals in ways congenial to the new constellation and ostentatious emphasis in public discourse on political renewal and economic greening 'enable policies of ecological modernization and sustainable development to function so as to simulate the possibility and desirability of environmental justice and integrity without genuinely aiming to address, let alone reverse, the fundamental unsustainability of late-modern society' (Bludhorn, 2002, p. 66). To the extent that this analysis reflects political reality, it again underscores the need for critical political awareness as a key element in evaluating the language of sustainability and in environmental education more generally.

ENVIRONMENTAL UNDERSTANDING, THE CURRICULUM AND THE CULTURE OF THE SCHOOL

Consistent with the above discussion, David Orr (1994) has made the point that in the context of Western-style education that increasingly focuses on producing students who are effective operators in a global market economy premised on perpetual growth environmental concern raises both problems *in* education and *of* education. For example, it raises such questions as: What *kind* of knowledge will best illuminate, and equip us to respond to, issues of sustainability? Is the arrangement frequently found in conventional curricula of primarily locating such understanding in the disciplines of science and geography adequate? Where does this leave the moral, social, economic, aesthetic, and spiritual dimensions of the issues that an adequate understanding of our relationship with our environment involves? And in any case should we simply assume that traditional subject domains are the appropriate vehicles for pursuing environmental issues when historically in the West many of their central motives were shaped in a cultural milieu preoccupied with subordinating and exploiting nature? Such questions suggest that we cannot simply assume that the tacit values operative in traditional subject domains will accord with at least some versions of sustainability, nor that study in these domains will reveal the holistic – and therefore perhaps interdisciplinary – nature of sustainability issues. At the very least, from the perspective of philosophy of education, an important area of investigation is opened up: What motives and attitudes towards nature are implicit in different areas of the school curriculum? And what curriculum structure will facilitate the kind of learning that our environmental predicament now requires?

To illustrate the first of these questions: there has been extensive discussion in the literature concerning the traditional assumption that science offers the most authentic insight into the reality of nature. Central elements of this debate include concern over the aggressive and manipulative motives taken by some to be inherent in modern experimental science – legitimized according to writers such as Caroline Merchant (1992, Ch. 2) by the feminine gendering of nature. Recognition of the need for more receptive-responsive, dialogical, forms of knowing sympathetic to the manifoldness of nature properly understood suggests that other portals must be sought and has been taken to open up wide-ranging implications for knowledge transformation, curriculum, pedagogy and the culture of the school. On such a view, regarding our relationship with nature, it is far from clear that Newton has as much to offer as Manley Hopkins. Such considerations have been interpreted as providing an entrée into educational debate for indigenous perspectives, romantic philosophy, as well as the views of early environmentalists such as Thoreau, Emerson, Leopold, Muir, and eco-feminist points concerning *inter alia* knowing dominated by a masculine rationality (Plumwood, 1995).

With regard to the second question, Stables and Scott (2002) have defended a discipline-based approach on the grounds that it would be a mistake to attempt to conceive of environmental education as some holistic cross-disciplinary element. Erroneously this would imply that there is, as it were, some single totalizing environmental grand narrative to be conveyed and risks a certain eco-fascism. Yet, there has been a recurring criticism of a discipline-based approach on the grounds that a curriculum intended to develop an understanding of an organic system must somehow reflect that organicism in its own structure. It has been argued that the atomistic understanding encouraged by a traditional curriculum inevitably both externalizes relevant factors and lacks cognizance of the greater whole. In his influential *Steps to an Ecology of Mind* Gregory Bateson (2000) argues that what is desperately required is a systemic wisdom that transcends the narrow purposive frameworks through which consciousness selectively samples events and processes. But how is the greater whole to be understood? What are the appropriate metaphors? Bateson favours that of a vast cybernetic system – a self-corrective information feedback system of which any individual mind is a variable localized part to be delineated by the phenomena that we wish to explain. Here the boundary between self and other is dissolved – a position quite frequently encountered in one form or another (see, for example, Matthews, 1994). But there have been other candidates: a created realm, a blind causal system, a realm governed by abstract laws, a domain of dialogical encounters attended by mystery. The helpfulness of any or all of these is a matter of ongoing debate, and certainly the radical revision of the landscape of human understanding required by Bateson's computer metaphor attracts philosophical scrutiny (see, for example, Bonnett, 2009).

Relevant to ideas of systemic wisdom, Stephen Gough (2002) draws on the 'co-evolutionary' approach of Richard Norgaard (1984) that posits the relationship between society and non-human nature as one of ongoing reciprocal change, each impacting on the other in ways that can never be fully anticipated. With regard to environmental planning, Gough suggests that this perspective in which uncertainty is systemic challenges us to look to keeping possibilities open and to consider the option value of aspects of the environment over a range of different decision points through time in a way that tends towards increasing the future option value of the environment and thus is permanently prepared for surprises in the way that things turn out. Hence the curriculum would need to develop the ability to conceive, recognize and manage an ever-increasing range of possibilities and to reverse the conventional attitude in which future options are systematically discounted in a political context that characteristically focuses on the short term. Education would need to prepare all to contribute to this in their decision-making in the different fields and institutions in which they work.

Chiming in with the theme of systemic uncertainty, John Foster (2002) argues that education for the environment requires a heuristic rather than economistic interpretation of the much-vaunted 'learning society'; the sense-giving frameworks that we employ in understanding the world need to be open to change and we must be prepared to surrender ourselves to 'the inescapable creativity and open-endedness of our grapple with the emergent'. He construes sustainability as living with the grain of a nature that is recognized as a well-spring of surprises as much as an object of prediction and this requires an outlook that is thus both radically open and radically precautionary in order to leave room for our fallibility and accommodation to the unexpected. This view seems entirely consistent with the previous construal of nature as the self-arising.

A strong theme to run through much thinking in the area is that of an integral connection with action. Indeed, it is possible to detect a clear tension in much environmental education policy between a perceived urgency to modify behaviour and respecting educational values: the impulse to action can be interpreted in either an essentially authoritarian or an essentially democratic way. The former – which has been termed 'environmentalism' – sets education up as a vehicle for achieving a set of prespecified environmentally friendly behaviours, such as certain levels of recycling and energy conservation, and has been seen to sit well with the school effectiveness movement (Elliott, 1999). While no doubt such behaviours are welcome, orientating schools in this way can bypass students' personal understanding, critical evaluation and commitment and thus not truly provide environmental *education*. As Bjorn Jensen and Karsten Schnack put it:

> A school does not become 'green' by conserving energy, collecting batteries or sorting waste. The crucial factor must be what the students learn from participating in such activities, or from deciding something else. (Jensen and Schnack, 1997)

The long-running OECD *Environment in Schools Initiative* (ENSI) is a good example of an approach that valorizes democratic action. It pursues 'ecologization' of schools by placing the notion of 'action competence' at the heart of the curriculum. This involves students identifying and addressing environmental problems as a member of the school and wider community and requires that pupils not only acquire relevant factual knowledge but also that they personally evaluate issues and the relevance of knowledge, and learn the practical ability to work effectively with others in a way that respects the views of all concerned. Here the aim is the acquisition neither of prespecified behaviours, nor of prespecified subject organized knowledge, but critically reflective environmental action framed in the context, of students' own life-worlds and understandings. In such a context, students are as likely to be the generators of knowledge as recipients. This approach has been viewed by those involved as radically 'transgressive' in the way it disrupts many boundaries that structure conventional education, such those between childhood dependency and adult responsibility, knowledge users and knowledge producers, knowing and acting and facts and values. It is argued that the inherently complex, contextualized, frequently controversial and often piecemeal occurrence of environmental issues in real-life situations precludes a traditional school curriculum and requires students to participate in shaping 'the social and economic conditions of their existence in society' (Elliot, 1999).

This highly dynamic model provides a powerful example of the extent to which environmental education might impact upon conventional understandings of pupils, teachers and educational institutions. There is clearly much philosophical work to be undertaken in reviewing such possibilities, including the adequacy of a student rationality tacitly conditioned by the previously discussed super-ordinate motivational climate to identify key issues. This leads to a further point concerning the kind of knowledge to be valorized by environmental education.

It is clear from the preceding discussion that pupils need to develop a range of understandings of our environmental predicament that includes that of the socio-political values and practices that have been heavy contributors to the current situation. Equally pressing would be a need to address the socio-political consequences of these values and practices. An important cluster of such ideas and their educational implications has been foregrounded through the notion of 'eco-justice pedagogy'. On C.A. Bowers (2002) account *inter alia* such pedagogy should seek to reveal the environmental racism and class discrimination involved in the way that the deleterious environmental impacts fall disproportionately on ethnically and economically marginalized groups, and to develop a sense of responsibility towards future generations and a corresponding self-limitation by an expansion of non-consumptive relationships. Following from this, he argues for the recovery of non-commodified aspects of community and a reversal of an ever-increasing dependency on meeting life's daily needs through consumerism rather than through self-reliance within the family and local networks of community support. Central to the realization of these aims, for Bowers, is to enable students to recognize how language carries forward culturally specific ways of thinking that are orchestrated by certain root metaphors. He argues that currently the dominant metaphors are those that underlay the industrial revolution such as 'individual' and 'linear progress' and that these are in conflict with the root metaphor underlying an eco-justice pedagogy, which is 'ecology'. In contrast to an emphasis on an autonomous individual, this 'foregrounds the relational and dependent nature of our existence as cultural and biological beings'. Through their implicit shaping of our understanding of the world, industrial metaphors have systematically undermined the value of tradition and therefore of inter-generational knowledge and continuity. If we can provoke students to reflect upon how cultural and environmental patterns connect, we might create a cultural space for criticizing the language patterns of different Western cultures that produce '… the individual psychology that accepts consumer dependency and environmental degradation as a necessary trade-off for achieving personal conveniences and material success'.

SUMMARY

If we are to enable pupils to address the causes of environmental problems rather than the symptoms we must engage them in those kinds of enquiry that reveal the dominant underlying motives, metaphors and interpretations that are in play in society and invite them to participate in shaping practices that are informed by the understandings that emerge. Several of the views considered above suggest that ultimately, this will involve an examination of motives that are inherent in our most fundamental ways of thinking about ourselves and the world – i.e. it will involve *metaphysical* considerations and action that is transformative. Thus, in significant ways the issues raised by the topic of education and the environment are not primarily matters of formal curriculum content but of the general culture of the school (and, of course, society). The focus moves to the underlying versions of human flourishing and the good life that are implicit in the ethos of the school as a community and how they connect with life more generally. This ethos conditions the character of participation in social practices, including the spirit in which the curriculum is taught and received. Insofar as a reflective examination of environmental concern disturbs the metaphysics to which societal and school life reverberates, its significance extends beyond the confines of any specific area of the curriculum designated 'environmental education'.

REFERENCES

Attfield, R. (1994) *Environmental Philosophy: Principles and Prospects.* Aldershot: Avebury.
Bateson, G. (2000) *Steps to an Ecology of Mind,* Pts V and VI. Chicago: IL: University of Chicago Press.

Beck, U. (1994) *Ecological Politics in an Age of Risk*. Cambridge: Polity.

Bell, D. (2004) Creating green citizens? Political liberalism and environmental education, *Journal of Philosophy of Education*, 38 (1), 37–53.

Bluhdorn, I. (2000) *Post-Ecologist Politics. Social Theory and the Abdication of the Ecologist Paradigm*. London: Routledge.

Bluhdorn, I (2002) Unsustainability as a frame of mind – and how we disguise it: the silent counter revolution and the politics of simulation, *The Trumpeter*, 18 (1), 59–69.

Bonnett, M. (2004) *Retrieving Nature. Education for a Post-Humanist Age*. Oxford: Blackwell.

Bonnett, M. (2007) Environmental education and the issue of nature, *Journal of Curriculum Studies*, 39 (6), 707–721.

Bonnett, M. (2009) Systemic wisdom, the 'selving' of nature, and knowledge transformation: education for the 'greater whole, *Studies in Philosophy and Education*, 28 (1), 39–49.

Bowers, C.A. (2002) Toward an eco-justice pedagogy, *Environmental Education Research*, 8 (1), 21–34.

Brundtland Commission (1987) *Our Common Future*. Milton Keynes: Open University Press.

Carr, D. (2004) Moral values and the arts in environmental education: towards an ethics of aesthetic appreciation, *Journal of Philosophy of Education*, 38 (2) 221–239.

Casey, E.S. (1997) *The Fate of Place: A Philosophical History*. Berkeley, CA: University of California Press.

Chapman, R.L. (2007) How to think about environmental studies, *Journal of Philosophy of Education*, 41 (1), 59–74.

Cooper, D. (1992) The idea of environment. In D. Cooper and J. Palmer (eds), *The Environment in Question*. London: Routledge.

Elliot, J. (1999) Sustainable society and environmental education: future perspectives and demands for the educational system, *Cambridge Journal of Education*, 29 (3), 325–340.

Foreman, D. (1993) Putting the earth first. In S. Armstrong and R. Botzler (eds), *Environmental Ethics*. New York: McGraw-Hill.

Foster, J. (2002) Sustainability, higher education and the learning society, *Environmental Education Research*, 8 (1).

Giddens, A. (1994) *Beyond Left and Right*. Cambridge: Polity Press.

Glacken, C.J. (1967) *Traces on the Rhodian Shore. Nature and Culture in Western Thought from Ancient Times to the End of the Eighteenth Century*. Berkeley, CA: University of California Press.

Gough, S. (2002) Increasing the value of the environment: a 'real options' metaphor for learning, *Environmental Education Research*, 8 (1), 61–72.

Haraway, D. (1991) *Simians, Cyborgs, and Women. The Reinvention of Nature*. London: Free Association Books.

Jensen, B.B. and Schnack, K. (1997) The action competence approach in environmental education, *Environmental Education Research*, 3 (2), 163–178.

McKibben, W. (1989) *The End of Nature*. New York: Random House.

Matthews, F. (1994) *The Ecological Self*. London: Routledge.

Merchant, C. (1992) *Radical Ecology*. London, Routledge.

Meyers, R. (2006) Environmental learning: reflections on practice, research and theory, *Environmental Education Research*, 12 (3–4), 459–470.

Mitchum, C. (1997) The sustainability question. In R. Gottlieb (ed.), *The Ecological Community*. London: Routledge.

Norgaard, R. (1984) Co-evolutionary agricultural development, *Economic Development and Cultural Change*, 32 (3), 525–546.

Ophuls, W. (1977) *Ecology and the Politics of Scarcity*. San Francisco, CA: W.H. Freeman.

Orr, D. (1994) *Earth in Mind: On Education, Environment, and the Human Prospect*. Washington, DC: Island Press.

Plumwood, V. (1995) Nature, self, and gender: feminism, environmental philosophy, and the critique of rationalism. In R. Elliot (ed.), *Environmental Ethics*. Oxford: Oxford University Press.

Postma, D. W. (2006) *Why Care for Nature? In Search of an Ethical Framework for Environmental Responsibility and Education*. Dordrecht, The Netherlands: Springer.

Rist, G. (1997) *The History of Development*. London: Zed Books.

Rorty, R. (1994) *Philosophy and the Mirror of Nature*. Oxford: Blackwell.

Ross, H. (2007) Environment in the curriculum: representation and development in the Scottish physical and social sciences, *Journal of Curriculum Studies*, 39 (6), 659–677.

Saward, M. (1995) Green democracy? In A. Dobson and P. Lucardie (eds), *The Politics of Nature*. London: Routledge.

Shiva, V. (1992) Recovering the real meaning of sustainability. In D. Cooper and J. Palmer (eds), *The Environment in Question*. London: Routledge.

Simmons, I. G. (1995) *Interpreting Nature*. London: Routledge.

Soper, K. (1995) *What is Nature?* Oxford: Blackwell.

Stables, A. (2001) Who drew the sky? Conflicting assumptions in environmental education, *Educational Philosophy and Theory*, 33 (2), 245–256.

Stables, A. (2007) *Living and Learning as Semiotic Engagement*. Lewiston, NY: Edwin Mellen.

Stables, A. and Scott, W. (2002) The quest for holism in education for sustainable development, *Environmental Education Research*, 8 (1), 53–60.

Taylor, P. (1986) *Respect for Nature: A Theory of Environmental Ethics*. New Jersey: Princeton University Press.

UNCED (1992) *Agenda 21*. New York: UNCED.

Vandeburg, W.H. (1995) Can a technical civilisation sustain human life? *Bulletin of Science, Technology and Society*, 15.

Winter, C. (2007) Education for sustainable development in English secondary schools, *Cambridge Journal of Education*, 37 (3), 337–354.

Index